OS X Mavericks
ALL-IN-ONE

FOR

DUMMIES®

A Wiley Brand

by Mark L. Chambers

FOR

DUMMIES®

A Wiley Brand

OS X® Mavericks All-in-One For Dummies®

Published by: **John Wiley & Sons, Inc.,** 111 River Street, Hoboken, NJ 07030-5774, www.wiley.com

Copyright © 2014 by John Wiley & Sons, Inc., Hoboken, New Jersey

Published simultaneously in Canada

For general information on our other products and services, please contact our Customer Care Department within the U.S. at 877-762-2974, outside the U.S. at 317-572-3993, or fax 317-572-4002. For technical support, please visit www.wiley.com/techsupport.

Wiley publishes in a variety of print and electronic formats and by print-on-demand. Some material included with standard print versions of this book may not be included in e-books or in print-on-demand. If this book refers to media such as a CD or DVD that is not included in the version you purchased, you may download this material at http://booksupport.wiley.com. For more information about Wiley products, visit www.wiley.com.

Library of Congress Control Number: 2013949059

ISBN 978-1-118-69181-6 (pbk); ISBN 978-1-118-70756-2 (ebk); ISBN 978-1-118-70765-4 (ebk)

Manufactured in the United States of America

10 9 8 7 6 5 4 3 2 1

Contents at a Glance

Table of Contents

Introduction

I remember the first moment I moved a mouse across an OS X Desktop. At that time, it was the beta of version 10.0 — and I very well remember the word *elegant* as my first impression. (My second impression was *Unix done better.*) That's really saying something because I'm an old personal computer operating system curmudgeon: I cut my computing teeth on Atari and TRS-80 Model III machines, and I still feel at home in the character-based environment of DOS and Unix. Of course, I've also used every version of Windows that His Gatesness has produced (everything from Microsoft Bob and Windows/286 to the much-maligned Windows 8). And yes, I've used Mac OS since before the days of System 7, using a Macintosh SE with a 9" monitor (and a built-in handle).

But out of this host of operating systems, could you really call one *elegant* before now? OS X — now at version 10.9, affectionately called *Mavericks* — is something different: a fine-cut diamond amongst a handful of semiprecious stones. It's the result of an unnatural marriage, I'll admit . . . the intuitive, graphical world of Mac paired with the character-based stability and efficient multitasking of Unix, along with the iOS operating system developed especially for Apple's mobile devices. Who would have thought that they would work together so well?

Therefore, you can imagine how I immediately jumped at the chance to write a comprehensive guide to Apple's masterpiece. (Although it's been a full decade ago now, I've never regretted the decision.) The book that you hold in your hands uses the classic *For Dummies* design; it provides you with the step-by-step instruction (plenty of which my editors grudgingly agree is somewhat humorous) on every major feature of OS X. It also goes a step further from time to time, delving into why something works the way it does or what's going on behind the scenes. You can chalk that up to my sincere admiration for everyone in Cupertino and what they've produced.

What you *won't* find in this *All-in-One* is wasted space. All the new features of version 10.9 are here, including the arrival of the Dynamic Duo from the iOS world: Maps and iBooks. You'll also find coverage of all the current iLife and iWork applications. Everything's explained from the ground up, just in case you've never touched an Apple computer before. By the time you reach the final pages, you'll have covered advanced topics, such as networking, AppleScript, Internet security . . . and yes, even an introduction to the powerful world of Unix that exists underneath.

I sincerely hope that you'll enjoy this book and that it will act as your guide while you discover all the wonderful features of OS X Mavericks that I use every day. Remember, if a Windows-minded acquaintance still titters about your Mac mini, I'll understand if you're tempted to drop this weighty tome on his foot. (Of course, you can also boot into Windows and watch him turn purple — truth is, he can't boot into OS X on his PC.)

The official name of the latest version is (portentous pause here, please) *OS X version 10.9 Mavericks*. But who wants to spit out that mouthful every time? Throughout this book, I refer to the operating system as *OS X* or simply *Mavericks*.

About This Book

No one expects a book in the *For Dummies* series to contain technojargon or ridiculous computer science semantics — especially a book about the Macintosh! Apple has always strived for simplicity and user friendliness. I hereby promise that I've done my absolute best to avoid unnecessary techno-talk. For those who are interested in what's happening under the hood, I provide sidebars that explain a little more about what's doing what to whom. If you'd rather just have fun and ignore the digital dirty work, please feel free to disregard these additions (but don't tear sidebars out of the book because there's likely to be important stuff on the opposite side of the page).

However, even *For Dummies* books have to get technical from time to time, usually involving commands that you have to type and menu items that you have to click. If you've read any of my other *For Dummies* books, you'll know that a helpful set of conventions is used to indicate what needs to be done or what you see onscreen:

✦ **Stuff you type:** When I ask you to type a command or enter something in a text field (such as your name or phone number), the text appears like this: **Type me.** Press the Return key to process the command or enter the text.

✦ **Menu commands:** When I give you a specific set of menu commands to use, they appear in the following format: Edit⇨Copy. In this example, you should click the Edit menu and then choose the Copy menu item.

✦ **Links:** URLs (web addresses) look like this: www.mlcbooks.com. I added plenty of them so you can quickly find cool products or helpful info online.

Foolish Assumptions

If you have a Mac that's either running OS X version 10.9 (Mavericks) or is ready to be upgraded to it, you're set to go. Despite what you might have heard, you *won't* require any of the following:

+ **A degree in computer science:** Apple designed OS X for regular people, and I designed this book for people of every experience level. Even if you've never used a Mac before, you'll find no hostile waters here.

+ **A fortune in hardware and software:** I do describe additional hardware and software that you can buy to expand the functionality of your Mac; however, that coverage is only five chapter's worth. *Everything else* covered in this book is included with OS X Mavericks — and by the size of this volume, you get a rough idea of just how complete OS X is! Heck, many folks buy Macs just because of the free software you get, such as iMovie and iPhoto.

+ **Full-time technical help:** Granted, you may need occasional professional technical support for specific hardware or software issues, but such instances will be rare — you won't have your smartphone constantly stuck to your ear as you wait for a human voice! Within the confines of this book, I try my best to cover all the bases, including troubleshooting you can perform on your own and possible pitfalls that you can avoid.

Oh, and you need to buy and download Mavericks from the Apple App Store, unless Mavericks came pre-installed on your Mac. Go figure.

Icons Used in This Book

The icons in this book are more than just attractive — they're also important visual cues for stuff that you don't want to miss.

My unique Mark's Maxims represent big-time-important stuff, so I call your attention to these nuggets in bold, like this:

Something *Really* Important Is Being Said that will likely affect your person in the near future.

Pay attention, commit these maxims to memory, and you'll avoid the pitfalls that the rest of us have hit on the way.

The Tip icons flag short snippets of information that will save you time or trouble (and, in some cases, even cash).

This icon highlights optional technical information. If you also used to disassemble alarm clocks for fun when you were six years old, you'll love this stuff.

Always read the information next to this icon first! Something looms ahead that could put your hardware or software at risk.

Look to the Remember icons for those tidbits that you need to file away in your mind. Just remember to remember.

Beyond the Book

I've written extra content that you won't find in this book. Go online to find the following:

✦ **Online articles covering additional topics at**

www.dummies.com/extras/osxmavericksaio

These "Web Extras" show you how to record audio, video, and screen activity in QuickTime Player, how to manipulate images in Pages, how to search for an Internet service provider, how to remotely control your Mac using VNC, and even how to display a virtual keyboard on your Mac's screen.

✦ **The Cheat Sheet for this book is at**

www.dummies.com/cheatsheet/osxmavericksaio

Here you'll find a listing of common Mavericks keyboard shortcuts, a schedule to help you keep track of OS X maintenance, and an explanation of the special symbols on your Mac keyboard.

✦ **Updates to this book, if there are any, can be found at**

www.dummies.com/go/osxmavericksaio

Where to Go from Here

The material in this book is divided into eight minibooks, each of which covers an entire area of OS X knowledge. For example, you'll find minibooks on networking, the Apple Digital Hub suite of applications known as iLife, Apple's iWork office productivity suite, customizing your Desktop, and Internet-related applications. Each self-contained chapter discusses a specific feature, application, connection, or cool thing about OS X.

You could read this book in a linear fashion, straight through from cover to cover — probably not in one session, mind you. (Then again, Diet Coke is cheap, so it *is* possible.) However, feel free to begin reading anywhere or to skip chapters at will. For example, if you're already using an Internet connection, you won't need the chapter on adding an Internet connection. However, I recommend that you read this book from the front to the back, as you do any good mystery novel. (Spoiler alert: For those who want to know right now, Microsoft did it.)

Book I
Getting Started with OS X

 Visit www.dummies.com for great Dummies content online.

Contents at a Glance

Chapter 1: Shaking Hands with OS X

In This Chapter

- ✔ Understanding the advantages of OS X
- ✔ Checking your system requirements
- ✔ Upgrading from earlier versions of Mac OS
- ✔ Installing OS X
- ✔ Running OS X for the first time

*I*t's human nature to require instant gratification from your software. I've seen it countless times: Someone runs a program, immediately feels comfortable with it, and then spends the rest of his days using that program religiously. Or another person plays with the same program for 120 seconds and dismisses it as too difficult or too confusing. It's rather like watching a fashion show runway in Rome or Paris: There had better be eye appeal pretty quickly, or the bucks won't flow.

Ditto for modern computer operating systems. An *operating system* (OS) is the basic software that determines the look and feel of your entire computer and usually extends to the programs that you run as well. Microsoft felt the pinch of an old-fashioned OS when Windows 98 and Windows Me (Millennium Edition) were starting to appear rather plain. Then came Windows XP, where menus fade in and out like fireflies on a summer night, puppies help you find files, and other animation abounds. With Windows Vista 7, and now 8, Microsoft is attempting to match some of the elegance and power of OS X Mavericks (and its predecessor, OS X Mountain Lion) in the PC world.

Sure, OS X looks doggone good. Forget the minimum requirement of shirt and shoes because this OS is wearing an Armani suit. What's really exciting for Macintosh owners around the world, however, is the heart that beats *beneath* the pretty form. At its introduction, OS X was an OS revolution, and it still delivers some of the most advanced features available on a personal computer while remaining easy to use. (And yes, I do own, use, and enjoy both PCs and Macs — in the end, what's important to me is which computer does the best job the fastest and easiest.)

Now, I'm not going to just haul off and proclaim that OS X can run rings around — well, you know, the *W* word — without solid proof. In this chapter, I introduce you to the advantages of OS X and why it's such a step ahead for those running Windows. I also cover the hardware requirements for running OS X version 10.9 (Mavericks) as well as guidelines on switching from Windows. Finally, I familiarize you with the steps you encounter the first time you fire up the Big X.

Convince Me: Why OS X?

Apple was one of the first to pioneer the graphical approach to personal computing with the first Macintosh, so you'd expect OS X to be simple to use — and indeed it is. For many folks, that's Job One. If you're one of those people, you can happily skip this section without need of further evidence because OS X is undoubtedly the easiest OS on the planet to use. (And believe me, I'm *not* knocking simplicity. Computers are supposed to be getting easier to use, and technonerds like me are supposed to be rendered unnecessary as computers advance.) Here is the mantra of the Mac — and the first of Mark's Maxims for this volume:

> Make it *easy.*

Still with me? Need more testimony? Or perhaps you're just curious about the engine under the hood. Then read on — and if you're a Macintosh owner, feel free to gloat! (If you're a PC owner, there's always eBay.)

Pretty to behold

They say a picture is worth a thousand words, so let me illustrate just how good OS X looks by showing you a screenshot. Figure 1-1 offers you a view of the latest version of the Big X, hard at work. As you can see, everything's streamlined in appearance, with maximum efficiency in mind. Tasteful 3-D abounds, from the drop-shadowed windows to the liquid-look toolbars. Icons look like miniature works of art. Macintosh owners appreciate outstanding design and recognize the value of a great computer, even if it's lime green, or the size of a ham sandwich, or looks like a silver picture frame. After all, many Mac owners are professionals in the graphic arts, and Apple provides the hardware they need — like the top-of-the-line display used with the 27" flat-panel Intel iMac or the killer performance of the latest Mac Pro with 12-core processing power.

Take a look at what's going on behind the curtain — the Great Oz is actually pretty busy back there.

Figure 1-1:
Eye-
catching?
You bet! OS
X Mavericks
is a
knockout.

The allure of Aqua

The Apple software developers who introduced us to OS X designed the
liquid look from the ground up. They call it *Aqua,* and it's the standard user
interface in Mavericks.

Whoops, I just realized that I slipped a ten-cent example of technobabble
into the preceding paragraph. Let me explain: A *user interface* (UI) design
determines how things look throughout both the OS itself and all applications written to run under it. The design includes the buttons you click, the
controls you click or move, and the appearance of the windows and menus.
For example, if you've already begun to use OS X, you've probably stopped
right in the middle of a task and exclaimed to yourself, "Why, Self, look at the
cool 3-D contour effect on the menu bar!" That shapely contour is a tiny part
of the Aqua user interface design.

Aqua also extends to the placement of controls and how they're shown to
you. For example:

✦ OS X uses Aqua *sheets* (which are like dialogs, but are attached to their
   parent windows) to prompt you for input, such as confirming when
   you're about to close a document without saving it. A dialog, on the
   other hand, can be moved around like a window, but it requires that
   you take an action before you can continue. I prefer sheets to dialogs
   because multiple programs can have multiple sheets open, so you can
   continue to work in other applications without being rudely forced to
   answer the query immediately. Like other things OS X, sheets just make
   more sense, and they're easier to use!

✦ OS X file selection controls, such as the one in Figure 1-2, make it much easier to navigate quickly to a specific file or folder from in an application.

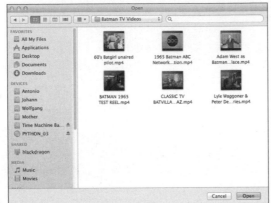

Figure 1-2: A typical file selection dialog (done right in Mavericks).

✦ The *Dock* is another Aqua favorite. The Dock launches your favorite applications, indicates what's running on your Mac, and allows you to switch between those programs — and all in a strip that you can relocate and customize at will. I talk about the Dock in greater detail in Book II, Chapter 2.

Consider Aqua as the *look and feel* of OS X and virtually all applications that it runs; you discover how to use these Aqua controls in the pages to come. Of course, Mac owners really don't have to worry about Aqua itself; the Aqua guidelines are a road map for those software developers writing applications for OS X. Programs written to the common Aqua interface standard will be easier for you to use, and you'll become a proficient power user of that program much faster because you're already familiar with Aqua controls.

The quality of Quartz

The second ingredient in the visual feast that is OS X is *Quartz Extreme.* Again, I must ask your forgiveness, good reader, because I have to get a tad technical again. Quartz Extreme is a *graphics engine:* the portion of OS X that draws what you see onscreen (in the Aqua interface, natch). Think of the engine in your car, which is responsible for making your car move. Whether your Mac is running Microsoft Word or simply idling at the Desktop waiting for you to finish your soda, Quartz Extreme is at work displaying icons, drawing shapes, exhibiting the windows you open, and animating things on the Dock.

What sets Quartz Extreme apart from the ho-hum graphics engine that Windows uses? It's all about international programming standards — you know, those things that Microsoft would much rather you forget. To wit:

✦ **PDF:** The Quartz Extreme engine is built around the Acrobat Portable Document Format (PDF) developed by Adobe. If you've spent any time at all on the Internet in the past 20 or so years, you know that PDF files have emerged as the standard for displaying and printing the highest-quality electronic documents. Plus, Adobe has released a version of the free Acrobat Reader (www.adobe.com) for just about every computer on this green Earth. As a result, text and graphics displayed in Quartz Extreme are razor sharp, resizable, and easily portable from one computer to another. OS X displays PDF files without even requiring Acrobat, using the built-in Preview application and Quick Look. Figure 1-3 shows a complex PDF document that I opened in OS X.

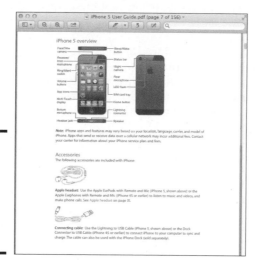

Figure 1-3: Yep, that's a PDF document, not a scanned image!

✦ **OpenGL:** Gamers will get really excited about the fact that Quartz Extreme also uses the OpenGL graphics acceleration standard, which delivers the fastest 3-D graphics on the planet. (Think photo-realistic, high-resolution graphics drawn in the blink of an eye.) This trick is a really cool — OpenGL is even used to produce the Desktop in OS X Mavericks.

In plain English? Today's top-of-the-line, 3-D gaming and 3-D graphics acceleration can take care of drawing *everything* — forget about waiting for windows to close or menus to appear even when you're creating the world's biggest honking spreadsheet or building a presentation the size of Baltimore. As the chairman of the board would've said, "We're talkin' fast, baby, like a rocket ship to the moon!"

✦ **Core Animation:** Mavericks includes functionality that Apple calls *Core Animation,* which makes it much easier for programmers to animate backgrounds and objects in their programs. Text, 3-D animation, and video now work seamlessly side by side, and eye-catching animations in applications, such as Time Machine, are the norm for Mac owners.

Stable, stable, stable

"So it's elegant in design. That's great, Mark, but what if OS X crashes? Aqua and Quartz Extreme aren't worth a plug nickel if my cursor doesn't move and I lose my document!" Believe me, I couldn't agree more; I make my living from computers, and every time a misbehaving program locks up one of my machines, I throw a tantrum that would make Godzilla back off. Lockups shouldn't be tolerated in this day and age.

Luckily, the folks who designed OS X were just as interested in producing a rock-solid OS as they were in designing an attractive look. (Think of Tom Cruise's face on The Rock's body.)

OS X is as hard to crash as the legendary Unix OS — that's right, the same reliable workhorse that technowizards around the world use to power the Internet, where stability is all-important. OS X is built on top of a Unix base that's well hidden, allowing you and me to focus on our programs and click with a mouse without knowing any of those obscure, arcane keyboard commands. You get the benefits of Unix without a pair of suspenders and a pocket protector, or the hassle of growing a beard. (Not to mention many, *many* years of computer programming experience.)

Apple has gone yet another step further in safeguarding your data in case of a power failure or misbehaving program: the *Auto Save* feature automatically saves all the changes you make to your document in the background while you work! You can revert to the document as it was when you last opened it whenever you need to. (I know one technology author who is downright thankful for Auto Save.)

Apple calls the Unix foundation at the heart of OS X by another nifty title: *Darwin.* I could tell you that Darwin provides the latest in 64-bit memory support and CPU management, but if you're a normal human being, your eyes would glaze over. Suffice it to say that Darwin makes the best use of your computer's memory (RAM) and your computer's brain (CPU) — Mavericks has been fine-tuned for processors with multiple cores, such as the Core i5, Core i7, and Xeon CPUs from Intel. Rest assured that your web server will stay up even if your misbehaving Virtual Birdcalling simulation decides to run amok. (Emus running amok — how dreadful.)

Don't forget QuickTime X!

If you've recorded or edited digital video (DV), you're probably already familiar with Apple's QuickTime MOV format. QuickTime movies are typically high resolution, relatively small, and easily created with iMovie, which I discuss in Book III, Chapter 4. Although QuickTime X isn't "on stage" all the time, as is Aqua or Quartz Extreme, it's still an important part of OS X: Every time you display a video clip that you've recorded or watch a streaming TV broadcast from a website, you use QuickTime X. (Note, however, that you don't use QuickTime X to watch DVD movies — that job is reserved for

Apple DVD Player.) QuickTime X includes support for AVC (Advanced Video Coding) for the best possible display of the latest HD (high definition) video signals from the expensive hardware now appearing at your local electronics Maze o' Wires chain store.

QuickTime has been around since the early 1990s, but the latest versions of OS X include QuickTime Player, which provides support for the latest broadcast and web video. You can set up your own TV station on the web with the tools included in the QuickTime Pro package.

Yes, yet another standard is at work here — uh-oh, Overlord Gates is truly angry now! Those who *do* have a beard and are curious about such things will want to know that Darwin uses a FreeBSD kernel, so it also inherits all the protocol standards that have made Unix the foundation of today's Internet. You can find more about FreeBSD at `www.freebsd.org`. Because much of the foundation code that underlies OS X is developed as an open source project, software engineers outside Apple can contribute ideas and code, just as Unix continues to evolve over time. (And yes, you'll even discover how to access the powerful Unix command prompt from OS X in Book VIII, Chapter 2!)

To get an idea of just how well armored OS X is, consider Figure 1-4. One program, which I call Titanic 1.0, has locked up like San Quentin. Under Mac OS 9 and older versions of Windows, your only chance at recovering anything would involve divine intervention. In OS X, however, my Pages application is unaffected because it plays in a protected area of system memory. (I show you how to force a misbehaving application to go away in Chapter 3 of this minibook.)

By the way, Darwin makes it easy for Unix software developers to quickly and easily port (or modify) all sorts of Unix applications to work under OS X. I think you'll agree that a wider selection of applications is a good thing.

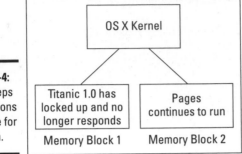

Figure 1-4:
OS X keeps applications separate for a reason.

Multitasking and multithreading for normal human beings

And now, for your entertainment, a short one-act play. (Yes, really. You'd be amazed at how popular this stage production has become among my readers.)

A Shakespearean Moment of Multitasking and Multithreading

Our play opens with Julius Caesar shaking his head in disgust at his Mac OS 9 Desktop.

Caesar: Anon, I am only one mortal, yet my Desktop doth abound with portals to applications of all different miens. Tell me, foul beast, why thy spirit seems slow and sluggish, and my Excel spreadsheet doth crawl on its belly!

[Enter Romeo, a cocky and rather brash young Apple software developer.]

Romeo: Dude, the problem is, like, your operating system. Y'see, older versions of both Mac OS and Windows ended up constantly, like, shifting your computer's attention from one app to another — Excel has to cooperate with everything else that's running in the background, like a good little corporate boy. It's less efficient and very, very '90s. Install OS X, and you get *preemptive multitasking* — the app you're using, like, gets the lion's share of the processing time, and everything runs smoother when you need it. That's the way Unix works.

Caesar: Verily, your strange tongue doth annoy me. Guards, behead him — then obtain for me this OS X.

Romeo: I'm outta here — I've got a hot surfing date — but don't forget, like, OS X also uses *multithreaded processing,* so your Mac can handle different operating system tasks at the same time. It's kind of like your computer can both walk and chew gum at the same time: fast, fast, fast!

[Exit Romeo — rather swiftly — stage right.]

Fin

When the play closes, we can only hope that Romeo is fast as well. (I told you it was a short play.)

The definition of Internet savvy

Remember the classic iMac advertisements that touted the one-plug approach to the Internet? That entire campaign was centered on one idea: The Internet was *supposed* to be easy to use. The folks at Microsoft sat up and took notice when the iMac proved so incredibly successful and (starting with Windows Vista) reduced some of the overwhelming folderol that you had to encounter just to connect to the Internet — but OS X still wipes the floor with Windows 8 when it comes to easy and complete Internet connectivity. For example:

+ **Easy configuration:** OS X sets up your entire Internet connection with a simple assistant. As long as you have the right information handy, which your Internet service provider (ISP) should supply, configuration is a snap.

+ **iCloud:** Apple's iCloud service provides you with a chunk of Internet-accessible space where you can automatically share documents, photos, and music with your other Apple devices and computers — from anywhere on Earth with an Internet connection! Absolutely, unbelievably, massively cool. I cover iCloud in detail in Book V, Chapter 4.

+ **All the Internet behind-the-scenes stuff:** The Internet is basically built on a number of *protocols* (read that as *rules for exchanging all sorts of data*) — and, as I mention earlier, Unix machines dominate the Internet. Ergo, OS X on your Macintosh also provides you with support for just about every Internet protocol on the planet. Even if you don't know these protocols by name or write your own software, the applications that you buy can use them.

+ **A gaggle of great Internet applications:** OS X ships with all sorts of Internet magic built in. For example, you'll get instant Internet and local network communication with Messages and the FaceTime video chat application (both of which I cover in Book V, Chapter 3), Safari (covered in Book V, Chapter 5), and Apple Mail, a standard-issue, battle-ready e-mail program (which I discuss in Book V, Chapter 2). Yup, it's all free.

Lots of free goodies

You don't just get Internet applications when you latch your fingers onto OS X — you can start doing all sorts of neat stuff without investing one extra dollar in more software!

What you receive along with OS X depends on whether you're upgrading from an older version of Mac OS or receiving the Big X already installed on a new Macintosh. With that in mind, check out these two "suite" possibilities (pun definitely intended):

✦ **This is the iLife:** This suite of easy-to-use integrated programs is included with a new Mac, and it's practically as well known as the computer itself these days: iPhoto, iTunes, GarageBand, and iMovie. Each of these stellar programs is covered in Book III. If you have a digital camera, an MP3 player, a USB musical keyboard, or a DV camcorder, you'll be a happy individual. I promise.

✦ **iWork to the rescue:** If you bought a new Macintosh with OS X preinstalled, you may have received a test-drive version of *iWork* (Apple's answer to Microsoft Office). Good stuff, indeed. If you don't want to spend the bucks on Office 2011, and you don't need the complex gewgaws and baroque architecture of Word, Excel, and PowerPoint, I can guarantee you that Pages, Numbers, and Keynote are powerful enough to satisfy your document and presentation yearnings.

What Do I Really Need to Run the Big X?

I've written well over a dozen other *For Dummies* books — I know, it's getting to be a habit (and a career) — and I always find the "Hardware Requirements" section a hard one to write. Why? Well, I know what Apple claims as the minimum hardware requirements necessary to run OS X. But I also know what *I* would consider the minimum hardware requirements, and they're substantially different. Oh, well, let me list the bare bones, and then I'll give you my take on what you really need. (Naturally, if OS X Mavericks is preinstalled on your computer, feel free to tear out this page and create a handful of celebratory confetti.)

From *The World According to Apple,* the minimum requirements are as follows:

✦ **Hardware:** You'll need any Mac with a 64-bit Intel Core 2 Duo, i3, i5, i7, or Xeon processor. This means that just about any recent desktop or laptop Mac is *technically* eligible to play (although you might find the performance of a Core 2 Duo Mac running Mavericks to be unacceptable). Note that no DVD drive is required for installation — you'll download your Mavericks upgrade directly from the Apple App Store! However, your Mac must already be running OS X Mountain Lion (10.8).

✦ **RAM:** You'll need at least 2GB of memory (RAM). At today's low prices, that purchase is like buying a pizza.

✦ **Hard drive territory:** Although svelte by Windows standards, OS X still needs about 8GB of free space on your hard drive.

From *The World According to Chambers,* the minimum requirements are as follows:

+ **Hardware:** I recommend a Mac with at least an Intel i3 processor. Remember, this is *my* opinion on what you'll need to really take advantage of OS X Mavericks, and again, I have to say that I don't think it performs well enough on Intel Core 2 Duo computers.

+ **RAM:** Don't settle for anything less than 4GB. Again, with memory as cheap as it is these days, this purchase is like adding extra cheese to that pizza.

Time for a Mark's Maxim:

Any technonerd worth the title will tell you that the *single most important key* to performance in today's operating systems is RAM — yep, it's more effective than a faster processor!

If you find some extra spending cash between your sofa cushions, spend it on RAM (up to an Earth-shaking 64GB of RAM on the latest Mac Pro racehorses).

+ **Hard drive territory:** I recommend having

  • 20GB free for just the OS

  • A minimum of an additional 60–100GB for any applications, digital video clips, photographs, and songs you'll be collecting

Upgrading from Earlier Versions of Mac OS

Because you install OS X Mavericks through the Apple App Store, everything about the upgrade process is practically automatic. The steps that you should take *before* you start the installation are important; I cover those in the next section. Pay heed, or pay later. I won't go into detail about the actual installation because there aren't any details to speak of — you'll answer a question or two and then hop up to get another cup of coffee or another caffeine-laden soda while the installer does the rest. Would anyone expect anything different from Apple?

But before you strike up the band, read the following sections to protect yourself against some common pitfalls.

Back up! — Please, back up!

I know you're anxious to join the In crowd, and Apple makes the upgrade process as noninvasive and as safe as possible, but snafus such as power loss and hard drive failures do happen. With a full backup of your system to an external hard drive (using Time Machine), you can rest assured that you'll get your precious files and folders back in pristine shape if tragedy strikes. You need to back up your system on a regular basis, anyway. Promise me *now* that you'll back up your system, won't you?

Snuff out disk errors

Before you upgrade, I recommend that you check that hard drive for errors one last time because upgrading a disk with directory errors takes longer. To give your drive a clean bill of health, use *Disk Utility,* which I cover in Chapter 9 of this minibook. Ain't technology grand?

Plug it, road warrior

You're on the road with your MacBook Pro, and you're thinking of buying your brand-spanking-new Mavericks OS upgrade — Stop! NOW.

Before you decide to upgrade your Mac notebook, consider what will happen if that magical vessel containing all your files should flicker and. . . . No, on second thought, don't even *visualize* it. (Even if the battery is fully charged.) If you're installing an OS X upgrade on a MacBook, MacBook Air, or MacBook Pro, make sure that it's plugged in and receiving its share of good, clean AC power from a handy, nearby wall socket. The installation process could take an hour, and you can expect constant hard drive activity — think "Attack of the Energy-Draining Installation from Planet Lithium." You *don't* want to try this while your notebook is operating on battery power.

Heck, a technopurist would probably recommend that you attach your Macintosh to an uninterruptible power supply (UPS) for the installation process, but I'm not quite *that* paranoid about power outages.

Keep one thing in mind while installing OS X: If you format the *destination drive* (the drive where you'll install OS X), you'll lose everything that it stored. No big surprise — and the installation program will warn you profusely beforehand. There's no reason to format the destination drive unless you just crave a *clean* installation (an installation of a new OS on a newly formatted drive, compared with an upgrade of your existing OS X System files). Oh, and if you do decide to format the drive, don't forget to use Mac OS Extended (Journaled) format when prompted by the OS X install application.

What's that, you say? You'd like a comprehensive guide to your classy new Apple MacBook Air or MacBook Pro laptop? Look no farther than the fourth edition of my bestselling *MacBook For Dummies,* published in both print and electronic format by the good folks at Wiley. With a copy in hand, any road warrior will find the answers to those Persistent Laptop Questions!

Personalizing the Big X

After the installation is complete and you've rebooted the beast, stand back and watch those beautiful rounded edges, brushed stainless-steel surfaces, and liquid colors appear. But wait — you're not quite done! You need to personalize OS X, just like your toothbrush or your SUV's six-way power seat. And to the rescue is Setup Assistant, which automatically appears the first time you boot OS X Mavericks.

These assistant screens change periodically — and they're completely self-explanatory — so I won't march you through each one step by step. However, here are a few tips for a bit of additional over-the-shoulder help while you're setting things up:

✦ **Set the language.** OS X defaults to U.S. formats and keyboard layouts. OS X does indeed provide full support for other languages and keyboard configurations, though. To display these options, click the Show All button at the bottom of the assistant screen.

✦ **Accounts are important.** When OS X asks you to create your account, don't forget to set your password. Your Mac password, by the way, is case sensitive, so *THIS* is different from *this* or *ThiS*. I recommend entering a password hint; just don't make that hint too easy to guess. For example, *My first dog's name* is probably preferable to *Plays Seinfeld on TV.* OS X uses the name and password that you enter to create your account, which you use to log in if you set up a multiuser system for several people (more on this in Book II, Chapter 4).

Never write down your passwords. Such crib sheets work just as well for others as for you.

✦ **I need to fix that.** You can click the Back button at any time to return to previous assistant screens. OS X, bright child that it is, automatically saves your choices, so when you click Continue to return, everything is as you left it.

✦ **Opt for extra stuff.** Whether or not you accept the news, offers, and related-product information from Apple is your decision. However, you can find this same information on the Apple website, so there's no need to engorge your e-mail Inbox unless you so desire. (In other words, I turned off this option.)

✦ **Set local area network (LAN) connections.** If you're connecting your Mac to a Transmission Control Protocol/Internet Protocol (TCP/IP) network (or you're using an Internet router that uses Dynamic Host Configuration Protocol [DHCP]), I recommend clicking Yes when you're asked whether you should use the configuration supplied by the existing server.

DHCP automatically provides the computers on the network with all the settings that they need to connect. If that sounds like ancient Sumerian, find out more in Book VI, Chapter 1.

✦ **Create your iCloud account.** Apple's iCloud service just plain rocks — especially the syncing between your Mac and your iOS devices. Again, more on this in Book V, Chapter 4, but take my word for it: Join up, trooper, and create your Apple ID during setup. The standard iCloud service is free, and upgrading to additional space is a breeze if you decide you like the service benefits.

✦ **Have your Mail settings handy.** If you set up your iCloud account, you can set up your @icloud.com address without any bother — again, this feature is a good thing. Mavericks will also try to configure your existing accounts automatically. However, if you're setting up an existing account, make sure you have all those silly settings and numbers and names that your ISP supplied you with when you signed up. (Just in case.) This stuff includes your e-mail address, mail server variety, user account ID, password, and outgoing mail server.

Chapter 2: Navigating and Running Programs

In This Chapter

✔ Restarting, sleeping, and shutting down OS X

✔ Using windows

✔ Using menus

✔ Recognizing and selecting icons

✔ Using the keyboard

✔ Running applications

✔ Switching between programs

✔ Opening, saving, and quitting an application

As the folks in Cupertino will tell you, "It's all about the graphics." And they're right, of course. OS X is a highly visual operating system, and using it without a mouse, trackball, or trackpad is like building Hoover Dam with a pocketknife. (And not a particularly sharp pocketknife, either.) Therefore, most of this chapter requires you to firmly grasp the little rodent, roll the ball, or finesse a trackpad. I introduce you to little graphical bits such as icons and menus, and you discover how to open windows that can display anything from the contents of a document to the contents of your hard drive.

On the other hand, any true Macintosh power user will tell you that the keyboard is still a useful piece of hardware. Because I want you to be a bona fide, well-rounded OS X power user, I also demonstrate the key combinations that can save you time, effort, and possible tennis elbow from all that mouse-wrangling.

Finally, I lead you through the basic training that you need to run your programs: how to start them, how to open and save documents, and how to quit an application as gracefully as Fred Astaire on his best day.

Restarting, Sleeping, and Shutting Down

First things first. As the guy on the rocket sled probably yelled, "This is neat, but how do you stop it?" Call 'em The Big Four — Sleep, Restart, Shut Down, and Log Out are the OS X commands that you use when you need to take care of business away from your computer. All four appear on the friendly Apple menu (⌘) at the top-left corner of your Desktop (as shown in friendly Figure 2-1).

Each option produces a different reaction from your Mac:

✦ **Sleep:** You don't need a glass of water or a bedtime story when you put OS X to *Sleep,* which is a power-saving mode that allows you to quickly return to your work later. (Waking your computer up from Sleep mode is much faster than booting or restarting it, and Sleep mode can conserve battery power on laptops.) Depending on the settings that you choose in System Preferences — which I discuss in Book II, Chapter 3 — your Mac can power-down the monitor and spin-down the hard drives to save wear and tear on your hardware. You can set OS X to automatically enter Sleep mode after a certain amount of mouse and keyboard inactivity.

To awaken your slumbering supercomputer, just click the mouse or press any key on the keyboard. MacBook owners can put their laptops to sleep by simply closing the computer; they can wake the beast by opening it back up again.

Figure 2-1:
Choose your path from the Apple menu.

The Power Nap feature in Mavericks allows your Mac to take care of business, even while it's in Sleep mode, because system updates are downloaded, iCloud data and documents are synchronized, and Time Machine continues to back up your hard drive.

✦ **Restart:** Use Restart if your Mac has suddenly decided to work "outside the box" and begins acting strangely — for instance, if your Universal Serial Bus (USB) ports suddenly lock up, or your Thunderbolt external hard drive no longer responds. First save any work that's open (unless your computer has locked up altogether). You also elect to restart OS X when you switch startup volumes or switch your Mac to a Windows partition using Boot Camp. (*Hint:* Some applications and Apple software updates require a restart after you install them.)

✦ **Shut Down:** When you're ready to return to the humdrum real world and you're done with your Mac for the time being, use the Shut Down option. Many Mac applications automatically prompt you to save any changes that you've made to open documents before the computer turns itself off. You can shut down OS X from the login screen as well.

Besides the Apple menu (🍎) command, MacBook laptops have a Power key on the keyboard that you can press to display a dialog with Sleep, Restart, and Shut Down buttons. If you change your mind and decide to tie up loose ends before you leave, click the Cancel button to return to OS X.

The Resume feature comes into play when you log out, restart, or shut down your Mac. Select the Reopen Windows When Logging Back In check box (as shown in Figure 2-2), and Mavericks automatically restores the state of your Desktop the next time you turn on your Mac, including all your open windows and selections! Resume also works with individual applications. For example, when you quit Preview, Mavericks saves the current state of that application's workspace. When you launch Preview again, it displays the windows you were viewing, documents and all. (Note that an application has to be written specifically for OS X Lion or later to support Resume.)

Figure 2-2:
Mavericks
can reopen
your
windows
for you.

We're not finished just yet

Don't forget the Log Out command (which you can find under the Apple menu, 🍎) and the Fast User Switching menu (at the right side of the Finder menu).

✔ Choose Log Out when you're running your Mac with multiple users and you want to completely pass control over to another person. All your programs will quit, and the other person can take over by logging in with his or her account. OS X then reconfigures with the other user's preferences.

✔ If you've enabled Fast User Switching, another user can log in from the Fast User

Switching menu. However, your applications don't quit, you don't have to formally log out, and you can take control back when the other user is finished. (Hence the words *Fast* and *Switching* in the name.) To turn on this feature, log in with an administrator account, display the Users & Groups pane in System Preferences, click Login Options, and then select the Show Fast User Switching Menu As check box. (More on Fast User Switching appears in Book II, Chapter 4.)

You can also hold down the Control key and press the Drive Eject key (which you use to load and eject discs) to display the same options.

A Window Is Much More Than a Frame: Navigating Windows

"And in the beginning, there was the window." Like with older Mac OSes, most of what you'll do in OS X occurs within these fancy frames. And, as you might imagine, a number of controls are at your disposal, which you can use to control the size, shape, and appearance of these potent portals. In this section, I — well, to be blunt, I do windows. (No squeegee jokes, if you please.)

Opening and closing windows

Windows are generally opened automatically by an application when you first run it, or it needs to display a document, or by OS X itself, such as when Finder opens a window to display the contents of your hard drive. *Finder*, by the way, is the application that OS X runs to display the OS X menus and windows.

Some programs even let you open new windows on the fly; for example, Figure 2-3 shows a window in its purest form: a new Finder window. To display this window on your own Mac, choose File⇨New Finder Window or press ⌘+N. From here, you can reach your files on your Mac or even venture to the Internet.

The Command (⌘) key usually has both an Apple (🍎) and a rather strange-looking symbol on it that I often call the Spirograph. (I'm told others have called it rather Celtic, but it's actually a Scandinavian character.)

When you're finished with a document or you no longer need a window open, close it to free that space on your Desktop. To close a window in OS X, move your cursor over the Close button; it's the red circular button at the top-left corner of the window (refer to Figure 2-3). An X appears on the button when you're in the zone. When the X appears, just click.

If you've been living the life of a hermit for the last two decades or so, pressing the left mouse button is called *clicking the mouse.* In the modern Apple universe, a Magic Mouse has no visible buttons, and neither do current MacBook trackpads (and the Magic Trackpad)! (You tap the top of the mouse or the trackpad surface with one finger to click.)

Close

Figure 2-3: You're ready to navigate with this Finder window.

If your Mac is equipped with a Magic Trackpad, **never use any object other than your finger on the trackpad!** That means no pencils (no, not even the eraser end), pens, or chopsticks; they can damage your trackpad in no time at all. And no, that doesn't bode well for ladies with long fingernails.

Most Mac applications don't want you closing a window willy-nilly if you've changed the contents without saving them. For example, try to close a document window in Word without saving the file first. The program asks you for confirmation before it closes the window containing your Great American Novel. Most programs also have a Close command on their File menu. (Here's another indicator: Most programs display a black dot in the center of the program's Close button to indicate that there are unsaved changes.)

To close all windows displayed by a particular program, hold down the Option key while you click the Close button on one of the windows. Whoosh! They're all gone.

Scrolling windows

Often, more stuff is in a document or more files are on your hard drive than you can see in the space available for a window. Guess that means it's time to delete stuff. No, no, *just joking!* You don't have to take such drastic measures to see more in a window.

Just use the scroll bars that you see in Figure 2-4 to move through the contents of the window. By default, scroll bars don't appear until you move your pointer close to them. You click the *scroll box* and drag it. For the uninitiated, that means clicking the darker portion of the bar and holding down the mouse button while you move the mouse in the desired direction. Alternatively, you can click in the empty area above or below the scroll box to scroll pages one at a time.

Depending on the type of application that you're using, you might be able to scroll a window with your arrow keys as well — or perhaps use the Page Up and Page Down keys to move through a window.

Minimizing and restoring windows

The multitalented Figure 2-4 also displays another control that you can use with a window: the Minimize button. When you *minimize* a window, you eliminate it from your Desktop and store it safely on the *Dock* — that strip of icons that appears along the bottom (or the side) of your OS X Desktop. A minimized window appears as a miniature icon on the Dock by default, so you can keep an eye on it (so to speak). Figure 2-5 illustrates a minimized window from Safari, which is displaying my website at www.mlcbooks.com. To minimize a window, move your mouse pointer over the yellow Minimize button at the top-left corner of the window — a minus sign appears on the button — and then click.

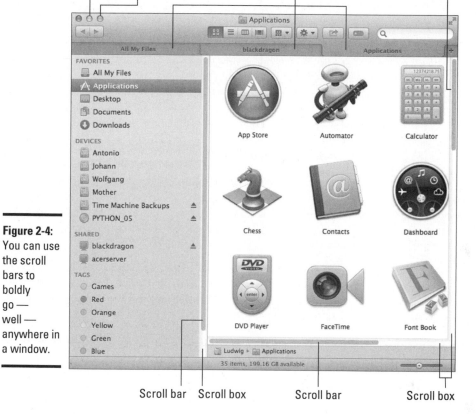

Figure 2-4:
You can use the scroll bars to boldly go — well — anywhere in a window.

Figure 2-5:
A minimized web page on the Dock.

You're gonna love this "Easter egg" hidden in OS X. If you hold down the Shift key whilst you minimize, the window shrinks in *cool* slow motion. (Who says operating systems have to be totally serious, anyway?)

When you're ready to display the window again on your Desktop — *restoring* the window — simply click the thumbnail icon representing the window on the Dock, and OS X automagically returns it to its former size and location.

By the way, some — note that I said *some* — applications continue to run when minimized, whereas others simply stop or pause until you return them to the Desktop. Such is the crazy world we live in.

Doing the full-screen dance

Mavericks provides system-wide support for *full-screen* operation — that's where a single application fills the entire screen, without displaying a window frame or traditional Finder menu bar.

The method you use to switch to full-screen mode varies depending on the application, so there's no One Menu Command or One Keyboard Shortcut that will always do the deed. Most of the applications included with OS X Mavericks use View⇨Enter Full Screen, and many applications have a button you can click in the window to switch back and forth. You may also see a button with a double-diagonal arrowhead icon in the upper-right corner of the window. Finder windows can also be switched to full-screen mode in Mavericks, and if you're using multiple monitors they can each be set to a different full-screen app!

So how do you switch between applications if they're all in full-screen mode?

- ✔ Move your cursor to the bottom of the screen to display the Dock, where you can click another application to switch to it.

- ✔ Invoke Mission Control and choose another application from there. (More about Mission Control in this chapter.)

- ✔ If you're working with a MacBook with a trackpad, a Mac with a Magic Trackpad, or a Mac with a Magic Mouse, swipe three fingers to the left or right across the surface of the pointing device.

- ✔ From the keyboard, use the ⌘+Tab shortcut to cycle through the applications you have running.

Zooming windows

Zooming windows has a kind of Flash Gordon sound to it, don't you think? It's nothing quite that exciting — no red tights or laser guns — still, when you're trying to view a larger portion of a document, *zooming* is a good thing because it expands the window to the maximum practical size for the application that you're using (and the content being displayed). In some cases, zooming a window fills almost the entire screen; in others, the extra space would be wasted, so the application zooms the window to the maximum size that shows as much content as possible (without any unnecessary white space). The Zoom button can even be disabled by an application that doesn't want you to muck about with the window; for example, I own some games that don't allow zooming.

To zoom a window, move your mouse pointer over the green Zoom button at the top-left corner of the window. Again, refer to Figure 2-4 (in the preceding section), which struts its stuff and illustrates the position. (Man, that is one versatile figure.) A plus sign appears on the Zoom button. Click to expand your horizons.

After you finish with a zoomed window, return it to its previous dimensions by clicking the Zoom button again.

Those hard-working toolbars

If you're wondering what those tiny icons are at the top of many OS X application windows, I won't leave you in suspense: They're called *toolbar buttons*. A *toolbar* is a strip of icons in a window (usually across the top) that you click to perform common commands, such as changing the display format or printing the current document. (The toolbar in Figure 2-4, for example, features icons to move Back and Forward, among others.) You'll encounter more toolbar technology throughout the book.

Most windows that include a toolbar also include some method of hiding the toolbar (to save screen real estate for your document). For example, you can toggle the display of the toolbar on and off in a Finder window from the View menu, or you can use the convenient ⌘+Option+T key shortcut to toggle the toolbar display on and off.

Moving windows

In contrast to the rather permanent windows in your home, you can cart a window to another portion of the Desktop. Typically, you do this when you're using more than one application and you need to see the contents of multiple windows. To grab a window and make off with it, click the window's *title bar* — the strip at the top of the window that usually bears a document or application name — and drag the window to the new location. Then release the mouse button to plant the window firmly in the new location.

By the way, some applications allow you to arrange multiple windows in a graceful swoop with a single click of a menu. Open the Window menu and choose Arrange All to perform this magic.

I talk about Mission Control and Spaces later, in the section "Switching 'Twixt Programs with Aplomb." Mission Control helps you organize a large number of open windows on your Desktop. You can use it to display all open application windows so that you can pick the one you want, or display all the windows opened by a specific application. Another Mission Control feature — Spaces — allows you to create custom virtual desktops. (Truly *cool*.) Each of your Spaces desktops can contain a different set of application windows that you use for different tasks!

Resizing windows

Next, consider how to change the width or height of your window. To change the dimensions of a window to your exact specifications, move your cursor over any edge of the window and then click and hold down the button to drag until the window is the size that you prefer.

Switching windows

Before I move on to other graphical wonders of OS X, it's important that you master how to switch between windows on your Desktop. First, remember this old Norwegian saying (or is it one of Mark's Maxims?):

Only *one* can be active at one time.

What our Oslo friends are communicating is that only one window can be active at any time. The active window appears on top of other windows, and it's the one that you can edit by typing or by moving your mouse. (It also sports Close, Minimize, and Zoom buttons in color, or it fills the entire screen if you're working in full-screen mode.) Other windows that you have opened might be minimized, as I describe earlier in the section, "Minimizing and restoring windows," or they can be inactive (mere ghosts of themselves) and remain on your Desktop. OS X dims the controls for inactive windows so that you can tell they're hanging around but can't be used at the moment. (Note that both active and inactive windows can contain Finder Tabs, which I discuss in the upcoming sidebar.) Figure 2-6 illustrates a number of open windows, with the iTunes window active.

I know you're going to get tired of hearing me say this, but here I go again: Certain applications, such as iTunes and File Transfer Protocol (FTP) clients, continue to run while their windows are inactive. Some programs, however, stop or pause until you make their window active.

Figure 2-6:
Many are open, but only one is active.

Using Tabs in Finder Windows

With the introduction of Mavericks, OS X now has a powerful new feature you can use to display multiple locations in the same window: *Finder Tabs,* which work just like the tabs in Safari (as well as other popular browsers for both Macs and PCs). To open a new tab in a Finder window, you have a wealth of choices:

- ✔ Click the desired location and press ⌘+T.

- ✔ Right-click the location and choose Open in New Tab.

- ✔ Select the location and click the New Tab button (which bears a plus sign) at the right side of the window.

- ✔ Click the Action icon (which bears a gear icon) in any Finder window toolbar and choose New Tab.

For example, if you're working on an iMovie project, you might create tabs using the Applications item in the Finder window sidebar and a folder (or even a DVD disc or shared drive) named Work that contains your video clips. The location appears as a new tab immediately under the toolbar. You can open as many tabs as you like — to close a tab, hover your cursor over it and click the X button that appears. The hardworking Figure 2-4 illustrates three Finder Tabs at work.

So why all the hullabaloo? Think about switching between multiple locations on your Mac *instantly*, and you start to understand why this crusty old Mac fanatic is so excited! Just click a tab to switch to that location; you can even drag files and folders from tab to tab. You can drag the Finder Tabs themselves to reorder them as you like.

You can also set new folders to open in tabs instead of windows — click the Finder menu at the top of your Desktop and choose Preferences, and then click the Open Folders in Tabs Instead of New Windows check box to enable it.

And how do you switch to — *activate* — a different window in OS X? Again, Mission Control allows you to activate another window, but if the window is currently visible, you can simply click any part of that window. I generally click the window's title bar if it's visible, but any part of the inactive window will do. (You can also right-click the application's icon on the Dock and choose the desired window from the menu.) The window that you click leaps like a proud stallion to the fore, and the previously active window now skulks in the background.

You can still use a window's Close, Minimize, and Zoom buttons even when the window is inactive.

Menu Mysteries Explained

Next, I move on to menu control in OS X. *Menus* are handy drop-down controls that allow you to select commands that are grouped logically. For example, an application's File menu usually allows you to create or open a document, save a document to disk, or print a document. To open a menu, click the desired menu group name on the bar at the top of the screen and then click the desired menu option from the extended menu.

Figure 2-7 illustrates the Safari menu. Submenus are designated by right-arrow icons. When you move your mouse pointer over a submenu command, you get another set of even more specific menu commands. In this case, the Services submenu command displays commands, such as Make New Sticky Note and Look Up in Dictionary.

Some applications allow you to create your own custom menus. Although configuring a new menu system takes some time to figure out, imagine the productivity gains that you'll enjoy! Custom menus are sleeker and easier to navigate. (However, you have to stop short of claiming that you wrote the application. Software developers get downright snippy about it.)

OS X also provides another type of menu: contextual. A *contextual* (or right-click, or shortcut) menu appears when you right-click certain items, revealing commands that relate specifically to those items. (Unfortunately, the items that sport contextual menus vary from application to application, so check the program's documentation before you spend countless hours right-clicking everything onscreen.) The same items in the right-click menu appear when you select an item and then click the Action pop-up menu, which looks like a mechanical gear. You can also hold down the Control key while clicking an item to display the contextual menu (or tap with two fingers, if you're using a trackpad).

Most manufacturers sell mice, trackballs, and other pointing things that include a secondary mouse button. And Button Number 2 is oft-called the "right-click button." Generally, if you have a pointing device with multiple buttons, the device displays contextual menus when you click the secondary button. Then again, you might launch Aunt Harriet into a geosynchronous orbit, so double-check the manual for your pointing thing on the default button assignment (and how to change it, if necessary). Note that you can set the behavior of the right button in the corresponding System Preferences pane (usually Mouse or Trackpad).

Many commands in menus have keyboard shortcuts. Because I hold forth on this subject in the upcoming section, "Keyboard Shortcuts for the True Power User," I hold off describing those shortcuts here.

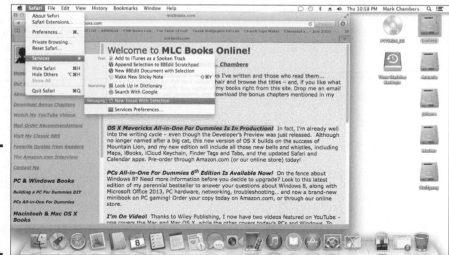

Figure 2-7:
Drilling
deeper into
Safari's
Services
menu.

Icons 'R Us

Icons are more than little pictures. They're, well, . . . I guess they're little pictures. However, these graphical WUDs (that's short for *Wonderful User Devices*) are really representations of the components of your OS X system, and therefore they deserve a section of their own.

For complete details on any icon, click it once to highlight it and then press ⌘+I. This displays an Info dialog like that in Figure 2-8, which tells you what kind of icon it is, where the item it represents is located, and how big it is. You also see a version number for applications — a handy way of quickly checking the version of a program you're running — and when the file was created and last modified. The Info dialog also offers other settings and options that you can display by clicking in the General section. (I cover them in other parts of the book.)

Figure 2-8:
The Info
dialog
provides the
complete
lowdown
on a Mac
application.

Hardware

OS X uses icons to represent the various hardware devices of your computer, including your

+ Hard drive

+ External hard drive

+ DVD drive (if a disc is loaded)

+ iPod

You get the idea. Just double-click a hardware icon to display the folders and files that it contains, as you do with your hard drive and a disc loaded in your DVD drive.

Generally, you'll encounter hardware icons only on your Desktop or in Finder windows, or in a device list or source list in applications such as iTunes and iPhoto. Figure 2-9 illustrates some of the hardware icons that live in my system.

Figure 2-9:
A wealth
of different
hardware
icons.

Programs and applications

Program and application icons are the fancy ones, folks. Most applications have their own custom icons, and double-clicking one will typically whisk you on your way. OS X also includes a generic icon or two for applications that don't include their own custom icon. Figure 2-10 illustrates a number of my favorite program icons from all sorts of OS X applications.

Running a program in OS X can be as simple as double-clicking the application icon — more on this later, in the section "Houston, We're Go to Launch Programs."

Figure 2-10:
Most
Mavericks
applications
are
represented
by custom
icons.

Files

Your hard drive will contain many thousands of individual files, and the Big X tries to make it as easy as possible to visually identify which application owns which file. Therefore, most applications use a special icon to indicate their data files. For example, Figure 2-11 illustrates several documents and data files created by a range of applications. Some cheeky applications even use more than one icon to differentiate among different file types, such as documents and templates in Microsoft Word.

Figure 2-11:
File icons
generally
give you a
visual clue
about their
origin.

A number of generic file icons indicate text files, including RTF (Rich Text Format) documents and PDF (Portable Document Format) documents, which use the Adobe Acrobat format.

You can open most documents and data files by double-clicking them, which automatically launches the proper application and loads the document.

TIP

I also recommend using the Quick Look feature for a lightning-fast peek at the contents of a file. Click the file once in a Finder window to select it; then press the spacebar to view the document — all without opening any applications!

Folders

Folders have a 3-D look in OS X — and, as you can see in Figure 2-12, some applications even customize their folder icon.

Figure 2-12: A selection of different generic and custom folder icons.

Major system folders — including Applications, Library, System, Users, Downloads, and Utilities — sport distinctive folder icons in Mavericks that help identify their contents.

To open a folder in OS X, just double-click the folder. (Alternatively, you can click it once to select it and then press ⌘+O.) Discover more about how to control the look of folder icons in Book II, Chapter 1.

Aliases

Essentially, an *alias* is a link to something else on your system. For example, an Adobe Photoshop alias can run Photoshop just as the program icon can, but the alias takes up only a scant few bytes on your hard drive. (If you're a switcher who's just crossed over from the Windows Wilderness, think *shortcut.*) The alias file yells at OS X: "Hey, the human wants you to run *this* or open *that thing* over there!"

An alias is a strange beast. Although it might look like a standard icon, upon closer examination, you'll notice that an alias icon sports a tiny curved arrow at the base. (In addition, the word *alias* often appears at the end of the icon name.) Figure 2-13 has roped in a variety of aliases for your enjoyment.

Figure 2-13:
An alias is
a pointer
to another
application,
file, or
folder.

Aliases come in handy for a number of reasons:

✦ **They allow you to launch applications and open files and folders from anywhere in your system.** For example, you might want an alias icon in your MP3 folder that runs the DVD-burning application Toast. With an alias icon, you can launch Toast and burn a data DVD without using Launchpad.

✦ **They can be easily deleted when no longer needed without wreaking havoc on the original application, file, or folder.** If you decide that you'd rather use iTunes to burn audio CDs, you can simply delete the Toast alias without trashing Toast itself.

✦ **Their tiny size allows you to add multiple aliases (and mucho convenience) for a single application without gulping down hard drive space.**

You might be wondering, "Why use aliases when I can just copy the actual application, file, or folder to the desired spot?" Well, indeed you can do that. However, the application might not work in its new location because you didn't copy the supporting files that most applications need to run. (An alias runs the original application or opens the original file or folder, so things should work just as if you'd double-clicked the original icon.) Additionally, remember that copying applications willy-nilly throughout your hard drive will eat up territory like a horde of angry Vikings. (Oh, and if the developer releases an update to the application, you'd have to manually track down and individually update all those copies. No, thank you!)

If you dislike the word *alias* hanging off the end of the icon name, feel free to rename it (as I show you in Chapter 3 of this minibook). The alias will continue to function nicely no matter what moniker you give it. (If you create an alias by holding down ⌘+Option whilst dragging the original icon to a new location, the alias name won't include the alias appendage.)

If the original file no longer exists, its alias no longer works, either. However, OS X is sharp enough to automatically "fix" an alias if you rename or move the original file, pointing the alias to the new location (as long as the original file remains on the same volume). *Slick!*

Selecting Icons for Fun and Profit

You'll often find yourself performing different actions on one icon — or a number of icons at one time. For example, you can copy or move files from one location on your hard drive to another or delete a group of files that you no longer need. (The idea of drag-and-drop file management using icons originated on the Mac, but I wait until Chapter 3 of this minibook to describe these operations in detail.) In this section, I focus on the basics of selecting one or more icons to specify the files and folders you want to use for whatever you're going to do next.

Selecting a single icon

First, here are the various ways that you can select a single icon for an impending action:

+ **Place your cursor over the file and click once.** OS X darkens the icon to indicate that it's selected — a mysterious process called *highlighting*.

+ **Type the first few letters of the icon's name.** After you type a letter, OS X highlights the first icon that matches that character.

+ **If an icon in a window is already highlighted, you can move the highlight to the next icon across by pressing the right-arrow key.** Likewise, the other three directional arrow keys move the highlight in the other directions. To move through the icons alphabetically, press Tab to go forward and Shift+Tab to go backward.

Selecting multiple icons

To select a gaggle of icons for an action, use one of these methods:

+ **Contiguous:** If the icons are next to each other, click and drag in a window (and not directly on a specific item) to highlight them all. As you drag, OS X displays a selection box, and any icons you touch with that box are highlighted when you release the button (as shown in Figure 2-14). Think "lasso" and you'll get the picture.

  You can also select multiple adjacent icons by clicking the first item to highlight it and then holding down the Shift key while clicking the last icon in the series that you want to select.

+ **Noncontiguous:** If the icons are *not* next to each other, you can hold down the ⌘ key while you click each item that you want to select.

Just selecting an icon doesn't launch or do anything. You're just marking your territory.

Figure 2-14:
Dragging
a selection
box in OS X.

Keyboard Shortcuts for the True Power User

Virtually all OS X applications have their own *keyboard shortcuts* — a ten-cent term for a key combination that performs the same operation as a menu command or a toolbar button. Although the mouse or trackpad might seem the easier path when controlling your Mac, it's not always the fastest. Those hardy souls who venture to learn common keyboard shortcuts can zip through a spreadsheet or warp through a complex outline at speeds that no mere rodent-wrangler could ever hope to attain.

With that in mind — and with the goal of "pumping you up" into a power user — I hereby present the most common keyboard shortcuts for the Big X in Table 2-1. I've also sprinkled other keyboard shortcuts liberally through the book when I discuss other applications, but these combinations are the classics that appear virtually everywhere.

Table 2-1	Common OS X Keyboard Shortcuts	
Combination Key	**Location**	**Action**
⌘+A	Edit menu	Selects all (works in Finder, too)
⌘+C	Edit menu	Copies the highlighted item to the Clipboard
⌘+H	Application menu	Hides the application
⌘+M	Window menu	Minimizes the active window to the Dock (works in Finder, too)

(continued)

Table 2-1 *(continued)*

Combination Key	Location	Action
⌘+O	File menu	Opens an existing document, file, or folder (works in Finder, too)
⌘+P	File menu	Prints the current document
⌘+Q	Application menu	Exits the application
⌘+T	File menu	Opens a new Finder Tab with the currently selected location
⌘+V	Edit menu	Pastes the contents of the Clipboard at the current cursor position
⌘+X	Edit menu	Cuts the highlighted item to the Clipboard
⌘+Z	Edit menu	Reverses the effect of the last action you took
⌘+?	Help menu	Displays the Help system (works in Finder, too)
⌘+Tab	Finder	Switches between open applications
⌘+`	Finder	Switches between open windows in the current application
⌘+Option+M	Finder	Minimizes all Finder windows to the Dock
⌘+Option+W	Finder	Closes all Finder windows

By the way, I should mention that many keyboard combinations use three keys instead of just two (and a few even use four). When these shortcuts appear in a menu, they look something akin to Egyptian hieroglyphics, but you need hold down only the first two keys simultaneously and press the third key. Common "strange" key symbols that you'll see in both Finder and most applications are shown in Table 2-2.

Table 2-2	**Arcane Key Symbols**
Key	*Symbol*
Control	⌃
Command	⌘
Del	⌫
Option	⌥
Shift	⇧

Houston, We're Go to Launch Programs

The next stop on your introductory tour of OS X is the starting point for your applications. Although Finder is useful, you'll likely want to actually *do* something with your Mac as well.

Starting applications from your hard drive

You can launch an application from your hard drive by

✦ Clicking the Launchpad icon on the Dock (it's the second one by default, just to the right of the Finder icon) to display all your application icons in a full-screen display. If you have more than one screen (or *page*) worth of applications, press the arrow keys to move between Launchpad pages. With a Magic Trackpad or Magic Mouse, swipe two fingers to the left or right. To launch an application, just click the icon. Figure 2-15 illustrates Launchpad in action. (If you're a proud owner of an iPhone, iPad, or iPod touch, you'll be familiar with Launchpad already because it corresponds directly to the *Home screen* on those devices.)

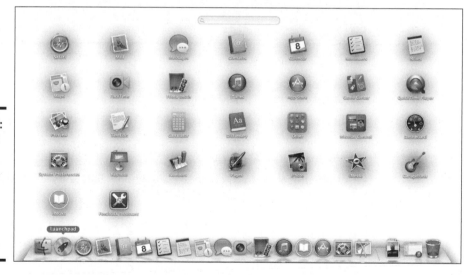

Figure 2-15: Launchpad is my favorite method of launching applications in Mavericks.

✦ Navigating to the corresponding application folder — by either clicking or double-clicking drive and folder icons — and double-clicking the application icon.

✦ Double-clicking a document or data file that's owned by the application. For example, double-clicking an MP3 audio file runs iTunes.

Dig that crazy Launchpad!

You can customize your Launchpad display by dragging icons into the order you prefer. For example, I have all the applications I use the most on the first Launchpad page. Drag an application icon to the right or left side of the screen to move it to another page.

Just like a Finder window, Launchpad also allows you to create folders to help you organize your applications. To create a folder in Launchpad, drag one application icon on top of another, and then add other icons by dragging them to the folder (or remove them by dragging them out of the folder). To run an application in a folder, click the folder icon to display the icons it contains, and then click the desired application.

Oh, and there's no need to stick with the boring folder names assigned by Launchpad! To change a folder name, click the folder to open it and then click the folder name to display a text-editing box. Type the new moniker for the folder and press Return.

If you want to remove an application from Launchpad — **which also deletes the application from your Mac entirely** — click the icon and hold down the button (or continue pressing on the trackpad) until the icon starts to wiggle. (Yes, you read that correctly, I said "wiggle." iPhone and iPad owners know what I mean.) Click the tiny Delete button that appears next to the icon — the one with the X — and the icon disappears. Press Esc to stop all that wiggling. (Note that the applications supplied with Mavericks can't be deleted this way.)

+ Double-clicking an alias that you've created for the application. (Get the skinny on aliases in the earlier section, "Aliases." I'll wait.)

+ Clicking the application's icon on the Dock (more on adding items to the Dock in Book II, Chapter 2).

+ Selecting the application icon and pressing the ⌘+O keyboard shortcut.

+ Adding the application to your Login Items list. (I cover the Login Items list in more detail in Book II, Chapter 3.)

Running applications from a CD-ROM or DVD-ROM

After you load a CD-ROM or DVD-ROM, you can display its contents by double-clicking the disc icon that appears on your Desktop. A Finder window opens and shows the files that reside on the disc, as shown in Figure 2-16.

After you locate the application you want to run on the disc, you can launch it by double-clicking it, or by selecting it and pressing ⌘+O.

Figure 2-16:
The Finder window shows the contents of a disc when you double-click its icon.

Switching 'Twixt Programs with Aplomb

You might think that juggling multiple applications will lead to confusion, fatigue, and dry mouth, but luckily OS X includes a number of features that make it easy to jump between programs that are running on your Mac. Use any of these methods to move from open application to application:

+ **Click anywhere in the desired window to make it the active window.**

+ **Click the application icon on the Dock.** All applications that are running have an icon on the Dock. Depending on the Dock settings in System Preferences, the icon may also have a shiny dot below it to indicate that the application is open.

+ **Press ⌘+Tab.** If you have a dozen windows open, this method can get a bit tedious, which leads me to one of the sassiest features in Mavericks, Mission Control. Figure 2-17 shows off the Mission Control screen.

Figure 2-17:
Mission Control is the desktop manager in Mavericks.

✦ **Press F3 (or Control+↑, depending on your keyboard) to show *all* open windows using Mission Control, grouped by application; then click the one you want.** Figure 2-17 illustrates the tiled All Windows display on my Mac after I press F9. Move the cursor on top of the window you want to activate — the window turns blue when it's selected — and click once to switch to that window. You can specify which keys you want to use in the Mission Control pane in System Preferences.

✦ **Press Ctrl+F3 (or Control+↓, depending on your keyboard) to show all open windows from the application that you're currently using; click the one that you want to activate.** This Mission Control function is great for choosing from all the images that you've opened in Photoshop or all the Safari web pages populating your Desktop!

Astute observers will notice that the application menu bar also changes to match the now-active application.

Besides the F3 and Control+F3 hot keys that I just discussed, Mission Control provides one more nifty function: Press ⌘+F3, and all your open windows scurry to the side of the screen. Now you can work with drives, files, and aliases on your Desktop — and when you're ready to confront those dozen application windows again, just press the keyboard shortcut a second time.

Although the Mission Control screen appears automatically when necessary, you can launch it at any time from your Mac's Launchpad display or by pressing the Mission Control key on your keyboard. If you're using a trackpad, display the Mission Control screen by swiping up with three fingers.

Ah, but what if you want to switch to a different set of applications? For example, suppose that you're slaving away at your pixel-pushing job — say, designing a magazine cover with Pages. Your page design desktop also includes Photoshop and Aperture, which you switch between often using one of the techniques I just described. Suddenly, however, you realize you need to schedule a meeting with others in your office, using Calendar, and you want to check your e-mail in Apple Mail. What to do?

Well, you could certainly open Launchpad and launch those two applications on top of your graphics applications and then minimize or close them. But with Mission Control's *Spaces* feature, you can press the Control+← or Control+→ sequences to switch to a different "communications" desktop, with Calendar and Apple Mail windows already open and in your favorite positions! Figure 2-17 illustrates multiple Spaces desktops at the top of the Mission Control screen.

When you've finished setting up your meeting and answering any important e-mail, simply press Control+← or Control+→ again to switch back to your "graphics" desktop, where all your work is exactly as you left it! (And yes, Virginia, Spaces does indeed work with full-screen applications.)

Now imagine that you've also created a custom "music" desktop for GarageBand and iTunes, or perhaps you paired Photoshop Elements and iPhoto together as a "graphics" desktop. See why everyone's so thrilled with Mavericks? (Let's see Windows 8 do *that* out of the box.)

To create a new desktop for use in Spaces, click the Launchpad icon on the Dock and then click the Mission Control icon. Now you can set up new Spaces desktops. Move your pointer to the top right of the Mission Control screen and click the Add button (with the plus sign) that appears. (If you've relocated your Dock to the right side of the screen, the Add button shows up in the upper-left corner instead.) Spaces creates a new empty desktop thumbnail. Switch to the new desktop by clicking the thumbnail at the top of the Mission Control screen, and then open those applications you want to include. (Alternatively, you can drag the applications from Mission Control onto the desired Desktop thumbnail.) That's all there is to it!

To switch an application window between Spaces desktops, drag the window to the edge of the desktop and hold it there. Spaces will automatically move the window to the next desktop. (Applications can also be dragged between desktops within the Mission Control screen.) You can also delete a desktop from the Mission Control screen. Just hover your cursor over the offending Spaces thumbnail and then click the Delete button (with the X) that appears.

You can jump directly to a specific Spaces desktop by clicking its thumbnail in your Mission Control screen or by holding down the Control key and pressing the number corresponding to that desktop. Finally, you can always use the Control+← or Control+→ shortcuts to move between desktops and full-screen applications.

Opening and Saving Your Stuff in an Application

Almost all OS X applications open and save documents in the same way, whether you're creating a presentation with Keynote or expressing your cinematic side with iMovie. Therefore, I take a moment to outline the common procedures for opening and saving documents. Believe me, you'll perform these two rituals dozens of times a week, so no nodding off.

Opening a document

First, the simple way to load a document: Double-click that document in a Finder window, and . . . well, that's it. (This is my preferred method because I'm an ALT — short for *Admitted Lazy Technowizard* — who would rather use complex hand movements to pour myself another Diet Coke.)

To open a document the hard way — from inside an application — here's the plan:

1. **Choose File⇨Open or press that handy ⌘+O key combination.**

Your OS X program is likely to display the attractive Open dialog that you see in Figure 2-18.

Many applications now allow you to open files that have been saved to your iCloud Library — click the iCloud button at the top-left corner of the Open dialog to display documents in your Library that you can open in this application, or click the On My Mac button to locate and open files on your Mac's drive or on your local network. Figure 2-18 illustrates the On My Mac face of the Open dialog.

Figure 2-18:
The soon-to-be-quite-familiar Open dialog.

2. **Navigate to the location of the document that you want to open.**

The pop-up menu allows you to jump directly to common locations — such as the Desktop, your Home folder, and your Documents folder — as well as places that you've recently accessed (Recent Places).

If the target folder isn't in your pop-up menu, it's time to use the Open dialog sidebar, where your hard drives, DVD drives, and network locations hang out.

You can quickly locate a document by clicking in the Search box at the upper right of the Open dialog and typing a portion of the filename or a phrase contained in the document.

3. **Click the habitat where the file will be found.**

If you're using Column view, you'll note that the right column(s) will change to show you the contents of the item that you just clicked. In this way, you can cruise through successive folders to find that elusive document. (This time-consuming process is derisively called "drilling," hence, the importance of using Recent Items, or dragging files, locations, and applications into the sidebar at the left of Finder.)

4. **When you sight the document that you want to load, either double-click it or click once to highlight the filename and then click Open.**

"Hey, the Open dialog can be resized!" That's right, good buddy. You can expand the Open dialog to show more columns and find things more easily. Click and drag any side or corner of the Open dialog to resize it. (You can also switch from Column view to List view or Icon view or Flow view, just as you can in a Finder window, using the buttons to the left of the pop-up location menu. I discuss setting view modes in a Finder window in Book II, Chapter 1.)

Saving a document

To save a document, follow these steps:

1. **Choose File⇔Save.**

   If you've previously saved this document, your application should immediately overwrite the existing document with the new copy, and you get to return to work . . . end of story. If you *haven't* saved this document, the program will display a Save dialog that's usually similar to the Open dialog; it generally has a few more options, however, so stay frosty.

2. **Navigate to the location where you'd like to save the document and then type a filename.**

   Often, you can use a default name provided by the thoughtful folks who developed the software. Note that you might be given the chance to save the document in one of several formats. For example, a word-processing application might allow you to save a document in RTF, HyperText Markup Language (HTML), and even bargain-basement text format. (Typically, I don't change the format unless I specifically need to change it.)

3. **Click Save (or OK, depending on the application).**

If an application offers a Save As menu option in the File menu, you can (in effect) copy the document by saving a new version of the document under another name. Save As comes in handy when you want to retain the original version of a document. Alternatively, use the Save menu option (in applications that support this Mavericks feature), and you can open different versions of the document instead.

Quitting Applications

If I had a twisted and warped sense of humor, I'd simply tell you to quit applications by pulling your Mac's power cord from the wall socket. (Luckily, I don't.) For a safer and saner way to exit an application, use one of these methods:

+ Press the ⌘+Q keyboard shortcut.

+ Choose the Application's named menu and then click Quit.

+ Control-click (or right-click) the application icon on the Dock and then choose Quit from the contextual menu that appears.

You can also click the Close button on the application window. Note, however, that this method doesn't always completely close down the application. For example, Safari stays running even if you close the browser window. In general, if the application works in a single window (such as System Preferences), closing the window also quits the application.

As I mention earlier in the chapter, if the application supports the Resume feature in Mavericks, the document you were working on will automatically be displayed when you launch the application again.

Chapter 3: Basic OS X Housekeeping

In This Chapter

- Copying, moving, and duplicating files
- Deleting and recovering files
- Renaming files
- Finding specific files
- Locking files
- Using Apple menu commands
- Using Services, the Go menu, and menu icons
- Listening to audio discs and recording data discs
- Printing in OS X applications

After you master basic Mac spell-casting — selecting items, using menus, opening and saving documents, working with windows, launching an application or two, and the like — it's time to delve deeper into OS X.

In this chapter, I discuss file management, showing you the hidden power behind the friendly Apple menu (). I also discuss some of the more advanced menu commands, how to print in most applications, and how to listen to an audio CD on your Mac. (It makes a doggone good stereo, especially with a good set of external speakers.) Finally, I introduce you to the built-in CD/DVD recording features in the Big X and show you how to add a standard USB printer to your system.

Finder: The Wind beneath Your Wings

So what exactly is Finder anyway? It's a rather nebulous term, but in essence, Finder gives OS X the basic functions that you'll use for the procedures I outline in this chapter. This über-OS has been around in one guise or another since the days of System 6 — the creaking old days when a Mac was an all-in-one computer with a built-in screen. Come to think of it, some things never change (as I glance at my iMac).

Finder is always running, so it's always available — and you can always switch to it, even when several other applications are open and chugging away. Figure 3-1 illustrates the Dock with the rather perspective-crazy Finder icon at the far left.

Is that icon supposed to be one face or two faces? I'm still confused, and I've been using the Mac now since 1989.

Don't forget that OS X gives you a second method of doing everything I cover in this chapter: You can use Terminal to uncover the text-based Unix core of OS X, employing your blazing typing speed to take care of things from the command line. Of course, that's not the focus of this book, but for those who want to boldly go where no Mac operating system has gone before, you'll find more in Book VIII, Chapter 2. Despite what you might have been led to believe, power and amazing speed are to be found in character-based computing.

Apple menu   Action

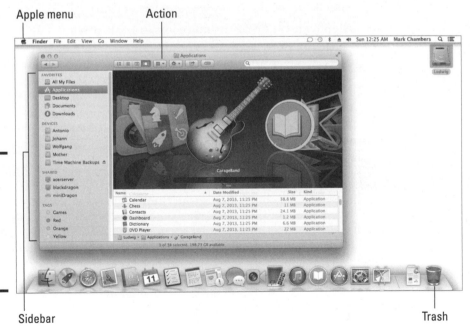

Figure 3-1: Finder is always there, supporting you with a unique smile.

Sidebar   Trash

Copying and Moving Files and Folders

Here's where drag-and-drop makes things about as easy as computing can get:

✦ **To copy a file or folder from one window to another location on the same drive:** Hold down the Option key and click and drag the icon from its current home to the new location. (*Note:* You can drop files and folders on top of other folders, which puts the copy inside that folder.) If you're copying multiple items, select them first (read how in Chapter 2 of this minibook) and then drag and drop the entire crew.

"Is the Desktop a valid target location for a file or folder?" You're darn tootin'! I recommend, though, that you avoid cluttering your Desktop with more than a handful of files. Instead, create a folder or two on your Desktop and then store those items in those folders. If you work with the contents of a specific folder often, drag it into the Favorites heading in the sidebar (the column on the left side of any Finder window), and you can open that folder from Finder with a single click — no matter where you are! (Alternatively, drag the folder to the right side of the Dock and drop it there, and you can open it with a single click from anywhere.)

✦ **To copy items from one window to a location on another drive:** Click and drag the icon from the window to a window displaying the contents of the target drive. Or, in the spirit of drag-and-drop, you can simply drag the items to the drive icon, which places them in the root folder of that drive.

✦ **To move items from one window to another location on the same drive:** Simply drag the icon to the new location, whether it be a window or a folder. (To move items to a different drive, hold down the key while dragging.)

OS X provides you with a number of visual cues to let you know what's being copied or moved. For example, dragging one or more items displays a ghost image of the items. When you've positioned the cursor over the target, OS X highlights that location to let you know that you're in the zone. If you're moving or copying items into another Finder window, the window border is highlighted to let you know that OS X understands the game plan.

In case you move the wrong thing or you port it to the wrong location, press +Z to undo the previous action.

If the item that you're dragging already exists in the target location, you get a confirmation dialog like the one you see in Figure 3-2. You can choose to replace the file, leave the existing file alone, keep both files, or stop the entire shooting match. (If you decide to keep both, OS X appends a numeric string to the new arrival's filename.)

Figure 3-2:
To replace
or not to
replace —
the choice
is yours.

Cloning Your Items — It's Happening Now!

No need for sci-fi equipment or billions in cash — you can create a duplicate of any item in the same folder. This technique is often handy when you need a simple backup of the same file in the same folder or when you're going to edit a document but you want to keep the original intact.

Click the item to select it and then choose File⇨Duplicate (or use the keyboard shortcut and press ⌘+D). To distinguish the duplicate from the original, OS X adds the word *copy* to the end of the duplicate's icon name; additional copies have a number added to the name as well.

Alternatively, drag-and-drop aficionados might want to hold down the Option key and drag the original item to another spot in the same window. When you release the button, the duplicate appears.

Heck, if you prefer the mouse (or trackpad), you can right-click the item and then choose Duplicate from the contextual menu that appears. Decisions, decisions. . . .

Oh, and don't forget that Action button on the Finder toolbar (labeled in Figure 3-1). You can also click the Action button and choose Duplicate from the pop-up menu.

When you duplicate a folder, OS X automatically duplicates all the contents of the folder as well. Remember that this process could take some time if the folder contains a large number of small files (or a small number of large files).

Deleting That Which Should Not Be

Even Leonardo da Vinci made the occasional design mistake. No doubt, his trash can was likely full of bunched-up pieces of parchment. Luckily, no trees will be wasted when you decide to toss your unneeded files and folders; this section shows you how to delete items from your system.

By the way, as you'll soon witness for yourself, moving items to the Trash doesn't necessarily mean that they're immediately history.

Dragging unruly files against their will

In OS X, the familiar Trash icon (a spiffy-looking wire can) appears on the right edge of the Dock. (Did you expect anything less from Mavericks?) You can click and drag the items that you've selected to the Trash and drop them on top of the wire can icon to delete them. When the Trash contains at least one item, the wire can icon changes to appear as if it were full of trash.

You can also add a Delete icon to your Finder toolbar. For all the details, see Book II, Chapter 1.

Deleting with the menus and the keyboard

The mouse isn't the only option when deleting items. Your other options for scrapping selected files include

+ Choosing File from the Finder menu and choosing the Move to Trash menu item

+ Pressing the +Delete keyboard shortcut

+ Clicking the Action button on the Finder toolbar and choosing Move to Trash from the pop-up menu

+ Right-clicking the item to display the contextual menu and then choosing Move to Trash from that menu

Emptying That Wastepaper Basket

As I mention earlier, moving items from your Mac's hard drive to the Trash doesn't delete them immediately from your system. Believe me, this fail-safe measure comes in handy when you've been banging away at the keyboard for several hours and you stop paying close attention to what you're doing. (I usually also blame the lack of Diet Coke.) More on how to rescue files from the Trash in the next section. If you connect to other computers and servers across your network, however, take heed: Moving items that reside on another computer to the Trash will display a warning dialog that the items will be immediately (and permanently) deleted.

As you can with any folder, you can check the contents of the Trash by clicking its icon on the Dock.

After you double-check the Trash contents and you're indeed absolutely sure that you want to delete its contents, use one of the following methods to nuke the digital Bit Bucket:

+ **If the contents of the Trash are still displayed in a Finder window, click the Empty button at the upper right of the window.**

+ **Choose the Empty Trash menu item from the Finder menu.**

+ **Choose Secure Empty Trash from the Finder menu.**

Believe it or not, if you use the standard Empty Trash command, you *still* haven't zapped that refuse! Some third-party hard drive repair and recovery programs will allow an uncool person to restore items from the Trash. Comparatively, use the Secure Empty Trash method for those sensitive files and folders that you want to immediately and irrevocably delete. The data is overwritten with random characters, making it impossible to recover without resorting to your backup. (A great idea for that Mac you want to sell on eBay, no? If you like, you can reinstall OS X before you ship the Mac, leaving the Setup Assistant ready-to-run for the new owner.)

+ **Press the ⌘+Shift+Delete keyboard shortcut.**

+ **Click the Trash icon on the Dock, hold down the mouse button, and choose Empty Trash from the menu that appears.**

+ **Right-click the Trash icon on the Dock and then choose Empty Trash from the contextual menu that appears.**

Depending on the method you select and the settings you choose in System Preferences (which I cover in Book II, Chapter 3), OS X might present you with a confirmation dialog to make sure that you want the Trash emptied.

Wait! I Need That After All!

In the adrenaline-inducing event that you need to rescue something that shouldn't have ended up in the scrap pile, first click the Trash icon on the Dock to display the contents of the Trash. Then rescue the items that you want to save by dragging them to the Desktop or a folder on your hard drive. (This is roughly analogous to rescuing your old baseball glove from the family garage sale.) You can also right-click any item in the Trash and choose Put Back from the menu that appears.

Feel free to gloat. If someone else is nearby, ask him or her to pat you on the back and call you a lifesaver.

Renaming Your Items

You wouldn't get far in today's spacious virtual world without being able to change a moniker for a file or folder. To rename an item in OS X, use one of these methods:

+ **With the mouse or trackpad:** Click once on an icon's name to highlight it, and then click the name again or press Return. OS X highlights the text in an edit box. Type the new name and then press Return when you're done.

  You want to wait a few seconds between clicks, as opposed to doing a rapid-fire double-click.

+ **From the Info dialog:** Select the item and press ⌘+I to display the Info dialog; then click the triangle next to Name & Extension. Click in the name field, drag the mouse to highlight the text that you want to change, and type the replacement text.

Naturally, the first method is the easiest, and it's the one that I use most often.

Adding a Dash of Color with Tags

In Mavericks, you can color-code files and folders to help you organize and recognize your data in a hurry using the Finder Tags feature. For example, why not assign the green Tag color to the files and folders that make up your current project? Or, if you need to mark a file for immediate attention, assign it the red Tag color.

To assign a Tag color to selected files and folders, you have five options:

+ Choose a Tag when you save a document.

+ Assign a Tag in the Info and Inspector dialogs (which I'll discuss in a page or two).

+ Click the Action button on the Finder toolbar and then click the desired Tag.

+ Right-click the selection and then choose the color from the pop-up menu.

+ From the File menu, choose that perfect shade from the menu.

Finder prompts you for a keyword when you create a new Tag, which is a great help when organizing your files and folders.

After you create at least one Tag, you'll notice that they are displayed in the Finder sidebar under the Tags heading. A single click on the Tag name in the sidebar displays all files with that Tag. Because Tags work in both your local drive and your iCloud Library, you can create documents using different applications and view them all at once, even if they're spread out in different locations and folders! You can also apply more than one Tag to an item.

You can search for items with specific Tags in the Spotlight search box, too — click in the Search box in any Finder window and type the Tag key-word or color. (From the Desktop, click the magnifying glass icon at the upper right corner of your Desktop and type the Tag keyword or color.) For more information on searching with Spotlight, flip to the next chapter.

Displaying the Facts on Files and Folders

Finder's Info dialog is the place to view the specifics on any highlighted item (including drives and aliases). You can display the Info dialog in a number of ways: Select an item and press +I, click the Action toolbar button and then select Get Info from the menu; right-click the item and choose Get Info; or open Finder's File menu and then choose Get Info. (See the results in Figure 3-3.) If you select more than one item, Mavericks opens a separate Info dialog for each item.

Figure 3-3:
The General information panel appears when you open the Info dialog.

You can also show an Info dialog that summarizes multiple items, and this is A Good Thing if you need to see the total size for several files or folders. To display the Summary Info dialog, select the desired items, hold down the Control key, and choose File⇨Get Summary Info. (Yep, in case you were wondering, some of the items on the File menu do change when you hold down Control. Display the File menu and try it yourself!)

There's yet another species of the Info dialog: *Inspector* displays the same data as the Summary Info dialog, but it's automatically updated when you click a different file or folder! (This feature is a great convenience if you're checking the information on a number of separate items in different locations on your MacBook.) To display Inspector, press ⌘+Option+I.

OS X displays the General information panel when you first open the Info dialog, but other panels are usually available (depending on the type of selected items).

For most types of files and folders, the Info dialog can tell you the following:

✦ **Kind:** What type of item it is — for example, whether it's a file, folder, drive, or alias

✦ **Open With:** What program launches automatically when you open the selected item

✦ **Size:** The total size of the item (or items, if there are more than ten) that you select

✦ **Where:** The path on your hard drive where the item is located

✦ **Dates:** When the item was created and was last modified

✦ **Version:** The application version number

✦ **Name & Extension:** The file's name and extension

✦ **Tags:** Any Finder Tags you've assigned to the item

✦ **Sharing & Permissions:** The privileges that control who can do what to the file (more on this later, in Book II, Chapter 6) and whether a file is locked in read-only mode

Some of this information you can change, and some can only be displayed. To banish the Info dialog from your Desktop, click the dialog's Close button.

You can hide or display various parts of the Info dialog by clicking the triangles next to each section heading.

For the rest of this section, I describe a number of tasks that you can accomplish from the Info dialog.

If you use a specific document over and over as a basis for different revisions, you can enable the Stationery Pad check box on the General information panel to use the file as stationery. Opening a stationery file automatically creates a new, untitled version of the file in the linked application, which can save you steps compared with duplicating the file.

Adding Spotlight comments

OS X provides you with a Spotlight Comments field in the Info dialog and Inspector, where you can add additional text that's stored along with the file (and can be matched with Spotlight). I use this feature to record the version number of manuscript chapters and programs that I create during the course of writing books.

To add a comment, follow these steps:

1. **Display the Info dialog for the item by pressing +I or choosing File⇨Get Info.**

2. **Click in the Comments box and type the comment text.**

    If you need to expand the Comments section of the Info dialog, click the triangle next to the Comments heading. The arrow rotates, and the Comments box appears.

3. **Close the Info dialog to save the comment.**

Displaying file extensions

File extensions are alien creatures to most Mac owners. However, these (usually) three- or four-character add-ons that follow a period at the end of a filename have been a mainstay in character-based operating systems like Unix for years. A file extension identifies what program owns a specific file, and therefore which application launches automatically when you double-click that file's icon. Examples of common extensions (and the applications that own them) include

+ .pdf: Preview, or Adobe Acrobat
+ .doc or .docx: Microsoft Word
+ .pages: Apple Pages
+ .key: Apple Keynote
+ .psd: Adobe Photoshop or Photoshop Elements
+ .jpeg or .jpg: Preview, or your image editor
+ .tiff or .tif: Preview, or your image editor
+ .htm or .html: Safari, or your web browser of choice

Why would someone want to see a file's extension? It comes in handy when a number of different types of files are linked to the same application. For example, both JPEG and TIFF images are displayed as thumbnails in a Finder window, so it's sometimes hard to tell one from the other. With extensions displayed, it's easy to tell what type of file you're looking at.

Follow this procedure to hide or display extensions with your filenames:

1. **Display the Info dialog for the item by pressing ⌘+I or choosing File⇨ Get Info.**

2. **If you need to expand the Name & Extension section of the Info dialog, click the triangle next to the Name & Extension heading.**

3. **To display the extension for the selected file, clear the Hide Extension check box to disable it.**

4. **Close the Info dialog to save your changes.**

Choosing the application with which to launch a file

So what's the plan if the wrong application launches when you double-click a file? Not a problem: You can also change the linked application from the Info dialog as well. (I told you this was a handy tool box, didn't I?) Follow these steps to choose another application to pair with a selected file:

1. **Click the Action button on the Finder toolbar and then click Get Info to display the Info dialog for the item.**

2. **Click the triangle next to the Open With heading to expand it.**

3. **Click the pop-up menu button.**

   OS X displays the applications that it feels are best suited to open this type of document.

4. **Select the application that should open the file.**

To go completely hog wild and choose a different application, select Other from the Open With pop-up menu. OS X displays a Choose Other Application dialog, where you can navigate to and select the application you want. (If the application isn't recognized as *recommended,* open the Enable pop-up menu and choose All Applications.) After you highlight the application, select the Always Open With check box and click the Add button.

If you don't have an application that can open a specific file type, you can also opt to search the App Store for an application you can purchase to open it. Just choose App Store from the Open With pop-up menu. (A sometimes pricey option, of course, but certainly convenient!)

5. **To globally update all the documents of the same type to launch the application that you chose, click the Change All button.**

   OS X displays a confirmation dialog asking whether you're sure about making this drastic change. Click Continue to update the other files of the same type or click Cancel to return to the Info dialog.

6. **Close the Info dialog to save your changes.**

Locking files against evildoers

"Holy Item Insurance, Batman!" That's right, Boy Wonder: Before I leave the friendly land of the Info dialog, every Mac owner needs to know how to protect files and folders from accidental deletion or editing. By locking a file, you allow it to be opened and copied — but not changed, renamed, or sent to the Trash. Locked items appear in Finder with a small padlock attached to the icon.

To lock or unlock a file, you have to have ownership of the file. I cover privileges in Book II, but on a Mac where you've configured only one administrator account, you should already have ownership.

If you're considering changing the ownership of a system-owned file, **don't do it.** You could throw a serious monkey wrench into your Mavericks system.

To lock a file, follow this procedure:

1. **Display the Info dialog for the item.**

2. **Select the Locked check box.**

   Find the Locked check box in the General section of the dialog. (Refer to Figure 3-3.)

3. **Close the Info dialog to save your changes.**

Creating an Alias

I mention aliases in Chapter 2 of this minibook. As I discuss in that chapter, an *alias* acts as a link to an application or document that exists elsewhere on your system (a handy trick to use when organizing items on your hard drive). You have a number of ways to conjure an alias after you select an item:

✦ From the Finder menu, choose File⇨Make Alias. You have to move the alias yourself.

✦ Press the ⌘+L keyboard shortcut. Again, you have to move the new alias to its new location.

✦ Click the Action button on the Finder toolbar and then click Make Alias.

✦ Right-click the selected item and then choose Make Alias from the contextual menu that appears.

In addition, you can hold down the ⌘+Option key combination and drag the item to the location where you want the alias.

Although OS X does a great job in tracking the movements of an original and updating an alias, some actions can break the link. For example, if you delete the original, the alias is left wandering in search of a home. However, all is not lost. When you double-click a broken alias, OS X offers to help you fix the alias. This involves browsing through your system to locate a new original.

Using the Apple Menu

The Apple menu (⌘) is a familiar sight to any Mac owner. Although Apple contemplated removing it during the original development and beta cycle for OS X version 10.0, the ruckus and cry from beta-testers ensured that it remained, and it's still present today. It's amazing how reassuring that little fellow can be when you boot the Big X for the first time.

In this section, I cover the important things that are parked under the Apple menu.

Using Recent Items

If you're like most of us — and I think I'm safe in assuming that you are — you tend to work on the same set of applications and files (and use the same network servers) during the day. Even with features such as Mission Control, Launchpad, and Stacks, you'll sometimes find yourself drilling down through at least one layer of folders to reach the stuff that you need. To make things easier on yourself, you could create a set of aliases on your Desktop that link to those servers, files, and applications . . . but as you move from project to project, you'd find yourself constantly updating the aliases. As Blackbeard the Pirate was wont to exclaim, "Arrgh!"

Ah, but OS X is one right-smart operating system, and several years ago, Apple created the Recent Items menu to save you the trouble of drilling for applications and files (and even network servers as well). Figure 3-4 illustrates the Recent Items menu from my system. Note that the menu is thoughtfully divided into Applications, Documents, and Servers. When you open documents or launch applications, they're added to the list. To launch an application or document from the Recent Items menu — or connect to a network server — just click it.

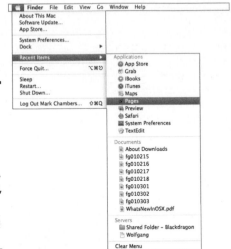

Figure 3-4:
Use the
Recent
Items
menu to
access files,
applications,
and servers
you've been
using.

To wipe the contents of the Recent Items menu — for example, if you've just finished a project and want to turn over a new digital leaf — click Recent Items and choose the Clear Menu item.

You can specify the number of recent items that will appear in the menu from System Preferences; display the General pane and click the list box next to the Recent Items field. (More on this in Book II, Chapter 3.)

Also, remember the trick that I mention earlier: You can drag any folder or server into the sidebar column at the left of a Finder window, adding it to that exclusive club that includes your Home folder, Applications folder, and media folders.

Playing with the Dock

You know how Air Force One acts as the mobile nerve center for the president? And how The Chief can jet all around the world and take all his stuff along with him? Well, the Dock is kind of like that. Sort of.

If you want your Dock to go mobile as well, click the Apple menu (🍎) and choose the Dock item to display the submenu. Here's a rundown of the options that you'll find:

✦ **Hiding:** Click Turn Hiding On/Off to toggle the automatic hiding of the Dock. With hiding on, the Dock disappears off the edge of the screen until you move the cursor to that edge. (This feature is great for those who want to make use of as much Desktop territory as possible for their applications.)

You can press +Option+D to toggle Dock hiding on and off from the keyboard.

✦ **Magnification:** Click Turn Magnification On/Off to toggle icon magnification when your cursor is selecting an icon from the Dock. With magnification on, the icons on the Dock get really, *really* big . . . a good thing for Mr. Magoo or those with grandiose schemes to take over the world. Check out the rather oversized icons in Figure 3-5. (You can control the amount of magnification from the System Preferences Dock settings, which I explain in Book II, Chapter 3.)

Figure 3-5:
Now those, my friend, are some pumped-up icons.

✦ **Position:** Click one of three choices (Position on Left, Bottom, or Right) to make the Dock appear on the left, bottom, or right of the screen, respectively.

✦ **Dock Preferences:** Click this option to display the System Preferences Dock settings, which I explain in Book II, Chapter 3.

Bad program! Quit!

Once in a while, you'll encounter a stubborn application that locks up, slows to a crawl, or gets stuck in an endless loop. Although OS X is a highly advanced OS, it can still fall prey to bad programming or corrupted data.

Luckily, you can easily shut down these troublemakers from the Apple menu. Just choose Force Quit to display the Force Quit Applications dialog that you see in Figure 3-6. (Keyboard types can press +Option+Esc.) Select the application that you want to banish and then click the Force Quit button; OS X requests confirmation, after which you click the Force Quit button again.

Figure 3-6:
Forcing an application to take a hike.

If you select Finder in the Force Quit Applications dialog, the button changes to Relaunch. This allows you to restart Finder, which comes in handy if your system appears to be unstable. This technique is much faster than restarting your Mac.

Forcing an application to quit will also close any open documents that you were working in that application, so *save your work beforehand* (if the program will allow you to save anything). This is not a good time to rely solely on the Resume feature, which may not work correctly if an application has locked up. If you relaunch Finder, some programs might restart as well.

Tracking down your version

If you choose About This Mac from the Apple menu, OS X displays the About This Mac dialog that you see in Figure 3-7 (in this example, proudly displaying my Mac Pro supercomputer). When you need to check the amount of memory or the processor in an unfamiliar Mac, the About This Mac dialog can display these facts in a twinkling. However, I primarily use it to check the OS X version and build number as well as to launch the Apple System Information utility (which I discuss in full in Chapter 9 of this minibook). Click the More Info button to launch System Information.

Figure 3-7:
Display your Mac's memory, processor, start-up disk, and Big X version.

Apple allows you to launch Software Update from three spots: the About This Mac dialog, the System Preferences window, and the Apple menu. Sheesh, they must really want you to keep your Big X up to date, I guess.

Visiting the App Store

If you haven't jumped into Apple's virtual storefront for Mac software, click the Apple menu and choose App Store, or click that handy App Store icon on the Dock. The App Store is a slick way to take care of the Big Three Points when shopping for software: finding the right application, installing the application, and keeping it updated. You can shop by categories, view the latest software additions to the App Store, or click in the App Store search box (at the upper right of the window) to find a specific title or type of application. Click the thumbnail for an application to view detailed information, including screenshots and user reviews. Click the Back arrow at the top left of the App Store window to return to the previous screen, just as you do on a web page in Safari.

Along the top of the App Store window, you'll see a number of toolbar buttons that let you jump directly to Apple's featured titles, as well as lists of the applications you've already purchased and a list of the software you've bought that needs updating.

When you locate the perfect application for your needs, click the price button to purchase the app. It's automatically downloaded to your Mac, and the App Store even adds an icon to your Launchpad so that you can try out your new software. You can install your App Store purchases on all of your Macs (using the same Apple ID), without having to buy additional copies or licenses. Leave it to Apple to Do Things the Right Way.

Specifying a location

OS X allows you to create multiple network locations. Think of a location as a separate configuration that you use when you connect to a different network from a different locale. For instance, if you travel to a branch office, you'd assign a location for your desk and a location for the remote branch. Or a student might assign one location for her home network and another for the college computer lab network.

Your Apple ID is your friend

Remember when you were offered the chance to create an Apple ID during the initial setup of Mavericks? (If you already had an Apple ID from using OS X Lion or Mountain Lion, or you created an ID while using your iPad or iPhone, you skipped ahead without a second thought.) If you're careful about your online travels, however, you may have passed up the chance to immediately create your Apple ID during Mavericks setup, thinking that you could probably take care of it later.

Unfortunately, you've probably realized by now that all sorts of OS X features and applications hinge on your Apple ID: your iCloud account, the App Store, Messages, the iTunes Store, and FaceTime come to mind. If you haven't created your Apple ID yet, take care of the chore now! It's free and painless, and marks you as one of the In Crowd.

Whenever you're prompted for an Apple ID by one of Mavericks's applications, click the Create Apple ID button to start the ball rolling, and the application will lead you through the process step by step. You can also create your ID through the App Store and the iTunes Store. Just click the Account link in either application's window and you'll be prompted to create your Apple ID.

A location saves all the specific values that you've entered in the System Preferences Network settings, including IP address, DNS servers, and proxy servers. If all this means diddly squat to you, don't worry; I explain it all in Book VI, Chapter 1. For now, just remember that you can switch between locations by choosing Location from the Apple menu, which displays a submenu of locations that you can choose among. You must, though, create at least a second location for the Location menu item to appear in the Apple menu. Makes sense, right?

Availing Yourself of OS X Services

In OS X, Services allow you to merge information from one application with another. To Mac old-timers, Services might sound suspiciously like the Clipboard; however, Services can also include functionality from an application, so you can create documents or complete tasks without running another program. Services can be used in both the Finder and OS X applications.

To illustrate, here's a fun example:

1. **Launch TextEdit from Launchpad and type your name.**

2. **Highlight your name.**

3. **Click the TextEdit menu — don't switch to Finder; use the TextEdit application menu — and choose Services.**

4. **From the Services submenu, choose Search with Google.**

After you've shaken your head at all the sites devoted to people with the same name, consider what you just did — you ran the Safari application from TextEdit, using selected words! Pretty slick, eh?

A glance at the other Services that show up in most applications gives you an idea of just how convenient and powerful OS X Services can be. I often use Services to take care of things such as

✦ **Sending an e-mail message from an e-mail address in a text file or Contacts (via the Mail Service)**

✦ **Capturing a screen snapshot in an application (using the Capture Selection from Screen Service)**

✦ **Sending a file to a Bluetooth-equipped tablet or cellphone in an application (using the Send File to Bluetooth Device service)**

    At the time of this writing, you can't use this Bluetooth file transfer feature with an iPhone, iPod touch, or iPad.

You can access the Services menu from an OS X application by selecting that program's application menu (sometimes called the *named menu*). For instance, in the demonstration earlier, I use the TextEdit menu that appears on the TextEdit menu bar. In Microsoft Word, I would click the Word menu.

Geez, I think the computing world needs another word for *menu* — don't you?

Many third-party applications that you install under OS X can add their own commands under the Services menu, so be sure to read the documentation for a new application to see what Services functionality it adds.

You can enable or disable menu items from the Services menu. For example, the Send File to Bluetooth Device service that I mention earlier is turned off by default. To make changes to your Services, display the Services menu from the Finder menu bar and choose Services Preferences. Mavericks displays the Services list in the Keyboard pane of System Preferences, and you can toggle the display of a service by selecting the check box next to it.

Get Thee Hence: Using the Go Menu

Remember the transporter from *Star Trek?* Step on the little platform, assume a brave pose, and whoosh! — you're transported instantaneously to another ship (or more likely to a badly designed planet exterior built inside a soundstage). Talk about convenience . . . that is, as long as the doggone thing didn't malfunction. (And you weren't wearing a red shirt.)

Finder's Go menu gives you the chance to play Captain Kirk: You can jump immediately to specific spots, both within the confines of your own system as well as external environments, such as your network or the Internet. (You can leave your phaser and tricorder in your cabin.)

The destinations that you can travel to using the Go menu are

+ **Back/Forward/Enclosing Folder:** I lump these three commands together because they're all basic navigation commands. For example, Back and Forward operate just as they do in Safari or your favorite web browser. If you're working in a folder, you can return to the parent folder by clicking Enclosing Folder.

+ **All My Files:** This window displays all the documents you've created or added, such as word-processing documents, images, and movies.

+ **Documents:** Yep, you guessed it: This window displays the contents of your Documents folder.

+ **Desktop:** This window displays the files and folders that you've stored on your Mavericks desktop.

+ **Downloads:** Here, you'll find the contents of your Downloads folder.

✦ **Home:** This window displays the home directory for the user currently logged in.

✦ **Library:** This window displays the contents of the Library folder for the user currently logged in. (The Library folder is located in the user's home directory but is hidden by default.) The Library entry in the Go menu appears only when you hold down the Option key.

✦ **Computer:** This window includes your hard drives, CD and DVD drives, and your network — the same places that appear when you open a new Finder window with the ⌘+N key shortcut.

✦ **Network:** Did you guess that this window displays a window with all your network's servers? Dead giveaway, that.

✦ **Applications:** This window includes all the applications that appear in your OS X Applications folder (a neat *Just the programs, ma'am* arrangement that really comes in handy).

✦ **Utilities:** This window displays the contents of your OS X Utilities folder.

✦ **Recent Folders:** This window displays a submenu that allows you to choose among the folders that you've recently opened.

You can also type the path for a specific folder (use the Go to Folder command) or connect to a specific network server (use the Connect to Server command).

Note that most of the Go menu commands include keyboard shortcuts, proving once again that the fingers are quicker than the mouse.

Monkeying with the Menu Bar

Ever stared at a menu bar for inspiration? Fortunately for Mac owners like you and me, smart people in Cupertino are paid to do just that, and these designers get the big bucks to make the OS X menu bar the best that it can be. Thus were born menu bar icons, which add useful controls in what would otherwise be a wasted expanse of white.

Using menu bar icons

Depending on your hardware, OS X might install several menu bar icons. The Spotlight, Notification Center, and Volume icons are always there by default, along with the Clock display, which is an icon in disguise. Figure 3-8 illustrates these standard icons, along with a few others.

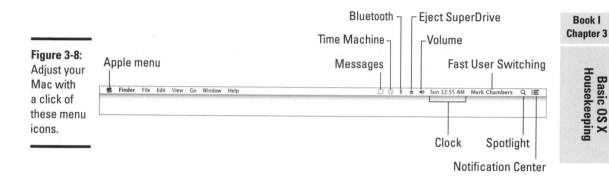

Figure 3-8:
Adjust your
Mac with
a click of
these menu
icons.

Some icons won't appear unless you turn them on. For instance, the Display icon won't appear unless you enable the Show Mirroring Options in the Menu Bar When Available check box in the Displays pane in System Preferences. The Display menu bar icon, which looks like a pair of monitors, allows you to choose from multiple monitors connected to your Mac (either by cable or wirelessly). You can also jump directly to the System Preferences Display settings by choosing Open Displays Preferences from the menu.

To quickly change the audio volume level in OS X, click the Volume icon (it looks like a speaker with emanating sound waves) to display its slider control; then click and drag the slider to adjust the level up or down. After you select a level by releasing the mouse button, your Mac thoughtfully plays the default system sound to help you gauge the new volume level.

Depending on the functionality that you're using with OS X, these other menu bar icons might also appear:

✦ **Modem status:** You can turn on the display of the Modem status icon from the corresponding modem panel on the Network pane in System Preferences, which I discuss in Book II, Chapter 3. The icon can be set to show the time that you've been connected to the Internet as well as the status of the connection procedure. (Naturally, your Mac will need a Mavericks–compatible external USB modem to use this status icon.)

✦ **Wi-Fi:** Because your Mac is equipped with an AirPort or AirPort Extreme card, you can enable the Show Wi-Fi Status in Menu Bar check box in System Preferences. To do so, click the Network icon and then choose your Wi-Fi connection in the column at the left. The Wi-Fi status icon displays the status of the connection; click the Wi-Fi icon to toggle your wireless hardware on or off. The icon displays the relative strength of your Wi-Fi signal, whether you're connected to a Base Station or a peer-to-peer computer network, or whether Wi-Fi is turned off. You can also switch between multiple Wi-Fi networks from the menu.

✦ **Sync:** If an iOS device is connected to your Mac and you sync the device, you'll see a rotating circle while the sync is in progress.

✦ **Bluetooth:** You can toggle Bluetooth networking on or off. You can also make your Mac discoverable or hidden to other Bluetooth devices, send a file to a Bluetooth device, or browse for new Bluetooth devices in your vicinity. Additionally, you can set up a Bluetooth device that's already recognized or open the Bluetooth pane in System Preferences. (If you don't see the angular Bluetooth icon in your menu bar, display the Bluetooth pane in System Preferences and make sure the Show Bluetooth Status in the Menu Bar check box is enabled.)

✦ **Messages:** You can monitor and change your online/offline status from the Messages menu bar icon, as well as check which of your Messages Buddies are online. You can also choose to compose a new message, which automatically launches Messages for you. This icon only appears if you launch Messages; choose Messages⇨Preferences, and select the Show Status in Menu Bar check box on the General pane.

✦ **Time Machine:** If you're using Time Machine to back up your Mac automatically, this icon displays the date of your last backup. You can also manually start a backup from the menu bar icon. To display the icon, open System Preferences and click the Time Machine icon; then select the Show Time Machine Status in the Menu Bar check box.

✦ **Open/Close SuperDrive:** If your Mac is equipped with a SuperDrive optical drive, click this icon (which bears the same familiar Eject symbol as your keyboard) to eject the disc.

✦ **PPPoE:** The display of this icon is controlled from the PPPoE settings on the Network pane in System Preferences. Click this icon to connect to or disconnect from the Internet using *Point-to-Point Protocol over Ethernet* (PPPoE), which is a type of Internet connection offered by some digital subscriber line (DSL) providers.

Doing timely things with the clock

Even the clock itself isn't static eye candy on the OS X menu bar. (I told you this was a hardworking operating system, didn't I?) Click the Clock display to toggle the icon between the default text display and a miniature analog clock. You'll also find the complete day and date at the top of the menu.

You can even open the System Preferences Date & Time settings from the icon. From the Date & Time settings, you can choose whether the seconds or day of the week are included, the separators should flash, or OS X should display the time in 24-hour (military) format. More on this in Book II, Chapter 3.

Eject, Tex, Eject!

OS X makes use of both static volumes (your Mac's magnetic or solid-state hard drive, which remains mummified inside your computer's case) and removable volumes (such as USB Flash drives, external hard drives, your iPod, and CDs/DVD-ROMs). OS X calls the process of loading and unloading a removable volume by old-fashioned terms — *mounting* and *unmounting* — but you and I call the procedure *loading* and *ejecting*.

Just to keep things clear, I should point out that we're talking hardware devices here, so static and removable volumes have nothing to do with the *sound* volume control on your menu bar.

I won't discuss loading/mounting a removable volume. The process differs depending on the computer because some Macs need a button pushed on the keyboard, others have buttons on the drive itself, and some drives have just a slot with no button at all. However, there are a number of standard ways of unloading/unmounting/ejecting a removable volume:

+ Drag the volume's icon from the Desktop to the Trash, which displays an Eject pop-up label to help underline the fact that you are *not* deleting the contents of the drive. Let me underline that with a Mark's Maxim because switchers from the Windows world are usually scared to death by the concept of dragging a volume to the Trash.

Have no fear. In the Apple universe, you *can* drag removable volumes to the Trash with aplomb.

+ Click the volume's icon and use the ⌘+E keyboard shortcut.

+ With the volume open in a Finder window, click the Action button and choose Eject from the pop-up menu.

+ Choose File⇨Eject.

+ Click the Eject button next to the device in the Finder window sidebar.

+ Right-click the volume's icon to display the contextual menu; then choose Eject.

+ Click the Eject icon on the Finder menu bar to eject a CD or DVD from your optical drive.

+ Press your keyboard Eject key (if it has one) to eject a CD or DVD from your built-in optical drive. (If you're using a keyboard without a Media Eject key, press and hold F12 instead.)

You can't unmount a static volume from the Desktop — you have to use the Disk Utility application — so your internal hard drive icon will stay where it is.

Mark's totally unnecessary Computer Trivia 1.0

"Where the heck did *mounting* come from, anyway? Sounds like a line from a John Wayne western!" Well, pardner, the term dates back to the heyday of Big Iron — the Mainframe Age, when giant IBM dinosaurs populated the computing world. Sherman, set the WayBack Machine. . . .

At the time, disks were big, heavy, removable cartridges about two feet in diameter (and about as tall as a 100-count spindle of CD-Rs). The acolytes of the mainframe, called computer *operators,* would have to trudge over to a cabinet and *mount* (or swap) disk cartridges whenever the program stopped and asked for them. That's right, those mainframes would stop calculating and print, "I need you to mount cartridge 12-A-34, or I can't go any further. Have a nice day." (Can you imagine what it'd be like loading and unloading a hard drive every time you needed to open a folder? Puts your iCloud Library in perspective, doesn't it?)

Anyway, even though eons passed and minicomputers appeared — which were only the size of a washing machine or a refrigerator — the terms *mounting* and *unmounting* still commonly appeared in programs. This time, the removable volumes were tape cartridges. Because Unix and its offspring Linux date from the Minicomputer Age, these operating systems still use the terms.

Common Tasks Aplenty

Okay, I admit it — this section is a grab bag of three common tasks: working with text files, listening to an audio CD, and recording a data CD. I present these three procedures here because I want to walk you through them early in the book. Mac owners with an internal or external optical drive will likely want to listen to and record CDs as soon as they start using Mavericks, and you'd be amazed how much information still flows across the Internet in plain, simple text.

Therefore, hang around and take care of business.

Opening and editing text files

Text files would seem to be another anachronism in this age of formatted web pages, rich text format (RTF) documents, and word processors galore. However, virtually every computer ever built can read and write in standard text, so text files are often used for

✦ **Information files on the Internet,** such as FAQs (Frequently Asked Questions files)

✦ **README and update** information by software developers

✦ **Swapping data between programs,** such as comma- and tab-delimited database files

Here's the quick skinny on opening, editing, and saving an existing text file:

1. **Navigate to your Applications folder and launch TextEdit.**

2. **Press +O to display the Open dialog.**

3. **Navigate to the desired text file and double-click the filename to
    load it.**

    You can easily switch between your iCloud Library and your Mac's local
    drives or network drives in the Open dialog. Click the iCloud button or
    the On My Mac button at the top of the Open dialog.

    You can also open an existing text file by dragging its icon from the
    Finder window to the TextEdit icon.

4. **Click the insertion cursor anywhere in the file and begin typing. Or,
    to edit existing text, drag the insertion cursor across the characters to
    highlight them and type the replacement text.**

    TextEdit automatically replaces the existing characters with those that
    you type. To simply delete text, highlight the characters and press
    Delete.

5. **After you finish editing the document, you can overwrite the original
    by pressing +S (the same as choosing File⇨Save).**

6. **Exit TextEdit by pressing +Q.**

I can't help but point out that the OS X Quick Look feature (which I discuss
in Book II, Chapter 1) displays this same text file with a single key! Just select
the file in the Finder window and press the spacebar. (However, you can't
edit a file using Quick Look.)

Listening to an audio CD

By default, Mavericks uses iTunes to play an audio CD. Although I cover
iTunes in great detail in Book III, Chapter 2, take a moment to see how to
master the common task of playing an audio CD (just in case you want to
jam while reading these early chapters). Follow these steps:

1. **Load the audio CD into your Mac's optical drive.**

    A CD volume icon appears on your Desktop. OS X automatically loads
    iTunes, displays its spiffy window, and begins playing the disc.

    The first time you run iTunes, you're asked to configure the program
    and specify whether OS X should automatically connect to the Internet
    to download the track titles for the disc you've loaded. I recommend
    that you accept all the default settings and that you allow automatic
    connection. Is simple, no?

2. **If iTunes doesn't automatically play the disc, manually start the music by clicking the Play button at the upper left of the iTunes window.**

   To play an individual track, double-click the track name in the iTunes window.

3. **If iTunes asks whether you'd like the music from the CD added (or *imported*) into your iTunes music library, accept or decline.**

   If you'd like to listen to the contents of the CD without having to load the physical disc in the future, feel free to import the CD tracks to your library — as long as the original CD is your property, of course!

4. **To adjust the volume from iTunes, drag the Volume slider to the left or right.**

   The slider is to the right of the Play and Fast Forward buttons.

5. **To eject the disc and load another audio CD, press &+E, click the Eject icon next to the CD entry in the Source list, or choose Controls⇨ Eject Disc.**

6. **Exit iTunes by pressing &+Q.**

Recording — nay, burning — a data CD

OS X offers a built-in CD-recording feature that allows you to burn the simplest form of CD: a standard data CD-ROM that can hold up to approximately 700MB of files and folders and can be read on both Macs and PCs running Windows, Unix, and Linux. (To burn an audio CD, use iTunes, as I show you in Book III, Chapter 2.) Of course, you'll need a Mac with a CD or DVD recorder.

Back to the story! To record a disc, follow these steps:

1. **Load a blank CD-R, CD-RW, DVD-R, or DVD-RW into your drive.**

   I assume for this demonstration that you're using a write-once CD-R.

   A dialog appears and prompts you for an action to take.

2. **For this demonstration, choose the default, Open Finder.**

   OS X displays an Untitled CD volume icon on your Desktop. (It's marked with the letters CDR so you know that the disc is recordable.)

3. **Double-click the Untitled CD icon to display the contents — it'll be empty, naturally.**

4. **Click and drag files and folders to the CD window as you normally do.**

5. **Rename any files or folders as necessary.**

After you've started recording, this stuff is etched in stone, so your disc window should look just like the volume window on the finished CD-ROM.

6. **Click the Burn button next to the disc heading in the Finder window sidebar, or click the Burn button in the CD window.**

   The Big X displays a confirmation dialog.

7. **If you've forgotten something, you can click the Cancel or Eject button. Otherwise, click the Burn button and sit back and watch the fun.**

Unfortunately, OS X doesn't support recording from Finder for some external and third-party drives available for the Macintosh. If you can't burn from Finder (or you're willing to pay for a lot of extra recording formats and features), I recommend that you buy a copy of Roxio Toast Titanium recording software (www.roxio.com).

All You Really Need to Know about Printing

To close out this chapter, I turn your attention to another task that most Mac owners need to tackle soon after buying a Mac or installing Mavericks: printing documents. Because basic printing is so important (and in most cases, so simple), allow me to use this final section to demonstrate how to print a document.

Most of us have a Universal Serial Bus (USB) printer — the USB being the favored hardware connection in OS X — so as long as your printer is supported by OS X, setting it up is as easy as plugging it into one of your Mac's USB ports. The Big X does the rest of the work, selecting the proper printer software driver from the Library/Printers folder and setting your printer as the default power of the universe.

Before you print, *preview!* Would you jump from an airplane without a parachute? Then why would you print a document without double-checking it first? Most applications now have their own built-in Preview thumbnails in the Print dialog, as shown in Figure 3-9 — this is definitely A Good Thing! However, if the application you're using doesn't have a Preview display in the Print dialog (or if it's too small to see clearly), I recommend that you click the Preview button with abandon. OS X opens the Preview application to show you what the printed document will look like, possibly saving you both paper and some of that hideously expensive ink or toner. When you've finished examining your handiwork, close the Preview application to return to your document.

Adding the perfect font with Font Book

Need to install a font in OS X, or perhaps you'd like to organize your fonts into collections based on their theme or their designer? If so, you're talking about *Font Book,* which is the font organizer that ships with Mavericks. To open Font Book, visit your Applications folder and double-click the Font Book icon.

Press ⌘+O (or choose File⇨Add Fonts) to import a new font into your system, or simply drag the font file from a Finder window into the Font Book window. Mavericks can accept TrueType, OpenType, and PostScript Type 1

fonts. When your new font has been added, it can be categorized by dragging it into one of your *collections,* thus making that font easier to locate and display. Individual fonts and entire collections can be enabled or disabled (by using the Enable and Disable items on the Edit menu) so that you can "turn on" only those fonts that you need for a specific application or project. The Font Book window also comes fully equipped with a Search box, so you can find any font by name.

To print from any application using the default page characteristics — standard 8½ x 11" paper, portrait mode, no scaling — follow these steps:

1. **In your application, choose File⇨ Print or press the ⌘+P keyboard shortcut.**

In most applications, OS X displays the simple version of the Print dialog. (To display all the fields that you see in Figure 3-9, click the Show Details button at the bottom of the sheet.) Some applications use their own custom Print dialogs, but you should see the same general settings.

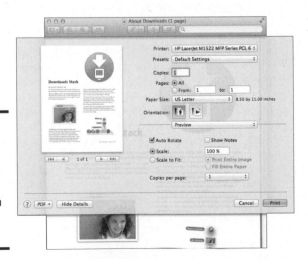

Figure 3-9: The Print dialog is available from any application with any real guts.

2. **Click in the Copies field and enter the number of copies that you need.**

   You can also enable or disable collation, just as you can with those oh-so-fancy copiers.

3. **Decide what you want to print.**

   - *The whole shootin' match:* To print the entire document, use the default Pages radio button setting of All.

   - *Anything less:* To print a range of selected pages, select the From radio button and enter the starting and ending pages (or, if the application allows it, a selection of individual pages).

4. **(Optional) Choose application-specific printing parameters.**

   Each OS X application provides different panes so that you can configure settings specific to that application. You don't have to display any of these extra settings to print a default document, but the power is there to change the look dramatically when necessary. To display these settings, open the pop-up menu in the center of the Print dialog and choose one of these panes. For example, if you're printing from Contacts, you can choose the Contacts entry from the pop-up menu and elect to print a phone list, an envelope, mailing labels, or an e-mail list.

5. **When everything is go for launch, click the Print button.**

Of course, there are more settings and more functionality to the printing system in OS X, and I cover more complex printing topics in much more detail in Book VII, Chapter 4. However, I can tell you from my experiences as a consultant and hardware technician that this short introduction to printing will likely suffice for 90 percent of the Mac owners on Earth. 'Nuff said.

Chapter 4: Searching Everything with Spotlight

In This Chapter

✔ Mastering basic Spotlight searching skills

✔ Selecting text and keywords for best results

✔ Displaying results in the Spotlight window

✔ Customizing Spotlight settings in System Preferences

Spotlight is Apple's desktop search technology that you can use to find files and folders on your computer as quickly as you can type. (Yep, you can search all the documents, Contacts cards, Mail messages, folders, and drives that your Mac can access.) The version of Spotlight included with Mavericks can even search other Macs across your network!

This chapter is your ticket to using this powerful search technology, from day one, like a professional technowizard. I discuss how Spotlight works and how you can use it to locate exactly what you want (and present those results as proudly as a wine steward showing off a fine vintage).

Doing a Basic Search

Figure 4-1 illustrates the Spotlight search field, which is always available from the Finder menu bar. Click the magnifying glass icon once (or press ⌘+Spacebar), and the Spotlight search box appears.

To run a search, simply click in the Spotlight box and begin typing. (The words you type that you want to match are called *keywords*.) Matching items appear as soon as you type, and the search results are continually refined while you type the rest of your search keywords. You don't need to press Return to begin the search.

Figure 4-1:
A lot of
power purrs
behind
this single
Spotlight
search box.

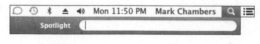

The results of your Spotlight search appear in the Spotlight menu, which is updated automatically in real time while you continue to type. The top 20 most-relevant items are grouped into categories — such as Messages, Definitions, Documents, Folders, Images, PDFs, and Contacts, on right on the Spotlight menu. Spotlight takes a guess at the item that's most likely the match you're looking for (based on your Search Results list in System Preferences, which I cover later in the chapter) and presents it in the special Top Hit category that always appears first.

Hover your cursor over an item in the Spotlight menu, and *shazam!* — Spotlight uses the Quick Look technology built into Mavericks to display either a thumbnail image of a document or information on the item! If the item is a song, you can even move your cursor on top of the thumbnail in the Quick Look display and click to play it — all without leaving the Spotlight menu.

To open the Top Hit item like a true Mavericks power user, just press Return. (My brothers and sisters, it just doesn't get any easier than that.)

Literally any text string is acceptable as a Spotlight search. However, here's a short list of the common search criteria I use every day:

✦ **Names and addresses:** Because Spotlight has access to the Contacts application in Mavericks, you can immediately display contact information using any portion of a name or an address.

✦ **E-mail message text:** Need to open a specific e-mail message, but you'd rather not launch Mail and spend time digging through the message list? Enter the person's e-mail address or any text string contained in the message you're looking for.

✦ **File and folder names:** A simple item name is the classic search favorite. Spotlight searches your entire system for that one file or folder in the blink of an eye.

✦ **Events and Reminder items:** Yep, Spotlight gives you access to your Calendar events and those all-important Reminders you've created.

+ **System Preferences:** Now things start to get *really* interesting! Try typing the word **background** in the Spotlight field. Some of the results will be System Preference panes! That's right: Every setting in System Preferences is referenced in Spotlight. (For example, the Desktop background setting resides in the Desktop & Screen Saver pane in System Preferences.)

+ **Web pages:** *Whoa.* Stand back, Google. You can use Spotlight to search the web pages you've recently displayed in Safari! (Note, however, that this feature doesn't let you search through all the Internet like Google does. Instead, you can search only the pages stored in your Safari web cache and any HTML files you've saved to your Mac's hard drive.)

+ **Metadata:** This category is pretty broad, but it fits. If you're not familiar with the term *metadata*, think of the information stored by your digital camera each time you take a photo — exposure setting, time and date, and even the location where the photo was taken, which are also transferred to iPhoto when you import. Here's another example: I like to locate Word documents on my system using the same metadata that's stored in the file, such as the contents of the Comments field in a Word document. Other supported applications include Adobe Photoshop images, Microsoft Excel spreadsheets, Keynote presentations, iTunes media, and other third-party applications that offer a Spotlight plug-in.

To reset the Spotlight search and try another text string, click the X icon that appears at the right side of the Spotlight box. Of course, you can also backspace to the beginning of the field, but that's a little less elegant, so try pressing ⌘+A to select the entire contents, and then press Delete.

After you find the item you're looking for, you can click it once to

+ Launch it (if the item is an application).

+ Open it in System Preferences (if it's a setting or description on a Preferences pane).

+ Open it within the associated application (if the item is a document or a data item).

+ Display it in a Finder window (if the item is a folder).

Here's another favorite timesaver: You can display all the files of a particular type on your system by using the file type as the keyword. For example, to provide a list of all images on your system, just use *images* as your keyword — the same goes for *movies* and *audio,* too.

How Cool Is That!? Discovering What Spotlight Can Do

Don't get fooled into simply using Spotlight as another file-'n-folder-name search tool. Sure, it can do that, but Spotlight can also search *inside* PDF, Pages, Word documents, and HTML files, finding matching text that doesn't appear in the name of the file! To wit: A search for *Mavericks* on my system pulls up all sorts of items with *Mavericks* not only in their names but also files with *Mavericks in* them:

+ Apple Store SF.ppt: A PowerPoint presentation with several slides containing the text *Mavericks*

+ bk01ch03.doc: A rather cryptically named Microsoft Word file chapter of this book that mentions Mavericks in several spots

+ Conference Call with Bob: A Calendar event pointing to a conference call with my editor about upcoming Mavericks book projects

Not one of these three examples has the words *Mavericks* occurring anywhere in the title or filename, yet Spotlight found them because they all contain the text *Mavericks* therein. That, dear reader, is the true power of Spotlight, and how it can literally guarantee you that you'll never lose another piece of information that Spotlight can locate in the hundreds of thousands of files and folders on your hard drive!

Heck, suppose that all you remember about a file is that you received it in your mail last week or last month. To find it, you can type time periods, such as *yesterday, last week,* or *last month,* to see every item that you saved or received within that period. (Boy, howdy, I *love* writing about TGIs — that's short for Truly Good Ideas.)

Is Spotlight secure?

So how about all those files, folders, contacts, and events that you *don't* want to appear in Spotlight? What if you're sharing your Mac as a multiuser computer or accessing other Macs remotely? Can others search for and access your personal information through Spotlight?

Definitely not! The results displayed by Spotlight are controlled by file and folder permissions as well as your account login, just as the applications that create and display your personal data are. For example, you can't access other users' calendars using Calendar, and they can't see your Mail messages. Only *you* have access to your data, and only after you've logged in with your username and password. Spotlight works the same way. If a user doesn't normally have access to an item, the item simply doesn't appear when that user performs a Spotlight search. (In other words, only you get to see your stuff.)

However, you can hide certain folders and disks from your own Spotlight searches if necessary. Check out the final section of this chapter for details on setting private locations on your system.

Be careful, however, when you're considering a search string. Don't forget that (by default) Spotlight matches only those items that have *all* the words you enter in the Spotlight box. To return the highest number of possible matches, use the fewest number of words that will identify the item; for example, use *horse* rather than *horse image,* and you're certain to be rewarded with more hits. On the other hand, if you're looking specifically for a picture of a knight on horseback, using a series of keywords — such as *horse knight image* — shortens your search considerably. It all depends on what you're looking for and how widely you want to cast your Spotlight net.

To allow greater flexibility in searches, Apple also includes those helpful Boolean friends that you may already be familiar with: AND, OR, and NOT. For example, you can perform Spotlight searches, such as

- ✦ Horse AND cow: Collects all references to both those barnyard animals into one search

- ✦ Batman OR Robin: Returns all references to either Batman or Robin

- ✦ Apple NOT PC: Displays all references to Apple that don't include any information about dastardly PCs

Because Spotlight functions are a core technology of OS X Mavericks — in other words, all sorts of applications can make use of Spotlight throughout the operating system, including Finder — the Finder window's Search box now shares many of the capabilities of Spotlight. You can use the time period trick that I mention earlier (entering *yesterday* as a keyword) in the Finder window Search box.

Expanding Your Search Horizons

I can just hear the announcer's voice now: "But wait, there's more! If you click the Show In Finder menu item at the beginning of your search results, we'll expand your Spotlight menu into the Spotlight window!" (Fortunately, you don't have to buy some ridiculous household doodad.)

Keyboard mavens will appreciate the Spotlight window shortcut key, and I show you where to specify this shortcut in the final section of this chapter.

Figure 4-2 illustrates the Spotlight window (which is a Finder window with extras). To further filter the search, click one of the buttons on the Spotlight window toolbar or create your own custom filter. Click the button with the plus sign to display the search criteria bar and then click the pop-up menus to choose from criteria, such as the type of file, the text content, or the location on your system (for example, your hard drive, your Home folder, or a network server). You can also filter your results listing by the date when the items were created or last saved. To add or delete criteria, click the Plus and Minus buttons at the right side of the search criteria bar. To save a custom filter that you've created, click the Save button.

Icon view   Add filters

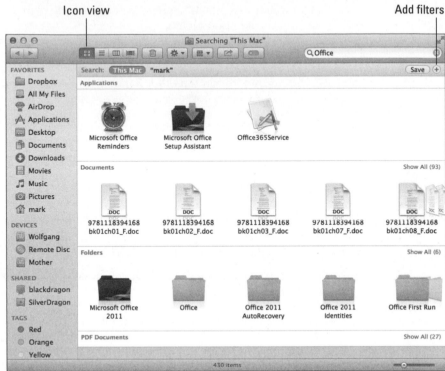

Figure 4-2:
The
spacious
borders of
the Spotlight
window.

Images appear as thumbnail icons, so you can use that most sophisticated search tool — the human eye — to find the picture you're looking for. (If you don't see thumbnail images, click the Icon view button on the toolbar.) Don't forget that you can increase or decrease the size of the icons by dragging the slider at the bottom right of the window.

To display the contents of an item in the list (without leaving the comfortable confines of the Spotlight window), click the item to select it and press the spacebar for a better view. Note that Mavericks must recognize the format of the file (and it must be supported by at least one application).

Again, when you're ready to open an item, just double-click it in the Spotlight window.

As I mention earlier, Spotlight can look for matching items on other Macs on your network only if those remote Macs are configured correctly. To allow another Mac running OS X Tiger 10.5 (or later) to be visible to Spotlight on your system, enable File Sharing on the other Mac. (Oh, and remember that you need an admin level account on that Mac — or access to a good friend who has an admin level account on that Mac.)

Follow these steps to enable file sharing on the other Mac:

1. **On the Dock, click the System Preferences icon (the gears).**

2. **Click the Sharing pane.**

3. **In the service list on the left side of the Sharing pane, select the On check box next to the File Sharing item to enable it.**

4. **Click the Close button in the System Preferences window.**

You can search only those items for which you have rights and permissions to view on the remote Mac (such as the contents of the Public folders on that computer). I discuss more about these limitations earlier in this chapter, in the "Is Spotlight secure?" sidebar.

Customizing Spotlight to Your Taste

You might wonder whether such an awesome OS X feature has its own pane in System Preferences — and you'd be right again. Figure 4-3 shows off the Spotlight pane in System Preferences: Click the System Preferences icon on the Dock and then click the Spotlight icon to display these settings.

Figure 4-3:
Fine-tune your Spotlight menu and Results window from System Preferences.

Click the Search Results tab to

✦ **Determine which categories appear in the Spotlight menu and Results window.** For example, if you don't use any presentation software on your Mac, you can clear the check box next to Presentations to disable this category (thereby making more room for other categories that you will use).

✦ **Determine the order that categories appear in the Spotlight menu and Results window.** Drag the categories to the order in which you want them to appear in the Spotlight menu and window. For example, I like the Documents and System Preferences categories higher in the list because I use those most often.

✦ **Specify the Spotlight menu and Spotlight Results window keyboard shortcuts.** You can enable or disable either keyboard shortcut and choose the key combination from the pop-up menu. By default, the menu keyboard shortcut is ⌘+Space, and the Results window keyboard shortcut is ⌘+Option+Space.

Click the Privacy tab (shown in Figure 4-4) to specify disks and folders that should never be listed as results in a Spotlight search. I know, I know — I said earlier that Spotlight respected your security, and it does. However, the disks and folders that you add to this list won't appear even if *you* are the one performing the search — a great idea for folders and removable hard drives that you use to store sensitive information, such as medical records.

Figure 4-4: When certain folders and disks must remain private (even from you!), add them to this list.

To add locations that you want to keep private, click the Add button (a plus sign) and navigate to the desired location. Click the location to select it, and then click Choose. Alternatively, you can drag folders or disks directly from a Finder window and drop them into the pane.

Chapter 5: Fun with Photo Booth

In This Chapter

✔ Using Photo Booth to take photos

✔ Adding effects to images and movie clips

✔ Capturing video with iMovie

Many Apple switchers and first-time owners quickly notice the built-in video camera that accompanies their iMacs, MacBooks, and Apple LED displays: a tiny square lens and LED light at the top of the screen. That square is the lens of your FaceTime HD camera (and the accompanying microphone), which allows audio and video chatting in Messages, video chatting in FaceTime, or a quick, fun series of photos or video clips via Mavericks's Photo Booth and iMovie applications. You can even take your user account photo with your FaceTime HD camera (in the System Preferences window)!

What's that you say? Your last computer didn't have a video camera? Well then, good reader, you've come to the right place! In this chapter, I show you how easy it is to produce photos and video with your FaceTime HD camera. *Sassy!*

Capturing the Moment with FaceTime HD and Photo Booth

As I mention earlier, every MacBook and iMac running Mavericks is ready to capture video, so pat yourself on the back and do the Technology Dance.

Previous MacBook and iMac models include an integrated camera that Apple called the *iSight* camera. Today's models use an improved version of the hardware, rechristened as the *FaceTime HD* camera (a name change aimed straight at Mavericks's FaceTime video-chatting application, which I describe in detail later in Book V, Chapter 3). If your older Mac has a built-in iSight camera, don't panic because if your Mac meets the other requirements for the FaceTime application, your onboard camera will work just fine. Naturally, a Mavericks–compatible USB webcam is perfect as well.

And if you're using a Mac mini or Mac Pro, you're not stuck out in the cold! The most elegant solution is an Apple LED display, which includes its own camera, microphone, speakers, and USB hub. If you already have a monitor, however, you can still add your own external camera; just check online at eBay or craigslist to pick up a used iSight camera. Many external USB and FireWire web cameras support OS X as well, and Mavericks automatically recognizes any supported external video camera.

Figure 5-1 illustrates a typical MacBook FaceTime HD camera. What can you do with your camera? Here's the rundown:

✦ With Messages, you can videoconference in style. Find everything you need to join the ranks of the Messages elite in Book V, Chapter 3.

✦ Book V, Chapter 3 also includes coverage of FaceTime, the video chat application you use to talk to owners of Mac computers and also iOS 5/6/7 devices, such as the iPhone, iPad, and iPod touch.

✦ You can capture video clips using iMovie and use the footage in all your iLife applications.

✦ Use Photo Booth to snap digital pictures just like you did in the old automatic photo booth at your local arcade — and Photo Booth comes complete with visual effects to add pizzazz and punch to your photos. (Oh, did I mention you can shoot video as well?) If you've used the Photo Booth application on an iPad, you're already familiar with how much fun you can have with your images and video clips!

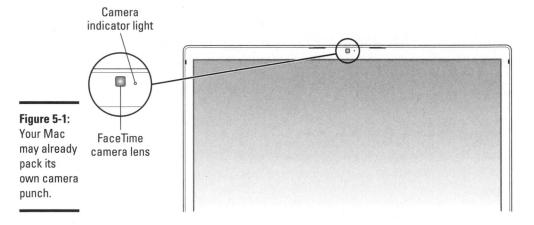

Figure 5-1: Your Mac may already pack its own camera punch.

The FaceTime HD camera's indicator light glows green whenever you're taking a snapshot or recording video . . . which, when you think about it, is A Good Thing (especially if you prefer chatting at home in Leisure Mode).

Need to quickly get a picture of yourself for use on your FaceBook page? Or perhaps your Messages icon needs an update to show off your new haircut? Photo Booth can capture images at 640 x 480 resolution and 32-bit color. Although today's digital cameras produce a much higher-quality photo, you can't beat the built-in convenience of Photo Booth for such a quick snapshot.

To snap an image in Photo Booth, follow these steps:

1. **From the Dock, launch Photo Booth (it looks like an old-fashioned arcade photo booth, complete with a strip of photos).**

You can launch Photo Booth also from Launchpad, and you'll find it in the Applications folder on your hard drive.

Figure 5-2 illustrates the application window that appears. (Ignore the rather silly gentleman who wandered into the frame. I doubt that he'll be in your Photo Booth window!)

Photo Booth features a different appearance in full-screen mode, complete with a fancy wooden stage and curtain. To try things out full-screen, click the Full Screen button at the top-right corner of the Photo Booth window, or choose View➪Enter Full Screen. From the keyboard, press ⌘+Control+F. To return to windowed mode, press Esc.

Figure 5-2:
Photo Booth does candid photography particularly well.

2. Choose to capture one image, four quick photos as a group, or digital video.

Use the three buttons at the lower left of the Photo Booth window to switch between taking four sequential photos (arranged as a group, like a photo strip from an arcade photo booth), one photo, or a movie clip.

3. (Optional) Click the Effects button to choose an effect you'd like to apply to your image.

Photo Booth displays a screen of thumbnail preview images so that you can see how each effect changes the photo. You can produce some of the simple effects you may be familiar with from Photoshop, such as a black-and-white image or a fancy color-pencil filter, or you can indulge in some mind-blowing distortion effects and even an Andy Warhol–style pop-art image.

To return the display to normal without choosing an effect, click the Normal thumbnail, which appears in the center. (Paul Lynde's spot, for those of you old enough to remember *Hollywood Squares*.)

Of course, you can always launch your favorite image editor afterward to use a filter or an effect on a photo — for example, the effects available in iPhoto. However, Photo Booth can apply these effects automatically as soon as you take the picture.

4. (Optional) Click a thumbnail to select the desired effect.

When you choose an effect, Photo Booth automatically closes the Effects display.

5. Click the Camera button to start the countdown, and you'll hear the "shutter" snap as the photo is taken.

The image (or video clip) automatically appears in the filmstrip at the bottom of the window. Photo Booth keeps a copy of all the images and clips you take in that filmstrip for easy access. Click a photo or film clip in the filmstrip, and a Share button appears above the filmstrip that allows you to

✦ Send the photo in an e-mail message.

✦ Send the photo in a Messages conversation.

✦ Upload the photo to Flickr, Twitter, or Facebook.

✦ Save the photo directly to iPhoto or Aperture.

✦ Use the image as your Mavericks user account icon.

To delete an image or a clip from the Photo Booth filmstrip, click the offending thumbnail, and then click the X button that appears at the left corner.

Who needs a fancy "green screen"?

Ever admired the animated background behind your favorite TV weather prognosticator? Believe it or not, you don't need an expensive "green screen" backdrop (and time in a video-editing application) to create the same effect. Just use Photo Booth to create those outrageous images and video clips. Both Messages and Photo Booth provide a surprising array of visual effects you can use.

Here's what to do, in Photo Booth:

1. Click the Effects button.

2. Click the right arrow next to the Effects button until you reach the series of thumbnails with names such as Clouds, Earthrise, Fish, and Rollercoaster.

These thumbnails are the animated backgrounds.

3. Click a background.

Photo Booth asks you to step outside the frame for a second so that your Mac can detect the patterns behind you.

4. When the background animation begins, step back into the frame and capture your image or video clip.

Hint: Just like a real green screen backdrop, you get the best results if you shoot your images and video in front of a blank white wall.

You're not limited to the Apple animated backgrounds, either. Use your own image or video clip by choosing one of the eight predefined User Backdrop thumbnails.

Producing Video on the Spot with iMovie

"Mark, am I limited to capturing stuff with Photo Booth?" Oh, pshaw on limitations . . . you're a Mac owner, after all! You can also use your FaceTime HD camera to snag video clips (complete with audio) in iMovie.

You don't need an expensive digital camcorder to produce video clips for use in iMovie! Your Mac's camera can capture those clips for you — think of the party possibilities! (Or the opportunity for practical jokes. But then again, you're not that kind of person, now, *are* you?) To capture video directly from your FaceTime HD camera into iMovie, follow these steps:

1. **Launch iMovie from the Dock or from the Applications folder.**

2. **Click the Open Camera Import Window button to switch to Import Video mode.**

The button is located at the far left of the toolbar running across the center of the iMovie window, and it sports a camera icon.

3. **Click the Camera pop-up menu at the bottom of the Import window and then click Built-in iSight.**

As I mention earlier in this chapter, the iSight camera is the ancestor of today's FaceTime HD camera. The name was changed after the release of iMovie '11, so you can choose this setting with a clear conscience, no matter what hardware you own.

4. **When you're ready to start recording video, click the Capture button.**

iMovie displays a sheet allowing you to select the location for the movie clip (including the approximate amount of time you can record). You can also choose to add the video to an existing iMovie Event or a brand-new Event. To help keep things steady in your clip, select the Analyze for Stabilization after Import check box to enable it. Enabling the stabilization process will significantly add to the time it takes for iMovie to save your clip to disk, though.

5. **When you're ready to start recording video, click the Capture button.**

iMovie automatically displays the incoming video in the monitor pane while it's recorded. (As you might expect, the goofy behavior on the part of the distinguished cast usually starts at about this moment.)

6. **Click the Stop button to stop recording.**

After you end the recording, iMovie creates the video clip and adds it to your Clips pane.

I go into much more detail on iMovie in Chapter 4 of Book III, but that's the gist of recording video clips.

Chapter 6: Using Reminders, Notes, and Notifications

In This Chapter

- ✔ Setting Reminders
- ✔ Making Notes
- ✔ Using Notification Center

A s I've said many times before in my books, "If it works in one place, it's likely to show up in another." In this case, three popular time-saving (and headache-preventing) apps have crossed over from the world of iOS devices — the iPhone, iPad, and iPod touch — and have securely landed on your Mavericks Desktop! Those apps are Reminders, Notes, and Notification Center.

That's not the only good news, though: These three Mac applications work seamlessly with an iCloud account you've already set up, so if you also use an iOS device (with the same Apple ID), the notes you take and the reminders you make are automatically synchronized among all your Apple computers and devices! (If you didn't create an Apple ID when you installed Mavericks, visit Chapter 3 of this minibook for the details.)

Because all three applications have a similar goal — namely, to keep you in touch with the information, daily tasks, and digital events that matter to you — I decided to cover them in one shiny chapter. Consider this chapter a guide that demonstrates how you can note, remind, and notify like a power user!

Remind Me to Use Reminders

You don't need to look far to find the new Reminders application on your Mac. Just click the Reminders icon on the Dock to display the main window, as shown in Figure 6-1.

Search box   Reminders sidebar   Reminders   Add Reminder

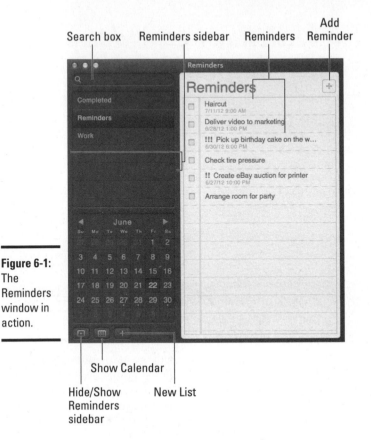

Figure 6-1:
The
Reminders
window in
action.

Show Calendar

Hide/Show
Reminders
sidebar

New List

The highlights of the Reminders window include

+ **Search box:** Click here and type a phrase or name to search for it among your reminders.

+ **Reminders sidebar:** You can add as many separate Reminder lists as you like in the application (one for work, for example, and another for your Mac user group). In the sidebar, you can switch quickly between your lists. (Note that two lists, Reminders and Completed, already appear.)

+ **Hide/Show Reminders Sidebar button:** Click this button to hide or show the Reminders sidebar. You save a significant amount of screen real estate when the display is hidden.

✦ **Calendar:** This handy calendar indicates which days of the current
month already have reminders pending: They're displayed with a dot
under the date. You can jump to any date by clicking it. To move forward and backward through the months, click the Previous and Next
buttons next to the month name. (Note that this calendar does not sync
or exchange reminder dates with the Calendar application that I cover in
Chapter 8 of this minibook.)

✦ **New List button:** Click this button to add a new Reminder list to the
sidebar; from the keyboard, press ⌘+L. The list name is highlighted in a
text box, so you can simply type the new name and then press Return.

✦ **Reminders:** These entries are the reminders themselves. Each is prefaced by a check box so you can select the check box when the reminder
is complete, thereby moving that reminder automatically to the
Completed list. And yes, if you select the Completed list in the sidebar
and deselect the check box for a reminder, it returns (like a bad penny)
to the original list.

✦ **Add Reminder button:** Click this button to add a new reminder to the
currently selected list; from the keyboard, press ⌘+N. In its simplest
form, a reminder is just a short phrase or sentence. Press Return afterward to save it to your list.

Adding a reminder is straightforward. First, click a date in the calendar
display to jump to that date, and then click the Add Reminder button. Type
a few words and press Return to create a basic reminder. However, if you
hover your cursor over the reminder you just created, an Info button (the
lowercase *i* in a circle icon) appears next to the text. The game is afoot! Click
the Info button to display the settings you see in Figure 6-2.

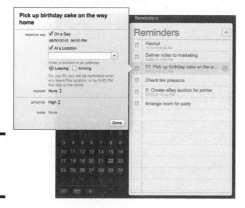

Figure 6-2:
Editing a
reminder.

The fields on the Edit sheet are

✦ **Reminder text:** Click this text to edit the reminder text itself.

✦ **On a Day:** Enable this check box if the reminder should appear in Notification Center on a particular day. By default, the date is the one selected when you created the reminder. You can click the Date and Time fields to change them.

✦ **At a Location:** Here's a powerful feature. Enable this check box, and you can choose a card from your Contacts application that includes an address (or simply type an address into the box). Now Reminders will monitor your current location on your iOS device and notify you when you're leaving or arriving at that location (and optionally, on the date and time you specify in the On a Day field). For example, you could create a reminder that notifies you on your iPhone when you're arriving at the mall on September 15 to pick up the watch that's being repaired. *Shazam!*

✦ **Repeat:** Set this reminder to automatically repeat every day, week, two weeks, month, or year at the same time.

✦ **Priority:** You can assign one of four priorities to the reminder: Low, Medium, High, or None. Assigning a priority prefaces the reminder text with one (Low), two (Medium), or three (High) red exclamation points so that the reminder stands out from the crowd.

✦ **Note:** Click next to the Note field to enter a free-form text note along with the reminder.

Click Done on the Edit sheet when you've finished making changes. You can edit a reminder as often as you like. For example, I sometimes have to change the date on a reminder multiple times as my schedule changes.

To delete a reminder from the list, right-click it and choose Delete from the menu that appears.

Taking Notes the Mavericks Way

Imagine a notepad of unlimited pages that's always available whenever you're around your Mac, iPhone, iPod touch, or iPad — that's the idea behind Notes, and it's superbly simple! To open the application, click the Notes icon on the Dock. The window shown in Figure 6-3 appears.

Folders list   Search box   Notes sidebar   Notes page

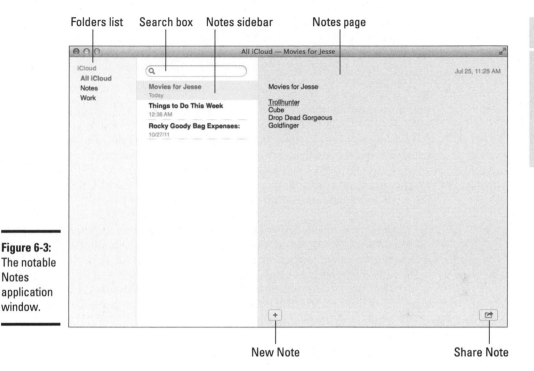

New Note   Share Note

Figure 6-3:
The notable Notes application window.

The salient stuff in the Notes window includes

✦ **Search box:** If you're hunting for a specific note, click in this box and type a phrase or name to search for it.

✦ **Folders list:** You can create new folders to hold specific kinds of notes. In Figure 6-3, for example, I added a Work folder. To add a new folder, choose File⇨New Folder or press ⌘+Shift+N, and then type the new folder name. To switch between folders, display the Folders list and click the desired folder.

✦ **Notes sidebar:** Each Note you create appears as a separate entry in the sidebar. You can click a Note to switch to it immediately.

✦ **New Note button:** Click this button to add a new Note. You can also right-click the Sidebar and choose New Note from the contextual menu. Notes uses the first line of text that you type as the title of the Note, which appears in the sidebar.

✦ **Note page:** This free-form pane is where you type the body of your note. You can also drag images from a Finder window and include them in the body of the note and even attach files by dragging them from a Finder window as well.

✦ **Share note icon:** Open this pop-up menu to share the contents of the current note, just like the Share button that appears on the Finder window toolbar. Sharing options can include a new e-mail message, a new message in the Messages application, and new postings to Twitter and Facebook.

To edit a note, click it to select it in the sidebar, and then simply make your changes or additions in the Note page. You can format the text from the Format menu — everything from different fonts and colors to inserting bulleted and numbered lists.

To delete a note you no longer need, right-click it in the sidebar and choose Delete from the menu that appears.

 If a note is particularly important and you'd like to keep it front and center on your Mavericks Desktop, double-click the note in the sidebar to open it in a separate window, and then choose Window⇨Float on Top. Now the note window will stay visible on your Desktop until you quit the Notes application. Even if other application windows are active and would normally be *on top* of the note window, it's downright stubborn and refuses to be hidden!

Staying Current with Notification Center

Unlike Reminders and Notes, Notification Center isn't an application you launch! Instead, the Notification Center icon appears at the far right side of the Finder menu bar, and it's always running.

Click the icon (or, if you're using a trackpad, swipe from the right edge to the left) to display your notifications, as shown in Figure 6-4. These notifications can be generated by a whole host of Mavericks applications and functions, including Calendar, Mail, FaceTime, Reminders, Game Center, Photo Stream, Messages, Safari, Facebook and even the Apple App Store.

I love how Notification Center doesn't interfere with open applications. It simply moves the entire desktop to the left so that you can see your notifications. You can close Notification Center at any time by clicking anywhere on the Desktop to the left, clicking the Notifications icon on the Finder menu bar again, or swiping in the opposite direction.

Notification entries that appear in Center are grouped under the application that created them. Many entries can be deleted from Center by clicking the Delete button that appears next to the application heading (the button bears an X symbol). Other entries, such as Calendar alerts, remain in Notification Center until a certain time has elapsed. (You'll read all about the OS X Calendar application in Chapter 8 of this minibook.)

Quick Message

System Preferences

Figure 6-4:
Notification
Center
muscles
your
desktop to
the side.

At the top of Notification Center is a Quick Message button — click it to display a pop-up dialog where you can specify the recipients of the message, type your message text, and then click Send (all without having to even launch the Messages application)! Depending on the Internet accounts you've added in System Preferences, you may see Facebook and LinkedIn Quick buttons at the top of Notification Center as well.

But wait, there's more to Notification Center than just a strip of happenings! Depending on the settings you choose, notifications can also appear without Notification Center being open at all. These notifications are displayed as pop-up *banners* (which disappear in a few seconds) and *alerts* (which must be dismissed by clicking a button). Figure 6-5 illustrates a typical alert notification.

Figure 6-5:
An alert
notification
appears
on your
Desktop.

Mavericks introduces *actions* in notifications — depending on the application or function that generates the notification, you may see buttons on a banner or an alert that allow you to take care of business (without requiring the application to be running). For example, if a new e-mail message is received in Apple Mail, you can choose to reply to or delete the message. Websites can display updates as notifications, and you can answer a FaceTime call directly from the notification.

You can configure the notifications for all your applications from the Notifications pane in System Preferences, which you can reach easily if Notification Center is open. Just click the gears icon at the lower right of the screen. I discuss the settings on the Notifications pane in Book II, Chapter 3.

Chapter 7: Keeping Track with Contacts and Maps

*A*re you still struggling with a well-thumbed address book stuck in a drawer of your office desk or an archaic folded map in your glove box? Are you fighting a wallet or purse crammed with sticky notes and odd scraps of paper, each of which bears an invaluable e-mail address, phone number, or scribbled directions? If so, you can finally set yourself free and enjoy the "Paperless Lifestyle" of the new millennium with the revolutionary new Rauncho Digital Buddy! Only $29.95 — and it doubles as an indestructible garden hose! But wait! There's more! And if you order in the next 10 minutes, we'll also send you. . . .

Of course, you and I would tune that stuff out as soon as we heard it, but believe it or not, the digital Address Book and Road Map do exist (after a fashion), and you already have both on your Mac — Contacts and Maps. In this chapter, I show you how to store and retrieve all your contact data, including Internet contact information, photographs, and much more. You'll also learn how to view and print travel directions and virtually tour a city!

(And before you ask, operators are *not* standing by.)

Hey, Isn't Contacts Just a Part of Mail?

In early versions of OS X, Contacts (then called Address Book) was relegated to the minor leagues and usually appeared only when you asked for it in Mail. Although it could be run as a separate application, many Mac owners never launched it as a standalone.

Now, however, the Contacts application appears in the limelight, earning a default location on the Dock and available whenever you need it. Although Contacts can still walk through a meadow hand-in-hand with Mail, it also flirts with other OS X applications and can even handle some basic telephony chores all by itself through the use of Services.

Figure 7-1 illustrates the default face of the Contacts application, complete with a personal address card: your own contact information, which you enter in Setup Assistant, as I mention in Book I, Chapter 1. This card carries a special me tag on your thumbnail image (indicating that it's your personal card) as well as your user thumbnail next to your name. Other OS X applications use the data in your card to automatically fill out your personal information in all sorts of documents. (In Figure 7-1, I added a number of well-known friends as well . . . a few TV characters, a composer or two. You know the drill.)

Figure 7-1: Greetings from the OS X Contacts application!

Add   Edit   Share

Entering Contact Information

Unless you actually meet and hire a group of Data Elves — see the sidebar, "I gotta type (or retype) that stuff?" — you do have to add contacts to Contacts manually, or import your contacts from another existing address book application. Allow me to demonstrate here how to create a new contact card:

1. **From the Dock, launch Contacts by clicking its icon.**

The icon looks like an old-fashioned paper address book with an @ symbol on the cover.

2. **Press the ⌘+N shortcut to create a new contact.**

Alternatively, choose File⇨New Card, or click the Add button (which carries a plus sign) at the bottom of the window and click New Contact from the menu that appears.

Contacts displays the template that you see in Figure 7-2, with the First Name field highlighted and ready for you to type.

3. **Enter the contact's first name and press Tab to move to the Last name field.**

4. **Continue entering the corresponding information in each field, pressing Tab to move through the fields.**

If a field isn't applicable (for example, if a person has no home page), just press Tab again to skip it. You can press Return to add extra lines to the Address field.

Figure 7-2: "Hey, I don't know anyone named *First Last!*"

Note the icons next to each field — the ones that look like up and down arrows. Contacts is telling you that there are additional versions of the field that you can enter as well. (Think home and work addresses.) Click the up/down icon and a pop-up menu appears, allowing you to choose which version of the field will be displayed. Depending on the field, Contacts may automatically display an additional version; for example, if you enter a work address for the contact, another field for the contact's home address appears. Click this new field and then you can enter the contact's home address, too.

You can also add new fields to a card, such as web addresses (also called URLs), birthdays, and maiden names. To add a new field, choose Card⇨Add Field and then choose the field you want to add from the menu that appears. You can also click the Add button at the bottom of the window to display the same menu.

5. **To add a photograph to the card, choose Card⇨Choose Custom Image (or drag an image from a Finder window on top of the thumbnail square).**

   If you choose to assign a custom image, click Defaults to select an image from the Mavericks thumbnail set (which is the same set you get when assigning a user account image). Click Photo Stream to choose an image from your Photo Stream, or click Faces to select an image of someone's face that you've tagged in iPhoto. You can also drag an image from a Finder window or paste an image you copied to your Clipboard.

   If your Mac has an iSight or a FaceTime HD camera, you can click the Camera tab to take a new image. You can also choose to add a Photo Booth effect to your new image!

6. **When you're done, click the Done button at the bottom of the Contacts window to save the card.**

You can edit the contents of a card at any time by displaying it and clicking the Edit button at the bottom (or by pressing ⌘+L, or even by clicking Edit on the Contacts menu bar and choosing the Edit Card menu item). When you're finished editing the card, click Done at the bottom of the Contacts window.

No need to edit a card to add information to the Note field. Just click and type.

You can also add contact cards directly to Contacts from the OS X Mail application, as well as a number of third-party e-mail applications — go figure. In Mail, click the message (to highlight it) from the person whom you want to add, click the friendly Message menu, and then click Add Sender to Contacts. Adding people this way doesn't add their supporting information — just their name and e-mail address (and, if they used Mail on their end to send the message and they have a photo attached to their personal card, their photo gets imported as well). Once again, your nimble fingers have to manually enter the rest. For more on Mail, see Book V, Chapter 2.

"I gotta type (or retype) that stuff?"

In my three-plus decades of travel through the personal computing world, I've noticed that computer owners share one lovely recurring fantasy that keeps cropping up over and over: I call it the *Data Elf Phenomenon.* You see, Data Elves are the hard-working, silicon-based gnomes in tiny green suspenders who magically enter into your database (or Contacts, or Quicken, or whatever) all the information that you want to track. They burrow into your papers and presto! — out pops all that data, neatly typed and . . . whoa, Nellie! Let's stop there.

For some reason, computer users seem to forget that *there are no Data Elves.* I wish I had a dime for every time I've heard a heartbroken computer owner say, "You mean I have to *type* all that stuff?" (My usual retort is, "Affirmative . . . unless you want to pay me a hideous amount to do it for you.") The arrival of iCloud certainly makes it easier to share contacts you've already entered into your iPhone, iPod touch, or iPad with the Contacts application on your Mac, but most folks don't add the entire contents of their paper address book into their iOS devices, so you're back to square one.

Therefore, make no mistake — adding a lifetime's worth of paper-based contact information into your Contacts application can be several hours of monotonous and mind-bendingly boring work, which is another reason why many computer owners still depend on paper to store all those addresses. But take my word for it, dear reader; your effort is worth it. The next time that you sit down to prepare a batch of Christmas cards or you have to find Uncle Milton's telephone number in a hurry, you *will* appreciate the effort that you made to enter contact information into Contacts. (Just make sure that you — say it with me — ***back up your hard drive.*** I recommend you back up using both Time Machine and iCloud, just for good measure.)

By the way, if you've already entered contact information in another PIM (short for Personal Information Manager), you can reuse that data without retyping everything — that is, as long as your old program can export contacts in vCard format. (More about vCards later in this chapter.) After you export the records, just drag the vCards into the Contacts window to add them, or import them by pressing ⌘+O. (More on this at the end of this chapter.) You can also export contact information in tab-delimited format with most PIMs, and import the file using Contacts from the File⇨Import menu path.

TIP

"Mark, I never use the Home Page field when I add a contact. Can't I get rid of it completely?" Indeed you can, good reader! To customize the default fields that appear when you create a new contact card, open the Contacts menu, choose Preferences, and then click the Template tab. Each field has a Delete icon (the red minus sign) and some have an Add icon (the green plus sign). To remove a field from your template, click the Delete icon. To add a new version of a field (for example, a home e-mail address), click the Add icon next to the existing field of the same type, and then click the up/down arrow icon to select the field name. To add a completely new field (such as Middle or Maiden Name), click the Add Field drop-down menu.

Don't forget to add those fax numbers! If you have an external USB analog modem that's compatible with OS X Mavericks, you can fax from any application. Just choose File⇨Print (or press ⌘+P) as you always have, and then click the PDF button at the bottom of the Print dialog and choose Fax PDF. OS X automatically fills in the address for you but only if the contact has a fax number entered as part of the contact card.

If someone sends you an e-mail message with a vCard (look for an attachment with a .vcf extension), consider yourself lucky. Just drag the vCard from the attachment window in Mail and drop it in your Contacts; any information that the person wants you to have is added automatically. Sweet!

To delete a card, right-click the unlucky name and then choose Delete Card.

Using Contact Information

Okay, after you have your contact information in Contacts, what can you actually *do* with it? Often, all you really need is a quick glance at an address. To display the card for any contact in Contacts, just click the desired entry in the Name column. You can move to the next and previous cards by using the up- and down-arrow keys on your keyboard. (Oh, and don't forget that you can right-click many items in a card to display menu commands specific to those items.)

But wait, there's more! You can also

✦ **Copy and paste.** The old favorites are still around. You can copy any data from a card (press ⌘+C) and paste it into another open application (press ⌘+V).

✦ **Visit a contact's home page**. Click the contact entry to select it, and then click the page link displayed in the card. Safari dutifully answers the call, and next thing you know, you're online and at the home page specified in the entry.

✦ **Send an e-mail message.** If you've already read through Chapter 3 of this minibook, you'll remember the OS X Services feature that I tell you about. Click and drag to select any e-mail address on a card; then choose Contacts⇨Services⇨New Email to Address. Bingo! Depending on the information that you select, other services might also be available.

✦ **Add a Messages buddy.** From Messages, choose Buddies⇨Add Buddy. From the dialog that appears, you can select a contact card that has an Instant Messenger address and add it to your Buddy list.

✦ **Export contacts.** From Contacts, select the contacts that you want to export and then choose File⇨Export⇨Export vCard. Contacts displays a Save sheet. Navigate to the location where you want to save the cards and click Save.

✦ **Send a contact through Mail or Messages.** Click the Share a Contact button (it looks like a box with an arrow) at the bottom of the Contacts window, and choose either Email Card or Message Card. The Contacts application automatically creates a new Mail message (or Messages conversation) with the contact information attached as a vCard.

✦ **Search amongst your contacts.** If you're searching for a specific person and all you have is a phone number or a fragment of an address, click in the Search field (which bears a magnifying glass icon) and type the text. While you continue to enter characters, Contacts shows you how many contact cards contain matching characters and displays just those entries in the Name column. Now that's *sassy!* (And convenient. And fast as all get-out.) Check out Figure 7-3; a couple of familiar folks share the same address in Gotham City, and I found them by using the Search field.

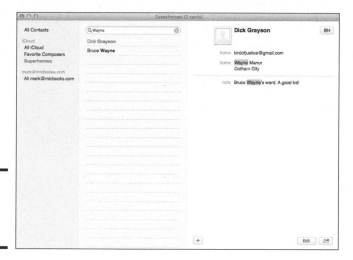

Figure 7-3:
Holy Text
Match,
Batman!

Speaking of searching using a contact card in Contacts, Spotlight is also at your beck and call. Click a contact to select it and then choose Edit➪Spotlight. *Whoosh!* Mavericks searches your entire system for everything related to that contact and displays it in the familiar Spotlight window.

Arranging Your Contact Cards

Contacts also provides you with a method of organizing your cards into groups. A *group* usually comprises folks with a common link, such as your family, friends, coworkers, and others who enjoy yodeling. For example, you could set up a Cellphone group that you can use when syncing data with your Bluetooth cellphone. You can hide or display the Groups list at the left of the Contacts window by choosing View⇨Hide/Show Groups (or by pressing ⌘+1).

To create a group, click the Add button at the bottom of the window and then click New Group. (You can also choose File⇨New Group or press ⌘+Shift+N.) Contacts adds a highlighted text box so that you can type the group name. After you type the group name, press Return to save it.

If you already selected the entries for those contacts that you want to add to a group, choose File⇨New Group from Selection instead. This saves you a step because the group is created, and the members are added automatically.

If you've created an empty group, it's easy to add folks manually. From the group list, click the All Contacts link to see a list of everyone in the Contacts database, and then click and drag the entries that you want to add to the desired group name.

After you create a New Group, you can instantly display members of that group by clicking its name in the group list. To return to the display of all your contacts, click the All Contacts link.

To further organize your groups, you can drag and drop a group on top of another group. It becomes a subgroup, which is handy for things such as branch offices in your company or perhaps relatives to whom you're not speaking at the moment.

Need an even harder-working group? Create a *smart group,* which — get this — automatically adds new contacts you create to the proper group or removes them from the group, depending on the criteria you specify! To create a smart group, follow these steps:

1. **Choose File⇨New Smart Group.**

2. **Type a name for the new smart group.**

3. **From the Card pop-up menu, choose the item that will trigger the action.**

   For example, you can choose to automate a smart group according to the contents of each new card, a company name, or a particular city or state.

4. **From the Contains pop-up menu, choose the criteria for the item.**

   An item might contain (or not contain) a specific string of characters, or it might have changed in a certain amount of time. To illustrate, one of my hardest-working smart groups automatically checks the Company field in every new card for my publisher's company name and adds that contact card to my Wiley Publishing group if a match occurs.

5. **To add another criteria line, click the button with the plus sign at the end of the first text field.**

   If you decide you have one criteria line too many, click the button with the minus sign next to the offending rule.

6. **After your smart group criteria are correct, click OK.**

   The smart group name appears in your group list. *Voilà!*

 Here's another handy feature of a Contacts group: You can send all the members of a group the same e-mail message at one time. In Mail, simply enter the Group name in the To field of the Compose window, and the same message is sent to everyone. Even Gandalf couldn't do that (but my copy editor bets that Dumbledore could).

Using Network Directories

I know, I know. I said earlier that you'd have to enter all your contacts yourself, but I was talking about your personal contacts. You can also access five types of external directories from Contacts:

✦ Mac users working in a Windows network environment can use Exchange 2007 (or later) or Outlook network directories.

✦ If you're a member of a company NetInfo network — and if you don't know, ask your wizened network administrator — you can search network directory servers from Contacts. These servers are available automatically, so no configuration is necessary. Sweet.

✦ OS X Mavericks Server offers a Contacts server feature for sharing directories across your network, using the CardDAV standard.

✦ Contacts can share contact information using your iCloud, Google, Facebook, LinkedIn, or Yahoo! account.

✦ You can search Internet-based LDAP directories. Again, suffice it to say that your network guru can tell you whether LDAP servers are available to you. (In another blazing display of technonerd acronym addiction, LDAP stands for *Lightweight Directory Access Protocol.*) With LDAP, you can search a central company directory from anywhere in the world as long as you have an Internet connection. Your network administrator or the LDAP server administrator can supply you with these settings.

To search any network directory, you need to create a corresponding directory account. Follow these steps to add a directory account:

1. **Choose Contacts⇨Preferences to display the Preferences window.**

2. **Click the Accounts tab.**

3. **Click the Add button at the bottom of the Accounts list to launch the Add Account assistant.**

4. **If you're using an Exchange directory, click Exchange from the list. If you're connecting to a CardDAV or LDAP directory, choose Other Contacts Account from the list.**

5. **Click Continue.**

    Type the required information in the fields that appear. (Your network administrator should be able to provide you with the necessary values.)

6. **Click Create.**

    You'll see the blue network directory entry appear in the Group column.

The rest is easy! Click the desired directory link in the group display and use the Search field as you normally would. Matching entries display the person's name, e-mail address, and phone number.

"But hey, Mark, what if I'm not online? My company's LDAP directory isn't much good then, right?" Normally, that's true. LDAP information is available to you only when you're online and the LDAP server is available. Ah, but here's a rocking power user tip that'll do the trick for MacBook owners: To make a person's information always available, search the LDAP database and drag the resulting entry from the contacts list to the desired group (or the All Contacts link) on the group display. You'll import the information to your local Contacts database — and you'll see it even when you're not online!

Printing Contacts with Flair

For those moments when you need an archaic hard copy of your contacts, Contacts offers a whopping four formats: mailing labels, envelopes, lists, and even a snappy pocket address book.

By default, Contacts prints on standard U.S. letter-size paper (8½ x 11") in portrait orientation. You can change these settings to, for example, legal-size paper or landscape orientation, right from the Print dialog (choose File⇨Print or press ⌘+P).

Follow these steps to print your contacts:

1. **Press ⌘+P.**

    Contacts displays the Print dialog. To show all the settings, click the Show Details button at the bottom of the sheet.

    If you need more than one copy, click in the Copies field to specify the desired number.

TIP

Need labels? We've got 'em! From the Style pop-up menu, choose Mailing Labels. Then, on the Layout pane, specify what type of label stock you're using. Click the Label button to sort your labels by name or postal code, choose a font, select a text color, and add an icon or image to your labels. To switch to a standard contact list, click Style again and then click Lists. (You can also print envelopes and pocket address book pages in a similar manner; just choose the desired entry from the Style pop-up menu.)

2. **Select the desired Attributes check boxes to specify which contact card fields you want to appear in your list.**

   The Attributes list appears only if you're printing contacts in either the Lists style or the pocket address book style.

3. **Click the Print button to send the job to the selected printer.**

   Alternatively, you can create a PDF file in a specified location, which is a handy trick to use if you'd rather not be burdened with paper, but you still need to consult the list or give it to others. (*PDF files* are a special document display format developed by Adobe; they are displayed like a printed document but take up minimal space.) To display the contents of a PDF file in OS X, you need only double-click it in the Finder window, and the built-in Preview application is happy to oblige. Even faster, select the PDF file in the Finder window and press the spacebar for a Quick Look.

Swapping Bytes with vCards

A *vCard* is a standard file format for exchanging contact information between programs such as Contacts, Microsoft Entourage, Microsoft Outlook, Eudora, and the Android operating system. (Heck, if you're sharp enough to have an iPod, iPhone, or iPad, you can even store vCard data there.) Think of a vCard as an electronic business card that you can attach to an e-mail message, send via File Transfer Protocol (FTP), or exchange with others by using your cellular phone and palmtop computer. vCard files end with the extension .vcf.

In Contacts, you can create a single vCard containing one or more selected entries by choosing File⇨Export⇨Export vCard. Then, as with any other OS X Save dialog, just navigate to the spot where you want the file saved, give it a name, and click Save.

Here are two ways to import vCards into Contacts:

✦ Drag the vCard files to Contacts and drop them in the application window.

✦ Choose File⇨Import (or press ⌘+O). From the Open dialog, navigate to the location of the vCard files that you want to add, select them, and then click Open.

TIP

The vCard tab in the Contacts Preferences window allows you to choose the format of your exported vCard files. Older devices work only with vCard 2.1 format, while newer applications recognize the improved vCard 3 format. You can also specify whether your exported vCard files will contain the contents of the Notes field and also whether they will include any photos you've attached. If you'd rather not provide the private data on your personal (or Me) card in a vCard, make sure that you select the Enable Private Me Card check box.

Introducing the Maps Window

If you're an owner of an iPad, iPhone or iPod touch, prepare yourself for a joyful state: With the arrival of OS X Mavericks, your beloved Maps application now resides on your Dock! As long as you have a connection to the Internet, Maps is ready to display locations, provide directions, and even allow for informal views of important sites worldwide! (Recognize the grand dame in Figure 7-4?)

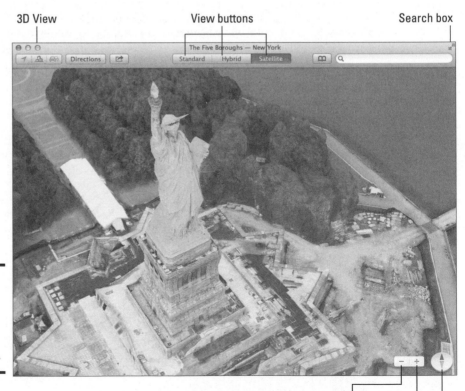

Figure 7-4: The Statue of Liberty shines in the Maps application.

Displaying an overhead view of an address is one of the simplest chores in all of OS X — from the Maps window, just click in the Search box at the top-right corner, type the address, and press Return. Maps displays the address with a red pushpin to help you locate it.

Depending on the location you've chosen, you may also see a tiny Info icon (which looks like a lowercase "i" within a circle) next to the name. To view more information, click the Info icon.

If you are using a MacBook, are in range of a Wi-Fi signal, and have turned Location Services on, you can quickly map your current location — just click View⇨Go to Current Location, or press ⌘+L.

Ah, but why stop with just a simple address? You can also enter information such as

✦ The name of a landmark, monument, or building (for example, *Statue of Liberty*).

✦ The name of a business or restaurant (or even a genre of food, such as *Chinese*) followed by the city name. Maps displays matching sites with pushpins (complete with reviews), and you can click any of the push-pins to find out more information on a location. Figure 7-5 illustrates a search for *pizza* — you can see the Info pop-up that appears when I click the Info icon next to the restaurant name, complete with a link to their website and reviews a-plenty.

✦ Attractions and services, followed by the city name. You can search for a gas station, movie theater, or a local park.

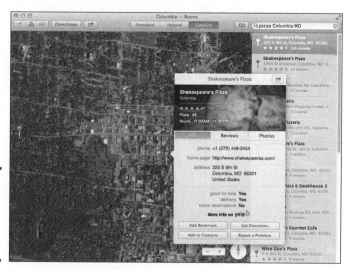

Figure 7-5:
Looks like this pizza joint is highly rated.

If you need to zoom in or zoom out on a Maps display, use the scroll function on your mouse, click the plus and minus buttons at the bottom-right corner of the Maps window, or use the ⌘+plus and ⌘+minus shortcuts. To move around the Maps window, click and drag the map in the desired direction.

Switching Views in Maps

A traditional printed map offers you only one view, which may be perfectly fine for determining a route but provides no visual interest. (The word *banal* comes to mind.) Maps, on the other hand, offers three types of views, each of which offers certain advantages:

✦ *Standard mode* is a familiar line map, with streets and highways marked. Standard mode is best for planning a road trip, just like your father's old-fashioned paper map.

✦ *Satellite mode* is a photographic overhead view without streets or highways marked, which is great for panoramic views of your neighborhood or a location and its surroundings.

✦ *Hybrid mode* is a photographic overhead view with streets and highways marked. (A friend of mine who's a Realtor loves Hybrid mode because she can display an overview of a neighborhood with identifying streets.)

To select your view, click one of the three buttons at the top of the Maps window, or press ⌘+1 for Standard, ⌘+2 for Hybrid, or ⌘+3 for Satellite. Figure 7-4 shown earlier illustrates Satellite view mode, while Figure 7-6 shows off Standard view.

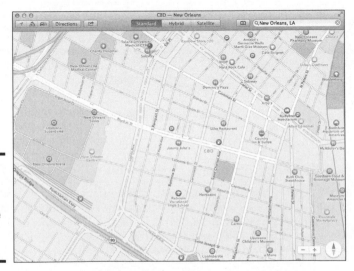

Figure 7-6: Standard view reminds me of an auto GPS unit.

For additional visual thrills, you can angle the Maps display with a slight 3D effect — nothing quite as grand as a 3D TV, but it does help add depth to Satellite and Hybrid views. To toggle 3D on and off, press ⌘+0, or press the button with the buildings icon in the upper-left corner of the Maps window.

By default, Maps is oriented with north at the top of the screen, but if you need to change the orientation, click the compass at the bottom-right corner of the screen and drag in the desired direction. To immediately return to north at the top of the screen, press ⌘+up or click View⇨Snap to North.

Getting Directions Over Yonder

My primary use for a map is getting directions from one point to another, and Maps doesn't disappoint when it comes to navigation. Click the Directions button to display the panel you see in Figure 7-7, and you're ready to plot your course.

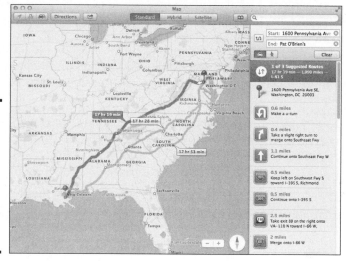

Figure 7-7:
The Directions panel is ready to provide directions to your next clambake.

Follow these steps to get directions between two addresses:

1. **In the Start box, type the starting address.**

As you type, Maps provides a pop-up list of suggestions taken from your recent locations, as well as addresses from your Contacts database and matching streets from around the globe. To choose one of these suggestions, just click it. To clear the contents of the field, click the X button that appears at the right side of the box.

2. **Press Tab to move to the End box.**

3. **In the End box, type the destination address.**

   Note that your destination doesn't have to be a specific address — for example, Memphis, TN works just fine.

4. **Click the Car button (which carries a car icon) for road directions, or the Walk button (which sports a pedestrian icon) for walking directions.**

5. **Press Return to generate your directions, or press Clear to start over.**

As you can see in Figure 7-7, Maps usually offers more than one route for your trip — the first route provided is typically the fastest or shortest, and it appears as a bright blue. To view one of the other routes, just click a light blue line and it turns bright blue to indicate it's now the selected route. (You can see the approximate mileage and time for the currently selected route at the top of the turn list.) The turn-by-turn list provides approximate mileage for each leg of the journey.

You can easily print the route map and directions by choosing File⇨Print (or by pressing ⌘+P), and then clicking the Show Details button at the bottom of the Print sheet to display all the options.

If you'd rather create a PDF document with your map and directions, choose File⇨Export as PDF.

Finally, Maps also allows you to share your maps and directions using Mail, Messages, Twitter, or Facebook. Click the Share button at the top of the window, and then select the desired sharing method.

Chapter 8: Marking Time with Calendar

In This Chapter

✔ **Entering and editing events**

✔ **Working with multiple calendars**

✔ **Sharing your calendars**

✔ **Subscribing to a WebDAV calendar**

✔ **Printing calendars**

What's so great about a computerized calendar? After all, you've probably been jotting events down on a paper calendar of one sort or another as long as you can remember. (These days, your insurance agent sends you one for free every year.) What if you're already using the Calendar app on your iPhone, iPod touch, or iPad? Isn't it more work to launch Calendar than to reach for that old paper standby?

Ah, good reader, there are indeed a number of good reasons to move from your old-fashioned paper calendar to the digital Calendar application in Mavericks! Sharing a common calendar with others in your home or office, for example — and imagine synchronizing the same calendar events between your Mac and your iPhone, iPod touch, and iPad. Suddenly those events become a lot more convenient, and your day becomes more organized. And don't forget that Calendar works hand in hand with other applications, such as Contacts, Notification Center, and Mail. (Read all about Contacts in Chapter 7 of this minibook, Notification Center in Chapter 6, and Mail in Book V, Chapter 2.)

In this chapter, I show you how to take full advantage of the OS X Calendar. You'll have to figure out how to recycle that tired old paper dinosaur yourself.

Shaking Hands with the Calendar Window

Launching Calendar requires only one click; Apple includes it as one of the default Dock icons. (You can launch the application also from Launchpad.) Figure 8-1 shows the Calendar window that appears — in this case, you're seeing my Calendar in Week display mode.

Significant stuff of note includes

✦ **Calendar List button:** Click this button to hide or show the Calendar list, which makes it easy to select from multiple calendars or choose a subscription, which I discuss later in the chapter. By default, Calendar uses your iCloud account and stores your calendars online, automatically syncing your OS X Calendar data with your iOS devices.

✦ **Quick Event button:** A click of this button displays the Quick Event pop-up text box, where you can enter a free-form event using three criteria: the event name, the time, and the day of the week. (For example, one of the events shown in my calendar in Figure 8-1 was created with the text *Lunch at noon on Friday.* Another example would be *Doctors Appointment at 3PM on 06/28.*) After you type the text and press Return, Calendar creates a one-hour named event at the time and on the day you specified, and displays the event in an Info dialog. Then all you have to do is click Done on the Info dialog to confirm.

✦ **Display mode buttons:** These buttons allow you to display your calendar in four different formats: by day, week, month, or year.

✦ **Search box:** Here's a familiar face! Click in the Search box to search the current calendar for events by name, time, contents of the Notes field, or those folks you've invited.

✦ **Navigation buttons:** Click the Previous button to switch to the previous day, week, month or year (depending on your display mode). Click the Next button to switch to the upcoming day, week, month, or year. You can always return to today's calendar by clicking the Today button.

If you appreciate menu controls, open the View menu and check out all the controls. Keyboard fans, you're not shorted either: Switch display modes using the ⌘+1 through ⌘+4 shortcuts. Pressing ⌘+→ acts the same as clicking the Next button, and ⌘+← works like the Previous button. To jump directly to today's date, press ⌘+T. You can also click Page Up and Page Down (although they're not listed on the View menu) to smoothly scroll through your Calendar events.

Maybe you don't want a view of a standard calendar arrangement — that is, a week starting on Sunday that lasts for seven days. You might prefer a work week view, (Monday–Friday). To make the change, choose Calendar➪Preferences and click the General tab to specify a number of important defaults: how many days you prefer in a week, when the week starts, and what time your day begins and ends.

Are you a Facebook fan? Perhaps Yahoo! or Google Calendar is your social mainstay instead? You can always add these calendars to your List (as well as your iCloud account) and view their events in Calendar! Choose Calendar➪Add Account, and then click the desired account and click Continue. Calendar will prompt you for the required sign-in information.

After the account is added, the corresponding calendar appears in your Calendar list. For instance, in Figure 8-1, you can see that I've added my Google and Facebook calendars. For those working in a company with shared Microsoft Exchange and CalDAV servers, you can easily include their calendars from the Add Account sheet as well.

Calendar List

Quick Event

Navigation buttons

Display modes

Search box

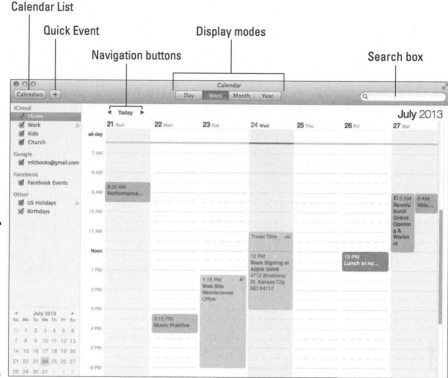

Figure 8-1:
The Calendar window can organize your very existence (well, almost).

Entering That Special Event

As I mention in the preceding section, the Quick Event button can create an event with just a short phrase. However, you can use even simpler (and more conventional) methods of adding events to your calendar. Besides clicking the Quick Event button, you can also start the ball rolling in three other ways:

✦ **Double-click a time or date.** Calendar automatically creates a one-hour event and opens a text box where you can type the event name. Press Return after you type the name, and you're done.

✦ **Right-click a time or date and choose New Event.** Again, you get a text box for the event name. After you enter it, press Return.

✦ **Choose File⇨New Event or press ⌘+N.** Calendar displays the Quick Event text box, where you can choose the event name, time, and date, as I describe earlier.

To delete an event from your calendar, just right-click the Event block and choose Delete from the contextual menu.

Editing Existing Events

As you might imagine, adding default events works perfectly if every occasion in your life lasts only one hour. But what if you need to change the duration, add information, or change an event after you create it?

First things first. In Day or Week display, changing the duration of an event couldn't be easier. Move your cursor over the top or bottom edge of any event block in your calendar, and it turns into a line with arrows pointing up and down, indicating that you can click and drag the edge of the event to change the starting or ending point. (In Month mode, events appear as a single line, so you'll have to edit the event to change the duration.)

As for adding information or changing an event, Calendar also allows you to edit any event to fine-tune it by following these steps:

1. **Click the event you want to change to select it and choose Edit⇨Edit Event from the menu.**

   You can also press ⌘+E or double-click the event. Figure 8-2 illustrates the pop-up dialog that appears.

2. **Click in a field to change it.**

   Some fields display text boxes, and others are pop-up menus or check boxes. I describe the available fields later in this section. Press Tab to move through the fields in succession.

   The icons that look like up and down arrows next to some fields are pop-up menus. Click the up/down icon, and a pop-up menu appears, where you can make your selection.

3. **After you finish your edits, click the event again to close it.**

   Click Revert to discard your changes and return the event to the original information.

Figure 8-2:
Edit info for
an event.

If you need to see the particulars for an event but don't want to change anything, right-click the event and choose Get Info from the menu that appears.
The Inspector that appears displays the same information as the Event Edit
sheet. (You can also edit from the Inspector, but that info is a highly protected Top Secret.)

Besides the event name, the fields you can change when editing are as follows (refer to Figure 8-2):

✦ **The location:** This field appears in the Event block under the Event
   name. If you enter a location that Mavericks recognizes (or a full street
   address), you'll even get a map in the Inspector!

✦ **All-Day:** If you click the date and time for the event and select this check
   box, Calendar automatically reserves the entire day for the event. If
   you're viewing your calendar in Week display mode, the application also
   moves the all-day event to the top of that day.

✦ **Time and Date:** Click the From/To dates for the event, and Calendar
   displays a nifty pop-up calendar, which you can use to select a new date.
   Click the From/To times and type a new starting and ending time for the
   event.

✦ **Repeat:** If this event is a regular occurrence, you can click the date and
   time for the event and specify that Calendar automatically repeat the
   event every day, week, month, or year at the same time. Alternatively,
   click Custom and then specify the frequency as well as how many days,
   weeks, months, or years to skip between events.

✦ **Travel time:** Need to allot time for traveling to the event location? Click the date and time for the event and then click this pop-up list to add travel time to the event — anywhere from five minutes to two hours — or click Custom and then specify the amount of time. Calendar displays the travel time as part of the event block.

✦ **Alert:** If you want your event to fire an alert, click the date and time for the event and open this pop-up menu to select the action your Mac should take. Mavericks can display a message using Notification Center (see Chapter 6 of this minibook) or display a message and play a sound to get your attention. You can also choose to receive an e-mail message sent automatically from Apple Mail, or open a file automatically on your Mac.

✦ **Calendar:** From this pop-up menu (which looks like a colored square), you can select which of your calendars should include this event. If you choose another calendar, the application automatically moves the event to the calendar you specified.

✦ **Invitees:** You can add individuals from your Contacts database or enter e-mail addresses directly to specify the invitees for this event. Calendar automatically sends an event invitation to each contact using Apple Mail — this trick works with Outlook too.

✦ **Attachments:** Click this link to associate one or more files with the event. (This feature is a great way to add a restaurant menu in PDF format for a lunch event or the minutes from a previous meeting.) The folks whom you've invited to the event can also open the attachments.

✦ **URL/Note:** These free-form text fields allow you to enter a web address for the event as well as notes regarding the event.

Keeping Track of Multiple Calendars

What's that you say? You need more than one calendar to keep your work, home, and school schedules in order? Luckily, Calendar allows you to create additional calendars at any time. The events from all your calendars will appear in the same display, so you can see the timeline of your upcoming days, weeks, and months at a glance.

To add a new calendar, choose File⇨New Calendar and select the desired account. By default, Calendar uses your iCloud account and stores your new calendar online. Type the name for your calendar and press Return, and your new calendar appears in the Calendar list. (If the Calendar list is hidden, click the Calendars button or choose View⇨Show Calendar List.) To delete a calendar, right-click the name in the Calendar list and choose Delete from the contextual menu.

Note that the events for each calendar can be individually enabled or disabled using the check box next to it. If you're on vacation, for example, you can easily disable the display of your Work calendar events until you get back.

I find it much easier to distinguish between multiple calendars when I color-code event blocks. (Changing the color of a calendar also changes the color of its check box in the List.) To change a calendar's color, right-click it in the Calendar list and choose Get Info from the menu that appears. Figure 8-3 illustrates the sheet that appears. Open the Color pop-up menu next to the Name text box and select just the right shade of magenta. While you're reviewing the Info for the calendar, you'll note that you can also change the name, add a description, or choose to ignore all upcoming alerts from this calendar. Click OK to save your changes.

Figure 8-3:
The Info
sheet for a
calendar.

Sharing Your Attractive Calendar

Calendar allows you to distribute your calendar information with others through its nifty sharing feature. Apple's iCloud service makes it easy to share calendars with an iPhone, iPad, or iPod touch. And, if you have already set up your iCloud account when you installed Mavericks, those calendars appear in your List right now. That's not all, though. You can also share calendars with other

✦ Macs running Mountain Lion or Mavericks (using the Calendar application)

✦ Macs running Lion (using the iCal application)

✦ Folks running Microsoft Outlook on PCs and Macs

To share a calendar, select it in the Calendar list and then choose Edit⇨Share Calendar. You'll see the Sharing pop-up dialog that appears in Figure 8-4.

Figure 8-4: Preparing to share a calendar.

From here, you can choose to share a *read-only* version of the calendar with everyone (no one else is allowed to edit the events), or invite specific people to share a *read-write* (editable) version of the calendar. To produce a public shared calendar that anyone can read (but not edit), just click the Public Calendar check box to select it.

To share a calendar with specific individuals, add names or e-mail addresses from Contacts to your read-write calendar by typing each name or e-mail address in the Share box (don't forget to press Return after entering each one). You can also click the Privilege pop-up menu next to each name or e-mail address to assign that person either full view and edit privileges or just the ability to view your calendar. (Naturally, if you invite individuals with read-write access, you want only those people who should have the ability to edit events.) Then click Done, and the shared calendar appears with a radio signal icon in the Calendar list.

You can view and change the sharing settings for a calendar at any time by right-clicking the calendar in the List and choosing Sharing Settings.

Why not subscribe?

Unlike calendar sharing, subscribing to a calendar depends on web-based calendars that reside on WebDAV servers. Such servers are usually maintained by companies or Internet service providers.

To *subscribe* to a calendar that someone else has published, choose File⇨New Calendar Subscription. Calendar prompts you for the WebDAV address (the person publishing the calendar should give this address to you), so

enter that address and then click Subscribe. You can now enter your own descriptive name and choose a color for your subscribed calendar. To distribute the subscribed calendar among all your iCloud devices, choose your iCloud account and specify whether you want to receive alerts and attachments along with the subscription's events. Click OK, and pause for a moment as Calendar downloads the subscription data. *Neat!*

Putting Your Calendar on Paper

I know, I know, I've spent the entire chapter telling you how much better an electronic calendar is than your old paper version, but I also know that everyone needs a hard copy from time to time. Choose File⇨Print (or press ⌘+P) to display the initial Setup dialog you see in Figure 8-5.

Figure 8-5:
Calendar
offers a
myriad
of print
configuration
options.

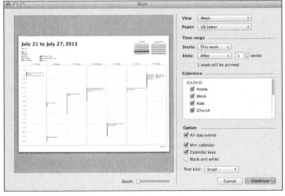

Unlike most other Mavericks applications, Calendar uses a two-step printing process. In the first Print dialog, you choose

✦ The calendar view you want: day, week, or month

✦ The type of paper to use

✦ The date range

✦ Which calendar events to print

After you set those choices, click Continue to move to the second step, where you encounter the more familiar Print dialog. From here, you can choose a printer, the number of copies, and specify which pages to print.

To show all available settings in the Print dialog, click the Show Details button, which appears at the bottom.

Don't forget the PDF feature in Mavericks! You can create a PDF file version of your calendar in a specified location, which is a handy trick if you need to check your calendar from time to time but don't want to carry around a paper copy. To display a PDF file, just double-click it in the Finder window to launch the built-in Preview application, or simply select the PDF file in the Finder window and then press the spacebar for a Quick Look. (PDFs can be used also with iBooks — *outstanding!*)

Chapter 9: The Joys of Maintenance

In This Chapter

✔ **Deleting applications**

✔ **Using Apple System Information**

✔ **Using Activity Monitor and Disk Utility**

✔ **Updating OS X and your drivers**

✔ **Backing up your system with Time Machine**

✔ **Using a disk defragmenter and start-up keys**

The title of this chapter really sounds like a contradiction in terms, doesn't it? The concepts of *joy* and *maintenance* are likely mutually exclusive to you — and it's true that most OS X owners would rather work or play than spend time under the hood, getting all grimy. I understand completely; maintenance is far less sexy than a game like *BioShock 2* or even an exciting productivity application like Pages.

However, if you do want to work or play uninterrupted by lockups and crashes — yes, believe it or not, the Big X can indeed take a dive if it's not cared for — and you'd like your Mac to perform like an Olympic athlete, you have to get your hands dirty. That means taking care of regular maintenance on your hardware, OS X, and your all-important applications, documents, and folders.

Like most techno types, I *enjoy* pushing my system to the limit and keeping it running in top form. And who knows — after you become a Mavericks power user, you could find yourself bitten by the maintenance bug as well. In this chapter, I cover how to take care of necessary tune-up chores, step by step.

Deleting Applications the Common-Sense Way

Nothing lasts forever, and that includes your applications. You might no longer need an application, or maybe you need to remove it to upgrade to a new version or to reinstall it. In contrast to Windows XP and Vista (which have the Add or Remove Programs utility in Control Panel) or Windows 7 and 8 (which have the Programs and Features utility), OS X doesn't have a stand-alone utility for uninstalling software — nor does it need one because virtually all Macintosh applications are self-contained in a single folder or series of nested folders. (And not by accident . . . keeping everything related to an application in a single folder has always been a rule for Apple software developers since the first days of the Macintosh.) Therefore, removing an application is usually as easy as deleting the contents of the installation folder from your hard drive (for example, removing the Quicken folder to uninstall Quicken). If an application does indeed sport an uninstall utility, that utility almost always appears in the same folder as well.

Always check the application's README file and documentation for any special instructions before you delete any application's folder! If you create any documents in that folder that you want to keep, don't forget to move them before you trash the folder and its contents. Some applications may come complete with their own uninstall utility, so checking the README and documentation may save you unnecessary steps.

Some applications can leave secondary files in other spots on your disk besides their home folder. When you're uninstalling a program that has support files in other areas, use Spotlight in the Finder menu bar to locate other files that might have been installed with the application. (I cover Spotlight in Chapter 4 of this minibook.) And make sure to check whether an application has an uninstall utility, or an uninstall option available through the original setup application.

For example, Figure 9-1 illustrates a Spotlight search that I ran on my Diablo 3 software. By searching for the words *Diablo 3,* I found a number of files created in other folders, such as log files, Web pages, and the language files that appear in a separate folder. Typically, you want to delete the main application folder and then remove these orphans.

Figure 9-1:
Use Spotlight to locate support files after uninstalling an application.

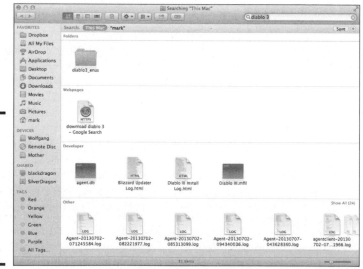

Popping the Hood: Using the System Information Utility

The day will likely come when you need hard information about your hardware. You might need to determine precisely what hardware is installed in your Mac for the following reasons:

✦ **You're working with a technical support person to solve a problem.** This person will usually request information about your system, such as what processor you're running and how much memory you have.

✦ **You're evaluating an application before you buy it.** You'll want to check its minimum system requirements against the hardware on your Mac.

✦ **You're considering an upgrade to your Mac.** You'll need to determine how much memory you have, what type it is, and which memory slots are filled. (The same goes for your hard drive and your video card, for those Macs with video card slots.) For more on upgrading your Mac, thumb through Book VII, Chapter 2.

Apple provides OS X with an all-in-one hardware and software display tool — System Information — which resides in the Utilities folder in your Applications folder. You can reach the System Information utility also via the Apple menu (). Just click About This Mac, click the More Info button, and then click System Report. System Information is also available from the Utilities (sometimes called Other or Extras) folder in Launchpad.

As with the folders in a Finder window in List view mode, you can expand or collapse each major heading that appears in an Information screen. Just click the triangle that appears to the left of each Contents heading to expand or collapse that heading.

The System Information major headings include

✦ **Hardware:** This heading tells you "volumes" about your hard drives (forgive me, I couldn't help that) as well as specifics concerning your memory; optical drives; modem; AirPort and Bluetooth hardware; printers; graphics and audio hardware; AC power settings; and any FireWire, Thunderbolt, eSATA, SCSI, and USB devices connected to your system. Figure 9-2 illustrates the information from my USB screen, with many of the devices expanded so that you can see them. (The text you see at the bottom half of the window is the detailed information on the selected item — my FaceTime HD camera, which uses an internal USB connection on my MacBook Air.)

Figure 9-2:
Display
information
about your
Mac's
ports and
connections.

✦ **Network:** This heading shows a listing of your network configuration, active network connections, and other assorted network paraphernalia. You'll probably need this screen only when asked by a technical support person for the network protocols that you're using, but it's handy nonetheless. (You'll find details on your network connection here that you can't find anywhere else in Mavericks.)

✦ **Software:** Okay, this heading shows something useful to the average human being! This screen lists all the applications, fonts, and preferences recognized on your start-up volume, along with their version numbers. (This list includes the fonts and preferences saved in your Home folder's Library folder.) If you're wondering whether you need to update an application with a *patch file* (to fix bugs in the software) or update a file from the developer, you can look here to check the current version number for the application. You also get a rather boring list of the *extensions* (or drivers) used by OS X applications. Logs are usually valuable only to tech support personnel; they document recent lockups, application crashes, and even system crashes.

Tracking Performance with Activity Monitor

Our next stop in Maintenance City is a useful little application dubbed *Activity Monitor,* which is specially designed to show you just how hard your CPU, hard drives, network equipment, and memory modules are working behind the scenes. (Activity Monitor is especially helpful in determining if your Mac is running low on system memory.) To run Activity Monitor, open the Utilities or Other folder in Launchpad and click the Activity Monitor icon.

To display each type of usage (CPU, system memory, and so on), click the buttons on the window toolbar; the lower pane changes to reflect the desired type (see Figure 9-3). For example, if you click Memory, you see the amount of unused memory; click CPU or Network to display real-time usage of your Mac's CPU and network connections.

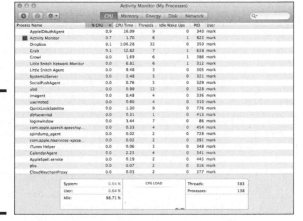

Figure 9-3: Keep tabs on Mavericks and what you're running.

You can also display a separate window with your CPU usage; choose Window⇨CPU Usage or press ⌘+2. And just to make things fun, three types of central processing unit (CPU, which is commonly called the "brain" of your Macintosh) displays are available from Activity Monitor:

✦ **CPU Usage window:** This display is the standard CPU monitoring window, which uses a blue thermometer-like display. The higher the CPU usage, the higher the reading on the monitor.

✦ **CPU History window:** This scrolling display uses different colors to help indicate the percentage of CPU time being used by your applications (green) and what percentage is being used by Mavericks to keep things running (red). You can use the History window to view CPU usage over time.

✦ **Dock icon:** This display of CPU usage is the smallest. Choose View⇨ Dock Icon; then choose what type of real-time graph you want to display in your Dock. (Feeling like a Mavericks power user yet? I thought so.) You can also monitor network, hard drive, or memory usage from the Dock.

Why do you have multiple bars in your CPU usage monitor? That's because you're running one of Apple's multiple-core Intel processors. More than one engine is under the hood!

Processes for Dummies

"Mark, what's that arcane looking list doing in the middle of the Activity Monitor window in Figure 9-3?" I'm glad you asked. That list contains processes. A *process* is a discrete task (visible or invisible) that Mavericks performs to run your applications. Some processes are executed by Mavericks just to keep itself running. For example, the Dock and Finder are processes, as are Adobe Acrobat and iPhoto.

In rare circumstances, you can — *can* — quit a specific process from Activity Monitor. Just click the offending process in the list and then click the Force a Process to Quit button on the Activity Monitor toolbar (which looks like a stop sign with an X in the middle). *Can* does not mean *should,* though. Tread carefully, Mr. Holmes, for there's danger afoot. For example, deleting a system process (such as the Dock or Finder) can result in *all* of OS X locking up! Therefore, delete a process ***only if instructed to do so by a support technician.*** If you need to terminate a misbehaving application, click the Apple menu and choose Force Quit instead.

If you're using the CPU Usage or History window, you can drag it anywhere that you like on your OS X Desktop. Use the real-time feedback to determine how well your system CPU is performing when you're running applications or performing tasks in OS X. If this meter stays peaked for long periods of time while you're using a range of applications, your processor(s) are running at full capacity.

Note, however, that seeing your CPU capacity at its max doesn't necessarily mean that you need a faster CPU or a new computer. For example, when I'm running memory-ravenous applications, such as Photoshop or Word, the Activity Monitor on my Mac mini is often pegged (indicating maximum use) for several seconds at a time. The rest of the time, it barely moves. Whether a computer is fast enough for you and the applications that you run is a subjective call.

Fixing Things with Disk Utility

Another important application in your maintenance toolbox is Disk Utility, which you find (no surprise here) in the Utilities folder in your Applications folder. When you first run this program, it looks something like Figure 9-4, displaying all the physical disks and volumes on your system.

The Disk Utility application has its own toolbar that you can toggle on and off. Choose Window⇨Hide/Show Toolbar to display or hide the toolbar, or Window⇨Customize Toolbar to select which icons inhabit the Disk Utility toolbar.

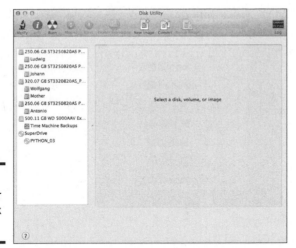

Figure 9-4:
The familiar
face of Disk
Utility.

Displaying the goods on your disks

The volume tree structure on the left of the Disk Utility window lists both
the physical disks and the partitions that you've set up. A *partition* is nothing
more than another word for *volume*, which is the formatted section of a disk
that contains data. A single physical hard drive can contain several partitions. The information display at the bottom of the Disk Utility window contains data about both the volumes and the partitions on your hard drive(s).

So what's a disk image?

Check out the New Image button on the Disk
Utility toolbar (or the image creation commands on the File⇨New submenu). If you're
wondering what a *disk image* is, you've come
to the right place. Think of a disk image as a file
that looks (and acts) like an external storage
device in Mavericks; for example, a mounted
disk image operates much like a DVD or flash
drive, and it can be ejected just like a disc can.
Images can be read-only (same as a standard
CD-ROM or DVD-ROM), or they can be created
blank (same as an empty hard drive), ready to
accept files and folders that you copy, using
Finder.

Images are great for storing data that would
normally have to be loaded from a CD or DVD
(a great convenience if you don't want to lug
optical media along with you during a vacation, or if your Mac lacks an optical drive).
Remember, a disk image acts just the same as
removable storage media as far as Mavericks
is concerned. Many Mac websites also offer
images as download files because a simple
double-click is all that's necessary to automatically mount a disk image. (Software developers
like words such as *fast* and *simple* when offering their shareware and demo applications to
the public.)

(continued)

(continued)

Finally, images are often used to create simple archives of little-used data: The images can be burned to CD/DVD or even copied to other hard drives. Oh, and don't forget the security aspect — you can choose to encrypt the data stored in an image, protecting it from prying eyes. (Having said that, I don't recommend using disk images to create full backups of your Mac's hard drives; more on this in the section "Hitching a ride on the Time Machine," later in the chapter.) To restore a disk image, you can use the Restore tab in Disk Utility.

If you're intrigued, I encourage you to click New Image on the Disk Utility toolbar and create a simple, unencrypted blank disk image on your Desktop. Then you can experiment with it. A disk image can be ejected to unmount it (same as with a CD/DVD, an iPod, or a USB Flash drive), and you can delete the image file at any time. (Just remember *not* to delete it if it contains anything you want to keep, of course . . . but you knew that already.)

To illustrate: On my system, clicking the physical internal hard drive at the top of the tree (the first drive labeled 250.06 GB) displays a description of the drive itself at the bottom of the window, including its total capacity, connection bus (the interface it uses), and whether the drive is internal or external (connection type). See Figure 9-5.

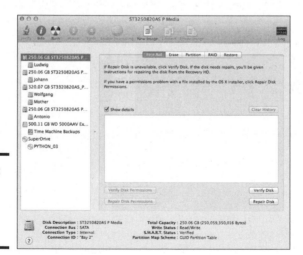

Figure 9-5: Display data on a physical drive.

However, clicking the tree entry for Ludwig (the name of the partition that I created when I formatted the drive) displays information about the type of formatting, the total capacity of the partition and how much of that is used, and the number of files and folders stored on the partition (as shown at the bottom of Figure 9-6).

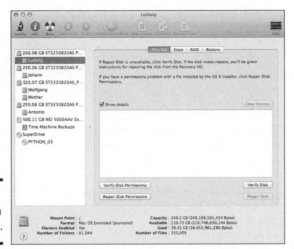

Figure 9-6:
Display data
on a volume.

Playing doctor with First Aid

From the First Aid pane, you can use Disk Utility to *verify* (or check) any disk (well, *almost* any disk) for errors, as well as repair any errors that it finds. Here are the two exceptions when the buttons are disabled:

+ **The start-up disk:** Disk Utility can't repair the *start-up disk* — that's Mac talk for the boot drive that contains the OS X Mavericks system you're using at the moment — which makes sense if you think about it, because that drive is being used!

   If you have multiple operating systems on multiple disks, you can boot from another OS X installation on another drive to check your current start-up disk. Or you can boot your system from the Recovery HD partition and run Disk Utility from the menu.

+ **Write-protected disks:** Although you can use Disk Utility to verify CDs and DVDs, Disk Utility can't repair them — um, because they're read-only. (Sound of my palm slapping my forehead.)

   You usually can't repair a disk that has *open* files that are currently being used. If you're running an application from a drive or you've opened a document that's stored on that drive, you probably can't repair that drive.

You can also elect to verify and repair the *permissions* (or *privileges*) on a disk (both permissions created by the Apple Installer and those created by the App Store); these are the read/write permissions that I discuss in detail in Book II, Chapter 6. If you can't save or move a file that you should be able to access, I recommend checking that drive for permissions problems. Although you can't fix disk errors on a boot drive, you can verify and repair permissions on any volume that contains an OS X installation (whether it was used to boot your Mac or not).

To verify or repair, you must be logged in as an admin-level user.

To verify or repair a drive, first select the target volume/partition in the list at the left. To check the contents of the drive and display any errors, click the Verify Disk button. Or, to verify the contents of the drive and fix any problems, click the Repair Disk button. (I usually just click Repair Disk because an error-free disk needs no repairs.) Disk Utility displays any status or error messages in the scrolling list; if you have eagle eyes, you'll note that the window can be resized so that you can expand it to display more messages. (You can also drag the dot between the left and right panes to expand the list.)

I generally check my disks once every two or three days. If your Mac is caught by a power failure or OS X locks up, however, immediately check the disks after you restart your Mac.

A number of very good commercial disk repair utilities are on the market. My favorite is Drive Genius 3 from Prosoft Engineering ($99; www.prosoft-eng.com). Disk Utility does a good job on its own, though, and it's free.

Erasing without seriously screwing up

"Danger, Will Robinson! Danger!" That's right, Robot, it is indeed very easy to seriously screw up and get "Lost in Erase." (Man, I can't believe I typed such a bad pun. I have no shame.) Anyway, it's time for another of Mark's Maxims. To paraphrase the rules for handling a firearm responsibly:

> **Never — and I do mean *never* — click the Erase tab unless you mean to use it.**

Figure 9-7 illustrates the Erase controls in Disk Utility. You need to erase a disk or volume only when you want to *completely wipe* the contents of that existing disk or volume. You can also erase a rewritable CD (CD-RW) or DVD (DVD-RW, DVD+RW, or DVD-RAM) from this pane.

✦ Erasing an *entire disk* deletes *all volumes* on the disk and creates a single new, empty volume.

✦ Erasing a *volume* wipes only the *contents of that specific volume,* leaving all other volumes on the physical disk untouched.

To erase, follow these steps:

1. **In the list on the left side of the screen, click the disk or volume icon that you want to erase.**

2. **Click the Erase tab.**

3. **In the Format pop-up menu, click the format that you want to use.**

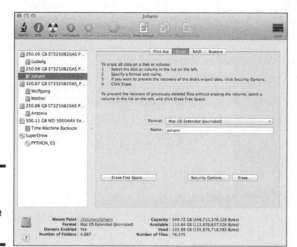

Figure 9-7:
The Disk
Utility Erase
controls.

Always choose Mac OS Extended (Journaled) entry from the Format list unless you have a specific reason to use the MS-DOS File System (for compatibility with PCs running Windows) or the ExFAT File System (for compatibility with high-capacity USB flash drives). In some cases, Disk Utility will force you to choose the Mac OS Extended entry instead, but the result is the same. Note that you do not need to format a disk or volume with the MS-DOS File System just to read a file from a PC system — OS X recognizes MS-DOS removable media (such as a USB drive formatted under Windows) without a problem. You can also choose to encrypt a volume when formatting it — not a necessity (in most cases) for a personal Mac, but often a requirement in business and government offices.

4. **In the Name field, type the name for the volume.**

   If you're erasing an existing volume, the default is the existing name.

5. **If you're worried about security, click Security Options and specify the Secure Erase method you want to use.**

   By default, this is set to Fastest, so Disk Utility doesn't overwrite any data while formatting; instead, it simply trashes the existing directory, rendering that data unreachable. *Or is it?* With some third-party disk utilities, an unscrupulous bum could recover your files after a simple Fast format, so you can specify alternative, more secure methods of erasing a disk or volume. Unfortunately, these more secure erasure methods can take a horrendous amount of time.

   So, using the Fast option is okay unless you want to make sure that nothing can be recovered, or use the Zero Out Data to take a more secure route with the least amount of extra waiting. For example, you'd want to use the next-slowest option (which writes a single pass of all zeros over the entire disk) if you're selling your Mac on eBay and you're formatting the drive for the new owner. If you're really set on the tightest, government-quality security, select Most Secure . . . but make sure you have plenty of time to spare!

You can even click Erase Free Space to wipe the supposedly "clean" areas of your drive *before* you format. Man, talk about airtight security!

6. **Click the Erase button.**

In the sheet that appears, click Erase to confirm that you do want to do the deleterious deed.

Partitioning the right way

From time to time, just about everyone wishes he had additional volumes handy for organizing files and folders, or at least a little extra space on a particular partition. If you find yourself needing another volume on a disk — or if you need to resize the total space on existing volumes on a disk — click the Partition tab in Disk Utility to display the controls that you see in Figure 9-8. (Make sure that you select a *disk* and not a volume.) From here, you can choose a volume scheme, creating anywhere from 1 to 16 volumes on a single disk.

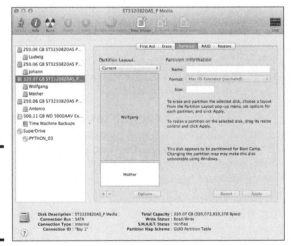

Figure 9-8:
The Disk Utility Partitioning controls.

You can't monkey around with the partitions on a start-up disk because OS X is currently running on that disk. (Think about removing your own appendix, and you get the idea.) Also, if you resize an existing volume, you may lose files and folders on that volume. Disk Utility will prompt you for permission, but always back up a partition before you resize it!

To set up the partitions on a disk, follow these steps:

1. **From the Partition panel in Disk Utility, click the disk icon (left side of the pane) that you want to partition.**

2. **Click the Partition Layout pop-up menu and choose the total number of volumes that you want on the selected disk.**

    To add a partition to an existing layout, click the Add button (plus sign).

3. **Click the first volume block in the partition list (under the Partition Layout pop-up menu) to select it.**

    I have two partitions set for this disk, as you can see.

4. **Click in the Name field and enter the name for the selected volume.**

5. **From the Format pop-up menu, choose a format for the volume.**

    Always use Mac OS Extended or Mac OS Extended (Journaled) from the Format menu unless you have a specific reason to use the MS-DOS file system (for compatibility with PCs running Windows) or the ExFAT file system (for compatibility with high-capacity USB flash drives).

6. **In the Size field, type a total size for this volume.**

7. **If you're creating multiple volumes, click the next volume block to select it and repeat Steps 4–6.**

    Some folks — like us author types — create multiple volumes so that they can boot from multiple versions of OS X.

8. **To delete a partition from your new scheme, click the unwanted volume and then click the Delete button (a minus sign) to remove it.**

9. **After everything is set to your liking, click the Apply button to begin the process.**

    If you suddenly decide against a partition change, click the Revert button to return to the original existing partition scheme.

    The Revert button is available only before you click the Apply button.

If you have more than one partition, check out the handles separating the volumes in the partition list — they appear as dashed lines in the lower-right corner of the partition. You can click and drag these handles to dynamically resize the volumes. This step makes it easy to adjust the individual volume sizes for the disk until you get precisely the arrangement you want.

RAID has nothing to do with insects

The next stop on the Disk Utility hayride isn't for everyone — as a matter of fact, only an OS X power user with a roomful of hardware is likely to use it. RAID (Redundant Array of Independent/Inexpensive Disks) is what it says.

In normal human English, a *RAID set* is a group of multiple separate disks, working together as a team. RAID can

✦ Improve the speed of your system

✦ Help prevent disk errors from compromising or corrupting your data

The RAID controls in Disk Utility are illustrated in Figure 9-9. You need at least two additional hard drives on your system besides the start-up disk, which I don't recommend that you use in a RAID set.

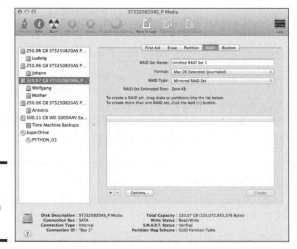

Figure 9-9:
The Disk
Utility RAID
controls.

To set up a RAID array in OS X, follow these steps:

1. **From the RAID tab of Disk Utility, click and drag the disks from the list at the left to the Disk box at the right.**

2. **Click the RAID Type pop-up menu to specify the type of RAID that you need.**

   • *Striped RAID Set:* Choosing this can speed up your hard drive performance by splitting data between multiple disks.

   • *Concatenated RAID Set:* Choosing this allows several volumes (or even multiple disks) to appear as one volume in Mavericks.

   • *Mirrored RAID Set:* Choosing this increases the reliability of your storage by creating a mirror backup of that data across multiple disks.

3. **Click in the RAID Set Name field and type the name for your RAID set.**

4. **In the Format pop-up menu, choose a format for the volumes.**

Always use Mac OS Extended or Mac OS Extended (Journaled) from the Format list unless you have a specific reason to use the MS-DOS File System (for compatibility with PCs running Windows). Journaling helps reduce the amount of disk fragmentation and also helps speed up your hard drive's performance.

5. **Click the Create button.**

Updating OS X

As any good software developer should, Apple constantly releases improvements to OS X in the form of software updates. These updates can include all sorts of fun stuff, like

+ Bug fixes

+ Improvements and new features

+ Enhanced drivers

+ Security upgrades

+ Firmware upgrades

Apple makes it easy to keep OS X up-to-date with the Software Update controls in System Preferences.

You don't even have to display the System Preferences window to check for new software updates manually. Click the Apple menu (🍎) on the menu bar and then choose Software Update to perform a manual check immediately.

To check for new updates periodically, display the App Store pane in System Preferences. Select the Automatically Check for Updates check box and choose whether you want to automatically download updates. For a manual check, make sure that your Mac is connected to the Internet and then click the Check Now button.

Mavericks also displays a Notification window alerting you to new updates. You can choose to continue with the update from the Notification window, or wait and update manually later.

To download updates automatically, mark the Download Newly Available Updates in the Background check box. (Note that you can also choose whether to install both new app updates and install system data and security updates. I suggest that you enable both these check boxes.) The Big X politely downloads the updates behind the scenes and then alerts you that they're ready to be installed. With automatic downloading disabled, OS X launches the Updates pane of the App Store and displays any available updates with short descriptions, and you can manually click the Update button next to a specific update.

If you own multiple Macs, you can even choose to automatically download those apps that you've purchased on your other Apple computers — remember, once you buy most apps from the App Store, they can be shared among all Macs that use the same Apple ID! The App Store pane displays the Apple ID you're using on this Mac.

I recommend installing all updates, even for hardware that you don't have yet. For example, I always install AirPort updates even though I don't have AirPort hardware in my Mac Pro. The reason? Often, the functionality covered by an update may include system software that you *do* use, so you still benefit from installing it.

You might have to reboot after everything has been installed, so shut down any open apps.

1 Demand That You Back Up Your Hard Drive

I know we're friends, but there's **no excuse** for not backing up your data. The more valuable and irreplaceable your documents are, the more heinous it is to risk losing them. (I don't get to use the word *heinous* in many of my books, but it fits *really* well here.)

Although Apple does include the capability to create disk images and restore them in Disk Utility (see the "So what's a disk image?" sidebar, earlier in this chapter), I don't recommend that you use disk images as your comprehensive backup solution. (Insert sound of stunned silence here.) The restore process can be confusing, and the disk image method doesn't offer the level of control that you need when it comes to backing up individual files and folders (or selectively backing up by date or recent use).

If you do create backup datasets using disk images, you can restore them from the Restore tab in Disk Utility. You can also restore from a volume — typically, a volume you want to restore would be saved on a DVD or an external hard drive.

"Okay, Mark, what do I use to back up my valuable data?" Well, good citizen, only a bona fide backup application gives you such flexibility and convenience . . . and that's why Mavericks power users turn to *Time Machine,* a feature that makes restoring files as easy as pointing and clicking!

Hitching a ride on Time Machine

If you enable backups through the Time Machine feature, you can literally move backward through the contents of your Mac's hard drive, selecting and restoring all sorts of data. Files and folders are ridiculously easy to restore — and I mean easier than *any* restore you've ever performed, no matter what the operating system or backup program. Time Machine can even handle things such as deleted Contacts entries and photos you've sent to the Trash from iPhoto! To be blunt, Time Machine should be an important and integral part of every Mac owner's existence.

You must have an external hard drive to use Time Machine — and if you travel often and you want to maintain a timely backup, you'll have to take that external drive with you on the road, so that it can stay connected whenever possible. Luckily, you can find countless portable hard drives on the market these days that take up less space than a paperback book. My Time Machine backup drive for my MacBook Air is the superfast 256GB Neutrino Thunderbolt Edition external drive from Akitio (www.akitio.com), which offers Thunderbolt connection speeds and the performance of a solid-state drive (or *SSD*). The Neutrino is light, rugged, and compact — and because the drive operates using power from thc Thunderbolt port, you don't need to pack yet another separate AC power cable!

Before you can use Time Machine, it must be enabled in the Time Machine pane in System Preferences. I cover these settings in detail in Book II, Chapter 3. I also recommend that you invest in an external USB, Thunderbolt, or FireWire hard drive to hold your Time Machine backups.

Here's how you can turn back time, step-by-step, to restore a file that you deleted or replaced in a folder:

1. **Open the folder that contained the file you want to restore.**

2. **In a separate window, open your Applications folder and launch the Time Machine application, or click the Time Machine icon on the menu bar and choose Enter Time Machine.**

   You can also click the Launchpad icon on the Dock and then click the Time Machine icon.

   The oh-so-ultra-cool Time Machine background appears behind your folder, complete with its own set of buttons at the bottom of the screen (as shown in Figure 9-10). On the right, you see a timeline that corresponds to the different days and months included in the backups that Mavericks has made.

3. **Click within the timeline to jump directly to a date (displaying the folder's contents on that date).**

    Alternatively, use the Forward and Back arrows at the right to move through the folder's contents through time. (You should see the faces of Windows users when you "riffle" through your folders to locate something you deleted several weeks ago!)

    The backup date of the items you're viewing appears in the button bar at the bottom of the screen.

4. **After you locate the file you want to restore, click it to select it.**

5. **Click the Restore button at the right side of the Time Machine button bar.**

    If you want to restore all the contents of the folder, click the Restore All button instead.

Time Machine returns you to Finder, with the newly restored file now appearing in the folder. *OUTstanding!*

To restore specific data from your Contacts or images from iPhoto, launch the desired application first and then launch Time Machine. Instead of riffling through a Finder window, you can move through time in the application window.

For simple backup and restore protection, Time Machine is all that a typical Mac owner at home is likely to ever need. Therefore, a very easy Mark's Maxim to predict:

Connect an external hard drive (or add a Time Capsule device to your system) and turn on Time Machine. *Do it now*. Don't make a heinous mistake.

How about that? I got to use *heinous* twice in one chapter.

Using other backup solutions

Time Machine is indeed awesome, but some Mac owners prefer a more traditional automated backup and restore process — one that doesn't involve running the Time Machine application and navigating through the files and folders on a drive. For example, a person backing up a Mac acting as a web server or iTunes media server would much rather restore the entire contents of a volume automatically, in bulk, or create a custom backup/restore schedule that safeguards only certain files and folders.

If you're dead-set against Time Machine, for your salvation you can turn to a commercial backup application such as SuperDuper! (from www.shirt-pocket.com), which can create a fully bootable image backup (often called a *clone*) of your Mac's hard drive.

If no other backup is available, you can always take a second to at least back up your most important documents by copying them to a rewriteable CD or a USB flash drive. With this poor man's backup, even if you lose your entire hard drive, you can still restore what matters the most.

1 Further Demand That You Defragment

Defragmenting your hard drive can significantly improve its performance. Using a defragmenter scans for little chunks of a file that are spread out across the surface of your hard drive and then arranges them to form a contiguous file. After a file has been optimized in this way, it's far easier and faster for OS X to read than reassembling a fragmented file.

However, Apple dropped the ball on this one and didn't include a defragmenter with OS X. Luckily, many third-party disk utilities (such as the aforementioned Drive Genius 3 from Prosoft Engineering) also include a defragmenting feature. If you have a defragmenter, I recommend that you use it once a month.

Special Start-Up Keys for Those Special Times

OS X includes a number of special keys that you can use during the boot process. These keys come in handy when you need to force your operating system to do something that it normally wouldn't, such as boot from a CD instead of the hard drive.

✦ **To boot from a CD or DVD:** Restart your Mac while pressing the C key. This is a great way to free your startup volume when you want to test it or optimize it using a commercial utility.

✦ **To boot from the Recovery HD partition:** Restart or boot OS X while pressing ⌘+R.

✦ **To eject a recalcitrant disc that doesn't show up on the Desktop:** Restart OS X and hold down the mouse button — or if you have a late-model Mac, press the Media Eject key as soon as you hear that magnificent startup chord.

✦ **To force your Mac to boot in OS X:** Hold down the X key while restarting or booting the Mac.

✦ **To display a system boot menu:** Hold down the Option key while restarting or booting the Mac, and you can choose which operating system you want to use.

✦ **To prevent start-up applications from running during login:** Hold down the Shift key while you click the Login button on the Login screen. If you don't see the Login screen during startup, just hold down Shift while OS X boots until the Finder menu appears.

Crave the Newest Drivers

No chapter on maintenance would be complete without a reminder to keep your hardware drivers current. *Drivers* are simply programs that allow your Mac to control hardware devices, such as a USB printer that you've added to your Mac Pro. The OS X Software Update feature that I discuss earlier, in the section "Updating OS X," provides most of the drivers you need for things such as printers, USB, Thunderbolt, and FireWire peripherals, and digital cameras, but it's still important to check those manufacturer websites.

Like the software updates from Apple, updated drivers can fix bugs and even add new features to your existing hardware, which is my definition of getting something for nothing.

Chapter 10: Getting Help for the Big X

In This Chapter

- ✔ Using the OS X Help Center
- ✔ Searching for specific help
- ✔ Getting help in applications
- ✔ Finding other help resources

*W*hether the voice echoes from a living room, home office, or college computer lab, it's all too familiar: a call for help. No matter how well written the application or how well designed the operating system, sooner or later, you're going to need support. That goes for everyone from the novice to the experienced Mac owner and from the occasional e-mail user to the most talented software developer.

In this short but oh-so-important chapter, I lead you through the various help resources available in OS X as well as native OS X applications. I show you how to tap additional resources from Apple, and I also point you to other suppliers of high-quality (as well as even questionable) assistance on the Internet and in your local area.

Displaying the Help Center Window

Your first line of defense is OS X Help Center, as shown in Figure 10-1. To display Help Center from the Finder menu, click Help and choose Help Center. This Help menu is context-sensitive, so it contains different menu items when you're working inside an application.

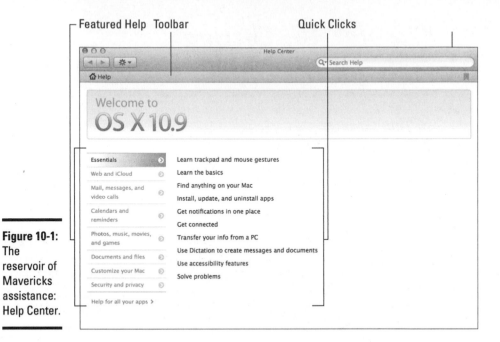

Figure 10-1:
The reservoir of Mavericks assistance: Help Center.

As shown in Figure 10-1, Help Center is divided into three sets of controls:

✦ **Toolbar:** The toolbar includes navigational controls (Back, Forward, and Home buttons), an Action button (where you can print a topic or change the text size), and the Ask a Question (or Search Help) text box.

✦ **Quick Clicks:** Clicking these links takes you directly to some of the most frequently asked Help topics for Finder (or the application you're using), such as Learn Trackpad and Mouse Gestures and Find Anything on Your Mac. You can display different Quick Click selections by clicking a different topic in the Featured Help list that appears at the left of the Help Center window — rather like the top level in an outline. To use a Quick Click, just click (once) the question that you want to pursue.

✦ **Featured Help:** Click any of these links to display specific help for an OS X application or a group of items on a similar topic. To see the comprehensive list of application help icons, click the Help for All Your Apps link at the bottom of the window.

I know that Help Center looks a little sparse at first glance. However, when you realize how much information has to be covered to help someone with an operating system — check out the size of the book you're holding, for instance — you get an idea of why OS X doesn't try to cover everything on one screen. Instead, you get the one tool that does it all: the Spotlight search box.

Searching for Specific Stuff

To search for the help topic you need, here are two paths to righteousness:

✦ **From the Finder Help menu:** Wowzers! In Mavericks, you don't even have to open Help Center to search for assistance on a specific topic. Just choose Help from the Finder menu (or press the ⌘+Shift+/ shortcut). Click in the Search field right there in the menu, and then type a keyword or two.

Although you can ask a full-sentence question, I find that the shorter and more concise your search criteria, the more relevant your results.

As when using the Spotlight Search box, you don't need to press Return; just click the topic that sounds the most helpful.

✦ **From Help Center:** Click in the Search Help text box at the right side of the toolbar, type one or two words that sum up your question, and then press Return. Figure 10-2 illustrates a typical set of topics concerning the Desktop.

Figure 10-2:
The results of a search in Help Center.

In the Help Center window, articles taken from the AppleCare Support section of the Apple website appear in the Product Support portion of the window. (Of course, because web stuff is going on in the background, you don't see these articles unless your Mac has an active Internet connection.)

You can double-click any topic to display the topic text, which looks like the text that you see in Figure 10-3. Note that if an extensive topic features major headings, you can reveal additional information by clicking the Show link next to each heading. To tidy up, click the Hide link, and any information displayed under that heading disappears.

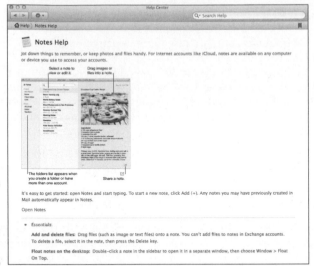

Figure 10-3:
A typical topic in Help Center.

To move back to the previous topic you viewed, click the Back button on the Help Center toolbar.

Prodding Apple for the Latest Gossip

I heartily recommend that you visit the Apple website at `www.apple.com` and surf wildly to and fro. You'll often pick up on news and reviews that you won't find anywhere else on the Internet.

From the opening web screen, don't forget to click the Hot News link at the bottom of the page and the Support tab during every visit to the Apple site. These pages give you

✦ Articles about the latest news from Cupertino

✦ Downloads of the latest OS X freeware, shareware, and demoware

✦ The *Knowledge Base* (an online searchable troubleshooting reference)

✦ News about upcoming versions of OS X and Apple applications galore

You'll also find OS X product manuals in Adobe Acrobat PDF format and online discussion forums that cover OS X.

Calling for Help Deep in the Heart of X

A number of different help avenues are available in OS X applications as well. They include

✦ **The Help button:** A number of otherwise upstanding OS X windows, dialogs, and System Preferences panes include a Help button, as shown in the lower right of Figure 10-4. Click the button marked with a question mark (?) to display the text for the settings in that dialog or window.

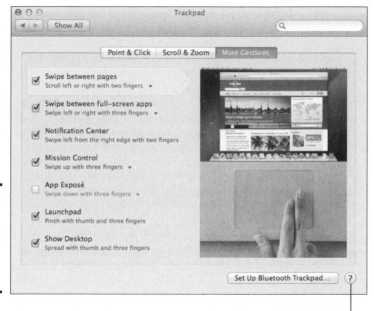

Figure 10-4:
Note the not-so-well-camou-flaged Help button.

Help

✦ **Pop-up help for fields and controls:** Most OS X applications display a short line of help text when you hover the mouse pointer on top of a field or control. Sometimes the text displays just the name of the item; sometimes it's a full descriptive line. Them's the breaks.

✦ **Application-specific help:** Applications typically have their own help system, which can use the Help Center window, a separate help display program, or a HyperText Markup Language (HTML; read that *web-based*) help system.

Other Resources to Chew On

Although Help Center can take care of just about any question that you might have about the basic controls and features of OS X, you might also want to turn to other forms of help when the going gets a little rougher. In this last section, I cover resources that you can call on when Help Center just isn't enough.

Voice support

As of this writing, Apple provides voice technical support for OS X. You can find the number to call in your Mac's printed manuals or online in the Support section of the Apple website. However, exactly when you qualify for voice support and exactly how long it lasts depends on a number of factors, such as whether you received OS X when you bought a new machine or whether you purchased a support plan from Apple.

Apple offers a support plan — One to One — for those Mac owners with an Apple retail store nearby. For a one-year, $99 membership, Apple techs can set up your Mac, provide personal support, demonstrate how to use your software, and provide you with training sessions.

You can also try the general online support site at `www.apple.com/support` — it's a great starting point for obtaining OS X help.

Mac publications and resource sites

You can refer to a number of great Mac-savvy publications and resources, both printed and online, for help. My favorites include

+ **Macworld** (`www.macworld.com`), both in archaic hard copy and oh-so-slick online versions.

+ **Inside Mac Games** (`www.insidemacgames.com`), the online gaming resource for the Macintosh.

+ **Download.com** (`www.versiontracker.com`), an online resource for the latest updates on all sorts of Macintosh third-party applications.

+ **MacFixIt** (`www.macfixit.com`), a well-respected troubleshooting site devoted to the Mac that offers downloads, news, and discussion areas. (A subscription may be required for some of the more useful sections of the site.)

In most of my books, I mention specific Internet newsgroups that cater to the topic I'm discussing; however, most Mac-specific newsgroups are devoted to illegally swapping pirated games and applications, so I don't cover them. Also, the help that you receive from individuals in newsgroups is sometimes misguided — and sometimes downright *wrong* — so take any claims with a grain of salt.

As a general rule, *never* identify yourself or provide your snail-mail or e-mail addresses in a newsgroup post! These messages are public, and they remain hanging around in cyberspace on newsgroup servers for years, leaving you a prime target for spam (or even worse).

Local Mac outlets and user groups

Finally, you can find local resources in any medium-size to large town or city: A shop that's authorized by Apple to sell and repair Macintosh computers can usually be counted on to answer a quick question over the phone or provide more substantial support for a fee. (For example, my local Mac outlet sponsors inexpensive classes for new Mac owners, and the Genius Bar is a great resource if you can reach an Apple Store.)

You might also be lucky enough to have a local Macintosh user group that you can join — members can be counted on for free answers to your support questions at meetings and demonstrations. To find a group near you, visit the Apple User Group Support site at www.apple.com/usergroups and click the Find a Group link.

Chapter 11: Troubleshooting the X

In This Chapter

✔ **Mastering the scientific approach**

✔ **Using troubleshooting techniques**

✔ **Performing radical solutions**

✔ **Checking troubleshooting resources**

*O*S X Mavericks is rugged, stable, and reliable — and as you can read in Chapter 9 of this minibook, practicing regular maintenance can help prevent problems caused by everything from power failures to faulty software drivers to cats on the keyboard. However, sooner or later you *will* encounter what I like to call The Dark Moments . . . a blank screen, a locked Mac, or an external device that sits there uselessly like an expensive paperweight.

How you handle The Dark Moments defines you as a true OS X power user because most computer owners seem to fall into one of two categories: Either you panic and beat your head against the wall (which really has little effect on the computer, when you think about it), or you set your brow in grim determination and follow the troubleshooting models that I provide in this chapter to locate (and, I hope, fix) the source of the problem.

Don't Panic!

My friend, this is the first — and *most important* — rule of troubleshooting, and yet another of Mark's Maxims:

> **Whatever the problem, you almost certainly *can* fix it (or get it fixed).**

Because they panic, most computer owners seem to forget the idea that a hardware or software error can be fixed. They simply see The Problem, and somehow they feel that they'll never be able to use their computer again.

Although the situation might look grim, don't ignore these facts:

✦ **You don't need to scrap your Mac.** As long as you haven't taken a hammer or a chainsaw to your Mac, the problem is only temporary. Sure, individual components do fail over time — heck, so do *people* — but the problem is usually something that can be tracked down and fixed without scrapping your entire computer.

✦ **Don't beat yourself up.** As long as you haven't installed a virus on purpose or deleted half your system files to spite yourself, the problem *isn't* your fault. Sure, it's possible that you might have done something by accident, but don't blame yourself — accidents happen to everybody. (Trust me, I do mean *everybody*. Even those Apple engineers, I'm told.)

✦ **Trust your Apple dealer.** As long as an Apple dealer is in your area, you can usually get your computer repaired professionally if a component's gone south. (In some cases, professional help is a necessity: For example, I'd be a fool to try to fix a power supply or a monitor on my own because both can pack a heavy electrical punch.)

✦ **Rely on your backup.** As long as you've made a backup, you won't lose much (if any) work. (You *did* back up your hard drive, didn't you? I harp about backups in Chapter 9 of this minibook.) I'm talking about a backup to an external hard drive here, using either an application such as Disk Utility or the Time Machine feature (also covered in Chapter 9). At the very least, make a "quickie" backup of your most important stuff, copied directly to a recordable DVD or USB flash drive.

Commit these facts to head and heart, and you can rest easy while you track down and attack the *real* enemy — whatever's causing the problem.

The Troubleshooting Process

When I first conceived this chapter, I decided to divide this section into separate hardware and software troubleshooting procedures. However, that approach is impractical because often you won't know whether a problem is caused by hardware or software until you're practically on top of it.

Therefore, here's the complete 12-step troubleshooting process that I designed while working as a consultant and Macintosh hardware technician for 20 years. Feel free to add your own embellishments in the margin or include reminders with sticky notes.

If you're not sure quite what's producing the error, this process is designed to be *linear* — followed in order — but if you already know that you're having a problem with one specific peripheral or one specific application, feel free to jump to the steps that concern only hardware or software.

I recommend creating a default user account for troubleshooting — what techs call a "vanilla" or "clean" account. You can use your vanilla account to test whether a problem occurs system-wide or is limited to a single user account. This is a great way to determine whether an application is misbehaving because of a corrupted preference file: If the same problem doesn't appear when you use the application with the vanilla account, the culprit is likely the user's copy of the application's preference file or a corrupt font. (Follow the instructions provided by the application for resetting or deleting the preference file it creates.)

Step 1: Always try a simple shutdown

You'd be amazed at how often a *reboot* (shutting down and restarting) can cure a temporary problem. For example, this can fix the occasional lockup in OS X or a keyboard that's not responding because of a power failure. If possible, make sure that you first close any open documents. As your first (and best) option for shutting down, click the Apple menu (◆) and then choose Shut Down.

When troubleshooting, always do a shutdown instead of simply restarting the computer because when OS X shuts down, all the hardware components that make up your system are reset.

If your Mac is locked tight and you can't use the Shut Down command, you have two choices. First, press and hold the Power button on your Mac for a few seconds. This will turn off your computer. If this doesn't work, you have to physically pull the power cord from the wall (or turn off the surge protector, if you're using one). This action is the Last Resort.

Step 2: Check all cable connections

Check all connections: the AC power cord and the keyboard cord, as well as any modem or network connections and all cable connections to external peripherals. Look for loose connectors, especially if you have a cat or dog — don't forget to check for chew marks. (Yep, this is the voice of experience talking.) If you've recently replaced a cable — especially a network, Universal Serial Bus (USB), or FireWire cable — replace it with a spare to see whether the problem still occurs.

Step 3: Retrace your steps

If the problem continues to occur, the next step is to consider what you've done in the immediate past that could have affected your Mac. Did you install any new software, or have you connected a new peripheral? If your Mac was working fine until you made the change to your system, the problem likely lies in the new hardware or software.

✦ **If you added an external device:** Shut down your Mac and disconnect the peripheral. Then turn on the computer to see whether all proceeds normally. If so, check the peripheral's documentation and make sure that you correctly installed the *driver* — the software provided by the device manufacturer — and that you connected it properly to the correct port. (You can also use the System Information utility, which I discuss later in this chapter, to check to see whether your Mac recognizes the external device.) To verify that the cable works, substitute another cable of the same type or try the peripheral on another Mac.

Make it a practice to check the manufacturer's website for the latest driver when you get new hardware. The software that ships in the box with your new toy could have been on the shelf for months before being sold, and the manufacturer has probably fine-tuned the driver in the interim. You should also run Software Update to verify that the drivers that Apple supplies are up-to-date. (Read about Software Update in Chapter 9 of this minibook.)

✦ **If you installed new software or applied an update or patch:** Follow the guidelines in Chapter 9 of this minibook to uninstall the application and search for any files that it might have created elsewhere. (Searching by date created and date modified can help you locate files that were recently created.) If this step fixes the problem, it's time to contact the developer and request technical support for the recalcitrant program; you can always reinstall the program after the problem has been solved by the developer.

Not all versions of OS X are created equal. If you recently upgraded to a major or minor new release of OS X, some of the applications that you've been using without trouble for months can suddenly go on the warpath and refuse to work (or exhibit quirky behavior). If this happens, visit the developer's website often to look for a *patch file* that will update the application to work with the new version of OS X.

✦ **If you recently made a change in System Preferences:** Maybe you inadvertently "bumped" something. For instance, you might have accidentally changed your modem or network settings or perhaps made a change to your login options. Verify the settings screens that you visited to make sure that everything looks okay.

Step 4: Run Disk Utility

Next, click the Launchpad icon on the Dock, click the Utilities (or Other) icon, and then run Disk Utility (as shown in Figure 11-1) to check for disk errors and permissions errors — especially permissions errors, which can wreak absolute havoc on just about any application on your hard drive. (From the Finder menu, you can also choose Go⇨Utilities and then double-click the Disk Utility icon to launch the application.) Chapter 9 of this minibook provides all the details on Disk Utility.

Step 5: Run antivirus software

Run your antivirus software and scan your entire system — including all system disks and removable disks — for viruses and other malware. Although OS X doesn't come with antivirus protection built in, the world-class program Intego VirusBarrier 2013 (www.intego.com) constantly scans each file that you open or download for infections. You can also run the great freeware ClamXav 2 virus scanner (available for downloading at www.clamxav.com).

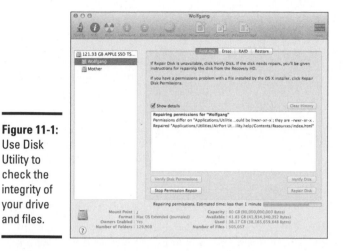

Figure 11-1:
Use Disk
Utility to
check the
integrity of
your drive
and files.

If you haven't already set your antivirus application to automatically update itself, download the latest virus update — usually called a *signature file* or *data file* — to keep your virus protection current.

Step 6: Check the Trash

Check the contents of your Trash to make sure that you haven't inadvertently tossed something important that could be causing trouble for an application. Click the Trash icon on the Dock to open the Trash window and peruse its contents. (To see the file types easier, switch to List view mode.) To restore items to their rightful place, drag them from the Trash back to the correct folder on your hard drive.

Step 7: Check online connections

If your Mac is connected to an Ethernet network, a cable modem, or a digital subscriber line (DSL), check your equipment to make sure that your system is currently online and receiving packets normally. Your network system administrator will be happy to help you with this, especially if you're blood relatives.

Step 8: Disable troublesome Login Items

Disable any Login Items that might be causing trouble. As you can read in Book II, Chapter 3, Login Items are launched automatically as soon as you log in. For example, an older application that doesn't fully support OS X Mavericks can cause problems if used as a Login Item. You can do this from the Login Items settings in the System Preferences Users & Groups pane (as shown in Figure 11-2); click the Apple menu (), choose System Preferences, click Users & Groups, and then click the Login Items tab.

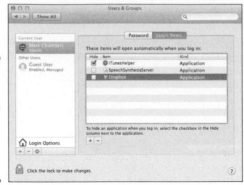

Figure 11-2:
A misbehaving Login Item can cause you a world of grief.

Unfortunately, if a Login Item doesn't display an error message, your old friend Trial-and-Error is just about the only sure-fire way to detect which item (if any) is causing the problem. Click an item to select it, click the Remove button (marked with a minus sign), and then press ⌘+Q to quit System Preferences. Log out to see whether the problem's solved. (If not, don't forget to add the item again to the Login Items list.)

You can also disable Login Items entirely when you reboot. If the login window appears when you reboot your computer, hold down the Shift key and then click the Login button. If you don't see the Login window when you reboot, hold down the Shift key when you see the James Bond–style twirling progress indicator in the startup window and continue to hold down the key until Finder appears.

Step 9: Turn off your screen saver

Another candidate for intermittent lockups is your screen saver, especially if you're running a shareware effort written by a 12-year-old with a limited attention span. Display your System Preferences, choose Desktop & Screen Saver, and click the Screen Saver tab. You can deactivate the saver entirely (by clicking the Start After pop-up menu and choosing Never) or choose the Computer Name saver (which is provided by Apple) from the Screen Savers list.

Step 10: Check for write protection

If you're running a multiuser ship, check to make sure that another user with administrator access hasn't accidentally write-protected your documents, your application, or its support files. If possible, log in with an administrator account yourself (as I describe in Book II, Chapter 5) and then try running the application or opening the document that you were unable to access under your own ID.

Trying an application under the aforementioned clean account is also a great way to determine whether your user-specific preference file for that application has been corrupted. If you can run the application using your clean account, contact the software developer to see how you can repair or delete a preference file that's causing problems.

Step 11: Check your System Information

If you've reached this point in the troubleshooting process and haven't found the culprit, you've probably experienced a hardware failure in your Macintosh. If possible, display the Hardware category in the Apple System Information utility (see Figure 11-3) and make sure that it can recognize and use all the internal drives, ports, and external devices on your Mac. To start System Information, click the Launchpad icon on the Dock, click the Utilities (or Other) folder icon, and then click the System Information icon. Alternatively, open your Utilities folder (inside the Applications folder) and double-click the System Information icon.

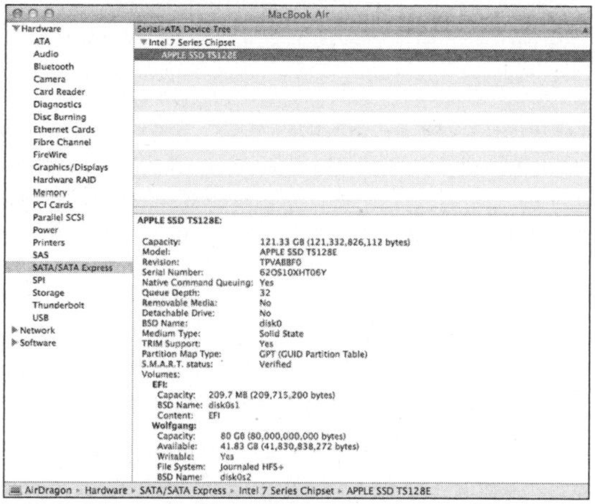

Figure 11-3:
Use System
Information
to check
the devices
and ports on
your system.

Step 12: Reboot with the OS X Recovery HD volume

In case your Mac is in seriously sad shape and won't even boot from its hard drive, here's a last step that you can take before you seek professional assistance: Check your Mac from the OS X Recovery HD volume. Reboot, hold down the ⌘+R keyboard shortcut immediately after you hear the startup chord, and then run Disk Utility from the window that appears. Because you've booted the system from the Recovery HD volume, you can verify and repair problems with your startup hard drive. (Some new Mac models also come with a diagnostic DVD that can help you pin down hardware problems.) After you're done, restart your system.

Booting from the Recovery HD volume also allows you to restore your system from your most recent Time Machine backup — a real lifesaver if your Mac's internal drive was the victim of catastrophe. (Think "accidental format." No, wait, don't even *think* it.)

Do I Need to Reinstall OS X?

To be honest, the question of whether or not you need to reinstall OS X is a difficult one to answer. Technically, you should never *need* to reinstall the Big X, but there's also no reason why you *can't.*

I can think of only two scenarios where reinstalling the operating system will *likely* solve a problem. One, if your system files have been so heavily corrupted — by a faulty hard drive or a rampaging virus, for example — that you can't boot OS X at all. Two, if the operating system encounters the death-dealing kernel panic on a regular basis. A *kernel panic* displays a dialog that instructs you to restart your Mac (in multiple languages, no less), usually overwriting whatever's on the monitor at the time. (This dialog is analogous to the infamous Windows Blue Screen of Death — I've grown to hate that shade of blue.)

If you receive kernel panics on an ongoing basis, something is really, *really* wrong. Make sure that your documents are copied to a rewriteable DVD or network drive, and don't overwrite any existing backup that you have with a new backup because the backup application is likely to lock up as well.

To reinstall, you can turn once again to Mavericks's Recovery HD volume. (That thing really comes in handy!) Reboot and hold down the ⌘+R startup shortcut immediately after you hear your Mac's startup chord, and then click the Reinstall OS X option in the window that appears.

It's Still Not Moving: Troubleshooting Resources

As I mention earlier in this chapter, you can pursue other avenues to get help when you can't solve a troubleshooting problem on your own. Mind you, I'm talking about professional help from sources that you can trust. Although you can find quite a bit of free advice on the Internet (usually on privately run websites and in the Internet newsgroups), most of it isn't worth your effort. In fact, some of it's downright wrong. That said, here are some sources that I *do* recommend.

OS X Help Center

Although most OS X owners tend to blow off Help Center when the trouble-shooting gets tough, that's never the best course of action. Always take a few moments to search the contents of Help Center — click Help on the Finder menu — to see whether any mention is made of the problem that you've encountered.

The Apple OS X Support site

Home to all manner of support questions and answers, the OS X Support section of the Apple website (www.apple.com/support) should be your next stop in case of trouble that you can't fix yourself. Topics include

✦ Startup issues

✦ Internet and networking problems

✦ Printing problems

You can search the Apple Knowledge Base, download the latest updates and electronic manuals, and participate in Apple-moderated discussion boards from this one central location.

Your local Apple dealer

An Apple dealer can provide just about any support that you're likely to need — for a price — but you can usually get the answers to important questions without any coinage changing hands. Your dealer is also well versed in the latest updates and patches that can fix those software incompatibility problems. Check your telephone book for your local dealer.

Book II
Customizing and Sharing

Contents at a Glance

Chapter 1: Building the Finder of Your Dreams

In This Chapter

✔ Choosing a view mode

✔ Modifying the toolbar

✔ Searching for files from the toolbar

✔ Searching for files with the Find command

✔ Changing view options

✔ Changing Finder preferences

*F*inder is the heart of OS X and, as you might expect, highly configurable. You can customize Finder to present icons, or you can peruse folders with a column view that can pack much more information onscreen at one time. Some folks prefer the default Finder toolbar, and others like to customize it with the applications and features that they use most often.

Decisions like these can help you transform Mavericks into *Your Personal Operating System* — and every OS X power user worth the title will take the time to apply these changes because an operating system (OS) that presents visual information the way that you want to see it is easier and more efficient to use.

No need for a hammer or saw — when you're building the Finder of your dreams, the only tools that you need are your cursor and keyboard!

Will That Be Icons or Lists or Columns . . . or Even a Flow?

The default appearance of a Finder window in OS X uses the familiar large-format icons that have been a hallmark of the Macintosh OS since Day One — but there's no reason you *have* to use them. (Most OS X power users I know consider the Icon view mode inefficient and slow.) Besides Icon view, as shown in Figure 1-1, OS X offers three other window view modes: List, Column, and Flow.

Figure 1-1:
A Finder
window in
default Icon
view mode.

To switch to any of the four view modes, click its button on the Finder window toolbar (the current view is highlighted), or choose View➪As Icons/ As List/As Columns/As Cover Flow. OS X places a helpful check mark next to the current view mode. Keyboard lovers can hold down ⌘ and press the 1, 2, 3, or 4 keys to switch views.

And now, without further ado, let me formally introduce you to each of the four Finder view modes:

✦ **Icon view:** OS X old-timers will thrill to the slider control at the bottom-right corner of Finder windows in Icon view mode. Check it out: Drag this control to the right to expand the size of the icons in the window, and drag the control to the left to reduce the icon size! (This feature A Big Thing for folks with less-than-perfect eyesight who prefer Icon view.) *Hint:* The Finder window status bar must be displayed to see the slider control, so if the status bar is hidden, choose View➪Show Status Bar.

✦ **List view:** Another feature familiar to long-time Mac owners, *List view* displays the folders on the volume in a hierarchical fashion. To display the contents of a folder, click the right-facing small triangle next to the folder name (called a *disclosure triangle*, believe it or not); the triangle rotates downward to indicate that you expanded the folder. Alternatively, double-click the folder icon to display the contents in a Finder window. To collapse the contents of the folder, click the disclosure triangle again; it rotates back to face the right. Figure 1-2 illustrates the same Finder window in List view.

To sort the items in the list by the field in a column heading — such as Size or Kind — click the heading. Click the heading again to sort the items in reverse order. And resize a column by dragging the right edge of the column heading.

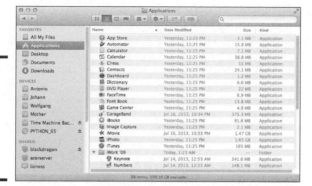

Figure 1-2:
The contents of a Finder window in List view mode.

✦ **Column view:** Figure 1-3 shows the same window in Column view, in which the volumes on your OS X system are displayed on the left. Each column on the right represents a lower level of subfolders. Click the volume in the Devices list and then click the desired folder in the first column on the right to display its contents, and so forth. (This is my favorite view — thanks, Apple! It's efficient and fast as all get-out.) When you drill deeper, the columns shift automatically to the left. When you click an item (instead of a folder), Finder displays a preview and a quick summary of the selected item in the rightmost column.

Figure 1-3:
Column view requires little scrolling.

Each column has its own scroll bar (for those really, really big folders), and you can drag the column handle at the bottom of the separators to resize the column width to the left. When you hold down Option and drag a column handle, all the columns are adjusted simultaneously.

✦ **Flow view:** When a new software feature or function turns out to be incredibly popular, a developer tries to use it wherever possible — hence, the Flow view shown in Figure 1-4, which Apple took directly from the Cover Flow view that proved so successful in iTunes. Flow view still displays the sidebar (that strip of locations and devices at the side of each Finder window), but each document or item is showcased in a preview pane (and with an accurate thumbnail, if possible). You can resize the preview pane by dragging the three-line handle on the bottom edge of the pane. The remainder of the Finder window in Flow view works similarly to List view, complete with the rotating triangles. However, if you like, you can click the scroll buttons or drag the scroll bar under the preview pane to move through the contents of your folder in a classy visual display!

Figure 1-4:
Wowzers!
Check out
the Flow
view for
Finder
windows!

TIP

You may notice that longer filenames appear with an ellipsis (. . .) in the name — the ellipsis indicates that the entire name can't be displayed in the amount of space provided. To view the full filename in List, Column, and Cover Flow views, you could resize the name column, but it's easier to move your cursor on top of the filename and leave it motionless for a few seconds. Like magic, Finder displays the full filename in a pop-up text box!

TIP

One of my pet peeves is cluttered disks. If you're continually having problems locating files and folders, ask yourself, "Self, do I need to organize? Am I (insert gasp) *cluttered*?" If your answer is yes, take an hour and organize your files logically into new folders.

I'm talking your documents and such — not your applications, which are usually where they need to be — in your Applications folder, and easily displayed using Launchpad. Often, documents that you create end up as stragglers, usually located in the root folder of your hard drive, which sooner or later ends up looking like a biker bar after Ladies' Night. (The same can be said of many OS X Desktops, too.)

REMEMBER

By keeping your root folder and Desktop clean and saving your files in organized folders, you waste less time searching for files and more time *using* them. It's also a good idea to take advantage of the All My Files feature in Mavericks, which I discuss in the sidebar, "All my files in one place." After all, organization leads to efficiency!

Doing the Toolbar Dance

In this section, I show you how to customize that strip of icons across the top of the Finder window that's affectionately called the *toolbar.* Or, if you like, you can dismiss it entirely to gain additional real estate for the contents of your Finder window.

Hiding and showing the toolbar

You can toggle the display of the toolbar in an active Finder window in one of three ways:

✦ Right-click the toolbar and choose Hide Toolbar.

✦ Press ⌘+Option+T.

✦ Choose View from the Finder menu and then choose Hide (or Show) Toolbar.

Hiding the toolbar also hides the sidebar.

Hiding and showing the status bar

The status bar appears either at the bottom or top of the Finder window, depending on whether the toolbar has been hidden, and it displays a number of helpful informational-type tidbits about the window's contents. Depending on what you've opened, the status bar can include

✦ **Statistics:** See the number of items in the window and the amount of free space remaining on the volume.

✦ **A Write-Protect icon:** This icon looks like a pencil with a line running through it, as shown in the lower left of Figure 1-5. The icon indicates that you don't have write permissions for the contents of the window or the volume where the contents reside. (Note that this doesn't necessarily mean that folders at a lower level are write-protected as well.) You'll typically see this icon when you're viewing the contents of a CD or DVD, where everything is write-protected.

To toggle the display of the status bar, choose View from the Finder menu and then choose Show/Hide Status Bar, or press ⌘+/.

The *path bar* (also shown in Figure 1-5) is a close relative of the status bar. If you turn it on, the path bar also resides at the bottom of every Finder window, and it shows the *system path* that leads to the selected file or folder (starting with the volume where the file resides, and following each enclosing folder). For example, if you select your Home folder in the Finder window sidebar, the path might read *Hard Drive > Users > mark.* I like this feature because it identifies the location of files and folders that I'm using. To view the path bar, choose View➪Show Path Bar. (Oh, and here's a neat trick: If you double-click at any specific point in the path, the Finder window jumps to that location!)

Back
Forward   View icons
Arrange   Action
Share
Edit Tags
Full Screen
New tab

Figure 1-5:
Check the status bar to scope out your write permissions.

Write-Protect   Status bar   Path bar

Giving your toolbar big tires and a loud exhaust

The default icons on the toolbar include

+ **Back and Forward:** As with a web browser, clicking the Back button moves you to the previous window's contents. If you use the Back button, the Forward button becomes enabled. Click this to return to the contents that you had before clicking the Back button.

+ **View icon buttons:** Click these to choose from the four view modes (Icon, List, Column, or Flow).

  Pssst. Selecting a folder and pressing the spacebar displays a summary of its size and last modification date. Pass it on.

+ **Arrange:** The items on this pop-up menu allow you to sort the elements in the Finder window by a number of criteria, from the file name to the size and date the file was last opened or modified.

+ **Action:** Open this pop-up menu to display context-sensitive commands for the selected items. In plain English, you'll see the commands that you'd see if you right-click the selection.

Book II
Chapter 1

Building the
Finder of Your
Dreams

Hey, where's my Quick Look icon?

New accounts you create in Mavericks are missing a good friend on the default toolbar: the Quick Look button, which was standard equipment on the Finder window toolbar in earlier versions of OS X. Luckily, you can easily add the Quick Look icon back to the toolbar using the instructions on customizing the toolbar in this section. (The Quick Look feature is also available as an item in the Action menu as well.)

After you add Quick Look to your toolbar, click the icon to display a window with the contents of the selected file or document without launching the corresponding application. Quick Look works with all sorts of images, video, and documents, allowing you to efficiently peruse files on your system without the hassle of

constantly launching and quitting applications. Quick Look works in any Finder window View mode, too. To activate Quick Look for a selected file from the keyboard, press the spacebar. To switch to a full-screen display, click the diagonal arrow icon at the upper right of the Quick Look window.

While Quick Look is active (and in full-screen mode), a number of format-specific buttons appear in the Quick Look window. For example, displaying an image file in Quick Look adds a button that can automatically import the image into iPhoto. These buttons vary with the format or type of document, but you'll always see a full-screen/exit full-screen button that toggles the Quick Look window between full-screen and regular size.

✦ **Share:** Open this pop-up menu to quickly send the selected items to a number of friendly destinations, such as Email (which creates a new Mail message with the items already attached) and Message (which sends the items to a buddy in the Messages application). Depending on the items you select and the available network connections you're using, you can also send items across an AirDrop connection or post them to Facebook, Twitter, Flickr, or Vimeo. (See Book VI, Chapter 2 and also Chapter 6 in this minibook for more on AirDrop.)

✦ **Edit Tags:** Click this icon to add or edit a Finder Tag on the currently selected items. (Finder Tags are discussed in detail in Book I, Chapter 3.)

✦ **Search:** Okay, I know it's not technically an icon, but the Search box is a member of the default toolbar family nonetheless. You can search for a file or folder using this box. More on this topic in the upcoming section, "Searching for Files from the Toolbar."

But, as one of my favorite bumper stickers so invitingly asks, "Why be normal?" Adding or deleting items from the toolbar is a great way to customize OS X. Follow these steps:

1. **From the active Finder window menu, choose View⇨Customize Toolbar to display the sheet that you see in Figure 1-6.**

Along with controls such as Back, Forward, and View, you find a number of system functions (such as Eject and Burn) and features you'd normally see on a contextual (right-click) menu (such as Get Info, Delete, and Quick Look).

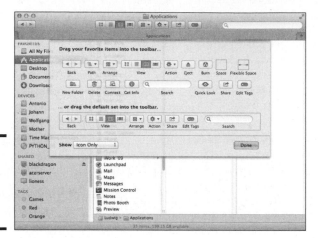

Figure 1-6: Changing the toolbar status quo in OS X.

2. **Add items to the toolbar by dragging them from the Customize Toolbar dialog up to the toolbar at the top of the window.**

   To add an item between existing buttons, drop it between the buttons, and they obligingly move aside. If you get exuberant about your toolbar and you add more icons than it can hold, a double-right arrow appears at the right side of the toolbar. A click of the arrow displays a pop-up menu with the icons that won't fit.

   Using the Customize Toolbar dialog isn't necessary for some toolbar modifications: You can also drag files, folders, and disk volumes directly from the Desktop or other Finder windows and add them to your toolbar at any time. To remove a file, folder, or disk volume from the toolbar, right-click the icon on the toolbar and choose Customize Toolbar, and then drag the icon off the toolbar. Watch it vanish like a CEO's ethics.

3. **Customize to your heart's content:**

   • *To remove an item from the toolbar:* Drag it off to the center of the window, amongst the other icons.

   • *To swap item positions:* Just click an item, drag it to its new spot, and then release the mouse button.

   • *To choose the default toolbar configuration or to start over:* Drag the default bar at the bottom of the dialog to the toolbar at the top. This is the toolbar equivalent of tapping your ruby slippers together three times and repeating, "There's no place like home."

All my files in one place

Mavericks includes a great timesaver for every Mac owner: the All My Files view, which appears in the Finder window sidebar under the Favorites heading. Click All My Files to display just your documents, grouped by category — images, PDF documents, music tracks, movies, and more. (No applications are included in All My Files, which avoids clutter and speeds up things.) While you're checking out the contents of All My Files, don't forget that you can use the Search box to locate specific files quickly, just like any other Finder window.

If you need different information in the All My Files view, right-click any of the major headings to display a menu of column choices. To add a column, click the desired data, and a checkmark appears. For example, I like to see the size of each file in my All My Files view. To hide a column, right-click a major heading, and then click the item to remove the check mark.

- *To toggle between displaying the icons with accompanying text (the default), the icon only, or a text button only:* Open the Show pop-up menu at the bottom of the Customize Toolbar dialog and make your decision there. (You can also right-click the toolbar and make the same changes.)

4. **After you arrange your toolbar as you like, click the Done button.**

If you don't want to customize the toolbar using the procedure I just explained, you can also hold down ⌘ and drag any item off the toolbar at any time, or hold down ⌘ and drag toolbar items to reorder them.

You can always drag a file or folder into the sidebar column at the left of the Finder window.

Searching for Files from the Toolbar

Need to find a file fast? The default toolbar has just what you need: the Search field, which you can use to perform a Spotlight search for a string of text in your files (including both filenames and contents). To locate a file with the Search field, follow these steps:

1. **Click in the Search box on the toolbar and type the text that you want to find.**

   Look for the text box on the right with the magnifying glass. (The folks at Apple are really, really into Sherlock Holmes . . . so am I!) If you need to clear the field and start over again, click the circular X button, which appears only when text is in the Search field.

Hey, who needs to press Return? Finder immediately displays the files with names (or contents) that include the text, as shown in Figure 1-7. Depending on what you enter, you may also see a pop-up menu option to display only those files with names that contain the text you specified, Finder Tags that match a keyword or color, or even specific file types that are related to the search text.

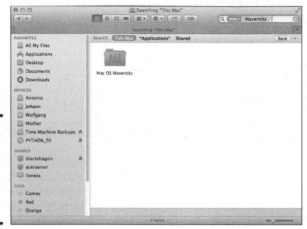

Figure 1-7:
Locating
a file or
folder with
the toolbar
Search box.

2. **To display the location of a file, click it once. To launch it, double-click the entry.**

   Files can also be moved or copied from the Search results list with the standard drag and Option+drag methods.

3. **To perform a new search, click the circular X button and type new text in the Search field.**

   To return to your original location in the Finder window, click the Back button on the toolbar.

Searching for Files from the Find Dialog

Although the Search box on the toolbar is all you usually need to find most files and folders, sometimes you need a little more flexibility and power to locate what you need on your system. To do so, add the Find controls, which you can use to create custom searches with more complex criteria. To locate a file by using the Find controls, follow these steps:

1. **With Finder active, display the Find controls by pressing ⌘+F (or choose Finder⇨File⇨Find).**

   OS X displays the controls that you see in Figure 1-8.

Figure 1-8:
The Find
controls add
a bit of extra
power to a
search.

2. **Click the buttons at the top of the list to specify where you want to search.**

   You can choose This Mac (your entire system, including network volumes) or a local volume.

3. **After you decide where to search, set the criteria of what to search for.**

   • *A specific filename:* Open the first pop-up menu in the Search Criteria strip at the top of the window and choose Name; type all or part of the filename in the Contains box.

   Mavericks automatically begins searching as soon as you type at least one character.

   After you locate the file or folder that you need, click the entry name to reveal the location of the matching file or folder in the path bar at the bottom of the window. You can also double-click it to launch (or display) it.

   • *A text string in the document itself:* Open the first pop-up menu in a row, choose Contents, and then type the string to match in the box.

   The text must appear just as you type it, so restrict what you're searching for to a minimum of words that you're fairly sure will cause a match. (Content searching is not case-sensitive, though.) Content searching works only when you've generated an index, which I explain later in this section, and only when Spotlight recognizes the file type.

   • *Additional search criteria lines:* Click the plus sign button next to the last criterion line.

You can limit your results based on all sorts of rules, including the date that the file or folder was last modified, when it was created, the file type, the size, the extension, or whether the file or folder is marked visible or hidden (such as a system file).

You can also remove a search criterion line by clicking the minus sign button.

4. **(Optional) To save the search criteria that you selected, click Save.**

   This creates a *smart folder*, which (you're gonna *love* this) Mavericks automatically updates (in real time) to contain whatever items match the criteria you saved! You can specify the location for your smart folder, and you can choose to add it to your Finder sidebar for the ultimate convenience. *Sweet.*

5. **When you're done canvassing your computer, click the Back button in the Find dialog to return to Finder.**

Configuring the View Options

As I discuss at the beginning of the chapter, you have a lot of control over how OS X presents files and folders in Finder. In this section, I cover how you can make further adjustments to the view from your windows. (Pardon me for the ghastly cliché posing as a pun.)

Setting Icon view options

First, allow me to provide a little detail on housekeeping in the Big X. After a few hours of work, a Finder window in Icon mode can look something like a teenager's room: stuff strewn all over the place, as I demonstrate with my Applications folder in Figure 1-9. To restore order to your Desktop, right-click in any open area of the active window, choose Clean Up By⇨Name. This command snaps the icons to an invisible grid so that they're aligned and sorted by name, as shown in Figure 1-10.

After things are in alignment, work with the icon view options. (Naturally, you'll want the active Finder window in Icon view first, so choose View⇨As Icons or press ⌘+1.) From the Finder menu, choose View⇨Show View Options or press that swingin' ⌘+J shortcut to display the View Options dialog that you see in Figure 1-11. (You might have noticed that the window name also appears as the title of the View Options dialog.) Remember that these are the options available for Icon view; I discuss the options for List, Column, and Cover Flow view later in this chapter.

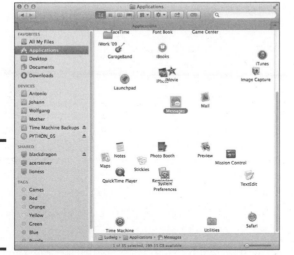

Figure 1-9:
Will
someone
please
clean up
this mess?

Figure 1-10:
Tidying up is
no problem.

Figure 1-11:
The settings available for Icon view.

Of course, OS X remembers the changes that you make in the View Options dialog, no matter which view mode you're configuring. Now, the changes that you can make from this dialog include

✦ **Always Open in Icon View:** Each Finder window that you open automatically uses Icon view. If this check box is deselected, the new window uses the last view mode you used.

✦ **Browse in Icon View:** As you browse through subfolders, Mavericks uses the current folder's view settings, not the view settings for those subfolders.

✦ **Arrange By:** Automatically separate items in a window with dividers, sorted by one of the following criteria from its pop-up menu: by name, kind (item type), application (the default application that opens each file or file type), date last opened, date added, date modified, date created, size, or the icon label you assigned.

✦ **Sort By:** If the Arrange By pop-up menu is set to None, you can open this pop-up menu and automatically align icons to a grid in the window, just as if you had used the Clean Up menu command. You can also sort the display of icons in a window by choosing one of the following criteria: by name, kind (item type), application (the default application that opens each file type), date last opened, date added, date modified, date created, size, or icon label.

✦ **Icon Size:** Click and drag this slider to shrink or expand the icons in the window. The icon size is displayed in pixels above the slider. (Remember, however, that Mavericks offers an icon resizing slider at the right side of the status bar of any Finder window in Icon view mode; it's much easier and more convenient just to drag the slider to expand or reduce the size of icons in a window.)

✦ **Grid Spacing:** Click and drag this slider to shrink or expand the size of the grid used to align icons in the window. The larger the grid, the more white space between icons.

✦ **Text Size:** Click the up and down arrows to the right of this pop-up menu to choose the font size (in points) for icon labels.

✦ **Label Position:** Select the Bottom (default) or the Right radio button to choose between displaying the text under your Desktop icons or to the right of the icons, respectively.

✦ **Show Item Info:** OS X displays the number of items in each folder in the window.

✦ **Show Icon Preview:** Finder displays icons for image files using a miniature of the actual picture. For those with digital cameras, this feature is cool, but it does take extra processing time because OS X has to load each image file and shrink it down to create the icon.

✦ **Background:** Select one of three radio buttons here:

  • *White:* This is the default.

  • *Color:* Click a color choice from the color block that appears if you make this selection.

  • *Picture:* Select this radio button and then click the Select button to display a standard Open dialog. Navigate to the location where the desired image is stored, click it once to select it, and then click Open.

✦ **Use as Defaults:** When you first open the View Options dialog, the changes you're making apply only to the Finder window that opens when you open the selected item — in other words, the item that appears in the window's title bar, such as a folder or drive.

For example, any changes made to the settings shown earlier in Figure 1-11 will affect only my Applications folder because it was the active Finder window when I pressed ⌘+J. However, you can decide to apply the changes that you make to *all* Finder windows that you view in your current mode. Simply click the Use as Defaults button.

After all your changes are made and you're ready to return to work, click the dialog's Close button to save your settings.

Setting List view options

If you're viewing the active window in List view, choose View⇨Show View Options to display the View Options dialog that you see in Figure 1-12.

Figure 1-12:
Here
are your
List view
settings.

As in Icon view, changes you make in this dialog typically apply only to this window, but you can click the Use as Defaults button to assign these settings to all windows that you view in List mode. The other List view settings are

✦ **Always Open in List View:** Mavericks will open all Finder windows in List view. If deselected, new windows use the last view mode you used.

✦ **Browse in List View:** As you browse through any subordinate folders, Mavericks uses the current folder's view settings, not the view settings for those subfolders.

✦ **Arrange By:** Automatically separate items in the window with dividers, sorted by one of the following criteria from its pop-up menu: by name, kind (item type), application (the default application that opens each file type), date last opened, date added, date modified, date created, size, or the icon label you assigned.

✦ **Sort By:** If the Arrange By pop-up menu is set to None, open this pop-up menu to automatically sort the display of icons in a window by choosing one of the following criteria: by name, kind (item type), application (the default application that opens each file type), date last opened, date added, date modified, date created, size, or icon label.

✦ **Icon Size:** You can choose between two icon sizes.

✦ **Text Size:** Click the up and down arrows to the right of the Text Size pop-up menu to choose the font size (in points) for icon labels.

✦ **Show Columns:** Select the check boxes under this heading to display additional columns in list view. These columns are the date that the item was modified, the creation date, the date the file was last opened, the date the file was added to your system, the size, the item type, the version (supplied by most applications), the label color, and any comments you added in the Info dialog for that item. (In my opinion, the more columns you add, the more unwieldy Finder gets, so I advise disabling the display of columns that you won't use.)

✦ **Use Relative Dates:** Display modification dates and creation dates with relative terms, such as *Today* or *Yesterday*. If this setting freaks you out, deselect this check box to force all dates to act like adults.

✦ **Calculate All Sizes:** Have OS X display the actual sizes of folders, including all the files and subfolders they contain. (Handy for figuring out where all your disk space went, no?) *Note:* Using this option takes processing time, so I recommend not using it unless you really need to see the size.

✦ **Show Icon Preview:** Display preview icons for image files. Again, this takes extra processing time, and the image preview icons are pretty doggone small in list view, so this feature may be of limited value to you.

To save your settings, click the dialog's Close button (or press ⌘+J).

Setting Column view options

To make changes to view options in any Finder window displaying items in Column view mode, choose View⇨Show View Options to display the View Options dialog that you see in Figure 1-13.

Figure 1-13: The glamorous Column view settings.

Any changes that you make to this dialog are *always* reflected in *every* Column view:

✦ **Always Open in Column View:** All Finder windows open in Column view. If deselected, new windows use the last view mode you used.

✦ **Browse in Column View:** As you browse through subfolders, Mavericks uses the current folder's view settings, not the view settings for those subfolders.

✦ **Arrange By:** Automatically separate items, sorted by one of the following criteria from its pop-up menu: by name, kind (item type), application (the default application that opens each file type), date last opened, date added, date modified, date created, size, or the icon label you assigned.

✦ **Sort By:** If the Arrange By pop-up menu is set to None, open this pop-up menu to automatically sort the display of icons in a window by choosing one of the following criteria: by name, kind (item type), application (the default application that opens each file type), date last opened, date added, date modified, date created, size, or icon label.

✦ **Text Size:** Open this pop-up menu to choose the font size (in points) for icon labels.

✦ **Show Icons:** Display icons in the columns. If this option is deselected, the icons don't appear, and you'll gain a little space.

✦ **Show Icon Preview:** Mavericks displays preview icons for image files — taking a little extra time to perform this service, naturally. As you find out in the next bullet, Column view mode can be set to automatically display a preview thumbnail in the last column when you click an image or a video file, and even some documents to boot. So, the usefulness of tiny icon previews in Column view mode may be limited for you.

✦ **Show Preview Column:** Clicking a file in Column view mode displays a thumbnail and preview information in the rightmost column, as shown in Figure 1-14.

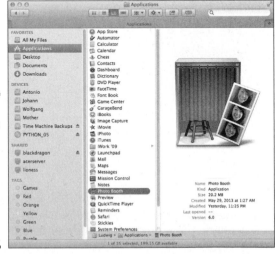

Figure 1-14: The Preview column provides more information on the selected file.

If you store a slew of smaller QuickTime movies and digital images on your drive, the Preview column is great. (You can even play a QuickTime movie from the Preview column.) Of course, longer movies and larger photos take more time to load — and those that are read from optical media or over the network take even longer!

Click the dialog's Close button to save your settings and return to Finder.

Setting Cover Flow view options

The view options for Cover Flow view are the same as those for List view that I cover earlier in this section, except for the Always Open in Cover Flow check box. Selecting this check box opens all new Finder windows in Cover Flow view. (If deselected, new windows use the last view mode you used.)

Setting Finder Preferences

Finally, you can change a number of settings to customize Finder itself. From the Finder menu, click Finder and choose the Preferences menu item to display the Finder Preferences dialog that you see in Figure 1-15.

**Book II
Chapter 1**

**Building the
Finder of Your
Dreams**

Figure 1-15:
You can configure your Finder preferences here.

In the General section, the preference settings are

✦ **Show These Items on the Desktop:** Display your internal hard disks, external hard drives, removable volumes (including CDs, DVDs, and iPods), and connected network servers.

✦ **New Finder Windows Show:** Specify where a new Finder window should open. By default, a new window displays the contents of the All My Files location.

✦ **Open Folders in Tabs Instead of New Window:** When this check box is selected, double-clicking a folder opens it in a Finder Tab instead of a new Finder window. (If deselected, the contents of the folder appear in a new Finder window.)

✦ **Spring-Loaded Folders and Windows:** This feature sounds a little wacky, but using it can definitely speed up file copying! If this check box is selected, you can drag an item on top of a folder — *without* releasing the button on your pointing device — and after a preset time (controlled by the Delay slider), a spring-loaded window appears to show you the folder's contents. At that point, you can either release the mouse button to drop the file inside the folder (upon which the window disappears), or you can drag the icon on top of another subfolder to spring it forth and drill even deeper.

The Finder Tags preference pane allows you to control which Finder Tags appear in the sidebar and in Finder menus (including Tags you've created). Add Tags to the sidebar by selecting the desired check boxes and to Finder menus by dragging them to the box at the bottom.

From the Sidebar preferences pane, you can choose which default items should appear in the Finder window sidebar column. Your choices include locations (such as your Home and Applications folders), network servers, removable media, the Desktop itself, and — naturally — your hard drives. To add a default item to the sidebar column, click the corresponding check box to select it; deselect the check box to banish that item forthwith.

The Advanced preference settings are

✦ **Show All Filename Extensions:** Finder displays the file extensions at the end of filenames. This feature comes in handy for some applications, where everything from a document to a preference file to the application itself shares the same icon. However, I usually find extensions distasteful and leave things set with the default of extensions off. (However, folks working with older Word files, which have the DOC extension instead of the newer DOCX extension, really appreciate this feature.)

✦ **Show Warning before Changing an Extension:** Also on by default, this setting forces Mavericks to display a confirmation dialog before allowing you to change the extension on a filename. Why? Well, changing an extension frequently results in a broken file association, so the file's corresponding application may not launch automatically any longer when you double-click the item. Double-clicking a Word document, for example, might not launch Word automatically as it used to do. If you show file extensions and you often change them, click this check box to disable the warning.

✦ **Show Warning before Emptying the Trash:** By default, this check box is selected, and OS X displays a confirmation dialog before allowing you to — in the words of OS X patrons around the world — *toss the Bit Bucket.* If you're interested in speed and trust your judgment (and your mouse finger), you can disable this setting.

✦ **Empty Trash Securely:** If you'd prefer to use the more secure method of emptying your Trash — where deleted items are far harder for anyone to recover — select this check box.

✦ **When Performing a Search:** Open this pop-up menu to specify whether the text you enter in the Finder window Search box should match everything on your Mac or whether the search should be limited to the current folder only. Choose Use the Previous Search Scope to use the scope setting you used during your last search.

After you make the desired changes to the Finder Preferences, click the dialog's Close button to save your settings and return to Finder.

**Book II
Chapter 1**

**Building the
Finder of Your
Dreams**

Chapter 2: Giving Your Desktop the Personal Touch

In This Chapter

✔ **Choosing your own background**

✔ **Adding and selecting a screen saver**

✔ **Choosing menu colors and highlights**

✔ **Keeping track of things with Stickies**

✔ **Customizing the Dock and using Dashboard**

✔ **Getting in the game with Game Center**

✔ **Cleaning and sorting the OS X Desktop**

"Tweak! Tweak!" It's not the cry of some exotic bird — that's the call of the wild Mac power users, who like to tweak their OS X Desktops just so, with *that* menu color, *this* background, and *those* applications on the Dock. Noncomputer types just can't understand the importance of the proper arrangement of your virtual workplace: When things are familiar and customized to your needs, you're more productive and things get done faster — just like the layout of your physical desktop in your home or office. (I'm told it's called "computer feng shui" by the elite.) If you've set up multiple users on your computer under OS X, the Big X automatically keeps track of each user's Desktop and restores it when that person logs in. (For example, when you use the Mac, you get that background photo of Farrah Fawcett from the '70s, whereas your daughter gets Justin Bieber.)

In this chapter, I show you what you can do to produce a Desktop that's uniquely your own, including tweaks that you can make to the background and your Desktop icons. I also show you how to use Desktop Stickies instead of a forest of paper slips covering your monitor.

With your OS X Desktop clad in the proper harmonious colors — yes, that can be your favorite photo of Elvis, himself — and your new Dock icons ready for action, you're indeed prepared for whatever lies ahead in your computing world!

Changing the Background

You might be asking, "Mark, do I really need a custom background?" That depends completely on your personal tastes, but I've yet to meet a computer owner who didn't change his background when presented with the opportunity (with one exception — an editor friend of mine, who has favored a plain white background for years!).

Favorite backgrounds usually include

- ✦ Humorous cartoons and photos that can bring a smile to your face (even during the worst workday)
- ✦ Scenic beauty
- ✦ Solid colors (relaxing and distraction-free)
- ✦ Photos of family and friends (or the latest Hollywood heartthrob)
- ✦ The company logo (not sure it does much for morale, but it does impress the boss)

If you do decide to spruce up your background, you have three choices: You can select one of the excellent default OS X background images, choose a solid color, or specify your own image. All three backgrounds are chosen from the Desktop & Screen Saver pane, located in System Preferences (as illustrated in Figure 2-1). Getting there is easy, too: Simply right-click any empty spot on your Desktop and choose Change Desktop Background from the menu that appears.

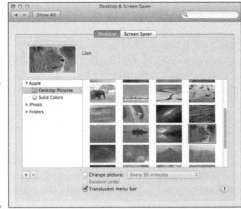

Figure 2-1: To select a background, get thee hence to System Preferences.

Book II
Chapter 2

Giving Your Desktop
the Personal Touch

How to annoy friends and confuse coworkers

Never let it be said that I can't dish out revenge when necessary. I don't know whether I should call this a *Tip* or a *Devilish Practical Joke That Will Drive People Nuts* — anyway, it's fun as all get-out. Right before you go to lunch, use the Grab utility (found in Launchpad in the Utilities folder) to take a snapshot of your Desktop with a number of windows open (or an error dialog with an OK or a Close button) and then save the image to your Pictures folder. Select the image as your Desktop background and then watch others go crazy trying to click those faux windows, buttons, and icons. For an archenemy, try the same trick on *his* Mac! Arrange a slightly embarrassing Desktop on his computer, use the Grab utility to capture it as an image, specify it as the background, and sit back while the fun begins. (Perhaps a web browser that's open to a somewhat unusual website?)

Picking something Apple

To choose a background from one of the collections provided by Apple, click one of these groups from the list at the left:

+ **Desktop Pictures:** These backgrounds feature scenic beauty, such as blades of grass, animals, sand dunes, snowy hills . . . that sort of thing. You also get close-up backgrounds of plant life. I especially recommend the green grass.

+ **Solid Colors:** This is for those who desire a soothing solid shade (and like their icons easily visible). More on this in the following section.

+ **iPhoto:** Choose an image of your own from your iPhoto Library.

+ **Folders:** Click the disclosure triangle next to the Folders entry, and you can display the images saved in the active user's Pictures folder, as well as any folder containing photos that you've added to the list. (I demonstrate how to add folders shortly.).

If you see something you like, click the thumbnail, and OS X displays it in the well (upper left of the pane) and automatically refreshes your background so that you can see what it looks like. (By the way, a *well* is a sunken square area that displays an image, color swatch or even a sound file icon — in this case, the background image that you select.)

OS X automatically manipulates how the background appears on your Desktop. If an image conforms to your screen resolution, fine. Otherwise, open the pop-up menu next to the well and make some tweaks.

This pop-up menu appears only if the Desktop picture that you select isn't one of the standard Apple images. All the pictures in the Apple Desktop Pictures and Solid Colors categories are scaled automatically to the size of your screen.

Your options for sizing your background image are

+ **Tile the background.** This option repeats the image to cover the Desktop. To produce a smooth, creamy, seamless look, use images with a pattern.

+ **Fill the screen.** Use this option with a solid color to get uniform coverage. The original aspect ratio of the image is preserved, so it's not stretched (although it might be cropped).

+ **Fit to screen.** Choose this option to resize the height or width of the image to fit your screen, keeping the original aspect ratio. (Fit to screen can result in solid color bars displayed at the top or sides of the image.)

+ **Stretch the background to fit the screen.** If your Desktop image is smaller than the Desktop acreage, this option works, but be forewarned: If you try to stretch too small of an image over too large a Desktop, the pixilated result can be pretty frightening. (Think of enlarging an old Kodak Instamatic negative to a 16 x 20 poster. Dots, dots, dots.) The original aspect ratio of the image isn't preserved, so you might end up with results that look like the funhouse mirrors at a carnival.

+ **Center the image on the screen.** This option is my favorite solution for Desktop images that are smaller than your resolution.

To change your Desktop background automatically on a regular basis, select the Change Picture check box and then choose the delay period from the corresponding pop-up menu. To display the images in random order, select the Random Order check box; otherwise, OS X displays them in the order that they appear in the pane. You can also select a translucent Finder menu bar, which (almost) blends in with your background. If you prefer a solid-color, matter-of-fact workman's menu bar, clear the Translucent Menu Bar check box.

I just gotta have lavender

As I mention earlier, for those who want their favorite color without the distraction of an image — even solid white — you can choose from a selection of solid colors. You can choose from these colors the same way that you'd pick a default OS X background image (as I describe in the preceding section).

To choose the exact color you're looking for, click the Custom Color button and then use the Color Picker dialog to find just the right match.

Selecting your own photo

Finally, you can drag your own image into the well from a Finder window to add your own work of art. To view thumbnails of an entire folder, click the disclosure triangle next to the Folder entry in the list at left. From here, you can display the contents of your personal Pictures folder, or any folder that you've added already. Speaking of adding a folder to this list, click the Add button (bearing the plus sign) at the lower left of the Desktop & Screen Saver pane to specify any folder containing photos on your system. Click the desired thumbnail to embellish your Desktop.

Changing the Screen Saver

Screen savers are another popular item. Because I cover the Screen Saver preferences in Chapter 3 of this minibook, I simply illustrate here how to choose one. Open System Preferences and click the Desktop & Screen Saver icon; then click the Screen Saver tab to display the settings that you see in Figure 2-2.

Figure 2-2:
A good
screen
saver can
almost
cancel the
effects of a
bad boss.

To add a third-party screen saver module so that everyone can use it on a multiuser system, copy it into the Screen Savers folder in the top-level Library folder. To selfishly keep that saver all to yourself, copy it into your user account's Screen Savers folder (which is located in the Library folder in your Home folder). To access your Library folder, hold down the Option key while clicking the Go menu on the Finder menu bar, and then click the Library menu item that appears.

Click one of the thumbnails in the column at the left to display a preview of the effect. If you choose one of the Slideshows screen savers, you can click the Source pop-up list to choose a default photo collection, or choose a folder of your own images. Selecting the Random thumbnail at the end of the list runs through 'em all, naturally.

To keep tabs on the current time, select the Show with Clock check box. Mavericks adds a clock display to any screen saver.

Many screen savers allow you to monkey with their settings. If the Screen Saver Options button is enabled (not dimmed), click it to see how you can change the effects.

Changing Colors in OS X

I can't understand it, but some people just don't appreciate menus with purple highlights! (You can tell a Louisiana State University graduate a mile away.) To specify your own colors for buttons, menus, and windows, follow these steps:

1. **Open System Preferences and click the General icon to display the settings, as shown in Figure 2-3.**

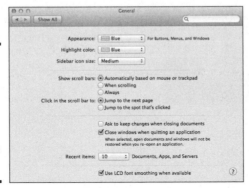

Figure 2-3: Okay, then, set up your own school colors with the Appearance settings!

2. **From the Appearance pop-up menu, choose the main color choice for your buttons and menus.**

3. **From the Highlight Color pop-up menu, choose the highlight color that appears when you select text in an application or select an item from a list.**

4. **Press ⌘+Q to exit System Preferences and save your changes.**

Adding Stickies

Stickies are interesting little beasts. I don't know their genus or phyla, but they're certainly handy to have around. To be technical for a moment, a *Sticky* is nothing more than a special type of document window, but these windows remain on your Desktop as long as the Stickies application is running.

I use Stickies for anything that a real-world sticky note can handle, such as jotting down someone's e-mail address or phone number, or even posting today's Dilbert cartoon from www.dilbert.com!

A Sticky can contain data pasted from the Clipboard, or you can simply type directly into the active Stickies document window. Sticky windows can include graphics and different fonts and colors. You can even locate specific text from somewhere in your vast collection of Stickies by using the Find command in the Stickies application. Just press ⌘+F while the Stickies menu is active to display the Stickies Find dialog. (And you don't use up our bark-covered friends of the forest, either.)

Book II Chapter 2

Giving Your Desktop the Personal Touch

In Book I, I discuss the OS X Services menu. You can make a Sticky note from the Services menu in many applications as well, such as Safari and TextEdit.

Follow these steps to stick your way to success:

1. **Click the Launchpad icon and click the Utilities/Other folder, and then click the Stickies icon to display the new window that you see in Figure 2-4.**

The text cursor is already idling in the new window.

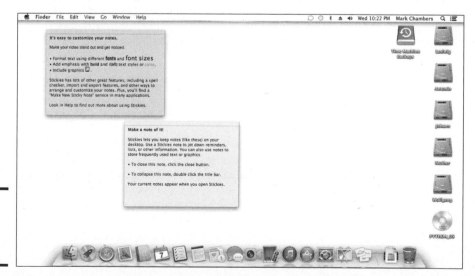

Figure 2-4:
"Look, Ma, it's a Sticky!"

2. **Type text in the window or press ⌘+V to paste the contents of the Clipboard into the window.**

   You can also import the contents of an existing file into a Sticky. Just choose File⇨Import Text to display a standard Open dialog.

3. **(Optional) Add text formatting, change the text font, and change font color from the Font menu.**

   From the Note menu, you can also choose to make the Sticky translucent. (No pressing reason; they just look cool.)

4. **(Optional) To change the Sticky color, open the Color menu and choose the appropriate hue.**

5. **Resize and drag the Sticky window to the desired location.**

   Press ⌘+M to toggle between a *miniaturized* view (showing only the title bar) and the expanded view.

To delete a Sticky, simply click the Close button at the upper-left corner of the Sticky window. Or click the Sticky to make it the active note and then click Close. Stickies display a dialog to confirm that you want to close the note; click Save to save the contents in a file or click the Don't Save button to close the note and discard its contents.

To close the Stickies application completely, click any note and press ⌘+Q. The application remembers the position and contents of each note for when you launch it again.

Customizing the Dock

In terms of importance, the *Dock* — the quick-access strip for applications and documents that appears on your Desktop — ranks right up there with the command center of a modern nuclear submarine. As such, it had better be easy to customize, and naturally, OS X doesn't let you down.

Adding applications and extras to the Dock

Why be satisfied with just the icons that Apple places on the Dock? You can add your own applications, files, and folders to the Dock as well.

✦ **Adding applications:** You can add any application to your Dock by simply dragging its icon into the area to the *left* side of the Dock (that's to the left side of the vertical dotted line on the Dock). You'll know when you're in the proper territory because the existing Dock icons obligingly move aside to make a space for it.

Attempting to place an application directly on the right side of the Dock sends it to the Trash (if the Trash icon is highlighted when you release the button), so beware. Note, however, that you can drop an application icon inside a Stack (more on that in a bit) or a folder that already exists at the right side of the Dock. (If you've repositioned the Dock to the left or right side of the screen, consider the top of the Dock as the "left side," and the bottom of the Dock as the "right side.")

+ **Adding individual files and volumes:** Individual files and volume icons can be added to the Dock by dragging the icon into the area to the *right* side of the Dock. (Attempting to place these to the left side of the Dock opens the application associated with the contents, which usually doesn't work.) Again, the existing Dock icons will move aside to create a space when you're in the right area.

To open the Dock item you've added in a Finder window, right-click the icon to display a Dock menu, where you can open documents, run applications, and have other assorted fun, depending on the item you choose.

+ **Adding several files or a folder:** Mavericks uses a feature called *Stacks,* which I discuss in a few paragraphs, to handle multiple files or add an entire folder to the Dock.

+ **Adding websites:** You can drag any URL from Safari directly into the area at the right of the Dock. Clicking that icon automatically opens your browser and displays that page. (Safari gets the treatment in Book V, Chapter 5.) Now that, my friends, is genuine *sassy!*

To remove an icon from the Dock, just click and drag it off the Dock. You get a rather silly (but somehow strangely satisfying) animated cloud of debris, and the icon is no more. Note, however, that the original application, folder, or volume is not deleted — just the Dock icon itself is permanently excused. If you like, you can delete almost any of the default icons that OS X installs on the Dock; only the Finder and Trash icons must remain on the Dock.

To set up a Dock icon as a Login Item — without the hassle of opening the Users & Groups pane in System Preferences — just click a Dock icon and hold the mouse button down until the pop-up menu appears. Select Options, and then select the Open at Login item from the submenu.

If you can't delete items from the Dock, you're using a *managed* account — meaning that your account is configured with Parental Controls turned on, and your administrator has selected the Prevent the Dock from Being Modified check box in your account. To delete Dock items, you'll need an admin-level user to log in; then visit the Users & Groups pane in System Preferences, click your account, and deselect the check box. For more information on user accounts, see Chapter 5 of this minibook.

Keeping track with Stacks

Mavericks offers *Stacks,* which are groups of items (documents, applications, and folders) that you want to place on the Dock for convenience — perhaps the files needed for a project you're working on, or your favorite game applications. For example, I have a Stack named Wiley on my Dock that holds all the project files I need for the book I'm currently writing.

To create a Stack, just select and drag the items you want to include to the right side of the Dock. As always, the Dock opens a spot on the right side of the Dock to indicate you're in the zone.

To display the items in a Stack, just click it:

✦ **If the Stack holds relatively few items,** they're displayed in a really cool-looking arc that Apple calls a *fan* (as shown in Figure 2-5), and you can click the item you want to open or launch.

✦ **If the Stack is stuffed full of many items,** the Stack opens in a grid display, allowing you to scroll through the contents to find what you need.

Mavericks provides a number of display and sorting options for a Stack. Right-click the Stack icon, and you can choose to sort the contents by name, date created or added, date modified, or file type. If you'd prefer a grid display (no matter how many items the Stack contains), you can choose Grid mode. Choose List to display the Stack's contents in much the same way as List view mode in a Finder window. List mode also allows you to view folders in a Stack as nested menu items. Choose Automatic to return to the default view mode.

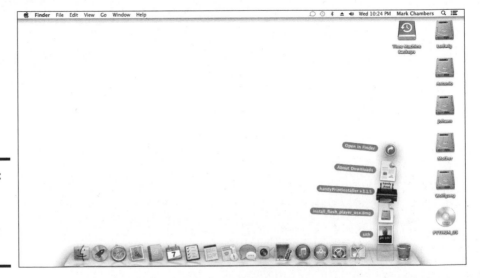

Figure 2-5: Click a Stack on the Dock to view its contents.

You can remove a Stack from the Dock by right-clicking the Stack icon and choosing Options from the menu that appears. Choose Remove from Dock from the submenu that appears. Alternatively, just drag that sucker right off the Dock.

You can also display the contents of a Stack in a Finder window. Right-click the Stack icon and choose the Open item at the bottom of the pop-up menu.

If you add a folder full of items, the Stack is named after the folder; otherwise, Mavericks does the best job it can in figuring out what to name the Stack.

Apple provides a Stack already set up for you: the Downloads folder, situated next to the Trash, is the default location for any new files that you download using Safari or receive in your e-mail. Mavericks bounces the Download Stack icon to indicate that you've received a new item.

Resizing the Dock

You can change the size of the Dock from the Dock settings in System Preferences — I explain this in more detail in Book II, Chapter 3 — but here's a simpler way to resize the Dock, right from the Desktop.

Move your cursor over the vertical solid line that separates the left side of the Dock from the right side; the cursor turns into a funky line with arrows pointing up and down. This is your cue to click and drag while moving up and down, which expands and shrinks the Dock, respectively.

You can also right-click when the funky line cursor is visible to display a menu of Dock preferences. This allows you to change your Dock preferences without the hassle of opening System Preferences and displaying the Dock settings.

Stick It on Dashboard

One of the most popular features in Mavericks is *Dashboard,* which you can use to hold widgets and display them with the press of a button. (Okay, I know that sounds a little wacky, but bear with me.) *Widgets* are small applications — dubbed by some as "applets" — that typically provide only one function. For example, Dashboard comes complete with a calculator, dictionary, clock, weather display, and quick-and-simple calendar. You can display and use these widgets at any time by pressing the Dashboard key; by default, that's F12 on older and non-Apple keyboards (and F4 on current Apple keyboard models), but you can modify the key on the Mission Control pane in System Preferences.

Dashboard appears as a desktop in the Spaces strip on the Mission Control screen, and as an icon in Launchpad. (I prefer pressing the F4 key to display my widgets. Geez, that sounds kind of racy. Best not to pursue it.)

Figure 2-6 illustrates Dashboard in action. Press the Dashboard key, and the widgets appear, ready for you to use. You can add widgets to your Dashboard by clicking the Add button (which bears a plus sign, naturally) at the lower-left corner of the Dashboard screen. Then, Dashboard displays your entire collection of widgets, and you can click a widget to add it directly onto your Dashboard.

Rearranging the widgets that are already populating Dashboard is easy: Drag them to the desired spot. After you finish customizing your Dashboard display, click the Dashboard background to return to your Dashboard. When it's time to go back to work (or play), you can return to your Mavericks Desktop by pressing the Dashboard key again, by clicking the button with the right arrow at the lower right of the screen, or by pressing the Esc key.

Care to add multiple copies of a widget? Go right ahead! If you often need to check the time around the world, I highly recommend a bank of World Clock widgets, each displaying the time in your favorite city. (The same goes for the Weather widget.)

Most widgets have an option button that allows you to change things, such as borders, ZIP codes, display columns, and the like; look for a tiny circle with a lowercase letter *i*. Click this information icon, and you can then tweak whatever options are available for that widget.

Figure 2-6: Dashboard proudly displays its widgets.

To remove a widget from the Dashboard display, just click the Delete button (which bears a minus sign) and you'll notice a tiny X button appears next to each widget on your Dashboard. Click the X button next to the widget you want to remove, and it vanishes from the display. Note, however, that deleting a widget doesn't remove it from your Mac entirely! You can add that deleted widget back again at any time by clicking the Add button.

While you're adding widgets, you can also click the More Widgets button, which jumps directly to the widget download area on the Apple website.

If you need to use a widget for only a second or two, press the Dashboard key and hold it. When you release the key, you're back to your Desktop.

Apple offers additional widgets that you can download on the OS X download site (www.apple.com/osx). Third-party software developers also provide both freeware and shareware widgets.

You can also modify the Dashboard key by turning it into a key sequence, trackpad gesture, or mouse button action, which is A Good Thing if you're already using an application that thrives on F12 (or F4, depending on your keyboard). Visit the Mission Control pane in System Preferences, and use the Shift, Control, Option, and ⌘ keys with the Dashboard key to specify a modifier, or choose a gesture or mouse button to activate Dashboard.

Oh, did I mention that Mavericks allows you to create your own Dashboard widgets? That's right. This feature is sure to be a winner amongst the In Crowd. Follow these steps to create a new WebClip Dashboard widget from your favorite website:

1. **Run Safari and navigate to the site you want to view as a widget.**

2. **Choose File⇨Open in Dashboard.**

3. **Select the portion of the page you want to include in your widget and then click Add.**

   Some web pages use frames to organize and separate sections of a page, so this step allows you to choose the frame with the desired content.

4. **Drag the handles at the edges of the selection border to resize your widget frame to the right size and then click Add.**

   Bam! Mavericks displays your new WebClip widget in Dashboard.

A WebClip widget can include text, graphics, and links, which Dashboard updates every time you display your widgets. Think about that for a second: Dynamic displays, such as weather maps, cartoons, even the Free Music Download image from the iTunes Store, are all good sources of WebClip widgets! (That last one is a real timesaver.)

If you click a link in a WebClip widget, Dashboard loads the full web page in Safari, so you can even use WebClips for surfing chores with sites you visit often.

Getting Social with Game Center

If you're the proud owner of an iPhone, iPad, or iPod touch, you've probably already joined the Apple Game Center community on your device. If not, a short introduction is certainly in order. Apple's Game Center (shown in Figure 2-7) is one part *leaderboard* (a gamer term for a central scoreboard that displays everyone's scores for a game) and one part social network (where you can add friends and challenge them to multiplayer games).

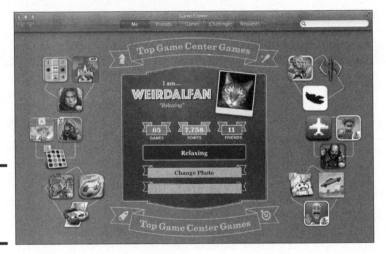

Figure 2-7:
The Game Center window.

To launch Game Center, click the Game Center icon in Launchpad. To use Game Center, you must have an Apple ID, which I discuss in Book I, Chapter 3. You're also prompted to enter a nickname (and optionally, a photo) when you join.

TIP

If you use the same Apple ID on Game Center on your Mac as you do on your iOS device, you'll be able to access all the friends and scores already on your iPhone, iPad, or iPod touch. However, you must purchase and download computer applications specifically created for OS X — your iOS games will not run on your Mac. Likewise, the OS X versions of your games will not run on your iOS devices.

From the Me pane of the Game Center window, you can see your personal vital stats — how many Games Center–enabled games you're participating in, how many Game Center points you've accumulated, and how many friends you've added. You can also change your Game Center account photo. Click the Apple ID account displayed on the Me pane, and you can view or sign out of the current account.

The other Game Center panes are

✦ **Friends:** Add friends (who may be using another Mac or any Game Center–compatible iOS device) to your list. You can compare scores with your friends, or even challenge them to multiplayer games. To see those folks from your Contacts database who may want to join you on Game Center, click the Get Friend Recommendations button.

✦ **Games:** Display the games you've downloaded and installed that support Game Center. Click the App Store button to automatically open the App Store and browse Game Center–compatible titles.

✦ **Challenges:** Challenge your friends to beat your top score (or complete the same achievements in a specific game) and accept their challenges.

✦ **Requests:** Monitor the status of friend requests you've made and also add friends (in the same manner as the Friends pane).

Click in the Search box to search for specific friends or games (depending on the pane you're using).

Book II
Chapter 2

Giving Your Desktop
the Personal Touch

Arranging Your Precious Desktop

Consider the layout of the Desktop itself. You can set the options for icon placement from the Finder View menu; choose View⇨Show View Options, or press ⌘+J. Just as you can with the options for Finder windows that I cover in Chapter 1 of this minibook, you can clean up and arrange your Desktop by name, date, size, or kind.

The View Options for the Desktop are different in two ways from the View Options for a Finder window in Icon view (which I discuss in Chapter 1 of this minibook):

✦ You choose a background for Finder from System Preferences.

✦ There's no Always Open check box. Your Desktop always opens in Icon view! (You can, however, navigate to your Home folder and open the contents of your Desktop in a Finder window, which allows you to change views in the window.)

A quick Desktop sort is always only two clicks away! If you need to sort the contents of your Desktop by name, type, date modified or created, size, or the label you've assigned, just right-click any empty section of the Desktop and then choose Clean Up By from the menu that appears.

Chapter 3: Delving under the Hood with System Preferences

In This Chapter

✔ **Displaying and customizing settings in System Preferences**

✔ **Saving your changes**

✔ **Changing settings**

The System Preferences window is the place to practice behavior modification in OS X. The settings that you specify in System Preferences affect the majority of the applications that you use as well as the hardware that you connect to your Mac; your Internet and network traffic; your iCloud Library and storage; the appearance and activity on your Desktop; and how Mavericks handles money, dates, and languages. Oh, and don't forget your screen saver — important stuff!

In this chapter, I discuss the many settings in System Preferences. You discover what does what and how you can customize the appearance and operation of OS X.

The Preferred Way to Display the Preferences

Apple has made it easy to open the System Preferences window. Just click the System Preferences icon (which looks like a number of gears) on the Dock, and the window shown in Figure 3-1 appears. You can also open the window by clicking the Apple menu ( ) and choosing the System Preferences item, or by clicking the System Preferences icon in Launchpad.

To display all the System Preferences icons at any time, click the Show All button. You can also use the Back and Forward buttons (on the toolbar's upper-left corner) to move backward and forward through the different panes you've accessed in System Preferences, just as you use the similar buttons in a web browser (yes, just like Safari!).

Figure 3-1:
The System
Preferences
window is
a familiar
face to any
Mavericks
user.

Although the System Preference panes are arranged by category (in rows) when you first install Mavericks, you can also display the panes in alphabetical order, which makes it easier to choose a pane if you're unsure what row it's in. To do so, choose View⇨Organize Alphabetically. Note that you can also select any pane directly from the View menu. Choose View⇨Customize, and you can hide specific icons from the System Preferences window. Just disable the check box next to each icon that you want hidden, and then click Done. You can still reach hidden icons from the System Preferences View menu, so they're not banished forever.

You can right-click the System Preferences icon on the Dock to jump to any pane from the contextual menu. *Wowzers!*

If a System Preference pane is locked, you won't be able to modify any of the settings on that pane unless you unlock the pane. Click the padlock icon and type your admin-level account password to unlock the pane. After you finish your tweaking, protect the settings from inadvertent changes by clicking the padlock icon again to close it.

Saving Your Preferences

The System Preferences window has no Save or Apply button. Illustrating the elegant design of OS X, simply quitting System Preferences automatically saves all the changes that you make. Some panes in System Preferences do sport an Apply button that you can click to apply your changes immediately. As with any other OS X application, you can quit the System Preferences window by pressing ⌘+Q or by choosing System Preferences⇨Quit System Preferences.

Hey, I got bonus icons in my window!

Some third-party applications and media plug-ins can install their own groups in your once-pristine System Preferences window. You'll see them at the bottom of the window. (For example, Adobe's Flash Player adds an icon, as shown in Figures 3-1 and 3-2.) Naturally, I can't document these invited guests in this chapter, but they work the same way as any other group in System Preferences. Click the icon, adjust any settings as necessary, and then close the System Preferences window to save your changes.

Searching for Specific Settings

Searching for a single button or check box amidst all the settings in System Preferences might seem like hunting for the proverbial needle in the pro-verbial haystack, but our friends at Apple have added a Search box to the upper-right of the window toolbar. Click in this Search box and type the setting name, such as **screen saver** (or even a word that's generally associated with a setting, such as **power** for the Energy Saver settings). Mavericks highlights all the icons in System Preferences that have anything to do with the search keywords you entered, as shown in Figure 3-2. You don't even have to press Return!

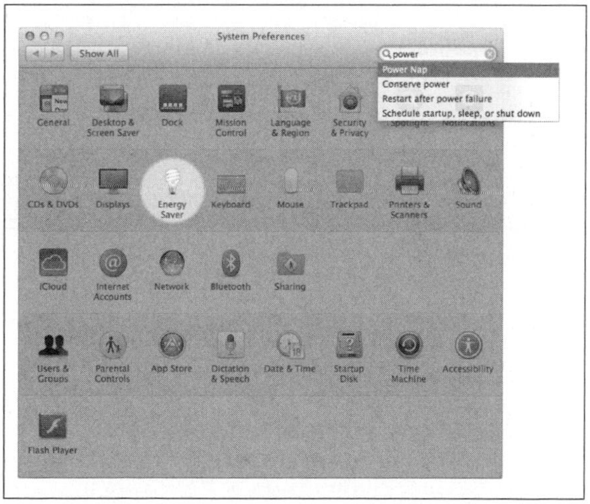

Figure 3-2: System Preferences highlights the panes that contain your search keywords.

To reset the Search field for a different keyword, click the X button that appears at the right of the Search box.

Getting Personal

The first stop on your tour of the System Preferences window is the Personal row. No singles ads here, though. This section is devoted to settings that you make to customize the appearance and operation of your Desktop and login account.

General preferences

The General pane appears in Figure 3-3.

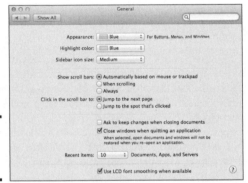

Figure 3-3:
The General pane.

These settings are

+ **Appearance:** Choose a color to use for buttons, menus, and windows.

+ **Highlight Color:** Choose a color to highlight selected text in fields and pop-up menus.

+ **Sidebar Icon Size:** Select the size of the icons in the Finder window *sidebar,* which is the strip to the left of the Finder window that displays your devices and favorite locations on your system. If you have a large number of hard drives or you've added several folders to the sidebar, reducing the size of the icons will allow you to display more of them without scrolling.

+ **Show Scroll Bars:** Specify when Mavericks should display scroll bars in a window. By default, they're placed automatically when necessary, but you can choose to display scroll bars always, or only when you're scrolling through a document. (If you used OS X before Lion, note that the familiar scroll arrows from those past versions of the operating system no longer appear in Mavericks.)

+ **Click in the Scroll Bar To:** By default, OS X jumps to the next or previous page when you click on an empty portion of the scroll bar. Select the Jump to the Spot That's Clicked radio button to scroll the document to the approximate position in relation to where you click.

✦ **Ask To Keep Changes When Closing Documents:** If you select this check box, Mavericks prompts you for confirmation if you attempt to close a document with unsaved changes. If the check box is deselected, Mavericks will allow the unsaved document to be closed without saving a new version.

✦ **Close Windows When Quitting an Application:** If this check box is deselected, Mavericks's Resume feature automatically saves the state of an application when you quit. When you launch the application again, Mavericks restores all application windows and opens the documents you were working on when you quit. In effect, you can continue using the application just as if you had never quit. If you select the check box, Mavericks will not restore your work, and you'll have to load your document again; this is the same action taken by earlier versions of OS X.

✦ **Recent Items:** The default number of recent applications, documents, and servers (available from the Recent Items item in the Apple menu [🍎], which you can read more about in Book I, Chapter 3) is 10. To change the default, open the pop-up menus here and choose up to 50. (I like 20 or 30.)

✦ **Use LCD Font Smoothing When Available:** By default, this check box is selected, making the text on your LCD/LED flat-panel monitor appear more like the printed page. If you're using an older CRT monitor, you can turn off this feature to speed up text display slightly.

Desktop and screen saver preferences

Figure 3-4 illustrates the settings in the Desktop & Screen Saver pane.

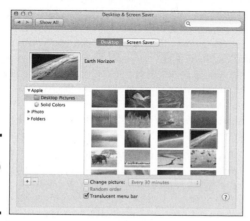

Figure 3-4:
The Desktop
& Screen
Saver pane.

**Book II
Chapter 3**

Delving under the
Hood with System
Preferences

The settings on the Desktop tab are

✦ **Current Desktop picture:** You can click a picture in the thumbnail list at the right half of the screen to use it as your Desktop background. The Desktop is immediately updated, and the thumbnail appears in the *well* (the upper-left square box in Figure 3-4). To display a different image collection or open a folder of your own images, click the Add Folder button at the lower left of the window (a plus sign) and browse for your heart's desire; then click Choose to select a folder and display the images it contains.

✦ **Layout:** As I explain in Chapter 2 of this minibook, you can tile your background image, center it, fill the screen with it, and stretch it to fill the screen. (Note that filling the screen may distort the image.) The layout pop-up menu appears only when you're using your own pictures, so you won't see it if you're using a Desktop image supplied by Apple.

✦ **Change Picture:** Change the Desktop background automatically after the delay period that you set, including each time you log in and each time your Mac wakes up from sleep mode.

✦ **Random Order:** To display screens randomly, enable the Random Order check box. Otherwise, the backgrounds are displayed in the sequence in which they appear in the thumbnail list.

✦ **Translucent Menu Bar:** When enabled, this feature turns your Finder and application menu bars semi-opaque, allowing them to blend in somewhat with your Desktop background. If you'd rather have a solid-color menu bar, deselect this check box.

Click the Screen Saver tab to see the following settings:

✦ **Screen Savers:** In the Screen Savers list at the left, click any screen saver to preview (on the right). To try out the screen saver in full-screen mode, click the Test button. (You can end the test by moving your cursor.) If the screen saver module that you select has any configurable settings, you can set them from the pane on the right (or, depending on the screen saver, you can also click the Screen Saver Options button to display them). Choose the Random screen saver to display a different screen saver module each time the screen saver is activated.

✦ **Start After:** Specify the period of inactivity that triggers the screen saver. To disable the screen saver, choose the Never setting at the top of the list. (**Note**: Your Start After delay should be a shorter time than the Display Sleep delay you set in the System Preferences Energy Saver pane. Otherwise, you won't see the great screen saver at all. I describe the Energy Saver pane in detail later in this chapter.)

✦ **Show with Clock:** If you want your selected screen saver to display the time as well, select this check box.

✦ **Hot Corners:** Click any of the four pop-up menus at the four corners of the screen to specify that corner as an *activation hot corner* (immediately activates the screen saver) or as a *disabling hot corner* (prevents the screen saver from activating). As long as the cursor stays in the disabling hot corner, the screen saver doesn't kick in, no matter how long a period of inactivity passes. Note that you can also set the Sleep, Mission Control, Launchpad, Notification Center, and Dashboard activation corners from here. (For the scoop on these features, see the upcoming section, "Mission Control preferences.")

Dock preferences

The Dock pane is shown in Figure 3-5.

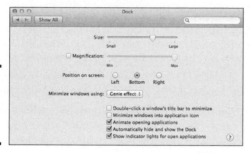

Figure 3-5:
The Dock preferences pane.

Settings here are

✦ **Size:** Move this slider to change the overall size of the Dock.

✦ **Magnification:** With this check box selected, a Dock icon magically expands (like the national deficit) when you move your cursor over it. You can move the Magnification slider to specify just how much magnification is right for you.

This feature is useful for helping you click a particular Dock icon if you've resized the Dock smaller than its default dimensions or if you have a large number of items on the Dock.

✦ **Position on Screen:** Choose from three radio buttons to make that crazy Dock appear at the left, bottom, or right edge of your Desktop.

- ✦ **Minimize Windows Using:** By default, OS X animates a window when it's shrunk into the Dock (and when it's expanded back into a full window). From the Minimize Windows Using pop-up menu, you can choose from a genie-in-a-bottle effect or a scale-up-or-down-incrementally effect. To demonstrate, choose an effect and then click the Minimize button (the yellow button in the upper-left corner) on the System Preferences window.

- ✦ **Double-Click a Window's Title Bar to Minimize:** Select this check box to minimize a Finder or application window by simply double-clicking the window's title bar.

- ✦ **Minimize Windows into Application Icon:** If this check box is not selected, minimized application windows appear as thumbnail icons on the Dock. To minimize application windows into the application icon on the Dock — which can save space on your Dock — select this check box. (To restore a window that's been minimized into the application icon, right-click the icon on the Dock and choose Restore from the menu that appears.)

- ✦ **Animate Opening Applications:** By default, OS X has that happy, slam-dancing feeling when you launch an application: The application's icon bounces up and down on the Dock two or three times to draw your attention and indicate that the application is loading. If you find this effervescence overly buoyant or distracting, deselect this check box.

- ✦ **Automatically Hide and Show the Dock:** If you like, the Dock can stay hidden until you need it, thus reclaiming a significant amount of Desktop space for your application windows. Select this check box to hide the Dock whenever you're not using it.

  To display a hidden Dock, move your cursor over the edge of the Desktop where it's hiding.

- ✦ **Show Indicator Lights for Open Applications:** OS X indicates which applications are running on the Dock with a small blue dot in front of the icon. To disable these indicators, deselect this check box.

You can also change most of these Dock preference settings from the Apple menu (🍎).

Mission Control preferences

Figure 3-6 illustrates the Mission Control, Spaces, and Dashboard settings that you can configure in this pane. You can use Mission Control to view all the application windows that you're using at one time so that you can select a new active window. Or you can move all windows aside so that you can see your Desktop. Dashboard presents a number of mini-applications (or *widgets*), which you can summon and hide with a single key.

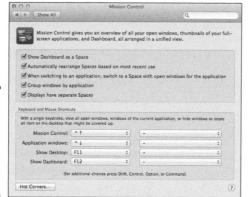

Figure 3-6:
Set your
Mission
Control
preferences
here.

The settings for Mission Control are

✦ **Hot Corners:** Click the button at the lower left to specify your hot corner settings. These four pop-up menus operate just like the Hot Corners/Active Screen Corners in the Desktop & Screen Savers pane, but they control the operation of Mavericks's screen management features. Click one to specify that corner as an All Windows corner (displays all windows on your Desktop), an Application Windows corner (displays only the windows from the active application), a Desktop corner (moves all windows to the outside of the screen to uncover your Desktop), a Dashboard corner (displays your Dashboard widgets), or a Notification Center corner (displays the Notification Center strip at the right side of your desktop). Choose Launchpad to activate the Launchpad screen. Note that you can also set the Screen Saver Start and Disable corners from here, as well as put your display to sleep.

✦ **Keyboard and Mouse Shortcuts:** From each pop-up menu, set the key sequences (and mouse button settings) for Mission Control, Application Windows, Show Desktop, and Show Dashboard.

You're not limited to just the keyboard and mouse shortcuts in the pop-up menus. Press Shift, Control, Option, and ⌘ keys while a pop-up menu is open, and you see these modifiers appear as menu choices! (Heck, you can even combine modifiers, such as ⌘+Shift+F9 instead of just F9.)

To display your Dashboard as a Space (a virtual desktop) in the Mission Control screen, select the Show Dashboard as a Space check box. If you prefer your Dashboard widgets to appear as an overlay (as in versions of OS X predating OS X 10.7 [Lion]), deselect this check box.

✦ **Automatically Rearrange Spaces Based on Most Recent Use:** If this check box is selected, Mission Control presents your most recently used Spaces first in the thumbnails at the top of the screen.

✦ **When Switching to an Application:** When selected, this check box allows you to switch applications between Spaces desktops by using the ⌘+Tab shortcut. Mavericks jumps to the Desktop that has an open window for the application you choose, even if that Desktop is not currently active.

✦ **Group Windows by Application:** When selected, this check box automatically arranges windows in the Mission Control screen by the application that created them.

✦ **Displays Have Separate Spaces:** If you have multiple monitors connected to your Mac, you can select this check box to create a separate Spaces display for each monitor.

Language & Region preferences

The Language & Region pane appears in Figure 3-7, and the settings for this pane are

✦ **Language:** Choose the preferred order for language use in menus and dialogs as well as the standards that OS X will use for sorted lists.

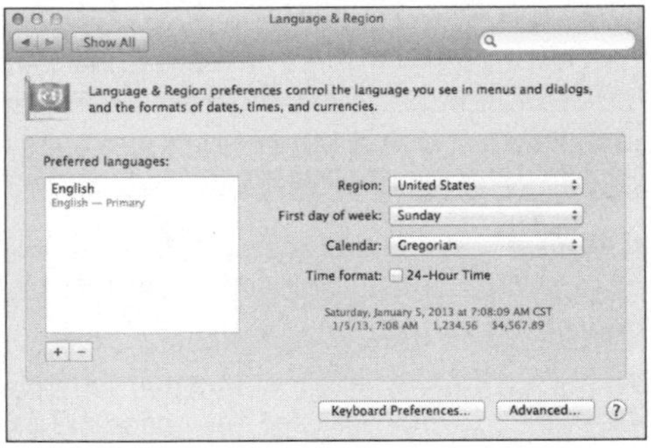

Figure 3-7: The Language & Region pane in System Preferences.

✦ **Region:** You can select your region of the world and specify the first day of your calendar week. Mavericks supports a number of different calendars, as well as the 12- and 24-hour (military) time format.

Click the Advanced button to change additional language and region settings:

• *Dates:* Select a region and use its date conventions (month-day-year versus day-month-year) or click the Customize button to build a custom format for the full date (Saturday, September 21, 2013), long date (September 21, 2013), medium date (Sep 21, 2013), and short date (9/24/2013) used throughout OS X.

- *Times:* You can configure the appearance of the full time (7:18:30 PM Central Standard), long time (7:18:30 PM CST), medium time (7:18:30 PM), and short time (7:18 PM) displayed in Mavericks. You can also specify different suffixes for morning (a.m.) and evening (p.m.).

- *General:* These convention settings determine the separators used for large numbers or numbers with decimals, as well as the currency symbol that you want to use and where it appears in a number. You can also choose between standard (U.S.) and metric measurement systems.

Security & Privacy preferences

The Security & Privacy pane is shown in Figure 3-8.

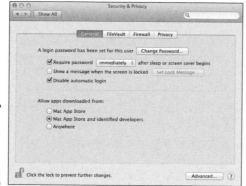

Figure 3-8:
Set Security preferences here.

Settings here are divided into four tabs:

✦ **General:** You can change your existing account password by clicking the Change Password button. To add an extra layer of password security to a laptop (or a Mac in a public area), select the Require Password After Sleep or Screen Saver Begins check box, then click the pop-up delay menu to specify when the password requirement will kick in (it's Immediately by default). OS X then requires that you enter your login password before the system returns from a sleep state or exits a screen saver. If you're an admin-level user, you can turn off automatic login and display a message when the screen is locked.

The Gatekeeper feature allows you to specify whether Mavericks runs only applications downloaded from the App Store or whether applications from Apple-approved developers can also be launched. Choose the Anywhere radio button, and Mavericks will launch any application you choose, no matter where it originated.

✦ **FileVault:** These controls allow you to turn on FileVault drive encryption, which makes it virtually impossible for others to access files from your drive on your Mac. Click the Turn On FileVault button to enter the passwords for each user. Even if you're using an Admin account, each user on your Mac must enter their password to enable their account for use with FileVault, which allows them access to data on the hard drive. Click Continue to display the recovery key — go ahead and write that key down and store it in a **very** safe place — and then click Continue to enable FileVault encryption for the user who's currently logged in; the user's Login password becomes his FileVault password as well.

If you forget both your login password and the recovery key, not even the technical experts at Apple can retrieve your data!

✦ **Firewall:** As I discuss in Book V, Chapter 6, OS X includes a built-in firewall, which you can enable from this pane.

To turn the firewall off entirely, simply click the Turn Off Firewall button. This is the very definition of Not a Good Thing, and I **always** recommend that any Mac hooked up to a network or the Internet have the system firewall turned **on**. (The only exception is if you're using a network that you *know* to be secure and your access to the Internet is through a router or sharing device with its own built-in firewall.)

When the firewall is enabled, click the Firewall Options button to set firewall options.

To turn on the firewall with only OS X application exclusions: Click Block All Incoming Connections, and only the sharing services you select from the Sharing pane in System Preferences are allowed through your firewall. This is a good choice for the most security-conscious Mac owner, but your firewall will block third-party applications that try to access your network or the Internet.

To turn on the firewall with exclusions: Click Automatically Allow Signed Software to Receive Incoming Connections. (Yep, this is the correct option for just about every Mac owner.) Any connection to a service (such as Web Sharing) or an application (such as Messages) that isn't listed is blocked, but you can enable access for third-party applications on an as-needed basis.

In firewall-speak, these entries are *rules* because they determine what's allowed to pass through to your Mac.

Enabling communications with an OS X service is easy: Just use the Sharing pane in System Preferences to turn on a service, and Mavericks automatically configures your firewall to allow communications. I describe the Sharing pane in detail later in this chapter.

To add a third-party application, click the Firewall Options button on the Firewall pane; then click the button with the plus sign. Navigate to the application that needs to communicate with the outside world. Click the application to select it and then click Add. To delete an application, select it in the list and click the button with the minus sign. Remember, you don't have to add any of the applications provided by Apple with Mavericks, such as Apple Mail, Messages, or Safari; only third-party applications that you install yourself need a firewall rule.

You can edit the rule for a specific service or application by clicking the rule at the right side of the entry. By default, the rule reads Allow Incoming Connections (including both your local network and the Internet); however, when you click the rule, you can also choose Block Incoming Connections to temporarily deny access to that application.

For heightened security, select the Enable Stealth Mode check box, which prevents your Mac from responding to attempts to identify it across your network and the Internet.

If you suddenly can't connect to other computers or share files that you originally could share, review the rules that you've enabled from this pane. You can also verify that everything's shipshape in the Sharing pane in System Preferences, which I cover later in this chapter.

✦ **Privacy:** From this pane, you can elect to send anonymous diagnostic and usage data behind the scenes to Apple to help squash bugs in OS X Mavericks and determine which features Mac owners use the most. You can also mark the Enable Location Services check box to activate the Location feature, allowing applications to request your Mac's current location. Click any of the entries in the list at the left, and System Preferences displays the applications you've used on your Mac that have requested access to that application.

Spotlight preferences

The Spotlight pane is shown in Figure 3-9. Settings here are

✦ **Search Results tab:** You can select or deselect the check boxes next to each of the categories to display or hide each category in the Spotlight search menu and dialog. Click and drag the categories to the order that you prefer. For example, I like to see matching documents before matching applications in the Spotlight dialog, so I dragged Documents to the first position in the list. You can also specify a different keyboard shortcut for both the Spotlight menu and window.

✦ **Privacy tab:** If you don't want to display the contents of certain folders in Spotlight — for instance, if you work in a hospital setting and you can't allow access to patient information and medical records — click the Add button (carries a plus sign) and specify the folder or disk you want to exclude from Spotlight searches. Alternatively, just drag the folders or disks to exclude into the list from a Finder window.

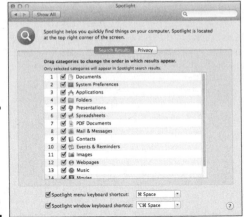

Figure 3-9:
Fine-tune
your
Spotlight
search
results here.

Notifications preferences

Mavericks' Notifications pane is shown in Figure 3-10.

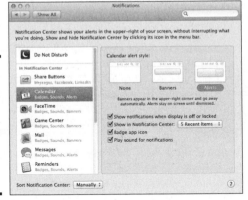

Figure 3-10:
Each
application
that uses
notifications
can be
individually
configured.

Click the Do Not Disturb entry in the list at the left to set Do Not Disturb
mode, where Notification banners, alerts, and sounds will be disabled. You
can specify a time period, turn on Do Not Disturb when your monitor is in
sleep mode, or turn on Do Not Disturb when you're mirroring (or sending)
the video from your Mac to a TV or projector. You can also optionally allow
FaceTime calls from anyone while Do Not Disturb is active or just from those
you've marked as Favorites in FaceTime. If you select Allow Repeated Calls,
the FaceTime callers you've approved can call a second time within three
minutes.

Each application that can display notifications appears in the list at the left of the pane. Click an application and then choose from these settings at the right:

+ **Alert Style:** These three buttons specify which type of alert should appear under the Notification Center icon in the Finder menu bar. You do not need to display Notification Center to see alerts, which appear on your Desktop. Choose None to disable alerts for this application. Choose Banners to display alert messages that will automatically disappear after a delay. Choose Alerts to display alert messages that remain onscreen until you click the confirmation button in the Alert box.

+ **Show Notifications when Display Is Off or Locked:** Select this check box to allow notifications even if your Mac's display is in sleep mode or displaying the Lock screen.

+ **Show in Notification Center:** To display notification messages from this application in Notification Center, select this check box. You can also specify how many recent messages from this application will be displayed.

+ **Badge App Icon:** This check box toggles the display of this application's icon on and off in alert boxes and Notification Center, as well as activating the numeric display of pending items on the icon itself (for example, unread mail and messages).

+ **Play Sound:** To play a sound when alerts appear, enable this check box.

Different applications display different options in the settings pane — in fact, the Share Buttons entry isn't an application at all, but a method of turning off the Share buttons for posting in Messages, Facebook, and LinkedIn that appear at the top of Notification Center.

It's All about the Hardware

The next row of icons, Hardware, allows you to specify settings that affect your Macintosh hardware.

CDs and DVDs preferences

The CDs & DVDs pane is shown in Figure 3-11.

**Book II
Chapter 3**

Delving under the
Hood with System
Preferences

Figure 3-11:
The CDs
& DVDs
preferences.

Choices here are

✦ **When You Insert a Blank CD:** From this pop-up menu, specify the action that OS X takes when you load a blank CD-R or CD-RW. You can choose to be prompted or to open Finder, iTunes, or Disk Utility. Additionally, you can open another application that you select, run an AppleScript that you select, or ignore the disc.

✦ **When You Insert a Blank DVD:** Use this feature to specify the action that your Mac takes when you load a recordable DVD.

✦ **When You Insert a Music CD:** Choices from this pop-up menu specify what action OS X takes when you load an audio CD. By default, iTunes launches.

✦ **When You Insert a Picture CD:** Choices from this pop-up menu specify what action OS X takes when you load a picture CD. By default, iPhoto launches.

✦ **When You Insert a Video DVD:** Choices from this pop-up menu specify what action OS X takes when you load a DVD movie. By default, DVD Player launches.

Displays preferences

The Displays pane is shown in Figure 3-12.

Figure 3-12: Configure your Mac's display settings from this pane.

The two tabs here are

✦ **Display:** To allow Mavericks to choose the best resolution for your display, select the Best for Display radio button. To manually select a resolution, select the Scaled radio button and then click the resolution that you want to use from the Resolutions list on the left. (In most cases, you want to use the highest resolution.) Depending on your monitor, you may also be able to choose a degree of rotation (for monitors that can rotate between landscape and portrait mode). Depending on the monitor your Mac is using, you may also be able to choose a refresh rate (from the, ahem, Refresh Rate pop-up menu). Generally, the higher the refresh rate, the better. Move the Brightness slider to adjust the brightness level of your display. These settings will differ, depending on what type of display you're using. For example, a Mac with a CRT monitor has more settings to choose from than a flat-panel iMac with an LED screen.

On the road again? Select the Show Mirroring Options in the Menu Bar When Available check box if you'll be using multiple monitors or a projector with your Mac. If you're using multiple monitors, each display has a dedicated Finder menu bar, and the Dock appears on whichever display you're using.

Ready to stream content to your TV directly from your Mac — *without cables*? You can use Mavericks's wireless AirPlay Mirroring feature to send the display from your Mac to your HD-TV. AirPlay Mirroring requires an Apple TV unit that supports this feature. You can also send the audio from your Mac directly to an AirPlay-enabled receiver or speaker system.

✦ **Color:** Click a display color profile to control the colors on your monitor. To load a profile, click the Open Profile button. To create a custom ColorSync profile and calibrate the colors that you see on your monitor, click the Calibrate button to launch the Display Calibrator. This easy-to-use assistant walks you step by step through creating a ColorSync profile matched to your monitor's gamma and white-point values.

Energy Saver preferences

The Energy Saver pane is shown in Figure 3-13.

Move the Computer Sleep slider to specify when OS X should switch to sleep mode. The Never setting here disables sleep mode entirely. To choose a separate delay period for blanking your monitor, drag the Display Sleep delay slider to the desired period. You can also power-down the hard drive to conserve energy and prevent wear and tear (an especially good feature for laptop owners).

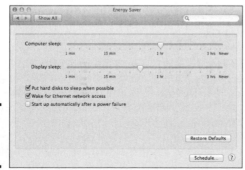

Figure 3-13:
The Energy
Saver pane.

Book II
Chapter 3

Delving under the
Hood with System
Preferences

If you want to start or shut down your Mac at a scheduled time, click the Schedule button. Mark the desired schedule (the Start Up or Wake check box and the Shut Down/Sleep check box) to enable them; then click the up and down arrows next to the time display to set the trigger time. Click OK to return to the Energy Saver pane.

Some of the settings can toggle events that control Mavericks's sleep mode, including a network connection by the network administrator (Wake for Ethernet Network Access). You can also set OS X to restart automatically after a power failure. If you're running a Mac laptop, select the Show Battery Status in the Menu Bar check box to show or hide the Battery Status icon.

Mac laptop owners can set two separate Energy Saver configurations:

✦ **Battery:** Applies when a Mac is running on battery power

✦ **Power Adapter:** Kicks in when a laptop is connected to an AC outlet

Keyboard preferences

The Keyboard group is shown in Figure 3-14.

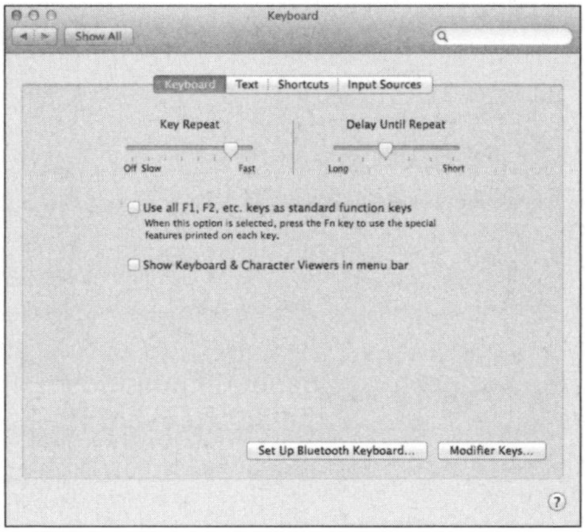

Figure 3-14:
The Keyboard preferences pane.

The four tabs are

✦ **Keyboard:** Move the Key Repeat slider to alter the rate at which a keystroke repeats. You can also adjust the Delay until Repeat slider to alter how long a key must be held down before it repeats. Enable the Show Keyboard & Character Viewers in Menu Bar check box to add the Viewer icon to your Finder menu bar, and click the Input Sources button to display the Language & Text settings that I describe earlier. If you change your keyboard, you can always run the Keyboard Setup Assistant by clicking the Change Keyboard Type button. You can also set up a wireless Bluetooth keyboard from this pane. Click the Modifier Keys button to assign different actions to your Caps Lock, Control, Option, and ⌘ keys.

Laptop owners (as well as Mac owners with newer Apple keyboards) can set the F1–F12 keys for applications by enabling the Use All F1–F12 Keys as Standard Function Keys check box. If you enable this feature, you have to hold down the Function (Fn) key while pressing the F1 through F12 keys to use the regular hardware keys.

✦ **Text:** Specify character combinations that will be automatically replaced with special characters. For example, Mavericks will automatically replace the combination **TM** with the special character ™. You can also toggle automatic spelling correction on and off, choose a language for spell-checking, and turn on "smart" quotes (where Mavericks chooses double or single quotation marks for you). Note that these settings can be overridden by preferences set in applications — for example, Microsoft Word.

✦ **Shortcuts:** If you're a power user who appreciates the lure of the keyboard shortcut, you can edit your shortcuts here. Click the key group you want to change in the list at the left, and then double-click the desired shortcut to change it.

Looking for even more keyboard customizing possibilities? Select the All Controls radio button on the Keyboard Shortcuts pane to see additional keys to use.

✦ **Input Sources:** Each check box here toggles the keyboard layouts available from the Input menu. (To display the Input menu on the Finder menu bar, select the Show Input Menu in Menu Bar check box.) If you select more than one input source, you can also click the Keyboard Shortcuts button to toggle the shortcuts for switching layouts and input methods.

Mouse preferences

Figure 3-15 illustrates the Mouse preferences pane.

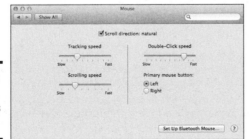

Figure 3-15:
The Mouse
preferences
panel.

The tabs you'll see on this pane depend on what type of mouse you have connected. The tabs are

✦ **Mouse:** To reverse the scroll direction for your mouse wheel, select the Scroll Direction: Natural check box. Drag the Tracking Speed slider to determine how fast the mouse tracks across your Desktop. You can also drag the Double-Click Speed slider to determine how fast you must click your mouse to cause a double-click. Drag the Scrolling Speed slider to specify the rate at which the contents of windows will scroll. Lefties might want to change the primary mouse button for their pointing device. To install a wireless Bluetooth mouse, click the Set Up Bluetooth Mouse button, which runs the Bluetooth device Set Up assistant.

✦ **(Optional) Bluetooth:** If you're using a wireless Bluetooth mouse or keyboard, you can check the battery level on these devices from this panel. You can also specify whether your Bluetooth keyboard or mouse wakes your Mac from sleep mode. If you don't have a Bluetooth mouse, this tab doesn't appear.

Trackpad preferences

The Trackpad pane was once a prime spot reserved for Mac laptop owners. However, now any Mac that can run Mavericks can use a Magic Trackpad. The settings on this pane allow the elite trackpad crowd to customize their tracking speed and the gestures recognized by Mavericks (see Figure 3-16); the settings you see here depend on the specific type of trackpad you're using. You can also monitor the battery level on a Magic Trackpad from this pane.

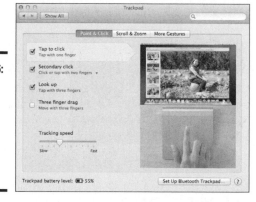

Figure 3-16: The Point & Click gesture settings in the Trackpad pane.

Each gesture is illustrated with a short video clip, demonstrating both the finger positions you've chosen for the selected gesture and the onscreen action it will perform. Click each tab (Point & Click, Scroll & Zoom, and More

Gestures) to display the gestures in that group. Each gesture can be individually toggled on or off, and many gestures allow you to configure the number of fingers or physical area on the trackpad that triggers the action. If you're using a desktop Mac, the settings on this pane are available only if you're using a Bluetooth trackpad.

Printers & Scanners preferences

Figure 3-17 illustrates the Printers & Scanners preferences.

Figure 3-17:
Configure faxing, scanning, and printing with these settings.

Click the Options & Supplies button to configure the selected printer's features, and click the Open Print Queue button to display the Print Queue window (no great shockers there). To add a new printer, scanner, or fax connection, click the Add button, which bears a plus sign — Mavericks launches the Browser. You can read more about printer, scanner, and fax setup in Book VII, Chapter 4.

The other settings here are

✦ **Share This Printer/Fax/Scanner on the Network:** Select this check box to share the selected device with other computers on your network. To specify who can use your shared device, click the Sharing Preferences button. System Preferences switches to the Sharing pane, where you can add or remove users from the permission list. (Note the separate Printer Sharing and Scanner Sharing services. Sharing a fax device is configured through the Printer Sharing service.)

✦ **Default Printer:** Open this pop-up menu to select the installed printer that acts as the default printer throughout your system. If you choose Last Printer Used, OS X uses the printer that received the last print job.

✦ **Default Paper Size:** Will that be US Letter or Tabloid? From this pop-up menu, specify the default paper size for future print jobs.

If you've added a fax entry to the list, click the entry to set up the fax send/receive functions built into Mavericks. To receive faxes on your Mac, you must first set up a fax connection; then, click the Receive Options button and select the Receive Faxes on This Computer check box.

After faxing is turned on, you can configure the other settings from the Printers & Scanners pane and the Receive Options sheet. These settings are

+ **Fax Number:** Enter the phone number that others call to reach your Mac.

+ **When a Fax Arrives:** You can determine how many times the phone rings before your Mac answers the incoming call. By default, OS X saves the incoming fax to your Shared Faxes folder, but you can change that location, or you can choose to print the incoming fax on the printer that you specify. Heck, if you like, you can send your fax to both destinations (a disk folder and a printer), or even mail the fax to the e-mail address you specify.

If you send and receive a large number of faxes, make sure you enable the Show Fax Status in Menu Bar check box.

You can also allow other computer users on your local network to send faxes through your Mac. Enable the Share This Fax on the Network check box, and your Mac's fax modem appears when the other users add a fax connection.

Sound preferences

The Sound pane is shown in Figure 3-18. To set the overall system audio volume, drag the Output Volume slider. To mute all sound from your Mac, select the Mute check box. I recommend that you select the Show Volume in Menu Bar check box, which displays a convenient volume slider menu bar icon.

Figure 3-18: The Sound preferences panel.

The three tabs here are

+ **Sound Effects:** From this pane, you can choose the system alert sound and the volume for alerts. You can also choose to mute user interface (application and Finder menu) sound effects as well as toggle the sample sound effect when the volume keys are pressed on your Mac's keyboard (or from the Volume slider).

+ **Output:** Use these settings to choose which audio controller your Mac uses for playing sound. Unless you've installed additional audio hardware, this remains set to Built-in Audio or Internal Speakers. You can adjust the balance between the left and right channels for the selected output controller.

+ **Input:** These settings allow you to specify an input source. Unless your Mac includes a Line In input source, leave this set to your Internal Microphone. Drag the Input Volume slider to increase or decrease the input signal volume; the input level display provides you with real-time sound levels.

Sharing the Joy: Internet and Wireless

Your Internet & Wireless connections are controlled from the settings in the Internet and Wireless row.

iCloud preferences

From Mavericks's iCloud Preference pane, you can specify which types of data will be automatically pushed to your MacBook and iOS devices (see Figure 3-19). If you haven't created an iCloud account yet — or if you signed out of an existing account earlier — System Preferences will prompt you to enter your Apple ID and password (which I discuss in Book I, Chapter 3). Click Sign In to display the contents of the iCloud pane.

Figure 3-19:
Control and configure your iCloud activity with these settings.

The check boxes for each category are

+ **Mail:** Synchronize your Mail messages between devices.

+ **Contacts:** Push your Contacts cards between devices.

+ **Calendars:** Push your calendar events to and from your iOS devices and other Macs.

+ **Reminders:** Push your reminders between iOS devices and other Macs.

+ **Notes:** Synchronize your notes between devices.

+ **Safari:** Synchronize your Safari bookmarks.

+ **Keychain:** Push your website passwords and credit card/payment information between devices.

+ **Photos:** Push the latest photos and video clips you've added in iPhoto to other devices, and update your iPhoto library with photos and video clips pushed from your iOS devices.

+ **Documents & Data:** Automatically synchronize the documents you create and your personal settings between your Mac and other iOS devices.

+ **Back to My Mac:** Control file and screen sharing across all the Macs sharing this iCloud account. Back to My Mac must be enabled on all computers that will use this feature.

+ **Find My Mac:** Locate your Mac from a web browser or your iOS device, and you can also choose to remotely lock your computer — or even *wipe your Mac's hard drive completely* to prevent someone from stealing your data!

Locking or wiping your Mac remotely will prevent it from being located in the future. These are drastic steps, indeed!

To display the storage currently being used by your mail, backups, documents, and application data, click the Manage button at the lower right of the pane. Apple provides each iCloud account 5GB of space for free, but you can also elect to buy additional storage from this sheet.

Internet Accounts preferences

The Internet Accounts pane is shown in Figure 3-20.

This pane is a central location for adding, editing, and configuring your Internet, social networking, iCloud, and local network accounts for e-mail, Contacts, Messages, and Calendar information. Accounts appear automatically in this pane when you create them in many applications. For example, creating a mail account in Apple Mail also automatically adds that account to the list in the Internet Accounts pane.

Figure 3-20:
Keep track of all your personal accounts from this pane.

To add a new account, click the New Account button (a plus sign) and then click the account type in the list at the right side of the pane. System Preferences displays a custom assistant that will lead you through the setup process for that specific account.

After you configure an account, it appears in the list at the left. Click an account in the list, and you can specify whether that account will be used with Apple Mail, Calendar, FaceTime, Messages and other Internet-savvy applications. You can also change account information — click the Details button, click in the desired field and type the new information. To delete the selected account entirely, click the Delete Account button (which bears a minus sign).

Network preferences

The Network group is shown in Figure 3-21.

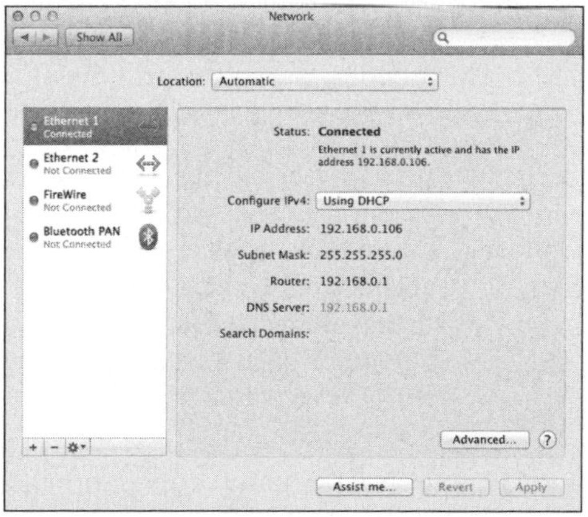

Figure 3-21:
The Network pane, showing the Ethernet status information.

You can choose an existing location from the Location pop-up menu at the top of the dialog, or you can create and edit your locations by choosing Edit Locations from this pop-up menu. (The default is Automatic, and it does a pretty good job of figuring out what settings you need.) As I mention in Book I, Chapter 3, creating a location makes it easy to completely reconfigure your Network preferences when you connect your computer to other networks — for example, when you take your laptop to a branch office. You can also set up locations to accommodate different ISP dial-up telephone numbers in different towns.

If you need to create a new location that's similar to an existing location, open the Location pop-up menu and choose Edit Locations. Then select the location that you want to copy, click the Action button (the gear symbol), and choose Duplicate Location from the pop-up menu. The new location that you create contains all the same settings (without several minutes of retyping), so you can easily edit it and make minor changes quickly.

You can choose locations from the Apple menu ( ) — a useful trick for laptop road warriors.

Ethernet network settings

When you select Ethernet from the list of connection types, the Status pane shows your connection information. Because most networks have a DHCP server to provide automatic settings, you probably don't have to change anything; Mavericks does a good job at making introductions automatic between your Mac and both a local network and the Internet.

Notice the very attractive Assist Me button at the bottom of the Network pane? It's there for a very good reason: Click it, and Mavericks launches a network connection and troubleshooting assistant that guides you step by step. If your ISP doesn't provide you with instructions on setting up your Internet connection — or that oh-so-smart Mr. Network Administrator is too busy to help connect your Mac to your office network — use both this book and the network assistant to do the job yourself!

Need to make manual changes to your network settings? Click the Advanced button (it's like opening the hood on your car). The tabs on the Advanced sheet are

+ **TCP/IP:** These settings are provided either automatically (by using DHCP) or manually (by using settings provided by your network administrator). For more details on TCP/IP settings, see Book V, Chapter 1 and Book VI, Chapter 2.

+ **DNS:** The settings that you enter here specify the DNS servers and search domains used by your ISP. Typically, any changes you make here are requested by your ISP or your network administrator. Click the Add buttons (with the plus signs) to add a new DNS server address or search domain.

✦ **WINS:** Dating back quite a few years, WINS is a name server required for computers running NetBIOS (practically dinosaurs in the computer timeline), and likely only those computers running a version of Windows older than Windows 2000. If that sounds like gobbledygook to you, you need to enter something on this tab only if instructed to do so by your network administrator.

✦ **802.1X:** This tab displays any wireless networking security protocols that you may need to connect to a third-party wireless base station or access point. Select the Enable Automatic Connection check box when making a wireless connection with an Apple Airport Extreme base station or Time Capsule backup unit.

✦ **Proxies:** Network proxy servers are used as part of a firewall configuration to help keep your network secure, but in most cases, changing them can cause you to lose Internet functionality if you enter the wrong settings.

Most folks using a telephone modem, cable modem, or DSL connection should leave these settings alone. Enable and change these settings only at the request of your network administrator, who should supply you with the location of a PAC file to automate the process.

If you've enabled your OS X firewall and you use FTP from the Terminal window to transfer files, enable the Passive FTP Mode check box on the Proxies pane. I recommend that you enable this setting to allow downloading from some web pages as well.

✦ **Hardware:** From this pane, you can configure the settings for your Ethernet network interface card. I *strongly* recommend that you leave the Configure pop-up menu set to Automatically (unless specifically told to set things manually by your system administrator or that nice person from Apple tech support).

Modem network settings

When you select Modem from the list of connection types, you can enter the telephone number, account name, and password provided by your ISP. In most cases, that's all the information you need. If you need to make a manual change, though, click the Advanced button to display these tabs:

✦ **Modem:** From the Modem pop-up menu, choose the brand and model of your modem.

I strongly recommend that you enable the Enable Error Correction and Compression in Modem check box; also choose Wait for Dial Tone before Dialing, from the Dial Mode pop-up menu. These settings provide you with the best performance and the fastest speeds.

You can also select tone or pulse dialing and whether you want to hear the two modems conversing. (If the caterwauling bothers you, turn off the Sound option.)

✦ **DNS:** These settings are the same as those I cover earlier, in the section "Ethernet network settings."

✦ **WINS:** Again, you're likely to never need these WINS settings, so make changes on this tab only if instructed to do so by your network administrator.

✦ **Proxies:** Some ISPs use proxy servers for their dial-up accounts to maintain security, but changing these settings willy-nilly is inviting disaster. Leave them disabled unless given specific instructions on what to set by your ISP.

✦ **PPP:** These settings are used for a Point-to-Point Protocol connection over a telephone modem. Again, your ISP provides you with the correct values to enter here.

If you're concerned about who's using your Internet connection — or you want to add an extra layer of security when you dial out — select the Prompt for Password after Dialing check box on the PPP tab, and OS X prompts you each time for your Internet account password.

I recommend that you select the Show Modem Status in Menu Bar check box on the Modem status pane, which gives you a visual reference on your connection status.

FireWire, Thunderbolt, and Wi-Fi network settings

The FireWire, Thunderbolt, and Wi-Fi settings are the same as those for Ethernet that I cover earlier in this chapter. In this section, I cover the following four settings on the Wi-Fi status pane:

✦ **Network Name:** Mavericks handles wireless connections automatically in most cases; if possible, it connects to the last wireless network you joined. If that network isn't available or there are others to choose from, Mavericks displays a dialog asking you which available network you want to join. If you want to join only one or more preferred networks (for security or convenience reasons), click the Advanced button and click the Add button (a plus sign) to enter the wireless network name and password.

✦ **Ask to Join New Networks:** Mavericks will always automatically join *known networks* in range — a network you've connected to in the past. This check box, however, controls what happens if no networks in range are known. If disabled, you must click the Wi-Fi icon in the Finder menu bar and select a network to use. If the check box is enabled, Mavericks automatically prompts you for confirmation before attempting to join a new network.

✦ **Turn Wi-Fi Off:** Okay, here's the honest truth — wireless networking is a significant drain on a laptop battery! If you're sure you're not going to use your MacBook's wireless network hardware in the near future, you can click this button to activate and deactivate your Mac's network hardware. (Alternatively, just click the Wi-Fi icon in the Finder menu bar and choose Turn Wi-Fi Off.) Turn off Wi-Fi if you don't need it, and your MacBook will thank you. (Just turn it back on using this same button when you need it or use the Wi-Fi status menu in the Finder menu bar. Naturally, without your Wi-Fi turned on, any application that accesses the Internet will have problems.)

✦ **Show Wi-Fi Status in Menu Bar:** Hey, speaking of the Wi-Fi status menu in the Finder menu bar, select this check box to display it! You can immediately see the relative signal strength of your connection, switch between available wireless networks, and turn off your Wi-Fi hardware to conserve your battery power (without digging this deep in System Preferences).

Bluetooth preferences

The Bluetooth group is shown in Figure 3-22.

Figure 3-22:
The
Bluetooth
pane.

The choices on this pane are

✦ **On/Off:** Click the Turn Bluetooth On/Off button to enable or disable your Bluetooth hardware. All recognized Bluetooth devices in range appear in the list, and you can disconnect them individually. Also, if you like, Mavericks can display a Bluetooth status menu in the Finder menu bar.

MacBook owners who want to conserve power can disable Bluetooth entirely. Just click the Turn Bluetooth Off button to save a significant amount of battery time!

✦ **Advanced sheet:** Click the Advanced button to display another group of settings. The two Open Bluetooth Setup Assistant check boxes determine whether Mavericks automatically launches the Bluetooth Setup Assistant when no Bluetooth keyboard, trackpad, or mouse are recognized. If you're using a Bluetooth mouse, keyboard, or trackpad, you can wake your Mac using these devices.

Sharing preferences

Figure 3-23 illustrates the Sharing preferences.

Figure 3-23: The Sharing preference settings.

Click the Edit button to change the default network name assigned to your Mac during the installation process. Your current network name is listed in the Computer Name text field.

Each entry in the services list controls a specific type of sharing, including DVD or CD Sharing, Screen Sharing, File Sharing (with other Macs and PCs running Windows), Printer Sharing, Scanner Sharing, Remote Login, Remote Management (using Apple Remote Desktop), Remote Apple Events, Internet Sharing, and Bluetooth Sharing. To turn on any of these services, select the On check box for that service. To turn off a service, click the corresponding On check box to deselect it. Options specific to the selected service appear to the right.

From a security standpoint, I highly recommend that you enable only those services that you use. Each service you enable automatically opens your Mavericks firewall for that service. A Mark's Maxim to remember:

Poking too many holes in your firewall is *not* A Good Thing.

When you click one of the services in the list, the right side of the Sharing pane changes to display the settings you can specify for that particular service.

Tweaking the System

The last row of the System Preferences window covers system-wide settings that affect all users and the overall operation of OS X.

Users & Groups preferences

The Users & Groups pane is illustrated in Figure 3-24.

**Book II
Chapter 3**

Delving under the
Hood with System
Preferences

Figure 3-24:
Configuring
user
accounts is
easy from
System
Preferences.

Each user on your system has an entry in this list. The panes and settings here change, depending on the access level of the selected account. They can include

✦ **Password tab:** You can edit the account's full name. Click the Change Password button to enter a new password and password hint for the selected user.

Click the Contacts Card Open button to edit the card that you mark in the Contacts application as My Card. OS X launches Contacts, and you can edit your card to your heart's content. (For the complete scoop on the OS X Contacts application, see Book I, Chapter 7.)

You can change the corresponding Apple ID for the selected user account from this pane. If you're sharing your Mac with a number of other users, each person can set up his or her own Apple ID account.

Enable the Allow User to Reset Password Using Apple ID check box to authorize the selected user to reset their password using their Apple ID. This is useful in case the selected user is locked out of System Preferences by Parental Controls.

If you have administrator access, you can in turn assign administrator access to the selected user account. An administrator account can edit other accounts and make global settings changes in System Preferences.

If you have administrator access, you can enable Parental Controls for the selected user account or open the Parental Controls pane. (More on Parental Controls earlier in this section as well as in Chapter 5 of this minibook.)

From the *Picture well* — the square area under the Password tab — you can choose one of the thumbnail images provided by Apple to represent the selected user, or drag a photo in from iPhoto or a Finder window. Click the well to display the thumbnails. Click Recents to view account images you've used recently, or click Camera to take a photo using your Mac's FaceTime HD camera. Click Faces to choose from photos with faces you've identified in iPhoto.

✦ **Login Items tab:** The applications and documents that you add to this list launch automatically each time that the current user logs in to OS X. To add an application or document, click the Add button (a plus sign), navigate to the desired item and select it, and then click the Add button. (Alternatively, you can simply drag an item from a Finder window into the Login Items list.) To remove an application from the list, click to select it and then click the Remove button (a minus sign). Each application can be launched in a *hidden state:* that is, its window doesn't appear on the Desktop. To toggle an item as hidden or visible, enable the Hide check box next to the desired application. The order that Login Items are launched can be changed by dragging entries in the list into the desired sequence.

Note that a user must be logged in to view and change the items on the Login Items pane. Even an Administrator-level user can't access another user account's Login items!

You can even set up Login Items directly from the Dock. Right-click the desired Dock icon to display the Options pop-up menu and choose Open at Login from the contextual menu.

✦ **Login Options button:** Look for the button with the little house icon at the lower left. Click it to set a number of global options that control how users log in. For example, you can choose to display either a Name and Password field on the Login screen (which means that the user must type in the correct username) or a list of users, from which a person can select a user ID. (If security is a consideration, use the Name and Password option.) The Password Hints feature can be enabled or disabled from this pane, and you can also add VoiceOver spoken interface support at the Login screen (making it easier for those with limited vision to log in to this Mac). Select the Show Input Menu in Login Window check box if you have multiple keyboards or assistive input devices connected to your Mac. If your office network provides a Network Account Server, you can join an Open Directory server or Active Directory domain by clicking the Join button.

If you choose, you can log in automatically as the selected user by opening the Automatic Login *<Username>* pop-up menu and choosing your account. This is not a particularly secure feature — especially for MacBook owners — but it's convenient as all get-out.

The Login Options tab also allows you to enable or disable Fast User Switching (which I discuss in Chapter 5 of this minibook), and you can prevent anyone from restarting or shutting down the Mac from the Login screen by deselecting the Show the Sleep, Restart and Shut Down Buttons check box.

Parental Controls preferences

Click a standard-level user account in the list to enable or configure Parental Controls for that user. Figure 3-25 shows the Parental Controls settings. (Parental Controls are disabled for administrator accounts and the Guest account.)

**Book II
Chapter 3**

Delving under the Hood with System Preferences

Figure 3-25: You can assign Parental Controls to any standard-level user account.

I discuss the Parental Control settings in detail in Chapter 5 of this minibook. You can use these settings to restrict a user's access to certain applications, or limit Mail and Messages communications to specific individuals. An administrator can also switch a user account to the Simple Finder, making Mavericks much easier to navigate (and limiting the amount of damage a mischievous or malicious user can inflict on your system).

You can create a new managed account directly from the Parental Controls pane by clicking the Add button (a plus sign) at the bottom of the account list. This saves you a trip to the Users & Groups pane.

App Store preferences

The App Store settings are shown in Figure 3-26. (Oh, and don't forget that you need an active Internet connection.)

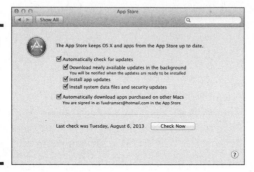

Figure 3-26:
Keep
Mavericks
up to date
with the
controls
in the App
Store pane.

These settings are

✦ **Automatically Check for Updates:** I strongly recommend selecting the Automatically Check for Updates, the Install App Updates, and the Install System Data Files and Security Updates check boxes. These settings provide you with the critical updates every Mac owner should apply, as well as updates to the applications you've downloaded. You can also elect to download new updates in the background automatically while you continue working.

✦ **Automatically Download Apps Purchased on Other Macs:** Select this check box to allow the App Store to automatically download all applications you've already installed on other Macintosh computers using the same Apple ID. (Consider this nifty feature as sharing the applications you've already bought and installed on other Macs.) The Apple ID you're using on this Mac for the App Store is displayed for convenience.

To manually search for updates, click Check Now.

Dictation and speech preferences

Figure 3-27 illustrates the Dictation & Speech settings. For a discussion of how these settings are used, visit Book VIII, Chapter 4.

Figure 3-27: Mavericks includes highly configurable dictation and speech features.

Book II
Chapter 3

Delving under the
Hood with System
Preferences

The two tabs here are

+ **Dictation:** With Dictation toggled on, you can use your voice to dictate to your Mac whenever you would normally type. To start Dictation mode, you can either press the keyboard shortcut you assign from the Shortcut pop-up menu or choose Edit⇨Start Dictation from the application's menu. Open the Language pop-up menu to select the language that Mavericks will recognize for Dictation mode.

  The Dictation icon at the left of the pane is more than just a pretty face. It also indicates the relative audio level of your voice, which can help you position your microphone (or adjust its sensitivity) for the best results. If you have more than one microphone, you can select which one you want to use by clicking the button under the Dictation icon.

+ **Text to Speech:** Here's a fun pane. Choose a voice from the System Voice pop-up menu, and OS X uses that voice to speak to you from dialogs and applications. You can set the Speaking Rate (from Slow to Fast) and play a sample by clicking the Play button. (Ready for something different? Click the Customize menu option and check a foreign language voice (or try novelty voices such as Zarvox, Bubbles, and Pipe Organ. Note that your Mac will have to download custom voices.)

  The Announce When Alerts Are Displayed feature speaks the text in alert dialogs; to configure spoken alerts, click the Set Alert Options button. You can optionally add a phrase before the text, which you can choose from the Phrase pop-up menu. To add a phrase to the list, such as *Don't Panic!,* choose Edit Phrase List from the list. Move the Delay slider to specify how much time your Mac waits before reading the dialog to you.

  You can also optionally announce when an application wants your attention, and Mavericks can speak the text that's selected in an application when you press a key that you specify.

This pane also provides a couple of convenient shortcut buttons that take you to other speech centers in System Preferences — specifically, the Date & Time and Accessibility panes.

Date and time preferences

Click the System Preferences Date & Time icon to display the settings that you see in Figure 3-28.

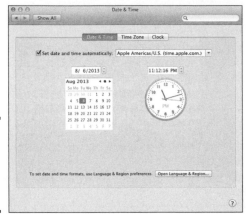

Figure 3-28:
The Date & Time preferences pane.

The three tabs here are

+ **Date & Time:** To set the current date, click the date in the minicalendar; to set the system time, click in the field above the clock and type the current time.

  You can't set these values manually if you use a network time server. To automatically set your Mac's system time and date from a network time server, select the Set Date and Time Automatically check box and then choose a server from the pop-up menu that corresponds to your location. (Of course, you need an Internet connection to use a network time server.)

+ **Time Zone:** Click your approximate location on the world map to choose a time zone or click the Closest City pop-up menu and choose the city that's closest to you (and shares your same time zone).

+ **Clock:** If you select the Show the Date and Time in Menu Bar check box, you can choose to view the time in text or icon format. You can also optionally display seconds, the date, AM/PM, and the day of the week; have the time separator characters flash; or use a clock based on 24 hours.

I get a big kick out of my Mac announcing the time on the hour . . . plus, it helps pull me back into the real world. (You have to eat sooner or later.) Anyway, if you'd like this helpful reminder as well, select the Announce the Time check box on the Clock pane, and click the pop-up menu to select an hour, half-hour, or quarter-hour announcement.

Startup Disk preferences

Figure 3-29 illustrates the Startup Disk pane.

Figure 3-29: The Startup Disk pane in System Preferences.

To select a start-up disk, click the desired start-up drive from the scrolling icon list.

OS X displays the version numbers of each system and the physical drives where each system resides. Select the Network Startup icon if you want to boot from a System folder on your local network; typically, such a folder is created by your network administrator. If you've set up a Windows partition on your hard drive using Boot Camp, the folder appears with a Windows logo.

If you're planning on rebooting with an external Universal Serial Bus (USB), Thunderbolt, eSATA, or FireWire start-up disk, that disk must be connected, powered on, and recognized by the system before you display these settings.

Click the Target Disk Mode button to restart your Mac as a FireWire or Thunderbolt external hard drive connected to another computer. (This feature comes in especially handy when you're upgrading to a new Mac and you need to move files between the two computers. I've also used it when the video card in one of my Macs decided to stop working. This option allowed me to make an updated backup copy of the ailing Mac's hard drive before I sent it off for repair.) You can also restart your Mac and hold down the T key to invoke Target Disk Mode.

After you click a disk to select it, click the Restart button. OS X confirms your choice, and your Mac reboots.

Time Machine preferences

The preferences pane shown in Figure 3-30 controls the automatic backups performed by Mavericks's Time Machine feature.

Figure 3-30:
Configure
your
backups
with these
Time
Machine
settings.

To enable Time Machine, click the On toggle switch and then select a disk
that will hold your Time Machine backup data on the sheet that appears;
click Use Disk to confirm your choice. If you choose an external Time
Capsule wireless unit, click Set Up instead.

By default, Time Machine backs up all the hard drives on your system; however, you may not need to back up some hard drives or folders on your Mac.
To save time and space on your backup hard drive, Time Machine allows
you to exclude specific drives and folders from the backup process. Click the
Options button and then click the Add button (with the plus sign) to select
the drives or folders you want to exclude, and they'll appear in the Exclude
These Items list.

To remove an exclusion, select it in the list and click the Delete button (with
the minus sign). Note the Estimated Size of Full Backup counter increases,
and Time Machine adds the item you deleted from the list to the next
backup.

By default, Mavericks warns you when deleting older backup files, but you
can turn this off from the Options sheet as well.

If you enable the Show Time Machine in Menu Bar check box, you can elect
to back up your Mac immediately by clicking the Time Machine icon in the
Finder menu bar and then choosing Back Up Now.

Accessibility preferences

The Accessibility preferences pane is shown in Figure 3-31. These settings
modify the display, input, and sound functions in OS X to make them friend-
lier to physically challenged users. Note that if you display the VoiceOver
entry in the list and then select the Enable VoiceOver check box, OS X
speaks the text for all text and buttons onscreen.

Figure 3-31:
The
Accessibility
pane.

You can elect to display the Accessibility status icon in the Finder menu bar.

The three categories in the list at the left are

+ **Seeing:** These settings make it easier for those with limited vision to use OS X. You can toggle VoiceOver on and off from here; I discuss more on this feature and these settings in Book VIII, Chapter 4.

  To turn on the display Zoom feature, click the Zoom item in the list and then select the Zoom On radio button or press ⌘+Option+8. From the keyboard, use ⌘+Option+= (equal sign) to zoom in and ⌘+Option+– (minus sign) to zoom out. You can specify a modifier key to activate the Zoom feature using your mouse or trackpad's scroll gesture.

  To specify how much magnification is used, click the More Options button. From the sheet that appears, you can set the minimum and maximum Zoom magnification increments. Optionally, you can display a preview rectangle of the area that's included when you zoom. OS X can smooth images to make them look better when zoomed; select the Smooth Images check box to enable this feature.

  You can also determine how the screen moves in relation to the cursor from the More Options sheet: By default, the zoomed screen moves with the cursor, but you can set it to move only when the cursor reaches the edge of the screen or maintain the cursor near the center of the zoomed image automatically.

  Click the Display item in the list to configure Accessibility graphics options. If you prefer white text on a black background, select the Invert Colors check box. Note that depending on your display settings, it'll probably be easier on the eyes to use grayscale display mode by selecting the Use Grayscale check box. Drag the Enhance Contrast slider to increase the contrast between text and background, and enlarge your cursor to make it easier to see using the Cursor Size slider.

✦ **Hearing:** If you need additional visual cues to supplement the spoken and audio alerts in OS X, click the Audio item in the list and select the Flash the Screen When an Alert Occurs check box. Two-channel stereo audio can be combined to single-channel mono audio with the Play Stereo Audio as Mono check box. To raise the overall sound volume in OS X, you can click the Open Sound Preferences button to display the Sound System Preferences settings, where you can drag the Volume slider to the right.

The Captions item allows you to set the style for subtitles in the DVD Player — you can also specify that closed captioning and subtitles for the deaf and hard of hearing be used instead of standard subtitles (when they are available).

✦ **Interacting:** The Keyboard item settings help those who have trouble pressing keyboard shortcuts or those who often trigger keyboard *repeats* (repetition of the same character) accidentally. If you select the Enable Sticky Keys check box, you can use *modifier keys* individually that are grouped together automatically as a single keyboard shortcut. In other words, you can press the modifier keys in a key sequence one after another instead of all together.

Click the Sticky Keys Options button to display additional settings. For example, Sticky Keys can be toggled on and off from the keyboard by pressing the Shift key five times. You can optionally specify that OS X sound a beep tone when a modifier key is pressed and whether the modifier keys are displayed onscreen.

Select the Enable Slow Keys check box to add a pause between when a key is pressed and when it's acted upon in OS X. Click the Slow Keys Options button to add a key-click sound each time you press a key; you can also specify the delay period from this sheet. To turn keyboard repeat off, click the Open Keyboard Preferences button, which opens the Keyboard preference settings that I discuss earlier in this chapter.

Click the Mouse & Trackpad item in the list to configure Accessibility input settings. With Mouse Keys active, you can use the numeric keypad to move the cursor across your screen. Drag the Double-Click Speed slider to specify the required delay between clicks to activate a double-click for your mouse or trackpad. Click the Mouse Keys Options button to display additional options. From this sheet, Mouse Keys can be toggled on and off by pressing the Option key five times, and you can drag the Initial Delay and Maximum Speed sliders to specify how long you must hold down a keypad key before the cursor starts to move as well as how fast the cursor should move across the screen. You can also disable the trackpad on a MacBook when using Mouse Keys.

You can also click the Trackpad Options or Mouse Options buttons to select a scrolling speed. Trackpad owners can optionally fine-tune scrolling and dragging gestures as well.

If you'd prefer to use an input device that's more comfortable to hold for navigating through Mavericks (as well as for selecting and using items), click the Switch Control entry in the list. From here, you can assign switches to functions, customize the functionality of the cursor, and set timings for switch recognition.

Click the Speakable Items entry in the list to configure spoken commands. You'll notice this item has three tabs of its own: Settings, Listening Key, and Commands.

- *Settings tab:* If you have more than one microphone, you can select which one you want to use as well as set the input volume with the Calibrate button. You can indicate what sound effect OS X plays when it recognizes a speech command. Optionally, Mavericks can confirm the command by speaking it if you select the Speak Command Acknowledgement check box.

- *Listening Key tab:* You can change the Listening key (Esc by default) and specify whether your Mac should listen only while the key is pressed or whether the Listening Key toggles listening on and off. You can also change the name of your computer (using the Keyword box) and whether that name is required before a command.

- *Commands tab:* Here you can select which types of spoken commands are available. Click the self-named button to open the Speakable Items Folder from this pane. Read more about these settings in Book VIII, Chapter 4.

Book II
Chapter 3

Delving under the
Hood with System
Preferences

Chapter 4: You Mean Others Can Use My Mac, Too?

In This Chapter

✔ Understanding how multiuser systems work

✔ Configuring login settings

✔ Changing the appearance of the login screen

✔ Tightening security during login

✔ Starting applications automatically when you log in

Whether you're setting up OS X for use in a public library or simply allowing your tweener to use your Mac in your home office, configuring Mavericks for multiple users is a simple task. However, you must also consider the possible downsides of a mismanaged multiuser system: files and folders being shared that you didn't want in the public domain, users logging in as one another, and the very real possibility of accidental file deletion (and worse).

Therefore, in this chapter, I show you how to take those first steps before you open Pandora's Box — setting login options, configuring the personal account that you created when you first installed the operating system, and protecting your stuff. Network administrators call this security checkup "locking things down." Better start using the terminology now, even before you buy your suspenders and pocket protector.

How Multiuser Works on OS X

When you create multiple users in OS X, each person who uses your Macintosh — hence the term *user* — has a separate account (much like an account that you might open at a bank). OS X creates a Home folder for each user and saves that user's preferences independently from those of other users. When you log in to OS X, you provide a username and a password, which identify you. The username and password combination tells OS X which user has logged in — and therefore which preferences and Home folder to use.

Each account also carries a specific access level, which determines how much control the user has over OS X and the computer itself. Without an account with the proper access level, for example, a user might not be able to display many of the panes in System Preferences.

The three most common account levels are

✦ **Root:** Also called *system administrator,* this über-account can change *anything* in OS X — and that's usually A ***Very*** Bad Thing, so this account is disabled by default. (This fact alone should tell you that the root account shouldn't be toyed with.) For instance, the root account can seriously screw up the Unix subsystem in OS X, and a root user can delete files in the OS X System Folder.

Enable the root account and use it only if told to do so by an Apple technical support technician.

✦ **Administrator:** This account level is the one that you're assigned when you install OS X. The administrator (or admin) account should *not* be confused with the root, or system administrator, account!

It's perfectly okay for you or anyone you assign to use an administrator account. An administrator can install applications anywhere on the system, create, edit, and delete user accounts, and make changes to all the settings in System Preferences. However, an administrator can't move or delete items from any other user's Home folder, and administrators are barred from modifying or deleting files in the OS X System folder. (You can use Unix commands from the Terminal application to work around these restrictions. However, I agree with Apple's thinking — these locations on your system are off-limits for good reason.)

A typical multiuser OS X computer has only one administrator — like a teacher in a classroom — but technically, you can create as many administrator accounts as you like. If you do need to give someone else this access level, assign it only to a competent, experienced user whom you trust.

✦ **Standard:** A standard user account is the default in OS X. Standard users can install software and save documents only in their Home folders, the Shared folder (which resides in the Users folder), and external drives (including USB Flash drives). Also, standard users can change only certain settings in System Preferences. Thus, they can do little damage to the system as a whole. For example, each of the students in a classroom should be given a standard-level account for the OS X system that they share.

If Parental Controls are applied to a standard account, it becomes a *managed* account, allowing you to fine-tune what a standard account user can do. (I discuss Parental Controls at length in Chapter 5 of this minibook.)

Working with the guest account

The *guest* account is a convenient method of granting someone temporary access to your Mac. Your guest doesn't even need a password to log in! The guest account has all the attributes of a standard account, so the visitor has little chance of accidentally (or purposefully) damaging your system. However, after the guest user logs out, the guest account is flushed, and all the data and files that person created using the account are deleted automatically. (This allows the next guest to start with a clean slate.) You can also give the guest user account access to the shared folders on your network.

By default, the guest account is disabled. To turn on this feature, open System Preferences, click Users & Groups, and then click the Guest User entry in the list. (You may have to click the lock icon in the lower-left corner of the Users & Groups pane and provide your admin password before you can continue.) Click the Allow Guests to Log In to This Computer check box to enable it.

Oh, and don't forget that you can enable specific Parental Controls for the guest account, just as you can for any other standard-level account. This feature should come in handy if your child has a slumber party coming up next weekend.

Configuring Your Login Screen

Take a look at the changes you can make to the login process. First, OS X provides two methods of displaying the login screen, as well as one automatic method that doesn't display the login screen at all:

✦ **Logging in with a list:** To log in, click your account username in the list, and the login screen displays the password prompt. Type your password — OS X displays bullet characters to ensure security — and then press Return (or click the Log In button).

✦ **Logging in with username and password:** Type your account username in the Name field and press Tab. Then type your password and press Return (or click the Log In button).

✦ **Automatic Login:** With Automatic Login set, OS X automatically logs in the specified account when you reboot. In effect, you never see the login screen unless you click Log Out from the Apple menu (), or you've enabled Fast User Switching (more on this in a bit). This is an attractive option to use if your computer is in a secure location, such as your home office, and you'll be the only one using your Mac.

To specify which type of login screen you see — if you see one at all — head to System Preferences, click Users & Groups, and then click the Login Options button.

✦ To set Automatic Login, display the Login Options settings, and click the Automatic Login pop-up menu. Choose the account that automatically logs in from the list. When OS X displays the Password sheet that you see in Figure 4-1, type the corresponding password and then click OK.

Figure 4-1: Configuring Automatic Login from the Users & Groups pane.

Never set the Automatic Login feature to an admin-level account unless you're sure to be the only one using your Mac. If the computer is rebooted, you're opening the door for anyone to simply sashay in and wreak havoc!

✦ To determine whether OS X uses a list login screen, you must again visit the Login Options settings pane (see Figure 4-2). Select the List of Users radio button for a list login screen or select the Name and Password radio button for a simple login screen where you must type your username and password. The latter option is more secure but also less convenient than going through the list login screen.

Figure 4-2: Will your login screen be simple or a list?

To change settings specific to your account — no matter what your access level — log in with your account, open System Preferences, and click Users & Groups. From here, you can change your account password and picture, the card marked as yours in the Contacts application, the Apple ID associated with your account and whether Parental Controls are set. You can also specify the Login Items that will be launched automatically when you log in. (Peruse more information on Contacts in Book I, Chapter 7, and read up on how to create your Apple ID in Book I, Chapter 3.)

To log out of OS X without restarting or shutting down the computer, start from the Apple menu (⌘) and then either choose Log Out or press ⌘+Shift+Q. You see the confirmation dialog, as shown in Figure 4-3.

**Book II
Chapter 4**

**You Mean
Others Can Use
My Mac, Too?**

Figure 4-3:
Always click
Log Out
before you
leave
your Mac!

OS X displays the login screen after one minute, but someone could still saunter up and click the Cancel button, thereby gaining access to your stuff. Therefore, make it a practice to always click the Log Out button on this screen before your hand leaves the mouse, or bypass the confirmation dialog altogether by holding down the Option key as you click Log Out from the menu!

If you want to use Mavericks' nifty Resume feature (which will restore your Desktop by reopening all your open documents and applications when you log back in), make sure that the Reopen Windows When Logging Back In check box is enabled. If you disable this feature, Mavericks will not automatically restore your Desktop when you log back in. (I love Resume, but Apple has wisely made it optional instead of mandatory.)

You can also enable Fast User Switching from the Login Options panel. This feature allows another user to sit down and log in while the previous user's applications are still running in the background. When you enable switching, Mavericks displays the active user's name or account icon at the right side of the Finder menu bar. Click the name, and a menu appears; click Login Window, and another user can then log in as usual. From the Login Options pane, you can also choose to display the current user by the account's short name or the account icon.

Even though you're playing musical chairs, the Big X remembers what's running and the state of your Desktop when you last left it. (When you decide to switch back, Mavericks prompts you for that account's login password for security . . . just in case, you understand.)

Locking Down Your Mac

If security is a potential problem and you still need to share a Mac between multiple users, lock down things. To protect OS X from unauthorized use, take care of these potential security holes immediately:

✦ **Hide the Sleep, Restart, and Shut Down buttons.** Any computer can be hacked when it's restarted or turned on, so hide the Sleep, Restart, and Shut Down buttons on the login screen. (After a user has successfully logged in, OS X can be shut down normally by using the menu item or the keyboard shortcuts that I cover earlier.) Open the Users & Groups pane in System Preferences, click the Login Options button, and deselect the Show the Sleep, Restart, and Shut Down Buttons check box. Press ⌘+Q to quit and save your changes. (Read more about restarting and shutting down in Book I, Chapter 2.)

✦ **Disable list logins.** With a list login, any potential hacker already knows half the information necessary to gain entry to your system — and often, the password is easy to guess. Be prudent and set OS X to ask for the username and password on the Login screen, as I describe earlier. This way, someone must guess both the username and the password, which is usually a much harder proposition.

✦ **Disable Automatic Login.** A true no-brainer. As I mention earlier in the chapter, Automatic Login is indeed convenient. However, all someone has to do is reboot your Mac, and the machine automatically logs in one lucky user! To disable Automatic Login, display the Users & Groups pane in System Preferences and click the Login Options button. Then, open the Automatic Login pop-up menu and choose the Off entry.

✦ **Disable the password hint.** By default, OS X obligingly displays the password hint for an account after three unsuccessful attempts at entering a password. Where security is an issue, this is like serving a hacker a piece of apple pie. Warmed, with ice cream. Head to System Preferences, display the Users & Groups settings, click the Login Options button, and make sure that the Show Password Hints check box is clear.

✦ **Select passwords intelligently.** Although using your mother's maiden name for a password might *seem* like a great idea, the best method of selecting a password is to use a random group of mixed letters and numbers. If you find a random password too hard to remember, at least add a number after your password, like dietcoke1 — and no, that isn't one of my passwords. (Nice try.) My editor suggests a favorite location spelled backward, with a number mixed in, which is easier to remember than a random sequence of characters!

For even greater security, make at least one password character upper-case, and use a number at the beginning and ending of the password (1dieTcoke2). Or, add a triplet number to replace characters with numbers, like this: dietc001ke.

Starting Applications Automatically after Login

Here's one other advantage to logins: Each account can have its own selection of applications that run automatically when that user logs in. These applications are Login Items, and they appear as a list in the Users & Groups pane (shown in Figure 4-4). A caveat or two:

✦ **The users setting their Login Items must be logged in.** Only the user can modify his or her own Login Items.

✦ **Users must have access to System Preferences or must be able to launch System Preferences.** If the person is using a standard-level account and wants to access the account's login items, the account must allow access to System Preferences. Alternatively, if the application icon appears on the Dock after you launch the application, the user can right-click the application icon on the Dock and choose Options➪Open at Login from the contextual menu.

Figure 4-4:
Preparing
to launch
Contacts
every time I
log in.

Ready? As example, I'm setting Contacts to launch every time I log in. Open System Preferences, click Users & Groups, click your account to select it, and then click the Login Items tab (refer to Figure 4-4).

Including an application in your Login Items list is easy: Click the button with the plus sign to navigate to the desired application, select it, and then click Add. (Alternatively, you can just drag items from a Finder window and drop them directly into the list.) Note that items in the list are launched in order. If something needs to run before something else, you can drag the item entries into any sequence. (Oh, and you can add an application that appears on the Dock to your Login Items list by just right-clicking the icon and choosing Options➪Open at Login from the menu!)

To launch the application in hidden mode — which might or might not display it on the Dock, depending on the application — click the list entry for the desired item and enable its Hide check box.

Chapter 5: Setting Up Multiuser Accounts

In This Chapter

✔ **Adding, modifying, and deleting users**

✔ **Establishing Parental Controls**

✔ **Configuring FileVault**

✔ **Avoiding keychains**

In Chapter 4 of this minibook, I introduce you to the different OS X multiuser account levels and the login process. In this chapter, if you're ready to share your Mac with others, you discover how to add new accounts and edit existing accounts. Oh, and yes, I also show you how to *frag* — that's multiplayer game-speak for "destroy" — accounts that you no longer need. I also demonstrate how to add optional limitations to an individual user account and how to avoid using a *keychain* (a tool that's supposed to make it easier to store that pocketful of passwords you've created on the Internet).

Yes, you read correctly. By all that's good and righteous, OS X actually has a feature that I *don't* want you to use. Read on to find out more.

Adding, Editing, and Deleting Users

Most multiuser account chores you'll encounter take place in a single System Preferences pane. (Cue James Bond theme song.) The Users & Groups pane is the star of this chapter, so open System Preferences and click the Users & Groups icon.

If you haven't added any users to your system yet, the Users list should look like Figure 5-1. You should see your account, which you set up when you installed OS X, set to administrator (admin) level.

You also have an entry for a *Guest* account, which anyone can use on an as-needed basis. To enable the Guest account, click the Guest entry in the list to the left and then select the Allow Guests to Log In to This Computer check box. Note that any files created or settings changed by the Guest user are automatically deleted when the Guest user logs out (or when you restart or reboot your Mac). If you like, you can also choose to apply Parental Controls to the Guest account. (I discuss Parental Controls later in this chapter.)

Figure 5-1:
A typical first look at the Users & Groups pane.

New User   Delete User

If you can't click the Guest User entry because it's dimmed, you need to unlock the Users & Groups pane first. Click the padlock icon in the lower-left corner, type your Admin user account password, and then click Unlock. Most panes in System Preferences have this lock feature, which prevents accidental changes to your Mavericks settings. A Good Thing. But now you won't be frustrated when you encounter a locked pane!

Adding a new user account

To add a new user account, follow these steps:

1. **In the Users & Groups pane (from System Preferences), click the New User button (plus sign) at the bottom of the accounts list (refer to Figure 5-1) to display an empty user record sheet like you see in Figure 5-2.**

If the New User button is disabled and you can't click it, click the padlock at the bottom left of the System Preferences pane and provide your admin password to unlock the Users & Groups pane.

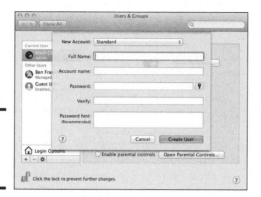

Figure 5-2:
Setting up
a new user
account.

2. In the New Account pop-up menu, select the access level for this user.

By default, the user receives a standard-level account. You can also choose an Administrator account, a managed standard account with Parental Controls already enabled, or a sharing-only account.

The sharing-only account allows the user to copy or open shared files from your Mac remotely (from another computer), but that user can't directly log in to your Mac.

3. In the Full Name text box, type the name that you want to display for this account (both in the Current User list and on the Login screen) and then press Tab to move to the next field.

OS X automatically generates a *short name* in the Account Name field for use as your screen name and Buddy name in Messages and various network applications. The short name is also the name of the folder that OS X creates on the computer's hard drive for this user. You can keep the default short name or type a new one, but it cannot contain any spaces. For more on Messages, jump to Book V, Chapter 3. (I'll wait for you here.)

4. Press Tab again.

5. In the Password text box, type the password for the new account.

Click the button with the key icon next to the Password field, and Mavericks is happy to display the Password Assistant, complete with a suggestion. Click the Suggestion pop-up menu to see additional suggestions. You can choose the length of the password and select among several types: letters and numbers, numbers only, memorable, completely random, or even government-quality. The Assistant automatically copies the current password you're considering into the Password text box.

As always, when you enter a password or its verification, OS X displays bullet characters for security.

6. **Press Tab, type the password in the Verify text box, and press Tab again.**

7. **(Optional) If you decide to use the password hint feature, which I describe in Chapter 4 of this minibook, you can enter a short sentence or question in the Password Hint text box.**

   The hint is displayed after three unsuccessful attempts at entering the account password.

   I recommend that you *do not* *use this option.* Think about it: Any hack could type in anything three times to get your hint to pop up! If you do use this option, at least make sure that the hint is sufficiently vague!

8. **Click the Create User button to finish and create the account.**

   The new account shows up in the Current User list and in the Login screen.

So you like your privacy . . .

These days, everyone's interested in securing personal files from prying eyes. Granted, this issue isn't a problem if you're the only one using your Mac. However, if you're sharing a computer in a multiuser environment, you might want a little more protection than just user permissions for those all-important Fantasy Football formations that you'll unleash next season.

Never fear! Mavericks offers *FileVault,* which provides disk encryption that prevents just about anyone except the NSA or FBI from gaining access to the files in your Home folder. (You'll notice that things slow down just a bit when logging in and out or working with files that are several gigabytes in size, but for those of us who need the peace of mind, this minimal performance hit is worth it.) You can enable the FileVault feature from the Security & Privacy pane in System Preferences. Two passwords control access to your drive when FileVault is active:

✔ The *Recovery Key* can unlock your drive if you forget your login password. Mavericks provides you with this key when you turn on the FileVault feature. **I highly recommend that you write down this key and store your copy in a safe place, away from your Mac.**

✔ Your *Login Password* unlocks the drive automatically when you log in.

I love this feature, and I use it on all my Macs running Mavericks. Yet a risk is involved (insert ominous chord here). To wit: ***DO NOT* forget your Login Password, and make doggone sure that your Admin user has access to a copy of that all-important Recovery Key!** OS X displays a dire warning for anyone who's considering using FileVault: If you forget these passwords, you can't retrieve any data from your Mac's drive. *Period.* As Jerry Reed used to say, "It's a gone pecan."

Editing an existing account

If you have administrator access, it's a cinch to make changes to an existing account from the Users & Groups pane in System Preferences. (Often, this change is assigning a personalized account picture, so I demonstrate that here.) Follow these steps:

1. **Click the account that you want to change in the list to the left of the window.**

If the accounts in the list are disabled and you can't select one, you must unlock the Users & Groups pane. Click the lock at the bottom left of the System Preferences pane (and type your password, if prompted).

2. **Edit the settings that you need to change.**

Examples include enabling administrator rights for an account temporarily (by selecting the Allow User to Administer This Computer check box), and changing the account password (by clicking the Reset Password button).

3. **Click the square picture well (the square that displays the image) to specify the thumbnail image that appears in the Login list next to the account name.**

Apple provides a number of good images in the preview collection. Just click a thumbnail to select it.

4. **To replace your account image, drag a new image from a Finder window or the iPhoto window and drop it in the picture well.**

- *To choose an image from the default set of Mavericks icons:* Click the picture well, click the Defaults tab, click the desired image, and then click Done.

- *To choose an icon image from your Photo Stream:* Click the picture well, click the Photo Stream tab, click the desired image, and then click Done. (If you use the iCloud Photo Stream feature on your iPhone, iPad, or iPod touch, this method is a great way to grab your latest candid photos.)

Alternatively, you can click the picture well and click the Camera tab to grab a picture from your FaceTime HD, iSight, or other video camera connected to your Mac. When you're set to take the photo, click the button with the camera icon and then click Done to accept it. *Most* cool.

5. **After you make the changes, press ⌘+Q to save them and close the System Preferences window.**

Deleting an existing account

To wipe an account from the face of the Earth, follow these steps:

1. **In the user list to the left of the window, click the account that you want to delete.**

2. **Click the Delete User button (which is smartly marked with a minus sign).**

OS X displays the confirmation sheet that you see in Figure 5-3.

Note that the contents of the user's Home folder can be saved in a disk image in the Deleted Users folder (just in case you need to retrieve something). That's what I opted for in the figure. Alternatively, you can choose to leave the deleted user's Home folder as is, without removing it.

Figure 5-3: Are you *quite* sure that you want to delete this user?

If you're absolutely sure you won't be dating that person again, select the Delete the Home Folder radio button (which doesn't save anything in the Deleted Users folder). You regain all the hard drive space that was being occupied by the contents of the deleted user's Home folder. As an extra measure of protection, you can also choose to securely erase the contents of the deleted user's Home folder.

3. **To verify and delete the account, click Delete User.**

If you're not sure, click the Cancel button to abort and return to the Accounts list.

Tightening Your Security Belt

Administrators are special people. Just ask one; you'll see. Anyway, when an administrator creates or edits the account for a standard-level user, OS X offers a number of levels of specific rights — *Parental Controls* — that can be assigned on an individual account basis. When Parental Controls are assigned to an account, it becomes a managed account.

Parental Controls are available only for standard-level users; administrators aren't affected by them because an administrator-level account already has access to everything covered by controls.

When do you need Parental Controls? Here are three likely scenarios:

- ✦ You're creating accounts for corporate or educational users, and you want to disable certain features of OS X to prevent those folks from doing something dumb. Just tell 'em you're "streamlining the operating system." (Yeah, that's it.) For example, you might not want that one particular kid making CD copies of *The Illustrated Anarchist's Cookbook* in the classroom while you're gone. Therefore, for that account, you disable the ability to burn CDs or DVDs.

- ✦ In the same environment, you might want to give a specific standard-level account the capability to administer printers. If Roger in Accounting is both helpful and knowledgeable — oh, and add *trustworthy* in there, too — you might want to give him this ability so that he can handle the print queues while you're on vacation.

- ✦ You want one or more users to access one — and only one — application on the system, or perhaps just two or three applications. To illustrate: In my years as a hospital hardware technician, we had a number of computers that were used solely to display patient records. No Word, no e-mail, nothing but the one program that accessed the medical records database. We called these machines "dumb terminals" although they were actually personal computers. (This trick also works well if you're a parent and you want to give your kids access without endangering your valuable files. Just don't call your computer a "dumb terminal" lest your kids take offense. That's experience talking there.) If you want to allow access to a *specified* selection of applications, you can set them in that account's controls.

Setting Parental Controls

Time to review what each setting does. (If the System Preferences window isn't open, click the System Preferences icon on the Dock, and then click the Users & Groups icon.) To display the controls for a standard account, click the account in the list and then click the Enable Parental Controls button, and (if necessary) click the lock icon in the lower-left corner to confirm your access. Click the Open Parental Controls button (which prompts you again for your password) to display the controls. Mavericks includes five categories (tabs) of controls, as shown in Figure 5-4:

✦ **Apps:** These settings (which I discuss in more detail in a second) affect what the user can do in Mavericks as well as what Finder looks like to that user.

Figure 5-4: You can restrict access to many functions in a Standard account.

✦ **Web:** Mavericks offers three levels of control for websites:

• *Allow Unrestricted Access:* Select this radio button to allow unfettered access for this user.

• *Try to Limit Access:* You can allow Safari to automatically block websites it deems adult. To specify particular sites that the automatic adult figure should allow or deny, click the Customize button.

• *Allow Access to Only These Websites:* Choose this radio button to specify which websites the user can view. To add a website, click the Add button (a plus sign), and Mavericks prompts you for a title and the website address.

✦ **People:** You can specify whether the user can join in Game Center multi-player games, as well as allow or prevent the user from adding friends in Game Center.

Select the Limit Mail and Limit Messages check boxes to specify the e-mail and instant messaging addresses with which this user can communicate. (Note that this affects only Apple Mail and Messages, so other mail clients, web-based mail, instant-messaging applications, and audio/video chat applications aren't controlled and must be restricted individually.) To add an address that the user can e-mail or chat with, click the Add button, which bears the familiar plus sign.

If you want a notification when the user is attempting to send an e-mail to someone not in the list, select the Send Requests To check box and then type your e-mail address in the text box.

✦ **Time Limits:** Parents, click the Time Limits button, and you'll shout with pure joy! Check out the options on this pane in Figure 5-5. You can limit an account to a certain number of hours of usage per weekday (Weekday Time Limits), to a specified number of hours of usage per weekend day (Weekend Time Limits), and you can set a bedtime computer curfew time for both weekdays (called "School Nights" here) and weekend days. Unfortunately, holidays and summer vacation days aren't tracked, so you may have to manually set and disable time limits from time to time.

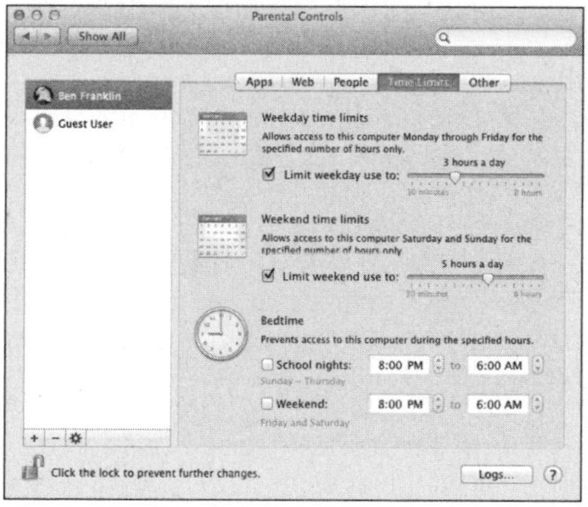

**Book II
Chapter 5**

**Setting Up
Multiuser Accounts**

Figure 5-5:
Mavericks
keeps track
of your kid's
computer
usage so that
you don't
have to.

✦ **Other:** These settings control the Dictionary and hardware devices such as your printer and DVD burner. They are

- *Disable Built-in Camera:* Select this check box to disable any built-in (internal) camera in your system. (Note, however, that this feature does **not** disable external cameras using your Mac's USB, Thunderbolt or FireWire port.)

- *Disable Dictation:* Select this check box to turn off the Dictation feature in Mavericks (which I discuss in more detail in Book VIII, Chapter 4).

- *Hide Profanity in Dictionary:* With this check box selected, profane terms are hidden in the Dictionary for this user.

- *Limit Printer Administration:* With this check box selected, the user cannot modify the printers and printer queues in the Print & Scan pane in System Preferences. If this option is enabled, the user can still print to the default printer and switch to other assigned printers but can't add or delete printers or manage the OS X print queue. (Of course, if the print job encounters a problem, that user has to bug you to fix things. Go figure.)

- *Limit CD and DVD Burning:* Select this check box to prevent the user from recording CDs or DVDs via the built-in disc-recording features in OS X. (Note, however, that if you load a third-party recording program, such as Toast, the user can still record discs with it.)

- *Disable Changing the Password:* Select this check box to prevent the user from changing the account password.

If you're creating a single standard-level account for an entire group of people to use — for example, you want to leave the machine in kiosk mode in one corner of the office, or everyone in a classroom will use the same account on the machine — I recommend disabling the ability to change the account password. (Oh, and please do me a favor — *don't* create a system with just one admin-level account that everyone is supposed to use! Instead, keep your one admin-level account close to your bosom and create a standard-level account for the Unwashed Horde.)

Mavericks keeps a number of different types of *text log files* (which track where the user goes on the Internet, which applications are launched by the account, and the contents of any Messages conversations where the user was a participant). Click the Logs button on any Parental Control screen to monitor all the logs for a particular account.

You can always tell whether an account has been assigned Parental Controls because the account description changes from Standard to Managed in the User list.

Of particular importance are the controls for Finder and applications. Click the Apps tab (refer to Figure 5-4) to modify these settings:

+ **Use Simple Finder:** I discuss the simple Finder in the following section because it's a great idea for families and classrooms with smaller children.

+ **Limit Applications:** When this option is selected, you can select the specific applications that appear to the user. These restrictions are in effect whether the user has access to the full Finder or just the simple Finder.

From the Allow App Store Apps pop-up menu, you can choose to block the account from launching any applications purchased from the Apple App Store or limit the user to installed App Store apps rated for specific ages.

To allow access to all the applications of a specific type — App Store, Other Apps (such as the iLife and iWork suites), Widgets, and Utilities — select the check box next to the desired group heading. To restrict access to all applications in a group, clear the check box next to any heading to deselect it. You can also toggle the restriction on and off for specific applications in these groups by clicking the triangle icon next to each group heading to expand the list and then marking or clearing the check box next to the desired applications. To locate a specific application, click in the Search box and type the application name.

Book II
Chapter 5

Setting Up
Multiuser Accounts

To add an application to the Allowed Apps list, drag its icon from Finder and drop it in the list in the Other Apps group. After you add an application, it appears in the Other Apps group, and you can toggle access to it just like the applications in the named groups.

These settings can work hand-in-hand with the Gatekeeper feature in Mavericks, which prevents anyone from launching applications that were not downloaded from the App Store (or are not Apple-approved). For more information on Gatekeeper, visit Chapter 3 of this minibook — you'll find it described as part of the Security & Privacy pane.

✦ **Prevent the Dock from Being Modified:** Select this check box, and the user will no longer be able to remove applications, documents, and folders from the Dock in the full Finder. (If you don't mind the contents of the Dock changing according to the whims of other users, go ahead and deselect this check box.)

Assigning the Simple Finder

You can restrict your standard-level users even further by assigning them the simple Finder set of limitations. The default simple Finder, as shown in Figure 5-6, is a highly simplified version of the regular OS X Finder. The simplified Dock contains only the following: the Finder icon; Trash; and the folders for the user's approved applications, documents, and shared files.

This is the network administrator's idea of a foolproof interface for OS X: A user can access only those system files and resources needed to do a job, with no room for tinkering or goofing off.

A simple Finder user can still make the jump to the full version of Finder by clicking the Finder menu and choosing Run Full Finder. The user has to enter a correct admin-level username and password.

Figure 5-6:
Whoa! It's the simple Finder — less filling; still runs great!

Using Keychains — Not!

Before I leave this chapter, I want to discuss an OS X feature that's been around for many years now: the keychain. Your *account keychain* stores all the username and password combinations for websites, file servers, File Transfer Protocol (FTP) servers, and the like, allowing you to simply waltz in and start using a service (whatever it is). Sounds downright convenient, doesn't it? And it can be, but you better watch your step.

With the debut of Mavericks, OS X now includes *two* keychains! To wit:

✦ **The local keychain (controlled from the Keychain Access utility):** Keychain Access allows you to create an account keychain for just your Mac, including passwords for websites, networks, and specific applications.

✦ **The iCloud keychain:** This new feature automatically shares your web passwords and credit card information among *all* of your Macs and iOS 7 devices! Think of the possibilities: the Safari app on your iPhone will automatically provide the password for your favorite online stores, and then enter your credit card information for you. (To use the iCloud keychain, your Mac computers must be running Mavericks, and your iOS devices must be running iOS 7 or later.)

Both keychains are managed in the Keychain Access application, but the iCloud Keychain feature must be toggled on from the iCloud pane in System Preferences — you'll find out more about the iCloud keychain in Book V, Chapter 4. I heartily recommend keeping the iCloud keychain turned off.

"What? Mark, why would I eschew such a neat feature?" I'll be perfectly honest here: I *hate* account keychains, whether they're based on your drive or stored in iCloud. With a passion, mind you. As a consultant, a support technician, a webmaster, and the SYSOP (an ancient Bulletin Board Service abbreviation meaning *System Operator*) of an Internet-based online system, I know what a hassle it is for users to remember separate passwords, and I feel that pain. (I use separate passwords for everything.) However, three massively big problems are inherent with using keychains:

✦ **Anyone can log in as you *without knowing your passwords*.** If your keychain is unlocked, which happens automatically when you log in, all someone has to do is sit at your desk, visit a site or connect with a server, and *bam!* They're on. As *you*. *Think about that.* And then think how many times you get up from your desk, just for a second, to grab another Diet Coke or a doughnut.

✦ **You'll forget your passwords.** If the keychain file is corrupted — and it can happen — your passwords have gone to Detroit without you. Unless you have them on paper hidden somewhere or they're on your recent Time Machine backup, it's time to change your online persona.

✦ **Keychains need yet another stinkin' password.** Yep, that's right. Your keychain can be locked (manually, or with the right settings, automatically), and you have to remember yet another password or passphrase to unlock your keychain. "When, oh, when will the madness end?"

From a security standpoint, keychains should be *completely off-limits* for anyone who's interested in maintaining a well–locked-down machine (whether the Mac is used in a company office or shared by a classroom). Unfortunately, Mavericks creates a keychain automatically for every user, so you have to monitor (and delete) your keychain data manually. (Sigh.)

However, if you're the only person using your Mac and it resides in your home — I'd prefer a bank vault — and you absolutely *must* use keychains, you can display them all for the current account from the Keychain Access application (see Figure 5-7), conveniently located in the Utilities/Other folder in Launchpad. Click the desired category, and then click an item in the keychain list to display or edit all its information.

Figure 5-7: Take my advice — stay away from the allure of the keychain.

Heck, just think about what I just wrote: Anyone can display and edit server and site information just by launching this application! That includes your nephew Damien — you know, the one who considers himself the hacker extraordinaire. (While I'm at it, I should mention that setting the Automatic Login feature — which I discuss earlier in this chapter — to an admin-level account is just as bad. One reboot, and you're rolling out the red carpet for the little rascal. For the inside information on Automatic Login, visit Chapter 4 in this very minibook.)

To help lock down things — at least when it comes to your Internet communications — flip to Book V, Chapter 5 and learn how you can remove saved web passwords from within Safari. You can also delete any password item from your iCloud keychain using Keychain Access. To display your iCloud keychain items, click the iCloud item in the Keychains list at the left. (Note that this entry won't appear in the list unless you've turned on the iCloud keychain in the iCloud pane in System Preferences.) Right-click any iCloud keychain item in the list and choose Delete to remove it. You're probably thinking, "Well, Mark, that pretty much eliminates the purpose of quick, convenient access without passwords, doesn't it?" Yes, indeed it does, but at least you can take fast action if your online identity is compromised.

To display *all* the keychains you can access, choose Edit⇨Keychain List. To create a new keychain, choose File⇨New Keychain. OS X prompts you for the filename for your new keychain file. In the New Keychain dialog that appears, enter a catchy name in the Save As text box. By default, the keychain file is created in the Keychains folder — a good idea — but if you want to store it elsewhere, click the down-arrow button next to the Save As text box and navigate to the desired folder. When you're ready, click the Create button. Now you need to enter yet another password, type it again to verify it, and then click OK.

To lock or unlock your login keychain, click the lock icon at the top-left of the Keychain Access window. (Unlocking your keychain requires you to enter your login password. Go figure.)

You might be saying to yourself, "Geez, this guy is more than a little paranoid." And yes, dear reader, I suppose I am. But then again, who's been uploading all those questionable images and MP3 files to the company server . . . using your account? And who wrote that tirade on your Facebook page?

**Book II
Chapter 5**

**Setting Up
Multiuser Accounts**

Chapter 6: Sharing Documents for Fun and Profit

In This Chapter

✓ Comparing network sharing with multiuser sharing

✓ Setting and changing permissions

✓ Sharing documents in Microsoft Office 2011 for the Mac

*N*ow here's a topic that any OS X power user can sink his teeth into — the idea that a document on a multiuser system can be *everyone's* property, allowing anyone in your family, workgroup, or highly competitive mob to make whatever changes are necessary, whenever they like.

Of course, potential pitfalls lurk — even in the Apple world, there's no such thing as an operating system that's both powerful *and* perfectly simple. However, I think you'll find that our dear friends from Cupertino have done just about as well as can be expected and that the settings that you use to share documents are fairly easy to understand.

Prepare to share!

Sharing over a Network versus Sharing on a Single Mac

First, allow me to clear up what I've found to be a common misconception by using another of Mark's Maxims.

Sharing documents on a single computer is fundamentally different from the file sharing you've used on a network.

True, multiple users can share a document over a network, which is a topic that I cover in Book VI. But although the results are the same, the way that you share that same document on a single machine betwixt multiple users is a completely different turn of the screw. In this section, I discuss the factoids behind the matter.

I'd be remiss if I didn't mention the *AirDrop* feature in Mavericks, which allows many folks with Macs running Lion, Mountain Lion, or Mavericks to transfer files wirelessly between their computers. AirDrop is easy and convenient to use, and I cover it in Book VI, Chapter 2.

No network is required

Although reiterating that no network is required is seemingly the most obvious of statements, many otherwise knowledgeable OS X power users seem to forget that sharing a document over a network requires an active network connection. (Note the word *active* there.) Unless you physically copy the document to your hard drive — which defeats the purpose of document sharing — any loss of network connectivity or any problem with your network account will result in a brick wall and a brightly painted (or flashing neon) sign reading, "No luck, Jack."

On the other hand, a document shared on a multiuser Mac in the home or classroom is available whenever you need it. As long as the file is located in the Shared folder, the file privileges are set correctly, and you know the password (if one is required by the application, such as a password-protected Word document), you're set to go regardless of whether your network connection is active.

Relying on a guaranteed lock

Sharing documents over a network can get a tad hairy when multiple users open and edit a document simultaneously. Applications, such as Office 2011 for the Mac, have methods of *locking* a document (giving one person exclusive access) when someone opens it or saves it. However, you always face the possibility that what you're seeing in a shared network document isn't exactly what's in the document at that moment.

A multiuser system doesn't need such exquisite complexity. *You're* the one sitting at the keyboard, and *you* have control: This is what network administrators call a *guaranteed lock* on that document file. Refreshing, isn't it?

But wait! OS X Mavericks includes a feature called *Fast User Switching* — I discuss it in Book I, Chapter 2 — that allows other users to remain logged in behind the scenes while another user is at the keyboard. Therefore, if you enable Fast User Switching, two users could have the same document open at the same time. To prevent this, you can simply turn off Fast User Switching from the Users & Groups pane in System Preferences. (Click Users & Groups, click Login Options, and clear the Enable Fast User Switching check box.)

It's also possible for someone to use Mavericks's Remote Login feature to log in to his or her account across the Internet. You can disable this feature by opening the System Preferences window, clicking the Share icon, and deselecting the Remote Login check box.

Most places are off-limits

Network users are often confident that they can blithely copy and move a document from one place to another with the greatest of ease, and that's true. Most shared network documents created by an application — such as a project outline created in Word, for example — carry their own sharing information and document settings internally. Thus, you can move that same file to another folder on your hard drive, and the rest of the network team can still open it — if they have the network rights to access the new folder, of course.

This isn't the case when it comes to multiuser documents. As you can read in Chapters 4 and 5 of this minibook, OS X places a tight fence around a standard-level user, allowing that person to access only the contents of certain folders. In this case, your document must be placed in the Shared folder for every standard-level user to be able to open it. If everyone using the document has administrator access, you can store the file in other spots on your system; as long as the permissions are set, you're set. And speaking of permissions. . . .

Permissions: Law Enforcement for Your Files

Files are shared in OS X according to a set of rules called *permissions,* the *ownership* of a file (typically the person who saved the document the first time), and an access level shared by multiple users who are specified as a *group.* The combination of privileges, ownership, and group determines who can do what with a file.

When you (or the person with the administrator account on your Mac) created your user account, you were automatically granted ownership of your Home folder and everything that it contains, as well as any files or folders that you store in the Shared folder or another user's Public folder.

Four possible actions are allowed through permissions:

✦ **Read Only:** The user can open and read the file, which includes copying it to another location.

✦ **Read & Write:** This permission grants full access to the file, including opening, reading, editing, saving, and deleting. Read & Write permission also allows the user to copy or move the file to another location.

✦ **Write Only (Drop Box):** This tight permission setting appears only with a folder, allowing access to copy an item to the folder but not to see any files it contains. Hence the informal name *Drop Box*, and the + (plus sign) icon added to the folder's icon to identify it. For example, a Drop Box is made to order for teachers: Students can submit homework by dragging their work to the teacher's Drop Box.

✦ **No Access:** This action is just what it sounds like: The user can't open the file, copy it, or move it.

No matter what permissions you've set, only the root user can copy items to another user's Home folder. Take my word for it on this one: Simply consider that this can't be done, and **stay as far away from the root account as possible.** (I repeat: Trust me on this.) Read all about the perils of enabling the root account in Chapter 4 of this minibook.

These permissions are set in the Info dialog or Inspector window for a file or folder (always accessible by pressing ⌘+I). If you're setting the permissions for a folder, you can also elect to apply those same settings to all the enclosed items in the folder.

To set permissions, follow these steps:

1. **Click the item to select it, press ⌘+I (or choose Finder⇨File), and then choose the Get Info menu item.**

   You can right-click the item and choose Get Info instead. Either way, OS X displays the Info dialog.

2. **Click the right-facing arrow next to the Sharing & Permissions heading to expand it, as shown in Figure 6-1.**

3. **To change your own permissions on the item, click the Privilege list next to your name — handily marked "(Me)" as well — and choose a new Ownership permissions level.**

   This is likely set to Read & Write, and it's a good idea to leave it alone. If you're the file's owner, you're likely not a security risk.

**Book II
Chapter 6**

Sharing Documents for Fun and Profit

Figure 6-1:
The Info dialog, expanded to show Sharing & Permissions.

Action button

Perhaps I should be a little less tactful here: *Never* choose an access level for yourself other than Read & Write without being absolutely sure of what you're doing because you could prevent yourself from accessing or deleting the file in the future! For example, if you simply want to lock an item to prevent changes being made, **don't** set your Ownership permission to Read Only. Instead, select the Locked check box in the General section of the Info dialog instead. You can easily clear the Locked check box later to make changes to the item.

If the Permissions fields in your Info dialog are disabled (they're dimmed and can't be clicked), the dialog is locked to prevent accidental changes. To unlock the dialog and make changes, click the tiny padlock icon at the lower-right corner of the Info dialog, type your user password, and then click OK. You can lock an Info dialog also by clicking the padlock icon again.

4. **To change permissions for someone else or a group, click the Privilege value for that user or group and then choose the appropriate value from the pop-up menu.**

Assigning permissions for an entire group is a good idea for limiting specific files and folders to only administrator access. (Note, however, that Mavericks reserves the group name *wheel* — a term from the Unix world that encompasses all administrator accounts — for internal tasks, so *never* alter any permissions for a group originally created by OS X.)

5. **If necessary, set the permission for the Everyone pop-up menu (otherwise known as "I'm going to lump everyone else into this category").**

If a user isn't the owner of an item and doesn't fit into any group that you selected, this access permission setting for this file applies to that user.

Need to apply the same permissions to all the contents of a folder — including subfolders within it? Select a folder, click the Action button at the bottom of the Info dialog (which carries a gear icon), and choose Apply to Enclosed Items from the pop-up menu that appears. After you confirm the action, Mavericks automatically changes the permissions for all the items in the folder to the same settings.

Generally, *do not* override the permissions for all the items in a folder, so use the Apply to Enclosed Items action only when necessary.

6. **After all the permissions are correct, click the Close button to save your changes and return to your friendly Finder.**

If a specific user or group doesn't appear already in the Privilege list, click the Add button (bearing the plus sign), and you can add a specific privilege level for that user or group. You can also delete a privilege level: Click the desired entry to select it and click the Delete button (which bears a minus sign).

Permission and Sharing Do's and Don'ts

After you get the basics of sharing files and assigning permissions under your belt, you need to master when to change permissions and why you should (and shouldn't) modify them. Follow these common-sense guidelines when saving documents, assigning permissions, and choosing access levels:

✦ *Do* **use the Shared folder.** The Shared folder is the center of proper document sharing. I know there's a strong urge to create a new document in your Home folder, but you're just making more work for yourself because you'll end up copying that document from your Home folder to the Shared folder. Instead of an extra step, store a document that's intended to be shared in the Shared folder — where it belongs in the first place.

✦ *Do* **review the contents of a folder before changing permissions for enclosed items.** That confirmation dialog doesn't appear just for kicks. For example, if you set a highly sensitive, private document with permissions of No Access for everyone but yourself and then you apply less-restrictive permissions globally to the folder that contains the document, you've just removed the No Access permissions, and anyone can open your dirty laundry hamper. (Ouch.) Therefore, make sure that you open the folder and double-check its contents first before applying global permissions to the items it contains.

✦ ***Don't* assign permissions just to protect a file from deletion.** If all you need to do is prevent anyone (including yourself) from deleting an item, you don't need to go to all the trouble of changing permissions. Instead, just display the Info dialog for the item and select the Locked check box, which prevents the item from being deleted from the Trash until the Lock status is turned off (or you specifically click Remove All Items when emptying the Trash).

✦ ***Don't* change permissions in the Applications or Utilities folders.** If you have administrator-level access, you can change the permissions for important applications such as Mail, Contacts, iTunes, and Safari, as well as their support files. This spells havoc for all users assigned to the standard-access level. Be polite and leave the permissions for these files alone.

✦ ***Definitely don't* change System ownership.** OS X is stable and reliable. Part of that stability comes from the protected state of the System folder, as well as a number of other folders on your hard drive. If you display the Info dialog for the System folder, you'll see that the Owner is set to *system,* and the Group is set to *wheel.* Now, promptly close that Info dialog, **without making any changes!**

✦ *Never, never, never* **change any permissions for any files owned by the System (including items with *wheel* group permissions) unless specifically told to do so by an Apple support technician. *Do not* monkey with System-owned items.**

This last one is quite striking for a reason, so heed the warning.

Sharing Stuff in Office 2011

Many OS X applications offer their own built-in document-sharing features. For example, Microsoft Office 2011 for the Mac includes both file-level and document-sharing features. Because Office 2011 is the most popular productivity suite available for OS X, I discuss these commands in this final section.

Document-sharing features

You'll find a number of commands that help multiple users keep track of changes that have been made in a shared Office document. Probably the most familiar is the Word revision-tracking feature (heavily used during the development of this book), but there are others as well:

✦ **Revision marks:** If several users edit a document, you can tell who did what by using *revision marks,* which apply different colors to changes made by different editors. Later, those additions and deletions can be accepted or rejected individually. If Johnson in Marketing adds incorrect material, you can easily remove just his changes. In a worst-case scenario, you can reject all changes and return the document to its pristine condition.

+ **Compare Documents:** Using this feature allows you to compare a revised document with the original (if, of course, you still have the original file handy). I use Compare Documents only if revision marks weren't turned on before editing began.

+ **Comments:** Editors can also converse in a document by using embedded Comments. These don't change the contents of the Word file the way revision marks do, but store commentary and notes in a behind-the-scenes kind of way. (Think of an OS X Sticky that appears in a document.) Again, the author of each comment is listed, allowing for (sometimes heated) communication in the body of a document.

+ **Highlighting:** You've heard the old joke about . . . Well, anyway, a traditional highlighter marker is useless on a computer monitor (leaving a nasty mess for the next user to clean), but Word allows multiple highlighting colors for identifying text. (And for the occasional practical joke — nothing like adding eight different highlighting colors to that important proposal. Just make sure that your résumé is up to date.)

File-level sharing features

Along with the document-level sharing commands, you'll find that Office 2011 applications also offer sharing features that control access to the document file itself.

Password protection

You can add password protection to any Office 2011 document. Follow these steps with a document created in Word, Excel, or PowerPoint:

1. **In the Office application, choose File⇨Save As.**

2. **In the Save As dialog that appears, click Options to display the Save Preferences pane.**

3. **Click the Show All toolbar button.**

4. **Click Security to display the Preferences pane.**

5. **To password-protect the document, enter a password in the Password to Open field.**

This password must be provided when opening the document.

If you like, you can enter another password in the Password to Modify field. This second password would then also be required to modify the document.

Both passwords are case-sensitive.

6. **Click OK to save the preference changes and return to your document.**

Document protection

Think of the Protect Document dialog in Word, from which you can effectively write-protect certain elements, as an extra level of security in a multiuser environment. In this Office application, you can protect revision marks, comments, and sections of a document containing forms. A password can be added if desired. To display the Protect Document dialog, click Tools in any of the Office 2011 applications and choose Protect Document from the menu.

**Book II
Chapter 6**

**Sharing Documents
for Fun and Profit**

Book III
The Digital Hub

Contents at a Glance

Chapter 1: The World According to Apple

In This Chapter

✔ **Doing things the hub way**

✔ **Digitizing your life**

✔ **Making your digital devices work together**

*I*f you're old enough to recall postage stamp–sized video, 256-color photos, and scratchy mono sound, you're old enough to remember the beginnings of computer digital media. Apple's success spanning the past decade has been due in large part to the Mac hardware and software revolution that brought professional-quality digital media within the reach of the home Mac owner.

And that recipe for digital success continues today. Using tightly integrated hardware and software (where everything works smoothly together), Apple gives you the ability to easily organize and produce your own multimedia with the iLife suite of digital tools, which includes iMovie, iPhoto, GarageBand, and iTunes. That same software also provides fantastic editing capabilities. Finally (and this is very important) — to paraphrase Will Smith in the movie *Men in Black,* "Apple makes these programs look *good.*"

First, Sliced Bread . . . and Now, the Digital Hub

In today's overloaded world of personal electronic devices, people may be juggling as many as five or six electronic wonders. Each device typically comes with its own software, power adapter, and connectors to the outside world. Although managing one or two devices isn't terribly difficult, as their number increases, so do the headaches. When you have a half-dozen cables and power adapters to cart around, the digital life can become pretty bleak. (And quite heavy. You'll need more than a backpack to lug all that gear around.)

To combat this confusion, Apple came up with the idea of a *digital hub,* whereby your Macintosh acts as the center of an array of electronic devices. By using standardized cables, power requirements, built-in software, and even wireless connections via *Bluetooth* (the standard for short-range wireless communications between devices) and 802.11x wireless (for connections to your Ethernet network and your Apple TV unit), the Macintosh — along with its operating system, OS X — goes a long way toward simplifying your interaction with all the electronic gadgets that you use.

Given the hub terminology, think of the digital hub as a wagon wheel. (See Figure 1-1.) At the center of the wheel is your Macintosh. At the end of each spoke is a digital device — and the spokes themselves are Apple's innovative iLife applications. Throughout the rest of this minibook, I give you the skinny on each application. This chapter gives you the overview and tells you how they all work together.

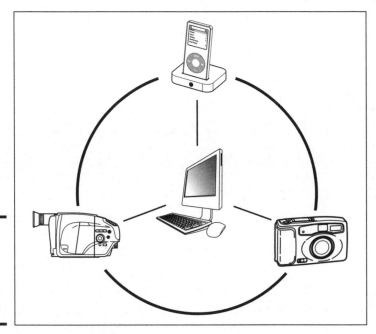

Figure 1-1:
Hey, look what's in the center of your digital hub!

What Can I Digitize?

As you've probably guessed by now, practically anything can be digitized. As long as you can represent something as numbers, you can digitize that data. Whether you have photographs, video, or audio, your Mac is adept at digitizing data and processing it.

Photographs

Perhaps the most popular of digital devices, the digital camera has transformed photography forever. By using sophisticated electronics, digital cameras convert the image that you see through the camera viewfinder into an image made purely of numbers.

After this numeric information is transferred to your Macintosh, your computer can cut, twist, fade, label, and paint your digital images. Because numbers are the only materials involved, you won't need scissors, paint, or adhesive tape to edit images. (Advertising photographers can say good-bye to the old-fashioned airbrush.) Your Macintosh does it all by manipulating those numbers. It cuts down on the messy art supplies and gives you the comfort of being able to go back in time — something that anyone who's not so handy with scissors can appreciate.

Music

Audio CDs are one application of music represented as digital data. The physical CD is just a piece of plastic with an embedded metal layer, but you don't even really need CDs any longer. Your Macintosh can digitize audio for storage on your internal drive, too, which brings up another important point. Digital information is not only palatable to a computer but also very portable. You can store it on any number of storage devices, such as an iPod, an iPad, an iPhone, a USB flash drive, or an external hard drive. (By the way, if you're a musician, you can use GarageBand and external instruments that will turn your Mac into a combination of synthesizer, amplifier, and backup band. Mozart would've loved this stuff.)

Video

When you photograph a scene multiple times per second and then replay the sequence, you get (tah-dah!) moving pictures. In the analog (as opposed to digital) world, these photographs would be a strip of celluloid film or magnetic tape. In the digital world, such a sequence of photographs is *DV*, or *digital video*. After you take your digital video, you can transfer that data to your Macintosh to further manipulate it: You can edit it and add transitions, text, and other effects.

DVD

Like a CD-ROM or a hard drive, a *DVD* is simply a means of storing digital data. Although you can use it to save many kinds of data, its most common use is for presenting video content. If your Mac is equipped with an internal DVD drive (or an external drive) and a third-party DVD authoring application, the Macintosh digital hub can produce DVDs by using any digital information you give it.

The Software That Drives the Hub

At the heart of your digital hub is your Macintosh. To use and manipulate all the data that arrives at your Mac, your computer needs software, which provides instructions on what to do with the information that you send.

Fortunately, Apple has fashioned some of the most attractive and easy-to-use software ever written to help you manipulate and manage your digital lifestyle. The list of software that belongs to the digital hub includes

✦ **iPhoto:** Use iPhoto to download, manipulate, and organize your favorite digital photographs. After everything is just so, iPhoto can print them, burn them to disc, or even help you design and order a hardbound album! (For way more on iPhoto, go to Chapter 3 of this minibook.)

✦ **iTunes:** iTunes offers the capability to manage your music and movie collections, along with sundry other media such as podcasts, Internet radio, audiobooks, and music videos. You can also purchase and download audio tracks and video from Apple's iTunes Store. iTunes can even burn audio CDs! (Head to Chapter 2 of this minibook for more.)

✦ **iMovie:** Every film director needs a movie-editing suite. iMovie gives you the chance to set up Hollywood in your living room with outstanding results, and then share your finished film in many different ways. (For more, see Chapter 4 of this minibook.)

✦ **GarageBand:** Call it a "music-building" application! Even if you can't play a note, GarageBand makes it easy to create your own original songs — and if you *are* a musician, you can turn your Mac into a production studio. The latest version can even help you learn how to play an instrument. (Turn to Chapter 5 of this minibook for more.)

iPhoto

What good is a camera without a photo album? *iPhoto,* Apple's photography software, serves as a digital photo album. Use it to help you arrange and manage your digital photos with advanced features, such as location tagging and facial recognition. Beyond its functions as a photo album, iPhoto also gives you the ability to touch up your images through cropping, retouching, scaling, rotating, and red-eye reduction (photographically speaking, not morning-after speaking).

Besides offering editing features, iPhoto also works automatically with your digital camera. Simply plug in the camera to your Mac's Universal Serial Bus (USB) port, and iPhoto knows the device is there. Need to transfer photos from the camera to your photo album? iPhoto can do that, too.

When you complete a collection of photographs that you find interesting, use iPhoto to help you publish them on the Internet or even to create your very own coffee-table book (the latest in high-tech: a paper book). And for those of you who still want that nifty wallet print to show off at work or a poster to hang on your wall, you can print your photos with your printer or order them online through iPhoto. Orders made with iPhoto show up in your mailbox — the U.S. Postal Service physical one outside your domicile — a few days later.

Isn't this a book about my Mac?

Why do I keep harping on the iPod? Well, as a proud owner of one, I'm glad you asked: Apple's iPod is a versatile, lightweight audio and video player with hidden extras that James Bond would covet. It has enough capacity to store your entire collection of music and several movies, but it's small enough to fit into your shirt pocket. With iTunes, you can instantly exchange media between your Macintosh and your iPod. And the iPod even works as honest-to-goodness, backup storage . . . you see, it also functions as a standard external USB 2.0 hard drive. A video-capable iPod can display text files and play games; you can carry even your Contacts cards and Calendar appointments with you with aplomb. (For the lowdown on iPod, peruse Chapter 2 of this minibook.) I should also mention that the iPad and iPhone offer the same functionality as the iPod (although they don't function as an external hard drive).

iTunes

To help you wrangle your enormous digital music and movie collection, Apple offers iTunes (see Figure 1-2). For starters, iTunes is a sophisticated audio player for all your digital audio files. But iTunes is also handy for converting audio tracks from audio CDs to a number of popular digital audio file formats, such as AAC and MP3. After you import or convert your music into computer files, iTunes helps you manage and maintain your music collection. You can even listen to streaming online radio stations 24 hours a day, as well as rent or buy videos, TV shows, and movies, either on your Mac, your iPhone or iPad, or on your video-capable iPod.

Figure 1-2:
With iTunes, you can buy music and video from the iTunes Store.

Plus, Apple throws in the iTunes Store, where you can preview hundreds of thousands of songs, TV shows, movies, and videos for up to 90 seconds each without spending a dime. (Podcast subscriptions and the first-class courseware available through iTunes U are usually free, bucko.) If you latch onto something that you'd like to buy, you can use your credit card to purchase and download your media (either as individual tracks or as a complete album or movie for a package price). After the media that you've bought is comfortably nestled in iTunes, you can play it on your Mac, burn music to an audio CD, or download it to your iPod, iPhone, or iPad.

iMovie

You needn't restrict yourself to still images: Hook up your digital camcorder to your Mac as well. Use *iMovie,* the video-editing application shown in Figure 1-3, to create and edit digital movies with ease.

With stunning video-editing candy such as transitions, sound effects, and video effects, iMovie turns your home movies into professional productions that you'll be proud to share with friends and family. Finally, you can have a home-movie night without putting everyone to sleep. (Don't forget to produce a professional-looking movie trailer for your vacation video!)

Figure 1-3: iMovie can turn you into Hollywood material — let's do lunch.

GarageBand

Imagine the freedom to create your own original music by simply dragging "digital instruments" onto a canvas . . . and then adding your own voice or the lead instrument! After the basic melody is in place, you'd want to be able to edit whatever you like, or even choose different instruments with the click of a mouse. As recently as ten years ago, dear reader, that concept was indeed just a dream. Then, software-based synthesizers and mixing applications brought musicians into the digital age. (The problem was that normal human beings couldn't afford the expensive software or the sample libraries of literally thousands of different instruments.) With the addition of GarageBand, however, the iLife suite provides everything you need to start making your own music (inexpensively) and then create MP3 files, ringtones, podcasts, or burn your own audio CDs. And believe me, if I can create a techno track that hit the speakers at a local dance club, *you* can, too!

Can I Use All This Stuff at One Time?

What makes the digital hub idea even juicier is that it's an *interoperable* model. Pause a sec to appreciate that. (What, you don't speak *engineer?* No problem!) In plain English, the digital hub allows you to use digital media from one part of the hub with another part of the hub. Thus, the individual parts of the digital hub can work together to complement each other. To illustrate, consider some digital-sharing scenarios:

✦ **You shoot a great photograph of your kids and store it in iPhoto.** It's so great that you want to use it as the title screen of your family's home movie. With the digital hub, you can use that same photograph in iMovie to create your home flick. One image just worked its way through three parts of the digital hub.

✦ **You just recorded a catchy song with GarageBand.** You add the song to the soundtrack of the music video that you're creating with iMovie. Then you create a fancy opening menu and upload that video to YouTube!

✦ **Your band becomes popular and starts to play some impressive gigs.** To document your band's rise to stardom, your friend films a concert with a DV camcorder. You use iMovie to transfer the video to your Macintosh and create clips of your favorite performances of the concert. After that, it's a simple matter to extract the audio from the video for use as an MP3 with iTunes, and grab an image from the video for a band scrapbook that you're creating with iPhoto. Oh, and don't forget the band podcast that you created with GarageBand, ready for distribution on your website. Now you've attained honest-to-goodness DHH (short-hand for *Digital Hub Heaven*). You've traversed the entire hub, easily sharing the media along the way.

Lest I forget, I should mention the other advantage of the digital hub: The media that you swap between all your "iApplications" *remains in digital form*, which is A Good Thing! In the previous example of shooting a concert, for instance, that concert footage remained practically pristine while it was being converted to MP3, pasted into your iPhoto album, or uploaded to YouTube. (Because some audio and video formats, such as MP3, are *compressed* to save space, a purist will argue that you lost a little something. It ain't much.) Unlike with archaic analog VHS tape, you don't have to worry about whether your source is second generation — and you can forget degradation and that silly tracking control. Make as many copies as you like of that band video, because the last one will look as good as the first!

Chapter 2: Browsing Your Library with iTunes and iBooks

In This Chapter

✔ Playing music with your Mac

✔ Arranging and organizing your music collection

✔ Tuning into the world with Internet radio

✔ Sharing your songs across a network

✔ Creating eye candy with Visualizer

✔ Reading e-books on the Mac

✔ Turning any electronic book into an audiobook

✔ Buying the good stuff from the iTunes and iBook Stores

Good news! Every installation of OS X comes with an unbeatable combination: *iTunes,* the finest stereophonic gadget in town, and *iBooks,* an easy-to-use electronic book reader. With iTunes, you can listen to your favorite songs and podcasts, organize your music collection, watch video or a full-length movie, listen to radio stations from around the world, buy music and video online, burn CDs and DVDs, and much more! In no time, you'll be pondering how much new speakers with a subwoofer will cost for your Mac. With iBooks, you can share your e-books across your iOS devices, and even listen as your Mac reads your e-books out loud!

In this chapter, I show you how to enjoy audio, video, and the written word, and you discover how to use your iTunes Library and iBooks Library to get one-click access to any song, movie, or book in your collection. I even show you how to enjoy free online lectures and educational presentations, as well as how to buy the latest hits and best-sellers from the iTunes Store.

What Can 1 Play on iTunes?

Simply put, iTunes is a media player that plays audio and video files. These files can be in any of many different formats. Some of the more common audio formats that iTunes supports are

- ✦ **MP3:** The small size of MP3 files has made them popular for file trading on the Internet. You can reduce MP3 files to a ridiculously small size (albeit at the expense of audio fidelity), but a typical CD-quality, three-minute pop song in MP3 format has a size of 3–5MB.

- ✦ **AAC:** Advanced Audio Coding is an audio format that's similar to MP3. AAC files typically offer better recording quality at the same file sizes. However, this format is less compatible with non-Apple MP3 players and software. (Luckily, you can still burn AAC tracks to an audio CD, just as you can MP3 tracks.) The tracks that you download from the iTunes Store are in AAC format.

    The iTunes Store's *iTunes Plus* tracks are also in AAC format, and encoded at a higher-quality 256 Kbps rate — hence, their higher price.

- ✦ **Apple Lossless:** Another format direct from Apple, *Apple Lossless* format provides the best compromise between file size and sound quality. These tracks are encoded without loss of quality although Apple Lossless tracks are somewhat larger than AAC. This format is generally the favorite of discerning audiophiles.

- ✦ **AIFF:** This standard Macintosh audio format produces sound of the absolute highest quality. This high quality, however, also means that the files are pretty doggone huge. AIFF recordings typically require about 10MB per minute of audio.

- ✦ **WAV:** Not to be outdone, Microsoft created its own audio file format (WAV) that works much like AIFF. It can reproduce sound at higher quality than MP3, but the file sizes are very large, similar in size to AIFF files.

- ✦ **CD audio:** iTunes can play audio CDs. Because you don't usually store CD audio anywhere but on an audio CD, file size is no big whoop — but once again, 10MB of space per minute of music is a good approximation.

- ✦ **MP2:** A close cousin of the far more popular MP3 format, MP2 is the preferred format in radio broadcasting and is a standard audio format for HDV camcorders. It produces file sizes similar to MP3 format.

- ✦ **Movies and video:** You can buy and download full-length movies, TV shows, music videos, and movie trailers from the iTunes Store . . . and, with an Apple TV unit connected to your home theater system, you can watch those movies and videos from the comfort of your sofa on the other side of your living room (or even from your bedroom on the other side of your house).

- ✦ **Podcasts:** These audio downloads are like radio programs for your iPod, but iTunes can play and organize them, too. Some podcasts include video and photos to boot.

- ✦ **iTunes U:** iTunes offers educational materials (think slideshows, presentations, and class recordings) from a wide variety of colleges and technical institutions — and virtually all free for the download.

✦ **Ringtones:** iPhone owners, rejoice! iTunes automatically offers to create ringtones for your iPhone (and iPad and iPod touch) from the tracks you bought from the iTunes Store or tunes you composed. You can even use these ringtones on your Mac, with the FaceTime and Messages applications.

✦ **Audiobooks:** No longer do you need cassettes or audio CDs to enjoy your spoken books. iTunes can play them for you, or you can send them to your iPod for listening on the go.

✦ **Streaming Internet radio:** You can listen to a continuous broadcast of songs from one of tens of thousands of Internet radio stations, with quality levels ranging from what you'd expect from FM radio to the full quality of an audio CD. You can't save the music in iTunes, but streaming radio is still great fun. (I run my own station . . . more on MLC Radio later in this chapter.)

Playing an Audio CD

Playing an audio CD in iTunes is simple. Just insert the CD in your Mac's optical drive, start iTunes by clicking its icon on the Dock, and click the Play button. (Note that your Mac might be set to automatically launch iTunes when you insert an audio CD.) The iTunes interface resembles that of a traditional cassette or CD player. The main playback controls of iTunes are Play, Previous, Next, and the Volume slider, as shown in Figure 2-1.

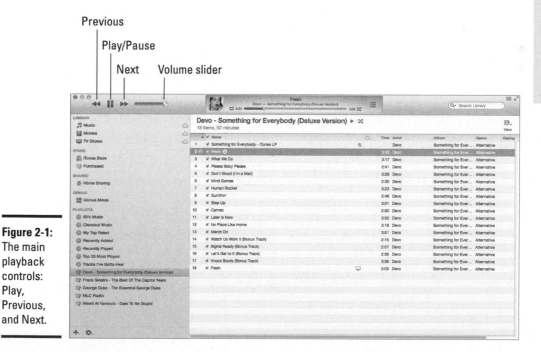

Previous
Play/Pause
Next   Volume slider

Figure 2-1:
The main
playback
controls:
Play,
Previous,
and Next.

Click the Play button to begin listening to a song. While a song is playing, the Play button toggles to a Pause button. As you might imagine, clicking that button again pauses the music. If you don't feel like messing around with a mouse or trackpad, you can always use the keyboard. The spacebar acts as the Play and Pause buttons. Press the spacebar to begin playback; press it again to stop.

Click the Next button to advance to the next song on the CD. The Previous button works like the Next button but with a slight twist: If a song is currently playing and you click the Previous button, iTunes first returns to the beginning of the current song (just like an audio CD player). To advance to the previous song, double-click the Previous button. To change the volume of your music, click and drag the volume slider.

As with other Macintosh applications, you can control much of iTunes with the keyboard. Table 2-1 lists some of the more common iTunes keyboard shortcuts.

Table 2-1	Common iTunes Keyboard Shortcuts
Press This Key Combination	*To Do This*
Spacebar	Play the currently selected song if iTunes is idle.
Spacebar	Pause a playing song.
→	Advance to the next song.
←	Go back to the beginning of a song. Press a second time to return to the previous song.
⌘+↑	Increase the volume of the music.
⌘+↓	Decrease the volume of the music.
⌘+Option+↓	Mute the audio if any is playing. Press again to play the audio.

Playing Digital Audio and Video

In addition to playing audio CDs, iTunes can play the digital audio files that you download from the Internet or obtain from other sources in the WAV, AAC, Apple Lossless, AIFF, MP2, and MP3 file formats.

Enjoying a digital audio file is just slightly more complicated than playing a CD. After downloading or saving your audio files to your Mac, open Finder and navigate to wherever you stored the files. Then simply drag the music files (or an entire folder of music) from Finder to the Music entry in the iTunes Source list, which appears in the iTunes sidebar at the left side of the window. The added files appear in the Music section of your iTunes Library. You can also drag a song file from a Finder window and drop it on the iTunes icon on the Dock, which adds it to your Music Library as well.

If the sidebar at the left side of the iTunes window isn't displayed as it is in Figures 2-1 and 2-2, click View➪Show Sidebar, or press ⌘+Option+S.

If you drop the file on top of a playlist name in the Source list, iTunes adds it to that particular *playlist* as well as the main Library. (More about playlists in a bit.)

Think of the Library as a master list of your audio and video media. To view the Music Library, select the Music entry in the left column of the iTunes player, as shown in Figure 2-2. (Go figure.) In a similar manner, you can view your movies and TV shows by clicking their entries in the Source list — right now, however, the focus is on music, so I'll discuss playing video in more depth later in the chapter.

To play a song, just double-click it in the Music list. Alternatively, you can use the playback controls (Play, Previous, and Next) that I discuss earlier in this chapter (refer to Figure 2-1).

Music entry   Source list

Figure 2-2:
The Music Library keeps track of all your audio files.

Playlist

The Source list of iTunes can list up to eight possible sources for music:

✦ **Library:** This section contains Music, Movies, TV Shows, Podcasts, Books, iTunes U, Apps (for iPhone and iPad), Ringtones (for iPhone), iPod Games, and Radio. (Think *Internet radio,* which I discuss further in the section "Internet Radio.")

✦ **Store:** I discuss this music source later, in the section "Buying Digital Media the Apple Way."

✦ **Shared:** If another Mac on your local network is running iTunes and is set to share part or all of its library, you can connect to the other computer for your music. (Shared music on another Mac appears as a separate named folder in the Source list.)

✦ **Devices:** If an iPod is connected, it appears in the list. (And yes, Virginia, other models of MP3 players from other companies will also appear in the list if they are supported in iTunes.) If you connect an iPhone or iPad to your Mac, it'll show up here as well.

✦ **Genius:** Click the Genius heading and then click the Turn On Genius button to allow iTunes to automatically create playlists from songs in your iTunes Music Library. You can also allow Genius to recommend music, movies, and TV shows based on the titles you already have in your iTunes Library. (More on this feature later in the chapter.)

✦ **Audio CD:** A standard audio CD . . . anything from the Bee Gees to Death Cab for Cutie will show up in the Source list if you load the CD into your optical drive.

✦ **Home Sharing:** You can turn on Home Sharing to share your Mac's media library across your wireless network with up to five other Mac computers, as well as iPhones, iPads, and the iPod touch. (More on Home Sharing later in this chapter.)

✦ **Playlists:** Think of playlists as folders you use to organize your music. (More on playlists later in this chapter.)

If you've invested in an Apple TV, it appears in the list as well, allowing iTunes to share media with your Apple TV, which in turn sends it to your ED- (enhanced definition) or HD- (high definition) TV.

Notice also that the Library lists information for each song that you add to it, such as

✦ **Name:** The title of the song

✦ **Time:** The length of the song

✦ **Artist:** The artist who performs the song

✦ **Album:** The album on which the song appears

If any song you're adding doesn't display anything for the title, album, or artist information, don't panic; most MP3 files have embedded data that iTunes can read. If a song doesn't include any data, you can always add the information to these fields manually. I show you how later, in the section "Setting or changing the song information manually."

Clicking any column heading in the Library list causes iTunes to reorder the Library according to that category. For example, clicking the Name column heading alphabetizes your Library by song title. I often click the Time heading to sort my Library according to the length of the songs. Oh, and you can drag column titles to reorder them any way you like (as long as the Name column remains at the far left).

You can browse your Music Library in a number of ways: first, click the Music Library entry in the Source list to select it. By default, the application uses the *songs* mode (refer to Figure 2-1), where each song is one entry. A click on the second mode button sorts your library into tracks by *album*. Click the third mode button (at the top of the iTunes window) to group tracks together by *artist*. Click the fourth mode button, and you're browsing by musical *genres*. (You can also view your iTunes Radio and Internet Radio stations, or see your iTunes Match library in iCloud — all three of these modes require an Internet connection, and I cover them later in the chapter.)

Browsing the Library

After you add a few dozen songs to iTunes, viewing the Library can become a task. Although a master list is nice for some purposes, it becomes as cumbersome as an elephant in a subway tunnel if the list is very long. To help out, iTunes can display your Library in another format, too: namely, browsing mode. To view the Library in browsing mode, click the View menu, hover your cursor over the Column Browser item, and click Show Browser. (Keyboard mavens can simply press the ⌘+B keyboard shortcut to switch to browsing mode.)

The Browse mode of iTunes displays your library in a compact fashion, organizing your tunes into up to five sections:

✦ Genres

✦ Artists

✦ Albums

✦ Composers

✦ Groupings

Selecting an artist from the Artist list causes iTunes to display that artist's albums in the Album list. Select an album from the Album list, and iTunes displays that album's songs in the bottom section of the Browse window.

(Those Apple software designers . . . always thinking of you and me.) You can also specify which sections you want included in Browse mode from the View⇨Column Browser menu item — click a section name to toggle the display of that section on or off.

Finding songs in your Music Library

After your collection of audio files grows large, you might have trouble locating that Swedish remix version of "I'm Your Boogie Man." To help you out, iTunes has a built-in Search function. To find a song, type some text into the search field of the main iTunes window. While you type, iTunes tries to find a selection that matches your search text. The search is thorough, showing any matching text from the artist, album, song title, and genre fields in the results. For example, if you type **Electronic** into the field, iTunes might return results for the band named *Electronic* or other tunes that you classified as *electronic* in the Genre field. (The section "Know Your Songs," later in this chapter, tells you how to classify your songs by genre, among other options.) Click the magnifying glass at the left side of the Search field to restrict the search even more: by Artists, Albums, Composers, and Songs.

Removing old music from the Library

After you spend some time playing songs with iTunes, you might decide that you didn't *really* want to add 40 versions of "Louie Louie" to your Library. (I prefer either the original or the cast from the movie *Animal House*.) To remove a song from the Library, click the song to select it and then press the Delete key on your keyboard.

You can also remove a song from the Library by dragging it to the Trash on the Dock.

Will I trash my Count Basie?

Novice iTunes users, take note: iTunes watches your back when you trash tracks.

To illustrate: Suppose you delete a song from the Library that's located only in the iTunes music folder (which you didn't copy into iTunes from another location on your hard drive). That means you're about to delete the song entirely, and there'll be no copy remaining on your Mac. Rest assured, though, that iTunes prompts you to make sure that you really want to move the file to the Trash. (I get fearful e-mail messages all the time from readers who are loath to delete anything from iTunes because they're afraid they'll trash their digital music files completely.)

Remember: If you delete a song from the Library that *also* exists elsewhere on your hard drive (outside the reach of the iTunes music folder), it isn't deleted from your hard drive. If you mistakenly remove a song that you meant to keep, just drag it back into iTunes from Finder, or even from the Trash. 'Nuff said.

Watching video

Watching video in iTunes is similar to listening to your music. To view your video collection, click the Movies or TV Shows entries in the Source list. iTunes displays your videos as thumbnails or in cover flow view. Music videos appear as a smart playlist. (Read more about these in the sidebar, "Some playlists are smarter than others.")

From your collection, you can

+ Double-click a video thumbnail or an entry in the list.

+ Drag a QuickTime–compatible video clip from the Finder window to the iTunes window. (These clips typically include video files ending in .mov, .mv4, or .mp4.)

iTunes plays video in the box below the Source list or in full-screen mode, depending on the settings you choose from the View⇨Video Playback menu item. In full-screen mode, move your mouse to display a control strip at the bottom of the screen, sporting the standard slider bar that you can drag to move through the video (as well as a volume control and Fast Forward/Reverse buttons). You can also pause the video by clicking the Pause button.

Keeping Slim Whitman and Slim Shady Apart: Organizing with Playlists

As I mention earlier, the iTunes Music Library can quickly become a fearsomely huge beastie. Each Library can contain thousands upon thousands of songs: If your Library grows anywhere near that large, finding all the songs in your lifelong collection of Paul Simon albums is *not* a fun task. Furthermore, with the Library, you're stuck playing songs in the order that iTunes lists them.

To help you organize your music into groups, use the iTunes playlist feature. A *playlist* is a collection of some of your favorite songs from the Library. You can create as many playlists as you want, and each playlist can contain any number of songs. Whereas the Library lists all available songs, a playlist displays only the songs that you add to it. Further, any changes that you make to a playlist affect only that playlist, leaving the Library untouched.

To create a playlist, you can do any of the following:

+ **Choose File⇨New⇨Playlist.**

+ **Press ⌘+N.**

✦ **Choose File⇨New⇨Playlist from Selection.** This creates a new playlist and automatically adds any tracks that are currently selected.

✦ **Right-click a song and click Create Genius Playlist from the menu that appears.** iTunes builds a playlist of songs that are similar in some way (typically by matching the genre of the selection or the beats per minute, but also based on recommendations from other iTunes members). Note that your Mac needs an Internet connection to create a Genius playlist, and the larger your music library the longer it will take iTunes to build your playlist. You'll also need to turn on the Genius feature by clicking Store⇨Turn on Genius and entering your Apple ID. (Note that Genius playlists can sometimes mix tracks containing explicit content with less objectionable material — especially in the comedy and rap genres.)

✦ **Drag a folder containing audio files from a Finder window onto the Playlists heading.**

✦ **Click the New button in the iTunes window (the plus sign button in the lower-left corner) and choose New Playlist.** You get a newly created empty playlist (the toe-tappin' *untitled playlist*).

All playlists appear in the Source list. To help organize your playlists, it's a good idea to . . . well, *name* them. (Aren't you glad now that you have this book?) For example, suppose that you want to plan a party for your polka-loving friends. Instead of running to your computer after each song to change the music, you could create a polka-only playlist. Select and start the playlist at the beginning of the party, and you won't have to worry about changing the music the whole night. (You can concentrate on the accordion.) To load a playlist, select it in the Source list; iTunes displays the songs for that playlist.

iTunes can display a playlist in three ways. By default, the application uses the List view, in which each song is one entry. You can click the View pop-up menu at the upper right of the iTunes window and choose Grid to group tracks together by album artwork. Finally, you can choose the Artist List view to quickly display playlists by artist.

The same song can appear in any number of playlists because the songs in a playlist are simply pointers to songs in your Music Library — not the songs themselves. Add and remove them at will to or from any playlist, secure in the knowledge that the songs remain safe in the Library. Removing a playlist is simple: Select the playlist in the Source list and then press Delete.

Removing a playlist does not delete any songs from your Library.

Some playlists are smarter than others

Click the File menu, and you'll see the New Smart Playlist menu command. You can also create a new smart playlist by clicking the Add button (a plus sign) at the bottom of the Source list.

The contents of a *smart playlist* are automatically created from a specific condition or set of conditions that you set via the Smart Playlist dialog: You can limit the track selection by mundane things, such as album, genre, or artist; or you can get funky and specify songs that were played last, or by the date you added tracks, or even by the sampling rate or total length of the song. For example, iTunes can create a playlist packed with songs that are shorter than three minutes, so you can fill your iPod Shuffle with more stuff! If you want to add another criterion, click the plus sign at the right side of the dialog and you get another condition field to refine your selection even further.

You can choose the maximum songs to add to the smart playlist, or limit the size of the playlist by the minutes or hours of play or the number of megabytes or gigabytes the playlist will occupy. (Again, great for automatically gathering as much from your KISS collection that will fit into a specific amount of space on a CD or your iPod.) Mark the Live Updating check box for the ultimate in convenience. iTunes automatically maintains the contents of the smart playlist to keep it current with your conditions at all times in the future. (If you remove tracks manually from a smart playlist, iTunes adds other tracks that match your conditions.)

Now think about what all these settings mean when combined . . . *whoa.* Here's an example yanked directly from my own iTunes library. I created a smart playlist that selects only those songs in the Rock genre. It's limited to 25 songs, selected by least often played, and live updating is turned on. The playlist is named Tracks I've Gotta Hear because it finds the 25 rock songs (from my collection of more than 7,000 songs) that I've heard least often! After I listen to a song from this smart playlist, iTunes automatically "freshens" it with another song, allowing me to catch up on the tracks I've been ignoring.

Know Your Songs

Besides organizing your music into Elvis and non-Elvis playlists, iTunes gives you the option to track your music at the song level. Each song that you add to the Music Library has a complete set of information associated with it. iTunes displays this information (see upcoming Figure 2-3) on the Info tab, including

✦ **Name:** The name of the song

✦ **Artist:** The name of the artist who performed the song

✦ **Album Artist:** The name of the artist responsible for a compilation or tribute album

✦ **Album:** The album where the song appears

✦ **Grouping:** A group type that you assign

✦ **Composer:** The name of the astute individual who *wrote* the song

✦ **Comments:** A text field that can contain any comments on the song

✦ **Genre:** The classification of the song (such as rock, jazz, or pop)

✦ **Year:** The year the artist recorded the song

✦ **Track Number:** The position of the song on the original album

✦ **Disc Number:** The original disc number in a multi-CD set

✦ **BPM:** The beats per minute (indicates the song's tempo)

You can display this information by clicking a song name and pressing ⌘+I. The fields appear on the Info tab.

Setting the song information automatically

Each song that you add to the iTunes Music Library might have song information included with it. If you add music from a commercial audio CD, iTunes connects to a server on the Internet and attempts to find the information for each song on the CD. If you download a song from the Internet, it often comes with some information embedded in the file already; the amount of included information depends on what the creator supplied. (And believe me, it's often misspelled as well — think *Leenard Skeenard*.) If you don't have an Internet connection, iTunes can't access the information and displays generic titles instead.

Setting or changing the song information manually

If iTunes can't find your CD in the online database or someone gives you an MP3 with incomplete or inaccurate information, you can change the information yourself — believe me, you want at least the artist and song name! To view and change the information for a song, perform the following steps:

1. **Select the song in either the Music Library list or a playlist.**

2. **Press ⌘+I or choose File⇨Get Info.**

3. **Edit the song's information on the Info tab, as shown in Figure 2-3.**

The more work you put into setting the information of the songs in your Music Library, the easier it is to browse and use iTunes. Incomplete song information can make it more difficult to find your songs in a hurry. If you prefer, you don't have to change all information about a song (it just makes life easier later if you do). Normally, you can get away with setting only a song's title, artist, and genre. The more information you put in, however, the faster you can locate songs and the easier they are to arrange. iTunes tries to help by automatically retrieving known song information, but sometimes you have to roll up your sleeves and do a little work. (Sorry, but some things just can't be automated.)

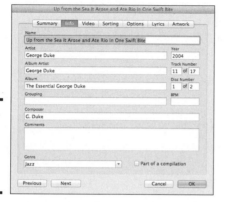

Figure 2-3:
View and edit song information here.

"What about cover art, Mark?" Well, I'm overjoyed that you asked! iTunes can try to locate artwork automatically for the tracks you select. (Note that embedding large images can significantly increase the size of the song file.) Follow these steps:

1. **Select the desired songs from the track list.**

2. **Choose File⇨Library⇨Get Album Artwork.**

You can set iTunes to automatically attempt the addition of album artwork every time you rip tracks from an audio CD, or when you add songs without artwork to your Music Library. Click iTunes and choose Preferences; then click the Store button and select the Automatically Download Album Artwork check box. (By the way, if you buy tracks or an album from the iTunes Store, Apple includes album covers automatically!)

Want to manually add album covers to your song info? If you select just one song in the track list, display the Info dialog and click the Artwork tab. If you select multiple songs from the same album, display the Info dialog. Now launch Safari, visit Amazon.com, and do a search on the same album (or search an online artwork library, such as AllCDCovers.com). Drag the cover image from the web page right into the Info dialog, and drop it on top of the "sunken square" Artwork image well. When you click OK, the image appears in the Summary pane, and you can display it while your music is playing by pressing ⌘+G, or by clicking the Show or Hide Song Artwork button at the lower left of the iTunes window.

Ripping Audio Files

You don't have to rely on Internet downloads to get audio files: You can create your own MP3, AAC, Apple Lossless, AIFF, and WAV files from your audio CDs with iTunes. The process of converting audio files to different formats is *ripping.* (Audiophiles with technical teeth also call this process *digital extraction,* but they're usually ignored at parties by the popular crowd.) Depending on what hardware or software you use, each has its own unique format preferences.

The most common type of ripping is to convert CD audio to MP3 (or AAC) format. To rip MP3s from an audio CD, follow these simple steps:

1. **Launch iTunes by clicking its icon on the Dock.**

   Alternatively, you can locate iTunes in your Applications folder or in Launchpad.

2. **Choose iTunes⇨Preferences.**

3. **In the Preferences window that appears, click the General toolbar button.**

4. **Click the Import Settings button that appears at the bottom of the Preferences dialog.**

5. **Choose MP3 Encoder from the Import Using pop-up menu.**

6. **Choose High Quality (160 Kbps) from the Setting pop-up menu and then click OK to return to the Preferences dialog; then click OK again to return to iTunes.**

   This bit rate setting provides the best compromise between quality (it gives you better than CD quality, which is 128 Kbps) and file size (tracks you rip will be significantly smaller than audiophile bit rates such as 192 Kbps or higher).

7. **Load an audio CD into your Mac's optical drive.**

   The CD title shows up in the iTunes Source list (under the Devices heading), which is on the left side of the iTunes window. The CD track listing appears on the right side of the window.

If iTunes asks you whether you want to import the contents of the CD into your Music Library, you can click Yes and skip the rest of the steps; however, if you've disabled this prompt, just continue with the remaining two steps.

8. **Clear the check box of any song that you don't want to import from the CD.**

   All songs on the CD have a check box next to their title by default. Unmarked songs aren't imported. The Browse button changes to Import CD.

9. **Click the Import CD button.**

Tweaking the Audio for Your Ears

Besides the standard volume controls that I mention earlier in this chapter, iTunes offers a full equalizer. An *equalizer* permits you to alter the volume of various frequencies in your music, allowing you to boost low sounds, lower high sounds, or anything in between.

To open the Equalizer, choose Window⇨Equalizer or Press ⌘+Option+2. Use the leftmost slider (Preamp) to set the overall level of the Equalizer. The remaining sliders represent various frequencies that the human ear can perceive. Setting a slider to a position in the middle of its travel causes that frequency to play back with no change. Move the slider above the midpoint to boost that frequency; conversely, move the slider below the midpoint to reduce the volume of that frequency.

Continue adjusting the equalizer sliders until your music sounds the way you like it. In case you prefer to leave frequencies to the experts, the iTunes Equalizer has several predefined settings to match most musical styles. Open the pop-up menu at the top of the Equalizer window to choose a genre. When you close the Equalizer window, iTunes remembers your settings until you change them again.

A New Kind of Radio Station

Besides playing back your favorite audio files, iTunes can also tune in Internet radio stations from around the globe. You can listen to any of a large number of preset stations, seek out lesser-known stations not recognized by iTunes, or even add your favorite stations to your playlists. You can also use the new iTunes Radio feature to create a custom station dedicated to just the genres and artists you prefer. This section shows you how to do it all.

What's with the numbers next to the station names?

When choosing an Internet radio station, keep your Internet connection speed in mind. If you're using a broadband DSL or cable connection — or if you're listening at work over your company's high-speed network — you can listen to stations broadcasting at 128 Kbps (or even higher). The higher the bit rate, the better the music sounds.

At 128 Kbps, for example, you're listening to sound that's as good as an audio CD.

However, if you're listening over a dial-up modem connection, iTunes can't keep up with audio streaming at higher bit rates, so you're limited to stations broadcasting at 56 Kbps or lower.

Internet Radio

Although it's not a radio tuner in the strictest sense, iTunes can locate virtual radio stations all over the world that send audio over the Internet — a process usually dubbed *streaming*. iTunes can track down hundreds of Internet radio stations in a variety of styles with only a few mouse clicks.

To begin listening to Internet radio with iTunes, click the Internet button located at the top of the window. The result is a list of more than 20 types of radio stations, organized by genre.

When you expand an Internet category by clicking its disclosure triangle, iTunes queries a tuning server and locates the name and address of dozens of radio stations for that category. Whether you like Elvis or not-Elvis (those passing fads, such as new wave, classical, or alternative), something's here for everyone. The Internet also offers news, sports, and talk radio.

After iTunes fetches the names and descriptions of radio stations, double-click one that you want to hear. iTunes immediately jumps into action, loads the station, and begins to play it.

Tuning in your own stations

Although iTunes offers you a large list of popular radio stations on the web, it's by no means comprehensive. Eventually, you might run across a radio station that you'd like to hear, but don't find listed in iTunes. Luckily, iTunes permits you to listen to other stations, too. To listen to a radio station that iTunes doesn't list, you need the station's web address.

In iTunes, choose Advanced⇨Open Stream (or press ⌘+U). In the Open Stream dialog that appears (as shown in Figure 2-4), enter the URL of your desired radio station and then click OK. In seconds, iTunes tunes in your station.

Figure 2-4:
Tuning into
MLC Radio,
my Internet
radio
station.

Radio stations in your playlists

If you find yourself visiting an online radio station more than once, you'll be glad to know that iTunes supports radio stations in its playlists. To add a radio station to a playlist from the Radio list, do the following:

1. **Open the category that contains the station you want to add to your playlist.**

2. **Locate the station that you want to add to your playlist and drag it from the Radio list to the desired playlist on the left.**

If you haven't created any playlists yet, see the section "Keeping Slim Whitman and Slim Shady Apart: Organizing with Playlists" earlier in this chapter to find out how.

Adding a radio station that doesn't appear in the Radio list is a bit trickier but possible nonetheless. Even though iTunes allows you to load a radio station URL manually by using the Open Stream command in the File menu, it doesn't give you an easy way to add it to the playlist. Follow these steps to add a specific radio station to a playlist:

1. **Add any radio station from the Radio list to your desired playlist.**

Any station in the list will do, as you'll immediately change both the station's URL and name to create your new station entry in the playlist.

2. **Press ⌘+I or choose File⇨Get Info to bring up the information dialog for that station.**

3. **Click the Summary section and change the URL by clicking the Edit URL button.**

4. **Enter the desired URL (refer to Figure 2-4) and click OK.**

5. **Click the Info tab, type the new station name, and then click OK.**

Have an itch to hear "Kung Fu Fighting"?

This particular technology author has a preference for a certain hot jam spot: *MLC Radio,* the Internet radio station I've been running for several years now. I call my station a '70s Time Machine because it includes hundreds of classic hits from 1970–1979, inclusive. You hear everything from "Rock and Roll Hoochie Koo" by Rick Derringer to "Moonlight Feels Right" by Starbuck. (Hey, I'm summing up a decade here, so be prepared for both Rush and the Captain and Tennille.) The station broadcasts at 128 Kbps (audio CD quality), so you need a broadband connection to listen. For the radio's Internet address or help connecting to MLC Radio, visit my website at `www.mlcbooks.com` — and then follow the steps in the "Radio stations in your playlists" section to add MLC Radio to your playlists!

Creating a custom radio station

The recent addition of i*Tunes Radio* makes it possible for you to listen to the artists, songs, and genres that you prefer in iTunes, without selecting a specific Internet radio station! To use iTunes Radio, click the Radio button at the top of the iTunes window, and then type the artist name, song name or genre you'd like to add to your station.

As you download new music from the iTunes Store (and add new artists and genres in iTunes Radio), the service learns more about your musical tastes and can automatically play and recommend new music, much like the Genius feature I discuss earlier in this chapter.

Like Internet radio, the iTunes Store, and Apple's iTunes Match subscription service, iTunes Radio requires an Internet connection and an Apple ID.

Your iTunes Radio station is automatically shared among all of your Macs running OS X Mavericks or later (as well as any devices you own running iOS 7 or later).

iTunes and iCloud Together

iTunes is connected closely with Apple's iCloud service, allowing you to share music betwixt all of your Macs and iOS devices. But how do you pull your audio and video out of that floating nimbus? Try this: Sign in with your Apple ID, select your Music Library in the Source list, and then click View⇨Show Music in the Cloud. Bam! All the audio and video that you've purchased from the iTunes Store appears in your Library. Note, however, that those items don't exist on your local drive — consider those entries as placeholders for the stuff you can download, allowing you to see (and search for) what's available through iCloud. (And, if you've purchased as much from the iTunes Store as I have, you'll save many, many gigabytes of storage space on your Mac's drive by just downloading certain songs.)

To download a local copy of any iCloud item, simply click the iCloud icon next to the item. After the local copy has been saved to your Mac's drive, the iCloud icon disappears and you're ready to listen or watch your purchase.

To hide the iCloud placeholder entries from your Library and display just the stuff you've got on your Mac's drive, click View⇨Hide Music in the Cloud.

Apple's iTunes Match subscription service builds on this same functionality, allowing you to store *all* your music in iCloud (including the songs you've ripped from audio CDs and downloaded from other sources) and listen to it on any of your Macs or iOS devices! When you join iTunes Match, all the songs that aren't available from the iTunes Store are automatically uploaded to iCloud.

At the time of this writing, the service is $25 a year and is limited to a maximum of 10 devices and 25,000 songs (note that purchases you make from the iTunes Store don't count toward that 25,000 song limit).

To subscribe to iTunes Match or manage your Match storage, click the Match button at the top of the iTunes window.

Sharing Your Media across Your Network

Ready to share your music, podcasts, and video — *legally*, mind you — with other folks on your local network? You can offer your digital media to other iTunes users across your home or office. Follow these steps:

1. **Choose iTunes⇨Preferences to open the Preferences dialog.**

2. **Click Sharing.**

3. **Select the Share My Library on My Local Network check box.**

4. **Specify whether you want to share your entire library or only selected playlists and files.**

   Sharing selected playlists is a good idea for those Meatmen and Sex Pistols fans who work at a cubicle farm in a big corporation.

5. **If you want to restrict access to just a few people, select the Require Password check box; then type a password in the text box.**

6. **Click OK.**

Your shared folder appears in the Source list for all iTunes users who enable the Shared Libraries check box on the General pane of their iTunes Preferences dialog. Note that the music you share with others can't be imported or copied, so everything stays legal.

Want to change that frumpy default name for your shared media library to something more exotic, like "Dan's Techno Beat Palace"? No problem — display the Preferences dialog again, click the General button and click in the Library Name text box. Edit your network entertainment persona to your heart's content.

You can also share your media library using *Home Sharing*, which allows up to five devices to join in the fun — including both Mac computers and iOS devices (your iPad, iPhone, and iPod touch, running iOS 4.3 or later). Home Sharing requires a network connection for all your devices, and you'll have to enter the same Apple ID information on each device — Book I, Chapter 3 contains information about creating your Apple ID. To turn on Home Sharing in iTunes, click File on the iTunes menu, hover your cursor over the Home Sharing submenu, and choose Turn On Home Sharing. (Don't forget to repeat this setup on each computer.) After Home Sharing is enabled, shared libraries will appear in the Source list under the Shared heading.

Sending music elsewhere with AirPlay

If you're using an AirPort Express portable wireless Base Station, you can ship your songs right to your Base Station from iTunes, and from there to your home stereo or boombox! Pick up an AirPlay-enabled sound system, and you can eliminate the stereo or boombox and the AirPort Express device entirely. (I get into some serious discussion of AirPort Express in Book VI, Chapter 3.)

After your AirPort Express Base Station is plugged in and you connect your home stereo (or a boombox or a pair of powered stereo speakers) to the stereo minijack on the Base Station, you see a Speakers pop-up list button appear at the bottom of the iTunes window. (If the Speakers button doesn't appear, choose iTunes⇨Preferences to open the Preferences dialog and then click the Devices button on the toolbar. Make sure that the Allow iTunes Audio Control from Remote Speakers check box is enabled.)

Click the Speakers button, and you can choose to broadcast the music you're playing in iTunes across your wireless network. Ain't technology truly *grand*?

Burning Music to Shiny Plastic Circles

Besides being a great audio player, iTunes is adept at creating CDs, too. iTunes makes the process of recording songs to a CD as simple as a few mouse clicks. Making the modern version of a compilation (or *mix*) tape is easier than getting a kid to eat ice cream. iTunes lets you burn CDs in one of three formats:

✦ **Audio CD:** This format is the typical kind of commercial music CD that you buy at a store. Most typical music audio CDs store up to 800MB of data, which translates into about 80 minutes of music.

✦ **Data CD or DVD:** A standard CD-ROM or DVD-ROM is recorded with the audio files. This disc can't be played in any standard audio CD player (even if it supports MP3 CDs, which I discuss next). Therefore, you can listen to these songs only by using your Mac and an audio player, such as iTunes or a PC running Windows.

✦ **MP3 CD:** As does the ordinary computer CD-ROM that I describe, an MP3 CD holds MP3 files in data format. However, the files are arranged in such a way that they can be recognized by audio CD players that support the MP3 CD format (especially boomboxes, DVD players, personal CD players, and car stereos). Because MP3 files are so much smaller than the digital audio tracks found on traditional audio CDs, you can fit as many as 160 typical four-minute songs on one disc. These discs can also be played on your Mac via iTunes.

Keep in mind that MP3 CDs aren't the same as the standard audio CDs that you buy at the store, and you can't play them in older audio CD players that don't support the MP3 CD format. Rather, this is the kind of archival disc that you burn at home for your own collection or for use in a CD/DVD player or car audio system that supports MP3 discs.

To begin the process, build a playlist (or select an existing playlist that you want to record). If necessary, create a new playlist and add to it whatever songs you would like to have on the CD. (See the earlier section, "Keeping Slim Whitman and Slim Shady Apart: Organizing with Playlists," if you need a refresher.) With the songs in the correct order, right-click the playlist and choose Burn Playlist to Disc to commence the disc-burning process. Click the desired recording format (again, usually Audio CD) in the Burn Settings dialog that appears.

To save yourself from sonic shock, I always recommend that you enable the Sound Check check box before you burn. iTunes adjusts the volume on all the songs on your audio CD so that they play at the same volume level.

Ready to go? Click Burn and load the blank disc. iTunes lets you know when the recording is complete.

Feasting on iTunes Visuals

By now, you know that iTunes is a feast for the ears, but did you know that it can provide you with eye candy as well? With just a click or two, you can view mind-bending graphics that stretch, move, and pulse with your music.

To begin viewing iTunes visuals, choose View⇨Show Visualizer (or press ⌘+T). Immediately, most of your iTunes interface disappears and begins displaying groovy lava lamp–style animations (like, *sassy,* man). To stop the visuals, choose View⇨Hide Visualizer (or press ⌘+T again). The usual sunny aluminum face of iTunes returns.

You can also change the viewing size of the iTunes visuals in the View menu. From the View menu item, choose Full Screen (or press ⌘+Control+F). To escape from the Full Screen mode, click or press Esc.

You can still control iTunes with the keyboard while the visuals are zooming around your screen. See Table 2-1 earlier in this chapter for a rundown on common keyboard shortcuts.

Exercising Parental Authority

Do young children use your Mac? I'll be honest here: A large amount of content in the iTunes Store, including audio, movies, and even apps, is stuff that I don't consider suitable for kids. And what about the media that others in the family may decide to share? Such is the world we live in today, and the good folks at Apple recognize that you may not want to inadvertently allow your kids to have access to explicit content.

Luckily, you can use the Parental settings in iTunes to build a secure fence around content that's for grown-ups only. Heck, you can even banish items from the Source list entirely. Figure 2-5 illustrates the Parental Preferences pane in the iTunes Preferences dialog.

You must log in with an Administrator account to change these settings, just like with the Parental Controls in the System Preferences dialog. If the settings are *locked* — the padlock icon at the bottom of the dialog is closed — click it and supply your administrator password to unlock them. (Read more about Parental Controls in Book II, Chapter 5.)

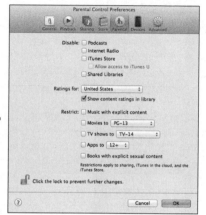

Figure 2-5:
Protect
your kids
from explicit
content.

To enable parental control, follow these steps:

1. **Choose iTunes➪Preferences.**

2. **Click the Parental tab.**

3. **Select any of the Disable check boxes to prevent access to those features.**

Disabling features in iTunes applies to *all* user accounts — no matter who is logged in! You'll notice that any features you disable disappear completely from the Source list at the left side of the iTunes window after you click OK at the end of these steps.

4. **Click the Ratings For pop-up menu and choose your country.**

Because Apple maintains separate iTunes Stores for different nations, you can choose which country's iTunes Store to monitor. If you like, you can disable the display of content ratings in your iTunes library by deselecting the Show Content Ratings in Library check box.

5. **To restrict specific content in the iTunes Store, select the check box next to the source, and then make choices from the corresponding pop-up menu to choose the restriction level.**

Note that these restrictions apply only to content in the iTunes Store and media shared with your Mac. Content in your iTunes library is never restricted.

6. **Click the padlock icon at the bottom of the dialog to close it and prevent any changes.**

7. **Click OK.**

Buying Digital Media the Apple Way

The hottest spot on the Internet for buying music and video is the iTunes Store, which you can reach from the cozy confines of iTunes. (That is, as long as you have an Internet connection. If you don't, it's time to turn the page to a different chapter.)

Click the iTunes Store item in the Source list, and after a few moments, you're presented with the latest offerings. Click a link in the store list to browse according to media type, or click the Power Search link to search by song title, artist, album, or composer. The Back and Forward buttons at the top of the iTunes Store window operate much the same as those in Safari, moving you backward or forward in sequence through pages you've already seen. Clicking the Home button (which, through no great coincidence, looks like a miniature house) takes you back to the Store's main page.

To display the details on a specific album, track, video, podcast, or audiobook (whew), just click it. If you're interested in buying just certain tracks (for that perfect road warrior mix), you get to listen to 90 seconds of any track — for free, no less, and at full sound quality. To add an item to your iTunes Store shopping cart, click the Add Song/Movie/Album/Video/Podcast/Audiobook button (sheesh!). When you're ready to buy, click the Shopping Cart item in the Source list and then click the Buy Now button. (At the time of this writing, tracks are usually 99 cents a pop, and an entire album is typically $9.99 . . . what a bargain!)

The iTunes Store creates an account for you based on your e-mail address, and it keeps secure track of your payment information for future purchases. After you use the iTunes Store once, you rarely have to log in or retype your credit card information again.

The tracks and files that you download are saved to a separate playlist called Purchased. After the download is finished, you can play them, copy them to other playlists, burn them to CD or DVD, share 'em over your network, or ship them to your iOS devices using iCloud, just as you can any other item in your iTunes Library.

iTunes can automatically download the media you purchase on another iCloud device (including another Mac and your iPhone, iPad, or iPod touch). To set up automatic downloading, choose iTunes⇨Preferences to open the Preferences dialog, and then click the Store tab. After you're signed in at the iTunes Store, you can choose to download music or app purchases, and you have the option to check for new downloads automatically. Click OK to save your changes.

Reading the Electronic Way

Before we wave goodbye to the happy residents of iTunes Central, I won't forget to mention that Mavericks introduces Mac owners to iBooks, the electronic book (or *e-book*) reading application that owners of the iPhone, iPad, and iPod touch have enjoyed for some time. Like iTunes, iBooks stores the books that you purchase from the iBook Store in iCloud, but you can download and read any of your books on any of your Macs or iOS devices that can run a version of iBooks.

Figure 2-6 illustrates my iBooks Library, with each thumbnail representing a different book cover. (The books that currently reside only in iCloud have an iCloud icon at the top-right corner of the thumbnail.) To download a local copy of a book, just click the cover.

iBook Store   Library view modes   Search box

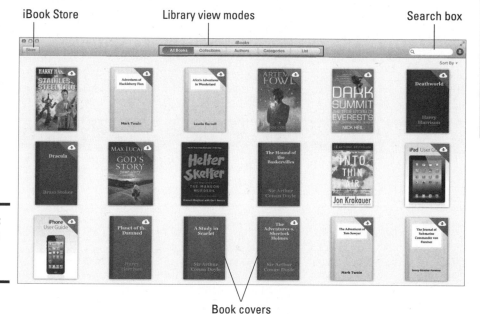

Figure 2-6:
My iBooks
Library
screen.

Book covers

At the top of the Library, you'll see buttons that enable you to display your library by collection, author, or category, or you can choose to list them. To search for a specific title, click in the Search box and type the text to match. To display the iBook Store and purchase more books, click the Store button on the left side of the Library toolbar.

After a book has been downloaded, you can open it and start reading by double-clicking the cover. iBooks displays pages across the full width of the application window, but you can display the iBooks toolbar you see in Figure 2-7 at any time — just move your cursor to the top of the iBooks window.

I prefer to read in full-screen mode. To enter full-screen mode, you can click the familiar double-arrow icon at the top right corner of the iBooks window, press ⌘+Control+F, or click View⇨Enter Full Screen. While the application is in full-screen mode, you can still display the iBooks toolbar by moving your cursor to the top of the window. To return to a windowed display, press Esc or click the double-arrow icon again.

Interested in reading two pages at once? Click View⇨Two Pages, or press ⌘+2. Press ⌘+1 to return to a single page of text.

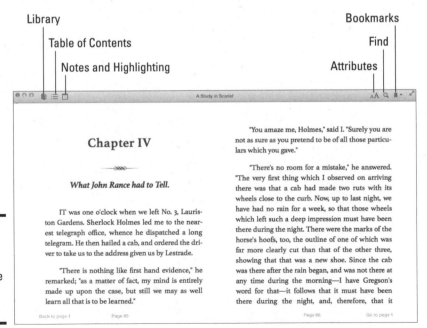

Library

Table of Contents

Notes and Highlighting

Bookmarks

Find

Attributes

Figure 2-7: Sherlock Holmes comes alive again in iBooks.

Navigating through your e-books

Turning pages in iBooks is as simple as pressing the left and right arrow keys (to move to the previous page or the next page, respectively). You can also click the arrows that appear at center of the left and right margins of the page (when you hover your cursor over those margins).

Ah, but iBooks gives you far more control over your reading than simply turning pages! You can

✦ **Display the table of contents:** Click the Table of Contents icon on the iBooks toolbar to display a pop-up list, and then click the desired chapter to start reading at that point.

✦ **Move by chapter:** Press ⌘+Shift+→ to skip ahead to the beginning of the next chapter, and ⌘+Shift+← to return to the beginning of the previous chapter.

✦ **Use a bookmark:** To add a bookmark for the current page, click the Bookmark icon on the far right side of the iBooks toolbar or press ⌘+D. After you've set a bookmark, you can return to it by clicking the down arrow next to the Bookmark icon and then clicking the desired bookmark. Your bookmarked pages are also synced automatically through iCloud. And if you open the same book on another Mac or another iOS device, iBooks automatically displays the page you were last reading! (This feature requires an Internet connection. Go figure.)

✦ **Find text:** Click the Find icon on the toolbar, click Edit⇨Find, or press ⌘+F to display the Find Search box. Type the desired words (without pressing Return) and iBooks displays a Spotlight-style list with all the matches. Click the desired match to jump to that spot in the book.

Tweaking the appearance of your e-book

You're stuck with the appearance of each page in a traditional printed volume, but in the world of e-books, dear reader, you can make changes to the

✦ Size of the onscreen font

✦ Color of the page background

✦ Font used to display text on the page

To view and change these attributes, click the Appearance icon on the iBooks toolbar (which bears two *A* characters). Note that any changes you make to the pop-up list affect the display of *all* your electronic books.

You can click the Notes icon on the iBooks toolbar to add highlights and notes to important passages — students, are you listening? Select the desired text, and then choose a highlight color from the pop-up dialog that appears or click Add Note to create a free-form text note. (Notes are indicated by yellow squares in the margin at the point you've selected in the text, but the Notes panel must be open for you to view the note you made.) From that same pop-up dialog, you can also copy the selected text, search the web or Wikipedia for a match, or share the text with others via Facebook or Twitter.

Turning any book into an audiobook

As I mention earlier in the chapter, you can purchase audiobooks from the iTunes Store and listen to them in iTunes just like any other audio. However, you can use a neat trick in iBooks to enable your Mac to read any book in your iBooks Library aloud! (The result won't be as smooth and polished as a professionally produced audiobook but it is *free* — just forgive your Mac if it stumbles over the occasional acronym or foreign language phrase.)

Open your book to the desired chapter, and then click Edit⇨Speech⇨Start Speaking. (Make sure that no text is currently selected.) To stop the reading, click Edit⇨Speech⇨Stop Speaking.

Buying new titles

Apple's iBook Store is similar in form and function to the iTunes Store. From the Library window, click the Store button, and then browse to your heart's content. You can choose a specific category using the Category pop-up list box at the right side of the window, under the Quick Links section.

Click a thumbnail to view a description of the book. From the screen you see in Figure 2-8, you can click Get Sample to download for free a few pages of the book, which appear in your iBooks Library with the word *Sample* on the thumbnail. Click Ratings and Reviews to read what others have said about this book, or peruse other books by the author by clicking the author's link under the title.

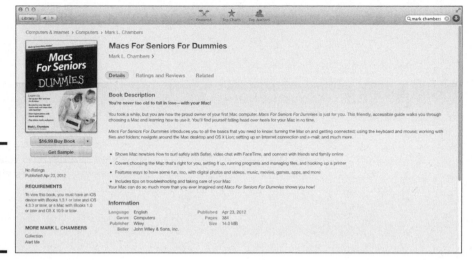

Figure 2-8:
Browsing
the iBook
Store for
some new
reading.

When you're ready to buy, click the Buy Book button — easier (and more convenient) than visiting your local brick-and-mortar bookstore!

**Book III
Chapter 2**

Browsing Your
Library with
iTunes and iBooks

Chapter 3: Focusing on iPhoto

*F*or years, the Macintosh has been the choice of professional photographers for working with digital images — not surprising, considering the Mac's graphical nature. Apple continues this tradition with *iPhoto,* its photography tool for the home user that can help you organize, edit, and even publish your photographs. (It sports more features than a handful of Swiss army knives.) After you shoot your photos with a digital camera, you can import them into iPhoto, edit them, and publish them. You're not limited to photos that you take yourself, either; you can edit, publish, and organize all kinds of digital image files. You can even create a photo album and use the iPhoto interface to order a handsome soft- or hard-bound copy shipped to you, or create a slideshow that you can upload to YouTube.

In this chapter, I walk you through an overview of what iPhoto can do. After that, I give you a brief tour of the controls in iPhoto so that you can see what features are available to you, including those for managing, printing, and publishing your photos.

Delving into iPhoto

In Figure 3-1, you can see most of the major controls offered in iPhoto. (Other controls automatically appear when you enter different modes; I cover them in upcoming sections of this chapter.)

Source list

Full Screen

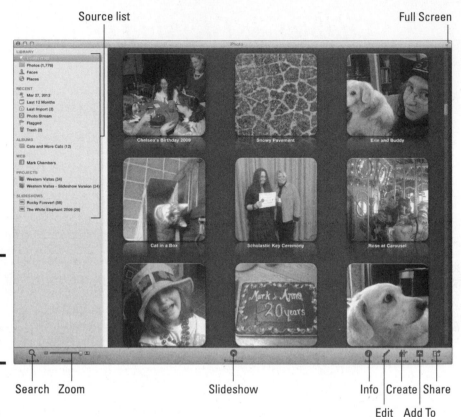

Figure 3-1:
iPhoto
greets you
with an
attractive
window.

Search Zoom

Slideshow

Info Create Share

Edit Add To

Although I cover these controls and sections of the window in more detail in the following sections, here's a quick rundown of what you're looking at when you first launch iPhoto:

✦ **Source list:** This list of image locations determines which photos iPhoto displays.

- You can choose to display either your entire image library or just the last set of digital images that you download from your camera.

- You can create new *albums* of your own that appear in the Source list; albums make it much easier to organize your photos.

- Photos can be grouped by *event* (when they were taken), *faces* (which appear in the photos), and *places* (where photos were taken).

- You can view the photos you've shared online using Facebook and Flickr.

- Photos synced with your iOS devices (such as your iPhone and iPad) appear in *Photo Stream*.

- You can create books, calendars, cards, and slideshows.

✦ **Viewer:** This pane displays the images from the currently selected photo source.

You can drag or click to select photos in Viewer for further tricks, such as assigning keywords and image editing.

✦ **Full Screen:** Click this button in the upper-right corner of the iPhoto window to switch to a full-screen display of your photos. In full-screen mode, the Source list disappears, and both images and events appear as thumbnails. You can double-click a thumbnail to view the image (or the contents, if it's an event) using your Mac's entire screen real estate. You can also use the same controls that I discuss later in this chapter for chores such as sharing and editing images; the toolbar is still available at the bottom of the screen.

✦ **Search:** Click the Search button to display the Search text box. Click in the Search box and start typing to locate photos by specific criteria or by description and title.

✦ **Zoom:** Drag this slider to the left to reduce the size of the thumbnails in Viewer. This allows you to see more thumbnails at one time, which is a great boon for quick visual searches. Drag the slider to the right to expand the size of the thumbnails, which makes it easier to differentiate details between similar photos in Viewer.

✦ **Play Slideshow:** Select an event, an album, a book, or a slideshow in the Source list (or multiple images you've selected in Viewer) and click this button to start a full-screen slideshow using those images.

✦ **Info:** Click this button to display information about the currently selected photos (or the item selected in the Source list).

✦ **Edit:** Click this button to edit the selected photos. (I cover editing in depth later in this chapter.)

✦ **Create:** Click this button to add a new blank album, book, calendar, card, or slideshow to your Source list.

✦ **Add To:** Click this button to add the currently selected photos to an existing album, slideshow, book, card, or calendar.

✦ **Share:** Click this button to share the currently selected photos on Flickr or Facebook as well as those from your other iOS devices via Photo Stream, if you're using Apple's iCloud feature. You can also order prints or e-mail the photos.

The toolbar buttons you see depend on which operation you're performing. For example, you see different toolbar buttons when you're editing a photo.

Working with Images in iPhoto

Even a superbly designed image display and image-editing application such as iPhoto would look overwhelming if everything were jammed into one window. Thus, Apple's developers provide different operational modes (such as editing and book creation) that you can use in the one iPhoto window. Each mode allows you to perform different tasks, and you can switch modes at just about any time by clicking the corresponding toolbar button.

In this section, I discuss three of these modes — import, organize, and edit — and what you can do when you're in them. Then I conclude the chapter with sections on publishing and sharing your images.

Import images 101

In *import* mode, you're ready to download images directly from your digital camera — as long as your specific camera model is supported in iPhoto. You can find out which cameras are known to be supported by visiting the Apple iPhoto support page at www.apple.com/support/iphoto. And you're not limited to cameras, of course: You can also import photos from a memory card reader (such as the SD or SDXC card slots sported by most current Macs, or even a Kodak PhotoCD).

Follow these steps to import images:

1. **Connect your digital camera to your Mac.**

   Plug one end of the camera's USB cable into your camera and the other end into your Mac's USB port.

2. **Prepare your camera to download images.**

   The procedure for downloading images varies by camera, but the process usually involves turning the camera on and choosing a Download or PC mode. Check your camera's user guide for details.

3. **Launch iPhoto.**

   Your Mac will probably launch iPhoto automatically when your camera is detected, but you can always launch iPhoto manually by clicking its icon on the Dock (or in your Applications folder or from Launchpad).

4. **Type an event name for the imported photos, such as** Birthday Party **or** Godzilla Ravages Tokyo.

5. **To allow iPhoto to automatically separate images into separate events based on the date they were taken, select the Split Events check box.**

6. **Click the Import All button to import your photographs from the camera.**

   To select specific images to import, hold down the ⌘ key and click each desired photo; click Import Selected instead of Import All. The images are added to your Photo Library, where you can organize them as you want.

   Depending on the camera, iPhoto may also import video clips.

7. **Specify whether the images you're importing should be deleted from the camera afterward.**

   If you don't expect to download these images again to another computer or another device, you can choose to delete the photos from your camera automatically. This saves you a step, frees space for new photos, and helps eliminate the guilt that can crop up when you nix your pix. (Sorry, I couldn't resist.)

"What's that about an event, Mark?" After you download the contents of your digital camera, those contents count as a virtual *event* in iPhoto — based on either the date that you imported them or the date they were taken. (Yet another reason to set your camera's internal clock!) For example, you can always display the last images you imported by clicking Last Import. If you want to see photos from your son's graduation, they appear as a separate event. (Events and Last Import both appear in the Source list.) Think about that . . . it's pretty tough to arrange old-fashioned film prints by the moment in time that they document, but iPhoto makes it easy for you to see just which photos are part of the same group! I explain more about events in the next section.

Here are four methods of organizing photos: by albums (which you may be familiar with from older versions of iPhoto), events, faces, and places.

Importing stored images

Adding images stored on your hard drive, a CD, a DVD, an external drive, or a USB flash drive is easy. If images are in a folder, just drag that folder from a Finder window and drop it into the Source list in the iPhoto window. iPhoto automatically creates a new album using the folder name, and you can sit back while the images are imported into that new album. iPhoto recognizes images in several formats: JPEG, GIF, RAW, PNG, PICT, PSD, PDF, and TIFF.

For individual images, drag and drop them as well. Select the images in a Finder window and drag them into the desired album in the Source list. To add them to the album displayed in Viewer, drag the selected photos and drop them in Viewer instead.

If you'd rather import images by using a standard Mac Open dialog, choose File⇔Import to Library. Simplicity strikes again!

Organize mode: Organizing and sorting your images

In the days of film prints, you could always stuff another shoebox with your latest photos or buy another sticky album to expand your library. Your digital camera, though, stores images as files instead, and many folks don't print their digital photographs. Instead, you can keep your entire collection of digital photographs and scanned images well ordered and easily retrieved by using iPhoto's *organize* mode. Then you can display them as a slideshow, print them to your system printer, order prints online, use them as Desktop backgrounds, or burn them to an archive disc.

A new kind of photo album

The most familiar method of organizing images in iPhoto is the album. Each album can represent any division you like, be it a year, a vacation, your daughter, or your daughter's ex-boyfriends. Follow these steps:

1. **Create a new album.**

You can either choose File⇨New Album (as shown in Figure 3-2) or press ⌘+N. iPhoto creates a new entry under the Albums heading in the Source list.

2. **Type the name for your new photo album.**

3. **Press Return.**

Figure 3-2: Add a new album in iPhoto.

iPhoto also offers a special type of album — a smart album — which you can create from the File menu (or from the keyboard by pressing Option+⌘+N). A *smart album* contains only photos that match certain criteria that you choose, including the keywords and rating that you assign to your images. Other criteria include text in the photo filenames, dates the images were added to iPhoto, and any comments you might have added as well as camera-specific data such as ISO and shutter speed. Now here's the really nifty angle: iPhoto *automatically* builds and maintains smart albums for you, adding new photos that match the criteria and deleting those that you remove from your Photo Library (as well as removing the photos that no longer match the smart album's criteria)! Smart albums' icons carry a gear symbol in the Source list.

You can display information about the currently selected item in the information pane at the far right of the window. Just click the Info button at the bottom of the iPhoto window, which sports the familiar "*i*-in-a-circle" logo. You can also type a short note or description in the Description box that appears in the Info pane, or add keywords to help you organize your photos.

You can also change information on an image by selecting it in Viewer and clicking the Info button. Click the Title heading in the pane and you can simply click in the box to type a new value.

You can drag images from Viewer into any album you choose. For example, you can copy an image to another album by dragging it from Viewer to the desired album in the Source list.

To remove a photo that has fallen out of favor, follow these steps:

1. **In the Source list, select the desired album.**

2. **In Viewer, select the photo (click it) that you want to remove.**

3. **Press Delete.**

When you remove a photo from an album, you *don't* remove the photo from your collection (which is represented by the Photos entry under the Library heading in the Source list). After all, an album is just a group of links to the images in your collection. To remove the offending photo from iPhoto, click the Photos entry under the Library heading to display your entire collection of images and delete the picture there. (This step removes the photo from any albums and projects that might have contained it as well.)

To remove an entire album from the Source list, just click it in the Source list to select it — in Viewer, you can see the images that it contains — and then press Delete. (Alternatively, right-click or Control-click the offending album and then choose Delete Album from the contextual menu.)

To rename an album, click the entry under the Albums heading in the Source list to select it and then click again to display a text box. Type the new album name and press Return.

Change your mind? Daughter's ex is back in the picture, so to speak? iPhoto comes complete with a handy-dandy Undo feature. Just press ⌘+Z, and it's as though your last action never happened. (A great trick for those moments when you realize you just deleted your only image of your first car.)

Arranging stuff by events

As I mention earlier, events are essentially a group of images that you shot or downloaded at the same time — iPhoto figures that those images belong together (which is usually a pretty safe assumption). Figure 3-3 illustrates some events I created in my iPhoto collection.

An event can be renamed, just as an album can — but you use a different procedure. Click the Events entry under the Library heading in the Source list to display your events in Viewer; click the existing event name in the caption below the thumbnail. A text box appears in which you can type a new name; click Return to update the event.

Figure 3-3: Events help you organize by what happened, not just when it happened!

Although a photo can appear in multiple albums, it can appear in only one event.

Try moving your cursor over an event thumbnail in Viewer, and you'll see that iPhoto displays the date range when the images were taken, as well as the total number of images in the event. Ah, but things get *really* cool when you move your cursor back and forth over an event with many images. The thumbnail animates and displays all the images in the event! (Why can't I think of this stuff? This is the future, dear readers.)

To display the contents of an event in Viewer, just double-click the event thumbnail. To return to the events thumbnails, click the All Events button at the top of Viewer.

Decided to merge those Prom event pictures with your daughter's Graduation event? No problem! You could drag one event thumbnail on top of another, but that's the easy way. Alternatively, click the Events entry under the Library heading in the Source list to display your events and then hold down ⌘ while you click the events that you want to merge. Heck, if the events you want to merge are selected, right-click one of them and choose Merge Events from the menu that appears; then click Merge in the confirmation dialog.

Whilst organizing, you can create a brand-new empty event by choosing Events⇨Create Event. Feel free to drag photos from albums, other events, or your Photo library into your new event.

Working with faces and places

iPhoto includes two organizational tools: Faces and Places. These two categories appear in the Library section of the Source list.

Putting names to faces

First, tackle Faces. (Well, don't literally tackle anyone's face, dear reader.) Faces is a sophisticated recognition system that automatically recognizes human faces in the photos that you add to your Library. (I don't know whether it works well with pets — but you can try, anyway.) You have to identify, or *tag*, faces before iPhoto can recognize them.

To tag a face, follow these steps:

1. **In the Source list, click the Photos item to display your image library.**

2. **In Viewer, click the photo with a person you want to tag.**

The photo is selected, as indicated by the yellow border.

3. **Click the Info button on the iPhoto toolbar at the bottom of the window.**

   iPhoto displays the Info pane you see in Figure 3-4.

4. **In the Faces section of the Info pane, click the Add a Face link.**

   Note that iPhoto has indicated each person's face in the photo with a label. If a face has already been tagged, the label will match the person's face.

5. **Choose a name option, depending on whether the face is recognized, unrecognized, or incorrectly identified:**

   • If iPhoto recognizes the face correctly and the name matches the person, click the check mark to confirm the tag.

   • If the face is unrecognized (labeled as Click to Name), click the label to open a text box and type the person's name.

   • If the face is incorrectly identified, click the X at the right of the text box and enter a new name.

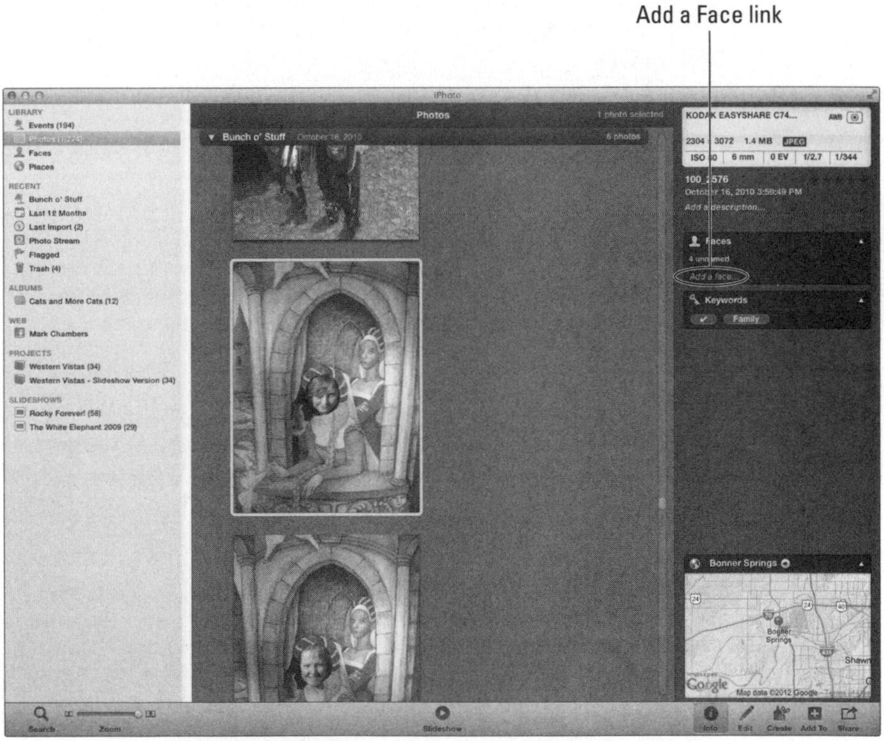

Add a Face link

Figure 3-4:
Adding another mug to my collection of faces. (That *still* doesn't sound right.)

If the name appears on a Contacts contact card — or is recognized as one of your Facebook friends — you can click the matching entry that appears to confirm the identity. Wowzers!

To delete a Face recognition box that isn't necessary, hover your cursor over the box and click the X button that appears at the top-left corner of the box.

If iPhoto doesn't recognize the face at all in the photo (which can happen if the person's face is turned at an angle to the camera, or is in a darker area of the photo), click the box border and drag the box over the person's face. If necessary, you can resize the box using the four handles at the corner of the box. Now you can click the label and type the person's name.

6. **After you've finished identifying faces in the photo, click the Info button to hide the Info pane.**

After you tag an image, it appears in your Faces collection, which you can view by clicking the Faces entry in the Source list. You can double-click a portrait in your Faces collection to see all the images that contain that person.

Notice the Confirm Additional Faces button that appears next to the person's name? Click it, and iPhoto displays other photos that may contain this person's face, allowing you to tag the person there as well. If a face is a match, click the thumbnail to confirm it.

As you might expect, the more tags you add for a specific person, the better iPhoto gets at recognizing that person!

Putting photos in their Places

Places makes it easy to track the location where photos were taken. For iPhoto to track location without your help, however, your digital camera must include GPS tracking information in the image metadata. (This feature is a relatively new one for digital cameras, so older models aren't likely to support GPS tracking.) Places also requires an Internet connection because it uses Google Maps.

Click the Places entry in the Source list to display a global map, with push-pins indicating where your photos were taken. You can switch the Places map between terrain and satellite modes, or choose a hybrid display. If you're familiar with Google Maps, these settings are old friends of yours.

If you click a specific photo (that includes location information) to select it and then click the Info button, you'll see a close-up map of the location where the photo was taken.

Alternatively, click the text Location buttons at the top of the map to display a character-based browser, where you can click country, state, city, and place names.

No matter which view mode you choose, clicking a pushpin or location displays the images taken in that area.

Organizing with keywords

"Okay, Mark, albums, events, faces, and places are great ideas, but there has to be a way to search my collection by category!" Never fear, good Mac owner. You can also assign descriptive *keywords* to images to help you organize your collection and locate certain pictures fast. iPhoto comes with a number of standard keywords, and you can create your own as well.

To illustrate, suppose you'd like to identify your images according to special events in your family. Birthday photos should have their own keyword, and anniversaries deserve another. By assigning keywords, you can search for Elsie's sixth birthday or your silver wedding anniversary (no matter what event or album they're in), and all related photos with those keywords appear like magic! (Well, *almost* like magic. You need to choose View⇨Keywords, which toggles the Keyword display on and off in Viewer.)

You're gonna need your own keywords

I'll bet you take photos of other things besides just kids and vacations — and that's why iPhoto allows you to create your own keywords. Display the iPhoto Keywords window by pressing ⌘+K, click the Edit Keywords button, and then click Add (the button with the plus sign). iPhoto adds a new unnamed keyword to the list as an edit box, ready for you to type its name.

You can rename an existing keyword from this same window, too. Click a keyword to select it and then click Rename. Remember, however,

that renaming a keyword affects *all the images that were tagged with that keyword.* That might be confusing when, for example, photos originally tagged as Family suddenly appear with the keyword Foodstuffs. (I recommend applying a new keyword and deleting the old one if this problem crops up.)

To change the keyboard shortcut assigned to a keyword, click the Shortcut button. To remove an existing keyword from the list, click the keyword to select it and then click the Delete button, which bears a minus sign.

iPhoto includes a number of keywords:

✦ Favorite

✦ Family

✦ Kids

✦ Vacation

✦ Birthday

✦ RAW

✦ Photo Booth

✦ Movie

✦ Checkmark

What's the Checkmark all about, you ask? It's a special case: Adding this keyword displays a tiny check mark icon in the bottom-right corner of the image. The *checkmark* keyword comes in handy for temporarily identifying specific images because you can search for just your check-marked photos.

To assign keywords to images (or remove keywords that have already been assigned), select one or more photos in Viewer. Choose Window➪Manage My Keywords or press ⌘+K to display the Keywords window, as shown in Figure 3-5.

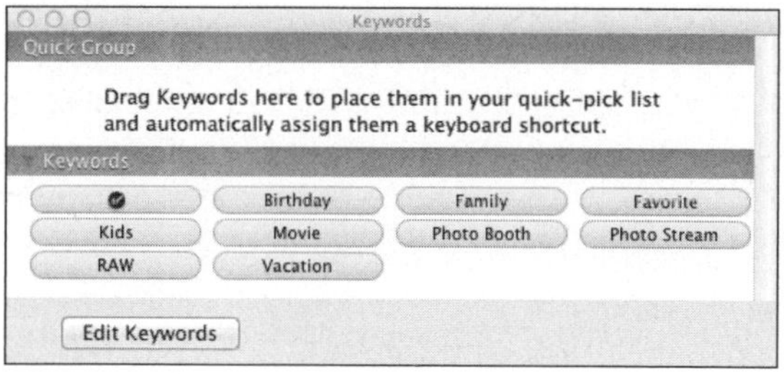

Figure 3-5:
Time to add keywords to these selected images.

Keywords
Quick Group
Drag Keywords here to place them in your quick-pick list and automatically assign them a keyboard shortcut.

Keywords			
⊘	Birthday	Family	Favorite
Kids	Movie	Photo Booth	Photo Stream
RAW	Vacation		

Edit Keywords

Click the keyword buttons that you want to attach to the selected images to mark them. Or click the highlighted keyword buttons that you want to remove from the selected images to disable them.

Drag the keyword buttons that you use the most to the Quick Group section of the Keywords window, and iPhoto automatically creates a keyboard shortcut for each keyword in the Quick Group. Now you don't even need to display the Keywords window to get business done!

Digging through your library with keywords

Behold the power of keywords! To sift through your entire collection of images by using keywords, click the Search button on the toolbar, and then click the magnifying glass button next to the Search box and choose Keyword from the pop-up menu. iPhoto displays a pop-up Keywords panel, and you can click one or more keyword buttons to display just the photos that carry those keywords.

The images that remain in Viewer after a search must have *all* the keywords that you specified. If an image is identified, for example, by only three of four keywords you choose, it isn't a match and it doesn't appear in Viewer. (You can create a smart album with specific keywords to get around this limitation — use *any* instead of *all* as the argument.)

To search for a photo by words in its description, just click in the Search box and start typing. You can also click that same magnifying glass by the Search box to search through your images by date and rating as well.

Speaking of ratings. . . .

Playing favorites by assigning ratings

Be your own critic! iPhoto allows you to assign any photo a rating of anywhere from zero to five stars. I use this system to help me keep track of the images that I feel are the best in my library. Select one image (or more) and then assign a rating using one of the following methods:

- ✦ Choose Photos⇨My Rating and then choose the desired rating from the pop-up submenu.
- ✦ Hover your cursor over the photo and click the More button that appears in the lower-right corner of the thumbnail, and then click the desired star rating in the menu that appears.
- ✦ Use the ⌘+0 through ⌘+5 shortcuts.

Sorting your images just so

The View menu provides an easy way to arrange your images in Viewer by a number of different criteria. Choose View⇨Sort Photos and then click the desired sort criteria from the pop-up submenu. You can arrange the display by date, keyword, title, or rating. If you select an album in the Source list, you can also choose to arrange photos manually, which means that you can drag and drop thumbnails in Viewer to place them in the precise order you want them.

Edit mode: Removing and fixing stuff the right way

Not every digital image is perfect — just look at my collection if you need proof. For those shots that need a pixel massage, iPhoto includes a number of editing tools that you can use to correct common problems.

The first step in any editing job is to select the image you want to fix in Viewer. Then click the Edit button on the iPhoto toolbar to display the Edit mode controls at the right side of the window, as shown in Figure 3-6. Now you're ready to fix problems, using the tools that I discuss in the rest of this section. (If you're editing a photo that's part of an event, an album, faces, or places, note the spiffy scrolling photo strip at the bottom, which allows you to switch to another image to edit from the same grouping.)

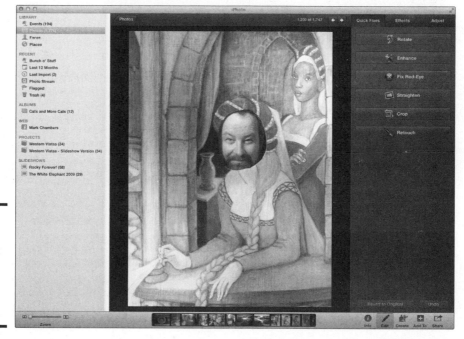

Book III Chapter 3

Focusing on iPhoto

Figure 3-6: iPhoto is now in edit mode — watch out, image problems!

If you'd prefer to edit images with more of your screen real estate, click the Full Screen button at the upper-right corner of the iPhoto window (refer to Figure 3-1). To switch back to the standard window arrangement, press Esc.

Need more features than iPhoto provides when editing a prized photograph? iPhoto even allows you to specify another image-editing application such as Photoshop Elements (in addition to the built-in editing controls that I cover in this section). First, choose iPhoto⇨Preferences⇨ Advanced. From the Edit Photos pop-up menu, opt for Choose App. Navigate to the image editor you want to use, select it, and click Open. Close the Preferences dialog, and iPhoto will automatically open the application you select when you click the Edit button. If you decide to return to iPhoto's built-in editing controls, just open the Advanced pane again, open the Edit Photos pop-up menu again, and choose In iPhoto.

When you're done with Edit mode, click the Edit button again to return to Viewer.

When you first enter editing mode, the Quick Fixes tab is selected, providing you with the tools I've already covered. (These are the changes you'll make most often, so having Quick Fixes as the default selection makes sense.) However, you can also choose to apply an effect from the Effects tab, or to make specific changes to the appearance of an image from the Adjust tab.

Rotating tipped-over shots

If an image is in the wrong orientation and needs to be turned to display correctly, click the Rotate button to turn it once in a counterclockwise direction. Hold down the Option key while you click the Rotate button to rotate in a clockwise direction.

Find yourself using that Option key often when rotating? Consider reversing the default direction. Choose iPhoto⇨Preferences, click the General tab, and then select the Rotate radio button to change the default direction.

While you're editing, you can use the Next and Previous buttons at the left of the tab button to move to the next image in the current group (or back to the previous image).

Crop 'til you drop

Does that photo have an intruder hovering around the edges of the subject? You can remove some of the border by *cropping* an image, just as folks once did with film prints and a pair of scissors. (We've come a long way.) With iPhoto, you can remove unwanted portions from the edges of an image; it's a great way to get Uncle Milton's stray head (complete with toupee) out of an otherwise perfect holiday snapshot.

Follow these steps to crop an image:

1. **Click the Crop button on the Edit toolbar.**

2. **Select the portion of the image that you want to keep.**

In Viewer, click and drag the handles on the rectangle to outline the part of the image that you want. Remember, whatever's outside this rectangle disappears after the crop is completed.

When you drag a corner or edge of the outline, a semi-opaque grid (familiar to amateur and professional photographers as the nine rectangles from the Rule of Thirds) appears to help you visualize what you're claiming. (Check it out in Figure 3-7.)

You can expand the outline to the full dimensions of the image at any time — just click the Reset button.

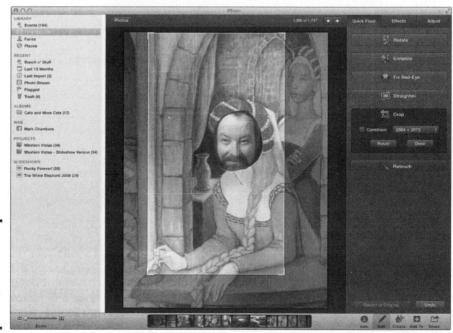

Figure 3-7:
Select the stuff that you want to keep in your photo.

**Book III
Chapter 3**

**Focusing
on iPhoto**

3. **(Optional) Choose a preset aspect ratio.**

   If you want to force your cropped selection to a specific aspect ratio — such as 4 x 3 or 16 x 9 for an iMovie project — select the Constrain check box and select that ratio from the Constrain pop-up menu.

4. **Click the Done button.**

   Oh, and don't forget that you can use iPhoto's Undo feature if you mess up and need to try again. Just press ⌘+Z.

iPhoto features multiple Undo levels, so you can press ⌘+Z several times to travel back through your last several changes. Alternatively, you can always return the image to its original form (before you did any editing) by clicking the Revert to Original button.

Straightening what's crooked

If your camera slightly tilted when you took the perfect shot, never fear! Click the Straighten button and then drag the Angle slider to tilt the image in the desired direction — iPhoto also slightly crops the image to return it to a rectangular shape. Click the Done button to return to Edit mode.

E-mailing photos to Aunt Mildred

iPhoto can help you send your images through e-mail by automating the process. The application can prepare your image and embed it automatically in a new message.

To send an image through e-mail, select it, click the Share button on the toolbar, and then click the Email menu item. Choose a theme for your message (complete with a background image and matching font selection). You can also specify the size of the images from the Photo Size pop-up menu, which can save considerable downloading time for those recipients who still use a dial-up connection. To add the images as attachments to the message, select the Attach Photos to Message check box.

Most ISP (Internet service provider) e-mail servers don't accept an e-mail message larger than 3MB to 5MB, so watch that Size display at the bottom of the window. (The encoding necessary to send images as attachments can *double* the size of each image!) If you're trying to send a number of images and the size goes over 3MB, try clicking the Photo Size pop-up menu and choosing a smaller size (reducing the image resolution) to get them all to fit in a single message.

When you're satisfied with the total file size and you're ready to create your message, click the Send button. iPhoto automatically creates a new message containing the images, ready for you to click Send!

Enhancing images to add pizzazz

If a photo looks washed out, click the Enhance button to increase (or decrease) the color saturation and improve the contrast. Enhance is automatic, so you don't have to set anything — but be prepared to use Undo if you're not satisfied with the changes.

Removing rampant red-eye

Unfortunately, today's digital cameras, like traditional film cameras, can still produce the same "zombies with red eyeballs." *Red-eye* is caused by a camera's flash reflecting off the retinas of a subject's eyes, and it can occur with both humans and animals. (I'm told that pets get *blue-eye* or *green-eye*, but iPhoto can handle that, too!)

iPhoto can remove that red- and green-eye and turn frightening zombies back into your family and friends! Click the Red-Eye button and then select a demonized eyeball by clicking in the center of it. (If the Red-Eye circular cursor is too small or too large, drag the Size slider to adjust the dimensions.) To complete the process, click the Done button.

Retouching like the stars

The iPhoto Retouch feature is perfect for removing minor flecks or lines in an image (especially those you've scanned from prints). When Retouch is active, the cursor turns into a circle; as with the Red-Eye tool, drag the Size slider to change the size of the Retouch cursor. Just drag the cursor across the imperfection and then click Done when you're finished touching up. Don't forget to take a moment and marvel at your editing skill!

Switching to black-and-white or sepia

Some shots look better in black-and-white (grayscale) or old-fashioned *sepia* tone (shades of copper and brown). It's fun to try. Just click the Effects tab, which offers nine effects you can apply to the photo, including black-and-white and sepia. You can also make "one-click" changes to your photo from the Effects tab, including lightening and darkening an image or enhancing the contrast.

Adjusting photo properties manually

Click the Adjust tab to perform manual adjustments to brightness and contrast (the light levels in your image), as well as attributes such as sharpness, shadow, and highlight levels. To adjust a value, make sure that nothing's selected in the image and then drag the corresponding slider until the image looks the way you want. Click the Close button to return to Edit mode.

Producing Your Own Coffee-Table Masterpiece

Book mode unleashes what I think is probably the coolest feature of iPhoto: the chance to design and print a high-quality bound photo book! After you complete an album — all the images have been edited just the way you want, and the album contains all the photos you want to include in your book — iPhoto can send your images as data over the Internet to a company that prints and binds your finished book for you. (No, they don't publish *For Dummies* titles, but then again, I don't get high-resolution color plates in most of my books, either.)

At the time of this writing, you can order many different sizes and bindings. The largest size is a 13" x 10" hardcover book with 20 double-sided pages for about $50 (extra pages cost $1.50 each). Smaller sizes include an 8.5" x 11" softcover book with 20 double-sided pages for about $20 and a hardcover 8.5" x 11" album with 20 double-sided pages for about $30 (shipping included for both). Extra pages can be added at $0.70 and $1.00 a pop, respectively.

You can also use iPhoto to produce and automatically order calendars and cards, using a process similar to the one I describe in this section for producing a book. Who needs that stationery store in the mall anymore? (You can even order old-fashioned prints from the Share toolbar menu.)

If you're going to create a photo book, make sure that the images have the highest quality and highest resolution. The higher the resolution, the better the photos look in the finished book. I try to use images of more than 1,200 pixels in the shortest dimension.

To create a photo book, follow these steps:

1. **In the Source list, click the desired album to select it.**

   Make sure that no individual photos are selected in Viewer. This way, iPhoto uses all the images in the chosen album.

2. **Click the Create toolbar button and then choose Book from the pop-up menu.**

3. **Select the type of book using the Binding buttons (Hardcover, Softcover, or Wire-bound) at the top of the window and the Size buttons (Small, Medium, Large, and Extra-Large, depending on the binding) at the left side of the window.**

   Your choices determine the number of pages and the size of the book. iPhoto displays the approximate cost of your book as you browse the options.

4. **Choose a theme.**

   Use the left- and right-arrow keys to cycle through the theme selections. The theme you choose determines both the layout scheme and the background graphics for each page. To change the color scheme for a theme, click one of the color swatches at the right side of the window.

5. **Click Create.**

   iPhoto adds your new book project under the Projects heading in the Source list, and you see the controls shown in Figure 3-8.

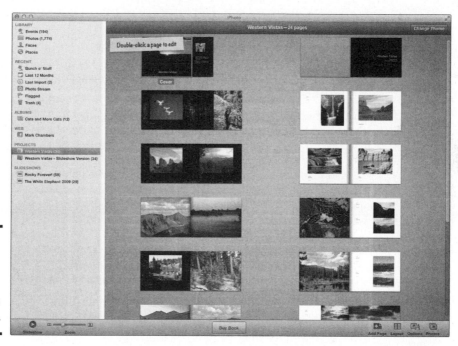

Book III Chapter 3

Focusing on iPhoto

Figure 3-8:
Preparing to publish my own coffee-table masterpiece.

In Book mode, Viewer displays a collection of thumbnail images, each of which represents a portion of your book — the front cover, internal pages, or the back cover. To display the photos you selected, click the Photos button on the toolbar. You can drag any image thumbnail into one of the photo placeholders to add it to the page.

Switch to another theme at any time by clicking the Change Theme button at the top of the window.

6. **Rearrange the page order to suit you by dragging the thumbnail of any page from one location to another.**

If you prefer a book without page numbers, right-click any page and choose Show Page Numbers to toggle it off. The check mark next to the menu item disappears.

7. **Need to change the look of a single page? Click either cover or a page to select it, and then click the Design button on the toolbar to change the color and design layout for that element.**

Clicking a design thumbnail automatically updates the page display.

8. **Double-click a page to edit captions and short descriptions.**

Click any one of the text boxes in the page display and begin typing to add text to that page. Some themes don't have captions or description text boxes, but you can add them by displaying the Design pane, clicking the desired photo placeholder, and then clicking one of the Border thumbnails that includes a text box.

When you've finished editing, click the All Pages button at the top of the window to return to your full spread.

9. **To add pages to your book, click the Add Page button on the toolbar.**

As I mention earlier, the price for additional pages varies according to the size and type of binding you choose.

10. **To view the book at any time, right-click any page and choose Preview Book.**

After a short wait, the Preview application opens, and you can then scroll through the contents of your book (or even print a quick copy). To close the Preview window, choose Preview⇨Quit Preview.

Why limit yourself to just paper copies of your publishing success? You can also right-click any page and choose Save Book as PDF to create a snazzy electronic version of your book.

11. **When you're ready to publish your book, click the Buy Book button.**

12. **In a series of dialogs that appears, iPhoto guides you through the final steps to order a bound book.**

You'll be asked for credit card information, so have that plastic ready.

I really need a slideshow

You can use iPhoto to create slideshows! Click the album or event you want to display in the Source list, and then click the Create button and choose Slideshow. Notice that iPhoto adds a Slideshows item in the Source list. A scrolling thumbnail strip appears at the top of Viewer, displaying the images in the album or event. Click and drag the thumbnails so that they appear in the desired order.

Click the Themes button on the Slideshow toolbar to choose the theme for your slideshow. The theme you choose controls the animation, transition type, and screen layout that iPhoto will use — everything from the classic Ken Burns "moving photo" animation to a really nifty Sliding Panels layout.

To choose background music for your slideshow, click the Music button on the Slideshow toolbar to display Apple's theme music, as well as the tracks from your iTunes library. To choose a standard theme, click the Source pop-up menu and choose Theme Music; select that perfect song and click Choose. To choose an iTunes song or playlist, click the Source pop-up menu and choose a playlist (or throw caution completely to the wind and choose one of your GarageBand compositions). (Read all about GarageBand in Chapter 5 of this mini-book.) You can also create a custom playlist by selecting the Custom Playlist for Slideshow check box. Then drag the individual songs you want to the song list at the bottom of the sheet. (You can drag them to rearrange their order in the list as well.) Click Choose to accept your song list.

To configure your slideshow, click the Settings button on the Slideshow toolbar and click the All Slides tab. In the dialog that appears, you can specify the amount of time that each slide remains on the screen, as well as an optional title slide. Widescreen Mac owners appreciate the Aspect Ratio pop-up menu, which allows you to choose a 16:9 widescreen display for your slideshow.

Click the This Slide tab to set the selected photo to display in black and white, sepia, or antique coloring.

To display a quick preview of your slideshow without leaving the iPhoto window, click Preview; this is a handy way of determining whether the theme and music you've selected are really what you want. When you're ready to play your slideshow, click the Play button, and iPhoto switches to full-screen mode. To create a movie file from your completed slideshow, click Export on the Slideshow toolbar.

Book III
Chapter 3

Focusing
on iPhoto

Putting Photo Stream to Work

iPhoto includes support for the iCloud *Photo Stream* feature that automatically shares the photos you take between your Mac, your PC, and any Apple device running iOS 5.0 or later (which includes iPhone 4/4S/5, second-through fourth-generation iPads, and iPod touch). Click Share and choose Photo Stream, and iPhoto automatically sends the selected images to all compatible devices over your Wi-Fi connection. (Note that all devices using Photo Stream must be configured iCloud accounts.)

You can also choose to share specific photos using *shared photo streams*, which you can turn on from the iPhoto Preferences dialog. Choose iPhoto⇨Preferences, click the Photo Stream tab on the toolbar, and then click the Shared Photo Streams check box to enable it. To subscribe to a shared photo stream invitation from another person, click the Photo Stream entry in the Source list, click the desired shared stream thumbnail, and then click Accept. To create your own shared photo stream, select the images you want to share, drag them to the Photo Stream entry in the Source list, and then click the New Photo Stream menu item that appears. iPhoto prompts you for the e-mail addresses of the folks you want to invite to your shared photo stream — after you have entered each address, click the Share button in the dialog to start the ball rolling.

Is that Facebook, Twitter, and Flickr I spy?

Indeed it is! iPhoto includes direct connections to both your Facebook and Twitter social networking accounts (www.facebook.com and www.twitter.com) and your Flickr online gallery account (www.flickr.com), allowing you to simply select one or more photos and send them automatically to any of these services! Click the Share button on the toolbar to select the type of account.

The first time you select photos in Viewer (or an album or event in the Source list) and choose either option, iPhoto prompts you for permission to set up your connection. (Of course, this will require you to enter your Facebook, Twitter, and Flickr account information — hence the confirmation request.) Click Set Up and provide the data that each site requires.

After you set up your accounts, simply select your photos, albums, or events, click the Share toolbar button, and then choose the menu item for the desired service. Apple, you absolutely *rock*!

When creating a shared photo stream, don't forget to select the Public Website check box if you want to share images with friends and family who don't own a Mac or an iOS device.

To turn on Photo Stream, choose iPhoto➪Preferences and click the Photo Stream toolbar button. Select the Enable Photo Stream check box.

You can also specify whether iPhoto should automatically import Photo Stream photos to you library, and also whether iPhoto should automatically upload the most recent 1,000 photos to Photo Stream for sharing with your other devices.

Chapter 4: Making Magic with iMovie

In This Chapter

✔ **Taking stock of the iMovie window**

✔ **Importing and adding media content**

✔ **Using transitions in your movie**

✔ **Creating a movie trailer**

✔ **Sharing your movie with others**

Alfred Hitchcock, Stanley Kubrick, George Lucas, and Ridley Scott — those guys are amateurs! Welcome to the exciting world of moviemaking on your Mac, where *you* call the shots. With iMovie, you can try your hand at all aspects of the movie-creating process, including editing and special effects. Built with ease-of-use in mind, iMovie lets you perform full-blown movie production on your Macintosh with a minimum of effort.

Don't let iMovie's fancy buttons and flashing lights fool you: This application is a feature-packed tool for serious movie production. The iMovie controls work the same as many top-notch, movie-editing tools that professionals use. From basic editing to audio and video effects, iMovie has everything that you need to get started creating high-quality movies.

The iMovie Window

If you've ever tried a professional-level video-editing application, you probably felt as though you were suddenly dropped in the cockpit of a jumbo jet. In iMovie, though, all the controls you need are easy to use and logically placed.

To launch iMovie, click the iMovie icon on the Dock or from Launchpad. (The icon looks like a star from the Hollywood Walk of Fame.) You can also click the Application folder in any Finder window sidebar and then double-click the iMovie icon.

To follow the examples I show you here, take these strenuous steps and create a new movie project:

1. **Choose File⇨New Project or press ⌘+N.**

iMovie displays the sheet you see in Figure 4-1.

2. Type a name for your project.

3. Select the aspect ratio (or screen dimensions) for your movie.

You can select a widescreen display (16:9) or a standard display (4:3). If compatibility with the familiar SDTV (standard definition TV) format is important, I recommend that you choose standard (4:3) ratio. If you're shooting in 16:9 format, choosing 16:9 for an SDTV set will result in letterboxing, those familiar black bars at the top and bottom of the screen, but you won't lose any content from the sides of the frame. On the other hand, choosing standard ratio for an HDTV results in pillarboxing, or black bars on the left and right sides of the screen.

4. Choose the frame rate.

The default frame rate is 30 frames per second (fps), which is normal for the North American NTSC video standard. However, you can choose a slower frame rate if necessary, such as the 25 fps setting for the international PAL and SECAM video standards.

5. Click a Project Theme thumbnail to select a theme to apply to your finished movie.

- *To theme:* iMovie automatically adds the transitions and titles that correspond to that theme. Typically, this is what you want. However, if you want to add transitions and titles manually, select the Automatically Add Transitions and Titles check box.

Figure 4-1:
Creating a new movie project within iMovie.

- *Or not to theme:* If you decide not to use a theme — opting for the No Theme thumbnail — iMovie can still add an automatic effect between clips. Select the Automatically Add check box and use the pop-up menu to choose the desired effect.

You can also create movie trailers in iMovie, which I demonstrate later in this chapter. Generally, however, I recommend that you create your trailer project *after* your movie project is complete — unless, of course, you're specifically creating just a trailer project. Why? For the same reason that studios create trailers when the filming is finished: After you complete your movie, you'll have all the clips imported already, and you'll have a better idea of what you want to include while "teasing" your audience!

6. Click Create.

iMovie adds the new project to the list in the Project Library pane, and you're on your way. Check out Figure 4-2: The whole enchilada is in one window.

Project Library/Project/
Trailer pane

Camera Input   Playhead   Playhead   Monitor

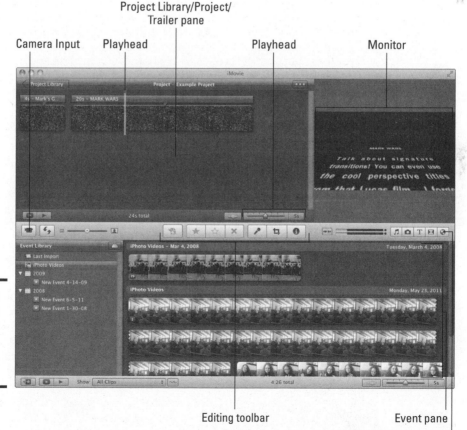

Figure 4-2:
iMovie is a
lean, mean
video-
producing
machine.

Editing toolbar   Event pane

Media Browser toolbar

**Book III
Chapter 4**

**Making Magic
with iMovie**

The controls and displays that you'll use most often are

+ **Monitor:** Think of this as being just like your TV or computer monitor. Your video clips, still images, and finished movie play here.

+ **Media Browser toolbar:** This row of buttons allows you to add media content (video clips, photos, and audio). The selected items fill the right side of the browser pane below the monitor.

+ **Event Library:** This list (lower left) displays all the video clips you can add to your project, including video clips you've created in iPhoto. These clips are organized as *events,* which I'll discuss later in this chapter.

+ **Event pane:** If you select a video clip in the Event Library list, iMovie displays a thumbnail of the content in the Event pane. If you decide to include it, you can add it to your project. I show you what each pane in the iMovie workspace looks like when you tackle different tasks in this chapter.

+ **Project Library/Project/Trailer pane:** iMovie displays the movie projects that you create in the *Project Library* pane. Note that when you double-click a project in the Project Library pane, it turns into the *Project* pane, which displays the elements you added to that specific project (such as video clips, still photos, and audio clips). If you drag an element into the Project Library pane, it turns into the Project pane for the selected project; if you're working on a movie trailer, the Project Library pane turns into the Trailer pane.

The Project Library pane displays different content, depending on the action you've taken.

+ **Playhead:** The red vertical line that you see in the Event and Project Library panes is the *playhead,* which indicates the current editing point while you're browsing your clips or creating your movie. When you're playing your movie, the playhead moves to follow your progress through the movie.

+ **Editing toolbar:** This strip of buttons allows you to control editing functions such as cropping, audio and video adjustments, voice-overs, and selecting items.

+ **Camera Import window:** Click this switch to import DV clips from your DV camcorder or FaceTime HD camera.

Those are the major highlights of the iMovie window. A director's chair and megaphone are optional, of course, but they do add to the mood.

A Bird's-Eye View of Moviemaking

I don't want to box in your creative skills here — after all, you can attack the moviemaking process from a number of angles (pun unfortunately intended). However, I've found that my movies turn out the best when I follow a linear process, so before I dive into specifics, allow me to provide you with an overview of moviemaking with iMovie.

Here's my take on the process, reduced to seven steps:

1. Import your video clips directly from your DV camcorder, FaceTime HD camera, iPhoto, or hard drive.

2. Drag your new selection of clips from the Event pane to the Project pane and arrange them in the desired order.

3. Import or record audio clips (from iTunes, GarageBand, or external sources, such as audio CDs or audio files that you've recorded yourself) and add them to your movie.

4. Import your photos (directly from iPhoto or from your hard drive) and place them where needed in your movie.

5. Add professional niceties, such as voice-overs, transitions, effects, and text to the project.

6. Preview your film and edit it further if necessary.

7. Share your finished film with others through the web, e-mail, your Apple TV, or an iOS device (an iPhone, iPad, or iPod touch).

That's the first step-by-step procedure in this chapter. I doubt that you'll even need to refer to it, however, because you'll soon see just how easy it is to use iMovie.

This chapter simply can't hold a description of all the settings and procedures in iMovie, but luckily, Tony Bove has done exactly that in his book *iLife '11 For Dummies.* Tony will take you from basics to all the in-depth features of each iLife application.

Importing the Building Blocks

Sure, you need video clips to create a movie of your own, but don't panic if you have but a short supply. You can certainly turn to the other iLife applications for additional raw material. (See, I told you that integration thing would come in handy.)

Along with video clips you import from your DV camcorder, FaceTime HD camera, and hard drive, you can also call on iPhoto for still images (think credits) and iTunes for background audio and effects. In this section, I show you how.

Pulling in video clips

Your Mac is probably equipped already with the extras that come in handy for video editing — namely, a large hard drive and both a USB port and a FireWire port. Most mini-DV camcorders today use a FireWire connection to transfer clips, whereas mass-storage camcorders use a USB connection. (Note that if your snazzy new DV camcorder uses a USB connection, you'll need to modify the steps I provide in this section for your particular device. Only a couple of steps are different, and I cover them shortly.) Oh, and if your Mac has a FaceTime HD camera on board, you're a self-contained movie studio!

Here's the drill if your clips are on a FireWire mini-DV camcorder or a mass-storage USB camcorder:

1. **Plug the proper cable into your Mac.**

2. **Set the camcorder to VTR (or VCR) mode.**

   Some camcorders call this Play mode.

3. **Click the Camera Import button (labeled in Figure 4-2).**

   iMovie opens a new window.

4. **Click the Camera pop-up menu (at the bottom of the Import window) and select your DV camcorder or FaceTime HD camera.**

   If you're using a tape-based camcorder, playback controls appear under the Camera Import window, mirroring the controls on your DV camcorder. This arrangement allows you to control the unit from iMovie. *Keen!* If you're using a mass-storage camcorder connected by USB, you instead get Import All and Import Checked buttons beneath the thumbnails of available clips.

   To capture video from your FaceTime HD camera, open the Video Size pop-up menu to choose the dimensions of the clip; then click Capture. On the sheet that appears, choose the location where the video will be saved and also whether to add this video to an existing event or to create a new event. Click Capture to start recording, and click Stop when your video is complete. (You can skip the rest of the steps in this section, which deal only with FireWire external camcorders.)

   iMovie can analyze your incoming video for one of three different post-recording procedures. Select the After Import Analyze For check box, and then choose Stabilization (which helps smooth shaky camera work), People (which marks a clip as including people, making it easier to locate) or Stabilization and People (which, predictably, does both). The Stabilization option is especially good if your camcorder doesn't have a built-in stabilization function (and you weren't shooting with a tripod), but beware: Any of these settings will add significant time to the import process!

5. **To import selected clips from your DV camcorder, set the Automatic/ Manual switch to Manual and advance the video to a couple of seconds before the point where you want to start your capture, and then click Import.**

   To import all clips, set the Automatic/Manual switch to Automatic and then click Import.

6. **(Optional) Clear the check boxes next to the clips that you don't want to import (to deselect them) and then click the Import Checked button.**

7. **From the Save To pop-up menu, choose the drive that should store your clips.**

   You can choose to add the new clips to an existing Event or create a new Event. Heck, if the event spanned more than one day, you can create a new Event for each day. (How do they think up these things?)

8. **Click OK and admire your handiwork.**

   iMovie begins transferring the footage to your Mac and automatically adds the imported clips to your Event Library.

If your clips are already on your hard drive, rest assured that iMovie can import them, including those in *high-definition video* (HDV) format. iMovie also recognizes a number of other video formats, as shown in Table 4-1.

Table 4-1	Video Formats Supported by iMovie
File Type	*Description*
DV	Standard 4:3 digital video
DV Widescreen	Widescreen 16:9 digital video
MOV	QuickTime movies
HDV, AVCHD	High-definition (popularly called *widescreen*) digital video, in 720p and 1080i
MPEG-2	Digital video format used for DVD movies
MPEG-4	A popular format for streaming Internet and wireless digital video, as well as for handheld iOS devices such as the iPad, iPhone, and iPod touch

It's easy to get lost in the morass of video formats and assorted standards in use today. Although I can't cover them all in a single chapter, I can recommend the wonderful website www.videohelp.com, which offers comprehensive information on video recording, optical hardware, and format-conversion software.

To import a movie file, follow this bouncing ball:

1. **Choose File⇨Import⇨Movies.**

   iMovie displays the familiar File Open sheet.

2. **If you're importing 1080i video clips, open the Optimize Video pop-up menu, choose the Full quality setting, and click OK.**

   If you're not importing 1080i video, use the default Large setting and click OK.

   The Large setting saves you a significant amount of hard drive space, but the Full setting preserves the original resolution and detail. The Full setting demands a significant chunk of the CPU and RAM resources from your Mac, though, so expect slower multitasking while importing.

3. **In the File Open sheet sidebar, click the drive that stores your clips and then navigate to the desired location.**

4. **Specify whether you want to add the imported video to an existing event or to create a new event.**

   If you choose to add the video to an existing event, open the pop-up menu and choose an event.

5. **Specify whether you want to copy the video (leaving the original movie intact) or whether the original movie should be moved (the original is deleted after a successful import).**

6. **Click Import.**

   Alternatively, you can also drag a video clip from a Finder window and drop it in the Project pane.

Making use of still images

Still images come in handy as impressive-looking titles or as ending credits to your movie. (Make sure you list a gaffer and a best boy to be truly professional.) However, you can use still images also to introduce scenes or to separate clips according to your whim. For example, I use stills when delineating the days of a vacation within a movie or different Christmas celebrations over time.

Here are two methods of adding stills to your movie:

✦ **Adding images and video clips from iPhoto:** Click the Photo Browser button on the Browser toolbar (or press ⌘+2) to experience the thrill that is your iPhoto Library, right from iMovie (as shown in Figure 4-3). You can elect to display your entire iPhoto Library or more selective picks, such as specific albums or events. When you find the image you want to add, just drag it to the correct spot in the Project pane. Videos from your iPhoto Library are automatically added to your iMovie Event Library — it doesn't get much easier than that.

✦ **Importing images from your hard drive:** If you're a member of the International Drag-and-Drop Society, you can drag TIFF, JPEG, GIF, PICT, PNG, and PSD images directly from a Finder window and drop them into the Project pane as well.

Transitions

Titles

Photo Browser

Music and Sound Effects

Play project full screen

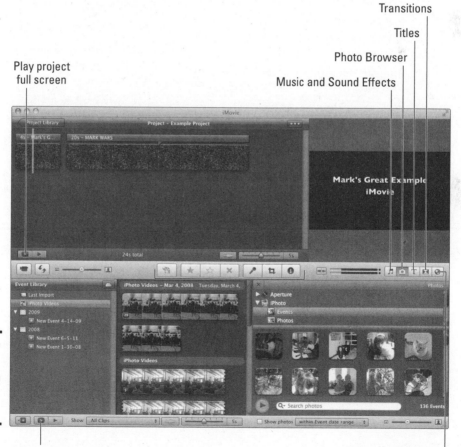

Book III Chapter 4

Making Magic with iMovie

Figure 4-3: Pulling still images from iPhoto is child's play.

Play event full screen

Map and Background

Narration the easy way

Ready to create that award-winning nature documentary? You can add voice-over narration to your iMovie project that would make Jacques Cousteau proud. You can record your voice while you watch your movie playing, allowing perfect synchronization with the action! To add narration, follow these steps:

1. **Click the Voiceover button on the Editing toolbar — it sports a microphone icon — to open the Voiceover window.**

2. **From the Record From pop-up menu, choose the input device.**

   Most Macs sport a decent internal microphone, but you can always add a USB microphone to your system.

3. **Drag the input volume slider to a comfortable level.**

   You can monitor the volume level of your voice with the left and right input meters. Try to keep the meters at 50 percent or so for the proper volume level.

4. **To block out ambient noise levels around you, drag the Noise Reduction slider to the right if necessary.**

If you'd like iMovie to enhance your voice electronically for a more professional sound, select the Voice Enhancement check box. If you need to hear the audio from your movie project while you speak, select the Play Project Audio While Recording check box. Note, however, that you'll need to listen to the audio while using a set of headphones (plugged into your Mac's headphone jack) to avoid feedback problems.

5. **Click in the desired spot within a clip in the Project pane where the narration should begin.**

6. **Begin speaking when prompted by iMovie.**

7. **Watch the video while you narrate so that you can coordinate your narration track with the action.**

8. **Click anywhere in the iMovie window to stop recording (or wait until the clip ends).**

   iMovie adds a tiny microphone icon to the Project pane underneath the video with the voice-over.

9. **Click the Close button in the Voiceover window.**

Importing and adding audio from all sorts of places

You can pull in everything from Wagner to Weezer as both background music and sound effects for your movie. In this section, I focus on how to get those notes into iMovie and then how to add them to your movie by dragging them to the Project pane.

You can add audio in a number of ways:

✦ **Adding songs from iTunes:** Click the Music and Sound Effects button on the Media Browser toolbar (or press ⌘+1) to display the contents of your iTunes Library. Click the desired playlist in the scrolling list box, such as the dynamite ABBA playlist I selected in Figure 4-4. (If you've exported any original music you've composed in GarageBand to your iTunes Library, you can use those songs in your own movie!) Add a track to your movie by dragging the song entry from the Music and Sound Effects list to the desired spot in the Project pane.

✦ **Adding sound effects:** Yep, if you need the sound of a horse galloping for your Rocky Mountain vacation clips, click iMovie Sound Effects or iLife Sound Effects in the scrolling list box. iMovie includes a number of top-shelf audio effects that you can use in the second audio track on the timeline viewer. This way, you can add sound effects even when you've already added a background song. Again, to add a sound effect, drag it to the perfect spot in the Project pane.

Figure 4-4:
Call on your iTunes Library to add tracks to your iMovie.

Book III
Chapter 4

Making Magic
with iMovie

If you have several gigabytes of music in your iTunes Library, it may be more of a challenge to locate Janis Joplin's rendition of "Me and Bobby McGee," especially if she's included in a compilation. Let your Mac do the digging for you! Click in the Search box below the track list and begin typing a song name. iMovie narrows the song titles displayed to those that match the characters you type. To reset the search box and display all your songs in the Library or selected playlist, click the X icon that appears to the right of the box.

+ **Ripping songs from an audio CD:** Load an audio CD and then choose Audio CD from the scrolling list box. iMovie displays the tracks from the CD, and you can add them at the current playhead position the same way as iTunes songs.

+ **Recording directly from a microphone:** Yep, if you're thinking voice-over narration, you've hit the nail on the head. Check out the "Narration the easy way" sidebar for the scoop.

You can fine-tune both the audio within a video clip or the audio clips that you add to your project. With the desired clip selected, click the Inspector button on the Editing toolbar (it bears a proud letter *i*) to display the Inspector window, and then click the Audio tab. The Audio Adjustments window that appears includes an array of audio controls that allow you to change the volume of the selected clip or to give that audio priority — or *ducking* — over other audio playing simultaneously (such as a sound effect that needs to be clearly heard over background music and the video clip).

If your clips dramatically vary in volume, click the Normalize Clip Volume button and then select each clip that you want to set to the same volume; click Normalize Clip Volume again for each clip. You can also set an automatic or manual Fade-in/Fade-out for the audio. When you're done tweaking, click Done. (Oh, and don't forget that you can always return the clip to its original volume; just open this window again and click Revert to Original.)

On the Video tab in the Inspector window, you can vary the exposure, brightness, contrast, and saturation of your clip. Click the Auto button, and iMovie will perform what it considers the best job of improving your video.

Building the Cinematic Basics

Time to dive in and add the building blocks you imported to create your movie. Along with video clips, audio tracks, and still images, you can add

Hollywood-quality transitions, optical effects, and animated text titles. In this section, I demonstrate how to elevate your collection of video clips into a real-life, honest-to-goodness *movie.*

Adding clips to your movie

You add clips to your movie via the Project pane and the Event pane. The Dynamic Duo works like this:

✦ **Project pane:** This displays the media you've added to your project so far, allowing you to rearrange the clips, titles, transitions, and still images in your movie. (If the pane is titled *Project Library,* remember that you have to double-click the desired project to select it. After you select a project, the Project Library pane turns into the Project pane.)

✦ **Event pane:** This displays your video clips arranged by event (the date they were shot or the date they were imported), acting as the source repository for all your clips. Movies pulled into iMovie, imported into iPhoto, or added manually from Finder appear here.

To add a clip to your movie, follow these steps:

1. **Move your cursor across clips in the Event pane to watch a preview of the video.**

2. **After you decide what to add to your project, you can add the entire clip or a selection.**

   • *To select an entire clip:* Right-click the clip's thumbnail and choose Select Entire Clip from the menu that appears.

   • *To select a portion of a clip:* Drag your cursor across the thumbnail. A yellow frame appears around your selection. To change the length of the selected video, drag the handles that appear on either side. If you make a mistake while selecting video, just click any empty space in the Event pane to remove the selection frame and try again.

3. **Drag the selection from the Event pane to where it belongs in the Project pane.**

   Alternatively, you can press the E key or click the Add to Project button (the first button on the Editing toolbar) to add the selection to the end of the current project.

Do this several times, and you have a movie, which you created just like the editors of old used to do by working with actual film clips. This is a good point to mention a moviemaking Mark's Maxim:

Preview your work — and often.

iMovie offers two Play Full Screen buttons: one under the Event Library and one under the Project Library. Select the project or Event you want to play and then click the corresponding button (or press ⌘+G). You can also choose View➪Play Full Screen to watch the selection. Press the spacebar to pause, and press Esc to return to iMovie. You can also move your mouse to display a filmstrip that you can click to skip forward or backward in the project or event.

To play a selection from the beginning, press \ (backslash). (If you've ever watched directors at work on today's movie sets, you may have noticed that they're constantly watching a monitor to see what things will look like for the audience. You have the same option in iMovie!)

While you're watching video in the Event pane, you may decide that a certain clip has a favorite scene or that another clip has material you don't want, such as Uncle Ed's shadow puppets. (Shudder.) iMovie features *Favorite* and *Rejected* frames, allowing you to view and use your best camera work (and ignore the worst stuff). To mark video, select a range of frames or an entire clip and then click the Mark as Favorite button on the Editing toolbar. Click the Reject button to hide the selected video or frames from view. (You can always unmark a Favorite or Rejected scene by using the Unmark button in the Editing toolbar; click the Show pop-up menu at the bottom of the window if the scenes aren't visible.)

Removing clips from your movie

Don't like a clip? Bah. To banish a clip from your movie, follow these steps:

1. **In the Project pane, click the offending clip to select it.**

2. **Press Delete.**

   Alternatively, you can right-click the clip (or a selection you've made by dragging) and choose either Delete Entire Clip or Delete Selection from the menu that appears. (*Note:* Deleting the video using either of these menu commands removes it from the Project, but the video clip still remains in the Event library.)

If you remove the wrong clip, don't panic. Instead, use iMovie's Undo feature (press ⌘+Z) to restore it.

Reordering clips in your movie

If Day One of your vacation appears after Day Two, you can easily reorder your clips and stills by dragging them to the proper space in the Project pane. When you take your finger off the mouse (or trackpad), iMovie automatically moves the rest of your movie aside with a minimum of fuss and bother.

iMovie allows you to switch to the familiar Timeline view, which many users of previous versions of the application will recognize (and many prefer, including this particular moviemaker). Click the Swap Events and Projects button — it's next to the Camera Import button, and it bears two arrows — to move the Project pane to the bottom of the window and the Event Library to the top, which switches you to Timeline view.

Editing clips in iMovie

If a clip has extra seconds of footage at the beginning or end (as it should to ensure you get all the action), you don't want that superfluous stuff in your masterpiece. Our favorite video editor gives you the following functions:

✦ **Crop:** Removes unwanted material from a video clip or still image, allowing you to change the aspect ratio of the media

✦ **Rotate:** Rotates a clip or image on its center axis

✦ **Trim:** Trims frames from a video clip

Before you can edit, however, you have to select a section of a clip. Follow these steps:

1. **Click a clip or image in either the Project pane (where changes you make are specific to this project) or the Event pane (where edits you make are reflected in any project using that footage).**

   iMovie displays the clip or image in the monitor.

2. **To select the entire clip or image, simply click it.**

3. **Drag your cursor across the thumbnail to select the section of the media you want to edit. (Note that some editing functions, such as Crop and Rotate, will automatically apply to the entire clip.)**

   The selected region is surrounded by a yellow frame. You're ready to edit that selected part of the clip.

**Book III
Chapter 4**

Making Magic with iMovie

Drag the handles that appear at the beginning or ending of the selection to make fine changes to the selected section.

✦ **To crop:** Click the Crop button on the Editing toolbar to display the frame in the Monitor pane and then click Crop at the top of the Monitor pane. Drag the edges of the frame and the handles to select the section you want to keep. To preview your selection, click the Play button at the top-right corner of the monitor. When you're ready, click Done, and everything but the selected region is removed.

✦ **To rotate:** Click the Crop button on the Edit toolbar and then click one of the two rotation buttons (which carry a curved arrow icon). Each click rotates the media 90 degrees in that direction. Click Done when the clip or image is properly oriented.

✦ **To trim:** Right-click the selection and choose Trim to Selection from the contextual menu. iMovie removes the frames from around the selected video.

Edits that you make to one clip or still image can be copied to multiple items! Select the edited clip and choose Edit⇨Copy from the iMovie menu. Now you can select one or more clips and choose Edit⇨Paste Adjustments to apply Video, Audio, or Crop edits. (To apply all three types of edits, just choose All.)

Transitions for the masses

Many iMovie owners approach transitions as visual bookends: They merely act as placeholders that appear between video clips. Nothing could be further from the truth because judicious use of transitions can make or break a scene. For example, which would you prefer after a wedding ceremony — an abrupt, jarring cut to the reception or a gradual fadeout to the reception?

Today's audiences are sensitive to transitions between scenes. Try not to overuse the same transition — pick two or three that match the mood of your film. Also, weigh the visual effect of a transition carefully. You may even decide that no transition is most effective; directors call this deliberate lack of a transition a *jump cut.*

iMovie includes a surprising array of transitions, including old favorites (such as Fade In and Dissolve) and some nifty stuff that you may not be familiar with (such as Cube and Page Curl). To display your transition collection (see Figure 4-5), click the Show Transitions button on the Media Browser toolbar (or press ⌘+4).

Figure 4-5:
Add transitions for flow between clips in iMovie.

To see what a particular transition looks like, move your cursor over the thumbnail to display the transition in miniature.

Adding a transition couldn't be easier: Drag the transition from the list in the Transitions Browser pane and drop it between clips or between a clip and a still image in the Project pane. In iMovie, transitions are applied in real time.

Even Gone with the Wind had titles

The next stop on our iMovie Hollywood Features Tour is Titles Browser, shown in Figure 4-6. You'll find it by clicking the Title button (which bears a big capital *T*) on the Media Browser toolbar or by pressing ⌘+3. You can add a title with a still image, but iMovie also includes everything you need to add basic animated text to your movie.

Most of the controls you can adjust are the same for each animation style. You can change the font, the size of the text, and the color of the text.

Figure 4-6:
Add titles
for your next
silent film.

To add a title manually, follow these steps:

1. **In the Titles Browser pane, select an animation thumbnail and drag it to the desired spot in the Project pane.**

2. **Click a background thumbnail to select a background for your title.**

These are the same backgrounds you'll see in the Map, Background, and Animatic Browser, which I discuss in the next section.

3. **Press ⌘+T (or choose Text➪Show Fonts) to make any changes to the fonts or text attributes.**

4. **Click in a text box to type your own line of text.**

5. **Click the Play button to preview your title.**

iMovie displays a preview of the effect in the monitor with the settings that you choose.

6. **Click Done.**

The title appears in the Project pane.

Adding Maps and Backgrounds

iMovie includes easy-to-use animated maps — think Indiana Jones traveling by airplane from place to place — and static backgrounds that can be used with your titles. To display them, click the Map, Background, and Animatic Browser button on the Media Browser toolbar, or press ⌘+5.

To use an animated map, drag one of the globe or map thumbnails to the Project pane. After the globe or map is created, click it to display the Inspector window, and now you can click the Start Location button (and optionally, the End Location button) to enter the start and stop points for the animation. Type a city or place name to see your choices. (Heck, you can even type in an airport code or decimal coordinates to specify the spot.) After you're done, click OK, and then click Done in the Inspector window. Now play the clip, and watch as iMovie animates your location (or your trip) in seconds!

To add a static background from the browser, drag it to the desired spot within the Project pane.

Creating an Honest-to-Goodness Movie Trailer

Yes, friends, you read that correctly! As I mention at the beginning of the chapter, iMovie includes a Movie Trailer feature that can turn your film clips into a Hollywood-class preview, complete with genre transitions and background music.

To create a trailer project, follow these steps:

1. **Choose File⇨New Project or press ⌘+N.**

2. **Type a name for your project.**

3. **Select the aspect ratio for your movie.**

   See the earlier section "The iMovie Window" for a discussion of standard (4:3) and widescreen (16:9) aspect ratios.

4. **Choose the frame rate.**

5. **Click a Movie Trailer thumbnail to select it.**

   iMovie displays a nifty preview of the trailer style that you selected. Click the thumbnails to preview their look before you make your decision. Choose a trailer style that most closely matches the mood you want to project with your movie.

Each trailer has a suggested number of cast members, and this number reflects the number of people that will appear in the clip placeholders during the editing process. (More on this feature in a page or two.)

6. Click Create.

iMovie replaces the Project Library pane with the Trailer pane, as shown in Figure 4-7. On the Outline tab, you can edit the titles used in the trailer as well as pop-up lists for information such as the gender of the star(s) and the logo style you want for your "studio" at the beginning of the trailer. To change a text field, click in it and type the new text. You'll see the changes you make in the Trailer display appear in the monitor in real time.

After you complete your edits to the titles, click the Storyboard tab. There, you can edit the text for each transition; simply click the text to display the edit box and type. You can also drag clips from your Event Library (or from a Finder window) to fill the storyboard's placeholders for video clips. To delete a clip from the storyboard, click it to select it and then press Delete.

To preserve the look and feel of the trailer storyboard, try to match your clips with the description and suggested activity indicated by the placeholder. (In other words, don't stick a wide-angle video clip of the family dog cavorting in the yard in a placeholder marked "Closeup" — you get the idea.)

The Storyboard tab might not look like an editing timeline, but you can move the cursor anywhere within the storyboard to preview your trailer. The playhead indicator appears wherever the cursor appears, allowing you to watch the clip or transition that it's resting upon. You'll soon be sweeping your cursor to the left or right to move through each section of your trailer.

For an overall listing of each clip required for the full trailer, click the Shot List tab. On this tab, clips are organized by type. For example, all the action clips appear in one section, and all the landscape and closeup clips are grouped together as well. If necessary, you can also add, delete, or swap video clips from the Shot List.

Figure 4-7:
Build your
movie trailer
from the
Trailer pane.

To preview your trailer in its entirety, click the Play Full-Screen button at the top-right corner of the Trailer pane. (Naturally, any storyboard placeholder that you haven't filled with a clip will display just the placeholder.)

After you're satisfied with your finished trailer — or if you'd like to work on another project — click the Project Library button at the top of the Trailer pane, and you'll see that iMovie has added your trailer as a new project in the Library list.

I bet all those hard-working Hollywood video editors are fuming at how easy it is to create a trailer in iMovie!

Sharing Your Finished Classic with Others

Your movie or trailer is complete, you've saved it to your hard drive, and now you're wondering where to go from here. Click Share on the application menu bar, and you'll see that iMovie can unleash your movie upon your unsuspecting family and friends (and even the entire world) in a number of ways:

✦ **iTunes:** Send your movie to your iTunes Library as a movie.

✦ **Media Browser:** Make your iMovie project available within other iLife applications, in five different sizes suited to different display devices. Note that the Media Browser is also available for other Apple applications, like Final Cut Pro X, and to third-party applications like Toast Titanium.

✦ **iDVD:** If you've installed this older iLife application (which is no longer available from Apple), you can send your movie to iDVD for use in a DVD project.

✦ **Podcast Producer:** You can send your movie to Apple's Podcast Producer application for incorporation into your newest podcasting epic.

✦ **YouTube/Facebook/Vimeo/CNN iReport:** Yep, you read right, you can send your iMovie directly to any of these websites! Can it get more convenient than that? (I think not.)

✦ **Export Movie:** Create a copy of your movie on your hard drive in one of five different sizes.

✦ **Export using QuickTime:** Create a QuickTime movie with your project using the QuickTime encoding engine (allowing greater control over the export process and the attributes of the finished movie file).

If you use this option, any computer with an installed copy of QuickTime can display your movies, and you can use QuickTime movies in Keynote presentations as well.

✦ **Export to Final Cut XML:** If you'd like to transfer your iMovie project to Final Cut Pro X, use this option to create a compatible XML file.

When you choose a sharing option, iMovie displays the video quality for the option and makes automatic changes to the movie attributes. (For example, choosing Tiny reduces the finished movie as far as possible in file size, and the audio is reduced to mono instead of stereo.)

Need to take a movie offline or stop sharing it? From the Sharing menu, you can remove a project from iTunes, your iLife Media Browser, and the YouTube, Facebook, Vimeo, and CNN iReport websites as well. Just click the corresponding Remove From menu item. (Of course, you can share the project again at any time.)

If you're worried about permanently reducing the quality of your project by sharing it in a smaller size, fear not! When you choose a sharing option to export your movie, your original project remains on your hard drive, unchanged, so you can share a better-quality version at any time in the future!

After you adjust any settings specific to the desired sharing option, click Publish (or Save) to start the ball rolling.

**Book III
Chapter 4**

Making Magic
with iMovie

Chapter 5: Becoming a Superstar with GarageBand

In This Chapter

- ✔ Navigating the GarageBand window
- ✔ Adding tracks and loops to your song
- ✔ Repeating loops and extending your song
- ✔ Building arrangements
- ✔ Adding effects to instruments
- ✔ Exporting your work to iTunes
- ✔ Burning your song to an audio CD

When I was a kid, I always thought that *real* rock stars trashed their instruments after a hard night's worth of jamming — you know, like The Who, Led Zeppelin, KISS, and the Rolling Stones. Guitars got set on fire, or pounded into the stage, or thrown into the crowd like beads during a Mardi Gras parade.

I can make my own music now, but you'll never see me trash my instrument! I compose music on my Mac with *GarageBand,* Apple's music-making component in the iLife application suite. You can solo on all sorts of instruments, and even add horns, drums, and a funky bass line for backup . . . all with no musical experience (and, in my case, little talent, to boot)!

Oh, and did I mention that you can use GarageBand to produce podcasts? That's right: You can record your voice and easily create your own show, and then share it with others from your website! Heck, add photos if you like. You'll be the talk of your family and friends and maybe even your Mac user group.

This chapter explains everything you need to know to create your first song (or podcast). I also show you how to import your hit record into iTunes so that you can listen to it on your iPod with a big, silly grin on your face (as I do) or add it to your next iMovie project as a royalty-free soundtrack. Heck, you can even turn that hit into your own personal iPhone or iPad ringtone!

Shaking Hands with Your Band

As you can see in Figure 5-1, the GarageBand window isn't complex at all, and that's good design. In this section, I list the most important controls so that you know your Play button from your Loop Browser button.

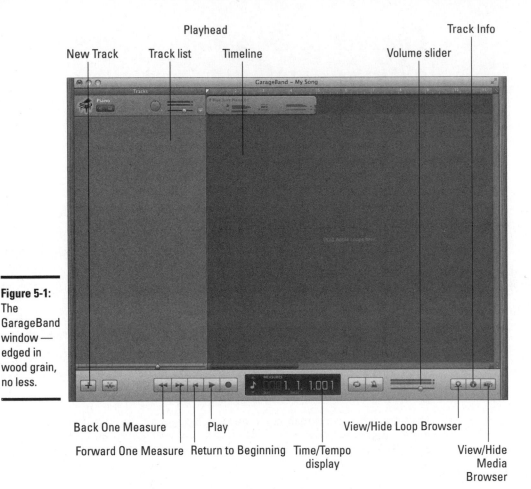

Playhead

Track Info

New Track   Track list   Timeline   Volume slider

Figure 5-1:
The
GarageBand
window —
edged in
wood grain,
no less.

Back One Measure   Play   View/Hide Loop Browser

Forward One Measure   Return to Beginning   Time/Tempo   View/Hide
display   Media
Browser

Your music-making machine includes

✦ **Track list:** In GarageBand, a *track* is a discrete instrument that you set
up to play one part of your song. For example, a track in a classical piece
for string quartet would have four component tracks — one each for
violin, viola, cello, and bass. This list contains all the tracks in your song
arranged so that you can easily see and modify them, like the rows in a
spreadsheet. A track begins in the list, stretching out to the right all the
way to the end of the song. As you can see in the upper left of Figure 5-1,
I already have one track defined — Piano.

If you're creating a podcast, a *Podcast artwork track* can also appear.

✦ **Timeline:** This scrolling area holds the loops (see the following bullet) that you add, compose, or record, allowing you to move and edit them easily. When a song plays, the Timeline scrolls to give you a visual look at your music. (Bear with me; you'll understand that cryptic statement in a page or two.)

✦ **Loop:** This element is a prerecorded short clip of an instrument being played in a specific style and tempo. Loops — the building blocks of your song — are only so long. Most are five seconds in length, and others are even shorter. You can drag loops from Loop Browser to a track and literally build a bass line or a guitar solo. (It's a little like adding video clips in iMovie to build a film.) Loops can also be repeated within a track, which I'll discuss further in a page or two.

✦ **Playhead:** This vertical line is a moving indicator that shows you the current position in your song while it scrolls by in the Timeline. You can drag the playhead to a new location at any time. The playhead also acts like the insertion cursor in a word-processing application: If you insert a section of a song or a loop from the Clipboard, it appears at the current location of the playhead. (More on copying and inserting loops later, so don't panic.)

✦ **New Track button:** Click this button to add a new track to your song.

✦ **Track Info button:** If you need to display the instrument used in a track, click the track to select it and then click this button. You can also control settings, such as Echo and Reverb, from the Edit pane of the Track Info display.

✦ **View/Hide Loop Browser button:** Click the button with the loop icon to display Loop Browser at the right side of the window; click it again to close it. You can see more of your tracks' contents without scrolling by closing Loop Browser.

✦ **View/Hide Media Browser button:** Click this button (which bears icons of a filmstrip, slide, and musical note) to display Media Browser at the right side of the window; click it again to close it. *Hint:* Close Media Browser to see more of your tracks. If you're already familiar with iMovie, you recognize this pane in the GarageBand window; it allows you to add media (in this case, digital song files, still images, or movies) to your GarageBand project for use in a podcast or as ringtones.

✦ **Return to Beginning button:** Clicking this button immediately moves the playhead back to the beginning of the Timeline.

✦ **Back and Forward One Measure buttons:** To move quickly through your song by jumping to the previous or next measure, click the corresponding button.

✦ **Play button:** Hey, old friend! At last, a control that you've probably used countless times before — and it works just like the same control on your audio CD player. Click Play, and GarageBand begins playing your entire song. Note that the Play button turns blue. To stop the music, click Play again; the button loses that sexy blue sheen and the playhead stops immediately. (If playback is paused, it begins again at the playhead position when you click Play.)

✦ **Time/Tempo display:** This cool-looking LCD display shows you the current playhead position in seconds.

You can click the icon at the left of the display to choose other modes, such as

- *Measures* (to display the current measure and mark the beat)
- *Chord* (to display note and chord names)
- *Project* (to show or change the key, tempo, and signature for the song)

✦ **Volume slider:** Here's another familiar face. Just drag the slider to raise or lower the volume.

Of course, more controls are scattered around the GarageBand window, but these are the main controls used to compose a song . . . which is the next stop!

Composing and Podcasting Made Easy

In this section, I cover the basics of composition in GarageBand, working from the beginning. Follow along with this running example:

1. **Close all existing GarageBand windows.**

   GarageBand displays the top-level New Project dialog shown in Figure 5-2.

2. **In the list at the left, click New Project.**

3. **Click the Piano icon and click Choose.**

   When you choose Piano, your new GarageBand project will have one track already in place — a grand piano. If you had chosen Electric Guitar or Voice, you'd have a project automatically created with an electric guitar track or male and female voice tracks, respectively. To create an empty project that you populate with tracks yourself, choose Loops.

   GarageBand displays the New Project from Template Save As dialog.

4. **Type a name for your new song and then drag the Tempo slider to select the beats per minute (bpm).**

   A GarageBand song can have only one *tempo* (or speed), expressed as beats per minute, throughout.

Figure 5-2:
Start
creating
your new
song here.

5. **If you want to adjust other settings for your song, you can select the**

   • *Time signature:* Expressed as beats per measure. (Again, a GarageBand song can have only one signature.)

   • *Key:* The Key box. (Think C major or D minor.)

   If you're new to music *theory* (the rules and syntax by which music is created and written), just use the defaults. Most of the toe-tappin' tunes that you and I are familiar with fit right in with these settings.

6. **Click the Create button.**

   You see the window shown earlier in Figure 5-1. (The Blue Jazz Piano 01 section at the top of Figure 5-1 — which I show you how to add in the next section — is an example of a typical loop.)

Adding tracks

Although I'm not a musician, I am a music lover, and I know that many classical composers approached a new work in the same way you approach a new song in GarageBand: by envisioning the instruments that they wanted to hear. (I imagine Mozart and Beethoven would've been thrilled to use GarageBand, but I think they did a decent job with quill and paper, too.)

GarageBand includes a *Songwriting* project (also available from the top-level New Project dialog). When you choose the Songwriting project, GarageBand presents you with a full set of four instrument tracks, plus a real instrument track for your voice. (More on software versus real instrument tracks in a page or two.) You're instantly ready to start adding loops and recording your own voice!

**Book III
Chapter 5**

Becoming
a Superstar
with GarageBand

If you've followed along to this point, you've noticed two issues with your GarageBand window:

✦ **There's no keyboard.** You can record the contents of a software instrument track by "playing" the keyboard, clicking the keys with your mouse. (As you might imagine, this isn't the best solution, especially with a track-pad.) If you're a musician, the best method of recording your own notes is with a MIDI instrument, which I discuss later in the chapter in the sidebar "Join in and jam . . . or talk!" For now, you can display the keyboard window by pressing ⌘+K. If the keyboard window is on the screen and you don't need it, banish the window by clicking the Close button.

Even if you're not interested in the "point-and-click" keyboard, GarageBand offers a musical typing keyboard, where you press the keys on your keyboard to simulate the keys on a musical keyboard. (Hey, if you don't have a MIDI instrument, at least it's better than nothing.) To display the musical typing keyboard window, press Shift+⌘+K.

✦ **The example song has only one track.** If you want to write the next classical masterpiece for Grand Piano, that's fine. Otherwise, on the GarageBand menu bar, choose Track⇨Delete Track to start with a clean slate. (I know, I could have started with a Loops project, but this way, you get to see how to delete a track.)

You can use the following five kinds of tracks in GarageBand:

✦ **Software instrument tracks:** These tracks aren't audio recordings. Rather, they're mathematically precise algorithms that your Mac *renders* (or builds) to fit your needs. If you have a MIDI instrument connected to your Mac, you can create your own software instrument tracks. (More on MIDI instruments later in this chapter.)

In this chapter, I focus on software instrument tracks, which are the easiest for a nonmusician to use.

✦ **Real instrument tracks:** A real instrument track is an audio recording, such as your voice or a physical instrument without a MIDI connection. (Think microphone.)

✦ **Electric guitar tracks:** GarageBand includes an instrument track especially made for an electric guitar, which allows you to use one of five different amplifiers and a number of stomp boxes (those effect pedals that electric guitarists are always poking with their foot to change the sound of their instruments).

✦ **Podcast artwork track:** You get only one of these; they hold photos that will appear on a video-capable iPod, iPhone, or iPad (or a window on your website) when your podcast is playing.

✦ **Video tracks:** The video sound track appears if you're *scoring* (adding music to) an iMovie movie. Along with the video sound track, you get a cool companion video track that shows the clips in your movie. (More on this in the "Look, I'm John Williams!" sidebar, later in this chapter.)

Time to add a software instrument track of your very own. Follow these steps:

1. **Click the New Track button (which carries a plus sign), labeled in the previously shown Figure 5-1.**

GarageBand displays the New Track dialog.

2. **Click the Software Instrument icon and then click Create.**

See all those great instruments in the Track Info pane on the right?

3. **Choose the general instrument category by clicking it.**

I chose Drum Kits.

4. **From the right column, choose your specific style of weapon, such as Rock Kit for an arena sound.**

Figure 5-3 illustrates the new track that appears in your list when you follow these steps.

Figure 5-3: The new track appears, ready to rock.

If you're creating a podcast and you want to add a series of still images that will appear on a device's screen (or on your web page), follow these steps:

1. **Click the View Media Browser button (labeled in Figure 5-1).**

2. **Click the Photos button.**

   GarageBand displays all the photos in your iPhoto library and Events.

3. **Drag an image from your iPhoto library in Media Browser to the Track list.**

   The Podcast track appears at the top of the Track list, and you can add and move images in the list at any time, just like the loops that you add to your instrument tracks. (More on adding and rearranging the contents of a track later in this section.)

Choosing loops

When you have a new, empty track, it's time to start adding something that you can hear. You do that by adding loops to your track from Loop Browser — Apple provides you with thousands of loops to choose from — and photos from your Media Browser. (Think of loops as snippets of a specific instrument that you hear in a song, such as a bass line or a drum beat.) Click the Loop Browser button (which bears a loop, somewhat like a roller coaster) to display your collection, as shown in Figure 5-4.

Figure 5-4:
Loop Browser, shown in button view.

Search

If your browser looks different from what you see in Figure 5-4, that's because of your view mode, just as with the different view modes available for a Finder window. The three-icon button in the upper-left corner of Loop Browser toggles the browser display between column, musical button, and podcast sounds view. Click the middle of the three buttons to switch to musical button mode.

Looking for just the right loop

The track in this running example uses a Rock drum kit, but I haven't added a loop yet. (Refer to Figure 5-3.) Follow these steps to search through your loop library for just the right rhythm:

1. Click the button that corresponds to the instrument you're using.

To follow along with the example, click the Kits button in Loop Browser. A list of different beats appears in the pane at the bottom of the Loop Browser window. (Refer to Figure 5-4.)

2. Click a loop with a green musical-note icon.

Go ahead; this is where things get fun! GarageBand begins playing the loop nonstop, allowing you to get a feel for how that particular loop sounds.

When you use only software instruments in a track (like I do throughout this chapter), choose only software instrument loops, which are identified by a green musical-note icon.

3. Click another entry in the list, and the application switches immediately to that loop.

Now you're beginning to understand why GarageBand is so cool for both musicians and the note-impaired. It's like having your own band, with members who never get tired, never miss a beat, and play whatever you want while you're composing. (Mozart would've *loved* this.)

If you want to search for a particular instrument, click in the Search box (labeled in the preceding Figure 5-4) and type the text you want to match. GarageBand returns the search results in the list.

4. Scroll down the list and continue to sample the different loops until you find one that fits like a glove.

For this reporter, it's Southern Rock Drums 01.

5. Drag the entry to your Rock Kit track and drop it at the very beginning of the Timeline (as indicated by the playhead).

Your window will look like Figure 5-5.

Figure 5-5:
A track
with a loop
added.

If you want that same beat throughout the song, you don't need to add any more loops to that track. (More on extending that beat in the next section.) However, if you want the drum's beat to change later in the song, you add a second loop after the first one in the *same* track. For now, leave this track as is.

Whoops! Did you do something that you regret? Don't forget that you can undo most actions in GarageBand by pressing the old standby ⌘+Z immediately afterward.

Second verse, same as the first

When you compose, you can add tracks for each instrument that you want in your song:

✦ Each track can have more than one loop.

✦ Loops *don't* have to start at the beginning; you can drop a loop anywhere in the Timeline.

For example, in Figure 5-6, you can see that my drum kit kicks in first, but my bass line doesn't begin until some time later (for a funkier opening).

Figure 5-6:
My Timeline
with a
synth and
an electric
bass
onboard.
Let's rock!

Look, I'm John Williams!

You, too, can be a famous composer of soundtracks . . . well, perhaps not quite as famous as Mr. Williams, but even he had to start somewhere. To add a GarageBand score to an iMovie, open the Track menu and then choose Show Movie Track to display the Movie track. Choose a movie to score from the familiar confines of Media Browser, and drag it to the Movie Track.

At this point, you add and modify instrument tracks and loops just as you would any other GarageBand project. The existing sound for the iMovie project appears in the Movie soundtrack. A Video Preview thumbnail appears within the Movie track. When you click the Play button, the video is shown as well so that you can check your work and tweak settings (as described later in the chapter).

After you finish composing, click Share on the menu bar to export your work as a QuickTime movie directly to your hard drive, or to iTunes as a movie. You can't return to iMovie with your project after you do this, though, so scoring should be a final step in the production of your movie.

You put loops on separate tracks so that they can play simultaneously on different instruments. If all your loops in a song are added on the same track, you hear only one loop at any one time, and all the loops use the same software instrument. By creating multiple tracks, you give yourself the elbow room to bring in the entire band at the same time. It's über-convenient to compose your song when you can see each instrument's loops and where they fall in the song.

Click the Reset button in Loop Browser to choose another instrument or genre category.

Resizing, repeating, and moving loops

If you haven't already tried listening to your entire song, try it now. You can click Play at any time without wreaking havoc on your carefully created tracks. Sounds pretty good, doesn't it?

But wait: I bet the song stopped after about five seconds, right? (You can watch the passing seconds using either the Time/Tempo display or the second rule that appears at the very top of the Timeline.) I'm sure that you want your song to last more than five seconds! After the playhead moves past the end of the last loop, your song is over. Click Play again to pause the playback; then click the Return to Beginning button (refer to Figure 5-1) to move the playhead back to the beginning of the song.

The music stops so soon because loops are only so long. Most are five seconds in length, and others are even shorter. To keep the groove going, you have to do one of three things:

✦ **Resize the loop.** Hover your mouse cursor over the left or right edge of most loops, and an interesting thing happens: Your cursor changes to a vertical line with an arrow pointing away from the loop. That's your cue to click and drag — and as you drag, most loops expand to fill the space you're making, repeating the beats in perfect time. When resizing a loop, you can drag the loop's edge as long as you like.

✦ **Repeat the loop.** Depending on the loop that you choose, you might find that resizing it doesn't repeat the measure. Instead, the new part of the loop is simply dead air. As I mention earlier, the length of many loops is limited to anywhere from one to five seconds. What to do? Move your cursor over the side of a loop that you want to extend, and if it turns into a circular arrow, you can click and *repeat* the loop. GarageBand adds multiple copies of the same loop automatically, for as far as you drag the loop. In Figure 5-7, I repeated the bass loop that you see in Figure 5-6.

✦ **Add a new loop.** You can switch to a different loop to change the flow of the music. Naturally, the instrument stays the same, but there's no reason you can't use a horn-riff loop in your violin track (as long as it sounds good played by a violin)! To GarageBand, a software instrument track is compatible with *any* software instrument loop that you add from Loop Browser — as long as that loop is marked with our old friend, the green musical note.

Figure 5-7:
By repeating the bass loop, you can keep the thump flowing.

You can also use the familiar keyboard shortcuts of cut (⌘+X), copy (⌘+C), and paste (⌘+V) to (um) cut, copy, and paste loops from place to place — both on the Timeline and from track to track. And you can click a loop and drag it anywhere. After all, you're working under Mac OS X.

Each track can be adjusted so that you can listen to the interplay between two or more tracks or hear how your song sounds without a specific track:

✦ Click the tiny speaker icon under the track name in the list, and the button turns blue to indicate that the track is muted. To turn off the mute, click the speaker icon again.

✦ You can change the volume or balance of each individual track by using the mixer that appears next to the track name. This comes in handy if you want an instrument to sound louder or to confine that instrument to the left or right speaker.

A track doesn't have to be filled for every second with one loop or another. Most of my songs have a number of repeating loops with empty space between them as different instruments perform solo.

Using the Arrange track

GarageBand includes another method you can use to monkey with your music: The *Arrange track* can be used to define specific sections of a song, allowing you to reorganize things by selecting, moving, and copying entire sections. For example, you're probably familiar with the chorus (or refrain) of a song and how often it appears during the course of the tune. With the Arrange track, you can reposition the entire chorus within your song, carrying all the loops and settings in the chorus along with it! If you need another chorus, just copy that arrangement.

To use the Arrange track, display it by choosing Track⊅Show Arrange Track. The Arrange track then appears as a thin strip at the top of the track list. In the Arrange track, click the Add Region button (which carries a plus sign) and you'll see a new, untitled region appear (as shown in Figure 5-8). You can drag the right side of the Arrangement region to resize it, or drag it to move it anywhere in the song.

Who wants an arrangement full of regions named "untitled"? To rename an Arrangement region, click the word *untitled* to select it (the Arrange track turns blue) and then click the title again to display a text box. Type a new name for the region and press Return.

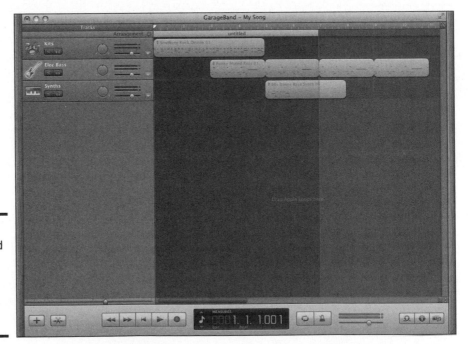

Figure 5-8: I just added a new region in my song's Arrange track.

Now, here's where Arrangement regions get *cool:*

✦ To move an entire Arrangement region, click the region's title in the Arrange track and then drag it anywhere you like in the song.

✦ To copy an Arrangement region, hold down the Option key and drag the desired region's title to the spot where you want the copy to appear.

✦ To delete an Arrangement region, select it and press ⌘+Option+Delete.

✦ To replace the contents of an Arrangement region with those of another Arrangement region, hold down the ⌘ key and drag the desired region's title on top of the offending region's title.

✦ To switch two Arrangement regions in your song — swapping the contents — drag one of the Arrangement region titles on top of the other and release the mouse button.

Join in and jam . . . or talk!

As I mention elsewhere in this chapter, GarageBand is even more fun if you happen to play an instrument! (And yes, I'm envious, no matter how much I enjoy the techno and jazz music that I create. After all, take away my Mac, and I'm back to playing the kazoo . . . at least until I absorb all the Learn to Play lessons for the guitar. More on this feature in the sidebar, "Hey, GarageBand, teach me how to play!")

Most musicians use MIDI instruments to play music on the computer. That pleasant sounding acronym stands for *Musical Instrument Digital Interface.* A wide variety of MIDI instruments is available these days, from traditional MIDI keyboards to more exotic fun, such as MIDI saxophones. For example, Apple sells a 49-key MIDI keyboard from M-Audio for around $100. Alternatively, the highly recommended Casio CTX-3000 offers 61 keys, and it's available online for about $130. (Both keyboards connect to your iMac via a USB cable.)

If you have an older instrument with traditional MIDI ports — they're round, so you'll never confuse them with USB connectors — you need a USB-to-MIDI converter. You can find this type of converter for around $50 on websites catering to musicians. (If you're recording your voice for a podcast, things are easier because you can use your Mac's built-in microphone.)

After your instrument is connected, you can record tracks using any software instrument. Create a new software instrument track as I demonstrate in this chapter, select it, and then play a few notes. Suddenly you're playing the instrument you chose! If nothing happens, check the MIDI status light — which appears in the time display — to see whether it blinks with each note you play. If not, check the installation of your MIDI connection and make sure you loaded any required drivers.

Drag the playhead to a beat or two before the spot in the Timeline where you want your recording to start. This gives you time to match the beat. Then click the big red Record button and start jamming or speaking! When you're finished, click the Play button to stop recording.

Tweaking the settings for a track

You don't think that John Mayer or U2 just "play and walk away," do you?
No, they spend hours after the recording session is over, tweaking their
music in the studio and on the mixing board until every note sounds just as
it should. You can adjust the settings for a track, too. The tweaks that you
can perform include adding effects (pull a Hendrix and add echo and reverb
to your electric guitar track) and kicking in an equalizer (for fine-tuning the
sound of your background horns).

To make adjustments to a track, follow these steps:

1. **In the track list, click the desired track to select it.**

2. **Click the Track Info button (refer to Figure 5-1).**

3. **Click the Edit tab to show the settings shown in Figure 5-9.**

4. **Click the button next to each effect you want to enable.**

(The button glows green when enabled.) Each effect has a modifier
setting. For example, you can adjust the amount of echo to add by
dragging its slider.

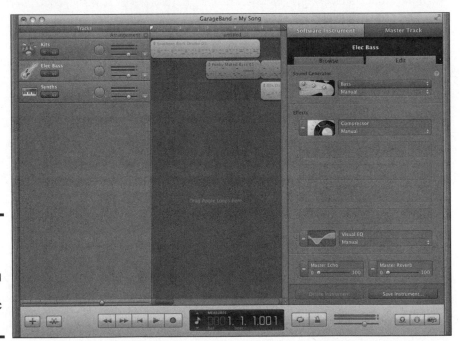

Figure 5-9:
Finesse
your tune
by tweaking
the sound
of a specific
track.

GarageBand offers a Visual Equalizer window that you can use to create a custom equalizer setting for each track. You can display the Visual EQ window by clicking the animated button next to the Visual EQ control on the Edit pane. To change the Bass, Low Mid, High Mid, or Treble setting for a track, click and drag the equalizer waveform in the desired direction. And yep, you can do this while your song is playing, so you can use both your eyes *and* ears to define the perfect settings!

5. **To save the instrument as a new custom instrument — so that you can choose it the next time you add a track — click the Save Instrument button.**

6. **Click the Track Info button again to return to GarageBand.**

Time for a Mark's Maxim:

Save your work often **in GarageBand, just as you do in other iLife applications. One power blackout, and you'll never forgive yourself. Press ⌘+S and enjoy the peace of mind — and use Time Machine with an external backup drive for good measure.**

Automatic Composition with Magic GarageBand

In a hurry? Too rushed to snag loops and tweak effects? Never fear, GarageBand can even compose a song *automatically!* The Magic GarageBand feature provides a wide range of nine different genres of music to choose from — everything from blues to reggae to funk and rock.

To create a song automatically, follow these steps:

1. **Close all GarageBand windows.**

   If you're currently working on a song, GarageBand will prompt you to save it before closing the window.

2. **Click the Magic GarageBand button in the New Project dialog (refer to Figure 5-2).**

3. **Click the desired genre button and click Choose.**

   Hover your mouse cursor over a genre button to get a preview of the song for that genre.

4. **To hear the entire song with the default instruments, click Entire Song and then click the Play button.**

   To hear a short sample of the song, click Snippet and then click Play.

   As shown in Figure 5-10, you see each instrument on stage. To choose a different musical style for an instrument (or a variation of the instrument), click it and then select the desired sound from the menu below the stage.

Figure 5-10:
Creating my
own arena-
rock classic
with Magic
GarageBand.

You'd like to join in and jam with Magic GarageBand? Click the instrument that appears at the front center of the stage to highlight it. GarageBand displays the My Instrument settings on the menu below the stage. Click the My Instrument pop-up menu at the lower-left corner of the window to add your own voice or instrumental using your Mac's keyboard, a microphone, or a MIDI instrument.

5. **When the song fits like a glove, click the Open in GarageBand button to open the song as a project in GarageBand.**

Now you can edit and tweak the song to your heart's delight as you can any other GarageBand project, adding other software or real instrument tracks as necessary.

Sharing Your Songs and Podcasts

After you finish your song, you can play it whenever you like through GarageBand. But then again, that isn't really what you want, is it? You want to share your music with others with an audio CD or download it to your iPod so that you can enjoy it yourself while walking through the mall.

Hey, GarageBand, teach me how to play!

In the early days of GarageBand, you were limited to creating music — and if you were a nonmusician like yours truly, GarageBand had no practical use as a tool for teaching yourself how to actually *play* an instrument.

Ah, but Apple's addition of Learn to Play turns GarageBand into your private video tutor for basic piano and guitar! From the New Project dialog, click the Learn to Play heading to display your lessons. Right out of the box, you have an Introduction to both instruments, but you can download more free lessons for each instrument from the Lesson Store. They cover more advanced topics, such as fingering and chords. Your onscreen instructor can even record what you play.

GarageBand also includes the How Did I Play feature, which can pinpoint the portions of a lesson that you played correctly and which spots in the song you need to work on. (I'm told musicians call such trouble spots *flubs* — having no musical talent, anything I attempt to play would be one giant flub.) To try How Did I Play, open your favorite lesson, move your pointer to the left side of the window, and then click the Play button that appears. Click the Record button (with the red dot in the center) and begin playing. To stop recording, click the Play button. Now you can see the portions of the song that you played correctly (where the notation area is green) and those spots where you flubbed (the notation area turns red). Oh, and make sure that your instrument is in tune because even correct notes played on an instrument that's out of tune produce errors for How Did I Play!

If you find the free Learn to Play lessons valuable, you can move up to the Artist lessons, which are taught by famous musicians (including favorites of mine, such as Alex Lifeson, John Fogerty, and Sting, who teaches you how to play "Roxanne")! Each Artist lesson is $4.99 — well worth the price.

iTunes to the rescue! As with the other iLife applications that I cover in this book, GarageBand can share the music you make through the digital hub that is your Mac.

Creating MP3 and AAC files and ringtones

You can create an MP3 audio file, an AAC audio file, or an M4R audio file (for an iPhone, iPod touch, or iPad ringtone, as well as for the Mavericks Messages and FaceTime applications) from your song or podcast project in just a few simple steps:

1. **Open the song that you want to share.**

2. **Choose Share➪Send Song to iTunes.**

   GarageBand displays the settings you see in Figure 5-11.

   To create a ringtone and send it to iTunes, choose Share➪Send Ringtones to iTunes.

Figure 5-11:
Tweaking
settings for
iTunes song
files.

3. **Click in each of the four text boxes to type the playlist, artist name, composer name, and album name for the tracks you create.**

   You can leave the defaults as they are, if you prefer. Each track that you export is named after the song's name in GarageBand.

4. **Click the Compress Using pop-up menu and choose the encoder GarageBand should use to compress your song file.**

   The default is AAC, but you can also choose MP3 encoding for compatibility with a wider range of devices.

5. **Click the Audio Settings pop-up menu to select the proper audio quality for the finished file.**

   The higher the quality, the larger the file. GarageBand displays the approximate file size and finished file information in the description box.

6. **Click Share.**

   After a second or two of hard work, your Mac opens the iTunes window and highlights the new (or existing) playlist that contains your new song.

Sending a podcast to iTunes

If you've prepared a new podcast episode in GarageBand, you can send it automatically to iTunes by following these steps:

1. **Open the podcast that you want to export.**

   Make sure that the Podcast track is displayed. If necessary, choose Track⇨Show Podcast Track to display it.

2. **Choose Share⇨Send Podcast to iTunes.**

3. **Click the Compress Using pop-up menu and choose the encoder that GarageBand should use to compress your podcast file.**

   Your choices are AAC and MP3 format.

4. **Click the Audio Settings pop-up menu to select the proper audio quality for the finished file.**

5. **Click Share.**

Burning an audio CD

Ready to create a demo CD with your latest GarageBand creation? Follow these steps to burn an audio disc from within GarageBand:

1. **Open the song that you want to record to disc.**

2. **Choose Share⇨Burn Song to CD.**

3. **Load a blank disc into your optical drive.**

Note that the CD you create only has one track, and by *track* I mean one song (not like a track in a song). To include more songs on the CD, add the song to your iTunes library (as described earlier), create a playlist containing the song, and burn that playlist in iTunes.

Chapter 6: No, It's Not Called iQuickTime

In This Chapter

✔ Viewing movies

✔ Listening to audio

✔ Converting media to different formats

✔ Keeping track of your favorite media

✔ Tweaking QuickTime preferences

QuickTime is a set of exciting technologies that gives you access to the greatest multimedia experience around. Despite its power, don't be surprised if you don't even realize that you're using it sometimes. Built with the average Joe in mind, QuickTime Player takes multimedia to new heights without forcing its users to become rocket scientists in the process.

QuickTime Can Do That?

QuickTime was created by Apple to perform all sorts of multimedia functions. Although normally associated with movie playback, QuickTime Player can do much more. Whether it's playing movies, audio, animation, or music, QuickTime acts as the main engine that drives all your multimedia needs. (It's even behind-the-scenes when Mavericks displays images on your screen.)

✦ **Media player:** QuickTime Player's main claim to fame is playing all sorts of media — and I do mean *all* sorts. Table 6-1 lists the most popular of the media types that QuickTime can play.

The real beauty of QuickTime Player is that it transparently handles playback of all these media formats and more. You don't even have to know what each of these formats is to play them. QuickTime Player takes care of that for you.

✦ **Recording utility:** QuickTime Player can record video, audio, and even activity on the screen.

✦ **Internet media tool:** When it comes to using media from the Internet, QuickTime is in a league all its own. In addition to playing the usual movies and audio files found on the web, QuickTime can play (or display) 3-D scenes and animations. As if that weren't enough, QuickTime even lets you interact with some media. For example, with QuickTime, you can navigate in 3-D worlds or play Flash games.

Table 6-1	QuickTime Playback Formats
Media Type	*File Types*
Movie	MOV*, AVI*, MPG, MPEG-1, DV, MP4/M4V, 3G (cellphones), H.263, H.264
Audio	AIFF, WAV, MP2, MP3, AU, SFIL, AAC, AMR
Image	JPEG, PNG, TIFF, GIF, BMP, PCX, TGA
Music	MID, KAR
3-D	QTVR (QuickTime Virtual Reality)
Animation	SWF

Movies in MOV and AVI formats use a wide range of compression schemes, many of them proprietary. For this reason, QuickTime might not be able to play some MOV or AVI movies that you download without the installation of a plug-in (called a "codec") for that scheme.

Playing Media with QuickTime

QuickTime makes a world of movies, audio, graphics, and music instantly available to you. Whether you want to view professional movie trailers or listen to a garage band's new single, QuickTime faithfully reproduces nearly any media format that you feed it.

To launch QuickTime Player, double-click its icon in Finder, or click the Launchpad icon on the Dock and then click the QuickTime Player icon that appears. You can launch QuickTime Player from Finder also by double-clicking a media file that QuickTime can play. (Refer to Table 6-1 for a listing of these file types.)

Don't make the mistake of thinking that QuickTime and QuickTime Player are the same thing: *QuickTime* is a technology that hides in the background waiting for instructions to do something with media; *QuickTime Player* is an application that uses the QuickTime technologies. You'll do recording, media conversions, playback, and editing with QuickTime Player. What you won't see is the QuickTime technology in action behind the scenes.

You can also launch QuickTime Player from an oh-so-convenient Dock icon. For more on adding stuff to the Dock, read Book II, Chapter 2.

Opening QuickTime movies

To begin viewing and hearing — aw, what the heck, how about *absorbing* — multimedia files, choose File⇨Open File from the QuickTime Player application. This isn't the only way to open a file with QuickTime Player, though. Some of the other ways to open files with QuickTime Player are

+ **Drag a file to the QuickTime Player icon on the Dock.**

+ **Right-click a movie and choose Open With; choose QuickTime Player from the pop-up menu.**

+ **Double-click the media file in Finder.**

Operating QuickTime Player

When you open a QuickTime file, QuickTime Player creates a new window to display it. All QuickTime Player windows have some common features:

+ **Close, Minimize, and Zoom controls:** These three controls appear at the top-left corner of most windows in Mac OS X. You probably recognize them by their colors: red, yellow, and green, respectively.

+ **Resizability:** Drag any corner or side of the QuickTime Player window to resize its movie for playback. Hold Shift while dragging to break free from constrained resizing. If the document contains only sound media, the window grows or shrinks in a horizontal direction when you resize it.

Any resizing that you perform makes no changes to the original file. QuickTime provides it for your convenience during playback.

Although some window features are common to all QuickTime Player windows, many features depend on the type of media that you want to play. Table 6-2 lists some of the window features that you might find and the media types associated with those features.

Table 6-2	QuickTime Player Window Features Based on Media
Window Feature	*Media Type That Uses This Feature*
Play	All time-based media: movies, audio, animations, and MIDI
Rewind	All time-based media: movies, audio, animations, and MIDI
Fast Forward	All time-based media: movies, audio, animations, and MIDI
Timeline	All time-based media: movies, audio, animations, and MIDI
Volume	All media with one or more audio tracks
Add to iTunes/Share	All media with audio or video
Toggle Full Screen	All movies and animations
Zoom	QTVR 3-D media
Rotate	QTVR 3-D media
Mute	All media with one or more audio tracks

To make your life easier, QuickTime does a lot of work for you behind the scenes each time it opens a media file. Although you might think that QuickTime Player has different combinations of controls, the various media windows are more similar than they are different. Figure 6-1 shows the location of various QuickTime Player controls when you're playing a video clip.

Playing media

Playback begins as you might suspect — by clicking the Play button. While a file is playing, the Play button toggles to a Pause button. Click that button to pause playback, which toggles the button back to Play.

Clicking the buttons that sport double arrows advances the playback head at high speed in the direction of the arrows. (Click once to advance at 2x speed; click again to increase the speed.) If the file contains audio, you hear the playback at high speed, which sounds like an episode of those helium-inhaling Chipmunks. (Remember? *Meee, I waaant a hooola hooop.*) Despite its comical sound, this feature enables you to quickly scan through a file.

You can also advance through the file by dragging the playback head — an action called *scrubbing* — in either direction. Scrubbing is allowed while the file is playing or when it's stopped. When you drag the playback head, however, you miss out on the high-speed sound and video that you would get if you used the buttons.

Figure 6-1:
QuickTime
Player
sports
different
controls,
depending
on the
media you
play.

To adjust the volume of a movie, simply move the volume slider left or right. To mute the volume, click the speaker icon to the left of the volume slider.

You can control playback by using the keyboard as well. Table 6-3 summarizes the keyboard shortcuts for playback.

**Book III
Chapter 6**

No, It's Not Called
iQuickTime

Table 6-3	Common Playback Keyboard Shortcuts
Keyboard Shortcut	*What It Does*
Spacebar	Starts or stops the player
←	Advances the playback head (one frame at a time or in slow motion)
→	Rewinds the playback head (one frame at a time or in slow motion)
Option+↑	Sets the volume to Maximum
Option+↓	Sets the volume to Minimum
↑	Increases the volume of the current movie
↓	Decreases the volume of the current movie

Sometimes you might want to play a piece of media more than once. In these situations, you need to loop the playback. To force a movie to loop, choose View⇨Loop or press ⌘+L. Press ⌘+L again to turn off looping.

Movie info

To see more information about the files that you're playing, ask the expert: QuickTime Player. To view basic information about a movie, choose Window⇨ Show Movie Inspector or press ⌘+I. The resulting window displays the following data:

✦ **Source:** Location of the file

✦ **Format:** Compressor and dimensions of the file

✦ **FPS:** Preferred rate of playback in frames per second (fps), shown only for video

✦ **Data size:** Size of the file

✦ **Data rate:** Preferred rate of playback (in bits per second)

✦ **Current time:** Position of the playback head (in units of time)

✦ **Current size:** Movie dimensions

These bits and pieces of information are *read-only* — you can't change them from the Movie Inspector window.

Chapter 7: Turning Your Mac into a DVD Theater

In This Chapter

✔ Understanding what you need to watch DVDs on your Macintosh

✔ Using the DVD Player software

✔ Unearthing the mysteries of the hidden controls

All the creative capabilities of the OS X digital hub are a lot of fun, but at some point, you'll want to take a break from work. Because of the now-familiar DVD, the idea of an honest-to-goodness theater in your home is now within the grasp of mere mortals (with, coincidentally, merely average budgets). OS X has everything that you'll need to enjoy a night at the movies without ever leaving home.

Getting the Right DVD Hardware

Before you watch one second of video, get your setup in order. Playing DVDs requires a bit of hardware; unfortunately, none of the latest entries in the Macintosh line come equipped with the optical drive that's necessary to watch DVDs. But don't panic just yet!

To play DVD movies, you need either an internal DVD-compatible drive in your older Macintosh or an external DVD drive with a FireWire, Thunderbolt, or USB connection. DVD-ROM drives can only play discs; others, such as the SuperDrive, can both play and record discs. Either type of drive works fine for watching movies on your Mac.

You can watch standard DVDs that you purchase at your local video store, as well as DVDs you've burned with applications such as Toast Titanium.

Watching Movies with DVD Player

To watch Frodo Baggins, Don Corleone, or James Bond, you also need DVD player software. OS X comes stocked with the perfect tool for the task: DVD Player.

Apple's DVD Player application is included with OS X; you can find it in the confines of your Applications folder or in Launchpad. But instead of rooting through Finder, you can launch DVD Player an even easier way: Simply insert a DVD into the drive. As soon as you do, your Mac recognizes the disc and launches DVD Player by default for you.

This automatic behavior can be curbed, however. You can control what action Mavericks takes (if any) when you load a DVD via the CDs & DVDs pane in System Preferences. For all the details, visit Book II, Chapter 3.

However you choose to start DVD Player, you'll notice that it offers two windows:

+ **Controller:** The small, silver-colored, remote control–looking interface that holds all the controls for Player. (See upcoming Figure 7-1.)

+ **Viewer:** The large window where you view your DVD movies.

In Full-Screen mode, you won't see the Viewer window, and the video takes up the entire screen. The controller appears as a floating opaque strip of controls along the bottom of the screen. To display the controls, move your cursor. Move the cursor to the top of the screen and you can switch chapters and jump to bookmarks. (I talk about both later in the chapter.)

If you're already using a traditional DVD player, you'll be right at home with Apple's DVD Player. Even if you've never used a traditional DVD player, you'll find that it's not much different from using a software-based audio player such as iTunes.

Using the Controller

The *Controller* is the command center of the DVD Player software. Arranged much the same as a VCR or tape deck, all the familiar controls are present. Check it out in Figure 7-1.

Figure 7-1:
Use the
Controller
for mundane
playback
chores.

Jumping right to the flying-monkey action

Movies on DVD usually are divided into *chapters* that enable you to jump directly to specific points. That way, you can jump right to the scene, say, where the flying monkey guards march into the Wicked Witch's castle in *The Wizard of Oz.* (Or skip that egg-hatching scene in *Alien* that always makes you nauseated.)

You can navigate to chapters, play the movie from the beginning, or check out special bonus features (such as trailers and documentaries) from the DVD's main menu. To switch to a different chapter in Full-Screen mode, move your cursor to the top of the screen.

Table 7-1 details the fundamental commands present in the DVD Player Controller. Apple software usually has some goodies hidden beneath the surface, and DVD Player is no exception. The controls in DVD Player have a few functions that might not be obvious to the casual user. These are listed in the third column of Table 7-1.

Table 7-1	Basic DVD Controls	
Control Name	*What It Does*	*Other Functions*
Play	Plays the DVD	Switches to a Pause button any time a movie is playing
Stop	Stops DVD playback	
Previous Chapter	Skips to the previous chapter	Click and hold down the button to quickly scan through the movie in reverse
Next Chapter	Skips to the next chapter	Click and hold down the button to quickly scan forward through the movie
Playback Volume	Adjusts DVD audio volume	
Arrow Buttons	Navigates through DVD menu items	
Enter	Selects the currently highlighted menu item	
Eject	Ejects the DVD from the drive	
Title	Jumps immediately to the DVD's title menu	
Menu	Displays current DVD menu	

Keeping your eyes on the Viewer

Although the DVD Player controls are neat, the Viewer window, shown in Figure 7-2, is where you'll actually watch your video.

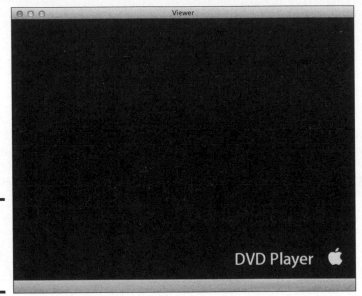

Figure 7-2:
The Viewer is the real star of DVD Player.

You can think of the Viewer window as a television inside your Macintosh, if it helps, but DVD Player goes one step further. Unlike a television screen, the Viewer has some nice tricks up its sleeve: For example, you can resize the Viewer window by using one of the five sizes listed in the View menu (Half, Actual Size, Double Size, Fit to Screen, and Full-Screen sizes). This feature is useful for watching a movie in a small window on your Desktop while you work with other applications. You can toggle your Viewer size from the keyboard; for example, select Half Size with ⌘+0 (zero), Actual Size with ⌘+1 (one), and Double Size with ⌘+2 (two).

If you're only in it for the entertainment factor, you'll probably want to resize the Viewer to fill the screen. I like to watch movies in Full-Screen mode, which you can toggle with the ⌘+F keyboard shortcut. If you want to take full advantage of all your screen space yet leave the Viewer window onscreen for occasional resizing, choose Fit to Screen mode with ⌘+3 (three).

Watching video in the raw

"Watching video in the raw" sounds a little racy, but I'm talking about viewing digital video directly from your hard drive to your HDTV! Many Mac owners prefer to leave their high-definition video content on a hard drive, instead of burning those huge clips and movies to DVD using Toast Titanium or another recording application — if you're one of this crowd, consider a peripheral such s the WD Elements Play from Western Digital (www.wdc.com/en), which connects directly to your TV's HDMI port.

Your Mac isn't involved at all because the device includes its own internal hard drive, and you can even plug in an external hard drive containing your video. Elements Play supports a bewildering range of video formats at up to AVCHD 1080p, including MPEG-1, MPEG-2, AVI (.divx, .xvid, and .avc), H.264, and MLV. Elements Play is available online for less than $100, complete with a remote control.

Taking Advantage of Additional DVD Features

As anyone with a little DVD experience knows, DVDs can do a lot more than those archaic tapes that you used to feed your VCR. Apple has included several functions that allow you to explore the extra features and content provided with a DVD movie.

Controller extras

To use the additional Controller features, double-click the small tab at the rightmost (or bottom) edge of the DVD Player Controller. After you do, a trick drawer slides out, displaying the extra controls. (See Figure 7-3.) You can also display or hide the drawer with the Controls⇨Open/Close Control Drawer menu command or by pressing ⌘+] (that's the right bracket key).

Figure 7-3:
Expand the
Controller
to view
additional
controls.

Are you interested in fine-tuning the audio from your DVD movies? If so, choose Window➪Audio Equalizer, and DVD Player displays a ten-band equalizer. (I often use this feature to add extra bass to a concert DVD.) To turn on the equalizer, select the On check box. Click the pop-up menu at the upper right of the Equalizer window, and you can choose a preset (such as Bass Boost or Vocal Boost), or even create custom audio presets.

Table 7-2 summarizes the functions that you can perform with these additional controls.

Table 7-2	Additional Controller Features
Control	*What It Does*
Slow Motion (half speed)	Plays a DVD in slow motion at half the original speed
Step (frame speed)	Steps through a DVD in ultraslow motion, one frame at a time
Return	Navigates to the previous menu
Subtitle/Closed Captioning	Displays alternate subtitles and closed captioning on the DVD
Audio	Plays alternate audio tracks on the DVD
Angle	Displays the current video footage from different camera angles

Although you won't find a Bookmark button on the Controller, DVD Player can set them nonetheless. A *bookmark* is a spot, like a favorite scene, that you specify in a movie so that you can return to it at any time. To set a bookmark at the current spot in the movie, choose Controls➪New Bookmark, or press ⌘+= (the equal sign key). DVD Player even allows you to name the bookmark so that it's easier to remember. To return to a bookmark, choose Go➪Bookmarks and click the desired bookmark. (If you're enjoying your movie in Full-Screen mode, move your cursor to the top of the screen to use the Bookmarks strip.)

DVD Player preferences

The DVD Player application has a variety of settings that you can access and adjust via its Preferences window. To open the Preferences window, choose DVD Player➪Preferences. This brings up the Preferences dialog.

This window consists of five panes:

✦ **Player:** Settings that affect how DVD Player operates

✦ **Disc Setup:** Settings for Audio, Subtitles, Language, and the web

✦ **Windows:** Settings for displaying onscreen information during playback

✦ **Previously Viewed:** Settings that determine what happens when you load a DVD that you watched (or have started watching) already

✦ **High Definition:** Settings that specify how high-definition video is displayed on your Mac

The advantage of these Preference settings is that you can customize your copy of DVD Player to match your needs or desires. (Thanks yet again to the Cupertino Crowd!)

Player

The Player settings take care of much of the automation in DVD Player:

✦ **When DVD Player Opens:** These two check boxes affect what happens when you launch the DVD Player application. You can force DVD Player to play in full-screen mode and automatically begin playback every time you start the application.

✦ **When DVD Player Is Inactive:** If you're multitasking while watching your movie in windowed mode, you can click another window to make it active. This check box determines whether DVD Player automatically pauses while you're working in that other application.

✦ **When a Disc Is Inserted:** Besides automatic playback on startup, you can also make DVD Player start playing a disc automatically when the application is running already. (To illustrate: If this check box is deselected, loading a new disc won't automatically start it playing if DVD Player is already running.)

✦ **When Playing Using Battery:** If you're using a MacBook, you can conserve power while using DVD Player by selecting this check box. The DVD Player will "spin down" the DVD whenever possible, which may cause a short delay when you fast-forward or rewind.

✦ **When Muted:** Do you answer a lot of telephone calls while you sneak a quick DVD movie at work? If so, be sure to enable this option. If you have to press the Mute button on your keyboard while a movie is playing, DVD Player automatically adds the subtitles/closed captions so that you can keep up with the dialog. *Super sassy!*

✦ **When Viewer Is Minimized:** Watching a DVD at the office, eh? Enable this check box, and DVD Player automatically pauses the movie when you minimize the DVD Player window. (Managers label this feature *downright sneaky.*)

Disc Setup

The second tab of the Player Preferences window, Disc Setup, consists of these controls:

✦ **Language:** *Sprechen Sie Deutsch?* DVDs are designed to be multi-language-aware. Feel like brushing up on your German, Spanish, or Chinese? You can control the language used for the audio, subtitling, and menus in this section.

✦ **Internet:** Some DVDs with DVD@CCESS support can access information on the Internet. Mark this check box to allow that function.

✦ **Audio:** Open this pop-up menu to specify the default audio output signal that you'd like to use. You can also choose to disable the Dolby dynamic range compression feature, which might enhance the sound for two-speaker systems; however, you don't want to damage the lower-output speakers on a MacBook or MacBook Pro, so I recommend that laptop owners leave dynamic range compression enabled.

Multiple languages and web access aren't mandatory features of a DVD, so don't be surprised if you see variations of support when it comes to these settings.

Windows

The Windows pane gives you the chance to configure the behavior of the Controller and status information for the Viewer window:

✦ **Status Information:** Mark the Display Status Information check box, and DVD Player adds a small text box at the top-left corner of the Viewer window. In this text box, you see the name of the last task that you performed with DVD Player. For example, click the Stop button to see the word *Stop* displayed in the Viewer on top of the video beneath it.

✦ **Fade Controller:** You can also set the Controller to fade away instead of just disappear. It's eye candy, but doggone it, it's *good* eye candy!

Previously Viewed

The Previously Viewed pane controls what happens when you load a disc that you've seen already . . . or perhaps your significant other watched it and didn't tell you. (Insert growling noise here.)

✦ **Start Playing Discs From:** If you have to quit DVD Player for some reason, the application is smart enough to remember where you were, and you can choose to begin watching from the beginning, from the last position (where you were when you stopped the last time), or from a default bookmark. Alternatively, just select Always Ask, and DVD Player will prompt you each time this situation crops up.

✦ **Always Use Disc Settings For:** Select these check boxes to specify whether DVD Player should use the same settings you used the last time you watched this disc.

High Definition

The final DVD Player Preferences panel, High Definition, specifies how both standard DV and high-definition video from a DVD are displayed in the Viewer window. (As I mention earlier, the Viewer window size can also be changed from the View menu, but the settings in this pane control what defaults DVD Player uses.)

✦ **For Standard Definition:** You can choose to display the actual video size by default or to use the default size provided by the DVD.

✦ **For High Definition:** These options affect how a high-definition video signal is displayed. Your choices are the actual video size, a height of 720 pixels, and a height of 1,080 pixels.

Don't forget to click OK to save any changes you make to your DVD Player preferences.

After you have your DVD Player customized to your liking, get out the popcorn, pull up your favorite recliner, and let the movies roll!

Book III
Chapter 7

Turning Your Mac into a DVD Theater

Book IV
Using iWork

Contents at a Glance

Chapter 1: Desktop Publishing with Pages

In This Chapter

- ✔ Creating a Pages document
- ✔ Entering and editing text
- ✔ Formatting text
- ✔ Inserting tables and graphics
- ✔ Resizing objects
- ✔ Checking your spelling
- ✔ Printing Pages documents
- ✔ Sharing your work

What's the difference between word processing and desktop publishing? In a nutshell, it's in how you *design* your document. Most folks use a word processor like an old-fashioned typewriter. Think Microsoft Word and a typical business letter. (Yawn.)

On the other hand, a desktop publishing application typically allows you far more creativity in choosing where you place your text, how you align graphics, and how you edit formats. I think desktop publishing is more visual and intuitive, allowing your imagination a free hand at creating a document.

In this chapter, I show you how to set your inner designer free from the tedious constraints of word processing! Whether you need a simple letter, a stunning brochure, or a multipage newsletter, Pages can handle the job with ease — and you'll be surprised at how simple it is to use.

Creating a New Pages Document

Every visual masterpiece starts somewhere, and with Pages, the first stop in creating your document is the Template Chooser window. To create a new Pages document from scratch, follow these steps:

1. **Click the Pages icon on the Dock.**

If Pages doesn't appear on your Dock, click the Launchpad icon and then click the Pages icon.

2. **Click the New Document button in the lower-left corner of the Open dialog.**

   Pages displays the Template Chooser window that you see in Figure 1-1.

Figure 1-1:
Select a
template
from the
Template
Chooser
window.

You can also create a new Pages document at any time from the File menu — just click New to display the Template Chooser window.

3. **In the list to the left, click the type of document you want to create.**

   The thumbnails on the right are updated with templates that match your choice.

4. **Click the template that most closely matches your needs.**

5. **Click the Choose button to open a new document in the template you selected.**

Opening an Existing Pages Document

You can always open an existing Pages document from a Finder window — just double-click the document icon. (The All My Files location in the Finder window sidebar makes it crazy-easy to track down a document.) However, you can also open a Pages document from within the program. Follow these steps:

1. **From Launchpad, click the Pages icon to run the program.**

2. **Press ⌘+O to display the Open dialog.**

The Open dialog operates much the same as a Finder window in Icon, List or Column view mode. To open a document that you've already saved in your iCloud folder, click the iCloud button in the top-left corner of the Open dialog.

3. **To open a document you've saved on your Mac's drive, click the On My Mac button, and then click the desired drive in the Devices list at the left of the dialog. Drill down through folders and subfolders until you locate the Pages document.**

Alternatively, you can use the Search box in the top-right corner of the Open dialog to locate the document. Click in the Search box and type a portion (or all) of the filename, and then choose Name Matches from the pop-up menu that appears. You can also search the contents of your files for a specific phrase. While searching, you can choose to search your drive, your iCloud folder, or both.

If you're using Icon view mode (or displaying the Preview column in Column view mode), you can hover your cursor over a document thumbnail and quickly flip through the different pages by clicking the left and right arrows that appear — this feature can help you identify a particular Pages document without even opening it.

4. **Double-click the thumbnail (or filename) to load it.**

If you want to open a Pages document that you've recently edited, things get even easier! Just choose File⇨Open Recent, and you can open the document with a single click from the submenu that appears.

Saving Your Work

Although Pages fully supports the Auto Save feature in Mavericks, you may feel the need to manually save your work after you finish it (or to take a break while designing). Follow these steps to save a document for the first time:

1. **With the Pages document open, press ⌘+S.**

2. **Type a filename for your new document.**

3. **Open the Where pop-up menu and choose a location for saving the document.**

   Note that Pages defaults to your iCloud folder as the target location. Alternatively, click the button sporting the down arrow to expand the Save As sheet. You can then navigate to a different location or create a new folder in which to store this Pages project.

4. **Click Save.**

After you save a Pages document for the first time, you can create a version of that document by choosing File⇨Save. To revert the current document to an older version, choose File⇨Revert To. Pages gives you the option of reverting to the last saved version, or you can click Browse All Versions to browse multiple versions of the document and choose one of those to revert to.

Touring the Pages Window

Before diving into any real work, take a quick tour of the Pages window! You'll find the following major components and controls, as shown in Figure 1-2:

+ **Pages list:** This thumbnail list displays all the pages you've created in your document. (For a single-page document, of course, the Page list will contain only a single thumbnail.) You can switch instantly between different pages in your document by clicking the desired thumbnail in the list.

+ **Layout pane:** This section, which takes up most of the Pages window, is where you design and edit each page in your document.

+ **Toolbar:** Yep, Pages has its own toolbar. The toolbar keeps all the most common application controls within easy one-click reach.

+ **Styles Drawer:** This window extension allows you to quickly switch the appearance of selected paragraphs, characters, and lists. You can hide and display the Styles Drawer from the View menu or from the View drop-down menu on the toolbar.

+ **Format bar:** This button strip runs below the Pages toolbar, with tools to format selected text, paragraphs, and lists on the fly.

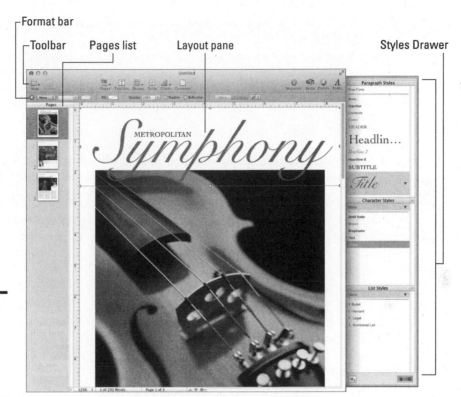

Format bar

Toolbar   Pages list   Layout pane   Styles Drawer

Figure 1-2:
The major
points of
interest in
the Pages
window.

Entering and Editing Text

If you've used a modern word-processing program on any computer —
including freebies such as TextEdit on a Mac or WordPad on a PC — you'll
feel right at home when typing in Pages. Just in case you've never used a text
editor, however, I'll review the high points:

✦ The bar-shaped text cursor, which looks like a capital letter *I,* indicates
where the text you enter will appear in a Pages document.

✦ To enter text, simply begin typing. Your characters appear at the text
cursor.

✦ To edit existing text in your Pages document, click the insertion cursor
at any point in the text and drag the insertion cursor across the characters to highlight them. Type the replacement text, and Pages automatically replaces the existing characters with the ones you type.

✦ To delete text, click and drag across the characters to highlight them;
then press Delete.

**Book IV
Chapter 1**

**Desktop Publishing
with Pages**

Using Text and Graphics Boxes

In Pages, text and graphics appear in boxes, which can be resized by clicking and dragging any handle that appears around the edges of the box. When you hover your cursor over one of the square handles and it changes to a double-sided arrow, Pages is ready to resize the box.

You can also move a box, including all the stuff it contains, to another location in the Layout pane. Click in the center of the box and drag the box to the desired spot, or hold down the Option key while you drag to create a copy in the new location. Pages displays blue alignment lines to help you align the box with other elements around it (or with regular divisions of the page, such as the vertical center of a poster or flyer). Figure 1-3 illustrates a box containing text that I'm moving; note the vertical alignment line that automatically appears.

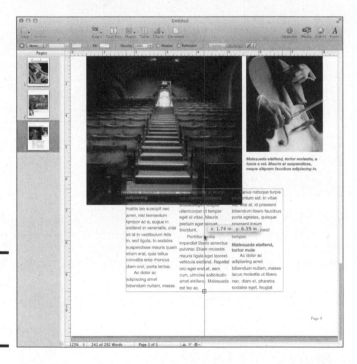

Figure 1-3: Moving a text box in the Layout pane.

To select text or graphics within a box, you must first click the box to select it and then click again on the line of text or the graphic that you want to change.

The Three Amigos: Cut, Copy, and Paste

"Hang on, Mark, you've covered moving stuff, but what if you want to *copy* a block of text or a photo to a second location? Or how about cutting something from a document open in another application?" Good questions, dear reader! That's when you can call on the power of the cut, copy, and paste features in Pages. The next few sections explain how you do these actions.

Cutting stuff

Cutting selected text or graphics removes it from your Pages document and places that material on your Clipboard. (Think of the Clipboard as a holding area for snippets of text and graphics that you want to manipulate.) To cut text or graphics, select some material and do one of the following:

- ✦ Choose Edit➪Cut.
- ✦ Press ⌘+X.

If you simply want to remove the selected material from your Pages document (and you don't plan to paste it somewhere else), just select the text and press the Delete key.

Copying text and images

When you copy text or graphics, the original selection remains untouched, but a copy of the selection is placed in the Clipboard. Select some text or graphics and do one of the following:

- ✦ Choose Edit➪Copy.
- ✦ Press ⌘+C.

If you cut or copy a new selection onto the Clipboard, it erases what was there. In other words, the Clipboard holds only the latest material you cut or copied.

You can also let your cursor do the work! Hold down the Option key while dragging selected items to copy them to a new location.

Pasting from the Clipboard

Are you wondering what you can do with stuff that's stored on your Clipboard? Pasting the contents of the Clipboard places the material at the current location of the insertion cursor. You can repeat a paste operation as often as you like because the contents of the Clipboard aren't cleared.

However, remember that the Clipboard holds only the contents of your *last* copy or cut operation, so you must paste the contents before you cut or copy again to avoid losing what's on the Clipboard.

To paste the Clipboard contents, click the insertion cursor at the location you want and do one of the following:

✦ Choose Edit⇨Paste.

✦ Press ⌘+V.

Formatting Text the Easy Way

If you feel that some (or all) of the text in your Pages document needs a face-lift, you can format that text any way you like. Formatting lets you change the color, font family, character size, and attributes as necessary.

After the text is selected, you can apply basic formatting in two ways:

✦ **Use the Format bar.** The Format bar appears directly below the Pages toolbar (refer to Figure 1-2). Click to select a font control to display a pop-up menu and then click your choice. For example, click the Font Family button and then change the font family from ho-hum Arial to a more daring font. You can also select characteristics, such as the font background color (perfect for "highlighting" items), or choose italicizing or bolding. The Format bar also provides buttons for text alignment (Align Left, Center, Align Right, and Justify).

✦ **Use the Format menu.** Most controls on the Format bar are also available on the Format menu. Click Format and hover the cursor over the Font menu item, and you can then apply bolding, italicizing, and underlining to the selected text. You can also make the text bigger or smaller. To change the alignment from the Format menu, click Format and hover the cursor over the Text menu item.

Adding a Spiffy Table

In the world of word processing, a *table* is a celled grid that holds text or graphics for easy comparison. Many computer owners think of a spreadsheet program such as Numbers when they think of a table (probably because of the rows and columns layout used in a spreadsheet), but you can create a custom table layout in Pages with a few simple mouse clicks.

Follow these steps:

1. **Click the insertion cursor at the location where you want the table to appear.**

2. **Click the Table button on the Pages toolbar.**

Pages inserts a simple table and displays the Table Inspector. (Both are visible in Figure 1-4.)

By default, Pages creates a table with three rows and three columns, with an extra row for headings at the top. You can change this layout from the Table Inspector by clicking in the Body Rows or Body Columns field and typing a number.

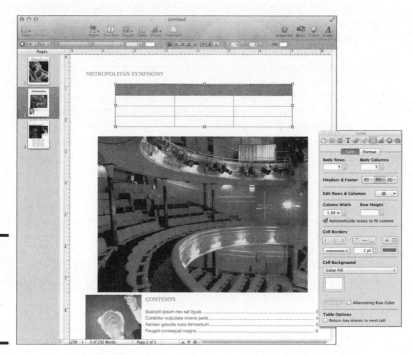

Figure 1-4: Preparing to tweak a table in my Pages document.

3. **Click within a cell in the table to enter text.**

The table cell automatically resizes and "wraps" the text you enter to fit.

You can paste material from the Clipboard into a table. See the earlier section "Pasting from the Clipboard" for details on pasting.

4. **To change the borders on a cell, click the cell to select it and then click one of the Cell Borders buttons to change the border.**

   Select multiple cells in a table by holding down Shift while you click.

5. **To add a background color (or even fill cells with an image for a background), open the Cell Background pop-up menu and choose a type of background.**

Adding Alluring Photos

You can choose from two methods of adding a picture in your Pages document: as a *floating* object, meaning that you can place the image in a particular spot and it doesn't move, even if you make changes to the text; and as an *inline* object, which flows with the surrounding text as you make layout changes.

✦ **Add a floating object.** Drag an image file from a Finder window and place it where you want in your document. Alternatively, click the Media button on the toolbar, click Photos, navigate to the location where the file is saved, and drag the image thumbnail to the spot you want in the document. Figure 1-5 illustrates the Media Browser in action.

Note that a floating object (such as a shape or an image) can be sent to the *background,* where text will not wrap around it. (Think shaded background shape or an image as a background.) To bring a background object back as a regular floating object, click the object to select it and choose Arrange➪Bring Background Objects to Front. (More about background objects later in this chapter.)

✦ **Add an inline object.** Hold down the ⌘ key while you drag an image file from a Finder window and place it where you want in your document. You can also click the Media toolbar button and click Photos to display Media Browser. Navigate to the location where the file is saved, hold down the ⌘ key, and drag the image thumbnail to the spot where you want it in the document.

To move either type of object to another spot on the page, click it to select it (handles will appear around the object) and then click in the center of the object and drag it to the new position.

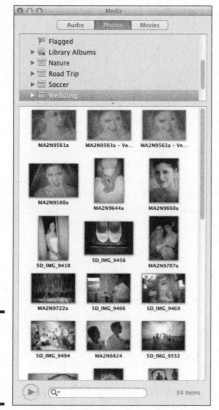

Figure 1-5:
Hey, isn't that Pages Media Browser?

Adding a Background Shape

To add a shape (such as a rectangle or circle) as a background for your text, follow these steps:

1. **Click the insertion cursor in the location you want.**

2. **Click the Shapes button on the Pages toolbar and choose a shape.**

   The shape appears in your document.

3. **Click the center of the shape and drag it to a new spot.**

   Like object boxes, shapes can be resized or moved.

4. **Before you can type over a shape, remember to select it and choose Arrange⇨Send Object to Background.**

Are You Sure About That Spelling?

Pages can check spelling as you type (the default setting) or check it after you complete your document. If you find automatic spell-checking distracting, you should definitely pick the latter method.

As my technical editor reminds us, spell-checking confirms only that a sequence of characters is a correctly spelled word — *not* that it's the correct word for the job! If you've ever "red" a document that someone else "rote," you know what he means, "deer" reader.

To check spelling as you type, follow these steps:

1. **Click Edit and hover the cursor over the Spelling menu item.**

2. **Click Check Spelling as You Type.**

If a possible misspelling is found, Pages underlines the word with a red, dashed line.

3. **Right-click the word to choose a possible correct spelling from the list, or ignore the word if it's spelled correctly.**

To turn off automatic spell checking, click the Check Spelling as You Type menu item again to toggle it off.

To check spelling manually, follow these steps:

1. **Click in the document to place the text insertion cursor where the spell check should begin.**

2. **Click Edit and hover the cursor over the Spelling menu item; then choose Check Spelling.**

3. **Right-click any possible misspellings and choose the correct spelling, or choose Ignore if the word is spelled correctly.**

Printing Your Pages Documents

Ready to start the presses? You can print your Pages document on real paper, of course, but don't forget that you can also save a tree by creating an electronic PDF-format document instead of a printout. (For the lowdown on PDF printing, visit Book VII, Chapter 4.)

To print your Pages document on old-fashioned paper, follow these steps:

1. **In Pages, choose File⇨Print.**

Pages displays the Print sheet you see in Figure 1-6.

2. **In the Copies field, enter the number of copies you need.**

3. **Select the pages to print.**

   • *To print the entire document:* Select the All radio button.

   • *To print a range of selected pages:* Select the From radio button and enter the starting and ending pages.

4. **Click the Print button to send the document to your printer.**

Figure 1-6: Preparing to print a work of art in Pages.

Sharing That Poster with Others

Besides printing — which is, after all, so passé — you can choose to share your Pages document electronically:

✦ **Share through e-mail.** Choose Share➪Send via Mail, and you can choose to add your Pages document to a Mail message in three formats: as a native Pages document file, as a Word format document, or as a PDF file. After you select a format, Pages obligingly launches Apple Mail for you automatically and creates a new message, ready for you to address and send!

✦ **Export.** Don't forget that Pages can export your work in one of five formats: a PDF document, a Word format document, an RTF (Rich Text Format) file, an ePub-format electronic book (suitable for reading with iBooks on your Mac or iOS devices), or plain text. Choose Share⇨Export, pick your format, click Next, and then select the location where Pages should save the file. Click Export and sit back while your favorite desktop publishing application does all the work.

To keep your document as close to how it appears in Pages as possible, I recommend PDF or Word. Your document will retain far more of your original formatting than an RTF or a plain-text document would.

Chapter 2: Creating Spreadsheets with Numbers

In This Chapter

✔ Opening, saving, and creating spreadsheets

✔ Selecting cells

✔ Entering and editing cell data

✔ Formatting cells

✔ Adding and removing rows and columns

✔ Creating simple calculations

✔ Adding charts to your spreadsheets

✔ Printing a Numbers spreadsheet

Are you downright afraid of spreadsheets? Does the idea of building a budget with charts and all sorts of fancy graphics send you running for the safety of the hall closet? Well, good Mac owner, Apple has once again taken something that everyone else considers super-complex and turned it into something that normal human beings can use! (Much like video editing, songwriting, and desktop publishing — heck, is there *any* type of software that Apple designers can't make intuitive and easy to use?)

In this chapter, I get to demonstrate how Numbers can help you organize data, analyze important financial decisions, and yes, even maintain a household budget! You'll soon see why the Numbers spreadsheet program is specifically designed with the home Mac owner in mind.

Before We Launch Numbers . . .

Just in case you're not familiar with applications such as Numbers and Microsoft Excel — and the documents they create — let me provide you with a little background information.

A *spreadsheet* organizes and calculates numbers of all kinds (including dates, times, and currency) by using a grid system of rows and columns. The intersection of each row and column is a *cell,* and cells can hold either text or numeric values (along with calculations that are usually linked to the contents of other surrounding cells).

Spreadsheets are wonderful tools for making decisions and comparisons because they let you "plug in" different numbers — such as interest rates or your monthly insurance premium — and instantly see the results. Some of my favorite spreadsheets that I use regularly are

✦ Car and mortgage loan comparisons

✦ A college planner

✦ My household budget (not that we pay any attention to it)

Creating a New Numbers Document

Like Pages, Apple's desktop publishing application, Numbers ships with a selection of templates that you can modify quickly to create a new spreadsheet. For example, after a few modifications, you can easily use the Budget, Loan Comparison, and Mortgage templates to create your own spreadsheets.

To create a spreadsheet project file, follow these steps:

1. **Click the Launchpad icon on the Dock.**

2. **Click the Numbers icon.**

3. **Click the New Document button in the lower-left corner of the Open dialog.**

Numbers displays the Template Chooser window you see in Figure 2-1. (To display the Template Chooser window and start a new Pages project at any time, just click File⇨New.)

4. **In the list to the left, click the type of document you want to create.**

The document thumbnails on the right are updated with templates that match your choice.

5. **Click the template that most closely matches your needs.**

6. **Click the Choose button to open a new document with the template you selected.**

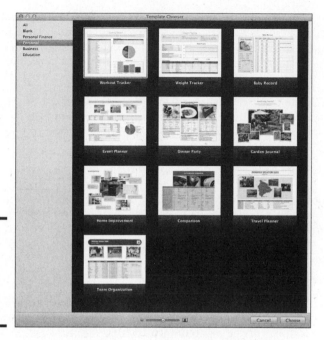

Figure 2-1:
Hey, these templates aren't frightening at all!

Opening an Existing Spreadsheet File

If a Numbers document appears in a Finder window (or you locate it using Spotlight or the All My Files location), you can just double-click the document icon to open it; Numbers automatically loads and displays the spreadsheet.

However, it's equally easy to open a Numbers document from within the program. Follow these steps:

1. **From Launchpad, click the Numbers icon to run the program.**

2. **Press ⌘+O to display the Open dialog.**

Because you're a Mac power user and you're running OS X Mavericks, you can now save and load Numbers documents directly to and from your iCloud folder! All three iWork applications include a new Open dialog that can display the contents of your iCloud folder as well as your drive. Click the iCloud or On My Mac button to switch locations.

3. **Click the On My Mac button, and then click the desired drive in the Devices list at the left of the dialog. Drill down through folders and subfolders until you locate the desired Numbers document.**

The Search box at the top-right corner of the Open dialog makes it easy to locate a document. Click in the Search box, type a portion (or all) of the filename, and then choose Name Matches from the pop-up menu that appears. (From the same pop-up menu, you can also search for text in your documents.) Note that you can choose to search your drive, your iCloud folder, or both.

4. **Double-click the spreadsheet to load it.**

If you want to open a spreadsheet you've been working on over the last few days, choose File⇨Open Recent to display recently used Numbers documents. Convenience is A Good Thing!

Save Those Spreadsheets!

Thanks to the AutoSave feature in Mavericks, you no longer have to fear losing a significant chunk of work because of a power failure or a coworker's mistake. However, if you're not a huge fan of retyping data, *period,* you can always save your spreadsheets manually after making a major change. Follow these steps the first time you save your spreadsheet to your hard drive:

1. **Press ⌘+S.**

If you're saving a document that hasn't yet been saved, the Save As sheet appears.

2. **Type a filename for your new spreadsheet.**

3. **On the Where pop-up menu, choose a location to save the file.**

You can select common locations, such as your Desktop, iCloud folder, Documents folder, or Home folder.

If the location you want isn't listed in the Where pop-up menu, you can also click the down-arrow button next to the Save As text box to display the full Save As dialog. Click the desired drive in the Devices list at the left of the dialog and then drill down through folders and subfolders until you reach the desired location. Alternatively, type the folder name in the Spotlight search box at the top right, and double-click the desired folder in the list of matching names. (Heck, you can even create a new folder in the full Save As dialog.)

4. **Click Save.**

After you save a Numbers document for the first time, you can create a version of that document by choosing File⇨Save. To revert the current document to an older version, choose File⇨Revert To. You can choose to revert to the last saved version, or you can click Browse All Versions to browse multiple versions of the document and choose one of those to revert to.

Exploring the Numbers Window

Apple has done a great job of minimizing the complexity of the Numbers window. Figure 2-2 illustrates these major points of interest:

✦ **Sheets list:** Because a Numbers project can contain multiple spreadsheets, they're displayed in the Sheets list at the left of the window. To switch between spreadsheets in a project, click the top-level headings (each of which has a spreadsheet icon).

✦ **Sheet canvas:** Numbers displays the rows and columns of your spreadsheet in this section of the window; you enter and edit cell values in the Sheet canvas.

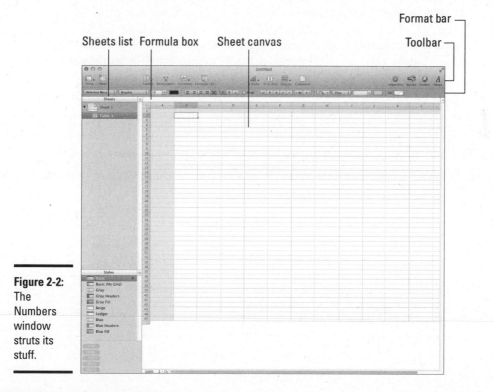

Sheets list Formula box Sheet canvas Format bar Toolbar

Figure 2-2: The Numbers window struts its stuff.

✦ **Toolbar:** The Numbers toolbar keeps the most common commands within easy reach.

✦ **Formula box:** Use the Formula box to enter formulas in a cell, allowing Numbers to automatically perform calculations based on the contents of other cells.

✦ **Format bar:** Located directly under the toolbar, the Format bar displays editing controls for the selected object. (If you enter an equal sign into the Formula box, the Format bar changes into the Formula bar. No, I'm not making this up.) My goodness, this is starting to sound like that classic movie about the chocolate tycoon and those kids!

Navigate and Select Cells in a Spreadsheet

Before you can enter data into a cell, you need to know how to get to the cell where you want to enter that data. You can use the scroll bars to move around in your spreadsheet, but when you enter data into cells, moving your fingers from the keyboard is a hassle. For this reason, Numbers has various movement shortcut keys that you can use to navigate, and I list them in Table 2-1. After you commit these keys to memory, your productivity shoots straight to the top.

Table 2-1	**Movement Shortcut Keys in Numbers**
Key or Key Combination	*Where the Cursor Moves*
←	One cell to the left
→	One cell to the right
↑	One cell up
↓	One cell down
Home	To the beginning of the active worksheet
End	To the end of the active worksheet
Page Down	Down one screen
Page Up	Up one screen
Return	One cell down (also works in a selection)
Tab	One cell to the right (also works in a selection)
Shift+Enter	One cell up (also works in a selection)
Shift+Tab	One cell to the left (also works in a selection)

You can use the mouse to select cells in a spreadsheet:

✦ To select a *single* cell, click it.

✦ To select a *range* of multiple adjacent cells, click a cell at any corner of the range you want and then drag the cursor in the direction you want.

✦ To select a *column* of cells, click the alphabetic heading button at the top of the column.

✦ To select a *row* of cells, click the numeric heading button on the far left side of the row.

Entering and Editing Data in a Spreadsheet

After you navigate to the cell in which you want to enter data, you're ready to type your data. Follow these steps to enter That Important Stuff:

1. **Either click the cell or press the spacebar.**

A cursor appears, indicating that the cell is ready to hold any data you type.

2. **Type in your data.**

Spreadsheets can use both numbers and alphabetic characters in a cell — either type of information is considered data in the Spreadsheet World.

3. **To edit data, click in the cell that contains the data to select it and then click the cell again to display the insertion cursor. Drag the insertion cursor across the characters to highlight them and then type the replacement data.**

4. **To delete characters, highlight the characters and press Delete.**

5. **When you're ready to move on, press Return (to save the data and move one cell down) or press Tab (to save the data and move one cell to the right).**

Selecting the Correct Number Format

After your data has been entered in a cell, row, or column, you still might need to format it before it appears correctly. Numbers gives you a healthy selection of formatting possibilities. *Number formatting* determines how a cell displays a number, such as a dollar amount, a percentage, or a date.

Characters and formatting rules, such as decimal places, commas, and dollar and percentage notations, are included in number formatting. So if your spreadsheet contains units of currency, such as dollars, format it as such. Then all you need to do is type the numbers, and the currency formatting is applied automatically.

To specify a number format, follow these steps:

1. **Select the cells, rows, or columns you want to format.**

2. **Click the Inspector toolbar button.**

3. **Click the Cells Inspector button on the Inspector toolbar to display the settings you see in Figure 2-3.**

4. **Open the Cell Format pop-up menu and choose the type of formatting you want to apply.**

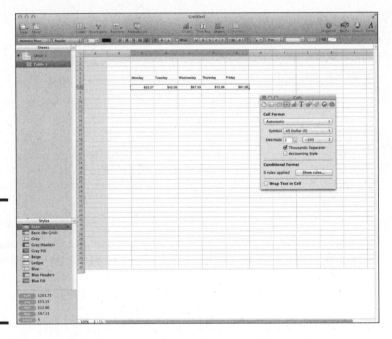

Figure 2-3:
You can format the data you enter from the Inspector.

Aligning Cell Text Just So

You can also change the alignment of text in the selected cells. (The default alignment for text is flush left.) Follow these steps:

1. **Select the cells, rows, or columns you want to format.**

   See "Navigate and Select Cells in a Spreadsheet," earlier in this chapter, for tips on selecting stuff.

2. **Click the Inspector toolbar button.**

3. **Click the Text Inspector button on the Inspector toolbar to display the settings you see in Figure 2-4.**

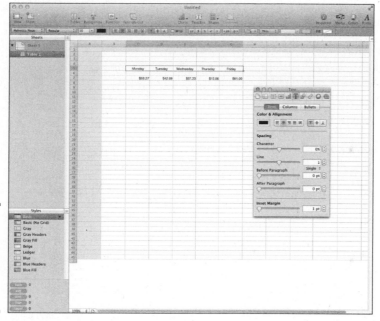

Figure 2-4: Use the Inspector to change text alignment in a cell.

4. **Click the corresponding alignment button to choose the type of formatting you want to apply.**

   You can choose from left, right, center, justified, and text left and numbers right. Text can also be aligned at the top, center, or bottom of a cell.

Do you need to set apart the contents of some cells? For example, you might need to create text headings for some columns and rows or to highlight the totals in a spreadsheet. To change the formatting of the data displayed in cells, select the cells, rows, or columns you want to format and then click the Font Family, Font Size, or Font Color buttons on the Format Bar.

Format with Shading

Shading the contents of a cell, row, or column is helpful when your spreadsheet contains subtotals or logical divisions. Follow these steps to shade cells, rows, or columns:

1. **Select the cells, rows, or columns you want to format.**

2. **Click the Inspector toolbar button.**

3. **Click the Graphic Inspector button on the Inspector toolbar.**

   Numbers displays the settings you see in Figure 2-5.

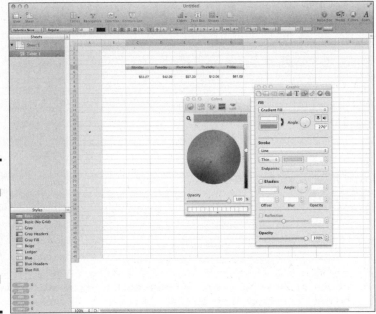

Figure 2-5: Add shading and colors to cells, rows, and columns to make them easy to read in Numbers.

4. **Open the Fill pop-up menu to select a shading option.**

5. **Click the color box to select a color for your shading.**

   Numbers displays a color picker (also shown in Figure 2-5).

6. **Click to select a color.**

7. **Click the Close button in the color picker.**

8. **Click the Inspector's Close button to return to your spreadsheet.**

Insert and Delete Rows and Columns

What's that? You forgot to add a row and now you're three pages into your data entry? No problem. You can easily add or delete rows and columns. Really — you can! First, select the row or column that you want to delete or that you want to insert a row or column next to, and do one of the following:

✦ **For a row:** Right-click and choose Add Row Above, Add Row Below, or Delete Row from the contextual menu that appears.

✦ **For a column:** Right-click and choose Add Columns Before, Add Columns After, or Delete Column from the contextual menu that appears.

If you select multiple rows or columns and choose Add, Numbers inserts the same number of new rows or columns as what you originally selected. Remember that you can also take care of this business from the Table menu. (I like to right-click.)

The Formula Is Your Friend

Sorry, but it's time to talk about *formulas*. These equations calculate values based on the contents of cells you specify in your spreadsheet. For example, if you designate cell A1 (the cell in column A at row 1) to hold your yearly salary and cell B1 to hold the number 12, you can divide the contents of cell A1 by cell B1 (to calculate your monthly salary) by typing this formula in any other cell:

=A1/B1

By the way, formulas in Numbers always start with an equal sign (=).

"So what's the big deal, Mark? Why not use a calculator?" Sure, but what if you then decide to calculate your weekly salary? Rather than grab a pencil and paper, you can simply change the contents of cell B1 to 52, and — boom! — the spreadsheet is updated to display your weekly salary.

That's a simple example, of course, but it demonstrates the basis of using formulas (and the reason that spreadsheets are often used to predict trends and forecast budgets).

To add a simple formula in your spreadsheet, follow these steps:

1. **Select the cell that will hold the result of your calculation.**

2. **Click inside the Formula box and type = (an equal sign).**

The Formula box appears to the right of the Sheets heading. Note that the Format bar changes to show a set of formula controls (also known as the Formula bar).

3. **Click the Function Browser button, which bears the *fx* label.**

It appears next to the red Cancel button on the Formula bar.

4. **In the window that appears, as shown in Figure 2-6, click the desired formula and then click the Insert Function button to add the formula to the Formula box.**

Function Browser   Accept   Formula box

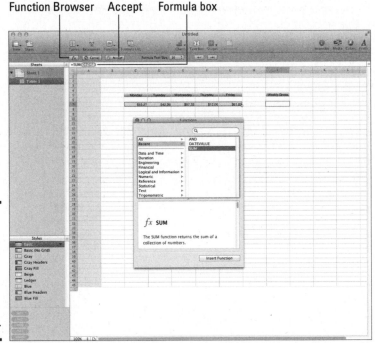

Figure 2-6:
If you have to use formulas, at least Numbers can enter them for you.

5. **After you finish, click the Accept button to add the formula to the cell.**

That's it! Your formula is now ready to work behind the scenes, doing math for you so that the correct numbers appear in the cell you specified.

To display all the formulas that you've added to a sheet, click the Formula List button on the toolbar.

Adding Visual Punch with a Chart

Sometimes you just have to see something to believe it — hence the capability to use the data you add to a spreadsheet to generate a professional-looking chart! Follow these steps to create a chart:

1. **Select the adjacent cells you want to chart by dragging the mouse.**

   To choose individual cells that aren't adjacent, you can hold down the ⌘ key while you click.

2. **Click the Charts button on the Numbers toolbar. The Charts button bears the symbol of a bar graph.**

   Numbers displays the thumbnail menu you see in Figure 2-7.

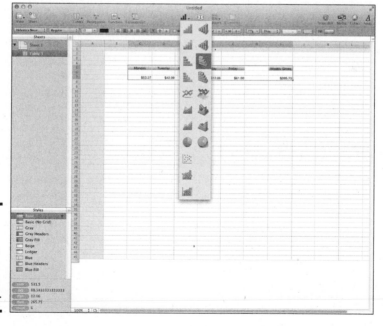

Figure 2-7: Numbers displays the range of chart styles you can use.

3. **Click the thumbnail for the chart type you want.**

   Numbers inserts the chart as an object in your spreadsheet so that you can move the chart. You can drag using the handles that appear on the outside of the object box to resize your chart. Figure 2-8 illustrates the 3-D chart I generated with just a couple of mouse clicks.

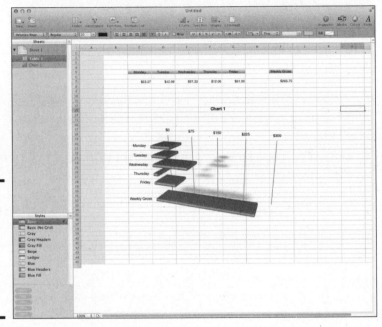

Figure 2-8: My finished chart looks like someone with talent drew it for me!

Click the Inspector toolbar button, and you can switch to the Chart Inspector dialog, where you can change the colors and add (or remove) the chart title and legend.

4. **To change the default title, click the title box once to select it; click it again to edit the text.**

After you add your chart to the sheet, it appears in the Sheets list as shown in Figure 2-8. To edit the chart at any time, just click the corresponding entry in the Sheets list.

Chapter 3: Building Presentations with Keynote

In This Chapter

- ✔ Creating a new presentation
- ✔ Adding slides
- ✔ Using selection boxes
- ✔ Entering and editing text
- ✔ Formatting text
- ✔ Adding presenter's notes
- ✔ Inserting media and shapes
- ✔ Running a slideshow
- ✔ Printing slides and notes

*I*t seems like only yesterday that I was giving business presentations with a klunky overhead projector and black-and-white acetate transparencies. Fancy color gradients and animation were unheard of, and the only sound my presentations made was the droning of the projector's fan. I might as well have been using tree bark and chalk.

Thank goodness those days are gone forever because cutting-edge presentation software such as Keynote makes slide creation easy and — believe it or not — *fun*! This is the application that Steve Jobs used for his Macworld keynotes every year, and there's so much visual candy available that you'll never need to shout to wake your audience again.

In this chapter, I demonstrate how simple it is to build a stunning Keynote presentation, and how to start and control your slide display from your keyboard (or even your iPhone, iPad, or iPod touch). And don't forget to print your slides and notes so that your audience can keep a copy of your brilliant work!

Creating a New Keynote Project

Like other applications in the iWork suite, Keynote begins the document-creation process with a Template Chooser window. To create a new presentation project, follow these steps:

1. **Click the Launchpad icon on the Dock.**

2. **Click the Keynote icon.**

3. **Click the New Document button at the lower-left corner of the Open dialog.**

   The Theme Chooser window that you see in Figure 3-1 appears. (Even now, years since the application debuted, I have to say that these are probably the most stunning visual building blocks I've ever seen in a presentation application. You should have heard the "oohs" and "ahhs" from the Macworld faithful when Steve Jobs demonstrated Keynote for the first time on the big screen!)

Figure 3-1: Select a template from the Theme Chooser window.

4. **At the bottom of the screen, open the Slide Size pop-up menu to choose the resolution for your completed slides.**

Although you don't necessarily need to select an exact match for the screen resolution of your Mac, I recommend opting for the closest value to the maximum resolution of your projector. (If someone else is providing the projector, the default value of 1024 x 768 is a good standard to use.) If you're using a second monitor during your presentation, select the native resolution for that monitor instead.

5. **Click the template that most closely matches your needs.**

6. **Click the Choose button to open a new document with the template you select.**

You can display the Template Chooser window and start a new Keynote project… just click File⇨New.

Opening a Keynote Presentation

If an existing Keynote presentation file is visible in a Finder window or on your Desktop, you can double-click the document icon to open the project. If Keynote is already running, however, follow these steps to load a project:

1. **Press ⌘+O to display the Open dialog.**

Like Pages and Numbers, Keynote presentations can be saved to and retrieved from your iCloud folder. To switch locations between your iCloud storage and your Mac's drive, click the iCloud or the On My Mac buttons.

2. **Click On My Mac, and then click the desired drive in the Devices list at the left of the dialog — now drill down through folders and subfolders until you locate the Keynote project.**

Alternatively, you can click the All My Files location in the Open dialog sidebar to display your documents, or click in the Search box at the upper-right side of the screen and type a portion of the filename (choose Name Matches from the pop-up menu that appears).

3. **Double-click the filename to load it.**

If you want to open a Keynote document that you've recently edited, things get even easier! Just choose File⇨Open Recent, and then open the document with a single click from the submenu that appears.

Saving Your Presentation

Because Keynote provides full support for the Auto Save feature in Mavericks, saving your work often isn't as critical as it used to be. But if you're the prudent type and want to safeguard your work in a world of power failures, follow these steps the first time you save a presentation:

1. **Press ⌘+S.**

If you're saving a document that hasn't yet been saved, the familiar Save As sheet appears.

2. **Type a filename for your new document.**

3. **From the Where pop-up menu, choose a location to save the document.**

To select a location not on the Where pop-up menu, click the button with the down-arrow symbol to expand the sheet. You can also create a new folder from the expanded sheet.

4. **Click Save.**

After you save a Keynote presentation for the first time, you can create a version of that document by choosing File⇨Save. To revert the current presentation to an older version, choose File⇨Revert To. You can revert to the last saved version, or you can click Browse All Versions to browse multiple versions of the presentation and choose one of those to revert to.

Putting Keynote to Work

Ready for the five-cent tour of the Keynote window? Launch the application and create or load a project, and you'll see the tourist attractions shown in Figure 3-2:

✦ **Slides list:** Use this thumbnail list of all the slides in your project to help you navigate quickly. Click a thumbnail to switch instantly to that slide.

The Slides list can also display your project in outline format, allowing you to check all your discussion points. (This is a great way to ferret out any "holes" in your presentation's flow.) While in outline mode, you can still jump directly to any slide by clicking the slide's title in the outline. To display the outline, choose View⇨Outline. You can switch back to the default Navigator Slide list by choosing View⇨Navigator.

✦ **Layout pane:** Your slide appears in its entirety in this pane. You can add elements and edit the content of the slide from the Layout pane.

Slides list   Layout lane

Toolbar
Format bar

Figure 3-2:
The Keynote
window is
dominated
by the
Layout
pane.

Notes pane

✦ **Toolbar:** Like the toolbar in Pages and Numbers, the Keynote toolbar makes it easy to find the most common controls you'll use while designing and editing your slides. Clicking an icon on the toolbar performs an action, just like selecting a menu item does.

✦ **Notes pane:** If you decide to add notes to one or more slides (either for your own use or to print as additional information for your audience), choose View➪Show Presenter Notes to open the Notes pane. This text box appears under the Layout pane.

✦ **Format bar:** Keynote displays this button strip below the Keynote toolbar, allowing you to format selected text, paragraphs, and lists on the fly.

Adding Slides

Sure, Keynote creates a single Title slide when you first create a project, but not many presentations are complete with just a single slide! To add more slides to your project, use one of these methods:

✦ Click the New button on the Keynote toolbar.

✦ Choose New Slide from the Slide menu.

**Book IV
Chapter 3**

**Building
Presentations
with Keynote**

✦ Press ⌘+Shift+N.

✦ Right-click (or Control-click) in the Slides list and choose New Slide from the contextual menu.

Keynote adds the new slide to your Slides list and automatically switches to the new slide in the Layout pane.

Need a slide that's similar to an existing slide? Right-click the existing slide and choose Duplicate to create a new slide just like it. (Consider it "cloning without the science.") Then edit the dupe.

To move a slide to a different position in the Slides list (and therefore a different order in your Keynote slideshow), drag that slide thumbnail to the new desired spot in the list.

Working with Text and Graphics Boxes

You've probably noticed that all the text in your first Title slide appears in boxes. Keynote uses boxes to manipulate text and graphics. You can resize a box (and its contents) by clicking and dragging one of the handles that appears around the edges of the box. (Your cursor changes into a double-sided arrow when you're "in the zone.") The side-selection handles drag only that edge of the frame, and the corner-selection handles resize both adjoining edges of the selection frame.

To keep the proportions of the box constrained, hold down Shift while dragging the corner handles.

Boxes make it easy to move text and graphics together (as a unit) to another location in the Layout pane. Click in the center of the box and drag the box to the desired spot; Keynote displays alignment lines to help you align the box with other elements around it (or with regular divisions of the slide, such as horizontal center). As you can see in Figure 3-3, I'm moving a box on the slide to a new location, and Keynote has supplied alignment lines to help me place it correctly.

To select text or graphics in a box, double-click the box.

If you're resizing a photo in a box, don't forget to hold down the Shift key while you drag the frame to preserve the aspect ratio of the image so that the vertical and horizontal proportions remain fixed. You can also flip images horizontally or vertically from the Arrange menu.

Figure 3-3:
Keynote provides alignment lines when you move boxes.

Adding and Editing Slide Text

Just like in Pages and Numbers — which use boxes for text layout — Keynote allows you to add or edit text with ease. For example, double-click in a box with the text *Double-click to edit,* and the placeholder text disappears, leaving the field ready to accept new text. Any new text you type appears at the blinking cursor in the box.

To edit existing text in your Keynote document, click using the bar-shaped cursor to select just the right spot in the text, and drag the insertion cursor across the characters to highlight them. Type the replacement text, and Keynote obligingly replaces the text that was there with the text you type.

If you want to delete existing text, click and drag across the characters to highlight them; press Delete. You can also delete an entire box and all its contents: Right-click (or Control-click) the offending box and choose Delete from the contextual menu that appears.

When the contents of a box are just right and you've finished entering or editing text, click anywhere outside the box to hide it from view. You can always click the text again to display the box later.

Formatting Slide Text for the Perfect Look

Keynote doesn't restrict you to the default fonts for the theme you choose. It's easy to format the text in your slides, choosing a different font family, font color, text alignment, and text attribute such as bolding or italicizing on the fly, whenever you like.

Select the desired text by double-clicking a box and then dragging the text cursor to highlight the characters. Now apply your formatting using one of these two methods:

+ **The Format bar:** The font controls on the Format bar work just like the controls on the toolbar: Either click a font control to display a pop-up menu or click a button to immediately perform an action. Opening the Font Size pop-up menu, for example, displays a range of sizes for the selected text; with a single click on the B (bold) button, you'll add the bold attribute to the highlighted characters.

+ **The Format menu:** The controls on the Format menu generally mirror those on the Format bar. To change the alignment from the Format menu, click Format and hover the cursor over the Text menu item. To change text attributes, click Format and hover your cursor over the Font menu.

Using Presenter's Notes in Your Project

As I mention earlier, you can type text notes in the Notes pane. I use them for displaying alternate topic points while presenting a slideshow. However, you can also print the notes for a project along with the slides, so presenter's notes are also great for including reminders and To Do points for your audience in handouts.

To type your notes, just click within the Notes pane; if it's hidden, choose View➪Show Presenter Notes. When you've finished adding notes, click in the Slides list or the Layout pane to return to editing mode.

To display your notes while practicing, use Keynote's Rehearsal feature. Click Play and choose Rehearse Slideshow, and you can scroll through the notes while the slideshow runs. (More on slideshows in a second.)

Every Good Presentation Needs Media

Adding audio, photos, and movies to a slideshow is drag-and-drop easy in Keynote! Simply drag an image, an audio, or a movie file from a Finder window and place it where you want in your document.

You can also use Media Browser. Click the Media button on the toolbar and then click the Audio, Photos, or Movies button to select the desired type. Keynote displays the contents of your various media collections — such as your iPhoto and iTunes libraries. You can also navigate to the file's location on your hard drive, or type a filename in the Search box at the bottom of the browser. When you find the file that you want to add, drag it to the spot you want in the document. Figure 3-4 illustrates Media Browser in action.

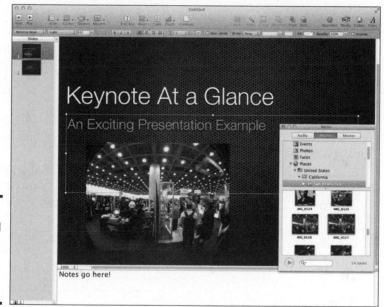

Figure 3-4:
You can add audio and movie clips to a slide, too!

Adding a Background Shape

Text often stands out on a slide when it sits on top of a background shape. To add a shape (such as a rectangle or circle) as a background for your text, follow these steps:

1. **Click the insertion cursor in the location you want.**

2. **Click the Shapes button on the Keynote toolbar and choose a shape.**

   The shape appears in your document. You can click in the Fill box on the Format bar to choose a different color and an opacity level.

3. **Click the center of the shape and drag it to a new spot.**

   Like image boxes, shapes can be resized or moved.

4. **When the shape is properly positioned and sized, select it and choose Arrange⇨Send to Back.**

Creating Your Keynote Slideshow

The heart of a Keynote presentation is the slideshow that you build from the slides you've created. A Keynote slideshow is typically presented full screen.

In its simplest form, you can always run a slideshow from a Keynote project by clicking the Play button on the toolbar, or by choosing Play⇨Play Slideshow. Advance to the next slide by clicking your mouse or by pressing the right bracket key, which looks like this:].

If you'd prefer a presentation that runs automatically by itself (often called *kiosk mode*), click the Inspector icon on the toolbar and then click the Document button (the first button at the top of the Inspector). Now open the Presentation pop-up menu and choose Self-Playing. Click the Close button to close the Inspector window, and you're all set!

Of course, other controls are available besides just the ones that advance to the next slide! Table 3-1 illustrates the key shortcuts you'll use most often during a slideshow.

Table 3-1	Keynote Slideshow Shortcut Keys
Key or Key Combination	**Action**
] (right bracket)	Next slide
P	Previous slide
Home	Jump to first slide
End	Jump to last slide
C	Show or hide the pointer
(number)	Jump to the corresponding slide in the Slides list
U	Scroll notes up
D	Scroll notes down
N	Show current slide number
H	Hide slideshow and display last application used (the presentation appears as a minimized icon on the Dock)
B	Pause slideshow and display a black screen (press any key to resume the slideshow)
Esc	Quit

Keynote offers a number of settings that you can tweak to fine-tune your slideshow. To display these settings, choose Keynote⇨Preferences and click the Slideshow button in the Preferences window.

If you have an iPhone or iPod touch handy and you've installed the Apple Keynote Remote application on your device, display the Preferences window and click the Remote button to link your iPhone or iPod touch to your Mac and Keynote. Now you can use your handheld device as a remote and use it during your slideshow!

Printing Your Slides and Notes

Okay, I'll be honest: I don't always print handouts for every presentation I give. Some of the slideshows I run are short introductions to hands-on demonstrations. However, if you're presenting a lengthy slideshow with plenty of information that you'd like your audience to remember, nothing beats handouts that include scaled-down images of your slides (and, optionally, your presenter's notes).

You can also use Keynote to create an electronic PDF-format document instead of a printed handout, which your audience members can download from your website. (For the lowdown on PDF printing, visit Chapter 4 in Book VII.)

To print a hard copy of your slides and notes, follow these steps:

1. Within Keynote, choose File⇨Print.

Keynote displays the Print sheet you see in Figure 3-5.

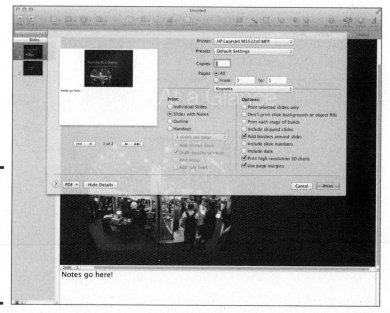

Figure 3-5:
Keynote offers a wide range of printing options for your slides and notes.

Book IV Chapter 3

Building Presentations with Keynote

2. **Click the desired format:**

   - *To print each slide on a separate page at full size:* Click Individual Slides.

   - *To print each slide on a separate page with the presenter's notes for that slide:* Click Slides with Notes.

   - *To print the contents of your Slides list in Outline view:* Click Outline.

   - *To print a handout with multiple slides per page (and, optionally, with presenter's notes):* Click Handout. Use the Slides per Page pop-up menu to specify the number of slides that Keynote should print on each page.

3. **Select the pages to print:**

   - *To print the entire document:* Select All.

   - *To print a range of selected slides:* Select the From radio button and enter the starting and ending pages.

4. **(Optional) Set specific options from the Options column.**

   You can include elements such as the date, borders around each slide, and the slide number as part of each page of the hard copy.

5. **Click the Print button to send the job to your printer.**

Book V
Typical Internet Stuff

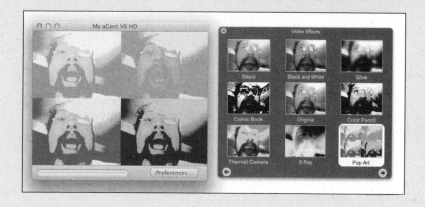

Contents at a Glance

Chapter 1: Getting on the Internet

In This Chapter

✔ Selecting an Internet service provider

✔ Understanding how your Mac gets on the Internet

✔ Setting up your Internet connection

I'll be honest — the Internet is a terribly complex monster of a network. If you tried to fathom all the data that's exchanged on the Internet and everything that takes place when you check your e-mail for Aunty Joan's fruitcake recipe, your brain would probably melt like a chocolate bar in the Sahara Desert. A shoebox *full* of archaic things is tucked under the Internet: communications protocols, routing addresses, packets, servers, and other hoo-hah that are beyond the grasp of just about everyone on the planet.

Luckily for regular folks like you and me, OS X Mavericks closes the trap-door on all these details, keeping them hidden (as they *should* be). You don't have to worry about them, and the obscure information that you need to establish an Internet connection is kept to a minimum. The happiest computer owners I've met think that the Internet is a little blinking light on their DSL or cable modem: If the light blinks in the proper manner, all is well. (I don't argue with them.)

In this chapter, I provide help and advice to those who are prepared to play games, download music, and chat with their friends — and I lead you through the procedure of adding an Internet connection under OS X. (In other words, you'll get your light blinking properly.)

If you entered your Internet configuration information while you were in Setup Assistant during the initial configuration of OS X, *you can skip this chapter!* The information contained herein is only for those who add or change their Internet connectivity *after* installing or upgrading OS X.

Shopping for an ISP

Before you can connect to the Internet, you must sign up for Internet access. (You may be able to find a location with free wireless Internet in your area, but this certainly won't satisfy your long-term need for Internet access in your home.) If you already have an ISP (acronym-speak for an *Internet service provider*) or your company or school provides Internet access, smile quietly to yourself and skip to the next section. Otherwise, hang around while I discuss what to look for in an ISP and how to locate one in your local area.

An *ISP* is simply the company you contract with so that you can connect to the Internet. You may be contracting with a cable company, such as Comcast, Bright House, or Mediacom, or you may be using a service such as AOL, Juno, or EarthLink. All these are ISPs.

ISPs are as thick as Louisiana mosquitoes these days, and often they're judged solely by the amount that they charge for basic access. Cost definitely is a factor, but it's not the *only* thing that should determine your choice in a service provider. Consider these guidelines when choosing or switching ISPs:

✦ **Broadband service:** Virtually all local ISPs, phone companies, and cable companies now offer digital subscriber line (DSL) or cable modem access. Collectively, these connections are called *broadband* because they offer the fastest method of transferring information to and from the Internet. If you have a home business, a large family, or students — or if you telecommute to your office — using broadband can make your life much simpler.

✦ **Quality technical support:** A 24-hour/7-day telephone support line is a godsend for the Internet novice; don't settle for voice support during business hours. Forget e-mail and web—based support, too; your e-mail and web browser applications will be dead and gone if your Internet connection gives you problems. (Sound of your palm whacking your forehead.)

✦ **Static IP addresses:** A *static IP address* — the unique number that identifies your computer on the Internet — allows you to set up a professional web server or File Transfer Protocol (FTP) server. Most ISPs charge an additional amount for a static IP address (considering it as a business account instead of a residential account), so it's not a good idea for a typical Mac owner at home. Suffice it to say, however, that a business or commercial organization running a web server or FTP server will benefit from using a static IP address.

✦ **E-mail accounts:** Investigate how many individual accounts you receive with various ISPs. Also, find out whether you can maintain them yourself through a website. If so, that's a good sign. Additionally, if the prospective ISP provides a website where you can read and send e-mail messages, you can stay on top of your e-mail even while you're on the road or vacationing halfway across the globe.

✦ **Local calling rates:** If you live in a rural area and you're using a dial-up modem, check to make sure that all prospective ISPs offer local calling rates. Believe me, no matter how much fun and how useful the Internet is, it's not worth hours of long-distance charges. (Oh, and don't forget to make sure that your ISP has local access numbers in the cities that you visit regularly.) To use a dial-up connection, you'll need to add an external Mavericks–compatible USB modem, which also allows you to send and receive faxes using Mavericks.

✦ **Web space:** If you want your ISP to host your website, the more space you get, the better. A minimum of 2GB is acceptable, but most ISPs provide 5GB or more these days. Also, beware of ISPs that charge you for your website if it receives a large amount of traffic: It can be expensive to host a popular website if you join one of these ISPs.

✦ **Domain name service:** Finally, the better class of ISP also offers a *domain name service,* which allows you to register something like *your-namehere*.com. For the most professional appearance, you can usually pay a yearly fee, and the ISP takes care of all the details in setting up your own .com or .org domain name.

Investigating Various Types of Connections

Consider the types of connections that are available under Mavericks to link your Mac to an ISP (see the preceding section for more about ISPs). You can choose among five pathways to digital freedom:

✦ **A dial-up connection:** Old-fashioned, yes. Slow as an arthritic burro, indeed. However, an *analog* (or telephone modem) connection is still a viable method for reaching the Internet for most computer owners. It's the cheapest method available, and all you need for this type of connection is a standard telephone jack and a modem. Apple used to include a modem with every computer, but no longer. These days, you'll have to buy an external USB modem to make the dial-up connection. (Any OS X Mavericks–compatible USB modem will work fine.)

✦ **A broadband connection:** Be it through DSL (which uses a typical telephone line) or cable (which uses your cable TV wiring), broadband Internet access is many times faster than a dial-up connection. Plus, both these technologies are *always on,* meaning that your computer is automatically connected to the Internet when you turn it on and that connection stays active. With DSL or cable, no squeaky, screeching whine accompanies your modem while it makes a connection each time you want to check your movie listings website. Both DSL and cable require a special piece of hardware (commonly called a *modem,* but it really isn't); this box is usually thrown in as part of your ISP charge. Broadband connections usually require a professional installation, too.

✦ **A cellular connection:** If you own a cellphone, you may already be using the Internet on your phone over a 3G or 4G connection. That same type of Internet connection is available for your desktop or laptop Mac from the major cellular providers. Sure, 3G and 4G connections are pricey compared to a typical broadband connection, but if you're a road warrior with a laptop — or if you can't get cable or DSL service in your area — cellular Internet may be the option for you.

✦ **A satellite connection:** If you're *really* out there — miles and miles away from any cable or DSL phone service, and even out of the range of a 3G/4G cellular network — you can still get high-speed Internet access. The price for a satellite connection is usually much steeper than a standard DSL or cable connection, but it's available anywhere you can plant your antenna dish with a clear view of the sky. Plus, a satellite connection is faster than other types of broadband access. Older satellite technologies required you to also use a dial-up connection — and the antenna could only receive, not send — but most ISPs that can handle satellite connections now offer satellite systems that both send and receive through the dish.

✦ **A network connection:** The last type of connection concerns those Macs that are part of a local area network (LAN) either at the office or in your home. If your Mac is connected to a LAN that already has Internet access, you don't need an ISP and no other hardware is required: Simply contact your network administrator, buy that important person a steak dinner, and ask to be connected to the Internet. On the other hand, if your network currently has no Internet access, you're back to square one: You'll need one of the previous four types of connections.

After you connect one of your computers on your network to the Internet, you can use an Internet sharing device to allow all the computers to share that Internet connection. Book VI, Chapter 4 goes into all the details on sharing an Internet connection on a network.

Setting Up Your Internet Connection

Okay, so you sign up for Internet access, and your ISP sends you a sheet of paper covered with indecipherable stuff that looks like Egyptian hieroglyphics. Don't worry; those are the settings that you need to connect to your ISP. After you get them in OS X, you should be surfing the web like an old pro.

Before you jump into this configuration, make sure that you've configured the Internet Accounts settings in System Preferences, as I discuss in Book II, Chapter 3. That way, you'll already have entered your default e-mail and web settings. You'll also need to be logged in using an Administrator account.

Using an external modem

Follow these steps to set up your Internet connection if you're using an external USB modem:

1. **Click the System Preferences icon on the Dock and choose Network.**

2. **Select External modem from the list at the left side of the pane.**

3. **Enter the settings for the type of connection that your ISP provides:**

   • *If your ISP tells you to use PPP (Point-to-Point Protocol):* Click the Configure IPv4 pop-up menu and choose Using PPP. If your ISP provided you with DNS Server or Search Domain addresses, type them now in the corresponding boxes.

   • *If you're using AOL:* Click the Configure IPv4 pop-up menu and choose AOL Dialup. If AOL provided you with DNS Server or Search Domain addresses, click in the corresponding boxes and type them now.

   • *If you're using a manual connection:* Click the Configure IPv4 pop-up menu and choose Manually. Then click in the IP Address, DNS Servers, and Search Domains fields and enter the respective settings provided by your ISP.

4. **If you need to enter PPP settings, click the Advanced button and enter the settings provided by your ISP.**

5. **In their respective fields, enter the account name, password, telephone number, and (optionally) the service provider name and an alternative telephone number provided by your ISP.**

I always like OS X to connect automatically when I'm using a modem. I hate excess cursor movements as much as the next technowizard. To automate your dial-up connection (allowing Mavericks to call your ISP whenever your system needs the Internet), select the Connect Automatically When Needed check box.

6. **Press ⌘+Q to exit System Preferences and save your changes.**

Your external USB modem must use a 64-bit driver to work with Mavericks, so make sure the modem you buy is listed as specifically supporting OS X Mavericks (10.9).

Using broadband or network hardware

Follow these steps to set up your Internet connection if you're using a network, cable modem, or DSL connection:

1. **Click the System Preferences icon on the Dock and choose Network.**

2. **Select Ethernet from the list on the left of the pane to display the settings that you see in Figure 1-1.**

Figure 1-1: The Network settings for an Ethernet Internet connection.

3. **Enter the settings for the type of connection that your ISP provides:**

   - *If your ISP tells you to use Dynamic Host Configuration Protocol (DHCP):* Choose Using DHCP from the Configure IPv4 pop-up menu, and your ISP can automatically set up virtually all the TCP/IP settings for you! (No wonder DHCP is so popular these days.)

   - *If you won't be using DHCP:* Choose Manually from the Configure IPv4 pop-up menu. Then enter the settings provided by your ISP in the IP Address, Subnet Mask, Router, and DNS Servers fields.

4. **If your ISP uses PPPoE (Point-to-Point Protocol over Ethernet), click the Configure IPv4 pop-up menu and choose Create PPPoE Service.**

   a. *Type an identifying name for the PPPoE service.*

   b. *Click Done.*

   c. *Enter the password for your PPPoE connection.*

5. **Press ⌘+Q to exit System Preferences and save your changes.**

Mavericks can get down-and-dirty in the configuration trenches as well! To launch an assistant to help with the configuration process, click the Assist Me button and then click Assistant.

Chapter 2: Using Apple Mail

In This Chapter

⯈ **Adding and configuring Mail accounts**

⯈ **Receiving, reading, and sending e-mail**

⯈ **Filtering junk mail**

⯈ **Opening attachments**

⯈ **Configuring and automating Apple Mail**

Okay, how many of you can function without e-mail? Raise your hands. Anyone? Anyone at all?

I suppose that I *can* function without my Internet e-mail, but why should I? OS X includes a very capable and reliable e-mail client, *Apple Mail* (affectionately called *Mail* by everyone but Bill Gates).

In this chapter, I discuss the features of Apple Mail and show you how everything hums at a perfect C pitch. However, you have to sing out, "You've got mail!" yourself. Personally, I think that's a plus, but I show you how you can add any sound you like.

Know Thy Mail Window

To begin our epic e-mail journey, click the Mail icon on the Dock. Don't worry if your display doesn't look just like Figure 2-1, which illustrates the Mail window after I've added an account — which I demonstrate in a page or two. What you'll see depends on whether you're using a new Mac with a fresh copy of Mavericks or upgrading from an earlier version of OS X, and also whether you provided e-mail account information in Setup Assistant.

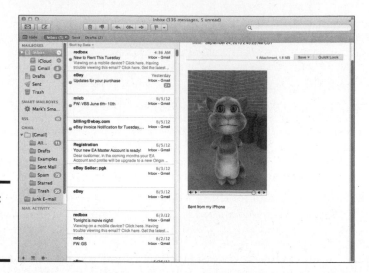

Figure 2-1:
The Apple
Mail
window.

Besides the familiar toolbar, which naturally carries buttons specific to Mail, you find the following:

✦ **Title bar:** This heading at the top of the Mail window displays information about the current inbox — typically, how many messages it contains, but other data can be included as well.

Like many other OS X Mavericks applications, you can switch Mail to a full-screen display (which hides the title bar, window controls, and menu bar). To switch to full screen, choose View⇨Enter Full Screen, or click the full-screen button at the top-right corner of the Mail window. If you need to use a menu command, move your cursor to the top of the screen, and the menu bar will temporarily reappear. To return Mail to a windowed display, display the menu bar and choose View⇨Exit Full Screen, or just press Esc.

✦ **Toolbar:** Yep, Mail has a high-powered, convenient-as-all-get-out toolbar of its own, and you can customize the Mail toolbar just like a Finder window toolbar! (Book II, Chapter 1 describes that process.) Choose View⇨Customize Toolbar and sit back in awe of the range of menu items and features that you can activate with just one click.

If you don't use the toolbar and you'd like to reclaim the space it takes in your Mail window, choose View⇨Hide Toolbar, or right-click the toolbar and choose Hide Toolbar from the menu that appears. For a "lite" version of the toolbar that takes less space, right-click the toolbar and choose Text Only.

✦ **Message list:** This resizable scrolling list box contains all the messages for the folder you choose. To resize the list larger or smaller, drag the handle on the bar that runs across the window. You can also resize the columns in the list by dragging the edges of the column heading buttons.

To specify which columns appear in the message list, choose View➪ Message Attributes. From the submenu that appears, you can toggle the display of specific columns. You can also sort the messages in the message list from the View menu; by default, messages are sorted by Date Received. (Alternatively, use Lazy Mark's method: Just click the column that you want to sort by. To reverse the sort order, click the column again.)

✦ **Mailboxes:** The pane at the left of the main Mail window is the Mailbox list. You can click any folder there to switch the display in the message list. The Mailbox list can be hidden or shown from the View menu by clicking the Show Mailboxes List item, or you can press the ⌘+Shift+M keyboard shortcut to hide or show it. There's even a Hide/Show button at the top-left corner of the Mailbox list. To widen or narrow the Mailboxes list, click the divider at the right side of the list. Your cursor turns to a line with double arrows, and you can drag it in the desired direction.

✦ **Preview pane:** This resizable scrolling pane displays the contents of the selected message, including both text and any graphics or attachments that Mail recognizes.

Mail uses the following folders (some of which appear only at certain times):

✦ **Inbox:** Mail you've received.

✦ **Outbox:** Messages that Mail is waiting to send.

✦ **Drafts:** Draft messages waiting to be completed.

✦ **Sent:** Mail you've sent.

✦ **Trash:** Deleted mail. Like with the Trash icon on the Dock, you can open this folder and retrieve items that you realize you still need. Alternatively, you can empty the contents of the Trash at any time by pressing the ⌘+K shortcut or by choosing Mailbox➪Erase Deleted Messages.

✦ **Junk:** Junk mail. You can review these messages and mark them as Not Junk or retrieve anything you want to keep by choosing Message➪Move To. After you're sure nothing of value is left, you can delete the remaining messages straight to the Trash. (Junk mail filtering must be enabled from the Junk Mail settings in Preferences before you see this box.)

✦ **RSS:** Messages from an RSS (really simple syndication) news feed that you've subscribed to. You find out more on RSS later in this chapter.

✦ **Notes:** This folder displays notes that you've made, like those all-important reminders about washing the car, paying taxes, and picking up dog food on the way home. I discuss how to create a new note later in this chapter.

You can add new personal folders to the Mailbox list to further organize your messages. Choose Mailbox⇨New Mailbox, or click the Add button (a plus sign) at the bottom of the Mailboxes list. Choose a location where the mailbox will appear in the list (for example, within the On My Mac section) and then type the name for your new folder in the Name box. Click OK to create the new personal folder.

What's a smart mailbox?

As I talk about in Book II, Chapter 1, you can create smart folders in Finder. Well, Apple Mail provides something similar for your e-mail messages: the *smart mailbox*. The contents of a smart mailbox are links to messages in your Mail folders; these links match the search criteria you specify, such as messages from a specific address or those that contain attachments. Other criteria include the date an item is received, the subject of a message, the mailbox a message is stored in, and so on. You can use smart mailboxes to organize your messages in different ways and identify those messages that require special (or **immediate!**) attention.

To set up a smart mailbox, choose Mailbox⇨ New Smart Mailbox, or click the Add (plus sign) button (in the lower-left corner of the Mail window) and choose New Smart Mailbox from the pop-up menu. Type a name to identify the mailbox and then click the Match pop-up menu to specify whether the search should match any or all of your criteria.

Now you can click the pop-up menus to specify what the search should find. To add a new criterion line, click the button with the plus sign. (To delete a criterion line that Should Not Be, click the button with the minus sign next to the offending line.) Note that you can also include messages from Mail's Trash and Sent folders. When you're ready, click OK, and the new smart mailbox appears in the Mailboxes list. It has a cool folder icon with a gear symbol, much like the gear symbol sported by smart folders in a Finder window.

If you've set up your smart folder, it automatically maintains itself when you receive, send, and delete messages, always showing whatever matches your criteria. Here's a mind-boggler: Imagine what Ben Franklin could've done if he'd been able to use smart folders!

Messages can be dragged from the message list and dropped into the desired folder in the Mailbox list to transfer them. Or you can move 'em from the Message list by selecting the messages that you want to move, choosing Message⇨Move To, and then clicking the desired destination folder. (You can also automate the transfer of messages from folder to folder using rules, which I'll cover later in the chapter.)

Also note that Spotlight has staked its claim with the Search box at the upper right in the Mail toolbar. You can use the Search box to locate text from subject lines, display messages from specific people, or even search for an attachment by name.

Setting Up Your Account

By default, Mail includes one (or more) of these accounts when you first run it:

✦ **The account that you entered when you first installed OS X:** Go to the beginning — literally, Book I, Chapter 1 — to read about Setup Assistant. If you entered the information for an e-mail account, it's available.

✦ **Your iCloud account:** If you registered for an iCloud service account, it's included.

✦ **Upgraded accounts:** If you upgraded an existing OS X system, your existing Mail accounts are added to the Accounts list in Mail.

Speaking of the Accounts list, choose Mail⇨Preferences and click the Accounts button to display the Accounts pane that you see in Figure 2-2. From here, you can add an account, edit an existing account, or remove an account from Mail. Note that the Mail accounts shown here are available also from the Mail, Contacts & Calendars pane in System Preferences. When you add, edit, or delete a Mail account from the Mail Accounts pane, Mavericks automatically performs the same operation in the Mail, Contacts & Calendars pane.

Although some folks still have only one e-mail account, you can use a passel of them. For example, you might use one account for your personal e-mail and one account for your business communications (plus that all-important account reserved for junk e-mail and spam). To switch accounts, just click the account that you want to use from this list to make it the active account.

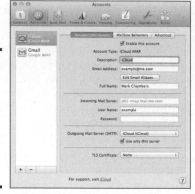

Figure 2-2:
The Accounts list, where all is made clear (about your e-mail accounts).

Add an account

To add a new account within Mail, choose File⇨Add Account to open an Accounts assistant that leads you through the process. 'Nuff said.

However, I'm a manual kind of guy — at least, that's what I'm told — so I should describe the process. For our demonstration, I'll add a typical ISP POP account from the Preferences dialog, which displays the same Add Account assistant.

Open the Preferences dialog by clicking Mail and choosing Preferences; click the Accounts button on the Preferences toolbar. Follow these steps:

1. **Click the Add (plus sign) button at the bottom-left corner of the window.**

    The Add Account assistant appears.

2. **In the Full Name field, type your full name — or, if this will be an anonymous account, enter whatever you like as your identity — and then press Tab.**

    Messages that you send appear with this name in the From field in the recipient's e-mail application.

3. **Type the e-mail address assigned to you by your ISP, and then press Tab.**

4. **In the Password field, type the password supplied by your ISP for login to your e-mail account.**

5. **Click Continue in the assistant — or, if Mail can automatically set up the account, click Create.**

   Yes, you read right: If Mail recognizes the type of account you're using, the assistant may offer to automatically complete all the required settings for you! (If the account is recognized, Mail displays the assistant's Account Summary screen with the configuration data it automatically entered. Smile proudly and click Create, and you're done. Sit back and watch as Mail downloads the existing messages.) If your account isn't recognized by Mail, it's no big deal — just continue with Step 6.

6. **From the Account Type pop-up menu, choose the protocol type to use for the account.**

   You can select an Apple iCloud account, a Post Office Protocol (POP) account, a Microsoft Exchange account, an Internet Message Access Protocol (IMAP) account, or a standard Microsoft Exchange IMAP account. If you're adding an account from an Internet service provider (ISP), refer to the setup information that you received to determine which account to use. Most ISP accounts are POP accounts.

   When you select an Account Type, the fields may change on the Add Account assistant, but they'll still follow the same general order I give in this POP account demonstration. (In fact, IMAP accounts have fewer fields to fill out!) Keep the account information provided by your ISP handy because that data should include everything covered in the assistant.

7. **In the Description field, name the account to identify it within Mail and then press Tab to move to the next field.**

   For example, *Work* and *Mom's ISP* are good choices.

8. **In the Incoming Mail Server text box, type the incoming mail server address supplied by your ISP.**

   If your ISP requires a login for security, you need to enter your server username and password.

9. **Click Continue.**

10. **On the Incoming Mail Security sheet, click the Authentication pop-up menu and choose the authentication scheme used by your incoming mail server.**

   Unless you're told differently by your ISP, the default choice — Password — is very likely correct already. Don't enable the Use Secure Sockets Layer (SSL) check box unless specifically instructed to do so by your ISP.

11. **Click Continue.**

12. **On the Outgoing Mail Server sheet, type a description for the server and press Tab.**

    I typically enter the ISP name.

13. **In the Outgoing Mail Server text box, type the outgoing mail server address supplied by your ISP.**

14. **If your ISP requires your e-mail application to authenticate the connection, select the Use Authentication check box and type the username and password supplied by your ISP into the corresponding fields.**

15. **Click Continue.**

16. **Click Continue on the Account Summary sheet.**

17. **Click Create on the Conclusion sheet.**

    You're done! The new account appears in the Accounts list.

You can specify advanced settings for an account. I cover those in the section "Fine-Tuning Your Post Office," later in this chapter.

When you add a new account in Mail — either automatically or manually — that account will appear also in the Mail, Contacts & Calendars pane in the System Preferences window.

Edit an existing account

Need to make changes to an existing account? Choose Mail⇨Preferences and click the account that you want to change. Mail displays the same settings that I explain in the preceding section.

Delete an account

If you change ISPs or you decide to drop an e-mail account, you can remove it from your Accounts list. Otherwise, Mail can annoy you with error messages when it can no longer connect to the server for that account. Display the Mail Preferences dialog, select the account that you want to delete, and then click the Remove button (which is graced by a minus sign).

Naturally, Mail requests confirmation before deleting the folders associated with that account. Click Remove to verify the deletion or click the Cancel button to prevent accidental catastrophe.

Receiving and Reading E-Mail Wisdom

The heart and soul of Mail — well, at least the heart, anyway — is receiving and reading stuff from your friends and family. (Later in this chapter, I show you how to avoid the stuff you get promising free prizes, low mortgage rates, and improved . . . um, performance. This is a family-oriented book, so that's enough of that.)

After you set up an account (or select an account from the Accounts list), it's time to check for mail. Use any of these methods to check for new mail:

+ **On the toolbar, click the Get Mail button, which bears a snazzy envelope icon.**

+ **If the Mail icon appears on the Dock, right-click it and choose Get New Mail from the menu that appears.**

+ **Choose Mailbox⇨Get All New Mail or press ⌘+Shift+N.**

+ **Choose Mailbox⇨Get New Mail and then choose the specific account to check from the submenu.**

This last method is a great way to check for new mail in another account without going through the trouble of making it active in the Preferences window.

Mail can also check for new messages automatically; you can find more on this topic in the "Check Mail automatically" section, later in this chapter.

You can receive a notification when you receive a new message — and Mavericks even allows you to conveniently read or delete the new message from the notification! For more information on notifications and how to set them for Apple Mail, visit the inviting shores of Book I, Chapter 6.

Displaying all Mail headers

Mail hides the majority of the heading lines that help identify and route an e-mail message to its rightful destination. By default, all you'll see is the *filtered heading,* which includes only the From, Date, To, and Subject fields. This is great unless (for some reason) you need to display the entire message header in all its arcane madness. If you do, press ⌘+Shift+H. You can toggle back to the filtered heading by pressing the same shortcut.

If you do have new mail in the active account, it appears in the Message list. As you can see in Figure 2-3, new unread messages appear marked with a snazzy blue dot in the first column. The number of unread messages is displayed next to the Inbox folder icon in the Mailboxes list.

Mail also displays the number of new messages that you've received on its Dock icon. If you've hidden the Mail window or sent it to the Dock, you can perform a quick visual check for new mail just by glancing at the Dock.

Figure 2-3:
A new message to read. Oh, joy, and no spam!

Reading and deleting messages

To read any message in the message list, you can either click the desired entry (which displays the contents of the message in the preview pane), or you can double-click the entry to open the message in a separate message window, complete with its own toolbar controls.

To quickly scan your mail, click the first message that you want to view in the message list and then press the down-arrow key when you're ready to move to the next message. Mail displays the content of each message in the preview pane. To display the previous message in the list, press the up-arrow key.

Mail also allows you to read your messages grouped within conversations (typically called *threads* within other e-mail applications). A *conversation* contains an original message and all related replies, which makes it easy to follow the flow of an e-mail discussion (without bouncing around in your

Inbox, searching for the next message in the conversation). Conversations are indicated in the Message list by numbers at the right side of the original message, indicating how many messages are included. Choose View⇨Organize by Conversation, and the replies in the current folder are all grouped under the original messages and sorted by date. To expand a thread, click the original message to select it; then press the right-arrow key (or choose View⇨Expand All Conversations). To collapse a thread, select the original message and press the left-arrow key (or choose View⇨Collapse All Conversations).

Hey, why not let Mail *read* you your mail? (That is, if you can drive and listen to your MacBook speak at the same time!) Simply select one message or a group of messages and then choose Edit⇨Speech⇨Start Speaking. *Wowsers!*

To delete a message from the message list, click the desired entry (or entries, by holding down the ⌘ key) to select them and then click the Delete button on the toolbar (or press the Del key). To delete a message from within a message window, click the Delete button on the toolbar.

Hey, what does MIME mean?

First, a note of explanation about Internet e-mail. (Don't worry about taking notes; you won't be tested on this stuff.) Decades back, Internet e-mail messages were pure text, composed only of ASCII characters — that means no fancy fonts, colors, stationery, or text formatting. However, as more and more folks started using e-mail, the clarion call rang forth across the land for more attractive messages (as well as attachments, which I cover in the section "Attachments on Parade"). Therefore, the MIME encoding standard was developed. In case you're interested, MIME stands for *Multipurpose Internet Mail Extensions* — a rather cool (and surprisingly understandable) acronym.

Originally, virtually all e-mail programs recognized one version of MIME, but then the Tower of Babel principle kicked in, and now multiple versions of MIME exist. Apple Mail uses the most common variant of MIME, so most folks who receive your e-mail can see them in all their glory (even under Windows).

However, if one of your addressees complains that he got a message containing unrecognizable gobbledygook and a heading that mentions MIME, he's using an e-mail client application that either doesn't support MIME or supports a different version. (Of course, that person could have unknowingly turned off MIME support.) You have two possible solutions: You can ask the addressee to double-check whether MIME is enabled on his end in the e-mail application, or you can disable MIME when sending a message to that particular person. When you're composing an original message or a reply, you can use pure text by choosing Format⇨Make Plain Text. (This choice prevents you from doing anything fancy, and files that you attach to a plain-text message might not be delivered correctly.)

Replying

What? Aunt Harriet sent you a message because she's forgotten where she parked her car last night? If you happen to know where her priceless '78 Pinto is, you can reply to her and save her the trouble of retracing her steps.

If Aunt Harriet isn't in your Contacts application yet, this is a good time to add her. With the message entry selected in the list, choose Message⇨Add Sender to Contacts or just press the convenient ⌘+Shift+Y keyboard short-cut. The person's name and e-mail address are added automatically to your Contacts database. To add more information in the new Contacts card, however, you have to open that application separately. (Read through Book I, Chapter 7 for the skinny on the Contacts application.)

But I digress. To reply to a message in Mail, follow these steps:

1. **Click the desired message entry in the message list and then click the Reply button (a single left arrow) on the toolbar.**

To respond to a message that you've opened in a message window, click the Reply button on the toolbar for the message window. (Or move your cursor on top of the dividing line between the header information and the body of the message, and click the Reply button that magically appears.)

If a message was addressed not just to you but also to a number of different people, you can send your reply to all of them. Click the Reply All button, which bears two left arrows, on the Mail window toolbar. (This is a great way to quickly facilitate a festive gathering, if you get my drift.)

You can also add carbon copies of your message to other new recipients, expanding the party exponentially; more on carbon copies later in the section, "Raise the Little Flag: Sending E-Mail."

Mail opens the Reply window that you see in Figure 2-4. Note that the address has been added automatically and that the default Subject is Re: *<the original subject>*. Mail automatically adds a separator line in the message body field that reads

On *<day><date>at<time>*, *<addressee>* wrote:

followed by the text of the original message, so the addressee can remember what the heck she wrote in the first place to get you so happy/sad/angry/indifferent. The original text is indented and prefaced by a vertical line to set it apart. If you like, you can click in the Subject line and change the default subject line; otherwise, the cursor is already sitting on the first line of the text box, so you can simply start typing your reply.

If you don't want to include the text of the original message in a reply, choose Mail⇔Preferences. Click the Composing button and clear the Quote the Text of the Original Message check box.

Figure 2-4:
Replying to an incoming e-mail message.

To choose the text from the original message that you want to include in a reply, select the desired text in the original message before you click the Reply button.

2. **After you complete typing your reply, you can select text in the message body and apply different fonts or formats.**

To change your reply's formatting, click the Format button (with the capital letter A) on the message window toolbar. From the buttons that appear, you can choose the font family, the type size, and formatting (such as italic or bold) for the selected text. You can also apply color to the selected text by clicking the Colors button — the black square — and then clicking anywhere in the color grid that appears to select that color. (You can set your default fonts and colors in the Fonts & Colors pane of Mail's Preferences window.)

Click the Format button again to hide these controls. (If you like menus, you can also choose Format from the menu and make changes from there.)

To create a list in your reply, choose Format⇔Lists and choose a bulleted or a numbered list. Mail thoughtfully prepares your first item for you. Press Return to add another item. Click outside the list item formatting to complete the list.

Care to chat directly with the recipients of your message? Just choose Message⇨Reply with Messages, and Mail automatically opens Messages and attempts to connect! (Note that this will work only with the recipients who have an instant-messaging address in their Contacts card.) This Chat feature also appears on the New Message window toolbar, which I discuss in a page or two.

3. **To add an attachment, click the Attach button (with the paper clip icon) on the toolbar.**

   Mail displays a familiar Open dialog. Navigate to the to-be-attached file, select it, and click the Open button to add it to the message. (More on attachments in the "Attachments on Parade" section, later in this chapter.) If the recipient is running Windows, make sure the Send Windows-Friendly Attachments check box is selected, which results in a slightly larger e-mail message size but helps ensure that PC e-mail programs, such as Outlook and Windows Live Mail, can correctly open your attachments.

   Because most folks end up sending photos through e-mail, Apple includes a Photo Browser button on the toolbar. Click this button on the Reply or New Message window toolbars, and you can choose a photo from your iPhoto library to insert directly into your message. Heck, you can even take a quick candid shot using Photo Booth! Naturally, your Mac will need a FaceTime HD camera (or other compatible video camera) to use the Photo Booth feature. You can also use iPhoto to post photos online. For more, check out the sidebar "Is that Facebook and Flickr I spy?" in Book III, Chapter 3.

4. **Choose the message priority.**

   By default, Mail adds a normal priority flag to your e-mail message. To decrease or increase the urgency, click the Priority icon at the right side of the Reply window toolbar and choose Low or High priority. Choosing a different priority won't send the message any faster or slower. It merely displays a High or Low priority notification in the recipient's e-mail application.

5. **When you're ready to send your reply, you have two options: send or save.**

   • *Send:* Click the Send button (which carries a cool paper airplane icon) to immediately add the message to your Outbox folder. After a message is moved to the Outbox folder, it's sent either immediately or at the next connection time that you specify in Mail Preferences. Read more on this in the upcoming section, "Check Mail automatically."

- *Save:* Click the Close button on the Reply window and store it in your Drafts folder for later editing. Saving the message to your Drafts folder doesn't send it. Read the following section for the skinny on how to send a message stored in your Drafts folder.

You can also forward a message or your reply to someone (other than the original sender). The new addressee receives a message containing both the text of the original message that you received and your reply. To forward a message, click the Forward button on the Mail toolbar (which bears a right arrow) instead of Reply or Reply to All.

By default, Mail checks your spelling while you type and also underlines any words that it doesn't recognize. (Very Microsoftian.) I like this feature, but if you find it irritating, you can turn it off or set Mail to check the spelling just once, when you click Send. Choose Mail⇨Preferences, click Composing, and open the Check Spelling as I Type pop-up menu to choose the desired option.

Raise the Little Flag: Sending E-Mail

To compose and send a new message to someone, follow these steps:

1. **Click the New Message button on the Mail toolbar or choose File⇨ New Message (or avail yourself of the handy ⌘+N keyboard shortcut).**

Mail opens the New Message window that you see in Figure 2-5.

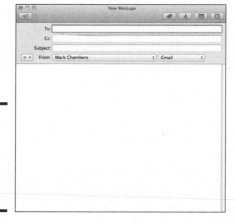

Figure 2-5:
An empty
Mail
message,
waiting to
be filled.

2. Enter the recipient's (To) address by

- *Typing it directly.*
- *Pasting it after copying it to the Clipboard.*
- *Dragging an e-mail address from your Contacts window.*
- *Choosing Window⇨Address Panel,* which shows you the scaled-down version of Contacts (the Addresses panel) that you see in Figure 2-6. This is my favorite method.

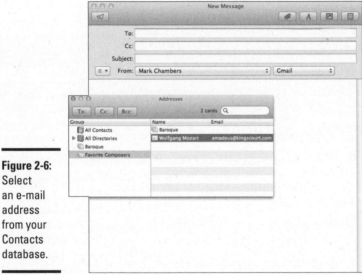

Figure 2-6:
Select
an e-mail
address
from your
Contacts
database.

From the Addresses panel, click the address that you want to use and then click the To button. To choose multiple recipients, hold down the ⌘ key while you click the multiple addresses. Click the Close button on the Addresses panel to close it; then, press Tab.

If you have a huge number of entries in your Contacts application, use the Search field on the Addresses panel toolbar, which operates just like the Finder window's Search box.

3. When Mail highlights the Cc field (the spot where you can send optional carbon copies of the message to additional recipients), you can type the addresses directly, use the contents of the Clipboard, or display the Addresses panel.

If you use the Addresses panel, select the addresses that you want to use and click the Cc button. Then click the Close button on the Addresses panel and press Tab.

Looking for the Blind Carbon Copy (Bcc) field? To display it, choose View⇨Bcc Address Field. A *blind carbon copy* is a message sent to multiple recipients, just like a regular carbon copy, but the recipients aren't listed when the message is displayed. (That way, the other recipients don't know who else got a copy of the message.) You can also click the small Field Display pop-up menu at the left side of the Subject field to toggle the display of the Bcc Address Field. Oh, and there's also a Bcc button on the Addresses panel — go figure.

4. **In the Subject field, enter the subject of the message. Then press Tab.**

   Your text cursor now rests in the first line of the message text area — type, my friend, type like the wind! It's considered good form to keep this line short and relatively to the point.

5. **(Optional) After you type your message, select any of the text that you've entered and use the toolbar features I describe in the earlier section "Replying" to apply different fonts or formatting.**

   Click the Format button in the message window toolbar to open a button bar of formatting choices. (Click the Format button again to hide the Format bar.) If you like menus, you can also click Format and make changes from there.

6. **(Optional) To add an attachment, click the Attach button on the toolbar, navigate to the to-be-attached file in the dialog that appears, select the file, and then click Open to add it to the message.**

   To include photos in your message, just click the Photo Browser toolbar button to select images from your iPhoto library, or take a photo with Photo Booth.

7. **When your new message is ready to post, either click the Send button to immediately add the message to your Outbox folder or click the Close button on the New Message window and then click Save to store it in your Drafts folder (without sending it).**

To send a message held in your Drafts folder, click the Drafts folder in the Mailbox list to display all draft messages. Double-click the message that you want to send, which displays the message window (you can make edits at this point, if you like), and then click the Send button on the message window toolbar.

If you don't have access to an Internet connection at the moment, Mail allows you to work offline. This way, you can read your unread messages and compose new ones on the road to send later. After you regain your Internet connection, you might need to choose Mailbox⇨Online Status (depending on the connection type).

Making an impression with Stationery

Stationery isn't required, but it really packs a visual wallop! Click the Show Stationery button on the toolbar to display the Stationery strip above the message text box (as shown in the nearby figure), where you can choose one of many backgrounds that Apple supplies.

Here's a few of the things you can do with Stationery:

- Double-click a thumbnail in the strip to add it to your message.

- To display a different category of stationery, such as a Greeting or Invitation, click the category buttons on the left side of the Stationery strip.

- This one will really knock your socks off: If you choose a Photo stationery background for your new message, you can even drag an image from Photo Browser, the iPhoto window, or a Finder window to fill the "placeholder" images on the background. (Which, when you think about it,

kind of makes sense . . . after all, why send an e-mail from sunny Italy that has stock photos of a strange couple at the top? Add your own travel shots instead!) The figure illustrates a Photo stationery background. Unfortunately, unless the recipient is using Apple Mail (or an iOS device), that Photo stationery background probably won't display correctly — and it will take quite a while to download.

I should repeat that: Not all e-mail applications on other computers correctly display a message with a stationery background. For the whole scoop, see the "Hey, what does MIME mean?" sidebar, earlier in this chapter. Also, remember that a message with a stationery background is going to be much larger than a simple text message, especially if it contains a number of photos. (And, as you guessed, that also means that it takes longer to send and receive, which is very important for those using a dial-up analog modem connection.)

What? You Get Junk Mail, Too?

Spam — it's the Crawling Crud of the Internet, and I hereby send out a lifetime of bad karma to those who spew it. However, chucking the First Amendment is *not* an option, so I guess we'll always have junk mail. (Come to think of it, my paper mailbox is just as full of the stuff.)

Thankfully, Apple Mail has a net that you can cast to collect junk mail before you have to read it. The two methods of handling junk mail are

✦ **Manually:** You can mark any message in the message list as Junk Mail. Select the unwanted flotsam in the message list and then click the Junk button (which carries the negative "thumbs down" icon) on the Mail window toolbar. Mail marks the message, as shown in Figure 2-7. (Ocean-front property in Kansas . . . yeah, right.) If a message is mistakenly marked as junk but you actually want it, display the message in the preview pane and then click the Not Junk button at the top of the preview pane.

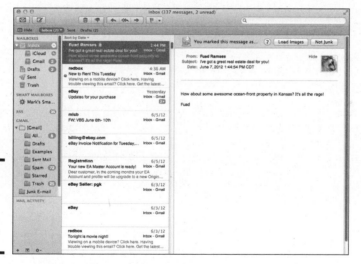

Figure 2-7: "Begone, sludge demons of Junk Mail!"

✦ **Automatically:** Apple Mail has a sophisticated Junk Mail filter that you train to better recognize what's junk. (Keep reading to discover how.) After you train Mail to recognize spam with a high degree of accuracy, turn it to full Automatic mode, and it moves all those worthless messages to your Junk folder.

You customize and train the Junk Mail filter from the Preferences dialog (available from your trusty Mail menu); click Junk Mail to show the settings. I recommend that you first try Mail in Training mode, using the Mark as Junk Mail, But Leave It in My Inbox option. Junk Mail then takes its best shot at determining what's junk. When you receive more mail and mark more messages as junk (or mark them as *not* junk), you're teaching the Junk Mail feature how to winnow the wheat from the chaff. In Training mode, junk messages aren't moved anywhere, and they're just marked with a particularly fitting, grungy brown color.

After you're satisfied that the Junk Mail filter is catching just about everything that it can (and not tagging messages it shouldn't), display the Mail preferences again and choose the Move It to the Junk Mailbox option. Mail creates a Junk folder and prompts you for permission to move all junk messages to this folder. After you review everything in the Junk folder, you can delete what it contains and send it to the Trash folder. To save a message from junkdom, click the Not Junk button in the preview window and then drag the message from the Junk folder message list to the desired folder in the Mailbox list.

Finally, you can create a complete set of custom *rules* for your Junk Mail filtering by clicking Perform Custom Actions. The Advanced button displays your Junk Mail rule set and allows you to edit your rules. I explain rules in more depth at the end of this chapter.

If you don't receive a lot of spam — or if you want to be absolutely sure that nothing gets labeled as junk until you review it — clear the Enable Junk Mail Filtering check box. (And good luck.)

By default, Mail exempts certain messages from Junk Mail status based on three criteria: if the sender is in your Contacts database, if you've sent the sender a message in the past, or if the message is addressed to you with your full name. To tighten up your Junk Mail filtering to the max, you might want to clear these check boxes as well.

To reset the Junk Mail filter and erase any training that you've done, visit the Junk Mail settings in Preferences again and click Reset. Then click the Yes button to confirm your choice.

Attachments on Parade

Attachments are a fun way to transfer files through e-mail. However, it's imperative that you remember these three important caveats:

+ **Attachments can contain viruses.** Even a message attachment that was sent by your best friend can contain a virus or malevolent macro — either because your friend unwittingly passed one along or because the virus took control of your friend's e-mail application and replicated itself automatically. (Ugh.)

✦ **Corpulent attachments don't make it.** Most corporate and ISP mail servers have a 4–6MB limit for the total size of a message, and the attachments (and any Photo stationery background you might have added) count toward that final message size. Therefore, I recommend sending a file as an attachment only if it's less than 3MB (or perhaps 4MB) in size. If the recipient's e-mail server sends you an automated message saying that the message was refused because it was too big, this is the problem.

✦ **Not all e-mail applications and firewalls accept attachments.** Not all e-mail programs support attachments in the same way, and others are simply set for pure text messages. Some corporate firewalls even reject messages with attachments. If the message recipient gets the message text but not the attachment, these are the likely reasons.

With all that said, it's back to attachments as a beneficial feature. Follow these steps to save an attachment that you receive:

1. **Click the message with an attachment in your message list.**

Messages with attachments appear with a tiny paper-clip icon in the Message list, but it's sometimes hard to spot them. Click the Sort By pop-up menu button at the top of the Message list and choose Attachments, and Mail places all messages with attachments at the top of the list.

If Mail recognizes the attachment format, it displays or plays the attachment in the body of the message; if not, the attachment is displayed as a file icon.

2. **To open an attachment that's displayed as a file icon, click the file icon and then choose Open Attachment from the pop-up menu that appears.**

If you know what application should be used to open the attachment, click the Open With button and choose the correct application from the submenu that appears.

To save an attachment, right-click the attachment (however it appears in the message) and then choose Save Attachment from the pop-up menu that appears. Then, in the Save dialog that appears, navigate to the location where you want to save the file and click Save.

Fine-Tuning Your Post Office

Like all other Apple software, Mail is easily customized to your liking. In this section, I discuss some preferences you might want to change.

Add an alert sound

To choose a sound that plays whenever you receive new mail, choose Mail⇨Preferences and click the General button. Either open the New Messages Sound pop-up menu and choose one of the sounds that Apple provides or choose Add/Remove from the pop-up menu to choose a sound file from the Sounds folder. (You can also add a sound to your Sound folder from this sheet.)

If you change your mind and long for silence again, choose None from the New Messages Sound pop-up menu to disable the new mail sound.

Check Mail automatically

By default, Mail automatically checks for new mail (and sends any mail in your Outbox folder) every five minutes. To change this delay period, display the General pane in the Preferences dialog, choose the Check for New Messages pop-up menu, and then choose one of the time periods.

To disable automatic mail checking, choose Manually; you can click the Get Mail toolbar button to manually check your mail any time you like. Disabling mail checking is handy for those folks using dial-up analog modem connections who may not fancy Mail taking control of the telephone line every five minutes.

Automate junk mail and message deletion

Mail can be set to automatically delete sent mail and Junk messages as well as permanently erase messages that you relegate to the Trash. To configure these settings, display the Accounts pane in the Preferences window, click the desired account, and then click the Mailbox Behaviors tab.

✦ **To delete Sent messages automatically:** Open the Delete Sent Messages When pop-up menu and choose the delay period or action. You can choose to delete mail after a day, a week, or a month, or immediately upon quitting Mail. If you leave this field set to Never, Mail never automatically deletes any messages from the Sent folder.

✦ **To delete Junk messages automatically:** Open the Delete Junk Messages When pop-up menu and choose the delay period or action. These are the same options available for Sent mail.

✦ **To delete messages from the Trash:** Open the Permanently Erase Deleted Messages When pop-up menu and choose the delay period or action. Again, the choices are the same as those for Sent messages.

Add a signature

To add a block of text to the bottom of your messages as your personal signature, follow these steps:

1. **Choose Mail⇨Preferences and click the Signatures button.**

2. **From the Signatures pane that appears, click the Add Signature button (a plus sign).**

3. **Type an identifying name.**

   Press Return to save the new name.

4. **Click inside the text entry box at the right to move the cursor.**

5. **Type the signature itself in the text entry box or copy the signature to the Clipboard and paste it into the text entry box.**

   It's considered good netiquette to keep your signature to three lines.

   Because downloading a graphic in a signature takes longer — and because some folks still use plain-text e-mail — avoid the temptation to include graphics in your signature. If you do use them, remember that a graphic used as a signature may be handled as an attachment by the recipient's e-mail application!

6. **If you have multiple signatures, click the Choose Signature pop-up menu to choose which one you want to use or to use them all randomly or in sequence.**

If you prefer the signature to appear above the quoted text in a reply, select the Place Signature above Quoted Text check box.

Changing the status of an account

Sometimes you can't reach one of your accounts. For example, maybe you're on the road with your laptop and you can't access your office network. Apple Mail allows you to enable and disable specific accounts without the hassle of deleting an account and then having to add it again.

To disable or enable an account, open the Preferences dialog, click the Accounts button, click the desired account, click the Advanced tab, and then select (or deselect) the Enable This Account check box as necessary.

If you disable an account, you should also deselect the Include When Automatically Checking for New Mail check box to make sure that Mail doesn't display an error message. You can always check any account for new mail by choosing Mailbox⇨Get New Mail and then choosing the desired account name from the submenu.

Automating Your Mail with Rules

Before I leave the beautiful shores of Mail Island, I'd be remiss if I didn't discuss one of its most powerful features: the capability to create *rules,* which are automated actions that Mail can take. With rules, you can specify criteria that can perform actions such as

✦ Transferring messages from one folder to another

✦ Forwarding messages to another address

✦ Highlighting or deleting messages

To set up a rule, follow these steps:

1. **Choose Mail⇨Preferences and then click the Rules button on the toolbar.**

   Mail displays the Rules pane.

2. **In the Description field, type a descriptive name for the new rule and then press Tab to move to the next field.**

3. **Open the If pop-up menu to specify whether the rule is triggered if any of the conditions are met or if all conditions must be met.**

4. **Because each rule requires at least one condition, click the Target pop-up menus to set the target for the condition.**

   These include whom the message is from or to, which account received the message, whether the message is marked as junk, and whether the message contains certain content. Select the target for the condition.

5. **Open the Criteria pop-up menu to choose the rule's criteria.**

   The contents of this pop-up menu change depending on the condition's target. For example, if you choose From as the target, the criteria include Contains, Does Not Contain, Begins With, and so forth.

6. **Click in the expression box and type the text to use for the condition.**

   For example, a completed condition might read

   ```
   Subject Contains Ocean-Front
   ```

   This particular condition is true if I get an e-mail message with a subject that contains the string Ocean-Front.

7. **Add more conditions by clicking the plus sign button at the right of the first condition.**

   To remove any condition from this rule, click the minus sign button next to it. Remember, however, that every rule needs at least one condition.

8. **To specify what action is taken after the condition (or conditions) is met, click the first Perform the Following Actions pop-up menu to see the action that this rule should perform. Then click the second pop-up menu and select the action for the rule.**

   Choices include transferring a message from one folder to another, playing a sound, automatically forwarding the message, deleting it, and marking it as read.

   Each rule requires at least one action.

9. **Depending on the action that you select, specify one or more criteria for the action.**

   For instance, if I select Set Color as my action, I must then choose whether to color the text or the background as well as what color to use.

   As with the plus button next to the conditions, you can also click the plus button next to the first action to perform more than one action. To remove an action, click the minus button next to it.

10. **When the rule is complete, click OK to save it.**

To save a little time, you can build a rule similar to an existing rule. From the Rules pane (choose Mail⇨Preferences⇨Rules), highlight the original in the list and then click the Duplicate button. Tweak to your heart's content, using the preceding steps.

Here's an example of a complex rule:

> If the message was sent by someone in my Contacts database *and* the Subject field contains the text FORWARD ME, forward the message to the e-mail address fuadramses@me.com.

This is a good example of an automated forwarding rule. With this rule in place and Mail running on OS X, any of my friends, family, or co-workers can forward urgent e-mail to my iCloud account while I'm on vacation. To trigger the rule, all the sender has to do is include the words *FORWARD ME* in the message subject. And if the sender isn't in my Contacts, the rule doesn't trigger, and I can read the message when I get home. Mondo *sassy*.

Each rule in the Rules dialog can be enabled or disabled by toggling the Active check box next to the rule in the Rules pane. You can also edit a rule by selecting it in the Rules pane and then clicking the Edit button. To delete a rule completely from the list, select it and then click the Remove button; Mail prompts you for confirmation before the deed is done.

If you decide to create a custom Junk mail processing rule, the process is the same, but you get to it from a different place. Click the Junk Mail button on the Preferences dialog toolbar and click the Perform Custom Actions radio button to select it. You see that the Advanced button is now enabled — click it and you can set up the custom Junk mail rules that handle stuff from any conceivable junk mail source!

Chapter 3: Staying in Touch with Messages and FaceTime

In This Chapter

✔ **Setting up Messages**

✔ **Changing modes in Messages**

✔ **Adding Buddies**

✔ **Chatting with others**

✔ **Sharing screens with another person**

✔ **Sending and receiving files through Messages**

✔ **Ignoring those who deserve to be shunned**

✔ **Adding visual pizzazz with video backgrounds and effects**

✔ **Chatting face-to-face with FaceTime**

*T*hroughout humankind's history, our drive has been toward communication, from the earliest cave paintings, through written language, to the telegraph, telephone, and now the ultimate in human interaction: the text message. Ah, technological rapture! Of course, the very same text messages that your family craves can also send your cellphone bill through the roof. (The classic Catch-22 quandary.)

Ah, but wait. Here are Apple and Mavericks to the rescue, so forget that silly cellular phone and your complicated calling plan! As long as you have Mac OS X and an Internet connection, you can instantly chat with your friends and family whether they're within shouting distance or halfway across the world. You can text anyone with a Mac or an iOS 5 or later device (such as an iPhone, iPad, or iPod touch) absolutely free. And, by golly, if the two of you have a FaceTime HD camera, Mac-compatible web camera, or digital video (DV) camcorder connected to your computers, you'll *see* each other in glorious, full-color video! These modern marvels are made possible by *Messages* and *FaceTime*, and they fulfill the decades-old promise of the video telephone quite well, thank you.

In this chapter, I show you how to gab with the following folks:

+ **Other Mac owners who use Messages (either on your local network or on the Internet)**

+ **Other Mac owners using iChat on an older version of OS X**

+ **Mac, iPhone 4 or later, iPod touch, and iPad 2nd generation or later owners**

  Sending and receiving iMessages requires iOS 5 or later, and FaceTime requires iOS 4.1 and later.

+ **Anyone who uses AIM (America Online [AOL] Instant Messaging), Jabber, Yahoo!, or Google Talk**

+ **Folks who participate in AOL chat rooms**

Configuring Messages

The first time you run Messages (click the Messages icon on the Dock or in Launchpad), you're prompted to sign in by entering your Apple ID (which you created while setting up Mavericks, or through the App Store as I demonstrate in Book I, Chapter 3). You use your iMessage account to send and receive free messages to others using either a Mac or an iOS 5 (or later) device such as an iPhone, iPod touch, or iPad. Messages also prompts you to select which phone numbers (for an iPhone) and e-mail addresses (for a Mac, an iPhone, an iPod touch, or an iPad) that you want to use with this account.

An *instant message* (IM, like those exchanged on AIM and Google Talk) is different from an *iMessage* (which can be exchanged only with others using Macs or Apple iOS devices). Messages can send and receive both types. If you used iChat in an earlier version of OS X, you were limited to just instant messages, audio chatting, and video chatting.

If you're already using AIM, Jabber, Yahoo!, or Google Talk and you want to use your existing IM account, choose File⇨Add Account, choose the correct type, and then click Continue. Messages prompts you to enter your existing account information.

To enter information for a Jabber account, click the Other Messages Account radio button, click Continue, and then click the Account Type pop-up list box and choose Jabber.

You can also choose to set up Bonjour messaging. Think of *Bonjour* as plug-and-play IM for your local network. In Messages, Bonjour allows you to see (and yak with) anyone on your local network without having to know his account information, because Bonjour automatically announces all the Messages users who are available on your network. If you have others using Messages, iChat, Jabber, Yahoo!, or AIM on your local network, go for this option; if you're not connected to a local network, however, Bonjour messaging isn't necessary. Also, if you're on a public Wi-Fi network or if you're connecting to the Internet with an external modem through dial-up, I recommend disabling Bonjour messaging. (For all that's cool about Wi-Fi, see Book VI, Chapter 3.) To turn on Bonjour messaging, choose Messages➪Preferences, click the Accounts tab, click the Bonjour account in the list to the left to select it, and then select the Enable Bonjour Instant Messaging check box.

Working with Messages

After you finish these configuration necessities, Messages displays the window that you see in Figure 3-1. Time for introductions all around!

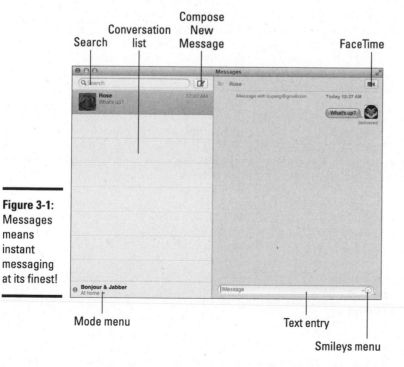

Figure 3-1: Messages means instant messaging at its finest!

If you want to send an iMessage to other Mac owners — or owners of iOS 5 (or later devices) — use the Messages window. If you already have an iPhone, iPod touch, or iPad running iOS 5 or later, you'll probably immediately recognize the Conversation list on the left, which displays each individual with whom you've recently exchanged iMessages. Click an individual in the list to review past conversations (and optionally continue them). The right side of the Messages window contains the iMessages sent back and forth, which I cover later in the chapter.

Only folks using either a Mac running Mountain Lion, Mavericks or an iOS 5 (or later) device can send and receive iMessages.

If you've used iChat in previous versions of OS X, you may be lamenting the demise of your old friend, the Buddies list — but don't despair, it's still around! You can display the familiar Buddies window (shown in Figure 3-2) at any time by pressing ⌘+1 or by choosing Window➪Buddies from the Messages menu bar. Use the Buddies window to invite others to chat using an instant-messaging program (such as AIM, Google Talk, and Jabber).

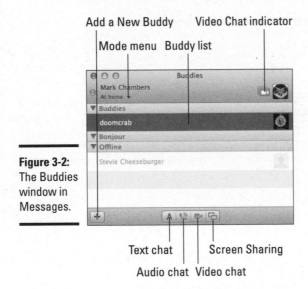

Add a New Buddy   Video Chat indicator

Mode menu   Buddy list

Figure 3-2:
The Buddies
window in
Messages.

Text chat   Screen Sharing

Audio chat   Video chat

A few things to note here about these two windows in Messages:

+ **If you don't like your picture, don't panic.** By default, Messages uses your user account thumbnail image as your visual persona. However, you can add a picture to your Messages by dragging an image to the well next to your name at the top of the Buddies window. If necessary, Messages asks you to position and size the image so that it fits in the (admittedly limited) space. This picture is then sent along with your words when you chat. In the figures for this chapter, I borrow the somewhat dour expression of a screech owl.

Click your image to display your recent thumbnails. This way, you can even use a different thumbnail image for each of your many moods. (Geez.) Also, you can click Camera from the pop-up menu and capture a new thumbnail with your FaceTime HD camera.

✦ **Check out the buttons along the bottom of the Buddies window.** In order, these buttons are

- *Add a New Buddy:* Covered in the following section
- *Start a Text Chat:* Plain, old-fashioned chatting via the keyboard
- *Start an Audio Chat:* Chatting with your voice, using microphones
- *Start a Video Chat:* The ultimate chat, where the parties can both see and hear each other
- *Start Screen Sharing:* Where you can view — or even remotely control — a Buddy's computer

Using these buttons can handle about 90 percent of the commands that you need to give while using Messages, so use 'em!

✦ **Hey, look, there's a Messages menu bar icon!** When you're running Messages, you can add a balloon menu bar icon in the upper-right corner of your screen. Click it to display the options that you see in Figure 3-3. You can change your online/offline status, immediately invite a Buddy for a chat, or display the Buddy list (which I discuss later in the section, "Will You Be My Buddy?"). The menu bar icon appears only if you select the Show Status in Menu Bar check box. Click Messages in the menu and choose Preferences; then click the General button in the Preference dialog.

Figure 3-3:
The Messages Finder menu icon leaps into action.

The Messages menu bar icon can even launch the application! Click the Messages icon in the Finder menu bar and choose New Message at the bottom of the menu, and Mavericks launches Messages automatically.

Changing Modes in Messages

Here's an important note: Just because Messages is running doesn't mean you're ready to converse! For those not familiar with the terms *online* and *offline,* here's the scoop: When you're *online,* folks can invite you to chat and communicate with you. When you're *offline,* you're disconnected: Messages isn't active, you can't be paged, you can't chat, and that is that. Your status applies only to IM and IM chat — iMessages can be sent and received at any time.

Switching modes is easy, and you can do it in several different ways:

+ Choose Available or Offline from the friendly Messages Finder menu bar icon, which looks like a speech bubble from a comic book.

+ If the Messages window is visible, open the Mode pop-up menu at the lower left of the window.

+ If the Buddies window is visible, open the Mode pop-up menu under your name at the upper left of the window.

+ If the Buddies window is visible, you can also click a Buddy name directly, which automatically switches Messages to online mode and starts a conversation with that Buddy.

You can use Away mode whenever Messages is running and you're still online but not available. For example, if I'm away from my Mac for a few minutes, I leave Messages running, but I switch myself to Away mode. My Buddies get a message saying that I'm Away, so they won't bother trying to contact me. When I return to my computer, I simply move my mouse, and Messages intelligently inquires as to whether I'd like to return to Available mode. You can also use the menu bar icon to switch from Away to Available (or my other favorite mode, Twiddling My Thumbs).

Messages can even display which iTunes song you're listening to. Choose Current iTunes Song from the menu and impress your friends with your digital audio technopowers.

Speaking of modes, you, too, can create a custom mode — like *Bored stiff!* or *Listening to the Pointy-Haired Boss* — and use it instead of the somewhat mundane choices of Available and Away. You can create your mode from the Messages or Buddies window: Open Mode pop-up menu in either window, and then click Custom Available or Custom Away to create your new mode. An edit box appears in which you can type the new mode; press Return to automatically add the newcomer to your mode list.

To choose an existing mode, click it; modes with a green bullet are online modes, and red bullet modes are offline modes. (Apple provides you with some starting choices, such as *Surfing the Web* for *Available* and *In a Meeting* for *Away*.) Note in Figure 3-3 that I created a custom mode called *Getting Another Diet Coke . . . cAfFeInE* fills my life.

If you decide your status list is getting a bit too lengthy with all those custom messages, open the Mode pop-up menu in either window and choose Edit Status Menu. Both the Available and Away list boxes have a Delete button (a minus sign). Just click the offending status message to select it and then click the Delete button to take care of business.

Will You Be My Buddy?

I know that asking whether you'll be my Buddy sounds a little personal, but in Messages, a *Buddy* is anyone with whom you want to chat using instant messaging, whether the topic is work- related or your personal life. Messages keeps track of your Buddies in the Buddy list. You can also add them to your Contacts database or use the AIM entry in a Contacts card to generate a new Buddy identity.

To add a new Buddy, follow these steps:

1. **With the Buddies window visible, choose Buddies⇨Add Buddy.**

   Alternatively, click the Add a New Buddy button at the bottom of the Buddies window and choose Add Buddy from the pop-up menu, or press ⌘+Shift+A.

   Messages displays a sheet where you can enter the instant-messaging account information for your new Buddy.

2. **To create a Buddy entry from a Contacts card that has an IM username, click the down-arrow button next to the Last Name box to display the Contacts list. Click the entry to select it.**

   As a shortcut, you can also click in the First Name box and then type the person's first name or click in the Account Name box and type the person's IM account name.

3. **To add a new person who's not already in your Contacts database, type the person's IM account name.**

4. **Click Add to save the Buddy information.**

Even when you add a new Buddy and that name appears in the Buddy list, don't be surprised if the name appears dimmed after a few seconds. The dimming indicates that the person is offline and unavailable. You can also tell when a person is available if his or her name appears with a green bullet in the Buddy list.

You can also specify a number of actions that Messages should take if a Buddy logs in or out of instant messaging, or if a Buddy changes status to Available. To display these actions, click the desired Buddy's entry in your Buddy list and then press ⌘+Shift+I. (From the menu, choose Buddies➪Show Info.) Click the Alerts button and then choose the event that should trigger the action from the Event pop-up menu. Select the desired check box to specify whether Messages should play the sound that you select, run an AppleScript, speak an announcement, or animate the Messages icon by "bouncing" it on the Dock.

Click the Address Card button on the Info dialog to enter or edit the person's

+ Real first and last names
+ Nickname
+ E-mail
+ Phone
+ Instant-messaging address
+ Buddy picture

The View menu offers a number of neat options to help you organize and customize your Buddy list. You can sort your Buddy list by first name, last name, or availability, and you can choose to display full names, short names (your Mavericks account name), or handles (nicknames). You can also toggle the display of offline Buddies.

Chat! Chat, I Say!

Turn your attention to getting the attention of others — through inviting others to chat. Good chatting etiquette implies inviting someone to a conversation rather than barging in unannounced. Note that you don't have to invite someone to start an iMessage conversation in the Messages window. I'm talking either an IM chat or an existing IM chat room here.

If you want to join a chat already in progress, choose File➪Go to Chat Room (or press ⌘+Control+G). Depending on the service being used, you might have to specify both the type of chat and the specific chat room name.

At this point, it's time to draw your attention to the green phone and video icons next to each person in your Buddy list (as well as next to your own name at the top of the list). If the green phone icon appears next to both your name and your Buddy's name, you can enjoy a two-way audio (or voice) chat. If both you and your Buddy (or Buddies) are lucky enough to have FaceTime HD, USB webcams, or DV cameras connected to your Macs, you can jump into a real-time, two-way video chat room, complete with audio. Time for a very important Mark's Maxim that's violated a surprising number of times:

Always wear a shirt while chatting with video, no matter your impressive physique. *Always.*

If your Mac has a microphone or video camera hooked up but you don't see these icons, click the Video menu and make sure that the Audio Chat Enabled and Video Chat Enabled menu items are selected.

To invite someone to a simple text-only IM chat, click the desired Buddy from the Buddy list, click Buddies, and then choose Start New Chat. (Using the mouse, right-click the Buddy in the list and choose Send Instant Message.)

To invite someone to an IM audio chat, choose Buddies⇨Invite to Audio Chat. To invite a Buddy to an IM video chat, choose Buddies⇨Invite to Video Chat. You can also click directly on the phone or camera icon next to the person's name in your Buddy list.

If you're ready to video-chat with a FaceTime-compatible Mac, iPhone, iPad, or iPod touch owner, check out the complete discussion of FaceTime at the end of this chapter. Unlike an IM video chat, you start a FaceTime conversation in one of two ways: Click the FaceTime icon on the Dock, or click the FaceTime icon at the top right of the Messages window. Both methods will launch the FaceTime application.

The recipient of your IM audio or video chat invitation can decline or accept your chat invitation. You're notified (as delicately as possible) if the chat has been declined. After you invite someone to chat (or you opt to simply send an IM), the action switches to the Messages window (for text chats) or to a separate window (for audio and video chats). For text chats, simply type in the text box at the bottom of the Messages window and then press Return to send the message.

Messages displays what type of conversation you're having in two spots — at the top of the window and in the text box — making it easier to differentiate between IM and iMessage conversations. For example, in Figure 3-4, you can see the word *iMessage* displayed at the top of the conversation and in the text box.

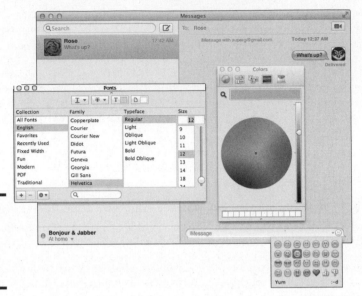

Figure 3-4:
Fonts,
colors, and
smileys —
oh my!

If you'd like to add a *smiley* (often called an "emoticon") to your message, click the Smileys drop-down menu at the right of the text box (as shown in Figure 3-4) and choose just the right symbol. (You can also choose Edit⇨ Insert Smiley.)

While text chatting, you don't have to alternate sending messages back and forth between participants because everyone in a chat can compose and send messages at the same time. Me, I like to alternate when I'm chatting one-on-one.

If someone invites you to an audio or a video chat, you get the opposite side of the coin: A prompt dialog appears, and you can choose to accept or decline the invitation. (If it's a video chat, you even get a video preview of the person inviting you.)

You can also change fonts and colors while composing a line of text. Simply select the text and then choose Format⇨Show Fonts or Format⇨Show Colors. (Press ⌘+T or ⌘+Shift+C to display the Font panel and Color Picker, respectively.) These windows can be resized and moved wherever you like, as shown earlier in Figure 3-4.

Messages doesn't limit you to just a chat between computers! You can also choose to ship off an e-mail message from Messages. Click a person in the Buddy list and click the Buddies menu; click Send Email to automatically launch Apple Mail (or your default e-mail application).

When the Messages window is active, you can make a number of display choices from the View menu. Click the Messages item in the View menu to display these options, including

✦ **Show as Text:** Each line that you write and receive in a chat can be displayed in *balloons* (just like your favorite comic) or as simple text. You can also choose to display text lines in the more traditional boxes or as compact text (allowing more room for more characters in the Messages window).

✦ **Show Names and Pictures:** Each line can be displayed with the individual's picture, just the name, or both the name and picture.

If you're tired of the default background for the chat window — or you want to select a default font and text color for either your messages or those from others — click Messages and choose Preferences from the menu, and then click the Messages toolbar button. Use the Background Color, Font Color, and Set Font controls to fine-tune things as you like.

Curious about the capabilities of your Mac hardware in Messages? Choose Video⇨Connection Doctor, where you can view statistics and information about your current chat, display the features of Messages that are supported by your Mac and your connection, and also view any error messages that are generated by Messages during this session.

If you're holding multiple conversations in the Messages window, you can switch between windows by clicking the desired conversation in the Conversation list to make it active. To close an IM chat or an iMessage conversation, click a conversation in the list to select it and then click the Close button that appears (it bears an X symbol).

Conversing with iMessages

So you'd like to send and receive those free iMessages I mention earlier with your sister in Poughkeepsie? As long as she has a Mac of her own (or a snazzy Apple device running iOS 5 or later) and a network, Wi-Fi, or 3G/4G/LTE connection, you're ready to go.

Click the Compose New Message icon at the top of the Messages window to start a new conversation. The cursor appears in the To field, and you can

✦ **Do things manually.** Type the person's name, e-mail address, or telephone number directly in the To field. The information you enter depends on the recipient's device — for example, sending an iMessage to an iPhone requires a telephone number, and an iPad or iPod touch needs an e-mail address — and whether that person has a card in your Contacts database that already has the required information.

✦ **Choose a Contact or Buddy.** Click the blue plus sign to display a pop-up menu, where you can select a Buddy from your list or a person from your Contacts database. To search for a specific person, click in the Search box and type a portion of the name.

From this point on, an iMessage conversation is similar to an IM chat; Figure 3-5 illustrates an iMessage conversation in progress. Type the desired text in the box at the bottom of the window and then press Return to send your iMessage. To close a conversation, right-click the offending conversation in the list and choose Close Conversation. (You can also select the conversation and click the Close button that appears, which carries an X.)

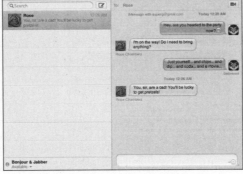

Figure 3-5: An iMessage conversation between a Mac and an iPod touch.

Sharing Screens with Aplomb

How often have you wanted to show someone a neat new application, or lead your Aunt Mildred through the paces of setting up an Apple TV connection on her system? That's the idea behind the ultimate collaboration tool *Sharing Screens,* where you can watch (or even remotely control) the display on another person's Mac, across any broadband Internet or local network connection.

Screen Sharing must be turned on for you to send or receive sharing invites. Choose Video⇨Screen Sharing Enabled. A check mark appears next to the menu item when the feature is enabled.

Sharing things with Theater

But wait. . . . What if you don't *want* to control Aunt Mildred's Mac? Perhaps you just want to share a document during an IM chat with her instead? For example, you could show off some photos or a movie you've just finished, or visit your family web page. That's the idea behind Theater, where you can share a document, web page, or video during a video chat and hold a conversation while viewing the content. Theater falls between Screen Sharing and a simple file download, which I cover in the next section.

After you've started an IM video chat, you can click the Invite button (a plus sign) and choose Share iPhoto with Theater (to share images from your iPhoto library), Share Webpage

with Theater (to share a web page in Safari), or Share a File with Theater (to share movies and other documents). Messages displays a standard Open dialog, in which you can select one or more items. Or, if you're showing a web page, you're prompted for the page's address (URL) to share. When you're ready to begin your Theater presentation, click Share. If you're using a video camera, your video appears as a thumbnail, while your content gets center stage. To stop sharing, click the Close button (which bears an X).

Theater works with anything that can be displayed in Quick Look or located with Spotlight, including slideshows from iPhoto, a Keynote presentation, or a QuickTime movie.

If a Buddy invites you to share a screen, you receive a prompt that you accept or decline. (You can also request to share a Buddy's screen by choosing Buddies⇨Ask to Share Screen.) If you accept the sharing invitation, Messages automatically initiates an audio chat (so that you can gab away to each other while things are happening onscreen). Suddenly, you're seeing the Desktop and applications that your Buddy is running, and you can both control the cursor and left- or right-click the mouse.

Throughout the screen-sharing session, Messages maintains a semi-opaque panel on your screen that has three buttons:

✦ **End the Shared Screen Session:** Click this button to exit shared screen mode.

✦ **Switch Desktops:** Click this button to swap between your Mac's screen and the remote Mac's screen. (Those Mac owners who have enabled Fast User Switching will recognize the cool screen swap animation.)

✦ **Mute Audio:** Click this button to mute the audio during the screen-sharing session.

To invite a Buddy to share your screen, choose Buddies⇨Share My Screen.

Okay, if sharing a screen with someone you don't absolutely know and trust doesn't set off alarm bells in your cranium, it **should.** Remember, anyone with shared screen access to you computer can perform most of the same actions on your Mac as you can, just as if that person were sitting in front of your Mac. Granted, most of the truly devastating things would require you to type your admin password, but a malicious individual could still delete files or wreak havoc any number of ways on your system. **Be careful with whom you share your screen!**

Sending Files with Messages

To send a file to a Buddy via instant messaging, click the desired entry in the Buddy list and then choose Buddies⇨Send File. Alternatively, you can

+ Use the ⌘+Option+F keyboard shortcut.

+ Right-click the Buddy in the list and choose Send a File.

+ Drag the file from a Finder window to the person's entry in the Buddy list.

+ Drag the file into the text-typing window.

How's that for convenience? No matter how you start the transfer, a dialog appears to indicate that the recipient is being offered a file transfer request. If the file transfer request is accepted by your Buddy, the transfer begins and is saved where the recipient specifies on his or her system.

If a Buddy sends you a file, the Incoming File Request pane appears. You can then either click the Decline button (to decline the file transfer) or the Save File button (to save the incoming file to any spot on your system).

To send a file during an iMessage conversation, choose Buddies⇨Send File, use the ⌘+Option+F keyboard shortcut, or drag the file from a Finder window and drop it into the text box in the Messages window.

Always check any files that you receive from Messages with your antivirus scanning software before you run them!

If you're looking for another easy method of sending files between Mac computers running Mavericks, don't forget to check out AirDrop. I discuss this feature in Book VI, Chapter 2. Messages does, however, have two important advantages over AirDrop: The two computers don't have to be within Wi-Fi range of each other, and Messages can transfer files with a wider range of computers (PCs running Windows, Macs running older versions of OS X, and PCs running Linux).

Eliminating the Riffraff

Here I need to explain something that I hope you won't have to use — what I like to call the Turkey Filter. Messages is a little more subtle. You just ignore people.

To ignore someone in a chat group, click the person's name in the list and choose Buddies⇨Ignore *<person>*. When someone is ignored in a chat group, you don't see anything that person types or have to respond to any file transfer requests from that person.

If only it were that easy to ignore someone when he or she is standing close to you.

Anyway, if the person becomes a royal pain, you can also choose to *block* that person entirely. That way, the offensive cur doesn't even know that you're online and can't reach you at all. Click the person in the list and choose Buddies⇨Block *<person>* — the deed is done.

Adding Visual Effects

Our esteemed Apple software developers decided to bring a little Hollywood special effects flash to Messages with video backdrops. You can also use many of the special effects filters provided by Photo Booth to keep your video chat room laughing!

To add a video backdrop to your video feed, choose Video⇨Video Preview to display your stunning self in a live video feed; then choose Video⇨ Show Video Effects. Use the scroll buttons to move to the backdrop thumbnails toward the end of the Effects library. When you click one, Messages prompts you to leave the frame for a few seconds so that the plain background behind you can be correctly masked (just like those blockbuster special effects used in today's films). When your background has been captured and masked, Messages prompts you to return to your spot, and you'll see that your new static or animated backdrop is in place. *Just plain cool!*

The plainer the background behind you, the better Messages can process and mask your background. A plain wall painted a single color works best.

"But, Mark, I want my *own* movies and photos for backgrounds!" No problem. Messages provides eight user-defined backdrop slots for your own selections at the end of the Video Effects collection. (Click the right scroll arrow in the Video Effects window until you reach the last couple of pages.) To add your own visuals, you can

✦ Drag a video from iMovie to an empty User Backdrop well in the Video Effects window.

✦ Drag a photo from iPhoto to an empty User Backdrop well in the Video Effects window.

✦ Drag a video or photo from a Finder window to an empty User Backdrop well in the Video Effects window.

As long as an item can be displayed in Quick Look, it can be used as a video background. Think of the possibilities!

To try out a Photo Booth effect in Messages, choose Video⇨Video Preview to display your live video feed; then choose Video⇨Show Video Effects (or press ⌘+Shift+E). Figure 3-6 illustrates the Video Preview and Video Effects windows; click a video effect thumbnail to see how it looks on you in the Preview window! Effects range from simple Black & White to a Thermal Camera look, an Andy Warhol–style Pop Art display, and a number of really cool optical distortions (such as Twirl and Light Tunnel).

Figure 3-6: Andy Warhol would be impressed by my Messages video effect!

After you find just the right video effect, close the two windows and start chatting. If you decide you'd rather return your video persona to something more conventional, display the Video Effects window again and click the Original thumbnail (which appears in the center of each screen of thumbnails).

Conversing with FaceTime

Although Messages' standard video chat is downright nifty, it has limits: You're confined to your IM buddies, and those folks may not have the necessary video hardware. With Apple's FaceTime technology, however, you can video-chat with owners of iOS devices and Macs without the constraints of instant-messaging accounts — and if they can run FaceTime, they're guaranteed to have the right video hardware.

At the time of this writing, FaceTime-compatible devices include

+ **Macs running Lion, Mountain Lion, and Mavericks**

  Mac owners running Snow Leopard 10.6.6 or later can also buy the FaceTime application from the App Store.

+ **An iPhone 4 or 4s running iOS 4.1 or higher or an iPhone 5 or later**

+ **A second, third, or fourth-generation iPad or an iPad mini running iOS 4.1 or higher**

+ **A fourth generation or later iPod touch running iOS 4.1 or higher**

If you're running a device under iOS 6 or later, you can use FaceTime over network, Wi-Fi, and 3G/4G/LTE connections. If you're using a device running iOS 5 or earlier, however, you'll need a Wi-Fi connection to use FaceTime with a mobile device. A 3G/4G/LTE cellular connection will not work. A Mac requires either a wired or Wi-Fi connection to the Internet to use FaceTime.

To launch FaceTime, click the jaunty-looking video camera icon on the Dock. The first time you use the application, you have to enter your Apple ID and your e-mail address. The folks you chat with on the other end use that same e-mail address to call you via FaceTime. (iPhone 4 or later owners can be called using their telephone numbers.)

To change the e-mail address that other FaceTime users use to call you, choose FaceTime⇨Preferences and then click the E-mail link under the heading You Can Be Reached for Calls At.

After you sign in, FaceTime displays your Contacts database by default. To initiate a call with any contact, click the name in the list, and FaceTime displays the e-mail and telephone numbers for the contact (once again, taken from your Contacts). Click the e-mail or telephone number that FaceTime should use, and the connection process begins. To return to the Contacts list and choose another person, click the All Contacts button at the top of the window.

Apple isn't satisfied with a mere Contacts list, however. You can use a number of other methods of selecting someone to call:

✦ **Recent Calls:** Click the Recents button to choose a contact that you've called (or attempted to call) in the recent past. Click the All or Missed buttons at the top of the window to further filter the Recents list.

✦ **Groups:** If you've set up one or more groups in your Contacts database, you can display them by clicking the Groups button. For example, if you've created a Contacts group containing all those fellow employees in your company, you can easily locate and call a specific person without wading through all your friends and family as well.

✦ **FaceTime Search:** Click in the familiar Search box and begin typing the contact's first or last name, and FaceTime displays the matching entries.

✦ **Favorites:** Sure, you have folks you like to chat with all the time, and it's easy to add them to the Favorites list. (Those who don't make the Favorites list don't have to know, right?) Click the desired contact, and then click the Add to Favorites button. To display your favorite contacts at any time, click the Favorites button in the FaceTime window.

When the call is accepted, you'll see a large video window with a smaller picture-in-picture display (you can drag the smaller display to any desired spot in the window). The video from the other person fills the large window, and the video that you're sending to them appears in the small display, as shown in Figure 3-7.

Figure 3-7:
The
FaceTime
window in
action.

Move your cursor into the FaceTime window, and you'll see the window controls appear, as well as three icons at the bottom of the window:

+ **Mute:** Click the mute icon to turn off the sound coming from your Mac. FaceTime displays a reminder that mute is enabled. (You'll continue to hear the audio from the other person.) To restore your audio feed, click the mute icon again.

+ **End:** Click this icon to end the FaceTime call.

+ **Full screen:** Click the full-screen icon (or press ⌘+Shift+F) to switch FaceTime into full-screen display mode. To return to window mode, press ⌘+Shift+F again, or move your mouse and click the full-screen icon again.

To switch FaceTime into landscape mode and take advantage of your Mac's widescreen display, choose Video➪Use Landscape, or press ⌘+R. (Why let the iPhone, iPod touch, and iPad owners have all the landscape fun?)

Chapter 4: Expanding Your Horizons with iCloud

In This Chapter

✔ **Introducing iCloud**

✔ **Setting iCloud preferences**

✔ **Managing iCloud storage**

If you ask the average Mac owner about what's available on the Internet, you likely hear benefits such as e-mail, drop box storage, web surfing, and Google searches. What you may *not* hear is "instant syncing and document sharing among all my Apple iOS devices."

If you have an iPhone, iPad, or iPod touch, you may have experienced what I like to call the "Synchronizing Blues" in the past: When you took a photo with your iPhone or created a new document with your iPad, your new additions just *sat* there (in their original location) until you had a chance to sync your device with your Mac. Ah, but with Apple's iCloud functionality, your stuff gets automatically synchronized across the Internet!

In this chapter, I show you what's *really* exciting about your Mac and that fancy Internet connection. With iCloud, you can automatically synchronize your stuff, access your documents with any Internet connection, and manage online backups of all your contacts, calendars, mail, bookmarks, and documents!

So How Does iCloud Work, Anyway?

Today's Apple iOS devices can all display or play the same media: photos, music, books, TV shows, and such. Heck, some iOS devices (such as your iPhone and iPod touch) can even share applications that you install. Therefore, it makes sense to effortlessly share all your digital media across these devices, and that's what iCloud is all about. Apple calls this synchronization "pushing."

Here's a look at how the pushing process works. Imagine that you just completed a Pages document on your iMac (an invitation for your son's birthday party), but you're at the office, and you need to get the document to your family so that they can edit and print it using your son's iPad.

Before iCloud, you had to attach the document to an e-mail message or upload it to some type of online storage such as Dropbox or Microsoft's SkyDrive, and then a family member had to download and save the document to the iPad before working with it. With iCloud, you simply save the document on your iMac to your iCloud Library, and OS X automatically pushes the document to the iPad! Your document appears on the iPad, ready to be opened, edited, and printed — and it appears on any other devices running iOS 5 or later (using the same Apple ID) as well. Figure 4-1 gives you an idea of what's happening in the background when one of your devices pushes data using iCloud.

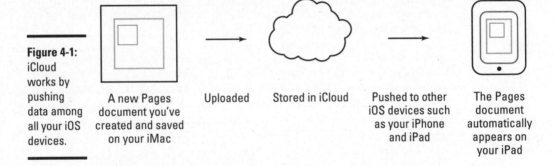

Figure 4-1: iCloud works by pushing data among all your iOS devices.

A new Pages document you've created and saved on your iMac | Uploaded | Stored in iCloud | Pushed to other iOS devices such as your iPhone and iPad | The Pages document automatically appears on your iPad

iCloud isn't limited to just digital media, though. Your Mac can also automatically synchronize your e-mail accounts, Calendar calendars, and Contacts entries with other iOS 5 or later devices across the Internet, so staying in touch is much easier (no matter where you are, or which device you happen to be using at the moment).

Apple also throws in 5GB of free online storage that you can use for all sorts of things: not only digital media files but also documents that you'd like to save online for safekeeping. Items you buy through the iTunes Store — music, video, and applications — do not count against your 5GB limit. (More on how you can expand that 5GB limit later in the chapter.)

To join the iCloud revolution, you need an Apple ID. If you didn't create one during the initial Mavericks setup, you can create an Apple ID from the App Store. To see how, read Book I, Chapter 3.

You can also access your documents through the web at www.icloud.com. Log in with your Apple ID and password to send mail, access your contacts and calendar, edit your notes and reminders, locate your devices, and use online versions of Pages, Numbers, and Keynote.

Saving and Opening iCloud Documents

iCloud online storage for your documents is definitely neat — however, if you're used to Dropbox, you'll find that the functionality of saving and opening files is somewhat different with iCloud. Dropbox allows you to use Finder to access your online Dropbox files (just like your Mac's internal drive), while iCloud allows you to save, open, move, and delete files from the Open dialog in Mavericks applications. (In other words, you can't copy a Numbers project from your iCloud Library. You can open it, delete it, or move it by dragging it from the Open dialog to your Mac's drive, but otherwise that document remains firmly entrenched in your iCloud Library.) You also can't copy files (such as an image file you create with Disk Utility) directly into your iCloud Library — you can save documents to your iCloud Library only from applications that support iCloud.

Figure 4-2 illustrates an iCloud Library Open dialog in action — in this case, the Open dialog from Pages.

Figure 4-2: I've stored three Pages documents in my iCloud Library.

Configuring iCloud

You control all the settings for iCloud from Mavericks' iCloud pane in System Preferences (shown in Figure 4-3). Click the System Preferences icon on the Dock and then click the iCloud icon. At the sign-in prompt, enter your Apple ID and your password. System Preferences will then guide you through basic iCloud configuration.

Figure 4-3:
The iCloud
pane
appears
in System
Preferences.

Most of the check boxes on the iCloud Preferences pane control whether a particular type of data — such as a Contacts entry, password, Mail message, or calendar in Calendar — is pushed among all your iOS devices. You can also disable the Documents and Data check box to return to the original File Open dialog, with no access to your iCloud Library. (Alternately, you can specify which applications will have access to your iCloud Library by clicking the Options button.)

Note, however, that you can enable three other unique features from this pane as well:

✦ **Photos:** Click the Options button and enable the My Photo Stream check box to allow your Mac to automatically receive photos from your iOS devices. Take a photo with your iPhone, for example, and that image is immediately pushed to your Mac, iPad, and iPod touch. On the Mac, however, Photo Stream goes one step further: The photos appear automatically in iPhoto or Aperture in a special album titled Photo Stream.

To turn on Photo Stream in iPhoto, choose iPhoto➪Preferences, click the Photo Stream button, and then select all three check boxes. My Photo Stream must also be selected in the iCloud Preferences pane.

✦ **Back to My Mac:** If you enable Back to My Mac, you can remotely control your Mac from another Mac computer (or vice versa) using Mavericks's Screen Sharing feature. (Read about that in the preceding chapter.) You can also transfer files between the two computers. Back to My Mac works over both a broadband Internet connection and a local network. Available Mac computers show up in the Shared section of the Finder window sidebar. Note that you must manually turn on Screen Sharing in the System Preferences Sharing pane before you can remotely control another Mac.

✦ **Find My Mac:** Talk about Buck Rogers! Imagine locating a lost or stolen Mac from your iPhone or iPad. Now think about this: With Find My Mac, you can even lock or completely wipe your Mac's hard drive *remotely*, preventing unauthorized use and erasing your private data! After you access your Mac from another iOS device, you can play a sound, send a message to be displayed onscreen, remotely lock the machine, or remotely wipe the drive.

After you lock or wipe the drive, though, you can't locate your Mac again.

Managing Your iCloud Storage

Apple knows that you're curious about how much space you've taken up in your personal iCloud. To monitor your iCloud storage, click the Manage button at the bottom-right corner of the iCloud Preferences pane. From the sheet that appears — as shown in Figure 4-4 — you can see how much space you're using for document and data storage.

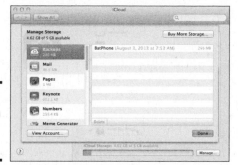

Figure 4-4:
Checking on
your iCloud
storage.

Click the data type in the left column, and iCloud displays the amount of storage space that's being used for that data. For instance, in Figure 4-4, I'm checking the amount taken by my iPhone backup. (I set my iPhone to back up wirelessly to my iCloud storage.) Other items that might appear in this sheet include Mail and selected iPad and iPhone apps that support iCloud.

If you find yourself running out of iCloud storage space, delete any stored item by selecting it in the list at the right side of the sheet and then click Delete.

And if you need more elbow room than 5GB, Apple is happy to provide 10GB, 20GB, or even 50GB of additional storage for an annual subscription fee of $20, $40, or $100 per year, respectively. Click the Manage button on the iCloud pane in System Preferences, and then click the Buy More Storage button.

Chapter 5: Going Places with Safari

In This Chapter

- Introducing the Safari window and controls
- Visiting websites with Safari
- Moving between sites
- Creating and using bookmarks
- Receiving files with Safari
- Surfing with your tabs showing
- Saving web pages to disk
- Protecting your privacy on the web
- Blocking those irritating pop-ups

*W*hen I was designing the Table of Contents for this book, I seriously considered leaving out this chapter. After all, more people already use a web browser now than any other software application. Who really needs a guide to mowing a lawn?

But then again, I suddenly thought of all the hidden features that folks don't know about Apple's Safari browser, such as all those handy tips and tricks to help you organize your online visits. It's a little like finding out more about the lawn mower itself, like learning how to remove the spark plug in the winter or how to sharpen the blade so that you can handle taller grass. To paraphrase a favorite author of mine, Arthur C. Clarke, *magic is nothing more than technology that someone understands.*

In this chapter, I show you how to use the myriad controls and toolbar buttons in Safari — you know, other than Forward and Back — and also how to keep track of where you've been and where you'd like to go. (Oh, and did I mention that you'll need a network connection?)

One note: I've got more ground to cover before dinner, so I don't include every Safari feature. However, the coverage here will explain all that you're likely to need for most surfing sessions.

Pretend You've Never Used This Thing

Figure 5-1 illustrates the Safari window. You can launch Safari directly from the Dock, or you can click the Safari icon in Launchpad.

Major sections of the Safari window are

✦ **The toolbar:** Here are the most often-used commands for tasks such as navigation, adding bookmarks, and searching Google (or Yahoo!, or Bing). Plus, here you can type or paste the address for websites that you'd like to visit. You can easily hide the toolbar to provide more real estate in your browser window for web content. To toggle hidden mode, choose View⇨Hide/Show Toolbar.

✦ **The Favorites bar:** Consider this a toolbar that allows you to jump directly to your favorite websites with but a single click or two. I show you later, in the section "Adding and Using Bookmarks," how to add and remove sites from your Favorites bar. For now, remember that you can toggle the display of the Bookmarks bar by choosing View⇨Hide/Show Favorites Bar or by pressing ⌘+Shift+B.

✦ **The Tab bar:** This toolbar allows you to quickly switch between multiple web pages that you've loaded, using what appear to be old-fashioned filing folder tabs. (Something familiar — familiar is good.) To hide or display the Tab bar, press ⌘+Shift+T or choose View⇨Hide/Show Tab Bar.

✦ **The Safari sidebar:** The sidebar pane allows you to organize and read your bookmarks, your reading list, and your shared links. To hide or display the sidebar, press ⌘+Shift+L or choose View⇨Hide/Show Sidebar.

✦ **The Content pane:** Congratulations! At last, you've waded through the pregame show and reached the area where web pages are displayed. The Content pane can be scrolled, and when you minimize the Safari window to the Dock, you get a *thumbnail* (minimized) image of the Content pane.

The Content pane often contains underlined text and graphics that transport you to other pages when you click them. These underlined words and icons are *links,* and they zip you right from one area of a site to another or to a different site. You can tell when your cursor is resting on a link because the cursor changes to that reassuring pointing-finger hand. Handy!

✦ **The status bar:** The status bar displays information about what the cursor is resting on, such as the address for a link or the name of an image; it also updates you about what's happening while a page is loading. To hide or display the status bar, press ⌘+/ (forward slash) or choose View⇨Hide/Show Status Bar.

Toolbar   Sidebar

Top Sites

iCloud Tabs   Downloads

Share   Address box   Favorites bar   Tab bar   Reload   New Tab

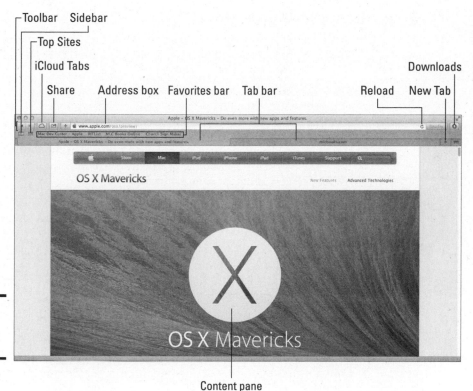

Content pane

Figure 5-1:
Safari at a
glance.

Visiting Websites

Here's the stuff that virtually everyone over the age of five knows how to
do . . . but I get paid by the word, and some folks might just not be aware
of the many ways to visit a site. You can load a web page from any of the
following methods:

✦ **Type (or paste) a website address in the Address box on the toolbar
and then press Return.** If you're typing in an address and Safari recognizes the site as one that you've visited in the past, it "helps" by auto-
completing the address for you. Press Return if you want to accept the
suggested site. If this is a new site, just keep typing.

The Safari Address box also acts as a *smart address* field, displaying a
new pop-up menu of sites that match the text you enter. Safari does this
by using sites taken from your History file and your bookmarks, as well
as sites returned from Google, Yahoo!, or Bing. If the site you want to
visit appears in the list, click it to jump there immediately.

✦ **Click a Bookmarks entry in Safari.**

✦ **If the Home button appears on your toolbar, click the button to go to the home page that you specify.** Read more on this in the upcoming section, "Setting Up Your Home Page."

✦ **Click the Show Top Sites button on the toolbar.** Safari displays a wall of preview thumbnail pages from your most frequently visited sites, and you can jump to a site just by clicking the preview. You can anchor a thumbnail to keep it onscreen permanently by clicking the pin icon next to the desired thumbnail. Click the Edit button on the Top Sites screen to delete a preview thumbnail (click the X). You can also choose the size of the preview thumbnails in Edit mode.

Because each thumbnail is updated with the most current content, the Top Sites wall makes a great timesaver. Quickly make a visual check of all your favorite haunts from one screen!

✦ **Click an item you saved earlier in the sidebar's Reading list.**

✦ **Click a link in the sidebar's Shared Links list.**

✦ **Click a page link in Apple Mail or another Internet-savvy application.** Some Mac applications require you to hold down ⌘ while clicking to open a web page.

✦ **Click a page link in another web page.**

✦ **Select a web address in a document, click the Services menu, and choose Open Page in Safari.**

✦ **Type a search term in the Address box.** By default, Safari uses Google as a search engine, but you can also use Yahoo! or Bing if you prefer. To set the default search engine, choose Safari⇨Preferences; then, on the General tab, open the Default Search Engine drop-down menu. (You can immediately switch to another engine from the bottom of the menu that appears as you're typing into the Address box.)

Click in the Address box, type the contents that you want to find, and then press Return. Safari presents you with the search results page on Google for the text that you enter. (In case you've been living under the Internet equivalent of a rock for the last several years, *Google* (www. google.com) is the preeminent search site on the web. People use Google to find everything from used auto parts to ex-spouses.)

✦ **Click a Safari page icon on the Dock or in a Finder window.** Drag a site from your Favorites bar (or drag the icon from the left side of the Address box) and drop it on the right side of the Dock. Clicking the icon that you add launches Safari and automatically loads that site.

This trick works only on the side of the Dock to the right of the vertical line. More on that all-important divider in a bit.

If you minimize Safari to the Dock, you'll see a thumbnail of the page with the Safari logo superimposed on it. Click this thumbnail on the Dock to restore the page to its full glory.

Speaking of full glory, Safari supports the same full-screen mode as many other Mavericks applications. Click the Full Screen icon at the top-right corner of the Safari window to switch to full-screen mode, or press the Control+⌘+F shortcut (a good shortcut to memorize because it works with virtually all Mavericks–compatible applications). To make things convenient for you, the Address box remains, as do the iCloud Tabs, Share, Reader, Downloads, Back, and Forward icons. To exit full-screen mode, press Esc or the Control+⌘+F shortcut again.

Navigating the Web

A typical web surfing session is a linear experience. You bop from one page to the next, absorbing the information that you want and discarding the rest. However, after you visit a few sites, you might find that you need to return to where you've been or head to the familiar ground of your home page. Safari offers these navigational controls on the toolbar:

✦ **Back:** Click the Back button (the left-facing arrow) on the toolbar to return to the last page you visited. Additional clicks take you to previous pages, in reverse order. The Back button is disabled if you haven't visited at least two sites.

✦ **Forward:** If you've clicked the Back button at least once, clicking the Forward button (the right-facing arrow) takes you to the next page (or through the pages) where you originally were, in forward order. The Forward button is disabled if you haven't used the Back button and haven't navigated to another page.

Safari supports a number of trackpad gestures. For example, you can swipe in either direction with two fingers to move backward and forward, just as you would move with the Forward and Back buttons. To zoom in and out on the Content pane, you can either double-tap the trackpad or pinch with two fingers — yes, just like an iPhone. (Ever get the notion that someday we'll just have a single box called "The Device" that does it all?)

✦ **Home:** Click this button (look for the little house) to return to your home page.

Not all these buttons and controls must appear on your toolbar — you may never see many of these toolbar controls unless you add them yourself. To display or hide toolbar controls, choose View➪Customize Toolbar. The sheet that appears works just like the Customize Toolbar sheet in a Finder window: Drag the control you want from the sheet to your Safari toolbar or drag a control that you don't want from the toolbar to the sheet.

+ **New Tab:** Click this button (it looks like a little tab with a plus sign) to open a new tab in the tab bar. I'll get knee-deep into tabbed browsing later in the chapter.

+ **AutoFill:** If you fill out a lot of forms online — when you're shopping at websites, for example — you can click the AutoFill button (which looks like a little text box and a pen) to complete these forms for you. You can set what information is used for AutoFill by choosing Safari⇨Preferences and clicking the AutoFill toolbar button.

To be honest, I'm not a big fan of releasing *any* of my personal information to *any* website, so I don't use AutoFill often. If you do decide to use this feature, make sure that the connection is secure (look for the padlock icon in the Address box) and read the site's Privacy Agreement page first to see how your identity data will be treated.

+ **Top Sites:** Click this button to display the Top Sites screen I discuss earlier. If you're having trouble finding it, the button bears a tiny, fashionable grid of squares.

+ **Zoom:** Shrink or expand the size of text on the page, offering smaller, space-saving characters (for the shrinking crowd) or larger, easier-to-read text (for the expanding crowd) by clicking the Zoom button, which is labeled with a small and large letter *A*. (From the keyboard, you can press ⌘++(plus sign) to expand and ⌘+– (minus sign) to shrink.

+ **Favorites bar:** Click this button (which carries the Bookmarks symbol sandwiched between two horizontal lines) to display or hide the Favorites bar.

+ **Stop/Reload:** Click Reload (which has a circular arrow in the Address box) to *refresh* (reload) the contents of the current page. Although most pages remain static, some pages change their content at regular intervals or after you fill out a form or click a button. By clicking Reload (look for the curvy arrow in the Address box), you can see what's changed on these pages. (I use Reload every hour or so with CNN.com, for example.) While a page is loading, the Reload button turns into the Stop button — with a little X mark — and you can click it to stop the loading of the content from the current page. This feature is a real boon when a download takes *foorrevverr,* which can happen when you're trying to visit a popular or slow website (especially if you're using a dial-up modem connection to the Internet). Using Stop is also handy if a page has a number of very large graphics that are likely to take a long time to load.

✦ **Bookmarks:** Click this toolbar button (which carries an open book icon) to hide or display the Safari sidebar. You'll find the complete description of the sidebar in an upcoming section.

✦ **History:** Click this button (which bears a clock symbol) to display or hide the History list, which I discuss later in this chapter.

✦ **Downloads:** Click this toolbar button to display the files you've downloaded recently. Click the Clear button to clear the contents of the Download list. Note that clearing the list does not delete the files you've downloaded; it simply cleans things up. You can also double-click a completed download in the list to open it immediately. (More on downloading in a couple pages.)

TIP

When you're downloading a file, a tiny progress bar appears in the Downloads button on the toolbar to show you how much you've received. Now that, good reader, is *progress*! (Let's see whether my editor allows such a horrible pun to remain.)

✦ **Open in Dashboard:** Click this button to create a Dashboard widget using the contents of the currently displayed web page. Safari prompts you to choose which clickable section of the page to be included in the widget's borders (such as the local radar map on your favorite weather website). Click Add, and Dashboard loads automatically with your new widget. (You learn more about widgets in Book II, Chapter 2.)

✦ **Mail:** Click this button (bearing an envelope icon) to send an e-mail message with a link to the current page, just as if you clicked the Share button and chose Email This Page. Safari automatically opens Apple Mail (or your default e-mail application) and creates a new message with the link already in the body. *Shazam!*

✦ **Add Bookmark:** Click this toolbar button (which carries a plus sign) to add a page to your Bookmarks bar or Bookmarks menu. (More on this in a tad.)

✦ **Print:** Click this convenient button to print the contents of the Safari window. (Dig that crazy printer icon!)

✦ **Share:** If you have an iPhone, iPod touch or iPad, you're probably already familiar with this button, which carries a rectangle and curved arrow symbol. Click the Share button to send the current page (or a link to it) to a number of different destinations, including your reading list, an e-mail message, your Messages application, Facebook, or Twitter. You can also add a bookmark to the current page using the Share button. Figure 5-2 illustrates the Share button in action.

Figure 5-2:
The Share button makes it easy to spread goodness and light!

Setting Up Your Home Page

Choosing a home page is one of the easiest methods of speeding up your web surfing, especially if you're using a dial-up modem connection. However, a large percentage of the Mac owners whom I've talked with have never set their own home page; instead, they simply use the default home page provided by their browser. Declare your independence! With Safari running, take a moment to follow these steps to declare your own freedom to choose your own home page:

1. **In Safari, display the web page that you want to become your new home page.**

I recommend selecting a page with few graphics, or a fast-loading popular site.

2. **Choose Safari⇨Preferences or press ⌘+, (comma).**

3. **Click the General button.**

You see the settings shown in Figure 5-3.

4. **Click the Set to Current Page button.**

5. **Click the Close button to exit the Preferences dialog.**

Alternatively, open the New Windows Open With pop-up menu and choose Empty Page if you want Safari to open a new window with a blank page. This choice is the fastest one for a home page.

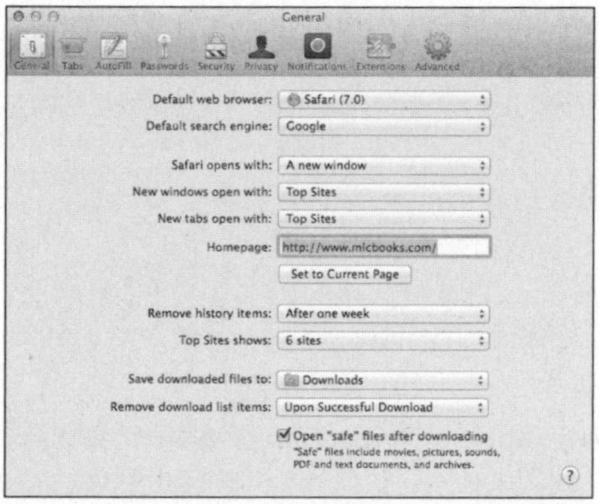

Figure 5-3:
Adding
your own
home page
is an easy
change you
can make.

Visit your home page at any time by pressing the Home button on the toolbar. If it doesn't appear on your toolbar, you can add it by choosing View⇨Customize Toolbar.

Adding and Using Bookmarks

No doubt about it: Bookmarks make the web a friendly place. As you collect bookmarks in Safari, you're able to immediately jump from one site to another with a single click of the Bookmarks menu or the buttons on the Favorites bar.

To add a bookmark, first navigate to the desired page and then do any of the following:

✦ **Choose Bookmarks⇨Add Bookmark.**

✦ **Press the ⌘+D keyboard shortcut.**

Safari displays a sheet where you can enter the name for the bookmark and also select where it appears (on the Favorites bar, Top Sites display, Bookmarks folder, or Bookmarks menu).

✦ **Drag the icon next to the web address from the Address field to the Favorites bar.**

This trick also works with other applications besides Safari, including in a Mail message or Messages conversation. Drag the icon from the Safari Address field to the other application window, and the web page link is added to your document.

You can also drag a link on the current page to the Favorites bar, but note that doing this adds a bookmark only for the page corresponding to the link — not the current page.

To jump to a bookmark, do one of the following:

+ **Choose it from the Bookmarks menu.** If the bookmark is contained in a folder, which I discuss later in this section, hover your cursor over the folder name to show its contents and then click the bookmark.

+ **Click the bookmark on the Favorites bar.**

  If you've added a large number of items to the Favorites bar, click the More icon on the edge of the Favorites bar to display the rest of the buttons.

+ **Click the Show Sidebar button (which looks like a small, opened book) on the Favorites bar, click the Bookmarks icon in the sidebar, and then click the desired bookmark.** The sidebar that you see in Figure 5-4 appears, where you can review each collection of bookmarks at your leisure.

+ **Click Bookmarks⇨Show Bookmarks (or press Option+⌘+B) to open the Bookmark list.** For those who prefer more information (and more onscreen elbow room) while selecting or organizing their bookmarks, the Bookmark list is the cat's meow. It displays both the name and web address for each bookmark in your collection.

The more bookmarks you add, the more unwieldy the Bookmarks menu and the sidebar can become. To keep things organized, choose Bookmarks⇨Add Bookmark Folder and then type a name for the new folder. With folders, you can organize your bookmarks into *collections,* which appear in the column at the left of the sidebar, as folders in the Bookmark list, and as menus on the Bookmarks bar. (Collections also appear as separate submenus in the Bookmarks menu on the Safari menu bar.) You can drag bookmarks into the new folder to help reduce the clutter.

Figure 5-4:
The sidebar puts all your bookmarks in easy reach.

To delete a bookmark or a folder from any of these locations, right-click it and then click Delete.

Working with the Reading List and Shared Links

Now that you know all about bookmarks, I'll introduce you to two other methods of loading, saving, and retrieving specific pages in Safari — and they're both hiding in the now-familiar confines of the Safari sidebar! These two sidebar celebrities are the reading list and your shared links.

Saving pages for later with the Reading List

The sidebar's Reading List pane allows you to save entire pages for later perusal. From the keyboard, press ⌘+Shift+L to display the sidebar, then click the Reading List button. Click Bookmarks⇨Add to Reading List or press ⌘+Shift+D to add the current page to the list; you can quickly add a snapshot of that page to the list by holding down the Shift key and clicking the link. (Oh, and don't forget that you can click the Sharing icon in the toolbar and choose Add to Reading List to achieve the same victory.)

Ah, but when you click one of those entries in the Reading List and then click the blue Reader button that appears at the right side of the Address box, the real magic begins! The Reader panel appears to display text articles free of advertisements and silly pop-ups. And if an article is continued over multiple web pages, the Reader panel automatically stitches them together to form a continuous block of text. (Think of an e-book displayed in iBooks on your Mac, and you get the idea.) You can also print or e-mail the article from in the Reader panel.

If the Reader button is blue in Safari's Address box — and you're *not* using the Reading List — don't panic! Because the page you're reading contains text articles, Safari is offering to display it in the Reader panel. (If a page has nothing to display in the Reader panel, the button remains gray.) To display the page in the Reader panel, click the blue Reader button in the Address box. To return to your mundane browsing experience, click the Reader icon again.

Visiting pages recommended by friends

If you're a fan of the Twitter or LinkedIn social media sites, listen up: Mavericks introduces shared links to Safari! After you've added your Twitter and LinkedIn account information in the Internet Accounts pane in System Preferences, Safari automatically adds links posted by your friends on both services on the sidebar's Shared Links pane.

To visit a shared link, just click it. To search for a specific shared link, click in the Search Links box at the top of the Shared Link list and type a portion of the link (or just type the person's name to see all the links they've posted).

The Shared Links pane won't appear in the sidebar unless you've successfully added your Twitter or LinkedIn account information in System Preferences.

Downloading Files

A huge chunk of the fun that you'll find on the web is the capability to download images and files. If you've visited a site that offers files for downloading, typically you just click the Download button or the download file link, and Safari takes care of the rest. While the file is downloading, feel free to continue browsing or even download additional files; the Downloads status list helps you keep track of what's going on and when everything will be finished transferring. To display the Downloads status list from the keyboard, press ⌘+Option+L. You can also click the Download button at the upper-right corner of the window to display the Download list.

By default, Safari saves any downloaded files to the Downloads folder on your Dock, which I like and use. To specify the location where downloaded files are stored — for example, if you'd like to scan them automatically with an antivirus program — follow these steps:

1. **Choose Safari⇨Preferences or press ⌘+, (comma).**
2. **Click the General tab (refer to Figure 5-3) and then open the Save Downloaded Files To pop-up menu.**
3. **Choose Other.**
4. **Navigate to the location where you want the files stored.**
5. **Click the Select button.**
6. **Click the Close button to exit Preferences.**

To download a specific image that appears on a web page, move your cursor over the image, right-click, and then choose Save Image As from the menu that appears. Safari prompts you for the location where you want to store the file.

You can choose to automatically open files that Safari considers safe — things like movies, text files, and PDF files that are *very* unlikely to store a virus or a damaging macro. By default, the Open "Safe" Files after Downloading check box is selected on the General pane. However, if you're interested in preventing *anything* you download from running until you've manually checked it with your antivirus application, you can deselect the check box and breathe easy.

Luckily, Safari has matured to the point that it can seamlessly handle most multimedia file types that it encounters. However, if you've downloaded a multimedia file and Safari doesn't seem to be able to play or display it, try loading the file in QuickTime Player. As you can read in Book III, Chapter 6, *QuickTime Player* is the Swiss Army knife of multimedia players, and it can recognize a huge number of audio, video, and image formats.

Using Subscriptions and History

To keep track of where you've been, you can display the History list by clicking the History menu. To return to a page in the list, just choose it from the History menu. Note that Safari also arranges older history items by the date you visited a site so you can easily jump back a couple of days to that page you forgot to bookmark!

Safari also searches the History list automatically, when it fills in an address that you're typing — that's the feature I mention in the earlier section, "Visiting Websites."

To view your Top Sites thumbnail screen, press ⌘+Option+1 or choose Show Top Sites from the History menu. You can also click the Top Sites button on the toolbar.

You can add a site manually to your Top Sites by dragging a bookmark from the sidebar to the Top Sites icon in the Favorites bar, or by dragging a link or URL address from another application to the Top Sites icon in the Favorites bar. (You'll see a plus sign appear next to your cursor to indicate the addition.) To rearrange screens in the Top Sites display, just drag a screen thumbnail to the desired location. If you prefer that a specific thumbnail remain in the same place, hover your cursor over the thumbnail and click the gray pushpin icon, which will turn blue to indicate that the thumbnail is pinned in place.

If you're worried about security and would rather not keep track of where you've been online, find out how to clear the contents of the History file in the upcoming section, "Handling ancient history."

Tabs Are Your Browsing Friends

Safari also offers *tabbed browsing,* which many folks use to display (and organize) multiple web pages at one time. For example, if you're doing a bit of comparison shopping for a new piece of hardware among different online stores, tabs are ideal. (Heck, tabbed browsing is so popular that Apple added tabs to Finder windows with the release of OS X Mavericks!)

When you hold down the ⌘ key and click a link or bookmark using tabs, a tab representing the new page appears at the top of the Safari window. Just click the tab to switch to that page. By holding down Shift+⌘, the tab is both created and opened. (If you don't hold down ⌘, things revert to business as usual, and Safari replaces the contents of the window with the new page.)

You can also open a new tab by clicking the plus sign that appears at the upper-right corner of the Safari window, or by pressing ⌘+T.

Trackpad owners will appreciate Safari's two new gestures that control tabs. With multiple tabs active, you can

✦ Pinch to display them all in a new *Tab view* (as shown in Figure 5-5).

✦ Swipe to switch between tabs.

Close

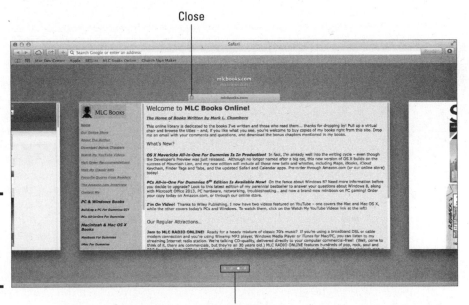

Figure 5-5:
Hang on,
Martha;
we've
struck tabs!

Tab navigation

To display your tabs in Tab view without a trackpad, click the Show All Tabs button that appears at the right side of the Safari window (next to the Open a New Tab button). From Tab view, you can click the white dots that appear below the thumbnails to view your tabs, and click any tab thumbnail to switch immediately to that tab. To close a tab in Tab view, click the Close button at the top of the thumbnail.

To fine-tune your tabbed browsing experience, choose Safari⇨Preferences to display the Preferences dialog; then click Tabs. From here, you can specify whether a new tab or window automatically becomes the active window in Safari.

Done with a page? You can remove a tabbed page by clicking the X button next to the tab's title.

Printing Web Pages

If you've encountered a page that you'd like to print, follow these steps:

1. **Display the desired page.**

2. **Choose File⇨Print or press ⌘+P.**

3. **In the Save As text field, type a name for the saved page.**

4. **Select the number of copies and specify whether you'd like to print the entire page, only the current page, or a range of pages.**

5. **Click Print.**

After the Save file has been created, double-click it to load it in Safari.

A quick word about printing a page in Safari: Some combinations of background and text colors might conspire to render your printed copy worthless. In a case like that, use your printer's grayscale setting (if it has one) or click the Show Details button and deselect the Print Backgrounds check box in the Print dialog (which can save you quite a bit of ink or toner). Alternatively, you can simply click and drag to select the text on the page, press ⌘+C to copy it, and then paste the text into TextEdit, Word, or Pages, where you can print the page on a less offensive background (while still keeping the text formatting largely untouched). You can also save the contents of a page as an electronic PDF file by clicking File⇨Export as PDF.

If you'd rather mail the contents of a web page to a friend, click the Share button and choose Email This Page. (If you've added the Mail button to your toolbar, one click does the job.) Mail loads automatically, complete with a prepared e-mail message. Just address it to the recipients and then click Send.

Protecting Your Privacy

No chapter on Safari would be complete without a discussion of security, against both outside intrusion from the Internet and prying eyes around your Mac. Hence this last section, which covers protecting your privacy.

Although diminutive, the padlock icon that appears at the left side of the Address box when you're connected to a secure website means a great deal! A *secure site* encrypts the information that you send and receive, making it much harder for those of unscrupulous ideals to obtain private data, such as credit card numbers and personal information. You can click the padlock icon (next to the site name) to display the security certificate in use on that particular site. A secure site web address begins with the prefix `https:` instead of `http:`. (The extra *s* stands for *secure*. A Good Thing.)

Yes, there are such things as bad cookies

First, a definition of this ridiculous term: A *cookie,* a small file that a website automatically saves on your hard drive, contains information that the site will use on your future visits. For example, a site might save a cookie to preserve your site preferences for the next time or — like shopping at Amazon. com — to identify you automatically and help customize the offerings that you see.

In and of themselves, cookies aren't bad things. Unlike a virus, a cookie file isn't going to replicate itself or wreak havoc on your system, and only the original site can read the cookie that it creates. However, many folks don't appreciate acting as a gracious host for a slew of little snippets of personal information. (Not to mention that some cookies have highly suggestive names, which can lead to all sorts of conclusions. End of story.)

You can choose to accept some or all cookies, or you can opt to disable cookies altogether. You can also set Safari to accept cookies only from the sites you choose to visit. To change your *Cookie Acceptance Plan* (or CAP, for those who absolutely crave acronyms), follow these steps:

1. **Choose Safari⇨Preferences.**

2. **Click the Privacy toolbar button.**

   Safari displays the preference settings shown in Figure 5-6.

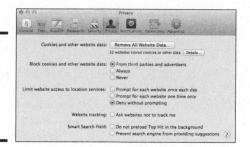

Figure 5-6:
Specifying
who's
welcome
in my
cookie jar.

3. **Choose how to block cookies via these radio button choices:**

   • *From Third Parties and Advertisers:* I use this option, which allows
   sites such as Amazon.com to work correctly without allowing a
   barrage of superfluous cookies.

   • *Always:* Block cookies entirely.

   • *Never:* Accept all cookies.

4. **To view the cookies currently on your system, click the Details button.**

   If a site's cookies are blocked, you might have to take care of things
   manually, such as by providing a password on the site that used to be
   read automatically from the cookie.

5. **Click the Close button to save your changes.**

Feeling nervous about the data stored by the websites you visit? You can
always delete *all* that stored information with a single click. From the
Privacy pane in the Safari Preferences window, click the Remove All Website
Data button. You'll be asked to confirm your draconian decision.

The Privacy pane also includes the Ask Websites Not To Track Me check
box, which works . . . *sometimes.* Unfortunately, it's up to a particular website whether to honor Safari's request for privacy. (Also, some sites — such
as Amazon.com — use tracking legitimately, to keep track of your likes and
purchases each time you return.) If you're especially worried about leaving a
trail of breadcrumbs behind you on the web, however, I recommend selecting this check box.

Cleaning your cache

Safari speeds up the loading of websites by storing often-used images and
multimedia files in a temporary storage, or cache, folder. The files in your

cache folder can be displayed (hint), which can lead to assumptions (hint, hint) about the sites you've been visiting (hint, hint, hint). (Tactful, ain't I?)

Luckily, Safari makes it easy to dump the contents of your cache file. Just choose Safari⇨Reset Safari, deselect all but the Clear History check box, and then click Reset to confirm that you want to clean up your cache.

Banishing pesky iCloud Keychain passwords

As you discover in Book II, Chapter 5, I am the world's biggest critic of *keychains,* which Mavericks uses to automatically provide all sorts of login information throughout the system. In Safari, for example, the password information is automatically entered for you whenever a website you've approved requires you to log in.

To be more specific, I'm sure many readers will adopt the new *iCloud Keychain*, which stores password and credit card information for Safari and wirelessly distributes that information automatically to other Macs and iOS devices using the same Apple ID. (Apple even says that the passwords generated by iCloud Keychain are more complex and harder to crack, which *sounds* more secure, right?)

I'd rather keep a pet piranha in a cereal bowl than use this feature! Why? Whenever you're logged in, *anyone* using your Mac gets control of your online persona (in the form of your passwords to secure websites). Safari, like an obedient puppy, will automatically provide access to sites with stored keychain passwords.

If you'd like to take the far-less-convenient-but-**much**-safer, old-fashioned route of remembering your passwords yourself, follow my lead: Visit the iCloud pane in System Preferences and deselect the Keychain check box to turn the iCloud Keychain feature off.

Now that I've warned you thoroughly, I feel better about mentioning the Passwords tab in Safari Preferences for those who *do* decide to use iCloud Keychain. From the Passwords tab, you can view the iCloud Keychain information that Safari uses, and either remove a specific password (or all passwords) from your iCloud Keychain.

Handling ancient history

As you might imagine, your History file leaves a very clear set of footprints indicating where you've been on the web. To delete the contents of the History menu, choose History⇨Clear History (at the very bottom of the History menu).

Safari also allows you to specify an amount of time to retain entries in your History file. Open the Safari Preferences dialog, click the General tab (refer to Figure 5-3), and then open the Remove History Items pop-up menu to specify the desired amount of time. Items can be rolled off daily, weekly, biweekly, monthly, or yearly.

Setting notifications

In Mavericks, Safari can allow websites you've approved to send you messages using Notification Center — you can control which sites have been given this functionality from the Notifications tab in Safari's Preferences dialog. To prevent a website from sending notifications, click the site in the list and click the Remove button.

Avoiding those @*!^%$ pop-up ads

I hate pop-up ads, and I'm sure you do, too. To block many of those pop-up windows with advertisements for everything from low-rate mortgages to "sure-thing" Internet casinos, open the Safari Preferences dialog, click the Security tab, and verify that Block Pop-Up Windows is selected.

Chapter 6: Staying Secure Online

In This Chapter

✔ Understanding the dangers of going online

✔ Using a firewall

✔ Avoiding trouble online

1 know that you've heard horror stories about hacking: Big corporations and big government installations seem to be as open to hackers as a public library. Often, you read that even entire identities are stolen online. When you consider that your Mac can contain sensitive and private information about your life — such as your Social Security number and financial information — it's enough to make you nervous about turning on your computer long enough to check your eBay auctions.

But how much of that is Hollywood? How truly real is the danger, especially to Mac owners? And how can you protect yourself? The good news is that you can *easily* secure your data from all but the most determined hacker. Depending on the hardware that you're using to connect to the Internet, you might be well guarded right now without even knowing it.

In this chapter, I continue a quest that I've pursued for over two decades now — to make my readers feel comfortable and secure in the online world by explaining the truth about what can happen and by telling you how you can protect your system from intrusions.

One quick note: This chapter is written with the home and small-business Mac owner in mind. Macs that access the Internet through a larger corporate network are likely already protected by that knight in shining armor, the network system administrator. (Insert applause here.) Of course, if you're using OS X in your office, you're still welcome to read and follow this material — especially if you have a laptop that could act as a carrier for viruses from home; however, check with your system administrator before you attempt to implement any of the recommendations that I make.

What Can Happen if I Don't Take Security Seriously?

Before I begin, I want to offer you a moment of reassurance and a little of my background to explain that I'm well qualified to be your guide through this online minefield. (After all, you don't want Andy Samberg lecturing you on how to maintain your Internet security. He's a *very* funny guy, though.)

✦ I've been running and managing all sorts of online systems since the days of the BBS (Bulletin Board System), the text-based dinosaurs that used to rule the online world in the early '80s to early '90s. (My first book was on this very subject — and it contained a chapter on viruses long before they were the darlings of the techno-media.)

✦ As a consultant, I run websites, remove spyware, and squash virus attacks for a number of individuals, companies, and organizations.

✦ I run a popular Internet radio station that serves up '70s hits in CD-quality to anyone with a high-speed DSL or cable Internet connection and a copy of iTunes. (More on this broadcasting revolution in Book III, Chapter 2.)

✦ I keep my own office network of six computers safe from attack while still providing readers all over the world with websites and the afore-mentioned radio station and BBS.

With that understood, here's what can happen to you online *without* the right safeguards, on *any* computer:

✦ **Hackers can access shared information on your network.** If you're running an unguarded network, others can gain access to your documents and applications or wreak havoc on your system.

✦ **Your system could be infected with a virus or dangerous macro.** Left to their own devices, these misbehaving programs and macro commands can delete files or turn your entire hard drive into an empty paperweight. (Although Mac viruses are very, *very* rare as I write this, they're starting to appear with more frequency, along with their malware brethren. Plus, if you dual-boot your Intel Mac into Windows, you've suddenly entered a veritable minefield of PC viruses, malware, and spyware. More on this in a page or two.)

✦ **Unsavory individuals could attempt to contact members of your family.** This kind of attack may take place through applications such as Messages, through e-mail conversations, or web discussion boards, putting your family's safety at risk.

✦ **Hackers can use your system to attack others.** Your computer can be tricked into helping hackers when they attempt to knock out web servers and public-access File Transfer Protocol (FTP) sites on the Internet. Along the same lines, that innocent web server you put online can be misused by spam-spewing, online "entrepreneurs." (Cute name, right?)

✦ **Criminals can attempt to con you out of your credit card number or personal information.** The Internet is a prime tool used by those trying to steal identities.

If it smells phishy . . .

Ever heard of the word *phishing?* Con artists and hackers create websites that look just like major online stores — including big names such as eBay, PayPal, and Amazon. These turkeys then send out junk e-mail messages that tell you that you must log on to this website to "refresh" or "correct" your personal information. As you've no doubt already guessed, that information is siphoned off and sold to the highest bidder. *Your* credit card number, *your* password, and *your* address. Luckily, if you follow the tips that I give later in this chapter in the section "A Dose of Common Sense: Things Not to Do Online," you'll avoid these phishing expeditions!

To be absolutely honest, some danger is indeed present every time you or any user of your Macintosh connects to the Internet. However, here's the good news. With the right safeguards, it's literally impossible for most of those worst-case scenarios to happen on your Macintosh, and what remains would be so difficult that even the most die-hard hacker would throw in the towel long before reaching your computer or network.

Using a Macintosh gives you an advantage: Hackers and virus developers (there's a career for you) are traditionally interested only in "having fun" with PCs running Windows, so the likelihood that Mavericks could pick up a virus is far less than it would be if you were using Windows. As I mention earlier, if you boot into Windows using the dual-boot feature on your Macintosh (which I discuss at length in Book VIII, Chapter 1), you need to pay heed to Windows security — the same warning also applies to those running Windows in a virtual machine (using programs like Parallels Desktop or VMware Fusion).

Because this is a book that focuses on OS X Mavericks, I won't be spending much time covering Windows. If you'd like a comprehensive guide to Windows 8 and the PC world, however, I can heartily recommend the sister volume to this book, *PCs All-in-One For Dummies,* 6th Edition, which (coincidentally) I wrote as well!

Heck, I even know a couple of fellow Mac owners who feel they just don't need antivirus protection — but believe me, this is *not* an area where you want to be lax and lazy, and you *still need* an antivirus application! (More on antivirus software later in this chapter.)

I also want to point out that virtually everyone reading this book — as well as the guy writing it — really doesn't have anything that's worth a malicious hacking campaign. Things like Quicken data files, saved games of Borderlands 2, and genealogical data might be priceless to us, of course, but most dedicated hackers are after bigger game. Unfortunately, the coverage that the media and Hollywood give to corporate and government attacks can turn even Aunt Harriet more than a little paranoid. Therefore, time for another of Mark's Maxims:

More of Mark's totally unnecessary computer trivia

The term *hacker* dates far back in the annals of the personal computer. Hacker originally had nothing to do with networks, the Internet, or illegal activities at all because In the Beginning, there was no public Internet!

"Explain yourself, Chambers!" All right. The original hackers were electronics buffs, ham radio operators, computer hobbyists, and engineers who built, or *hacked,* a working computer from individual components with a soldering gun and a whole lotta guts. At the time, you didn't simply order a computer from Apple or visit your local Maze o' Wires store in the mall to select your favorite system. You built it from a kit, or even from scratch!

Remember, I'm talking about the mid-'70s, in the halcyon time before IBM even introduced the IBM PC (and when the only folks using the Internet, which wasn't called that back then, were military folks, academics, and researchers). Even the simplest computer — really nothing more than a glorified calculator by today's standards — had to be lovingly assembled by hand. These early personal computers didn't run software as we know it. Instead, you programmed them manually through a bank of switches on the front, and they responded with codes displayed on a bank of lights. (Think about that the next time you launch Microsoft Word with a single click of a Dock icon.)

Today, of course, the need to assemble a computer from individual transistors is nonexistent, and the word *hacker* has an entirely different connotation — but don't be surprised if you meet an older member of your Macintosh user's group who's proud to be an old-fashioned hacker! (Look for the soldering gun, usually worn in a holster like a sidearm.)

It's not necessary to fear The Bad Guys each time you poke your Mac's power button. A few simple precautions are all that are required.

"Shields Up, Chekov!"

"Okay, Mark, now I know the real story on what can happen to my computer online. So what do I do to safeguard my Macintosh?" You need but two essential tools to protect your hardware (besides a healthy amount of common sense, which I cover in the upcoming section "A Dose of Common Sense: Things Not to Do Online"): a firewall and an antivirus program.

Firewall basics

First, a definition: A *firewall* is a piece of hardware or software that essentially builds an impermeable barrier between the computers on your side of the wall (meaning your Mac and any other computers on your network) and all external computers on the other side of the wall (meaning the rest of the Internet).

"But wait a second — if other computers can't reach me and my Mac can't reach them, how can I use the Internet at all?" Ah, that's the beauty of today's firewalls. By using a series of techniques designed to thwart attacks from the outside, a firewall allows you to communicate safely, even monitoring what you send and what you receive for later examination. Figure 6-1 illustrates the basics of a firewall.

A firewall sounds grand and incredibly complex and highly technical — and sometimes it is — but it can also be incredibly simple. For example:

✦ You can spend anywhere from fifty to thousands of dollars installing sophisticated firewall hardware or software or both.

or

✦ You can "activate" your firewall by disconnecting your Mac's dial-up, digital subscriber line (DSL), or cable modem from the wall socket. (In this same fashion, one of my favorite editors never connects his PCs running Windows to the Internet. *Ever.*)

Believe it or not, both of those examples technically involve a firewall. In the first case, the firewall is a physical, tangible presence on the network; in the second case, the lack of a connection to the Internet acts as a firewall. (Think of it as the Air Firewall.) I've spoken to a number of readers who do this; however, if you're running a website or downloading a file from your company's FTP site, yanking the connection when you head to bed isn't an option. Therefore, most of us will install a physical firewall through hardware or software.

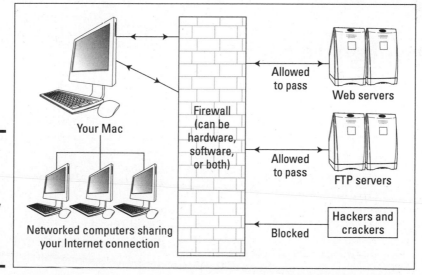

Figure 6-1:
A firewall,
hard at
work. (It's
not actually
made
of brick,
though.)

Do I already have a firewall?

In some cases, you might already be using a hardware firewall and not even
know it. For example, many Internet-sharing devices include a built-in NAT
firewall. Network Address Translation (NAT) is the most effective and popular hardware firewall standard in use by consumer devices. If you're using
an Internet-sharing hub or router, check its manual to determine whether it
offers NAT as a firewall feature — and if so, turn it on if NAT isn't enabled by
default. (See Book VI, Chapter 2 for more on Internet sharing, routers, and
firewalls.)

For instance, Figure 6-2 illustrates the configuration screen for my Internet
router. Note the options to disable port scanning and ping responses, which
are two tricks that hackers often use to detect what's often called a "hot
computer" — meaning that the computer can be identified and is accessible
to attack. Wireless networks are notoriously hot. For more information on
securing your wireless connections, visit Book VI, Chapter 4.

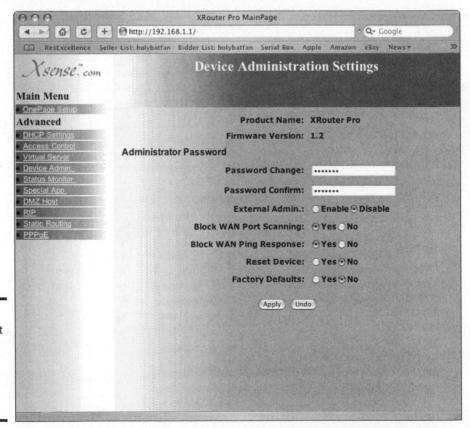

Figure 6-2:
My Internet
router is
set to be
downright
rude to
hackers.

Using the internal OS X firewall

OS X includes a powerful internal firewall, which Mavericks makes simple to use. Most Mac owners will be perfectly satisfied with this built-in firewall, which is configured through System Preferences. Find more information on setting up your firewall in Book VI, Chapter 2.

Using a commercial software firewall

You'll also find a number of popular alternatives to the Mavericks built-in firewall that offer more control over individual applications and more configuration options. For example, consider these commercial software firewall applications:

✦ **Symantec, Norton Internet Security 5 for Mac, $70 per year** (www.symantec.com)**:** Frequent updates and top-of-the-line technical support ensure that your firewall stays current and that you can get help when you need it.

✦ **Intego, Mac Internet Security 2013, about $40 per year** (www.intego.com)**:** Along with antispam and antiphishing features, Mac Internet Security 2013 comes with a number of preset configurations that allow you to choose a basic firewall for your network environment with a single click.

Whether you set up the internal firewall, a shareware firewall, or a commercial firewall, visit a favorite site of mine on the web: www.grc.com, the home of Gibson Research Corporation. There you'll find the free online utility ShieldsUP!!, which automatically tests just how tight your firewall is and how susceptible your Mac could be to hacker attacks. Visit this site often because this service is updated periodically to reflect new hacking techniques.

Antivirus basics

Next, consider your antivirus protection (under both Mavericks and Windows XP, Vista, 7, or 8 if you're running Boot Camp on an Intel-based Mac). *Viruses* are typically transmitted through applications. You run a program, and the virus is activated. Although they don't meet the traditional definition of a virus, both scripts and macros can be used to take control of your system and cause trouble, as well. Therefore, you need to closely monitor what I call The Big Three:

✦ **Web downloads:** Consider every file that you receive from the Internet a possible viral threat.

✦ **Removable media:** Viruses can be stored on everything from CD-ROMs and DVD-ROMs to USB flash drives.

✦ **E-mail file attachments:** A Trojan horse or worm application sent to you as an e-mail attachment is an easy doorway to your system.

Horrors! OS X has no built-in antivirus support. (Then again, until the arrival of Windows 8, neither did Windows.) However, a good antivirus program will take care of any application that's carrying a virus. Some even handle destructive macros in documents. Make sure that the antivirus program you choose offers *real-time scanning,* which operates when you download or open a file. Periodic scanning of your entire system is important, too, but only a real-time scanning application such as VirusBarrier 2013 can immediately ensure that the StuffIt or Zip archive or the application you just received in your e-mail Inbox is free from viruses. (Oh, and don't forget that many of the software updates released by Apple for Mavericks will plug security holes in our favorite operating system — yet another reason to keep your system updated.)

Virus technology continues to evolve over time, just as more beneficial application development does. For example, viruses have been developed that are contained in both JPEG image files and e-books. Nasty business, indeed. With a good antivirus application that offers regular updates, you'll continue to keep your system safe from viral attack.

I heartily recommend both ClamXav 2 (free for personal use at www. clamxav.com) and Intego's VirusBarrier 2013 for Mac (which is included as part of the Mac Internet Security 2013 suite I mentioned earlier) for antivirus protection. Both programs include automatic updates delivered while you're online to make sure that you're covered against the latest viruses.

A Dose of Common Sense: Things Not to Do Online

You can use one more powerful weapon to make sure that your Mac stays safe from unlawful intrusion: common sense. Practicing common sense on the Internet is just as important as adding a firewall and an antivirus application to your Mac.

With this in mind, here's a checklist of things that you should never do while you're online:

✦ **Never download a file from a site you don't trust.** And make sure that your antivirus software is configured to check downloaded files before you open them.

✦ **Never open an e-mail attachment until it has been checked.** Don't give in to temptation, even if the person who sent the message is someone you trust. (Many macro viruses replicate themselves by sending copies to the addresses found through the victim's e-mail program. This problem crops up regularly in the Windows world but has been known to happen in the Macintosh community as well.)

✦ **Never enter any personal information in an e-mail message unless you know the recipient.** I send my mailing address to friends and family but to no one else. E-mail can be intercepted by a determined hacker, so if you're sending something truly important such as personal or company data, use an encryption application, such as PGP Personal Desktop (www.pgp.com).

✦ **Never enter any personal information on a website provided as a link in an e-mail message.** Don't fall prey to phishing expeditions. Some of these e-mail message–website combinations look authentic enough to fool anyone! *No reputable online company or store will demand or solicit your personal information through e-mail or through a linked website.* Feel free to contact the company through its *real* website and report the phishing attempt!

✦ **Never include any personal information in an Internet newsgroup post.** In case you're not familiar with the term, *newsgroups* are public Internet message bases, often called Usenet groups. Many ISPs offer a selection of newsgroups that you can access. Newsgroup posts can be viewed by anyone, so there's no such thing as privacy in a newsgroup. (For a glimpse of just how long one of these posts can linger in the great Internet continuum, visit www.google.com, click the Groups button, and search for your name. I can pull up newsgroup messages that I posted back in 1995!)

✦ **Never buy from an online store that doesn't offer a secure, encrypted connection when you're prompted for your personal information and credit card number.** If you're using Apple's Safari browser, the padlock icon appears next to the site name in the title bar. When the padlock icon appears in the title bar, the connection is encrypted and secure — you'll also note that the web address begins with https: rather than http:.

✦ **Never divulge personal information to others over a Messages connection.**

✦ **Never use the same password for all your electronic business.** Use different passwords that include both letters and numbers, change them often, and never divulge them to anyone else.

✦ **Never give anyone else administrative access to your web server.**

✦ **Never allow any type of remote access (such as sharing screens) to your Macintosh or your network without testing that access first.** It's very important to restrict remote access to visitors whom you trust.

Find more details on securing your network from intrusion — including Internet hacker attacks — in Book VI. In Book II, I cover System Preferences that can affect the security of your system.

Book VI
Networking in OS X

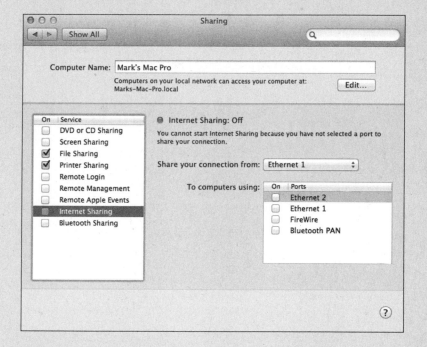

Discover how to remotely control your Mac from other computers and devices in the "Taking Charge of Your Mac... Remotely" article at www.dummies.com/extras/osxmavericksaio.

Contents at a Glance

Chapter 1: Setting Up a Small Network

In This Chapter

✔ **Finding out what a network is and why you might want one**

✔ **Setting up the network hardware**

✔ **Configuring network system preferences**

✔ **Troubleshooting your network**

In the not-so-distant past — I'm talking a generation ago — networks were found only in huge companies that had the money and the workforce to pay for and maintain them. But now, as technology rolls on, a home or small office network is both affordable and relatively easy to create.

Networks can be used for many things. Computers exchange all types of data over a network: files that you want to send between computers or to networked printers, streaming audio or video, data for multiplayer computer games, or even a private company website (typically called an *intranet*). Anything that you can imagine that would involve moving data between multiple computers can be done by using a network.

In this chapter, I introduce you to what networks are, what you can do with them, and how to set up a small Mac-based network of your own for your home or small business.

What Do I Need to Set Up My Network?

In a nutshell, a *network* is a combination of hardware, cables, and software that allows computers, printers, and other devices to talk with one another. (Heck, you don't even need cables with a wireless network, as I show you in Chapter 3 of this minibook.) To build a wired network, you need the right hardware and software. Some of the hardware and all the software that you'll need probably came with your Mac, depending on which Mac you have. As you progress through this chapter, you'll discover everything that's required to set up your network so that you can pick up any additional parts you need. Any good-sized computer store (either the brick-and-mortar or online variety) has everything that you need to get up and running.

Now, back to the requirements: You need the right hardware and software to make your wired network sing. This section covers each component with a description about the role that each part plays on the network and other good stuff you'll want to know to get your network right the first time.

Something to network

Okay, this might be obvious, but I'm nothing if not thorough. The first thing that you need to build a network is . . . well, *stuff!* That's right — you need to have devices that you want to network. Most times these are computers (whether Macs or other PCs running Windows, Linux, or Unix), printers, personal digital assistants (PDAs), cellphones, iOS devices (such as the iPad, iPhone, and iPod touch) and other standalone, network-capable devices (such as file servers and shared backup drives).

Network interface card (NIC)

A *network interface card* (NIC) is a hardware device that your computer uses to talk to the rest of the network. The NIC connects to the network cabling, and it speaks the language of electronics, sending data around the network. Nowadays, most networks use the Ethernet networking protocol, and most NICs are Ethernet-compatible. All Mavericks–compatible Mac models have Ethernet NIC hardware built right onto the Mac's main system board. *Note:* The MacBook Air and the MacBook Pro with Retina display offer only wireless hardware built in, but you can add a wired Ethernet port to either model using an external USB or Thunderbolt adapter.

Switch

So you have an assortment of devices in your home or small office that you decide to network. How do you make them all interconnect? You could connect just two computers by using nothing more than a single Ethernet cable. But to connect more than two computers, you need fancier hardware: namely, a switch. The switch is used to connect everything, so it's the focal point of the network. No switch, no network.

Thirty-nine flavors of Ethernet . . . but no Rocky Road

Ethernet standards allow for operation at different speeds. Because the Ethernet standard has improved over time, some older Ethernet devices support only the older (slower) speeds. Ethernet's speed is rated by how much data it can transfer in a second — usually in millions of bits per second, or megabits per second (Mbps). Originally, Ethernet was designed to run at 10 Mbps. Now Ethernet is available in different speeds: 10 Mbps, 100 Mbps, 1000 Mbps, and even faster.

1000 Mbps Ethernet — also called *gigabit Ethernet* or just *gigabit* for short — is the best choice for small home or office networks. All consumer-level gigabit Ethernet NICs also support running at 10 Mbps or 100 Mbps, so you will hear them called *10/100/1000 Ethernet NICs*. All current Mac models (except the MacBook Air and the MacBook Pro with Retina display) come with a 10/100/1000 Ethernet NIC built in, including the standard display MacBook Pro and Mac mini. Gigabit switches are now priced less than $50, and most devices that can connect Gigabit NICs now cost about the same as their 10/100 counterparts.

Virtually all modern NICs and other Ethernet hardware support both 10 Mbps and 100 Mbps. Most times, you'll see this labeled as *10/100 Ethernet*. For your home networking, you probably want to invest in hardware that can deliver gigabit speeds.

Time for a quick hardware introduction: A *port* is like an Ethernet NIC on your computer. A *switch* is really just a small box that has a bunch of Ethernet ports on it. Inside, all those Ethernet ports are arranged so that the talking (sending) wires from each port connect to the listening (receiving) wires on all other ports. Therefore, when one computer talks, all others listen.

Setting up a switch (and therefore giving birth to your network, which sounds more painful than it is) is usually no more difficult than connecting a power cable to the device and then plugging in your computers with their own Ethernet cables. You'll see various lights on the box — usually a power light indicating that the switch is powered on and operational. You'll also see lights that correspond to each port on the switch; these lights tell you what's going on in the box. For instance, you normally see the following types of lights:

✦ **Link light:** Each port on a switch should have a *link light,* which simply tells you which ports have something alive connected to a given port — that is, a device is connected and powered on.

✦ **Speed light:** Each port on the switch should have a *speed light,* which tells you the speed of the device at the other end. Some switches have different lights for different speeds, and some use a single light that changes color at different speeds.

✦ **Activity light:** When one computer speaks, they all hear it. Typically, an entire switch has only one *activity light* for the entire network, indicating that someone is speaking. With heavy traffic, the light can appear solid.

Bear with me whilst I spew technotalk for a paragraph or two. When an Ethernet switch receives a *frame* — that's the name for a standard unit, or *packet,* of network data — it reads the label on the frame to see the return address of the computer that sent the frame. In a short amount of time (after being turned on and watching the data move around), a switch figures out which computer is located on which port. Then, whenever data comes into the switch, it looks at the *header* (some information on the front of all frames, much like a mailing label on a package that you send) and sees which computer should receive the frame. The switch then sends the frame out the port for that computer only. This process is A Good Thing. Instead of forcing all computers on the network to listen while one Mac speaks (as antique network hubs did) — known as *half-duplex* — a switch sends the data directly to the only computer that needs to hear it.

Cables

Cables are the ties that bind . . . literally. *Cables* are used to connect the Ethernet port on each computer to the switch, the central hardware of the network. With a little experience, you'll be a cable-wielding superhero with hundreds of feet of cable draped across every piece of furniture in your place for your first LAN party. (A *LAN party,* by the way, is when way too many techies bring their computers into a small space, connect them, and play games for 48 hours straight. Oh, and we eat a lot, too. Good stuff!)

Here's the scoop on what kind of cables to use. Technically, you can run 100 Mbps Ethernet over Cat-5 cable (like a super-version of the wire that you use for your telephones).

Although you can do 10/100 Mbps Ethernet over Cat-5 cable, any new cables that you buy should be Cat-5e or Cat-6 — which I talk about in the following section — because these types of cables are specifically meant for use with 1000 Mbps (gigabit) Ethernet. I'm sure you noticed that the common denominator here is the Cat-5 cable. That's because fiber optic cable, although supporting speeds of 100 Mbps, 1 Gbps, and even 10 Gbps, is much more expensive and more difficult to install.

Hey, did I mention that you can eschew cables entirely? For more information on the lean, mean (but significantly slower) world of wireless networking, see Chapter 3 of this minibook.

Be sure to buy *straight-through* Cat-5e/Cat-6 cables (also called *patch* cables) and not *crossover* cables, which are used only in certain circumstances. Crossover cables are mainly used to connect two computers directly (to form a tiny, two-computer network), to connect a cable/DSL modem directly to a computer, or to connect multiple switches.

Cat-5 cable supports speeds of 100 Mbps. 1000 Mbps Ethernet, of course, is designed to run ten times faster than that; luckily enough, it was engineered to be compatible with 90 percent of Cat-5 installations. Having said that, I must also point out that some Cat-5 cables don't stick to the stringent specifications that 1000 Mbps Ethernet requires. The newer version of Cat-5 cable is *Category 5 Enhanced*, or Cat-5e for short. Cat-5e is recommended for any new installation because it can easily handle 10/100 Mbps Ethernet as well as 1000 Mbps Ethernet. Even if you're using 10/100 Mbps Ethernet, you can upgrade someday to 1000 Mbps without having to worry about upgrading your cabling. In your network travels, you may also find Cat-6 cabling, which can also easily handle 1000 Mbps speeds.

Setting Up Your Network

After you collect the hardware components I list earlier in this chapter, you're ready to connect things. Here's a quick list of things to do to get your network fired up:

1. **Find the best location for placing your switch.**

To keep costs down, try to place the switch in a location close to a centrally located power outlet so that you use the least amount of cable. If cost isn't an issue, hide the unit in a closet and just run all the cables along the walls to the hub or switch. And if cost *really* isn't an issue, get your house fully wired with Cat-5e or Cat-6 cable.

2. **Plug the switch into the power socket.**

   Some switches come on automatically when you plug them in and can never be turned off. Others have a power switch that you need to turn on the first time that you plug them in.

3. **Verify that the switch is working by looking at the lights on the front. Check the manual that came with the switch to see what light configuration is normal for that particular unit.**

   Until you have computers or printers attached to it, the switch might just have a status light that shows that the switch is powered on. But if the lights on your unit don't match up with what the manual says, you could have a bum unit that you need to return.

4. **Verify that all your devices are near enough to the switch to be connected by your cables; then turn them all on.**

5. **Get one of your Cat-5e or Cat-6 cables and connect one cable from the Ethernet jack on your computer, usually on the side or back, to an open port on the switch.**

   You should see a link light or speed light come on that verifies that the two devices sense each other. (And, depending on the Mac, you might also have a link light on the NIC where you plug in the cable.)

6. **Repeat Step 5 until each device is attached to the switch.**

Congratulations! You're a network technician! (Don't forget to call your friends and brag.) The first phase of the network, the physical connection, is complete; the next step is the configuration of OS X.

Understanding the Basics of Network Configuration

Take a deep breath; there's no need to panic — configuring your network software basically involves entering a lot of numbers and other stuff in dialogs. (Most folks can just allow Mavericks to take care of network settings automatically.) But just so that you'll understand what's involved, this section explains what those numbers are, what they do, and why you ought to know what they do. Because this is an OS X book, I stick with configuring Macs running the Big X.

TCP/IP

First things first: TCP/IP stands for *Transmission Control Protocol/Internet Protocol*. Second, a *protocol* is just the technonerd word for a set of rules or a language that computers use to communicate. Without protocols, the computers on your network would never be able to speak to one another even though you have NICs, cables, and a hub or a switch. The Internet Protocol (IP) part of the TCP/IP suite is what you're really interested in because it's the most important part of your network configuration chore.

IP addresses

IP addresses are like street addresses for computers on a network. Each computer on the network has an IP address, and this address needs to be unique because no other computer can share it. When a computer wants to communicate with another computer, it can simply send the data on the network in a nice package that has its address as well as the address of the computer that it's trying to talk to. (Remember frames? If not, take a refresher in the earlier section "Switch.")

An IP address is just a number, but it's written in a strange way. (Go figure.) All IP addresses are currently written as four sets of numerals between 0 and 255 with a dot (period) between each set. For instance, a common IP address that you might run into is 192.168.0.1. As everyone knows, engineers can't sleep unless they have three or four ways to write the same thing, including IP addresses. The form shown here — which is by far the most common — is *dotted notation.* Each number, such as 192, is an *octet.*

Book VI
Chapter 1

Setting Up a Small Network

Don't worry too much about this stuff: You don't have to remember terms like *octet* to create your own network. These terms could be helpful, however, if something goes wrong and you need to place a call to tech support. Plus, you can impress the computer salesperson (gleefully called a *wonk* by Mac power users) at your local Maze 'o Wires store with your mastery of technobabble.

IP addresses at home versus on the Internet

One important thing to keep in mind is that the Almighty IP Address Police — Internet Assigned Numbers Authority (IANA; www.iana.org) — has broken IP addresses into groups. The two main types of IP addresses are public and private:

✦ **Public IP addresses** can be used on the Internet and are unique throughout the whole world.

✦ **Private IP addresses** are used in homes or businesses and can't be used to talk to the public Internet. Private IP addresses are used over and over by many people and most commonly take the form 192.168.*x.x,* 172.16.*x.x,* or 10.0.*x.x.* (Apple routers, such as Time Capsule or AirPort Extreme, set up private networks in the last range.)

You'll almost always get a public IP address from your Internet service provider (ISP), whether you're using a cable modem, digital subscriber line (DSL), or a regular dial-up modem. If you use a cable/DSL router or Mavericks's built-in sharing software to share your Internet connection among multiple computers, you'll be using private IP addresses on your network while using a single public IP address to talk to the Internet. (More on that in Chapter 4 of this minibook.)

"Great! I get an IP address, put it into my Network settings in System Preferences, and off I go. Right?" Well, you're close, but here are a few other pieces of information that you might need before you can go surfing around the world:

✦ **Default gateway:** When you send information to other networks — whether in another building or around the world on the Internet — your computer needs to know the IP address of the gateway that will forward your data down the line. The *default gateway* is really just the IP address of a *router,* which is a device that connects multiple networks. A *gateway* gets its name because it really is your gateway to all other networks.

✦ **Subnet mask:** A *subnet mask* is a number that helps your computer know when it needs to send stuff through the router. It's a group of four octets with dots, just like an IP address, but almost always uses 0 or 255 for each of the four octets. Most often, the subnet mask is 255.255.255.0. If the wrong number is entered for the subnet mask, it could keep you from talking to the Internet or even to computers on your own network.

Software applications

After you have the hardware in place and you've chosen and configured a protocol to allow the computers to all talk to one another, you need software to make use of your new network connections. Time for more good news: A lot of the software that you need to move data on your network is included already in OS X! Here are brief descriptions of some of the network software and protocols already built in to OS X and what they're used for:

✦ **FTP:** *File Transfer Protocol* (FTP), part of the TCP/IP protocol suite, allows computers of any type — Mac, PC, Linux, Unix, mainframe, or whatever — to transfer files back and forth. You can use either a third-party FTP application — several are available for Maverick — or open a Terminal window and use text commands to transfer files. (You'll learn more about the Terminal application and how to use it in Book VIII, Chapter 2.)

+ **Telnet:** *Telnet* is also part of the TCP/IP suite — you can use it to remotely connect to a computer and execute commands on the remote machine.

+ **Samba:** *Samba* (or *SMB*) enables OS X users to share files with people using Windows computers and allows the Mac users to connect to files that the Windows computers share.

+ **HTTP:** *HyperText Transfer Protocol* (HTTP), also part of the TCP/IP suite, is used by web browsers to provide access to all the various pages on the World Wide Web.

Configuring Network System Preferences

In this section, I show you how to configure your Mac to communicate with other computers on a local network.

Leave it to Mavericks to provide you with assistance — in this case, when you first open the Network pane, you might be greeted with a dialog offering you assistance on setting up the stuff I cover in this section. (Whether you get this *absolutely free* offer of aid depends on whether you upgraded your Mac from a previous version of OS X or whether you entered your network and Internet settings in the Mavericks Setup Assistant.) If you do decide to allow the Mavericks Internet/Network Assistant to guide you through your network setup, I'll meet back up with you at the next section. (Note that you can also start the assistant manually at any time by clicking the Assist Me button at the bottom of the Network pane.)

Using DHCP for automatic IP address assignment

Now I'd like to introduce you to a *very* dear friend of mine — an abbreviation that you will soon grow to love, as does everyone else who's set up a small Mac network. *Dynamic Host Configuration Protocol* (DHCP) enables a computer to automatically get all the information that I've talked about to this point. (Check in your *Webster's* . . . this protocol is the very definition of the word *godsend*.)

You're saying, "Mark, there's gotta be a catch, right?" Well, here's the bad news: Before you can use DHCP, you have to add a *DHCP server,* which provides other computers on the network with their configuration settings. Here's the good news: Most Internet connection-sharing hardware devices (and software-sharing implementations as well) provide a DHCP server as part of the price of admission. (*Internet connection sharing* allows all your networked computers to access the Internet through a single Internet connection. I cover it more in Chapter 4 of this minibook.) Most wired and wireless routers can provide DHCP services these days. Technology marches on.

If you plan to use Internet connection sharing or you know that you have a DHCP server on your network, you can set up your Mac to automatically obtain the required IP address and information by following these steps:

1. **Open System Preferences from the Dock or the Apple menu () and choose Network.**

2. **From the Network dialog that appears, click the Ethernet entry in the list on the left.**

3. **On the Configure IPv4 pop-up menu, choose Using DHCP; click the Apply button.**

    OS X contacts the DHCP server to obtain an IP address, a subnet mask, a gateway router IP address, and a Domain Name System (DNS) address. (*DNS servers* convert a human-friendly address, such as www.yahoo.com, to a computer-friendly IP address, such as 66.218.71.86.)

A few seconds after clicking the Apply button, you should see the information, as provided by the DHCP server, which lets you know that the process worked and configuration is complete. You might also notice that the DNS Server information is empty (or dimmed). Fear not: OS X is really using DNS information provided by the DHCP server. Press ⌘+Q to quit System Preferences and save your settings.

If you ever make a network change that screws things up, such as entering the wrong subnet mask or an IP address that isn't in the same range as others on your LAN, you can always click the Revert button to get back your old settings.

One DHCP server on a network is princely, but two or more DHCP servers on a single network will fight like alley cats and grind everything to a halt. Therefore, if you're considering adding a DHCP server to an existing network, make *doggone* sure that you're not treading on another server's toes. (Ask that network administrator person.)

Manually choosing an IP address range

You say you don't have a DHCP server, and you need to manually assign IP addresses? Oh, rapture — this configuration requires you to manually configure the TCP/IP properties. Keep in mind that for now, you are concerned not with the Internet — just with computers on the local network.

A result of being on a *local* network — because it's not connected to the Internet, it's also called a *private* network — is that you must use IP addresses that are reserved for private network use. You can use a few different ranges of IP addresses, but I recommend that you choose an address range from the 192.168.*x.x* networks. In the next section, I show you how.

Down to business: *I recommend that you use IP addresses in the 192.168.x.x range.* What does this mean exactly? Well, here's the scoop:

✦ **Use IP addresses where the first two octets are 192 and 168 (192.168).**

   Octet numbers are conjoined by periods.

✦ **For the third octet, select any number between 1 and 254.**

   It doesn't matter which one you choose as long as you use this same third number on all computers on your network.

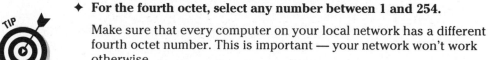

✦ **For the fourth octet, select any number between 1 and 254.**

   Make sure that every computer on your local network has a different fourth octet number. This is important — your network won't work otherwise.

✦ **Use 255.255.255.0 as your subnet mask.**

For instance, suppose that you're using three computers on your network. All the IP addresses that you use will start with *192.168.* Next, suppose you choose *123* for the third octet. (Remember that you can choose any number between 1 and 254.) Finally, for the fourth octet, choose the numbers 100, 105, and 110 for the three computers, respectively. (Again, you can choose any numbers between 1 and 254.) The resulting IP addresses used on the three computers are

   192.168.123.100

   192.168.123.105

   192.168.123.110

By the way, I should mention that there are other range possibilities for reserved private networks — AirPort and AirPort Extreme hardware typically use a 10.*x.x.x* network range, for example — but the 192.168.*x.x* range is the most popular and the most common default on Ethernet network hardware.

After you know the IP addresses and the subnet mask that you're going to use, start setting up each computer. Being a nice guy, I walk you through the process of configuring OS X with the 192.168.0.106 address as an example.

Be sure that you have all the physical portion of your network powered up and connected as I outline in the earlier section, "Setting Up Your Network."

1. **Select any of your Macs to start with and open System Preferences (either from the Apple menu or from the Dock).**

2. **From the System Preferences dialog, choose Network.**

    The Network pane appears.

3. **Click Ethernet in the list.**

4. **On the Configure IPv4 pop-up menu, choose Manually.**

5. **In the IP Address text box, enter the IP address for this machine (192.168.0.106 in this example).**

6. **In the Subnet Mask text box, enter the subnet mask (255.255.255.0 in this example).**

7. **If you're using a router or hardware Internet-sharing device, enter the IP address used by the router in the Router text box.**

    Figure 1-1 shows how things should look at this point.

Figure 1-1: Manually configuring TCP/IP settings.

8. **Click the Apply button.**

   Your new network settings take effect.

9. **Press ⌘+Q to quit System Preferences.**

   Repeat this procedure with the other IP addresses for each of the other Macs that are connected to your network.

Most ISPs also supply DNS server addresses and search domains. If your ISP included DNS server addresses or search domains, don't forget to type them in the corresponding boxes on the TCP/IP panel.

Verifying Connectivity

After you have your Macs connected and your TCP/IP configuration is done, check to make sure that everything is working. After you have at least two computers on your network, each with a TCP/IP address, you can use a simple little utility called *ping* to test the connection.

The ping application is a simple but extremely helpful utility that's the first connectivity-testing tool out of the box, even for network professionals. When you use the ping utility — referred to as *pinging* something — the application sends a small packet of data to whatever destination you're trying to reach. When the receiving computer hears the ping, it answers with a ping reply. If the original computer receives the ping reply, you know that the connection between the computers is good.

To ping a computer, you use a little application built in to OS X called *Network Utility,* which allows you to work various network wonders (including checking connectivity, watching the route that your computer takes to get to another computer, and looking up information about Internet domain names). To use Network Utility to check network connectivity, follow these steps:

1. **Click the Spotlight icon in the Finder menu, and then type** Network Utility **in the Search box.**

2. **Click the Network Utility entry in the Results menu to launch the application.**

3. **Click the Ping tab (see Figure 1-2).**

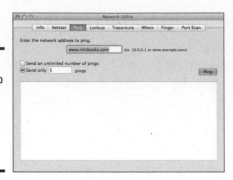

Figure 1-2:
Preparing to
ping. (Can
you say
that with
a straight
face?)

4. **In the Enter the Network Address to Ping text field, enter the IP address (or web address) of the computer that you want to ping.**

5. **To simply verify connectivity, select the Send Only *x* Pings radio button and then enter a low number, such as 5, in the text field.**

   Five or ten pings are plenty to see whether the connection is working.

6. **Click the Ping button.**

   Your Mac sends ping packets to the IP address that you entered.

If the pings are successful, text appears in the text box at the bottom of the Ping tab: one line for each ping reply received from the other computer. The end of each line reads `time=` *number*. That number is the amount of time, in $1/1000$ of a second (milliseconds [ms]), that it took for the ping packet to go from your computer to the other computer and back.

If your ping is unsuccessful, you see nothing, at least for a little bit. Each ping that you send takes two seconds before it's considered missing in action. So, if you choose five pings, wait ten seconds before you see the results. After all the pings time out — a ping *times out* when it doesn't get returned in the proper amount of time — you see a line of text appear that reads `ping: sendto: No route to host` or `100% packet loss`. Both error messages mean the same thing: All the ping packets that you sent out are now in the packet graveyard, never to be seen again. As you've likely guessed already, this is *not* A Good Sign for your network connectivity. Look to the following section, "Troubleshooting Your New Network," to find out where to begin troubleshooting this problem.

If you can ping all the other computers on your network from one of the computers, you don't need to go to each computer and ping all the others. You can logically assume that all the computers can communicate. For instance, if you can ping computers B, C, and D from computer A, you don't need to bother with ping tests from computer B, C, or D.

After you have your computers configured and you've verified connectivity among them, start doing the fun stuff that a network allows you to do, such as sharing data, printing, and (most important) playing games with users on other computers.

Troubleshooting Your New Network

After a network is set up and operating, it rarely has problems. Still, Murphy sometimes takes charge, and the darn thing just won't work right. When you do have problems with the network, I recommend using a standard, consistent approach to finding and fixing the problem. This section breaks down troubleshooting into two areas:

✦ **The hardware:** The best place to start troubleshooting a network problem is with the actual equipment, such as the NICs, the cables, and the switches. (See earlier sections on each equipment type.)

✦ **The software:** The second place to check for problems is in the configuration of the computers on the network, specifically the configuration on the computer(s) having the problem that you're troubleshooting.

Physical problems with your network

Although many things on a network can go bad or cause problems, network problems are typically caused by faulty equipment or wiring. Sometimes it's something as simple as a cable not being plugged in snugly. Looking at the physical cables, connections, and equipment is always the best place to start looking for problems. The following steps will help you check physical things that can cause network problems:

1. **Make sure that both ends of the network cable are firmly connected.**

Check the end that plugs into the computer first — and then check the end that connects to the switch.

2. **Turn on the problematic computer to make sure that it's connected to a hub or switch.**

Check the port on the switch to see whether the link or speed light is lit. (Depending on the switch that you have, you might not have a link light. Many switches use a speed light to indicate a link. Check the manufacturer's manual for your model.) If your computer is on and connected but no link or speed light is lit, try replacing the network cable.

3. **If you replace the network cable and the light still isn't lit, try unplugging the cable from the switch and plug it into another port.**

Choose one of the other computers connected to the switch that works, unplug it, and plug the broken computer into that port for testing. Occasionally, a single port on a switch goes bad; if that happens, just mark it as bad and don't use it anymore. But if all computers connected to the switch stop working, it's probably the switch that's gone south. If the switch is still under warranty, I recommend getting it fixed or replaced. If the warranty has expired, it's usually more cost-effective to replace a switch than fix it.

4. **If you replace the cable, try a different port on the switch.**

If other computers work fine on that switch, the NIC inside your computer has possibly gone bad.

If you reach this determination, call your local service center to have it looked at and repaired. If you have an older model on which the NIC was added instead of built in, you can simply replace the NIC yourself.

The key when troubleshooting physical problems is the link or speed light on the switch. If the link or speed light still doesn't work, the problem likely isn't physical. Start troubleshooting the network configuration on the computer itself.

Network configuration problems

After checking the hardware, look for problems in the network settings. When using TCP/IP on your network, look for these specific things: the TCP/IP configuration mode, IP address, subnet mask, and router IP address (if you're using a router to connect to the Internet or other networks). To check these settings, open System Preferences and click the Network icon to bring up the Network pane. Click the Ethernet entry in the list and then follow these steps:

1. **Make sure that the Configure IPv4 pop-up menu is set to the appropriate option.**

   - *Using DHCP:* Select the Using DHCP option only if you're using a cable/DSL modem/router or other DHCP server. Otherwise, set this option to Manually.

   - *Manually:* If the configuration is set to Manually, check the IP Address, DNS Servers, Router, and Subnet Mask fields to make sure that they're correct. If you're not sure whether your Subnet Mask field entry is correct, you can usually make it the same as other computers on the same network with you. Most times, the subnet mask is 255.255.255.0.

2. **To check your Internet connectivity to the rest of the Internet, try pinging** www.apple.com.

   This step checks the router and DNS settings.

3. **If you're set up for DHCP and your TCP/IP settings remain blank, make sure that your DHCP server — which could be your cable, DSL modem, or router — is turned on and working properly.**

Book VI Chapter 1

Setting Up a Small Network

Chapter 2: Using Your Network

In This Chapter

✔ **Finding out what you can do with your network**

✔ **Sharing your files and printers with other Macs**

✔ **Sharing your files with Windows computers**

✔ **Accessing files on Windows computers**

✔ **Configuring the built-in firewall**

✔ **Remote-controlling your Mac**

*H*ere's one of those incredibly complex concepts that you always find in these computer books: After you have your network set up and ready to go, you can do *all kinds of really cool things with it.* (Highly technical.) You can use your network to share files, share printers, remotely control your Mac, or even play multiuser games against friends. To keep your files safe from unwanted snoops, you can configure the OS X built-in firewall. In this chapter, I cover the basics of file sharing, printer sharing, and using the firewall to protect yourself from intruders.

It's All about (File) Sharing

One of the main reasons for building a network is sharing files between computers. You might even want to set up a *server,* which is a computer with shared files that are always available to anyone on the network. Think of a server as a common file storage area for the rest of the network. Really, any computer that shares files is technically a server because it's serving, so to speak. But most people use the word *server* only to mean a computer that's dedicated solely to serving files, printers, and so on for the rest of the network.

Creating an account

Sharing files on your Mac with other Mac users is a piece of cake. Remember, however, that you need to create an account for anyone that you want to have access to your files. Each person assigned an account is called a *user*. By default, the user accounts that you create can open and save files in the three folders shown in Figure 2-1 (as well as in external hard drives and USB Flash drives).

Figure 2-1: The location of user folders and the Shared folder on your hard drive.

Those three folders are

+ **The account's Home folder:** The specific account's Home folder carries a short version of the username in the Users folder on your hard drive. Figure 2-1 shows the Home folder, which is noted with an icon that looks like a house, for the mark account (where *mark* is the short account name for Mark Chambers, and *ben* is the name for one of my example users). (If you create a Sharing Only account — see Book II, Chapter 5 — Mavericks doesn't create a Home folder for that account.)

+ **Each account's Public folder:** Each admin, standard, or managed user account you create also has a Public folder located in its Home folder. Any files you place in the Public folder can be accessed by any user on your Mac, local or remote. (Once again, Sharing Only accounts don't have a Public folder.)

+ **The Shared folder:** This folder is also in the Users folder on your hard drive. Anyone with an admin-level account on your Mac can access the Shared folder across the network, and any user account on your Mac can access the Shared folder locally, so it's a great place to keep common files that everyone wants to copy or use.

If you create a Sharing Only account, the user of that account can use only the contents of the Shared folder. (Go figure.)

To create an account, you need to be logged in as an admin user. I cover creating accounts in greater detail in Book II, Chapter 5, but here's the short version:

1. **Open System Preferences from the Apple menu (⌘) or the Dock.**

2. **Click the Users & Groups icon.**

3. **Click the New User button, which carries a plus sign.**

If the New User button is dimmed, you need to unlock the Users & Groups pane first. Click the padlock icon in the lower-left corner, type your admin user account password, and then click Unlock.

4. **Open the New Account pop-up menu and choose the account type.**

Your choices are Administrator (Admin), Standard, Managed with Parental Controls, and Sharing Only.

5. **Fill in the appropriate information, including the name for the account and a password.**

The name that appears as the short name determines the name of that user's Home folder.

6. **Click Create User.**

7. **Press ⌘+Q to exit System Preferences.**

Enabling file sharing

When you enable file sharing, your files are exchanged over Transmission Control Protocol/Internet Protocol (TCP/IP).

As I discuss in more dry detail in Chapter 1 of this minibook, TCP/IP is a protocol suite used for Internet data transfer.

Follow these steps to turn on sharing:

1. **Open System Preferences.**

2. **Click the Sharing icon to open the Sharing Preferences pane.**

3. **Select the File Sharing check box to turn on File Sharing.**

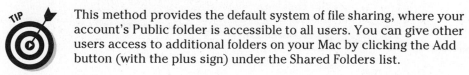

This method provides the default system of file sharing, where your account's Public folder is accessible to all users. You can give other users access to additional folders on your Mac by clicking the Add button (with the plus sign) under the Shared Folders list.

Connecting to a shared resource

At the top of the Sharing pane, you can see that other Macintosh users can access your computer at `afp://<ip address>`, where *ip address* is the IP address for your specific computer. When another Mac user wants to connect to your shared files, that person can do the following:

1. **From the Finder menu bar, choose Go⇨Connect to Server.**

   The Connect to Server dialog opens.

2. **In the Server Address box, type** afp://*<ip address>* **(where *ip address* is the IP address of your Mac), and then click the Connect button.**

Transferring files the easy AirDrop way

AirDrop is the local Mac-to-Mac file transfer feature built-in to OS X Mavericks, and it couldn't be much easier to use, with no setup and no passwords! However, here are three caveats (aren't there always?):

✔ AirDrop works only with Macs running Lion, Mountain Lion, and Mavericks, and only with specific models: MacBook Pro (late 2008 or newer), MacBook Air (late 2010 or newer), and MacBook (late 2010 and newer). The 17" MacBook Pro (late 2008) doesn't support AirDrop.

✔ AirDrop uses the Wi-Fi hardware built into today's Mac laptops and desktops, so don't forget to turn on Wi-Fi first. (If you're displaying the Wi-Fi status icon on your Finder menu bar, click the icon and choose Turn Wi-Fi On.)

✔ You have to be within Wi-Fi signal range of another Mac to use AirDrop. Note, however, that the two computers *don't* have to be using the same Wi-Fi network. (For example, my iMac uses a wired connection to my network, but because the iMac has internal Wi-Fi hardware, I can use AirDrop to send files to my MacBook Pro.) Because AirDrop uses a Wi-Fi connection, file transfers are significantly slower than they would be over a wired Ethernet network.

To use AirDrop to transfer files to another Mac, both users should click the AirDrop icon in any Finder window sidebar to join the AirDrop group. After a short delay, you'll see the account pictures for all the Macs within signal range that have AirDrop open. Just drag the files you want to transfer to the person's picture. Both you and the recipient are prompted for confirmation before the transfer begins. After the transfer is completed, the files you sent are saved in the recipient's Downloads folder.

When you're done using AirDrop, just close the Finder window displaying the account pictures (or click another location in the Finder window sidebar), and you'll exit from the AirDrop group. Don't forget that you have to open AirDrop again if someone wants to send you files, so I leave my AirDrop Finder window open and minimized to the Dock.

You can also browse for a shared resource in the Connect to Server dialog. Choose Go⇨Connect to Server or press ⌘+K, and then click Browse to locate the shared computer. You might be prompted to choose whether you want to connect as a guest or a registered user. To connect to the server as a registered user, you must supply the username and password. If you connect as guest, you don't have to supply a password, but you will have restricted access to only the Public folder for each account on the system that you connect to. If you need to connect as a registered user, ask an admin user who controls that Mac to supply you with the username and password.

Give the username and password that you created to the person using the other Mac, and he or she can now access files in that account's Home folder as well as any other Public folders on your computer.

The sidebar that appears in Finder windows offers a Shared heading. (If nothing is listed under the Shared heading, click the Show button next to it.) The Shared heading displays other shared resources on your network, just as if you had clicked Browse from the Connect to Server dialog. (I'm starting to think *Mavericks* might be a synonym for *convenience*.)

Sharing a Connected Printer

Sharing your printer for others to use is one of the best reasons to have a network. Setting up your Mac to share your printer is easy under OS X. Here's a quick rundown of what you need to do:

1. **Open System Preferences.**

2. **Click the Sharing icon to open the Sharing Preferences pane.**

3. **Select the Printer Sharing check box.**

By default, when you turn on Printer Sharing, Mavericks automatically shares all the current printers connected to your Mac. To select which printers can be used for shared printing from the Sharing pane, select the check box next to each printer: that is, select the check box to share that printer, or deselect it to block others from using it. (Alternatively, you can click the Print & Scan icon in System Preferences. From this pane, you can also enable and disable sharing of individual printers.)

After Printer Sharing is enabled, follow these steps to connect to that printer from other computers on your network:

1. **Click System Preferences on the Dock.**

2. **Click the Printers & Scanners icon.**

3. **Click the Add button (plus sign) under the Printers list at the left side of the pane.**

If the Add button is disabled, click the padlock icon in the lower-left corner, type your admin user account password, and then click Unlock.

If you're prompted to add a printer automatically when the Printer Setup Utility opens, click the Add button to begin the addition. (For more on adding a printer with the Printer Setup Utility, see Book VII, Chapter 4.)

4. **From the Browser window that opens, click the Default button on the toolbar.**

5. **Click the shared printer you want to use and then click the Add button.**

Already have the Printer Browser open? Then follow the easier path: Clicking the Default toolbar button displays all the available local shared printers. Click the desired printer and then click Add.

Sharing Files with Windows Computers

If you've deigned to allow PCs running Windows access to your network (a generous gesture indeed), you'll probably want to also share files with those computers. Sharing files with a Windows PC — actually a Windows *user* — is similar to sharing files with other Mac users.

To allow file sharing with Windows computers, follow these steps:

1. **Click the System Preferences icon on the Dock.**

2. **Click the Sharing icon to open the Sharing Preferences pane.**

3. **Click the File Sharing entry.**

4. **Click the Options button to display the Options sheet.**

5. **Select the Share Files and Folders Using SMB check box.**

6. **Select the On check box next to the user account (or accounts) that will be accessible by Windows PCs.**

Mavericks will growl while you try to enable SMB sharing because you have to enable Windows access on the desired account before it can be used. (SMB is short for Server Message Block, which is a file-sharing protocol used by Windows.) Mavericks prompts you for your password, smugly informing you that the account password will be stored "in a less secure manner." Generally, this isn't a problem, but never enable an account for Windows access unless only trusted individuals will use it.

7. **Click Done to exit the Options sheet, and close the System Preferences window to save the changes.**

Book VI Chapter 2

Using Your Network

Accessing File Shares on Windows Computers

Fair is fair: If you allow a Windows PC to access your files, you'll also probably want to putter around with files on that Windows PC. Easy!

Accessing files on Windows computers relies on the Samba component (a part of the Unix foundation of OS X). Follow these steps:

1. **From Finder, choose Go⇨Connect to Server.**

   The Connect to Server dialog opens.

2. **In the Address box, enter** smb://<*ip address*>, **where *ip address* is the IP address of the Windows computer that you want to connect to.**

   Don't forget that you can also use the Browse button to search for Macs and PCs with shared files on your network.

3. **Click the Connect button.**

   Depending on the type of account you have on the Windows PC, OS X might display an SMB authentication dialog in which you can enter your username and password. (Think security for the Windows crowd.)

4. **Choose the desired shared folder or drive to mount from the pop-up menu.**

5. **Mount the shared folder or drive according to the Windows version:**

   • *If you're accessing a file shared on a Windows 98 or Me computer:* Simply click OK to mount the share.

   • *If you're accessing a file shared on a Windows 2000, XP, Vista, 7, or 8 computer:* Click the Authenticate button. Then enter your username and password, click OK, and then click OK again to mount the share.

After you mount the shared location, you'll see it on your Desktop, just as you see a Mac volume. You can use this drive just as you do any other drive on your system. To disconnect from the Windows share, you can do one of the following:

✦ Drag the icon to the Trash on the Dock (which changes to an Eject icon when you start dragging).

✦ Press ⌘+E.

✦ Right-click the icon, and then choose Eject from the menu that appears.

Using FTP to Access Files

FTP — *File Transfer Protocol* — is part of the TCP/IP protocol suite. FTP is one of the oldest methods for sharing files between computers; however, because it's part of the TCP/IP protocol suite, it can be used on many different kinds of computers, including those running just about any type of strange and arcane operating system. You can still manage to exchange files regardless of whether you're using OS X, Windows, Linux, or Unix. (Heck, even dinosaurs like DOS can join the party.) FTP transfers are also faster than downloading the same file from a web server.

FTP is a client/server application. In plain English, this means that two pieces make things tick: the *server* (which hosts the connection, rather like a file server) and the *client* (which connects to the server, and which you control). OS X, thanks to its Unix foundation, has an FTP client built in. To use FTP, you need a computer running the FTP server software to give others access to files; then the other computer, or client, can connect to the FTP server. After the connection is made, the client can either send files to the server *(uploading)* or get files from the server *(downloading)*.

In this section, I cover how to use FTP to access files on a server.

You can use FTP to transfer files with an FTP server by using the command line interface, in a Terminal (or shell) session. I discuss Terminal and the Unix command line in detail in Book VIII, Chapter 2.

Start by clicking the Launchpad icon on the Dock. Click the Other group, and then click the Terminal icon. (Or, from a Finder window, double-click the Terminal icon in the Utilities folder inside the Applications folder.) When you open a Terminal session, you're presented with a window that accepts text commands. You'll see a prompt that consists of your computer's name and the folder that you're in, followed by your user ID. It's at this prompt where you type various FTP commands.

After you're in the Terminal session, you'll use a series of commands to connect to another computer, move in and out of folders, and transfer files.

Many FTP servers will limit you to sending files only to certain folders. Most times this folder is named *Upload, Uploads,* or something similar.

Here is a list of the basic commands to use FTP as well as a brief description of what each command does:

Book VI
Chapter 2

✦ ftp: This command starts the FTP command line interface session. You can tell that you're in the FTP client application when you see ftp> as your command prompt. The command prompt is where you type all other FTP commands to do things.

✦ open: This command is used to start your connection to another computer. Type this command followed by the IP address of the FTP server to which you want to connect.

✦ ls: Use this command to see a listing of all files and folders in the current folder on the FTP server.

✦ cd: This command allows you to change the folder that you're in. Type **cd <*folder*>** (where *folder* is a specific folder name) to move to a subfolder on the FTP server. Type **cd ..** (that's cd, space, and two periods) to go back out a folder level.

✦ lcd: This command acts exactly like cd except that it changes the folder that you're currently in on your local system, not the FTP server. Use this command to move to the folder on the local drive that you want to transfer files to and from.

✦ bin: Type this command to get in binary mode to transfer files that aren't plain-text files. *Important:* Always use binary mode unless you're specifically transferring plain-text files.

✦ ascii: This command puts you in ASCII mode for transferring text files.

✦ get or mget: To retrieve a single file, use the get command followed by the filename of the file that you want to retrieve. If you want to get multiple files at one time, use the mget command followed by a filename, possibly containing * and/or ? as wildcards.

✦ put or mput: To send a single file, use the put command followed by the filename to send a file to the FTP server. To send multiple files, use the mput command followed by a filename, possibly containing * and/or ? as wildcards.

✦ quit: Use the quit command to end your FTP session.

To end a Terminal session and exit Terminal at any time, press ⌘+Q. Terminal prompts you for confirmation if necessary.

Using Your Network

Using FTP on the Internet

Because File Transfer Protocol (FTP) is a part of the TCP/IP suite, it works on virtually every type of computer, over both the Internet and your local area network (LAN). So, assuming that you have your computer connected to the Internet through a modem or a LAN connection, everything that I discuss about FTP and how to use it applies to connecting to FTP servers on the Internet as well. When you connect to FTP servers on the Internet, you can use the Fully Qualified Domain Name (or FQDN for short), such as `ftp.apple.com`, instead of an actual IP address.

Here's an example of how to use these commands in the Terminal window:

1. **In Terminal, type** ftp **to get into FTP mode.**

2. **Type** open *<ip address>* **(where** *ip address* **is the server's network IP address) to open your connection to the FTP server.**

3. **Enter your username and password.**

For many FTP servers, using the username *anonymous* and your e-mail address as the password is enough to get you logged in. Some sites even allow you to log in without any username or password at all. On secure sites, however, you must use an assigned username and password provided by the administrator of that particular server.

4. **Type** lcd *<folder>* **(where** *folder* **is a specific folder name) to change into the folder on your local drive that you want files to come to or from.**

5. **Type the** ls **and** cd **commands to place yourself into the desired folder on the FTP server.**

6. **Type the** ascii **or** bin **command to set your file transfer mode to ASCII or binary, respectively.**

This is important because choosing the wrong type will likely cause the transfer to fail. Unless it's a plain-text file, always use binary mode.

7. **Type the** get, mget, put, **and** mput **commands to receive or send the desired files.**

8. **Type the** quit **command to close the connection and exit the FTP session.**

If you'd rather use a drag-and-drop graphical client application for transfer-ring files using FTP, I recommend the freeware FileZilla application (available at `http://filezilla-project.org`).

Using the Built-in Firewall

A *firewall* watches all the network communications coming into your Mac. It automatically plays the role of security guard, blocking (denying) certain network traffic that you want to prevent from reaching your Mac. It acts as another layer of security to help keep you safe from unwanted attacks. That's all well and good, but you must be careful to set up your firewall cor-rectly before you turn it on because a configuration mistake could make your Mac inaccessible from the network.

For instance, if you want to enable screen sharing on your Mac (which I discuss in the next section) but you also want to keep all other traffic from coming into your Mac, you can tell the built-in firewall to allow only screen sharing. The firewall on the Mac will follow the rules you set up on what to block or allow.

If your network already has either a hardware or software firewall in place — for example, a built-in firewall on your router or Internet sharing device — turning on your OS X Mavericks firewall can result in conflicts or stability problems.

When enabled, the firewall blocks all traffic that comes into your Mac. By default, however, the firewall is turned off. So, your first job is to activate the firewall, which you can do by following these steps:

1. **Click the System Preferences icon on the Dock.**

2. **Click the Security & Privacy icon.**

3. **Click the Firewall tab.**

4. **Click the Turn On Firewall button to turn on your firewall.**

Is the Turn On Firewall button disabled? Don't panic! Just click the pad-lock icon in the lower-left corner, type your admin user account pass-word, and then click Unlock.

This step enables the firewall. And, by default, virtually all incoming TCP/IP traffic is blocked.

5. **Click the Firewall Options button to show the settings that you see in Figure 2-2.**

Figure 2-2:
You can help protect your Mac by using Mavericks' built-in firewall.

6. **Select the Automatically Allow Signed Software to Receive Incoming Connections check box.**

    As I mention earlier, you must enable each sharing method that you want to be able to use. However, when you enable different sharing methods from the Sharing pane in System Preferences (such as File Sharing or Screen Sharing), you'll notice that those types of traffic now appear in the Firewall list. (In other words, when you turn on a sharing method, the firewall automatically allows traffic for that sharing method, which Mavericks calls a *service*. **Most** excellent.)

    Sometimes, you might want to allow other traffic through your firewall that isn't on the firewall list of recognized services and applications. At that point, you can click the Add button (which bears a plus sign) to specify the application that your firewall should allow. Mavericks presents you with the familiar Add dialog, and you can choose the application that needs access.

7. **Click OK to save your changes and return to the Security & Privacy pane, and then click the Close button to close the System Preferences window.**

Remote Control of Your Mac

Forgive me whilst I wax technonerd here: One of the coolest advantages to a network is the capability to take control of one computer from another computer. For example, sometimes you might need to access files on your

Mac while you're on a trip, but you don't have File Sharing enabled. What can you do? You can remotely connect into your Mac and then — just as if you were sitting in front of it — enable File Sharing (as I demonstrate earlier in the chapter). Perhaps you have a file on your computer with someone's phone number that you suddenly need on the road. With remote control, it's at your fingertips! (Sigh . . . ah, technology.)

Mavericks' Screen Sharing feature, which is available from Messages, can be turned on for individual users from the Sharing pane in System Preferences. You can allow access for all user accounts on your Mac or limit remote access to selected users. Screen Sharing is Apple's implementation of virtual network computing (VNC) technology.

To set up Screen Sharing, follow these steps:

**Book VI
Chapter 2**

**Using Your
Network**

1. **Click the System Preferences icon on the Dock.**

2. **Click the Sharing icon to open the Sharing Preferences pane.**

3. **Select the Screen Sharing check box.**

4. **To limit remote access for specific accounts, select the Only These Users radio button and then click the Add button (a plus sign) to select a user.**

5. **Close the System Preferences window to save the change.**

After you enable screen sharing, you can use the Buddies⇨Share My Screen menu item in Messages to share your screen with another person. To view another person's screen, use the Buddies⇨Ask to Share Remote Screen menu item. (For the details on Messages and Screen Sharing, see Book V, Chapter 3.)

Chapter 3: Going Wireless

In This Chapter

- ✔ Finding out how wireless networking works
- ✔ Discovering wireless security
- ✔ Connecting to other Macs without a wireless access point
- ✔ Connecting to and disconnecting from AirPort networks

Nowadays, wireless connectivity is king. For example, mobile phones have gone from being a toy of the technological elite to a permanent fixture on the hip of *homo sapiens.* The shorts that I'm wearing right now have a special pocket just for a cellphone to ride in; when I'm without my phone, the pocket usually carries a 5th Avenue candy bar. (Perhaps that was too personal . . . sorry.)

Because people have become accustomed to being able to keep in touch wherever they are, they also want to be able to have access to their network, at least in their house or workplace, without the hassle of cables (which are magnets for pets that enjoy a good chew toy). This desire for convenience and the advances in wireless technology have combined to bring you the wireless network — as well as wireless coffee shops, wireless access providers, and even wireless gaming centers. (Apple's iPad is a wireless Internet marvel, with instant connectivity to any Wi-Fi–enabled Mac and full-featured e-mail and browsing that'll knock your socks off.)

Now you can be connected to your home local area network (LAN) and your shared Internet connection (which I cover in Chapter 4 of this minibook) from your balcony, lounge chair in the yard, or even your bedroom. (And yes, you can go wireless in your office too.) In this chapter, I talk about how wireless networks work, and then I give you a lot of information to help you get the right pieces to free yourself — *securely,* mind you — from the world of the wired.

Speaking the Wireless Lingo

Wireless networks aren't all that different from their wired siblings. In this chapter, I discuss some of the features and limitations of wireless networking, but you must first be familiar with a foundation of information.

Because of the technology involved in wireless networks and how things are changing rapidly in this area, you'll find yourself swimming in a sea of acronyms and other technobabble. Although you don't need to know every little detail to be able to set up your own wireless network, you should know some of these terms so that you can avoid getting stung by hackers or stuck with equipment that's on the verge of obsolescence.

Here's a quick list of terms that you'll see on your road to becoming a wireless network guru:

✦ **WLAN:** Wireless LAN. If you've read earlier chapters in this minibook, you know that a LAN is just a bunch of connected computers and other devices.

✦ **IEEE:** Institute of Electrical and Electronics Engineers. This organization approves standards that allow computers, network equipment, and just about anything else electronic to play nicely together. Sometimes IEEE helps create these standards before approving them, and sometimes it just approves standards that others have produced.

✦ **802.11:** This term refers to the part of the IEEE standards that deals with wireless networking.

Although wireless is usually generically referred to as *wireless networks* (Apple uses the term *Wi-Fi*), it's all really a wireless form of Ethernet.

✦ **Wireless access point:** WAP. This device allows wireless network devices to connect to a wired Ethernet network.

✦ **Service Set Identifier:** SSID. This text tells your computer the name of the wireless network that you want to use.

✦ **Wired Equivalency Privacy:** WEP. This encryption can be used by wireless networks to keep your wireless network more secure from snoopers and hackers.

✦ **Wi-Fi Protected Access:** Usually referred to as WPA. This security protocol is more robust and harder to crack than WEP. The latest version, WPA2, is a common security feature on today's wireless hardware.

+ **Ad Hoc mode:** In this type of wireless network, each wireless device talks directly with all other wireless devices.

Apple calls Ad Hoc mode a *computer-to-computer network*.

+ **Infrastructure mode:** All wireless devices talk to a WAP, and the WAP then talks to other wireless devices and the wired network.

As I cover the different parts of wireless networking and how to set it up, you'll find yourself using these terms over and over. Before you know it, you'll be spouting these wireless-related acronyms like a pro. (Really. I'm not kidding.)

Figuring Out the Different Flavors of Wireless Ethernet

One of the first things that you might notice when you start looking into wireless networking is the existence of different wireless standards. You should at least be aware that these standards exist: That way, you can be sure to get wireless network components that will work together because *some of the wireless standards are not compatible*. (Feel free to photocopy this list and stick it on your fridge door.)

Basic Wi-Fi: 802.11b

IEEE 802.11b has another name that you'll likely see on product advertisements, literature, or boxes in stores: *Wi-Fi*, which stands for Wireless Fidelity. (Kinda like that cutting-edge Hi-Fi stereo from the '60s and '70s, where *Hi-Fi* stands for *High Fidelity*.) Most folks proclaim Wi-Fi as only 802.11b, but Apple has adopted the term to describe *all* flavors of wireless Ethernet.

Don't be confused when you see "Wi-Fi" in the Network pane in System Preferences. To Apple, *any* wireless Ethernet — including the much faster 802.11n and 802.11ac that are standard equipment on Macs today — is Wi-Fi hardware.

802.11b was the first version of wireless Ethernet. This version of wireless runs at speeds up to 11 million bits per second, or 11 Mbps — roughly the equivalent of the original 10 Mbps wired Ethernet standard. The reason I say that it runs at speeds *up to* 11 Mbps is because the actual speed at which the data is transferred depends on things such as signal strength and quality. When the conditions are such that your signal strength or quality is decreased — an inconvenient concrete wall or a circuit breaker box between you and your AirPort Base Station — you might find that your wireless connection changes down to 5.5 Mbps, 2 Mbps, or even as slow as 1 Mbps.

802.11b has been largely supplanted in current wireless networking, and almost all the equipment you can buy today is either 802.11n or 802.11ac (both of which I cover in a moment). However, if you're working with older computers and existing 802.11b hardware, any new networking equipment you buy today should be backward-compatible with 802.11b.

Apple's original AirPort network cards and standard-issue AirPort Base Station used 802.11b. It's time for Mac owners to swell with pride yet again: Apple was the first computer company to ship 802.11b hardware. (Back then, in 1999, it was the original AirPort Base Station.) Now, of course, Apple has raised the bar with AirPort Extreme, which I discuss later in this chapter, and the AirPort Express mobile Base Station.

In theory, 802.11b network cards have the capability to communicate with other wireless Ethernet devices and WAPs that are up to 1,000 feet away. Having said that, realize that 1,000 feet is a generous estimate (and that's outdoors on a clear day with no wind blowing) — you see what I'm getting at. In reality, when you set up your wireless network, things such as walls — especially concrete walls, as in basements — and areas with lots of electrical wiring decrease the distance that you can cover. If you use a WAP, plan on no more than 150 feet between wireless computers and the WAP. However, your mileage might vary.

That 11 Mbps bandwidth is shared between all computers using it. Collisions can also occur if more than one computer tries to communicate at the same time. If you have a lot of people on your wireless network, the network will become noticeably slower because of increased collisions. Remember that the total bandwidth is shared among the computers on the wireless network. This applies not only to 802.11b but also to the 802.11a (which I cover in the nearby sidebar) and the 802.11g standards.

One last thing about 802.11b networking: It uses the 2.4 GHz frequency range. (It uses 11 different channels, but they're all around the 2.4 GHz range.) So if you're using a 2.4 GHz cordless phone or even a microwave, either device can interfere with or even shut down your wireless network. Keep this in mind when you buy your next phone or wonder why your file transfers stop when you're communing with Orville Redenbacher in the microwave.

802.11a networks

802.11a was a newer version of wireless Ethernet than 802.11b. 802.11b came out first, and 802.11a came out next. (I know what you're thinking, but it's not true: No one ran into a doorframe. The engineers just finished the 802.11b standard first.) 802.11a doesn't have a generally recognized handy nickname like *Wi-Fi*, so just call it 802.11a.

802.11a equipment isn't compatible with Wi-Fi or older 802.11b AirPort Base Stations, so don't make the mistake of buying both 802.11b and 802.11a network equipment. Instead, I strongly recommend that you follow the AirPort Extreme course charted by Apple and use the 802.11n or 802.11ac standards (which are backward-compatible with Wi-Fi). Just in case, the current AirPort Extreme Base Station and the Time Capsule wireless backup device (both of which use 802.11ac) do support 802.11a — hats off again to the folks in Cupertino!

802.11a can run at speeds up to 54 Mbps — almost *five times* faster than Wi-Fi — because 802.11a uses the 5 GHz frequency range instead of the cluttered 2.4 GHz range that Wi-Fi uses. The powers that be set aside the 5 GHz range just for wireless networking, so cordless phones and microwaves (or any other wireless devices, for that matter) can't interfere with the network. The downside to using the higher 5 GHz range, though, is that the distances that can be covered are even less than that of Wi-Fi — no more than about 60 feet to maintain the highest speeds.

Because of the incompatibilities with 802.11b and the arrival of 802.11n and 802.11ac, 802.11a equipment has all but disappeared, and you should steer clear of it with a wide berth. (Good luck finding 802.11a hardware anywhere but on eBay and craigslist.)

Let's get Extreme: 802.11g

Apple's release of the first generation of AirPort Extreme provided both the speed of 802.11a and the compatibility with Wi-Fi. That's because it used the *802.11g* standard, which operates at speeds up to 54 Mbps (as did 802.11a) but will also operate at the same frequency ranges and play nicely with existing 802.11b equipment. (Notice that we're heading in the right direction again when it comes to naming conventions. Go figure.)

Apple was once again the *first* company to offer 802.11g hardware as standard equipment. Feel free to enjoy the Superiority Dance yet again.

Naturally, there's a downside: 802.11g returned to that pesky 2.4 GHz range, so your cordless phone and microwave can also wreak the same havoc that they did with your original AirPort equipment.

The current standard: 802.11n

The 802.11n standard is currently the most popular wireless flavor. Most third-party manufacturers now offer only 802.11n wireless equipment. 802.11n is supported by the entire range of current Apple products, including the AirPort Extreme Base Station, the AirPort Express, the AirPort Extreme hardware in most of the Macintosh computer line, the iPod touch, iPad and iPhone, and the spiffy Apple TV.

802.11n offers throughput in excess of 100 Mbps — roughly equivalent to a 100 Mbps wired Ethernet connection — but don't bet your house that you'll get that kind of speed, though. (As with the other members of the 802.11 family, that's likely to be a theoretical maximum speed.)

Although no longer the fastest horse on the track, the 802.11n standard offers compatibility with virtually all current wireless networking hardware. Only 802.11ac offers a better connection . . . speaking of which . . .

Raising the bar to 802.11ac

I would be remiss if I didn't mention the latest wireless standard from IEEE: 802.11ac. (I know, I know, these engineers seem to have lost their way in Alphabet Land. Just concentrate on the good things they do.) Anyway, Apple's latest Macs, the AirPort Time Capsule, and the AirPort Extreme offer 802.11ac wireless compatibility, which is — get this — almost *three times* as fast as 802.11n! Of course, before you invest your retirement income in 802.11ac hardware, don't forget my SWD (*Standard Wireless Disclaimer*): In most real-world situations, you won't get anywhere near that maximum speed or range. At the time of this writing, 802.11ac isn't widely available, but that will change in a hurry.

The guy with the turquoise teeth

I should also mention *Bluetooth* — a strange name for a wireless standard, I admit, but it works like a charm. Bluetooth devices use 2.4 GHz as well, but they're designed only for very short distances — only about 30 feet. Bluetooth is the future for linking mobile devices (such as personal digital assistants and cellphones) and external peripherals (such as wireless keyboards and mice) to your Mac. Bluetooth is built in to all current Macs, which can turn your iMac or Mac Pro into a completely cordless machine — except for the power cord, of course. Mavericks provides built-in support for Bluetooth through the Bluetooth pane in System Preferences.

Keeping Your Wireless Network Secure

Are you worried about the security of your AirPort wireless network? You should be, bunkie. Imagine someone in the next apartment or house — or standing right in your street — intercepting and monitoring your data from your wireless network.

But before you decide to toss the idea of a wireless network, keep this in mind: Even though it is technically *possible* that someone might camp out on your doorstep to gain access to your wireless network, this possibility isn't very probable for most home networks. Even if someone tries to gain access to your wireless network and perhaps even *sniff* your network — a technon-erd term meaning to record all the data flying around a network — there isn't a whole lot someone can do with that information.

If a friend invites you for an evening of war driving, think "recreational mobile hacking." *War driving* is the act of driving through neighborhoods in a car equipped with a laptop computer and a wireless network card. The payoff? If the hacker is lucky enough to locate a house with an open wireless network, we're talking free wireless Internet access, from the comfort of his car! (Not to mention any shared files or information available on that network.) Again, keep security in mind when installing wireless hardware, and these bozos will get nothing from your network.

You might say, "But I use my credit card on the Internet to buy stuff." Sure, this is a valid concern; however, if you purchase things on the Internet with your credit card, you should already be using a secure connection provided by the website for your personal information so that the data you're sending across your wireless network is encrypted and relatively safe from thieves. (You can find more on this when I discuss Safari in detail in Book V, Chapter 5.)

"I have shared my files on my computer. Can the Bad Guys access those shared files?" Another good question, but if you read Chapter 2 of this mini-book, you know that you have to create an account for those whom you want to access your files. Unless the would-be hacker is very good at guessing usernames and passwords, your files are pretty safe, too.

This is not to say that you bear absolutely no risk of being hacked. If a legitimate user on your wireless network connects to your computer and starts transferring a file, a would-be hacker could potentially record all the traffic and then reconstruct the file that was sent from the data that was recorded. In other words, a hacker could grab that user's username and password. That's where the following encryption standards come in handy!

Book VI Chapter 3

Going Wireless

WPA and WPA2

Wi-Fi Protected Access (WPA) is A Good Thing (even if it makes for a silly-sounding acronym). It's currently the standard encryption protocol offered for home wireless networking — WPA2 standard is the latest version — and is even better at defending your wireless network. As you might expect, all of Apple's current AirPort wireless hardware supports WPA2 security, as does most of the wireless hardware you'll find on the shelf at your local Hardware Heaven electronics store. (It's still a good idea to check the specifications on the box, though, to make sure that WPA2 is supported.)

WPA2 works well as a deterrent to keep the wrong people out of your stuff. Although WPA2 isn't going to ward off the spies at the National Security Agency, it's good enough to protect home and small-business networks.

WEP

Wired Equivalency Privacy (WEP) is an old friend of mine (albeit another ridiculous acronym for another wireless security system). WEP was one of the first widely supported wireless encryption schemes, but in today's world, WEP is now outdated and pretty easy for a hacker to outwit. I strongly recommend that your network use WPA2 whenever possible.

Apple's implementation of WEP comes in two varieties: 40 bit and 128 bit. The more bits used in the encryption, the more secure (and the better) it is.

To use WEP, you need to select a WEP *key,* which is really just a code word. And speaking of keys:

+ The longer the key, the better.

+ When making a key, use something undecipherable, such as *ab8sher7234ksief87* (something with random letters and numbers as opposed to something that's easily guessed, like *mykey*).

If you're using an Ad Hoc wireless network, all the computers need to have their wireless network card configured with the same WEP key to communicate. If you're using a wireless access point to connect to the rest of the network, your computers need to use the same key that you've configured on your wireless access point.

One thing to note about WEP is that it's been *broken,* meaning that someone has figured out how to undo the encryption that WEP provides. For businesses, especially those with sensitive data, WEP isn't a good security solution.

The LEAP security standard

Lightweight Extensible Authentication Protocol (LEAP) is an encryption protocol developed by Cisco Systems for superior security in the business world. To use LEAP, you need to have a server that's set up to enable users to log in to gain permission to the wireless network. After you initially log in (*authenticate*) to your network, LEAP changes encryption keys on the fly at a time interval that you determine. You could set it so that every 15 minutes your encryption key is changed: Even if someone is in that hypothetical tent on your front lawn, he could never record enough packets to figure out your key because it changes so often.

Setting up a server so that you can use LEAP isn't something for the novice to attempt. I would encourage you to read up on LEAP only if you're very serious about airtight security on your WLAN. The Cisco website (www.cisco.com) is a good place to read about LEAP.

All current AirPort Extreme wireless network hardware and the Apple AirPort Time Capsule are compatible with the Cisco LEAP standard for higher security.

Setting Up Your Wireless Network

On to the good stuff. This section describes how to set up an Ad Hoc or infrastructure-based WLAN (wireless LAN).

In case you have any issues using AirPort or need more information about anything related to AirPort, check this page at the Apple website: www.apple.com/support/airport.

Setting up an Ad Hoc wireless network

Using an Ad Hoc network — also called a *computer-to-computer* network — is a fairly easy thing to accomplish in OS X. Plus, you're not limited to just Macs: With an Ad Hoc network, you can also swap niceties with PCs, tablets, and phones that have 802.11b/g/n/ac network hardware installed. This Ad Hoc network is great for setting up an impromptu network in a classroom, exchanging recipes and pictures at a family reunion in a park, or blowing your friend up while gaming across the aisle of a Greyhound bus at 70 mph.

Using non-Apple wireless equipment with AirPort Extreme equipment

Because of Apple's implementation of wireless standards in the AirPort Extreme product line, keep in mind some things when trying to mix Apple wireless equipment with other vendors' 802.11b, 802.11g, 802.11n or 802.11ac equipment. As you discover elsewhere in this chapter, using AirPort wireless networks can require a WEP password that corresponds to the 802.11b/g/n/ac WEP key for encryption. However, the password that you enter for AirPort networks isn't exactly the same as the WEP key for that same network.

If you're using an AirPort network card and are trying to connect to a non-Apple WAP, you need to follow a specific procedure. You can find this procedure by going to `http://search.info.apple.com` and searching on the words *802.11 Compatibility*. You'll also find helpful information at this same spot if you're using a non-Apple 802.11b/g/n/ac network card and are trying to connect to an Apple AirPort Base Station. (If you're using WPA2 encryption, no special configuration is needed. Go figure.)

You want my opinion? Because of the issues of using non-AirPort 802.11b/g/n/ac hardware with The Real Thing (AirPort/AirPort Extreme stuff), I recommend that you stick with Apple equipment if possible.

To set up an Ad Hoc network, you first have to create the computer-to-computer network on one of your Macs. This process takes advantage of the AirPort Software Base Station that's built into Mavericks.

To create a computer-to-computer network, follow these steps:

1. **Click the Wi-Fi status icon on the menu bar.**

    If you haven't set Mavericks to display your Wi-Fi status in the Finder menu bar, follow these steps:

    a. *Open the Network pane in System Preferences and choose the Wi-Fi entry in the list at the left of the pane.*

    b. *Enable the Show Wi-Fi Status in Menu Bar check box.*

    c. *Close the System Preferences window to save your changes.*

2. **Click Create Network to display the dialog that you see in Figure 3-1.**

Figure 3-1:
Creating a
computer-
to-computer
wireless
network
through
software.
Excellent.

3. **Enter a name for your network.**

4. **From the Security pop-up menu, choose 128-bit WEP to turn on WEP encryption.**

5. **Enter a password for your network and then enter it again to confirm it.**

   Although you can leave encryption disabled, I highly recommend that you turn it on and choose a password for that extra bit of security. (Just call me Security Man.) Note that the password must be an exact length, which is determined by whether you chose a 40-bit (5-character) key or a 128-bit (13-character) key.

6. **(Optional) Select a channel for the connection.**

   In general, channels 1, 6, and 11 are the only ones that don't overlap other channels — and are therefore the best choices to use. If you're close to other wireless access points (including Time Capsule devices, AirPort Base Stations, or other Ad Hoc networks), try to find a channel that's not being used; otherwise, performance can be degraded. (If you have only one access point, the channel you select doesn't matter — just allow Mavericks to select a channel, which is typically channel 11.)

7. **Click Create.**

Creating a computer-to-computer network gives the illusion of having an AirPort Base Station. So for people to join your network, they would follow the same steps as those they would use to join any other AirPort Wi-Fi network, as I cover in the next section.

Setting up wireless networks

After one computer is running a computer-to-computer network or you've set up and configured an AirPort Extreme Base Station, AirPort Express, or AirPort Time Capsule, you're ready to invite other computers with wireless hardware to the party.

Joining in an existing Wi-Fi network

After you have a network set up on one of your wireless-enabled computers, you just need to have the other wireless-enabled computers join that network. You can use the same process, as I describe here, to join any wireless network (think your local coffee shop or your hotel room on your next trip):

1. **Click the Wi-Fi status icon on the menu bar.**

   A list of existing network connections appears in the AirPort menu.

2. **Select an existing network connection that you'd like to join.**

   If you want to join a network whose name doesn't appear in the list — a *closed network* — follow these steps:

   a. *Select Join Other Network from the Wi-Fi status menu.*

   b. *Enter the name of the network that you want to join.*

   c. *If the network uses security encryption, click the Security pop-up menu, choose the proper encryption format — the administrator of the network should be able to tell you the correct format — and then type the password. If you plan on using the network in the future, make sure the Remember This Network check box is enabled.*

   d. *Click Join.*

   A closed network is another added measure of security — one that's good enough for most people because it's very unlikely that a hacker is going to try to break into a hidden network.

Disconnecting from a Wi-Fi network

To disconnect from a Wi-Fi network, you can turn off your Wi-Fi hardware, which I cover in the next section. (Simplicity, they say, is an art.) Another way is to connect to another Wi-Fi network, but this option is useful only if you *want* to connect to another network.

Turning your Wi-Fi hardware on or off

Being able to turn your Wi-Fi hardware on and off has its uses:

✦ **Freedom:** You might want to use your Mac, usually your MacBook, in a place where your wireless hardware shouldn't be used, such as in an airplane (when they tell you to turn off all cellphones) or in a hospital area that doesn't allow cellphones or other wireless devices.

✦ **Conservation:** Turning off your Wi-Fi hardware conserves your MacBook's battery life.

To turn your Wi-Fi equipment on or off using the Wi-Fi status icon on the menu bar, give it a click and then choose Turn Wi-Fi On/Off from the resulting menu.

Chapter 4: Sharing That Precious Internet Thing

In This Chapter

✔ Finding out how Internet sharing works

✔ Choosing between hardware and software Internet sharing

✔ Connecting your Macs to a cable/DSL router

✔ Adding wireless support to a shared Internet connection

Although in previous chapters I discuss lots of fun stuff that you can do with your network, my favorite networking activity is sharing a single Internet connection among *all* the computers on your network. If you have more than one computer, I'm sure that you've had to deal with the dilemma that pops up whenever more than one person wants or needs to access the Internet at the same time.

Luckily, because small home and office local area networks (LANs) use our old friend TCP/IP for network communications, connecting an entire network to the Internet isn't as troublesome a task as you might think. In this chapter, I talk about different hardware and software options for sharing your Internet connection as well as how to include your wireless devices. (Read Chapter 1 of this minibook for the lowdown on TCP/IP and LANs.)

Sharing the Internet

Sharing a single Internet connection among all your computers can be a boon simply because of the reduced chances of random acts of violence. (Internet deprivation can be an ugly thing, you know.) Although I won't claim that Internet sharing will save lives, it can indeed save you from headaches and arguments when more than one person wants to use the Internet at a time.

Throughout this chapter, I talk a lot about *cable* modems and *Asymmetric Digital Subscriber Line* (ADSL) modems. Both are high-speed and relatively inexpensive Internet connections typically offered by your local cable company and your local phone company, respectively. The phone company offers different kinds of digital subscriber line (DSL) connections, the most common of which is ADSL. However, because different kinds of DSL connections exist, in this chapter I refer to them all generically as *DSL*.

To share your Internet connection, you need a few things, so here's a brief checklist:

✦ **An Internet connection:** Typically, this connection is a cable or DSL modem connection, but older versions of the AirPort Base Station can use a dial-up Internet connection that's accessed via a standard v.90/v.92 analog telephone modem. (Note that recent models of the AirPort Extreme Base Station do not have the capability to use analog dial-up connections.)

✦ **A LAN:** You need a standard LAN (which is connected with cables) or a wireless LAN, which Apple calls a *Wi-Fi* network. (Heck, you can even have a hybrid with wired *and* wireless access.) See Chapter 1 of this minibook for more information about setting up a LAN and Chapter 3 for more on setting up a wireless LAN (WLAN).

✦ **An Internet-sharing device:** I use the word *device* because the method that you use to share your Internet connection could be through software that you run on one of your computers or stand-alone hardware, depending on how you connect to the Internet and what best fits your needs.

When you have these three things ready to go, you can share your Internet connection. However, you need to know some background information to help you choose the right components and get everything up and running.

Using Network Address Translation

You must determine one thing before you start your Internet-sharing quest: the set of network Internet Protocol (IP) addresses that you'll use. As I discuss in Chapter 1 of this minibook on setting up and configuring a LAN, I suggest a specific range of IP addresses to use. Here's a quick recap:

When talking about IP addresses, the ruling body that tracks IP addresses and where they're used has divided all IP addresses into two parts:

✦ **Public IP addresses:** *Public* IP addresses are used to communicate on the Internet, and only one device in the entire world can use a given public IP address at any given time.

✦ **Private IP addresses:** *Private* addresses, on the other hand, are supposed to be used only on networks (such as your home LAN) and do *not* connect directly to the Internet. Lots of people can use the same private address on different networks because their networks never go public; that is, they never directly access the Internet, so their IP addresses never conflict.

Only one computer can use a specific private address at one time on your network. An IP address *must* be unique, or all Hades breaks loose.

AirPort Extreme routers and Time Capsule wireless backup devices use private addresses in the form of 10.0.*x.x* by default; however, if you're using non-Apple hardware, you'll likely use addresses in the form of 192.168.*x.x* on your LAN. See Chapter 1 of this minibook for an overview of IP addresses and how they work.

Book VI Chapter 4

Sharing That Precious Internet Thing

You might be wondering to yourself thusly: "If I use private IP addresses on my LAN at home or in the office and I have to use a public IP address to communicate on the Internet, how can my private IP addresses on my LAN communicate with public IP addresses on the Internet?" That is an excellent question, and the answer is Network Address Translation (NAT).

NAT acts as a gatekeeper between your private IP addresses on your LAN and the public IP addresses on the Internet. When you connect to the Internet, your Internet service provider (ISP) gives you one — and usually *only* one — public IP address that can be used on the Internet. Instead of one of your computers using that public IP address and depriving all the other computers on the LAN, the hardware or software that you use to share the Internet will take control of that public IP address. Then, when any computer on your LAN tries to communicate on the Internet, your NAT software/ hardware intercepts your communications and readdresses the traffic so that it appears to be coming from your allotted public IP address. (Think of a funnel that collects water from several different sources and then directs all the water into a single stream.)

When the website, File Transfer Protocol (FTP) server, or whatever strange Internet intelligence you're using on the Internet replies, it replies to your NAT device. The NAT device remembers which private IP address it should go to on the LAN and sends the information to that computer. See NAT at work in Figure 4-1.

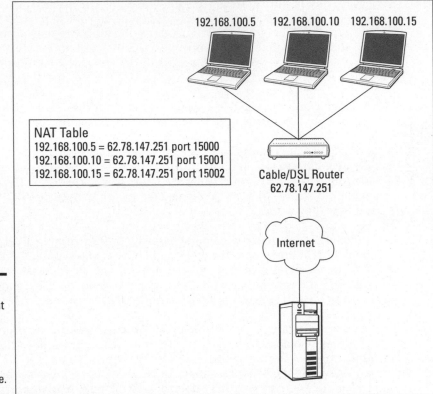

192.168.100.5   192.168.100.10   192.168.100.15

NAT Table
192.168.100.5 = 62.78.147.251 port 15000
192.168.100.10 = 62.78.147.251 port 15001
192.168.100.15 = 62.78.147.251 port 15002

Cable/DSL Router
62.78.147.251

Internet

Figure 4-1:
NAT hard at
work —
for the
betterment
of Macs
everywhere.

Ways to Share Your Internet Connection

After you have an Internet connection and your LAN is set up, you need
something to make this NAT thing work. You have two options to take care
of NAT for your shared Internet connection: hardware or software. (Go
figure.) Each has pros and cons, so take a look at each option individually.

If you read Chapter 3 of this minibook, you know that Mavericks has Wi-Fi
software built in. So, if you have an AirPort Extreme wireless network card
in your Mac and you're using Mavericks, you can have your Mac act like an
AirPort Extreme Base Station for all the wireless computers on your network, which in turn can use a software NAT.

Using hardware for sharing an Internet connection

Probably the most popular way to share an Internet connection is to buy a
hardware device that connects to your Internet connection, which then

connects to your LAN. These devices are referred to as *cable/DSL routers*. The main downside to a hardware Internet connection-sharing device is that it costs more than a software solution.

Cable/DSL routers are nice because they're easy to set up and configure. You can also leave them on, which means constant Internet access for those on your LAN. You don't have to worry about turning on another computer to connect to the Internet as you do with a software solution. Sounds like a good spot for a Mark's Maxim:

Hardware routers are the best choice for sharing your Internet connection, so you should get one if you can afford it!

Apple's AirPort Extreme Base Station and Time Capsule backup device are both *wireless access points* (WAPs) for your network, as I discuss in Chapter 3 of this minibook. They also act as Internet connection-sharing devices. (AirPort Express can't share an Internet connection, though. Sorry.) Some older flavors of AirPort Base Station even have a built-in v.90 modem for sharing a single 56 Kbps connection using a dial-up account! A base station typically has several Ethernet connections for sharing a high-speed Internet connection, including a dedicated port to connect to a cable/DSL router and two or four ports to connect to other computers on the LAN. Along with acting as a wireless access point, Apple's Time Capsule also includes a built-in hard drive, allowing it to back up data from your Mac wirelessly.

If you think that a cable/DSL router, a Time Capsule device, or an AirPort Extreme Base Station could be the karmic pathway for you to achieve your goal of sharing your Internet connection, here are some things to consider when deciding which device to buy for your LAN:

✦ **Do you need a switch?** Most cable/DSL routers have a small 3-, 4-, or 5-port switch built in. See Chapter 1 of this minibook to discover more about switches. This multiport capability is nice because the same cable/DSL router that shares your Internet connection is also the centerpiece of your LAN where all your connections meet, thus saving you from having to buy a switch on top of the cost of the cable/DSL router.

Some cable/DSL routers, however, have only a single Ethernet connection to connect to your LAN. So keep in mind that if you choose a device with a single LAN connection, you must supply your own switch that would then connect the cable/DSL router to the rest of your LAN.

✦ **Got modem?** If your only Internet connection is through a dial-up modem account, look for a built-in analog telephone modem on your cable/DSL router. You must have this feature if you want to use a hardware device to share your Internet connection. (Again, older versions of the AirPort Base Station are great for this because the modem is built in, but you'll have to do some shopping on eBay or craigslist, and these older AirPort Base Stations aren't guaranteed to work with OS X Mavericks.) Even if you have cable/DSL service, some ISPs also include a dial-up account with your broadband access. With such a bountiful selection of connections, you can plug in your cable or DSL service to the cable/DSL router as well as use the dial-up account as a backup in case your main service has problems.

✦ **Want a printer with that?** Some cable/DSL routers also have a port for connecting a printer — a great feature because it allows you to leave the printer connected and turned on so that anyone on the network can print to it at any time. (This is much better than connecting the printer to a computer and sharing it because then the computer doing the sharing must be always on to make the printer available.) OS X can send a print job to a printer by using Bonjour or TCP/IP, so just make sure that your printer is compatible with TCP/IP printing, also called *LPR* (Line Printer Remote).

Using software for sharing an Internet connection

As I mention earlier, if you're using OS X Mavericks, your Mac can act like an AirPort or AirPort Extreme Base Station, providing both wireless Ethernet connectivity for other computers on the LAN *and* a shared Internet connection.

Mavericks also has built-in software that allows a single computer on your network to share its Internet connection with others on the LAN. To share your Internet connection, follow these quick steps:

1. **Click the System Preferences icon on the Dock.**

2. **Click the Sharing icon.**

3. **Click the Internet Sharing entry in the list on the left side of the pane.**

The settings shown in Figure 4-2 appear.

Figure 4-2: Turning on Internet sharing with Mavericks.

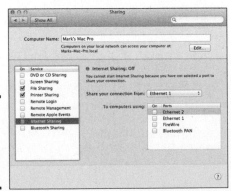

4. **Click the Share Your Connection From pop-up menu and choose Ethernet.**

   If you're using an older Mac Pro, don't be surprised to see Ethernet 1 and Ethernet 2 listed — your Mac has support for *two* Ethernet ports built in! Choose Ethernet 1 from the pop-up menu, and make certain that your Ethernet connection to the Internet is plugged in to Ethernet port 1.

5. **Select the Ethernet check box (in the To Computers Using list) to enable it.**

   When you do, you're issued a warning that enabling this could affect your ISP or violate your agreement with your ISP. In my experiences, this step has never caused any networking problems. However, if you have any doubts, contact your ISP and verify this.

6. **Click OK in the warning dialog to continue.**

   You go back to the Sharing dialog, where you'll notice that the Internet Sharing check box (in the list at the left) is conveniently ready for you to select it — feel free to click it now.

If you're using a dial-up modem to access the Internet, you need to also make sure that the computer that has the modem also has an Ethernet or wireless LAN connection. Unfortunately, no Mac that can run Mavericks has a built-in modem, but if you buy a Mavericks-compatible external USB modem, you can still use this feature.

If you're using a cable or DSL modem for your Internet connection, the Mac that you want to run the sharing software on should have two Ethernet connections: one to connect to the cable/DSL modem and one to connect to the rest of the LAN.

The main disadvantage to using a software solution for Internet connection sharing is that the computer that connects to the Internet must be turned on and ready to go all the time so that others on the network can get to the Internet. And although the sharing software operates in the background on the machine it's running on, it still chews up some of that Mac's processing power and memory, so it could slow down other applications that you're running on that computer.

Connecting Everything for Wired Sharing

After you decide whether to use a software or hardware solution, it's time to get your hands dirty: All the pieces of the puzzle must be set up and connected. In this section, I tell you how to connect things for the software and hardware methods of sharing the Internet connection.

Using the software method

When you use the software method to share your Internet connection, one of the computers on your network has both the connection to the Internet and a connection to the LAN. Figure 4-3 shows a typical setup for software Internet sharing, whether you're using a dial-up modem account or a cable/DSL modem for your Internet connection.

Keep in mind, though, that when using a cable/DSL modem for your Internet connection, the computer running the sharing software *must* have two Ethernet connections.

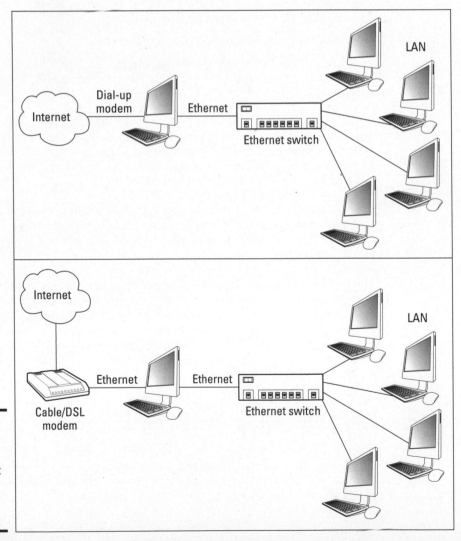

Figure 4-3: Two configurations for Internet sharing through software.

Using the hardware method

Not only does using a dedicated piece of hardware free one of the Macs on your network from the onerous job of hosting the shared connection, but it also keeps you from having to have more than one Ethernet connection on a single computer if you're using a cable/DSL modem for your Internet access. Figure 4-4 shows how you would connect your devices for hardware Internet sharing by using a cable/DSL router with either a built-in Ethernet switch or a stand-alone Ethernet switch.

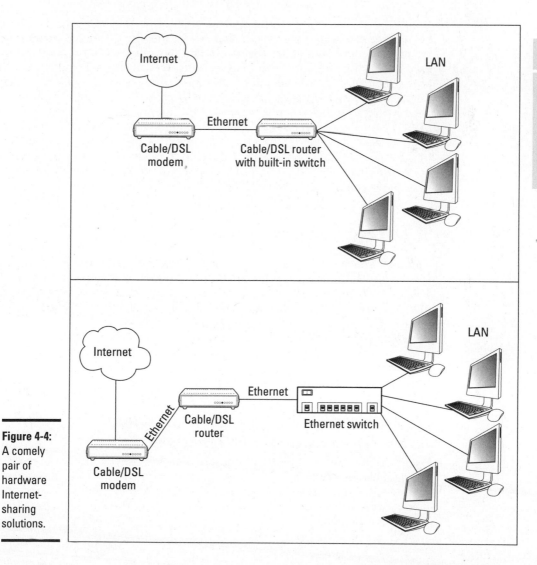

Figure 4-4: A comely pair of hardware Internet-sharing solutions.

If you choose to buy a cable/DSL router with a built-in Ethernet switch, you can simply connect all your computers on the LAN to the built-in switch. However, if you buy a cable/DSL router with only a single LAN connection — like older versions of the AirPort Base Station — you must connect that single LAN connection to an external switch to get all the computers on the same network.

We're talking wired Ethernet here. Of course, wireless connections don't require a port on your router or base station. (More on this in the next section.)

Regardless of whether you use the hardware or software method to share your Internet connection, all the computers on your LAN — except the one that's doing the sharing, if you're using software sharing — should be configured to obtain its IP address automatically through our old friend, Dynamic Host Configuration Protocol (DHCP). (See Chapter 1 of this minibook for details on how to do this in Mavericks.) Setting up your other devices with DHCP is not a requirement but is recommended unless you understand the IP addressing scheme required by your cable/DSL router and you're willing to set up the addresses manually. You need to follow the instructions that come with the cable/DSL router or software that you purchase for detailed information on how to configure that.

Adding Wireless Support

You might have noticed that I mention *wireless* here and there in this chapter. This section covers in a bit more detail how you can add wireless capabilities to your shared Internet party. To discover more about how wireless networks work and how to set up one, see Chapter 3 of this minibook.

Basically, you can encounter a couple of situations when trying to add wireless capabilities into the mix. Either you already have an Internet connection-sharing mechanism in place (either hardware or software), or you don't yet have your Internet connection shared.

If you already have a cable/DSL router or are using software Internet sharing

If you already have a cable/DSL router or if you're using software Internet sharing, like that built into Mavericks, you can simply buy a wireless access point (WAP) and connect it to your LAN. Adding a WAP enables anyone using wireless Ethernet access to your network and thus to your shared Internet connection.

There are many WAPs that you can buy to add wireless to your network. AirPort Extreme is a good example; however, because AirPort Extreme also can do Internet sharing, make sure that you *don't* enable Internet sharing through software on your Mac! (In this case, you don't want or need this feature because it can conflict with your cable/DSL router operation.)

If you do not have a hardware-sharing device

If you don't have a cable/DSL router, a Time Capsule device, or an AirPort Extreme Base Station for Internet sharing, you have a few options. Each option has an upside and a downside.

One option is to get either an AirPort Extreme Base Station or a Time Capsule, either of which will provide both wireless access for computers with Wi-Fi hardware and Internet sharing for the entire network. Because both the AirPort Extreme Base Station and the Time Capsule also feature three built-in Ethernet ports for wired connections, you can connect up to three Macs (or PCs, or printers, or even network file servers) using Ethernet cables without buying an additional switch. The other option is to buy a combination cable/DSL router, which has a built-in WAP. Most cable/DSL routers — including the ones that have wireless built in — also have multiple Ethernet ports on them, so connecting computers by using wired Ethernet can be done without buying an external switch.

The final option is that you can use the AirPort software built into Mavericks to turn your Mac into an AirPort or AirPort Extreme Base Station, as I discuss earlier. This is a great, low-cost way to add wireless and Internet sharing to your network, but remember that the software will still eat up processor time and memory, and your Mac must remain turned on to supply the connection to your network. For more on wireless networking, read Chapter 3 of this minibook.

Book VII
Expanding Your System

Contents at a Glance

Chapter 1: Hardware That Will Make You Giddy

In This Chapter

- Using digital cameras, digital video camcorders, and scanners
- Adding keyboards, trackballs, joysticks, and drawing tablets
- Using optical recorders
- Adding speakers, subwoofers, and an iPod

Hardware. We love it. To a Mac power user, new hardware holds all the promise of Christmas morning, whether your new toys are used for business or for pleasure. We pore over magazines and visit our favorite Mac websites like clockwork to check on new technology.

These hardware devices don't come cheap, however, forcing you to make the painful decision regarding which new hardware you really need to accomplish what you want and which hardware is a luxury. Also, if you're a new Mac owner, you might not know what's available. For example, I constantly get e-mail from readers, asking, "What can I connect to my new computer?" I guess I could reply, "Why, the kitchen sink!" To that end, I decided to add this chapter to the book to let you know how you can expand the hardware for your OS X Mavericks powerhouse.

Each section in this chapter provides a description of what a particular device does, an idea of how much it costs, and a set of guidelines that you can use when shopping. Although the coverage isn't in-depth — after all, this book is supposed to be about Mavericks — it will serve to get you started if you've just become a Mac owner. And for those interested in a specific piece of hardware, I recommend other books that you can read for the exhaustive details.

Ready? To quote a great line from the 1989 *Batman* film: "Alfred, let's go shopping!"

Parading Pixels: Digital Cameras, DV Camcorders, and Scanners

The first category of hardware toys revolves around images — hardware for creating original images, capturing images in real time, and reading images from hard copy.

Digital cameras

A digital camera shares most of the characteristics of a traditional film camera. It looks the same, and you use the same techniques while shooting photographs. The difference is in the result. With a digital camera, instead of a roll of film that has to be developed, you have an image in JPEG, RAW, or TIFF format stored in the camera's built-in memory or on a removable memory media. You can download the contents of the memory card to your Mac via iPhoto (which I discuss with great pleasure in Book III, Chapter 3) — and then the real fun begins. Here are some things that you can do with a digital photograph:

✦ Edit it with an image editor such as iPhoto or Adobe Photoshop Elements (or their more professional-level brethren, Aperture and Photoshop).

✦ Print it.

✦ Record it to a CD or DVD (if your Mac has an internal or external optical drive).

✦ Add it to a web page.

✦ Upload it to a social website such as Facebook or Flickr.

✦ Print several of them in a coffee-table book (using iPhoto or Photoshop Elements).

✦ Mail it to friends and family.

What they cost

Consumer-level digital cameras typically sell for anywhere from around $100 (for a 10-megapixel [MP] model) to less than $300 (for a 14MP point-and-shoot camera). *Megapixel* is a general reference to the *resolution* (the size of the image, measured in individual dots called *pixels*) and detail delivered by the camera. This class of digital camera can produce photographs well suited for just about any casual shutterbug.

Professional digital cameras — a digital SLR, for example — capture far more detail, sport more advanced features, and offer designs that resemble the best SLR film camera. These puppies can set you back $600–$1,000. Because of their cost and complexity, I wouldn't recommend them to someone who's just discovered digital photography.

What to look for

Here are some general guidelines that I recommend when selecting a digital camera:

✦ **At least 10MP:** As a general rule, the higher the megapixel value, the better the camera.

✦ **A built-in lithium-ion (Li-ion) battery:** Why spend money on batteries when you can charge your camera, as you do your iPhone and iPad?

✦ **At least a 4GB internal memory card:** The memory card stores your images — and the more memory, the more images!

✦ **Waterproof body or case:** For those with an active lifestyle who spend plenty of time by the water (or under it).

✦ **A Universal Serial Bus (USB) connection to your Macintosh:** I cover USB in all its glory in Chapter 3 of this minibook.

✦ **A burst mode feature:** A digital camera with burst mode can take a number of consecutive images quickly, without the shutter lag that other cameras experience.

✦ **An optical zoom feature:** *Optical zoom* allows you to draw closer to subjects that are farther away.

Eschew digital zoom. Essentially, *digital zoom* is a silly feature that simply resizes a portion of your image, providing a blocky close-up. An image editor such as Photoshop Elements can produce the same result as a camera with digital zoom . . . and it looks almost as bad. Only an optical zoom truly results in a sharper magnification of the subject.

✦ **A self-timer:** With a self-timer, your camera can snap a photo automatically, allowing you to finally be seen in your own pictures!

✦ **A manual flash setting:** Although automatic flash is a good thing most of the time, a manual setting allows you to disable your camera's flash for artistic shots (or just to prevent red-eye or the glare on subjects with polished surfaces).

DV camcorders

Like digital cameras, digital video (DV) camcorders are the counterpart to the familiar video camcorder. A DV camcorder looks and operates like a smaller version of an analog camcorder, but you can connect it to your Macintosh via a FireWire or USB cable and download your video clips directly into iMovie. Today's crop of DV camcorders can also record in High

**Book VII
Chapter 1**

Hardware That Will
Make You Giddy

Definition (HD for short) for your widescreen TV or monitor. (Chapter 4 of Book III explains all about iMovie, and both FireWire and USB connections are tackled in Chapter 3 of this minibook.)

Digital video offers higher quality as well as a number of other real advantages over analog video:

✦ Edit DV with applications, such as iMovie or Final Cut Pro X.

✦ Record DV to a DVD (using applications such as Toast Titanium and Adobe Premiere Elements).

✦ Copy DV endlessly with no loss of quality.

✦ Post DV for downloading on a web page.

What they cost

The least expensive DV camcorders start at about $50. You'll find camcorders that record in HD for less than $100.

What to look for

I recommend the following when shopping for a DV camcorder:

✦ **The highest optical zoom in your price range:** Again, as with a digital camera, a good zoom can help you capture subjects and action when you can't get any closer — think the bear exhibit at the zoo, or those school plays.

✦ **Image stabilization:** This feature helps steady the picture when you're holding the camcorder without a tripod.

✦ **Onboard effects:** These effects generally include some snazzy things such as black-and-white footage, fades, and wipes.

✦ **AV connectors:** Display your video by connecting the camcorder directly to your TV.

✦ **Digital still mode:** This feature is handy when you want to take still photographs when your digital camera isn't handy. *Note:* The image quality isn't as good as from a bona fide digital camera.

For a closer look at digital video, iMovie, and iDVD, check out *iLife '11 For Dummies* by Tony Bove (Wiley).

Scanners

Figure 1-1 illustrates a typical flatbed scanner, which is the tool of choice when digitizing images and text from printed materials. Flatbed models are much more versatile and produce better-quality scans than sheet-fed models (the upright ones that look like a fax machine).

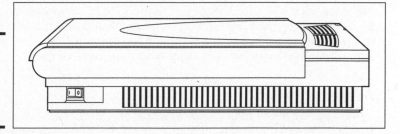

Figure 1-1:
The flatbed scanner, King of Digitizing.

Like a digital camera, a scanner produces digital images that can be edited, e-mailed, displayed on the web, or added to your own documents.

What they cost

A good-quality scanner can cost anywhere from $50–$200. The best models — featuring the fastest scanning speeds, best color depth, and highest resolutions, or those meant for scanning film negatives — go for around $400. Many multifunction printers can also perform good-quality scanning.

What to look for

Try to get the following features in a scanner:

+ **The highest color depth that you can afford:** Get a minimum of 48 bits.

+ **The highest resolution that you can afford:** Get a minimum of 2400 dots per inch (dpi) (optical).

+ **Single-pass scanning:** This feature results in a faster scan with less chance of error.

+ **Transparency adapter for scanning film negatives:** If you're a traditional film photographer, you'll find that a transparency adapter turns a standard flatbed scanner into an acceptable negative scanner.

+ **One-touch buttons for e-mailing your scanned images or uploading them to the web:** With these controls of convenience, one button press automatically scans the item and prepares the image to be e-mailed or uploaded to a website.

+ **USB 3.0:** I cover the advantages of this faster version of USB in Chapter 3 of this minibook.

Incredible Input: Keyboards, Trackballs, Joysticks, and Drawing Tablets

Although your Mac probably came equipped with a keyboard and a Magic Mouse or Magic Trackpad, you can replace them with enhanced hardware that will add functionality and precision to your work. (Or you can buy a joystick and spend your days wreaking havoc on your enemies.)

Keyboards

If you're using a Mac mini (which requires an external keyboard) or a MacBook laptop and you want to add an external keyboard — you can take advantage of the convenience of a USB keyboard. My favorite Mac USB keyboard appears in Figure 1-2: It's the Tactile Pro keyboard from Matias Corporation (www.matias.ca), which uses mechanical key switches for speed, durability, and that awesome tactile feedback! If you remember the typing speeds possible on older models of Apple keyboards, adding this keyboard to your system is like renewing an old friendship. The Tactile Pro also offers dedicated function keys for OS X, as well as a built-in 3-port USB hub.

Figure 1-2: An ergonomic upgrade — the USB Tactile Pro keyboard from Matias.

What they cost

Aftermarket (nonstandard-issue) keyboards generally cost anywhere from $30–$150.

What to look for

Look for the following keyboard features when shopping for a keyboard:

+ **Programmable buttons:** Configure these buttons to launch applications or run macros.

+ **Additional USB ports:** Use these ports to turn your keyboard into a USB hub. The best keyboards offer powered USB hubs, where you can connect devices that draw their power from the USB port (and therefore don't require a separate power supply).

+ **One-touch buttons to launch your browser or e-mail application:** Press one of these buttons to launch your web browser or Mail.

+ **Ergonomic wrist pad:** Use this accessory to help prevent wrist strain and repetitive joint injuries.

Trackballs

Some folks prefer using a trackball, like the one shown in Figure 1-3, over a mouse . . . even the Magic Mouse now included with Mac desktops. Graphic artists find that trackballs are more precise and offer better control.

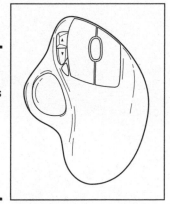

Figure 1-3: Many Mac power users (myself included) favor a trackball over a mouse.

What they cost

Trackballs range in price from $20–$90. Most are optical (see the following section), so they need little cleaning, and they'll last for many years of precise pointing at things.

What to look for

Look for the following features when shopping for a trackball:

+ **More programmable buttons:** Opt for at least two buttons, of course, but the more the merrier! Most include a secondary button to display right-click menus. (One model on the market has eight buttons. Who needs a keyboard?)

+ **Optical tracking:** An *optical* trackball — one that uses a photo-sensitive sensor instead of rollers to record the movement of the ball — is more precise and easier to keep clean.

+ **A scroll wheel:** Use this gizmo to scroll documents up and down.

+ **Ergonomic design:** Look for a wrist pad or slanted buttons.

Joysticks and steering wheels

Game players, unite! For arcade and sports games, using a joystick results in increased maneuverability, more realistic action, higher scores, less wear and tear on your keyboard . . . and just plain more fun. Joysticks range from the traditional USB aircraft controller, as shown in Figure 1-4, to USB arcade controllers, steering wheels, and gamepads that rival anything offered on today's console game machines.

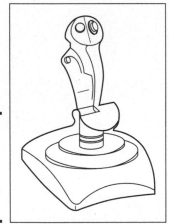

Figure 1-4:
The secret weapon of Mac gaming — a joystick.

What they cost

Joysticks vary in price from $30–$120. At the low end, you'll usually find the gamepad-type controllers, whereas aircraft controllers carry the highest price tag.

What to look for

Get the following features in a joystick:

+ **Yet even more programmable buttons.**

+ **Pitch and yaw controls.** These controls are for the flight simulator crowd.

+ **Force feedback.** A *force feedback* joystick or gamepad rumbles and moves in tandem with the action in the game, providing an extra feeling of realism.

Drawing tablets

A drawing tablet (see Figure 1-5) might be pricey, but if you're a graphic artist or a designer, using a tablet will revolutionize the way that you work with your Mac. Rather than use a mouse or trackball to sketch, you can draw on the tablet freehand, just as you would draw on paper or canvas. Tablets can recognize different levels of pressure, allowing applications such as Photoshop and Painter to re-create all sorts of photo-realistic brush effects. Most drawing tablets will also allow you to use Ink (the handwriting recognition feature built into Mavericks, which I discuss in Book VIII, Chapter 3).

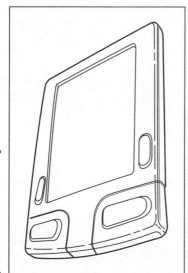

Figure 1-5:
Professional artists and designers swear by the graphics tablet.

What they cost

Depending on the size of the tablet and the pressure levels that you need, you'll pay anywhere from just under $100 to a whopping $1000.

What to look for

I recommend the following tablet features:

+ **Programmable buttons:** See a trend here?

+ **Accessory mouse:** Some high-end tablets include a mouse that you can use along with the tablet.

+ **A cordless stylus:** Make sure that it doesn't require batteries.

+ **The highest number of pressure levels possible:** The more levels that the tablet offers, the more subtle and precise your control over painting effects.

Sublime Storage Devices: DVD/Blu-Ray and Flash Drives

Ready to talk storage? Consider using a rewriteable DVD-RW drive, which can store 4.7GB on a single disc, or dual-layer drives, which can store 8.5GB! (And don't even get me started on the latest generation of optical technology — the Blu-ray recorders — which can store 50GB on a single disc!)

If you're using a Mac without an internal optical drive (or you want the latest Blu-ray storage capacity, or the capability to burn or read odd-sized media), you can always add an external model.

If you're stuck in 1985 (did a flock of seagulls just fly over?) and like to store and trade data on unreliable floppy disks, sure — you *can* pick up an external USB floppy drive for about $50. However, I eschew floppy disks, which are unreliable and carry a mere 1.44MB of data. Pick up a USB flash drive instead.

What they cost

A USB 3.0 DVD-RW drive averages about $100, and a typical 64GB USB 2.0 flash drive costs about $30.

What to look for

Get the following features in an external DVD recorder:

✦ **An internal buffer of at least 8MB:** The larger the buffer, the less chance that you'll encounter recording errors and the faster your drive will burn.

✦ **At least 16X DVD recording speed:** A no-brainer here. The faster the recording speed, the less time you'll wait for the finished disc.

✦ **AC power through the USB or FireWire cable:** This capability eliminates the need for a separate AC power supply.

✦ **Thunderbolt, USB 3.0, or FireWire 800 speed:** If your Mac offers one of these ports (which are all faster than USB 2.0 or FireWire 400), make sure your recorder can use that port.

✦ **Burn-proof technology:** This feature virtually eliminates recording errors due to multitasking, so that you can continue to work on other applications while you record.

For a USB flash drive, look for these features while shopping:

✦ **A minimum capacity of at least 16MB:** Naturally, the higher the capacity the better, but costs tend to get pretty steep when you reach 128GB of storage (or more).

✦ **USB 3.0 if you need it:** If your Mac sports USB 3.0 ports, don't settle for USB 2.0 speeds.

Awesome Audio: Subwoofer Systems and MP3 Hardware

Although virtually all Macs ship with speakers, I'll be honest: the stock speakers don't measure up to the standards of a true audiophile. Those who enjoy their music and their game audio will want to read this last section, which covers the world of Macintosh aftermarket sonic enjoyment.

Subwoofer speaker systems

You want a subwoofer, which simply plugs in to a handy USB port. In case you've never heard a subwoofer — think chest-rattling *thump, thump, thump* — you should know that they provide the basement-level bass that can add power and punch to both your music and your games. Being hit by an asteroid is a flat, tinny experience with a pair of battery-powered speakers that you salvaged from your Walkman years ago. With a new set of speakers and a subwoofer, you'll swear that Han Solo is sitting in the cockpit chair next to you!

With the growing importance of the computer as a replacement for your home entertainment center, investing in a more powerful set of speakers will help you enjoy all those audio CDs and MP3s that you've added to your iTunes playlists. (Read all about iTunes in Book III, Chapter 2.)

What they cost

Most USB-powered speakers with a subwoofer are priced less than $100, but true audiophiles looking for surround sound can spring for a better $300 system that includes five satellite speakers and a subwoofer.

What to look for

Get these features in a subwoofer:

+ **At least 30 watts of power:** The higher the wattage rating, the more powerful the speakers (and the louder your music can be).

+ **Additional headphone jacks and stereo mini-plug input jacks:** Use these jacks for connecting your iPod or MP3 player directly to your speaker system. (Read all about iPods in the next section.)

+ **Magnetic shielding:** This feature helps prevent your speakers from distorting your monitor display.

MP3 players (well, actually, just the iPod)

I've lusted after Apple's iPod MP3 player ever since it arrived on campus. Depending on which model you get, this incredible device can hold up to 160GB of digital audio — that's 40,000 songs — as well as digital photographs and full-length movies! Plus, the iPod also acts as your personal data butler by carrying your files; it's an honest-to-goodness, external USB 2.0 hard drive. You can download your contacts and appointments from OS X and view them wherever you go. Just think: Carry your files to and from your office *and* carry DEVO and the Dead Kennedys *and* watch a movie you downloaded as well! Oh, and did I mention that you can play games and use all sorts of applications with the iPod touch model?

All this fits into a beautiful, stylish package about the size of a cellphone, with up to a 36-hour lithium rechargeable battery, high-quality earbud headphones, and automatic synchronization with your iTunes music library. (The iPod shuffle is the smallest member of the iPod family — it's just a little over an inch square.) Life just doesn't get any better for a technoid like me. If you think that your Mac is a well-designed piece of equipment, you'll understand why this little box is so alluring. (And why I have one now.)

Sure, other MP3 players are out there, but many of them share the following problems:

✦ They use digital memory cards, which offer far less capacity than the iPod Classic's built-in hard drive.

✦ They use standard batteries, or you have to furnish rechargeable batteries (which certainly don't last 36 hours).

✦ They don't operate as an external hard drive, photo slideshow repository, game machine, movie theater, or contacts/appointment database.

I say, forget 'em. The iPod is worth every penny.

The 2GB iPod shuffle runs about $50 at the time of this writing, the 16GB iPod nano runs $149, and the 160GB iPod Classic model costs $249. Finally, you can opt for the svelte and sexy iPod touch, which runs $299 for the 32GB model.

Chapter 2: Add RAM, Hard Drive Space, and Stir

In This Chapter

✔ **Understanding the advantages of extra RAM**

✔ **Shopping for a RAM upgrade**

✔ **Choosing between internal and external hard drives**

✔ **Determining your hard drive needs**

✔ **Shopping for a new hard drive**

✔ **Installing your upgrades**

M̲ost Macintosh owners will make two upgrades — adding more memory (RAM) and adding additional hard drive space — during the lifetime of their computers. These two improvements have the greatest effect on the overall performance of OS X. By adding RAM and additional hard drive space, not only do you make more elbow room for your applications and documents, but everything runs faster: Think of the Six Million Dollar Man, only a heck of a lot cheaper to operate (and no strange noises accompanying your every move).

In this chapter — meant for those of you who aren't well versed in selecting memory modules or weighing the advantages of different types of hard drives — I steer you around the hidden potholes along the way. However, if you buy the wrong piece of hardware, remember that using a hammer to make it fit is *not* a workable option.

Adding Memory: Reasons for More RAM

Of all the possible upgrades that you can make to your Macintosh, adding more random access memory (RAM) is the single most cost-effective method of improving the performance of OS X. (Your machine will likely run faster with more memory than a reasonably faster processor!) OS X uses available RAM for the following:

✦ **Applications:** Naturally, OS X needs system RAM to run the applications that you launch. The more memory in your machine, the larger the applications that you can open and the faster they'll run.

✦ **Overhead:** This category includes the operating system (OS) itself, as well as various and sundry buffers and memory areas devoted for temporary work. As you would guess, the more memory here, the merrier.

"But Mark, what happens if my Mac runs out of system memory?" A-ha! Great question, and the answer is *virtual memory* — something that I mention lightly and politely in Book I, but hasn't really amounted to a hill of beans until this moment. (Can you tell I'm a big fan of Bing Crosby?) Virtual memory allows OS X to use empty hard drive space as temporary system memory, as shown in Figure 2-1. Data is written to your hard drive instead of being stored in RAM, and then is erased when it's no longer needed. This neat trick is also used by Windows and Linux. Virtual memory works automatically in OS X.

Figure 2-1: The mysterious beauty of virtual memory — but it still doesn't beat real RAM!

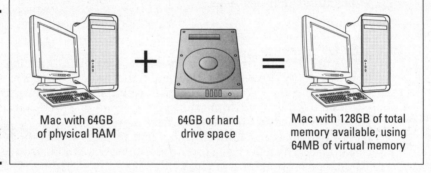

Mac with 64GB of physical RAM

64GB of hard drive space

Mac with 128GB of total memory available, using 64MB of virtual memory

At first, virtual memory sounds like absolute bliss, and it does indeed allow your Macintosh to do things that would otherwise be impossible, such as running an application that requires 4GB of RAM in just 2GB of physical RAM. However, here come the caveats:

✦ **Virtual memory is as slow as molasses in December.** Today's fastest magnetic hard drive is many, *many* times slower than RAM (and even solid-state hard drives, which use memory chips as well, are still much slower than your Mac's system RAM), so any use of virtual memory instead of RAM slows down OS X significantly.

✦ **Virtual memory abuses your hard drive.** If you've ever run Photoshop on a Windows PC with 2GB of RAM, you're having flashbacks right now. Whenever your Macintosh is using virtual memory, your hard drive remains almost constantly active. (Hardware types, myself included, call this phenomenon *thrashing* because we know what's happening inside that poor hard drive.) Over time, running any computer with insufficient RAM and behemoth applications will result in a significant increase in hard drive wear and tear.

✦ **Virtual memory costs you processing power.** With sufficient RAM, OS X gleefully runs as efficiently as it can. When virtual memory kicks in, however, your Mac has to spend part of its quality time shuttling data to and from the hard drive, which robs your computer of processing power.

The moral of the story is very simple, so it's time for another of Mark's Maxims:

The less OS X needs to use virtual memory, the better.

To put it another way, *physical memory* (meaning memory modules) is always a better choice than virtual memory. This is why power users and techno-types crave as much system memory as possible — and why my Mac Pro boasts 12GB of RAM. (Someday I hope to win the lottery and add more!)

About ten years ago, 256MB of RAM was a quite comfortable figure for most folks. All current Macs can use at least a whopping 4GB (that's short for *gigabyte,* or 1,024 megabytes) of system RAM. (At the extreme end of the scale, the King Kahuna — Apple's latest Mac Pro — can now accommodate an unbelievable minimum of *64GB* of RAM!) The MacBook Pro Retina and MacBook Air come from Apple preconfigured with RAM, and they are sealed units (so the RAM can't be expanded).

If you'll be keeping your Macintosh for a few years, order it with as much memory as you can afford (or install more later) — you'll thank me every time OS X Mavericks boots.

Shopping for a RAM Upgrade

Before you click some online computer store's Buy button, you need to determine two things that will help you determine which memory module to buy: how much RAM you already have and how much more your system can handle.

Finding out the current memory in your Mac

Memory modules are made in standard sizes, so you need to determine how much memory you already have and which of your memory slots are filled.

To do this, click the Apple menu (🍎) and choose About This Mac. In the dialog that appears, click the More Info button, and then click the Memory toolbar button.

Here you can see exactly how many memory modules you have, what type they are, and how much memory each provides. For example, in Figure 2-2, my Mac Pro has eight memory slots, each of which uses an 800 MHz DDR2 module. Four of those slots are filled with a 1GB module each, and the other four slots are filled with a 2GB module each, giving me a total physical memory of 12,288MB, or 12GB. Jot down the name and contents of each slot on a piece of paper — or, if you're a real OS X power user, add a Sticky to your Desktop with this information. (Stickies are covered in Book II, Chapter 2.)

Figure 2-2: Look under the hood with Apple's About This Mac dialog.

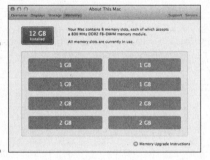

Click the Memory Upgrade Instructions link at the bottom of the dialog, and OS X Mavericks automatically opens a Safari browser window with online instructions on how to upgrade the RAM in your specific Mac model. If you're confident about your technical skills, you can use this documentation as a guide to removing and installing memory modules. (Because I can't cover the process for every Mac model, I highly recommend that you review these instructions closely!)

Unfortunately, on some machines, only one memory module can be upgraded by a mere mortal — and as I mention earlier, the memory in the MacBook Air and Retina MacBook Pro laptops can't be upgraded at all.

Potentially confusing? You bet. This arrangement differs on just about every model of Macintosh ever made: Some have more memory slots, and others allow you to upgrade all the system memory instead of just one module. The only way to determine which modules are accessible on your Mac is to identify the exact model of your computer.

Determining the exact model of your computer

Most folks know the type and model of their computers, but there's a catch here, too: Sometimes the memory that you need varies by the processor in your Macintosh. For instance, many different versions of iMacs have been made since the Bondi Blue Beast debuted, and over the course of those years, Apple has made a slew of changes inside. Your eye should be on the actual processor speed and *bus speed* — the transfer speed that data reaches whilst speeding across your motherboard — because they're the identifying factors here. An older iMac with a 2.93 GHz Intel Core 2 Duo processor, for example, will use a different type of memory than an iMac with a 3.4 GHz Intel Core i7 processor.

Again, your salvation turns out to be the About This Mac dialog. Just click the Overview toolbar button to display both the machine speed (processor speed) and the common identifier that Apple uses to refer to your specific model. For example, my Mac Pro has two quad-core 2.8 GHz Intel Xeon processors, and it's identified as an Early 2008 model. Grab that same piece of paper (or open that same Sticky) and add these two figures to your list.

Now armed with the information you need, go online and buy the right memory — or, if you'd rather work directly with a human being, you can visit your local Apple dealer, present that most august personage with the list, and have the memory upgrade ordered for you.

Buying memory online is much cheaper, though. I recommend the following online stores:

+ **MacMall:** www.macmall.com

+ **Other World Computing:** www.macsales.com

+ **MacConnection:** www.macconnection.com

The Tao of Adding Hard Drive Territory

Next, turn your attention to the other popular Mac upgrade — adding extra hard drive space. With today's cutting-edge, 3-D games using several gigabytes of space each and Photoshop CS6 expanding to a minimum of 16GB, IDC (short for *Insidious Data Creep*) is a growing problem. (Bad pun most certainly intended.)

Of course, you can always reclaim wasted space by deleting those files and folders you don't need. And yes, you guessed it, you can even determine how much free space remains on a hard drive from the About This Mac dialog! Click the More Info button and then click the Storage toolbar button to display all your glorious hard drive information, as shown in Figure 2-3. (I'm a major-league Mozart fan-boy, hence the name of my internal hard drive — my other drives are named after other composers as well.)

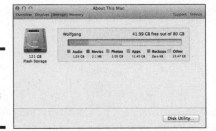

Figure 2-3:
Checking your drive's free space.

As a general rule, the following factors indicate that you're ready to upgrade your hard drive territory:

✦ You have less than 20GB of space on your hard drive.

✦ You've cleaned *all* unnecessary files, and your Mac is still lagging behind in storage.

✦ You need to share a large amount of data between computers that aren't on the same network. (Read on to discover why.)

Internal versus External Storage

Most people who upgrade their existing hard drive do so because they need extra space; however, you might also need to add a hard drive to your system that can go mobile whenever necessary. Unlike an *internal* drive (residing hidden inside your Mac's case), an *external* drive is a lean, mean, self-contained traveling storage machine that's perfect for road warriors.

External drives

Although most external drives carry their own power supply, some models don't need a separate power supply because they draw their power through your Mac's Universal Serial Bus (USB), FireWire port, or Thunderbolt port. (The next chapter in this minibook tells all about Thunderbolt, USB, and FireWire.) If you have an older MacBook Pro with an ExpressCard/34 slot and an external SATA (eSATA) card adapter — or if you're using a Mac Pro with an eSATA expansion card — you can also use an external SATA drive.

⚡ Thunderbolt

Ψ USB

ʚ FireWire

External drives also have a number of other advantages:

✦ **No installation hassle:** You can easily install a Thunderbolt, USB, or FireWire drive in seconds. Simply plug in the drive to the proper connector on the side or back of your Mac, connect the power supply (if necessary), and turn it on. (No software installation necessary. As the folks in Cupertino are fond of saying, "Look, Ma — no drivers!")

✦ **No extra space needed:** Many Macs simply don't have the internal space for another drive — laptops and iMacs are good examples. Therefore, if you want to keep your existing internal drive as-is while you're adding more storage, an external drive is your only choice.

✦ **File sharing with ease:** With an external drive, you can share your data among multiple computers or bring your files with you on your next trip.

✦ **Safe from prying eyes:** Unlike an internal drive, external drives are easy to secure. Take your sensitive information home with you or lock it in a safe.

After you plug in an external drive, OS X displays it just like any other hard drive volume. Figure 2-4 illustrates my 500GB USB external drive in action with Time Machine, as shown in the Storage pane — note the drive bears the USB symbol as an icon, marking it as an external drive.

**Book VII
Chapter 2**

**Add RAM,
Hard Drive Space,
and Stir**

Figure 2-4:
A typical
USB
external
drive.

I'd be remiss if I didn't mention that iMac, Mac mini, and MacBook models and older Mac Pro models have a DVD-R drive, which makes it easy to send up to 8.5GB of data through the mail on a single recordable disc. No one wants to box up an expensive external hard drive to transport 4GB worth of photos to Aunt Martha!

Internal drives

Your other alternative is to upgrade your internal drive, which can be a hassle. Like undertaking a memory upgrade, adding or swapping an internal drive involves opening your Mac's case. The procedure is somewhat more complex than adding memory.

I usually recommend adding a second drive rather than swapping out an existing drive. You'll avoid the hassle of backing up and restoring your system on a new drive or (even worse) reinstalling OS X and then reinstalling all the applications that you use. (Swapping a hard drive should be the definition of the word *hassle*.) Instead, add a second drive and leave your current hard drive as-is.

However, here are some important reasons why many Mac owners choose updating internal drives, even with the hassle of swapping:

+ **Cost:** You'll spend significantly less on an internal drive because it doesn't need the case and additional electronics required by an external drive.

+ **Speed:** A typical USB 3.0 or FireWire 800 drive isn't as fast as an internal drive.

+ **Space:** An internal drive eliminates the space taken by an external drive, which can range anywhere from the size of a deck of cards to the size of a hardback book.

After you establish that you are ready for more space — and you've decided whether you want to add an internal drive, an external drive, or (if you enjoy punishment) upgrade your existing internal drive — you're ready to consider how big a drive you need.

Determining How Much Space You Need

Your next step is to decide just how much hard drive space is enough. I suppose that if your last name is Zuckerberg and you had something to do with that Facebook thing, you can probably choose just about any drive on the market. However, I have a family, a mortgage, a car payment, and lust in my heart for the latest computer games; therefore, I must be a little more selective.

I have two hard-and-fast rules that I follow when I'm determining the capacity of a new drive:

+ **If you're buying a replacement for your** *existing drive,* **shop for a drive with at least twice the capacity of the existing drive (if possible).**

+ **If you're buying an** *external drive,* **shop for a drive with at least the same capacity as your existing internal drive (if possible).** One exception: If you're adding an external drive for use with Time Machine, you'll want at least twice the capacity of your existing drive.

Those rules seem to work pretty doggone well in most circumstances, with two exceptions: gamers and digital video gurus. These folks need to shoehorn as much space as they possibly can into their systems. If you're a hard-core gamer or if you work primarily with digital video, you need a wheelbarrow's worth of hard drive capacity. Trust me: Buy the biggest hard drive that you can afford.

Shopping for a Hard Drive

Ready to brave the local Wireless Shed superstore (or perhaps its website)? Here's a list of guidelines to keep handy while you're shopping for a new internal or external hard drive:

+ **Faster is indeed better.** You'll pay more for a 10,000 revolutions per minute (rpm) drive than a slower 5,400 or 7,200 rpm drive, but the extra expense is worth it. Faster drives can transfer more data to your Mac in less time, especially if you're replacing your Mac's internal Serial ATA drive.

  Faster drives are especially important for storing digital video.

+ **Serial ATA and EIDE drives are different.** If you're replacing your internal drive, you have to get the same type of drive that you already have: EIDE or Serial ATA. (EIDE, short for *Enhanced Integrated Drive Electronics,* is a common parallel ATA standard hard drive used in PCs and older Macs.) Again, the About This Mac dialog can tell you which type of drive your Mac is using. Click the Overview button in the toolbar and then click the System Report button to launch the System Information utility. Your drive will be listed under either the Serial ATA heading or the Parallel ATA heading.

+ **Solid state drives (SSD) are hot.** An SSD drive has no moving parts. It uses RAM modules to store your data, much like the USB flash drives so common today. Silicon storage allows for superfast performance (and avoids the possibility of a hard drive crash, where the internal moving parts in a traditional magnetic hard drive decide to take a permanent vacation). Unfortunately, at the time of this writing, you'll pay more for a solid-state drive than a standard magnetic hard drive. (Go figure.) Check the specifications on any SSD drive you're considering to make sure it's compatible with your Mac.

+ **Avoid used or refurbished drives.** Hard drives are one of the few components in your computer that still have a large number of moving parts. (Again, the exception is a solid-state drive.) Therefore, buying a used drive isn't a good idea unless it's priced very low.

Because the prices on new hard drives are constantly dropping, make sure that you check on the price for a new, faster drive of the same capacity before you buy that "bargain" used drive.

+ **Choose FireWire over USB.** Compared with a FireWire 400 connection, a USB 2.0 external hard drive is less efficient and slightly slower. Because most Macs with USB ports also have FireWire ports, make very sure that you buy a FireWire drive! (Of course, you can buy a USB 2.0 drive without being embarrassed. Or invest in a drive that has both FireWire and USB 2.0 connectors! Heck, if you're running one of the latest Mac models with a Thunderbolt port or a USB 3.0 port, you can invest in some of the fastest external performance on the planet — but you'll pay a higher price for Thunderbolt devices.)

A FireWire 800 port is roughly twice as fast as either a USB 2.0 port or the older FireWire 400 port, but a FireWire 800 port is far slower than a USB 3.0 port. (For a complete discussion of USB, FireWire, and Thunderbolt, turn to the next chapter in this minibook. It's *thrilling* reading, let me tell you.)

+ **Watch the size of the drive when buying internal drives.** Most SATA (Serial ATA) and EIDE drives are standard half-height 3.5" units, but check to make sure that you're not investing in a laptop drive — unless, of course, you're upgrading a laptop.

Installing Your New Stuff

After you get your memory modules or hard drive, choose one of two methods of installing them: easy or hard. Guess which method will cost you money?

The easy way

Your Apple dealer can perform either type of hardware installation for you. You can rest easy knowing that the job will be done right, but money will definitely change hands.

I always recommend that MacBook Air and MacBook Pro laptop owners allow their dealers to install hard drives because these laptops are much more complex than a desktop and much easier to damage. (The Mac mini is a bear to work on, as well.)

The hard way

If you're familiar with the inside of your Macintosh, you can install your own upgrade and save that cash. A memory upgrade is one of the simpler chores to perform, but that doesn't mean that everyone feels comfortable taking the cover off and plunging their hands inside a computer; hard drives are a tad more complex.

If you have a knowledgeable friend or family member who can help you install your hardware, buy him or her in your cause with the purchase of the proverbial NSD (*Nice Steak Dinner*). Even if you still do the work yourself, it's always better to have a second pair of experienced eyes watching, especially if you're a little nervous.

Because the installation procedures for both memory modules and hard drives are different for *every* model of Mac — heck, even removing the cover on each model of Macintosh involves a different challenge — I can't provide you with any step-by-step procedures in this chapter. (As I mentioned earlier, Apple provides instructions for upgrading memory in the About This Mac dialog.) Many online stores include installation instructions with their hardware. Other sources for installation instructions include the Apple website (`www.apple.com/usergroups`) and your Apple dealer. You can use Safari's Google search feature to scan the Internet for installation information for your particular model. However, here are guidelines to follow during the installation:

✦ **Watch out for static electricity.** When opening your Macintosh and handling hardware, make certain that you've touched a metal surface beforehand to discharge any static electricity on your body. (You can also buy a static wrist strap that you can wear while working in the bowels of your Mac.)

✦ **Check the notch on the memory module.** Most types of memory modules have a notch cut into the connector. This notch makes sure that you can install the module only one way, so make certain that the notch aligns properly with the slot.

✦ **Make sure you're using the right memory slot.** As I mention earlier in this chapter, most Macs have multiple memory slots, so check the label on the circuit board to make sure that you're adding the memory to the correct slot. (Naturally, this won't be a problem if you're installing a module into an unoccupied slot.)

✦ **Take good care of older hardware.** If you replace an existing memory module or hard drive with a new one, put the old hardware in the leftover antistatic bag from your new hardware and immediately start thinking of how you'll word your eBay auction . . . *Used 1GB Memory Module for Intel iMac,* for example. (Heck, some online stores will even give you a rebate if you return the original Apple memory modules.)

✦ **Check your hard drive jumper settings.** If your Mac uses EIDE hard drives, you must set the master and slave jumpers correctly on the back (or underside) of the new drive. A *jumper* is simply a tiny metal-and-plastic connector that is used to change the configuration on a hard drive. Setting jumpers indicates to your Mac which drive is the primary drive and which is the secondary drive. (I don't know how engineers came up with the whole master/slave thing . . . they're normally not quite so exotic when naming things.)

If you're adding a second drive to a desktop with an EIDE drive, you'll probably have to change the jumper settings on the original drive as well. (If you're replacing the existing drive, you're in luck; simply duplicate the jumper settings from the old drive and use them on the new drive.) Because the configuration settings are different for each hard drive model, check the drive's documentation for the correct jumper position.

To determine whether a memory upgrade was successful, you can again turn to the About This Mac dialog. Display the dialog again and click the Memory toolbar button; then compare the memory overview specifications with the original list that you made earlier. If the total amount of memory has increased and the memory module is recognized, you've done your job well. If not, switch off the Mac and check the module to make sure it's completely seated in the slot.

Chapter 3: Port-o-Rama: Using Thunderbolt, USB, and FireWire

In This Chapter

✔ Using FireWire, USB, and Thunderbolt with OS X

✔ Adding a USB or FireWire hub

✔ Troubleshooting external connections

✔ Adding and updating drivers

Apple's list of successes continues to grow — hardware, applications, and (of course) OS X — but the FireWire standard for connecting computers to all sorts of different devices is in a class by itself. For many years, FireWire was the port of choice for all sorts of digital devices that need a high-speed connection.

And let us not forget that Apple was the first major computer manufacturer to include Intel's Universal Serial Bus (USB) ports as standard equipment — and the Thunderbolt external port first appeared on the MacBook Pro. (The arrival of the new Mac Pro will introduce Thunderbolt 2, which provides the fastest connection speed *ever* to an external device!) A Thunderbolt port is now standard equipment on virtually all current Mac models.

In this chapter, I discuss the importance of all three connections to the digital hub (described in Book III), and I compare FireWire with Thunderbolt, USB version 2.0, and USB version 3.0 connection technology. I also talk troubleshooting and expansion using a hub.

Appreciating the Advantage of a FireWire Connection

So what's so special about FireWire, anyway? Why does Apple stuff at least one FireWire port in almost every current Macintosh model? (The exceptions are the MacBook Air and MacBook Pro models.) Heck, even the iPod (Apple's MP3 player, which you can read more about in Book III, Chapter 2) originally used only a FireWire connection. (The FireWire *official* name is IEEE 1394, but even the Cupertino crew doesn't call it that — at least not very often.)

First things first. As countless racing fans will tell you, it's all about the *speed,* my friend. The original FireWire 400 port delivered 400 Mbps (megabits per second), which proved fast enough for most peripherals of the day to communicate with a Macintosh. The following list includes a number of hardware toys that are well known for transferring prodigious file sizes:

✦ Digital video (DV) camcorders

✦ High-resolution digital cameras

✦ Scanners and some printers

✦ External hard drives and CD/DVD recorders

✦ Networking between computers

For example, consider the sheer size of a typical digital video clip captured by one of today's DV camcorders. DV buffs commonly transfer hundreds of gigabytes of footage to their computers at one time. Check out the relative speeds of the different types of ports in Table 3-1, and you'll see the big attraction of FireWire 800, USB 3.0, and Thunderbolt connections.

Table 3-1	Transfer Speeds for Ports through the Ages	
Port	*Date Appeared on Personal Computers*	*Transfer Speed (in Megabits)*
PC Serial	1981	Less than 1 Mbps
PC Parallel	1981	1 Mbps
USB (version 1.1)	1996	12 Mbps
FireWire 400	1996	400 Mbps (version 1)
USB (version 2.0)	2001	480 Mbps
FireWire 800	2002	800 Mbps
USB (version 3.0)	2010	5 Gbps (5,000 Mbps)
Thunderbolt	2011	10 Gbps (10,000 Mbps)
Thunderbolt 2	2013	20 Gbps

Ouch! Not too hard to figure that one out. Here are three other important benefits to FireWire:

✦ **Control over connection:** This is a ten-cent term that engineers use, meaning that you can control whatever gadget you've connected using FireWire from your computer. This feature is pretty neat when you think about it; for example, you can control your mini-DV camcorder from the comfort of your computer keyboard, just as though you were pressing the buttons on the camcorder.

✦ **Hot-swapped:** You don't have to reboot your Mac or restart OS X every time that you plug in (or unplug) a FireWire device. Instead, the FireWire peripheral is automatically recognized (as long as the operating system has the correct driver) and is ready to transfer.

✦ **Power through the port:** FireWire can provide power to a device through the same wire — typically, enough power is available for an external drive or recorder — so you don't need an external AC power cord for some FireWire devices. (Apologies to owners of DV camcorders, but those things eat power like a pig eats slop.)

You'll note from Table 3-1 that FireWire 800 (okay, really named *IEEE 1394bB,* but no one calls it that) delivers a respectable 800 Mbps. Although nowhere near as fast as a USB 3.0 or Thunderbolt connection, FireWire 800 peripherals are much easier to find (and are much cheaper) at the time of this writing than Thunderbolt devices. If your Mac sports USB 3.0 connectors, a USB 3.0 external device makes a nice compromise: much faster than FireWire 800 but much less expensive than Thunderbolt peripherals (and much easier to find, at least for now).

Oh, and as you would expect from Apple, FireWire 800 ports are backward-compatible with older FireWire 400 hardware. However, the ports aren't exactly the same, so you'll need a plastic port converter to connect FireWire 400 devices to a FireWire 800 port. (Such important little conversion fixtures are commonly called *dongles.* No, I'm not making that up. Ask your favorite technowizard.)

Travelling at Warp Speed with Thunderbolt

Thunderbolt 2, Apple's latest external connection, is listed at 20 Gbps (giga-bits per second), and the original Thunderbolt port can deliver 10 Gbps; (refer to Table 3-1). Here's your technonerd trivia for the day: Data on a 1 Gbps connection is moving as fast as data on a 1,000 Mbps connection. That means the original Thunderbolt port is more than *12 times faster* than FireWire 800! Heck, Thunderbolt trumps even USB 3.0 technology, which has a maximum speed of only 5 Gbps.

Thunderbolt's sheer jump-to-warp speed performance allows something that's never been possible before: Mac owners can edit uncompressed digital video in real time on an external Thunderbolt hard drive! (That's a chore that requires moving huge amounts of data very quickly between your computer's processor and hard drive, which until now simply wasn't possible on an external drive.) Thunderbolt is also versatile — it even provides a direct high-definition connection between your Mac and your HDMI flat-screen TV or a superfast high-resolution monitor such as the Apple LED Cinema Display.

A single Thunderbolt port can handle up to six peripherals, including a mixture of a high-resolution display and devices such as hard drives and Blu-ray recorders. And, like FireWire, Thunderbolt can provide plenty of power to a connected device as well. Probably the only downside to Thunderbolt 2 (at least at the time of this writing) is that Thunderbolt 2 devices are not generally available yet, and are likely to be significantly more expensive than their older counterparts. Such is the lament of the early adopter of cutting-edge computer hardware!

Understanding USB and the Tale of Two Point Oh

The other resident port on today's Apple computers is the ubiquitous USB 3.0 (found on the latest models) and its older brother USB 2.0. Those consumed by curiosity might want to know that *USB* is short for *Universal Serial Bus.* (By the way, *ubiquitous* means *ever-present* or *universal,* which I quickly discovered by using my Dictionary widget — read all about widgets in Book II, Chapter 2.) USB has taken the world by storm. It's used for everything from mice to keyboards, speakers, digital cameras, and even external drives and DVD recorders. (A friend of mine never misses the chance to point out that USB — which was originally developed by Intel, the makers of the Core i5 and i7 processors — was given its first widespread implementation on the original iMac. *You're welcome,* Intel.)

USB 3.0 delivers a superfast 5 Gbps connection, and USB 2.0 delivers performance comparable to the original FireWire standard: USB 2.0 can transfer 480 Mbps, although far less efficiently than FireWire, so the FireWire connection is still faster overall. (Don't call Apple snobbish; at the time of this writing, the Mac mini, iMac, MacBook Air, and MacBook Pro models feature USB 3.0 ports, while the new cylindrical Mac Pro has USB 3.0 ports.)

Like FireWire, USB connections are hot-swappable and *may* provide power over the connection. (Some USB ports don't supply all the power that devices need — more on this later in this chapter.) A USB port offers a more limited version of control over connection as well, making it a good choice for virtually all digital cameras.

Speaking of digital cameras. . . . Smaller devices that use a USB connection to your Mac may not have standard USB ports. For example, digital cameras and cellphones are notorious for featuring *mini-USB* connectors, which are much smaller than a standard USB port. If you're wondering why your device needs a special cable (supplied by the manufacturer), here's why: One end looks like a standard USB connector and plugs into your Mac, and the other is deliberately tiny and shaped differently, and plugs into the device.

Owners of older Mac Pro desktop models can add a USB 3.0 adapter card to use the faster peripherals.

Hey, You Need a Hub!

Suppose that you've embraced FireWire and USB and you now have two USB drives hanging off the rear end of your Mac — and suddenly you buy an iPod. (Or you get another USB device that's as much fun as an iPod, if that's possible.) Now you're faced with too many devices for too few ports. You *could* eject a drive and unhook it each time that you want to connect your iPod, but there *must* be a more elegant way to connect. Help!

Enter the hub. Both the FireWire and USB specifications allow you to connect a device called a *hub,* which is really nothing more than a glorified splitter adapter that provides you with additional ports. With a FireWire or USB hub at work, you do lose a port on your Mac; however, most hubs multiply that dedicated port into four or eight ports. Again, all this is transparent, and you don't need to hide anything up your sleeve. Adding a hub is just as plug-and-play easy as adding a regular FireWire or USB device.

When shopping for a USB hub, make sure you choose a model that provides full power to each port. As I discuss later in the chapter, many USB peripherals draw their AC power from the port itself — these devices won't work with a cheaper hub that doesn't supply that juice. Oh, and one more shopping tip: If your Mac sports USB 3.0 ports, you'll naturally need a hub that can handle USB 3.0 connections.

I should also mention that FireWire supports *daisy-chaining* — a word that stretches all the way back to the days of the Atari and Commodore computers, when devices had extra ports in the back so that additional stuff could be plugged in. However, not every FireWire drive has a daisy-chain port (also called a *pass-through port*). With daisy-chaining, you can theoretically add 63 FireWire devices (or 127 USB devices) to your Mac — talk about impressing the folks at your next Mac user group meeting!

Uh, My External Device Is Just Sitting There: Troubleshooting

Man, I *hate* it when FireWire and USB devices act like boat anchors. FireWire and USB peripherals are so doggone simple that when something goes wrong, it's really aggravating. Fortunately, I've been down those roads many a time before, so in this section, I unleash my experience. (That sounds a little frightening, but it's a *good* thing. Really.)

Common FireWire and USB headaches

Because FireWire and USB are so alike in so many ways, I can handle possible troubleshooting solutions for both types of hardware at one time:

✦ **Problem:** *Every time I turn off or unplug my external peripheral, OS X gets irritated and displays a nasty message saying that I haven't properly disconnected the device.*

Solution: This happens because you haven't *ejected* the peripheral. I know that sounds a little strange for a device such as an external hard drive or a digital camera, but it's essentially the same reasoning as ejecting a CD or DVD from your Desktop. When you click your USB or FireWire device and hold down the mouse button, the Trash icon turns into an Eject icon. Just drag the device icon to the Eject icon and drop it, and the external device disappears from your Desktop. (You can also click the device icon to select it and press ⌘+E. And don't forget the right-click menu — right-click the device and choose Eject.) At that point, you're then safe to turn off the device or unplug the FireWire or USB cable.

If Mavericks recognizes the device as an external drive, which is usually the case with a digital camera, an external hard drive, or an external DVD or Blu-ray recorder, you can simply click the Eject button next to the device icon in the Finder window's sidebar.

✦ **Problem:** *The device doesn't show a power light.*

Solution: Check to make sure that the power cable is connected — unless you have a device that's powered through the connection itself, which can pose its own share of problems when using USB devices. Not all USB ports provide power to devices because some ports are designed only for connecting mice, keyboards, and joysticks.

To check whether an unpowered USB port is your problem, either connect the device directly to a USB port on your Mac or connect it to a powered hub or another computer. If the device works when it's connected to another port, you've found the culprit.

✦ **Problem:** *The device shows a power light but just doesn't work.*

Solution: This problem can occur because of issues with your cable or your hub. To check, borrow a friend's cables and see whether the device works. If you're testing the hub, try connecting the device directly to your Mac using the same cable to see whether it works without the hub.

If you're attempting to connect a FireWire device through another FireWire device, try connecting that first device directly to see whether it works. If so, the middleman device either needs to be switched on to pass the data through or it doesn't support daisy-chaining — in which case, you may be able to place the "problem" device at the *end* of the chain. Of course, you can always connect both devices to a powered FireWire hub.

✦ **Problem:** *OS X reports that I have a missing driver.*

Solution: Check the manufacturer's website and download a new copy of the USB or FireWire driver for your device because the driver has been corrupted, overwritten, or erased. Because OS X loads the driver for a USB or FireWire device when it's connected, sometimes just unplugging and reconnecting a peripheral will do the trick.

Check those drivers

Speaking of drivers . . . antique hardware drivers are a sore spot with me. *Drivers* are simply programs that tell OS X how to communicate with your external device. Each new version of OS X contains updated drivers, but make certain that you check for new updates on a regular basis. That means using both the Software Update feature in OS X (which I cover briefly in Book II, Chapter 3 and much more in Book I, Chapter 7) *and* going to the websites provided by your USB and FireWire hardware manufacturers.

Chapter 4: I'm Okay, You're a Printer

In This Chapter

✔ Adding a local printer

✔ Adding a non-USB printer

✔ Managing print jobs

✔ Sending and receiving faxes

✔ Setting up a shared printer

*O*f all the features Mac owners appreciate in Mavericks, one of the most important is the support the operating system provides for Universal Serial Bus (USB), network, and Bluetooth printers. As I discuss in Book I, Chapter 3, if Mavericks recognizes your USB printer, you can print within seconds of plugging it in, with no muss or fuss. A USB printer is connected physically to your Mac, but you can also send print jobs over the network to a network printer or even to a wireless printer. (Unfortunately, if that network printer is in another room, you do have to get out of your comfortable chair to retrieve your printed document . . . not even Mavericks is *that* powerful.)

But what if you want to send documents to a printer over TCP/IP (Transmission Control Protocol/Internet Protocol)? To take care of tasks like that, you need to dig a little further — and I do so in this chapter. You also discover here how to use the features of the System Preferences Printers & Scanners pane and how to juggle print jobs like a circus performer.

Meet Printer Browser

Printer Browser runs automatically whenever it's needed by Mavericks, but you can always summon it at any time by clicking the plus sign (or Add) button on the Printers & Scanners pane in System Preferences.

If your USB printer is *natively supported* (has a preloaded driver in Mavericks), you might not need to go through the trouble of clicking the Add button on the Printers & Scanners pane. OS X can add a new USB printer automatically, so don't be surprised if your Mac swoops in and does it for you as soon as you plug in a new printer. Also, the manufacturer's installation program for your printer might add the printer for you in a behind-the-scenes way, even if OS X lies dormant.

PDF printing

In the Windows world, Adobe Acrobat is the most popular program for creating electronic PDF documents. Although you certainly can install Adobe Acrobat under Mavericks, I'd be remiss if I didn't mention that you don't *have* to! OS X Mavericks provides built-in support for printing documents in Adobe PDF format (which can then be viewed and printed on any other computer with Acrobat Reader or added to your website for downloading). Acrobat has

more features, naturally, but — wait for it — don't pay for Acrobat unless you need it.

You don't even have to install a PDF print driver or display Printer Browser. To print a document as a file in PDF format, click the PDF drop-down button in the application's Print dialog, click Save as PDF from the menu, navigate to the desired folder and enter a filename, and then click Save.

Although Printer Browser doesn't look like much (as shown in Figure 4-1), power lurks underneath.

Figure 4-1: The rather plain-looking Printer Browser is actually a rugged adventurer.

Along the top of Printer Browser are four toolbar icons that display the printer connections possible in Mavericks that you can add to your system:

✦ **Default:** Click this button to add or display the entry for the default printer.

To choose as default a printer that you've already added, click System Preferences and click the Printers & Scanners icon. Click the Default Printer pop-up menu in the Printers & Scanners pane and choose that printer. You can also choose the Last Printer Used option from the pop-up menu, which automatically makes the default printer the last printer you used.

✦ **Fax:** Click this button to add an external USB fax connection as a printer selection.

✦ **IP:** Click this button to add a remote printer to your Mac through an Internet connection or a local network connection. Sending a job to an Internet Protocol (IP) printer shoots the document across a network or Internet connection by using a target IP address or domain name. Generally, it's best to have a *static* (unchanging) IP address for a network printer; if the IP address changes often, for example, you have to reconfigure your connection to your IP printer each time it changes.

If you're using Apple's AirPrint feature on your iPhone, iPad, or iPod touch to wirelessly print (using your AirPrint-compatible printer), consider using the fine handyPrint application from Netputing (www. netputing.com). The app does require iOS 4.3 or later. After installing handyPrint on your Mac, you can then use AirPrint to print to virtually *any* networked or shared printer, regardless of the manufacturer. The handyPrint app is free to try, but the authors require a donation if you want to fully license the software.

✦ **Windows:** Click this button to add a shared printer that's connected to a PC on your local network. "Hey, I get to use the enemy's printers, too?" That's right, as long as a Windows user on your network has shared his or her printer (via the ubiquitous Windows File and Printer Sharing feature). *Sweet.*

Oh, and one additional important control on the toolbar isn't actually a button: You can click in the Search field and type text to locate a particular printer in any of these dialog lists. (I don't have that many printers on my network, but in a larger company, this field can save you the trouble of scrolling through several pages of shared printers.)

Adding a Funky Printer

"And what," you might ask, "is a *funky* printer?" Well, you have a number of possibilities, but they all add up to a non-USB connection. (Remember, I said that USB connections to a printer are generally automatic, or at least handled by the printer's installation software.) Some of the non-USB connections I mention in the preceding section include Windows shared printers and IP printers.

No matter which type of funky printer you add, it needs a driver installed in the Printers folder, which resides in your Library folder. (A *driver* is a software program provided by the printer manufacturer that tells OS X how to communicate with your printer.) Also, if the printer is PostScript-compatible, it needs a Postscript Printer Description (PPD) file installed in your PPD folder, which also appears in the Printers folder. Luckily, Mavericks comes complete with a long list of drivers and PPD files already installed and available — bravo, Apple dudes and dudettes!

To add a funky printer that supports Mavericks, follow these steps:

1. **Launch the manufacturer's installation application, which should copy the driver and PPD files for you.**

   If you have to do things the hard way, manually copy the driver file into the Library/Printers folder and then copy the PPD file (if required) into the Library/Printers/PPD folder.

2. **If you're adding a physical printer — instead of an application printer driver — verify that the printer is turned on and accessible.**

   If you're printing to a shared printer connected to another Mac or PC, that computer has to be on. Luckily, most network printers (and their computer hosts) remain on all the time.

3. **Display the Printers & Scanners pane in System Preferences and click the Add button.**

   You see the familiar Printer Browser (refer to Figure 4-1). Shared printers should show up on the default list, so you can click the printer to select it.

4. **To add an IP printer, click the IP Printer button on the browser toolbar.**

   Click the Protocol pop-up menu to choose the IP printing protocol (typically either IPP or the manufacturer-specific socket protocol). If you have a choice, it's always a good idea to use the manufacturer-specific socket.

   Click in the Address box and type the printer's IP address or Domain Name System (DNS) name, which should be provided by your network administrator or the person running the print server. You can use the default queue on the server by leaving the Queue box blank — which I recommend — or select the Queue text box and type a valid queue name for the server.

   If you don't know a valid queue name, you're up a creek — hence, my recommendation to use the default queue.

   If you like, you can type a name and location for the remote printer; this is purely for identification. Finally, click the Use pop-up menu, choose the brand and model of the remote printer, and then click Add.

5. **To add a Windows printer, click the Windows button on the Printer Browser toolbar.**

   Click the correct Windows workgroup that includes the printer(s) that you want to use in the left column. After a scan of the specified workgroup, Printer Browser displays the list of printers that it can access. (Don't forget to thank His Billness later.)

6. **After everything is tuned correctly, click the Use pop-up menu and choose the brand and model of the remote printer.**

7. **Click Add to complete the process and admire your new printer on the Printers & Scanners panel in System Preferences.**

Heck, Mavericks even allows you to *order supplies* for your printer from the comfort of System Preferences! Sure, you'll pay a premium price, but think of the technonerd bragging rights you'll enjoy at your next Mac user group meeting! Click a printer in the Printers & Scanners pane, click the Options & Supplies button, and then click the Supply Levels tab. When you click the Supplies button, System Preferences automatically launches Safari with the proper web page from the Apple Store.

Managing Your Printing Jobs

You can also exercise some control over the documents — or, in technoid, *print jobs* — that you send to your printer. To display the jobs that are *active* (in line and preparing to print), open the Printers & Scanners pane in System Preferences and click the Open Print Queue button (as shown in Figure 4-2).

Figure 4-2:
Click the
Open Print
Queue
button to
control your
print jobs
like puppets.

Where's the chapter on faxing?

Good question, and here's the answer: Mavericks handles faxing so seamlessly that you don't need a chapter's worth of instruction! As long as your Mac has an external analog (dial-up) modem (or a multifunction printer) connected to a phone line, you're a lean faxing machine.

To fax any open document in an active application, just choose File⇨Print or press ⌘+P. Click the PDF button at the bottom of the Print dialog and click Fax PDF — remember, this item appears only if you have a dial-up modem or a printer with fax support connected. Type the destination telephone number in the To field. Next, type a dialing prefix if one is necessary to reach an outside line.

If you need a spiffy-looking cover page, select the Use Cover Page check box. Click in the Message box directly below it and type whatever you like. You can optionally type a subject as well. When all is ready, throw caution utterly to the wind and click the Fax button. The Printer Browser treats a fax just as it does any other printed document, so you can cancel it or monitor its progress, as I discuss in the section, "Managing Your Printing Jobs."

Your Mac can also receive faxes. To enable this feature, open System Preferences and click the Printers & Scanners icon. Click the entry for your fax in the list, click the Receive Options button, and then select the Receive Faxes on This Computer check box. Set the number of rings Mavericks should wait before answering the call. You can save your incoming faxes as files in a folder you specify or e-mail the contents automatically to any e-mail address you like. (Perfect for vacations!) If you like, you can even take the mundane route and print them on your system printer.

If you're going to use your Mac as a fax machine often, I definitely recommend selecting the Show Fax Status in Menu Bar check box, which appears when you click the entry for your fax modem in the list. That way, you can monitor what's happening as your Mac sends and receives throughout the day.

The icons available from the Print Queue window are

✦ **Pause:** Click this icon to stop all printing to this printer. Note that Pause doesn't *remove* any print jobs from the list. When jobs are stopped, the Pause icon morphs into Resume — click it to restart all jobs in the queue list from the beginning.

This is a good feature to use when your printer is about to run out of paper.

✦ **Settings:** If your printer supports remote supply monitoring, you can click this icon and click the Supply Levels tab to display the current levels of ink and paper in your printer (thus saving your feet from the wear and tear of walking). Click the General tab on the Settings sheet, and Mavericks displays the model-specific configuration settings and features (if any) available for the active printer. These settings vary for every printer produced by the hand of Man — they're determined by the manufacturer's printer driver — but they usually include actions (such as cleaning and alignment) and settings (such as print quality).

Sharing a Printer across That There Network

Before we leave the Island of Big X Printing, I'd like to show you how to share a printer with others on your local network, using the super-easy Bonjour network sharing feature in Mavericks. (Earlier in this chapter, I show you how to connect to other shared printers around you. Here, you're going to share a printer that's connected directly to your Mac.)

If you share printers, don't be surprised if OS X seems to slow down slightly from time to time. This is because of the processing time necessary for your Mac to store queued documents from other computers. The hard drive activity on your Mac is likely to significantly increase as well.

Once again, turn to System Preferences! Click the Sharing icon; then select the Printer Sharing check box. (When it comes to printing, Mavericks gives you more than one way to take care of business.) To share a printer, select the check box next to the desired printer (as shown in Figure 4-3) and click the Add button to select which users will have access to the shared printer. (By default, a shared printer can be accessed by everyone.) To prevent someone from printing, click that user's entry in the list and click the Delete button (look for the minus sign). *Voilà!* You're the guru!

Figure 4-3:
Mavericks
takes
care of
everything
when you
want to
share a
printer.

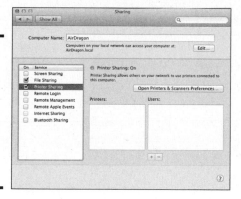

"Hey, what about my firewall?" Remember, you're using Mavericks, and everything is set *automatically* for you the moment you click the Printer Sharing check box! Mavericks automatically opens the correct port in your firewall to allow printer sharing. (And yes, if you decide not to share your printers and you deselect the Printer Sharing check box later, Mavericks cleans up after you. It closes the port in your firewall for you.) Super-flippin' *sweet*.

The printers that you specify are available to other computers in the same IP subnet. In other words, someone in your local network can use your printers, but no one outside your network has access.

If you haven't already assigned a printer a descriptive name, open System Preferences and click the Printers & Scanners icon. Click the desired printer from the list in the Printers & Scanners pane and then click the Options & Supplies button. Click the General button on the sheet that appears and enter a descriptive name in the Name text field. You can also identify that printer's location in the Location text field. For example, in an office environment, I like to add the room number to a shared printer name (as well as the Location field).

Chapter 5: Applications That You've (Probably) Gotta Have

In This Chapter

☑ Using Microsoft Office for Mac 2011

☑ Using disk repair applications

☑ Editing images

☑ Editing digital video

☑ Using Internet applications

☑ Burning discs with Toast

☑ Running Windows with Parallels Desktop

☑ Adding third-party utilities

☑ Playing games with OS X

In Chapter 1 of this minibook, I present you with an overview of the most popular hardware that you can add to your Mac — and where there's hardware, software can't be far behind. (Somebody famous said that — I think it was Mark Twain.)

And as I talk about in Book I, Chapter 1, a new Mac comes with a full suite of software tools right out of the box. You get Internet connectivity, disk repair, a digital audio and video player, image editing and cataloging, digital video editing, and — depending on the price that you pay or the Mac model configuration that you buy — even a complete set of productivity applications. However, if you're willing to pay for additional features and a manual (at least what passes for a manual in the manufacturer's opinion), you can make all these tasks easier and accomplish them in even shorter time by purchasing other software.

Read on for an overview of the most popular third-party software applications for OS X: what everyone's using, how much they cost, and why they're (usually) better. However, before you drop a wad of cash on a fancy new application (or even an expensive upgrade to an existing application), remember yet another of Mark's Maxims:

If an application you already have does everything you really need — and you like the way it works — you *don't* have to buy a new application. Honest and truly.

The Trundling Microsoft Mammoth

Yes, I know I've been poking fun at Microsoft for much of this book — you have to admit, it's a pretty good target in the Apple world — but His Gatesness and the rest of Microsoft *did* pull PC owners out of the character-based world of DOS, and I'll be the first to say that they do get things right on a regular basis. (Witness my bestselling book *PCs All-in-One For Dummies*, recently revised for a sixth edition!)

For example, I've always been a fan of Microsoft Office. Office has long been the productivity suite of choice in the Windows world, and it's also been favorite for even longer on the Macintosh side. Perhaps this is a good spot to remind everyone that Excel originated on the Mac!

A lot of hard work was put into the latest Mac version of Microsoft Office, and it shows. Office 2011 for Mac more closely mirrors the design of the PC version of Office (as you can see by Microsoft Word for Mac in Figure 5-1), but it still includes everything you'd demand from a native OS X application (such as Pages from *iWork*, which is Apple's competing office productivity suite).

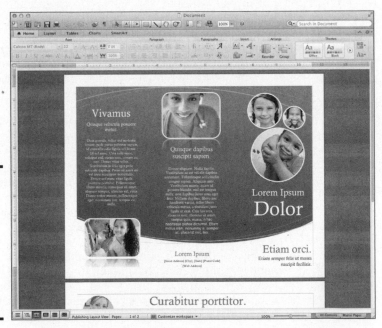

Figure 5-1: Man, that is one good-looking Office. Thanks, Microsoft (and I mean that).

However, as with OS X itself, Office 2011 for Mac isn't just an attractive exterior. Consider some of the advantages of Office 2011:

✦ **Perfect document compatibility with the Windows version of Office:** You can both read and write documents with transparent ease, no matter which platform gets the file. Documents can be shared between platforms on the same network.

✦ **Mirrored commands:** Office 2013 and Office for Mac 2011 have similar menu items, dialogs, and settings, thus making OS X instantly familiar to anyone who's used Office on a Windows PC.

✦ **Support for native Aqua features:** These features include transparent graphics in your documents, input and confirmation sheets, and palettes for formatting.

✦ **Tons of templates, samples, and support files:** Microsoft doesn't scrimp on ready-to-use documents and templates, as well as additional fonts, clip art, and web samples.

✦ **Outlook:** Office for Mac 2011 now includes a version of Outlook that's similar to the Windows version in scope and power. It combines most of the features that you'll find in the Apple Mail, Calendar, and Contacts applications. (Read about Apple Mail in Book V, Chapter 2; read about Calendar in Book I, Chapter 8; read about Contacts in Book I, Chapter 7.)

Besides Outlook, Office for Mac 2011 includes three applications:

✦ **Word:** The word-processing application that rules the planet

✦ **Excel:** The leading spreadsheet application

✦ **PowerPoint:** A favorite presentation development application

The Office for Mac 2011 suite costs about $150 at the time of this writing. You might save a few dollars if you buy it online from a web store such as MacMall (www.macmall.com).

Your OS X Toolbox: Drive Genius 3

My favorite native OS X disk repair application is Drive Genius 3 from Prosoft Engineering (www.prosofteng.com).

More than just about any other type of application, use a disk maintenance program built "from the ground up" for OS X. *Never* attempt to repair an OS X disk using an older repair utility that wasn't designed for Mavericks.

With Drive Genius 3 (as shown in Figure 5-2), you can thoroughly check a hard drive for both *physical* errors (such as faulty electronics or a bad sector on the disk surface) and *logical* errors (incorrect folder data and glitches in the file structure). Disk Utility, which is included with OS X, does a fine job of checking the latter, but it doesn't perform the physical testing — and Drive Genius 3 does both.

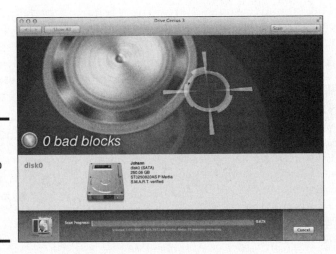

Figure 5-2: Use Drive Genius 3 to check for all sorts of hardware errors.

Drive Genius 3 doesn't take care of viruses. For that kind of protection, pick up a copy of VirusBarrier 2013 (`www.intego.com`) or the excellent freeware application ClamXav 2 (`www.clamxav.com`) to thwart viral attacks.

Drive Genius 3 also takes care of disk optimization, which is a feature that's been conspicuously absent from OS X since the beginning. As I explain in Book I, Chapter 9, defragmenting your disk will result in better performance and a faster system overall.

Drive Genius 3, which will set you back about $100, comes as both an application (that you download and use directly) and as a disc image that you can use to create a self-booting DVD-ROM; so if your Mac has an optical drive, you can easily fix your start-up volume by booting your system from the Drive Genius 3 disc.

Image Editing for the Masses

The only one true King of the Retouching Hill in OS X, Adobe Photoshop (www.adobe.com/products/photoshop) has been the digital-image–editing favorite of Mac owners for many years now. As does Office for Mac 2011, the latest version of Photoshop (CC) takes full advantage of the Aqua standard.

You can find more three-pound Photoshop books on the shelf than politicians in trouble, so it's no surprise that I can't provide you with a sweeping list of its features in this section. However, here's a summary of what you can expect from Adobe's crown jewel:

+ **Superior editing:** The most sophisticated image editing possible for a digital photograph. If you can accomplish an image-editing task in software, it's very likely that Photoshop can do it. You can even combine and splice parts of different images to produce a new work of art or distort and liquefy an image to produce a new look.

+ **Image-retouching tools:** These tools help you rescue images with problems, such as overexposure and color imbalance. (You can also use tools such as the Healing brush to erase imperfections in a photograph's subject.)

+ **Plug-ins:** Photoshop has been a standard for plug-in functionality since it first appeared. If you need features that aren't in the application out of the box, you can add them through third-party plug-ins.

+ **Web posting:** Prepare images for use on the web.

+ **Painting tools:** Use these gems to simulate different types of inks, paints, and brushes on different types of media.

 Although Photoshop CC is a hefty $20 a month for the full package, Adobe has also created a kid brother, Photoshop Elements 12, which sells for a mere $99. Designed for the novice or intermediate-level photographer, Elements has most of the functionality of the full package that you're likely to need. Elements can also automate the most common image-editing tasks, as well as provide one of the most comprehensive Help systems I've ever used.

The Morass of Digital Video

Two types of applications make up the DV market: *digital video editing* (in which you create a movie) and *DVD mastering* (in which you take that movie and create a DVD movie). You can find a number of great applications on the market in both these categories, all at different price points and different levels of complexity. The offerings from Apple include

✦ **iMovie:** I cover this easy-to-use video-editing iApp in Book III, Chapter 4. A good choice for any novice, it's bundled for free with today's new Mac models, and it's also available from the App Store.

✦ **Final Cut Pro X:** If you assume that Final Cut Pro X is a first-rate DV-editing package for OS X, you won't get any argument from me. At $299 (and available in the App Store), it offers far more features and power than iMovie, yet it's still easy to use. *Sassy.*

Yes, It's Really Called "Toast"

Time to turn your attention to a subject near and dear to my heart: recording data CDs, audio CDs, and DVDs on the Macintosh. Of course, OS X can burn basic data CDs that you can share with your Windows and Unix friends without any add-on software. If you have a Mac equipped with a SuperDrive (either internal or external), you can create standard, cross-platform data DVDs, too. But what if you need an exotic format, such as CD Extra, that allows data and digital audio tracks to co-exist peacefully on one disc? Or perhaps you need a self-booting disc, or you just got a Blu-ray external recorder?

There's one clear choice: When you're ready to seriously burn, you're ready for Roxio Toast Titanium (www.roxio.com), the CD and DVD recording choice for millions of Mac owners. (No snickering about the name, please.) Figure 5-3 illustrates this powerhouse of an application, which has an elegant design that's both simple to use and perfectly Aqua. Files, folders, and digital audio tracks that you want to record are simply dropped into the application window.

As for exotic formats, here's a list of some types of discs you can record with Toast:

✦ Standard data CDs and DVDs

✦ Standard audio CDs

✦ Video CDs

✦ Super Video CDs

✦ MP3 discs (which store MP3 audio tracks)

- ✦ Discs recorded from an image file
- ✦ Mac volumes
- ✦ Hybrid PC/Mac discs
- ✦ ISO 9660 discs
- ✦ Multisession discs
- ✦ CD Extra discs

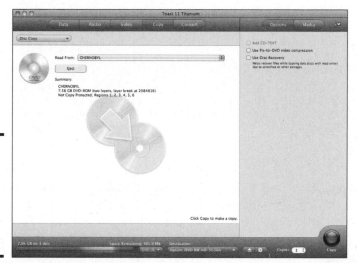

Figure 5-3:
Toast is the classic Mac CD- and DVD-recording application.

Toast works with both internal and external CD, DVD, and Blu-ray recorders, taking advantage of the latest features on today's drives. You can also copy existing discs, using one or multiple drives.

Toast is quite affordable at $80. You can buy it directly from the Roxio online store at www.roxio.com.

If You Positively Have to Run Windows...

Here's where Mac power users usually start grinning from ear to ear like Santa's elves on the day after Christmas, because — get this — many of the great Unwashed Windows Horde still think that you *can't* run Windows on a Macintosh! Can you believe that? Obviously, they haven't heard of Boot

Camp, which is built into Mavericks (and covered in Book VIII, Chapter 1). But what if you don't want to reboot to switch operating systems? What if you need to share data between both Mac and PC applications running simultaneously? Well, that's where Parallels Desktop from Parallels (www. parallels.com) comes in, which is without a doubt one of the coolest applications ever written for the Mac.

Check out the screen on my Mac Pro in Figure 5-4. No, my friend, your eyes aren't deceiving you — you're indeed looking at Windows 8 running along with OS X, in blissful cohabitation. Parallels Desktop (which requires OS X) provides a near-perfect PC environment for any version of Windows from 95 all the way up to Windows 8. Literally, Windows has *no* idea that it's not running on a typical piece of PC iron.

Parallels Desktop simulates everything necessary for you to get the full functionality out of Windows. For example, this jewel automatically (and transparently) handles your Windows Internet connection, network tasks, and CD and DVD access. You can run full-screen or run Windows in a window (pun joyfully intended).

As if that weren't enough, you can also run multiple operating systems. So if you need Red Hat Linux, Ubuntu, or Windows 2000 along with your Windows 8 system, no problem — all it takes is the install disc for those operating systems and the hard drive space to hold 'em. Outstanding!

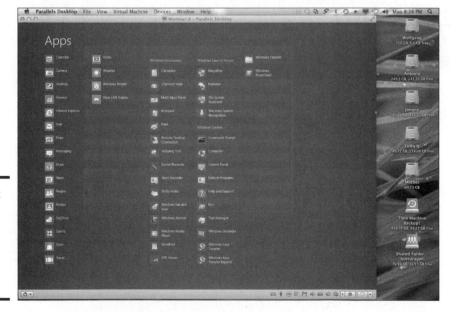

Figure 5-4:
Take *that*, Bill! I get to play in your pool, without rebooting!

Naturally, performance is an issue — and, to be honest, Parallels Desktop isn't for the PC gamer, even with the newest Macs and their super-duper GeForce and Radeon video cards. Because today's most demanding PC games push an actual PC to the limit, they just run too sluggishly on a Mac emulating a PC — they do run, just slowly. (Also, virtually all of today's blockbuster PC games are also being ported to OS X, so why not just run the Mac version?) If I must run a Windows game on my Mac, I almost always use Boot Camp to boot directly into Windows, which allows my system to devote all its resources to the game at hand.

However, when it comes to just about any other type of application, Parallels Desktop running on a late-model Intel-based Mac can deliver performance equal to a typical Intel PC. The more memory that your Mac has, the more you can give your virtual PC, so it also pays to have 8GB or more of RAM. I use this application with niche Windows programs that have never appeared on the Mac as well as native Mac versions of all other applications. Again, you don't need to use Mac to run the Windows version of Photoshop CS6 because Photoshop CS6 is also available as a native application for the Mac.

If you're tired of the undeserved taunts from your clueless Windows friends — you know, the ones who say that you can't run both Mac and Windows programs at the same time — head to your browser and order a copy of Parallels Desktop. The program is an affordable $70, but don't forget that you have to supply your own copy of Windows. (I should also mention the popular VMware Fusion 5, which is a direct competitor with Parallels Desktop and cheaper at $50 — visit www.vmware.com for more information on Fusion.)

For a free taste of virtual computing, try VirtualBox at www.virtualbox.org.

All Hail FileMaker Pro

If databases are the name of your game, you've already been using FileMaker Pro for years (on both Mac and Windows, more than likely). For the unitiated, FileMaker Pro (www.filemaker.com) is the premier database creation, editing, and maintenance application for OS X. It comes with dozens of ready-made database templates for business, home, and education use, or you can construct your own database in surprisingly short order. If you use AppleScript, you'll also be glad to hear that FileMaker Pro is a highly scriptable application.

Right out of the box, you can use FileMaker Pro to create

✦ Business databases and forms for inventory, personnel, purchase orders, and product catalogs

✦ Home databases for budgeting, recipes, music CDs, DVD movies, family medical records, and event planning

✦ Education databases for student records, expense reports, field trip planning, book and multimedia libraries, and class scheduling

In FileMaker Pro 12, you can add images and multimedia to your database, and you can quickly and easily publish your databases on your website by using one of the built-in theme designs. Visitors to your website can update your database online, if you like. FileMaker Pro can also allow multiple users to share data across your network, no matter whether they're running the Mac or Windows version. You can even run scripts automatically based on user input and extract data directly from websites.

At $299, FileMaker Pro 12 is one of the least expensive — and most powerful — applications that you can buy for the Big X.

Utilities That Rock

The next stop on this Cavalcade of Software is an assortment of the absolute best you've-got-to-get-this utility applications. Sooner or later, you're likely going to buy (or register) these utilities because you'll use them every day.

StuffIt

In the Windows world, the zip archive is the king of archiving formats. A *zip archive* contains one or more compressed files that you can uncompress whenever you need them. Folks store files in archives to save space on their hard drives; archiving is also a neat way to package an entire folder's worth of files in a single convenient file, which you can attach to an e-mail message or send via File Transfer Protocol (FTP). OS X includes built-in support for zip files.

Manage your archives with StuffIt Deluxe, from Smith Micro Software (`http://mysmithmicro.com`). StuffIt Deluxe can both archive and unarchive `.sit` files (the common name for StuffIt archives) as well as zip archives from your Windows friends. You can also encrypt the contents of a StuffIt archive for those "sensitive" transfers. The application runs $50 at the Smith Micro Software online store.

BBEdit

Although we all know and love OS X as a graphical operating system, folks still need a powerful text editor for creating and modifying text files. For example, software developers and webmasters still use text editors daily to write applications or to apply a quick fix to the HyperText Markup Language (HTML) that makes up a web page. (I use a text editor to make minor changes to my website, MLC Books Online, without firing up a horrendous web design application. Talk about overkill!)

At first, you might think of TextEdit, which is the free application that ships with OS X. It's not a bad editor, either, with features that far surpass Notepad in the Windows environment. However, serious text and code editing requires a more powerful tool, and the text editor of choice for Mac owners is universally considered to be BBEdit, from Bare Bones Software (www.barebones.com). Figure 5-5 shows a document open in BBEdit 10.

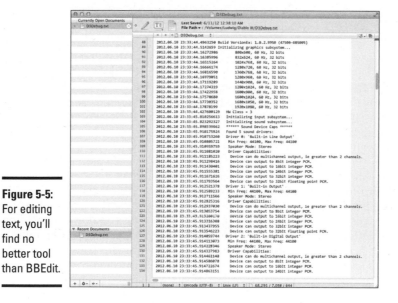

Figure 5-5: For editing text, you'll find no better tool than BBEdit.

Bare Bones Software pulls no punches in describing BBEdit — its advertising still proclaims, "It (still) doesn't suck." Gotta give Bare Bones credit; this incredibly popular editor includes features such as

+ **Support for DOS/Windows, Mac, and Unix text files:** Yes, differences do exist among the platforms, even with a so-called *pure* text file.

+ **Support for massive text files larger than 2GB:** Try that with TextEdit. Hmm. . . . On second thought, *please* don't.

+ **HTML tools for web design:** These tools include syntax checking and browser preview.

+ **grep pattern-based, multifile search and replace:** In nonprogrammer and non-Unix English, a sophisticated search-and-replace function can span more than one text file.

+ **Syntax coloring:** Use this feature to quickly locate commands and qualifiers in programming languages.

+ **Built-in FTP transfer commands:** No need to launch a separate FTP application because you can send your files right from BBEdit.

You can even expand the functionality of BBEdit with plug-ins, many of which are free extensions written by programmers and developers for languages such as C/C++, Java and JavaScript, Perl, and Pascal.

BBEdit 10.5 is available from the Bare Bones Software site for $50.

Xojo Desktop

The final application that I want to mention isn't a utility as such; however, you can use it to write your own software, so I guess that it should qualify. As an ex-COBOL programmer, reluctant Visual Basic shareware developer, and recalcitrant dBASE coder, I can tell you that Xojo Desktop (from Xojo) is definitely the easiest visual drag-and-drop programming environment that I've ever used on a personal computer. If you want to develop your own productivity applications, OS X utilities, or — dare I say it? — your own game, award-winning Xojo Desktop is the way to go.

Development in Xojo Desktop is as simple as designing the application window by first simply adding controls, text, and multimedia wherever you like. Then just fill in the blanks, such as by setting variables and specifying what happens when the controls are triggered, which you do by using a new implementation of the tried-and-true BASIC language. Some programming knowledge is required, but far less than you'd need with Visual Basic. And the results look as good as anything you can accomplish in those so-called real programming languages.

Check out these features:

+ **Cross-platform support so that you can write your program once and compile it for Linux, OS X,** *and* **Windows.** Code it once; then release three versions with no extra work. This is a *very* superb thing.

+ **Support for all sorts of multimedia,** including QuickTime.

+ **Capability to animate and rotate text and objects,** or tap the 3-D power of OpenGL graphics.

✦ **Capability to allow printing, network, and Internet communications** in your application.

✦ **Automation of Microsoft Office applications** and connection of your Real Studio application to business databases (such as FileMaker Pro).

✦ **Royalty-free applications,** so you can give them away or release them as shareware.

Xojo has been such a popular development tool on the Macintosh for so many years that dozens of user-supported websites and mailing lists have sprung up, offering all sorts of plug-ins, tutorials, and sample code for you to use in your own projects.

I recommend the Desktop Edition of Xojo for programming novices. It's $300, and you can order it from http://www.xojo.com/.

At Least One Game

To be completely accurate, OS X comes with at least one game — a very good version of chess, which I cover in the next section — but the Macintosh has never been considered a true gaming platform by most computer owners. Until recently, many popular Windows games were never ported (or converted) for the Mac, and only the most expensive Mac models had the one important component that determines the quality of today's games: a first-rate, 3-D video card.

However, within the last four or five years, all that has changed dramatically. *All* of today's Mac models feature muscle car–quality video cards that use the NVIDIA GeForce or ATI Radeon chipsets; they can handle the most complex 3-D graphics with ease. Match that with the renewed popularity of the Macintosh as a home computer and the performance of the current crop of Intel-based processors, and wham! Suddenly you have the best game developers in the business — id Software (www.idsoftware.com) and Blizzard (www.blizzard.com), to name two — releasing Macintosh versions of their newest games concurrently with the Windows versions.

For the gamer in you, allow me to take you on a tour of the best of the new generation of entertainment.

OS X Chess

No mercenaries, no rail guns, and no cities to raze — but chess is still the world's most popular game, and OS X even includes a little 3-D as well. Figure 5-6 illustrates the Chess application at play; you'll find it in your Applications folder.

Mark Chambers – Computer   (White to Move)

Figure 5-6:
Mavericks
says, "How
about a nice
game of
chess?"

The game features speech recognition, move hints, take back (or undo) for your last move, and a 2-D or 3-D board. You can also list your games in text form and print them or save games in progress. Maybe it's not a complete set of bells and whistles as commercial chess games offer, but the price is right, and the play can be quite challenging (and a bit slower) when you set it at the higher skill levels.

World of WarCraft

I end this chapter with Blizzard's best: the online megahit that is *World of WarCraft*. This MMORPG (short for *massive multiplayer online role-playing game*) is yet another wrinkle in the popular WarCraft game series. *World of WarCraft* puts the character you create in the boots of human princes, Orc battle generals, undead champions, trolls, gnomes, and elfin lords — you can create multiple characters and play them as you choose. My recommendation: Stick with the Undead, my friend.

Combat, however, is only half the job. By finishing quests and killing various nasties, you earn experience, upgrade your armor and weapons, and build a reputation with various groups throughout the land. You can take to the air, buy goods from mercenaries, and even hone your skills with a trade such as leatherworking or enchanting. Spells abound, and you can join a guild and chat with the new friends you make online. I've played for years now, and I'm still excited by this incredible game.

Control is by both keyboard and mouse; the game is easy to understand, but you'll always find someone to kick your posterior in battlegrounds or dungeons over the Internet.

You'll pay about $50 online for *World of WarCraft,* and then you'll be charged a set fee for each month's subscription . . . and it'll be worth every single penny you spend. (Remember, this is a program you'd buy on your own; it doesn't come with your Mac or with Mavericks.) For all the details and some great desktop backgrounds, check the official site at www.blizzard.com.

I'm also a huge pinball fan, and I can heartily recommend the wonderful pinball games available from LittleWing (www.littlewingpinball.com) — you can try the games in demo mode for free! Don't forget to check the compatibility notes for any LittleWing game before you download it because some of those games run only on Macs running older versions of OS X.

Chapter 6: Putting Bluetooth to Work

In This Chapter

✔ Using Bluetooth for wireless connections

✔ Adding wireless keyboards and mice

✔ Adding third-party utilities

✔ Printing over a Bluetooth wireless connection

T ime to talk cordless. Today's MacBooks and the iMac are already pretty doggone all-inclusive because the elements that most computers string together with cords, including the monitor and speakers, have been integrated into the computer's case. However, here's another reason to celebrate the disappearance of cords: Every Mac model capable of running Mavericks includes built-in Bluetooth wireless technology — and Bluetooth is officially Hot Stuff.

For most of us, Bluetooth introduces new possibilities — which result in more questions. Exactly how do other wireless devices communicate with your Mac? Can you really share the data on your Mac with a cellphone or tablet that doesn't carry a striking Apple logo?

In this chapter, I describe what's cooking in the world of wireless devices. I don't delve into wireless Ethernet networking between your Mac and other computers; I cover that topic in depth in the confines of Book VI, Chapter 3. However, I *do* cover the wireless Bluetooth connections that you can make with devices other than computers.

Bluetooth: What a Silly Name for Such Cool Technology

Originally, wireless computer connections were limited to IR (infrared) and 802.11b (the original Wi-Fi specification for wireless Ethernet networks).

This constraint was fine; after all, what were you gonna connect to your Mac besides other computers? Ah, but progress marches on.

Bluetooth has been incorporated into a range of peripherals and devices, including

✦ Smartphones

✦ Laptops

✦ Wireless computer peripherals such as keyboards and mice

✦ Printers

✦ Headphones

Mavericks and Bluetooth, together forever

You'd expect a modern, high-tech operating system such as OS X to come with Bluetooth drivers. You'd be right, but Apple goes a step further: Mavericks comes with a Bluetooth pane in System Preferences and a utility application to help you get your laptop connected with the Bluetooth devices that are likely hanging out in your coat pockets.

A little Danish history

In 1998, a consortium of big-name phone, PDA, and computer laptop manufacturers decided that their products needed a method of communicating with each other. This new wireless standard needed to be inexpensive and consume as little battery power as possible, so designers decided to keep the operational distance limited to a maximum of about 30 feet. Plus, the idea was to keep this new wireless system as hassle free as possible: Everyone agreed that when you're using one device, you should simply be able to walk within range of another device for the two to link up immediately and automatically. Thus, Bluetooth was born.

If the name "Bluetooth" sounds faintly like Viking-speak to you, it should. For some ridiculous reason, the companies that developed the Bluetooth standard decided to name their creation after the tenth-century Danish king Harald Blatand, nicknamed Bluetooth, who succeeded in joining Denmark and Norway in a political alliance. Hence the rather Viking and runic-looking Bluetooth symbol. (Geez, these folks need to take a day off. Read comic books or play with a Slinky. *Something*.)

Start by clicking the System Preferences icon on the Dock, and then click the Bluetooth icon in the System Preferences pane. From the Bluetooth pane that appears (shown in Figure 6-1), you can

✦ **Turn Bluetooth hardware on or off.** Click the Turn Bluetooth On/Off button to enable or disable your Bluetooth hardware.

I recommend that you enable the Show Bluetooth in the Menu Bar check box. If you're using a MacBook, the Bluetooth menu lets you conserve power by turning off your Bluetooth hardware until you need it. You can also conveniently toggle your Mac's discovery status as well as set up a device or send and browse files. (You can even see what devices are connected to your Mac with the click of a menu icon. 'Nuff said.)

✦ **Connect or disconnect Bluetooth devices.** All recognized Bluetooth devices in range appear in the list, and you can connect or disconnect them individually. Click the Pair button next to the device you want to add to your list of recognized Bluetooth devices, and follow the onscreen prompt to enter the code number that identifies your Mac to the device.

Make sure that your Bluetooth device is in range and *discoverable* (available for connections with other Bluetooth devices) before you open the Bluetooth pane in System Preferences. Check your user manual to determine how to set your Bluetooth device as discoverable, and make sure that you're about 20 feet (or fewer) away from your Mac.

Figure 6-1: The Bluetooth pane in System Preferences.

If you know you won't be using Bluetooth devices while you're on the road, disabling a Bluetooth service on a MacBook can help conserve battery power.

The other Bluetooth resource that you can use is the stand-alone Bluetooth File Exchange application. (Yes, you can call it BFE if you like. I do whenever possible.) You have to launch BFE the old-fashioned way; it's available from the Utilities folder (which can also be named Extras or Other) in Launchpad. Launching the application presents you with a file selection dialog in which you choose the file(s) you want to send to the connected Bluetooth device. You can also elect to browse the files on a networked Bluetooth device so that you can see what the owner of that device is offering. (Note, however, that BFE doesn't work with iPhones, iPads, or the iPod touch as of this writing.)

You can also set up your defaults for file exchanges from the Sharing pane in System Preferences. While you're in the Bluetooth pane, click the Show All button, and then click the Sharing icon. Select the Bluetooth Sharing check box (left side) to display the settings shown in Figure 6-2. Here, you can control what Mavericks does when you receive files or Personal Information Manager (PIM) data through BFE. For instance, with these settings, Mavericks can

✦ Prompt you for permission to receive each file or PIM item

✦ Accept all files and PIM items without restriction or prompting

✦ Save all incoming files and items to the folder that you specify

✦ Prompt you for permission when other devices want to browse your Mac

✦ Offer only the files and items in the folder that you specify when other Bluetooth items browse your Mac

Figure 6-2:
Configure file exchanges in System Preferences.

I'm all for the defaults in Mavericks for file exchanges:

✦ **When Receiving Items:** Stick with Ask What to Do so you can know when someone is sending you something.

✦ **Folder for Accepted Items:** I recommend that anything you receive be saved in your Downloads folder.

✦ **When Other Devices Browse:** I prefer to authorize other devices when they attempt to browse my Mac, so I leave this set to Ask What to Do.

✦ **Folder Others Can Browse:** If you allow a device to browse, it can access the contents of only your Public folder.

However, feel free to adjust, enable, and disable to your heart's content.

Adding Wireless Keyboards and Mice to Your Mac

The current crop of Macs arrives at your doorstep with full wireless support: Apple includes both internal Bluetooth hardware and internal AirPort Extreme wireless hardware. You can indeed work keyboard and mouse magic from across the room from your Mac, with a wireless keyboard and mouse — either the wireless keyboard and mouse (or trackpad) that come with specific Mac models or models you buy on your own. Even if you're a MacBook owner, perhaps you just want a full-size keyboard and an external pointing device to use when you're working from your home or office.

A number of wireless Bluetooth keyboard/mouse packages are on the market, and any one of 'em should work fine with your Mac. You can buy Apple's wireless Bluetooth keyboard and mouse separately, for about $140. Other offerings from Logitech and our old buddy Microsoft run about the same amount.

When shopping for a Bluetooth keyboard/mouse desktop, keep these facts in mind:

✦ **Some keyboards are created more than equal.** Many of today's third-party keyboards are encrusted with extra function buttons that do everything from open your e-mail application to search your kitchen cabinets for another can of spray cheese.

I like these programmable function keys because they're handy for bringing up your favorite applications with a single keystroke while you're relaxing 20 feet away. I recommend that you look for the keyboard in your price range that offers the most programmable keys.

✦ **Rodents crave energy.** If the wireless mouse or trackpad comes with its own recharging stand, that's a big plus. Depending on how much you use your laptop, a pointing device that runs on standard batteries can go through a set in as little as a month's time! (Not surprisingly, many computer owners use rechargeable batteries in their wireless mice.) Some wireless mice and trackpads (including those from Apple) feature an on/off switch to help conserve battery power.

✦ **Wireless doesn't always mean Bluetooth.** Just because a keyboard or mouse is wireless doesn't automatically make it a Bluetooth device. Plenty of wireless RF (radio frequency) devices are out there, too. These toys need their own transmitters, which are usually USB-based as well. Therefore, read the box or technical specifications carefully to make sure you're buying Bluetooth.

✦ **Wireless stuff isn't self-cleaning.** Sure, your new wireless keyboard and mouse can hang out with you on the sofa, but that doesn't mean they're happy sharing your nacho puffs and grape soda. Look for an optical mouse that doesn't use a ball, and check whether a prospective keyboard or trackpad can be easily cleaned and maintained before you buy it.

Most Bluetooth devices are installed and controlled through the Bluetooth pane in System Preferences. However, wireless keyboards, trackpads, and mice are special cases because they're installed via the Bluetooth controls in the Keyboard, Trackpad, or Mouse pane, respectively. (Geez, those Apple designers give you a dozen roads to the same spot on the map, don't they?) You can read more about each of these System Preferences panes in Book II, Chapter 3.

The Magic of Wireless Printing

To your Mac, a wireless Bluetooth printer might be just another Bluetooth connection, but to you, it's the very definition of convenience, especially if desk space is limited next to your Mac. Just set that paper-producing puppy up anywhere in the 30–40 foot range, plug it in, set up the printer in Mavericks, and let 'er rip.

Not all printer manufacturers produce Bluetooth models that communicate properly with your Mac. Make sure that the Bluetooth printer you buy supports HCRP. (Great, another jawbreaker acronym. This time it stands for Hardcopy Cable Replacement Profile.)

You have two options when installing a Bluetooth printer:

✦ Whenever possible, use the printer manufacturer's software. A printer might require a driver that a typical Bluetooth device doesn't need.

✦ You can usually successfully set up a printer via the Bluetooth pane of System Preferences (as I discuss earlier in this chapter) by following these steps:

1. *Make sure your printer is set as discoverable.*

   Check your printer manual to determine how to switch your printer to discoverable mode. This mode allows other Bluetooth devices within range (including your Mac) to recognize and make a connection to your printer.

2. *Choose the printer from the list of discovered Bluetooth devices.*

3. *Click the Pair button.*

4. *Follow the onscreen instructions.*

Luckily, after you successfully set up a Bluetooth printer, you can just press ⌘+P to open the Print dialog and choose that printer from the Printer pop-up menu. No big whoop . . . and that's the way it *should* be.

Book VIII

Advanced OS X

Contents at a Glance

Chapter 1: Running Windows on Your Mac with Boot Camp

In This Chapter

- ✔ Introducing Boot Camp
- ✔ Comparing Boot Camp with software emulation
- ✔ Creating your Windows partition
- ✔ Switching to your Windows system
- ✔ Updating Apple software in Windows

Do you sometimes miss that (cough) *other* operating system? Would you like to run legacy Windows programs on your Mac? Do you miss the familiar confines of the Microsoft world?

No need to be furtive about your Windows yearnings. Although I'm an enthusiastic Mac owner, I also own two smooth-running PCs, and all my computers cohabitate quite well in my office. I use both Windows 7 and Windows 8 every day for a number of tasks. So, dear reader, what if I told you that both OS X Mavericks and Windows 7 or 8 can live together in peace and harmony, *all on the same hard drive inside your Mac?*

In this chapter, I discuss the wonder that is Boot Camp — the free utility included with Mavericks that allows you to install and run Windows on your Mac's hard drive. I explain why Boot Camp is superior in performance to Windows emulator software and how to switch between OSes with a simple reboot.

Hold on to your hat, Mac owners: You're about to take a wild trip that proves you can indeed have the best of both worlds.

Figuring Out How Boot Camp Works

First, a bit of technobabble, but I promise it'll be over soon, and I'll try to keep things from getting too boring. In years past, you may have heard that a Mac computer couldn't run Windows out of the box (without expensive hardware or software), and that Mac software was off-limits to PCs . . .

and you'd have heard correctly, at least for all but the recent history of the Macintosh computer. The incompatibility was a result of Apple using a series of Motorola processors (CPUs) that didn't speak the same language as the Intel CPUs used in PCs. Consider a person speaking Korean trying to read a book in Arabic, and you get the general idea.

Then Apple began using Intel processors in Macs, and the ground rules changed. Apple hardware was suddenly compatible with Windows. All that was needed was a bridge to help keep both OSes separate on the same hard drive — and Apple developed Boot Camp. Of course, that bridge works only in one direction because you still can't run Macintosh software on a PC. (Go figure.)

Boot Camp accomplishes this magic by creating a separate Windows partition on your Mac's hard drive. The partition holds all your Windows data, including the OS, your program files, and the documents you create while running Windows. Consider this partition as completely separate from your OS X data even though both partitions exist on the same physical hard drive.

Think of it this way: When you reboot your Mac using Boot Camp, it's similar to changing the station on an FM radio. The hardware is the same, but you switch to a different station (Windows instead of OS X), and you're listening to different music (country instead of rock). How's *that* for a comparison, Dr. Science?

Naturally, you need free space on your Mac's hard drive to install Boot Camp. Apple recommends having 10GB of free space, but I'd bump that up to 40GB. A new Boot Camp installation in Mavericks requires Windows 7 or Windows 8.

When your Mac is running Windows, it's just as susceptible to virus and spyware attack as any other Windows PC. Make sure to invest in quality antivirus and antispyware protection for your Windows side!

Comparing Boot Camp to Windows Emulators

"But Mark, what about Windows emulators?" you ask. Ah, that's a good point: A number of excellent Mac applications let you run Windows in what's called a *virtual machine.* Although your Mac is still running OS X, these emulators create an environment where Windows can share system resources such as hard drives, RAM, and even peripherals. I discuss my favorite, Parallels Desktop, in Book VII, Chapter 5.

These Windows emulators have four big advantages over Boot Camp:

✦ **Versatility:** Unlike Boot Camp, where you're restricted to creating only one Windows partition, Parallels Desktop allows you to create as many virtual machines as you have hard drive space. Plus, you can run multiple versions of Windows, or even other operating systems such as Unix, Linux, and DOS.

✦ **Portability:** An emulator allows you to store your Windows installation on a separate hard drive — even a large-capacity USB flash drive! With Boot Camp, the Windows partition you create must reside on your Mavericks boot drive (which can sometimes eat up space on smaller-capacity MacBook drives).

✦ **Shared data:** If you have Windows and OS X applications that you must run concurrently (such as FileMaker Pro on the Mac side and Microsoft Access on the Windows side) and they use the same data with both Mavericks and Windows, an emulator is your only option.

✦ **No need to reboot:** With Boot Camp, you must reboot to run your Mac under Windows. Windows emulators don't need a reboot.

"Okay then, Mark, why are you such a fan of Boot Camp?" I'm glad you asked! Here are two major reasons to choose Boot Camp over a Windows emulator:

✦ **Performance:** One word, dear reader: *speed.* No software Windows emulator will ever run as fast or perform as trouble-free as Boot Camp. A Mac running Boot Camp is *actually running as a true Windows PC,* able to access all the system resources Windows demands without an emulator slowing things down. It makes sense when you think about it. Because you're running Parallels Desktop or VMWare Fusion on top of Mavericks, your Mac has to devote a significant amount of computing time to just keeping OS X running. Some Windows applications simply won't run well under emulation, such as today's memory- and processor-hungry 3-D games.

✦ **Peripheral control:** If you're running a software Windows emulator and you plug a USB flash drive into your Mac, which OS gets to use it? How about your digital camera or that external Blu-ray recorder? Although Parallels Desktop has all sorts of automatic and manual controls you can set to determine which operating system gets to use what, a Mac running Boot Camp owns everything you plug into it free and clear, with no troublesome conflicts between operating systems arguing over peripherals.

**Book VIII
Chapter 1**

Running Windows on Your Mac with Boot Camp

Oh, and I don't want to forget what many Mac owners consider the most important advantage for Boot Camp: It's free. You need a licensed copy of the version of Windows you want to run, but there's nothing else to buy.

Remember what I said about Boot Camp modifying your hard drive? **Do not install Boot Camp without backing up your existing data on your Mac's hard drive!** I've never had a problem with Boot Camp, but there's always a first time. In case of catastrophe, you can always use your Time Machine backup to restore your Mac's operating system and all your data — yes, that's yet *another* good reason for you to pick up an external drive and use Time Machine on your Mac, as I describe in Book I, Chapter 9!

Configuring Boot Camp

Installing Boot Camp is surprisingly easy and takes far less time than it takes to install Windows afterward. Follow these steps:

1. **Launch the Boot Camp Assistant.**

   You can find the Assistant in your Utilities folder, which is in your Applications folder. I use Launchpad to reach it quickly: Click the Launchpad icon on the Dock, click the Utilities folder icon, and then click the Boot Camp Assistant icon.

   Click the Print Installation & Setup Guide button on the Introduction screen. Keep this additional documentation handy just in case you have questions about running Windows that aren't covered in this chapter.

2. **Click Continue on the Introduction screen.**

   Figure 1-1 illustrates the Boot Camp Assistant Support Software screen that appears.

Figure 1-1: Yes, you want the Windows support software. Trust me.

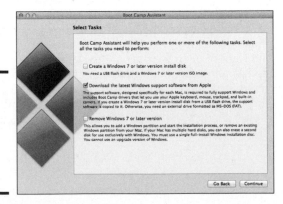

3. **Make sure the Download the Latest Windows Support Software from Apple check box is selected and then click Continue.**

   Boot Camp Assistant can copy these drivers to a blank CD or DVD or an external USB flash drive. I think a disc (which you can hang on to in case you need it later) is the easiest choice, but most Mac models no longer have an optical drive, so the USB flash drive may be a better choice. You load this software after your Windows installation is complete, and it provides all the drivers that Windows needs for your Mac's hardware.

4. **Choose the size of your Windows partition and then click Create.**

   Again, you can devote more hard drive space to your Windows partition than the amount recommended by the assistant, but don't forget this important fact: What you reserve for use in Windows cannot be used by OS X Mavericks! Therefore, I always suggest a conservative amount. (In other words, don't devote 300GB of your 500GB drive to your Windows partition because you'll cramp your style in OS X.)

5. **Reboot if required.**

   You may be prompted to launch the assistant again.

6. **Click Start the Windows Installer and then click Continue.**

   From this point on, you're running the Windows installation program, just as you would be if you were using a PC. (Well, actually you *are* using a PC now.) Follow the onscreen prompts, which differ for each version of Windows.

When prompted by the Windows Installer to choose the partition to format, choose the partition named BOOTCAMP. Formatting any other partition will likely result in the loss of all your OS X files and data. (Again, this is why you should always back up your existing system before putting Boot Camp to work.)

After Windows has been installed, load the disc or USB flash drive you created with the drivers and support software. Windows should automatically run the Boot Camp driver installation program for you. After the drivers are in place, you're ready to do the Microsoft dance.

Are you moving your stuff from Windows (running on your old PC) to . . . well, Windows (running on your Mac)? Brings an entirely new meaning to the term *switcher,* doesn't it? If so, the files and folders on your existing PC can be copied directly to Windows running on your Mac by using the Windows Easy Transfer utility.

Using the Boot Camp Control Panel

Besides the capability to restart your Mac in OS X Mavericks, the Windows Boot Camp notification icon is also your gateway to a number of other features. Right-click the icon and choose Boot Camp Control Panel from the contextual menu to display the settings; these will vary depending on the version of Windows you're using and the type of Mac you're running. On the Control Panel, you will find these tabs:

✔ **Startup Disk tab:** From this tab, which is essentially a Windows version of Mountain Lion's Startup Disk pane in System Preferences, you can choose to reboot in OS X Mavericks by clicking the Mac OS X folder and then clicking Restart.

✔ **Brightness tab:** Use the Brightness slider here to dim or brighten your display.

✔ **Remote tab:** Enable or disable remote control by an Apple Remote.

✔ **Power tab:** Specify whether your Mac should restart automatically after a power failure.

If you make any changes in the Boot Camp Control Panel, click OK to save your changes and return to Windows.

Switching to Windows

Here are three methods for switching back and forth between your OS X partition and your Windows partition:

✦ **From OS X Mavericks:** To restart your Mac in Windows, click System Preferences on the Dock and then click the Startup Disk icon to display the settings you see in Figure 1-2. Click the Windows partition you created in the list to select it. (The folder icon will bear the Windows logo, and it will be labeled Windows as well.) Click Restart and then click Restart again when asked for confirmation. Your Mac reboots and loads Windows, and continues to run Windows when started or rebooted until you follow one of the next two methods of returning to OS X.

✦ **From Windows:** Right-click the Boot Camp icon in the notification area at the right side of your Windows taskbar — it looks like a slanted square — and choose Restart in Mac OS X from the menu that appears. Again, you'll be asked to confirm your choice. After you click OK, your Mac reboots and returns to Mountain Lion.

✦ **During the boot process:** Need a temporary fix from your other OS? You can reboot from either Mavericks or Windows and hold down the Option key when you see the Apple logo appear. Your Mac displays a nifty row of icons, each representing a bootable OS that your Mac can use. To boot OS X, click the Mavericks partition icon. To choose Windows, click the Windows partition icon. Note that when you turn on or reboot your Mac, it returns to the OS you last selected in the System Preferences Startup Disk pane.

Figure 1-2:
Preparing to
jump ship to
Windows.

Checking for Apple Updates

Apple sometimes releases updates for Boot Camp software and drivers. From an active Internet connection, you can easily check for updates in Windows using the Apple Software Update program.

To run Update, click the Start button and click Apple Software Update. The program automatically connects to Apple's servers and displays any updates (including those for the Windows versions of programs like Safari and iTunes). Select the check box for each update you want to apply and then click the Install button to start the ball rolling.

Although this is a shameless plug, it fits very well at the end of a chapter dedicated to Windows: If you'd like a handy companion guide to Windows 8, Microsoft Office 2013, and the world of PCs, I can highly recommend the book *PCs All-in-One For Dummies,* 6th Edition, written by yours truly. (As I said at the beginning of this chapter, I draw no favorites between PC and Mac.)

Chapter 2: . . . And Unix Lurks Beneath

As I mention in the first chapter of the book — at the beginning of our Mavericks odyssey — Unix lurks deep beneath the shiny Aqua exterior of OS X. Unix is a tried-and-true operating system (OS) that's been around for decades, since the days when minicomputers were king. If you don't believe that it's a powerful (and popular) OS, consider that more than half of all web servers on the Internet run using some variety of Unix.

Besides being battle-tested and having a long history, Unix offers some fantastic features. Unlike in the graphical world of OS X, the keyboard plays an integral role in using Unix. Because Unix is text-based, it's evolved a large set of useful keyboard-driven commands that can perform powerful feats that a mouse user just can't easily equal, such as moving a huge number of specific files (such as Word documents) from one folder to another. This chapter examines the role of the keyboard in Unix and describes how to execute standard file system commands. You also discover how to use a number of simple programs and how to retrieve information from the Internet.

Why Use the Keyboard?

To begin benefiting from the Unix underpinnings of OS X, get used to doing things with the keyboard. Although mouse skills can be applied to using Unix, you'll generally find performing Unix functions to be faster and easier with the keyboard.

Unix keyboarding is fast

Why on Earth would any red-blooded Macintosh owner want to leave the comfort of the mouse to use a keyboard? After all, the graphical user interface (GUI) is what made the Macintosh great in the first place. After all, with Finder, you can navigate and manage the various files on your hard drive with a few clicks. This sounds simple enough. For some tasks, though, using the keyboard can be just as fast — if not faster.

Suppose, for example, that you need to copy a file on your hard drive to somewhere on that same drive. In the traditional manner using Finder, it's a click-and-drag trek: Open a Finder window, navigate to the file to copy, open another Finder window (⌘+N, because clicking the Finder icon on the Dock doesn't open a second Finder window), navigate to the folder where you want to copy the file, duplicate the original file, and *then* drag that copy to its intended destination.

Comparatively, by using the keyboard and the power of Unix, you can accomplish the same task with a one-line command. For some tasks, the mouse is definitely the way to go, but you can perform some other tasks just as quickly, if not faster, with the keyboard. For the skinny on one-line commands, skip to the section, "Uncovering the Terminal."

The Unix keyboard is a powerful beast

So maybe you're not an expert typist, and using the mouse still sounds inviting. For many scenarios, you'd be correct in assuming that a mouse can handle the job just as quickly and easily as a bunch of commands that you have to memorize. Using the keyboard, however, offers some other distinct advantages over the mouse. To allow you to control your computer from the keyboard, Unix offers a command line tool that you use to enter commands one line at a time. OS X ships with Terminal, its command line application. From Launchpad, you can find the Terminal icon in the Utilities folder (depending on how you installed OS X, the folder may also be called Other). You can also find it here:

```
/Applications/Utilities/Terminal
```

One shining feature of the command line is its efficiency. One mouse click is equal to one command. When you use the command line, you can combine commands into a kind of super command (minus the silly cape, but with bulging muscles intact), with each command performing some action of the combined whole. From the command line, you can string together a whole bunch of commands to do a complex task.

For example, consider how many times you'd have to click a mouse in Finder to complete these steps:

1. Find all files that begin with the letters *MyDocument.*

2. From this list of files, add a number to the beginning of the filename, indicating its size in kilobytes.

3. Save the names of all altered files to a text file.

From the command line, you could accomplish all these tasks by typing only one *super command:* a collection of three simple commands combined to form one instruction. The built-in Terminal program that ships with OS X Mavericks gives you everything you need to start using the command line. I show you how in the section, "Uncovering the Terminal," later in this chapter.

Delving further into super commands isn't for the faint-hearted; things get pretty ugly pretty quickly, and this chapter can show you only the very beginning of the Unix Yellow Brick Road. Therefore, if your thirst for Unix dominance so compels you, I invite you to do a little independent study to bone up on the OS. Pick up a copy of the great book of lore entitled *UNIX For Dummies,* 5th Edition, written by John R. Levine and Margaret Levine Young (Wiley).

Go where no mouse has gone before

Finder is generally a helpful tool, but it makes many assumptions about how you work. One of these assumptions is that you don't have any need to handle some of the files on your hard drive. As I mention in Book II, Chapter 6, OS X ships with its system files marked "off limits," and I generally agree with that policy (which keeps anyone from screwing up the delicate innards of OS X). To secure your system files, Apple purposely hides some files from view.

But what road do you take if you need to modify those system files? Yep, you guessed it: The command line comes to the rescue! You can use the command line to peer inside every nook and cranny of your Mac's vast directory structure on your hard drive. It also has the power to edit files that aren't typically accessible to you. From the command line, you can pretend to be other users — even users with more permissions. By temporarily acting as a more powerful user, you can perform actions with the command line that would be impossible in Finder. (Just remember to make sure that you know *exactly* what you're doing, or that you're working with an Apple technical support person — one wrong move, and it'll be time for an ominous chord.)

Automate to elevate

If all these benefits are beginning to excite you, hold on to your socks! Not only can you perform complex commands with the command line, but you can go even one step further: *automation.* If you find yourself using the same set of commands more than once — say, to copy a folder of images to another location and rename them all — you're a likely candidate for using automation to save time. Instead of typing the list of commands each time, you can save them to a text file and execute the entire file with only one command. Now that's power, right up there with the dynamic duo of AppleScript and Automator! (Granted, it's not graphical like Automator, but then again, Unix has been around for decades.)

Of course, you probably don't like doing housekeeping tasks while you're busy on other things, so schedule that list of commands to run in the middle of the night while you're fast asleep. And of course, the command line lets you do that, too.

Automation of Unix commands is separate from automation of OS X applications with AppleScript and Automator, which I cover in Chapter 3 of this minibook.

Remote control

"So, Mark, the command line is the cat's meow for efficiently accessing and working with files on my Mac, and I can use it to automate many operations. Anything else?" I'm glad you asked! From the command line, you can also send commands to another computer anywhere in the world (as long as you know the right login and password). And after you log in to another computer, you can use the same commands for the remote computer.

Unix was created with multiple users in mind. Because computers used to be expensive (and honking *huge* machines to boot), Unix was designed so that multiple users could remotely use the same machine simultaneously. If OS X is your first encounter with Unix, you might be surprised to know that many Unix beginners of the past weren't even in the same room, building, state, or even country as the computer that they were using.

Not only can you work with a computer that's in a different physical location, but it's also very fast to do so. Instead of the bandwidth hog that is the Internet, the command line is lean and mean, permitting you to use a remote computer nearly as fast as if it were sitting on the desk in front of you. (This is a great advantage for road warriors who need to tweak a web server or an e-mail server from a continent away.)

Uncovering the Terminal

The best way to find out how to use the command line is to jump right into the Terminal application, which (as I mention earlier) comes with OS X. Click the Launchpad icon on the Dock, click the Utilities folder, and then click the Terminal icon.

You can also jump directly to the Utilities folder from the keyboard by pressing Shift+⌘+U (which displays the Utilities folder in a Finder window, as shown in Figure 2-1). Double-click the Terminal icon there. By the way, feel free to make Terminal more accessible by dragging its icon from the Utilities folder to the Dock.

Consider yourself prompted

Upon launch of the Terminal application, you'll immediately notice some text in the window that appears onscreen. For example

```
Last login: Sun Jun 23 17:51:14 on console
WHITEDRAGON:~ markchambers$
```

This text details the last time that you logged in to Terminal. The last line, however, is the more important one: It's the *prompt*.

Figure 2-1:
Find the Terminal application in your Utilities folder.

The prompt serves some important functions. First, it lists the current directory, which is listed as ~ in the preceding example. A tilde character (~) denotes a user's Home directory. By default, you're always in your Home folder each time you begin a new session on Terminal. After the current directory, Terminal displays the name of the current user, which is markchambers in this example.

As you've probably surmised, a folder and a directory are two different names for the same thing. *Folder* is the name with which most Mac users are familiar, and *directory* is a term that Unix power users prefer. I use the terms interchangeably throughout the remainder of this chapter.

The final character of the prompt is a $. Consider this your cue because immediately after this character is where you enter any command that you wish to execute.

Go ahead; don't be shy. Try out your first command by typing **uptime** in Terminal. This will show you a listing of how long your Mac has been running since the last reboot or login. (It's a good idea to type Unix commands in lowercase because case-sensitivity is all-important in Unix.) Your text appears at the location of the cursor, denoted by a small square. If you make a mistake while entering the command, no worries. Just press Delete to back up and then type the characters again. If the typing error is stuck deep in a longer command, press the left- or right-arrow key to move the cursor immediately after the incorrect character and press Delete to back up; then type the correct characters. After you type the command, press Return to execute it.

```
WHITEDRAGON:~ markchambers$ uptime
6:24PM up  2:42, 4 users, load averages: 2.44, 2.38, 1.90
WHITEDRAGON:~ markchambers$
```

In the preceding example, the computer has been running for 2 hours and 42 minutes (2:42 in line 2). Simple, eh? Immediately following the listing of the uptime command (line 3), the Terminal displays another prompt for you to enter more commands. I examine many more commands later in this chapter.

Prefer a different appearance for the Terminal window? Click the Terminal menu and choose Preferences; then click the Settings toolbar button to choose the color combinations for the Terminal window background and text.

A few commands to get started

As you use the command line to navigate through the various folders on your hard drive, you'll lean on two vital commands: ls and cd. The ls command is shorthand for *list,* and it does just that: It lists the contents of the current directory. Enter **ls** at the prompt, and you see a listing of your Home folder.

The complementary `cd` command (again, note the lowercase) — *change directory* — opens any folder that you specify. It works much the same as double-clicking a folder in Finder: The difference is that following the `cd` command, you don't immediately see the entire folder's content. Too, the `cd` command requires a *parameter* (extra options or information that appear after the command) so that your Mac knows which folder to open.

For example, to open the Documents folder in your Home directory, type **cd Documents** and press Return. Hmm. Another prompt is displayed immediately. So where are all the files in the Documents folder? You must enter another command to see what items are in the folder that you just opened. Type your old friend **ls** again to see the contents of the Documents folder.

The preceding example works for a folder named with just one word. To open a folder with any spaces in its name, make sure to enclose the folder's name in quotation marks, like this:

```
cd "My Picture Folder"
```

Read more about spaces and using quotation marks in your commands in the upcoming section, "Command line gotchas." You can also precede a space (or any other character that the command line treats as special, such as an *) in a name with a backslash, like this:

```
cd My\ Picture\ Folder
```

To return to your Home folder in this example, enter a modified version of the `cd` command:

```
cd ..
```

This causes your Mac to move back up the folder hierarchy one folder to your Home directory. By using these three simple commands — `ls`, `cd` *foldername*, and `cd ..` — you can traverse your entire hard drive (or at least those locations where you have permission to peruse).

After you successfully enter a command, you can recall it by pressing the up-arrow key. Press the up-arrow key again to see the command prior to that, and so forth. This is an extremely useful trick for retyping extra long file paths.

Using the mouse skills you already have

Just because the Terminal is text-based doesn't mean that it doesn't act like a good Macintosh citizen. All the usual Mac features that you know and love are there for you to use. The familiar Copy function works anywhere, as you might expect. Paste, however, works only at the prompt position.

Drag-and-drop is also at your disposal. After you play around with the Terminal for a while, you'll find yourself bored to tears typing the long paths that represent the files on your hard drive. To automatically enter the path of a file or folder to a command, simply drag it to the active Terminal window, as shown in Figure 2-2. The file's full path instantly appears at the location of your cursor. (Thanks, Apple!)

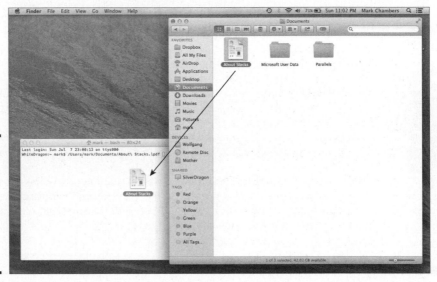

Figure 2-2:
Drag a
file from
a Finder
window into
Terminal to
display its
path.

You can even use the mouse while entering commands in the Terminal. Click and drag your mouse over text to select it. From there, you can copy to the Clipboard as you might expect with any other application.

Unix Commands 101

To use the command line effectively, familiarize yourself with other Unix commands. After all, how can you use a tool without knowing what it can do? You might have to memorize a few commands, but Unix makes it easy on you by abbreviating commands, following a standard grammar (so to speak), and providing you with extensive documentation for each command.

Anatomy of a Unix command

Unix commands can perform many amazing feats. Despite their vast capabilities, all commands follow a similar structure. Note the spaces between the command, the flags, and the operands:

```
command <optional flag(s)> <optional operand(s)>
```

The simplest form of a Unix command is the command itself. (For a basic discussion on Unix commands, such as `ls`, see the earlier section, "A few commands to get started.") You can expand your use of the `ls` command by appending various *flags,* which are settings that enable or disable optional features for the command. Most flags are preceded by a dash (-) and always follow the command. For instance, you can display the contents of a directory as a column of names by tacking on a `-1` flag after the `ls` command.

```
ls -1
```

Besides flags, Unix commands sometimes also have *operands,* which are something that is acted upon. For example, instead of just entering the `ls` command (which lists the current directory), you can add an operand to list a specific directory:

```
ls ~/Documents/myProject/
```

The tilde (~) denotes the user's Home directory.

Sometimes a command can take multiple operands, as is the case when you copy a file. The two operands represent the source file and the destination of the file that you want to copy, separated by a space. The following example using the `cp` command (short for *copy*) copies a file from the Documents folder to the Desktop folder.

```
cp ~/Documents/MyDocument ~/Desktop/MyDocument
```

You can also combine flags and operands in the same command. This example displays the contents of a specific folder in list format:

```
ls -1 ~/Documents/myProject/
```

Command line gotchas

In earlier sections, I describe a few simple command line functions. You might not have noticed, but every example thus far involves folder names and filenames that contain only alphabetic characters. As I discuss earlier, remember what happens if you have a folder name with a space in it. Try the following example, but don't worry when it doesn't work.

As you can read earlier in this chapter, the `cd` command stands for *change directory*.

```
cd /Example Folder
```

The result is an error message:

```
-bash: cd: /Example: No such file or directory
```

The problem is that a space character isn't allowed in a path. To get around this problem, simply enclose the path in double quotation marks, like this:

```
cd "/Example Folder"
```

OS X lets you use either double *or* single quotation marks to enclose a path with spaces in it. Standard Unix OSes, however, use double quotation marks for this purpose.

As I mention earlier, you can get the space character to be accepted by a command by adding an escape character. (In this case, the escape character acts as a marker that skips over the space.) To escape a character, add a backslash (\) immediately prior to the character in question. To illustrate, try the last command with an escape character instead. Note that this time, no quotation marks are necessary.

```
cd /Desktop\ Folder
```

You can use either quotation marks or escape characters; they're interchangeable. Note that the backslash (\) is the escape character, not the forward slash (/).

Help is on the way!

By now, you might be wondering how a computer technowizard is supposed to keep all these commands straight. Fortunately, you can find generous documentation for nearly every command available. To access this built-in help, use the man command. Using the man command (short for *manual*) will display a help file for any command that it knows about. For example, to read the available help information for the ls command, simply type **man ls** at the prompt. Figure 2-3 illustrates the result.

Figure 2-3:
Use the
man
command to
display help
information.

Autocompletion

To speed things along, the bash shell can automagically complete your input for you while you type. A *shell* takes the commands you type and submits them to the OS, which then performs the tasks. Although the Terminal permits you to enter commands via the keyboard, it is the shell that interprets those commands. Many kinds of shells are available to Unix users. The shell that Mavericks uses by default is bash, and another common shell is tcsh. Use the autocompletion features of bash to autocomplete both commands and filenames. To demonstrate, begin by typing the following:

```
cd ~/De
```

Then press Tab, and the shell predicts what you want to type:

```
cd ~/Desktop/
```

Of course, if you have another folder that begins with the letters *De* in the same folder, you might need to type a few additional characters because otherwise the shell returns the first hit it encounters. This gives the autocompletion feature more information to help it decide which characters you want to type. In other words, if you don't type enough characters, autocompletion ends up like a detective without enough clues to figure things out.

Working with Files

If you've used a computer for any time at all, you're no doubt familiar with the idea of files. Even before the first floppy drive appeared in personal computers, OSes have stored data in files, dating back to when a mainframe computer system could occupy an entire floor of an office building. OS X is no exception, and it's important to understand how OS X arranges files into folders and how you go about accessing them via the command line. This section describes the basic file and folder information you need to know to tame the beast that is Unix.

Paths

Before you dive into Unix commands, you should first know a few facts . . . nasty things, facts, but you can't earn your pair of technowizard suspenders without 'em. For starters, as a Mac user, you might not be familiar with how paths work in Unix. A *path* is simply a textual representation of a folder or file. The simplest paths are the root, denoted by the forward slash (/), and your Home directory, denoted by a tilde character (~), which acts as the equivalent of /Users/<*your short account name*> (in my case, /Users/markchambers). Any folder in the Home directory is represented by the folder's name preceded by a forward slash (/). For example, a document entitled myDoc that resides in the current user's Documents folder would have a path like this:

~/Documents/myDoc

Similarly, a folder named myFolder that resides in the current user's Documents folder would have a path like this:

~/Documents/myFolder/

As I mention earlier, a *folder* (Mac-speak) and a *directory* (Unix-speak) are simply two different names for the same thing.

Because OS X is a multiuser environment, you might sometimes want to work with folders or files somewhere other than in your Home folder. Starting from your Home folder, enter the following command:

cd ..

This moves you to the folder right above your Home folder, which happens to be the Users folder. Using another quick ls command will show you all users who are permitted to use the machine. (By the way, Shared isn't a user — it's a folder with privileges set so that any user can access its contents.)

Enter **cd ..** once again, and you find yourself at the root of your main hard drive. The *root directory* is what you see in Finder when you double-click your hard drive icon on the Desktop. Remember that a user's Home directory is represented by a tilde character (~), and the root of the hard drive is denoted by a forward slash (/), as displayed by the prompt:

WHITEDRAGON:/ markchambers$

Skip right back to your Home directory by following this sequence:

WHITEDRAGON:/ markchambers$ cd Users
WHITEDRAGON:/Users markchambers$ cd markchambers
WHITEDRAGON:~ markchambers$

And here's an even faster way. Instead of moving through each successive folder until you reach your intended destination, you can specify the path by using just one cd command:

WHITEDRAGON:/ markchambers$ cd /Users/markchambers
WHITEDRAGON:~ markchambers$

The Home directory is a special folder in that you can also navigate there by simply entering **cd ~**, but the main point here is that you can navigate directly to specific folders by using a folder's path in conjunction with the cd command.

Furthermore, when you navigate your hard drive by using paths, you can jump directly to your desired destination from any place. When you enter **cd ..**, it's in relation to your current position, whereas entering

```
cd /Users/markchambers
```

always takes you to the same directory, regardless of your starting point.

Copying, moving, renaming, and deleting files

After you're comfortable moving around the hierarchy of your hard drive, it's a cinch to copy, move, and rename files and folders.

To copy files from the command line, use the cp command. Because using the cp command copies a file from one place to another, it requires two operands: first the source and then the destination. For instance, to copy a file from your Home folder to your Documents folder, use the cp command like this:

```
cp ~/MyDocument ~/Documents
```

Keep in mind that when you copy files, **you must have proper account permissions to do so!** Here's what happens when I try to copy a file from my Desktop to another user's Desktop (an account named fuad):

```
WHITEDRAGON:~ mark$ cp ~/Desktop/MyDocument ~/Users/fuad/Desktop/MyDocument
```

Denied! Thwarted! Refused!

```
cp: /Users/fuad/Desktop/MyDocument: Permission denied
```

If you can't copy to the destination you desire, you need to precede the cp command with sudo. Using the sudo command allows you to perform functions as another user. The idea here is that the other user whom you're emulating has the necessary privileges to execute the desired copy operation. When you execute the command, the command line asks you for a password. If you don't know the password, you probably shouldn't be using sudo. Your computer's administrator should've given you an appropriate password to use. After you enter the correct password, the command executes as desired.

The curious reader might want to know that sudo stands for *set user and do*. It sets the user to the one that you specify and performs the command that follows the username.

```
sudo cp ~/Desktop/MyDocument ~/Users/fuad/Desktop/MyDocument
Password:
```

A close cousin to the cp (copy) command is the mv (move) command. As you can probably guess, the mv command moves a folder or file from one location to another. (I told you that all this character-based stuff would start to make sense, didn't I?) To demonstrate, this command moves MyDocument from the Desktop folder to the current user's Home folder:

```
mv ~/Desktop/MyDocument ~/MyDocument
```

Ah, but here's the hidden surprise: The mv command can be used as a rename command. For instance, to rename a file MyDocument on the Desktop to MyNewDocument, do this:

```
mv ~/Desktop/MyDocument ~/Desktop/MyNewDocument
```

Because both folders in this example reside in the same folder (~/Desktop/), it appears as though the mv command has renamed the file.

Again, like the cp command, the mv command requires that you have proper permissions for the action you want to perform. Use the sudo command to perform any commands that your current user (displayed in the prompt) isn't allowed to execute. On Unix systems, not all users are necessarily equal. Some users can perform functions that others can't (handy for keeping your child's mitts off important files on your computer). It also creates a hurdle should you choose to work on files while using your child's restricted user account. The sudo command lets you temporarily become another user — presumably one that has permission to perform some function that the current user can't.

What would file manipulation be without the capability to delete files? Never fear; Unix can delete anything you throw at it. Use the rm (remove) or rmdir (remove directory) command to delete a folder or file. For example, to delete MyNewDocument from the Desktop folder, execute the rm command like this:

```
rm ~/Desktop/MyNewDocument
```

Again, deleting files and folders requires that you have permission. In other words, any time you manipulate files with the command line, you're required to have the proper permission. If your current user lacks these permissions, using sudo helps. You should also check to make sure that your target is correctly spelled and that no pesky spaces that could wreak carnage are lurking in the command.

Opening documents and launching applications

Launching applications and opening documents is child's play for a Unix pro like you. The `open` command does it all. For example, to bring Finder to the foreground without touching the mouse, use

```
open /System/Library/CoreServices/Finder.app
```

To open a document from the command line, follow a similar scheme. For example, to view an image named `myImage.tif` that's stored in your Documents folder, try this:

```
open ~/Documents/myImage.tif
```

Useful Commands

Manipulating files and viewing folder content is fun, but the command line is capable of so much more! Now focus your attention on some of the other useful tasks that you can perform with the command line.

OS X comes stocked with a full set of useful commands. You can discover many of the commands that are installed by viewing the files in `/usr/bin`. Type **cd /usr/bin** to navigate there. Other locations to peruse include `/bin` and `/usr/local/bin`.

Calendar

One of my favorite command line functions is the `cal` command, which displays a calendar in text form. Simply entering **cal** at the prompt displays a calendar for the current month, as shown in Figure 2-4.

Figure 2-4:
View a
calendar for
the current
month.

Append a number to the `cal` command to display a 12-month calendar for a specific year. For example, to view a calendar for 1970, type **cal 1970**. The result appears in Figure 2-5.

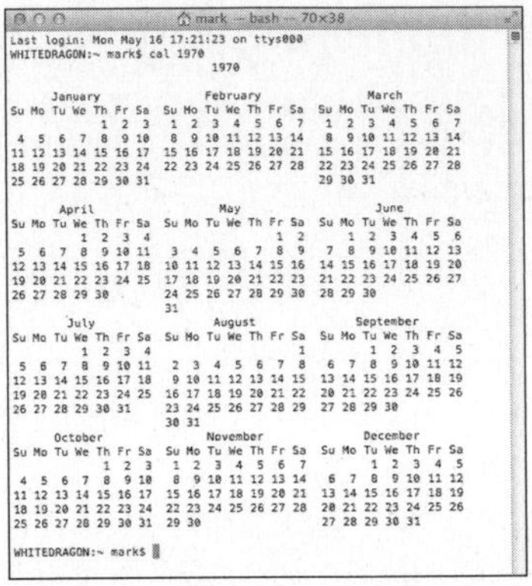

Figure 2-5: Type **cal** followed by a year to view the 12 months of that year.

Append a month number and a year number to display the calendar for that month. For example, to view a calendar for April 2014, type **cal 04 2014**.

Another useful command that's related to the cal command is date. Type **date** at the command line to display the day, date, time, and year based on your computer's settings.

```
WHITEDRAGON:~ markchambers$ date
Sun May 18 11:32:20 CDT 2014
```

Processes

Have you ever been curious about why your hard drive seems to spin and grind on occasion while your system is seemingly inactive? OS X sometimes has a lot of stuff going on behind the scenes. To discover what your computer is busy doing at any time, use the top command to display all the actions that your computer is currently performing, as shown in Figure 2-6. These activities are *processes;* some are created when you launch applications, and others are simply tasks that OS X has to take care of to keep things running smoothly.

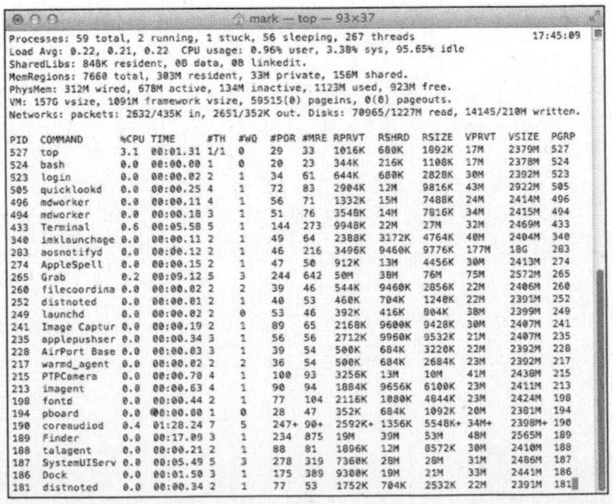

Figure 2-6: The top command displays all running processes.

Besides listing the names of the various processes currently in use, `top` tells you how much of your CPU is being devoted to each process. This lets you know what process is currently hogging all your computing power.

Sometimes a process stalls, effectively freezing that action. By using the `top` command to find the Process ID (PID) of the offending process, you can halt the process. Simply use the `kill` command followed by the PID of the process you want to stop. (The `man` help page for the `kill` command gives more options that may help terminate stubborn processes with prejudice.)

Do *not* take a cavalier attitude when killing processes! Although OS X is extremely stable, removing the wrong process — such as `init` or `mach_ init` — is rather like removing a leg from one of those deep-sea drilling platforms: the very definition of Not Good. You could lock up your system and lose whatever you're doing in other applications. If you simply want to shut down a misbehaving program, go graphical again (at least for a moment) and use the Force Quit menu command from the Apple menu (🍎).

Like `top`, another handy command for examining process info is `ps` (short for *process status*). Most often, you'll want to append a few flags to the `ps` command to get the information that you desire. For example, try the following command, which displays additional information for each process:

```
ps -M
```

The `man` page for `ps` explains what each flag means. (Read more about using the `man` command in the earlier section, "Help is on the way!")

Unix Cadillac Commands

Besides working with files and processes, the command line has all kinds of sophisticated commands. For example, with the command line, you have instant access to a variety of tools for finding files or even stringing together commands.

Finding files

The command line gives you a number of ways to search for files on your hard drive. The two most commonly used commands are `find` and `locate`.

To use `find`, specify a starting point for the search followed by the name of the file or folder that you want to find. For example, to find the Fonts folder that belongs to your user, enter the command like this:

```
find ~/ -name "Fonts"
```

You should see at least one result of the find command.

```
/Users/markchambers/Library/Fonts
```

One great feature of the find command is that you can look for a file or folder in more than one location. Suppose you want to find a file named MyDocument that you know resides either in your Documents folder or on your Desktop. For this kind of search, use the find command like this:

```
find ~/Documents ~/Desktop -name "MyDocument"
```

In this example, you're telling the find command which folders it should search when looking for the file named MyDocument.

Using pipes

Nearly all Unix commands can take on greater capabilities by using a construct called the *pipe*. A pipe is represented by that funny little vertical line (|) that shows up when you press Shift+\. The pipe routes data from one command to another one that follows — for example, many Unix commands produce large amounts of information that can't all fit on one page. (You might have noticed this behavior when you used the locate command.) Joining two commands or functions together with the pipe command is *piping*. To tame the screens full of text, pipe the find function to the less command. The less command provides data one page at a time.

```
find ~/ -name "Fonts" | less
```

When the results fill up one page, the data stops and waits for you to press any key (except the Q key) to continue. When you reach the end of the results, press Q to quit and return to a command line prompt.

Handy Unix Programs

As a Macintosh user, you might be surprised to know that many applications on your hard drive don't reside in one of the typical Applications folders of OS X. These applications don't have a GUI like what you're accustomed to. They're accessible only from the command line. The remainder of this chapter covers some of these applications.

Text editors

Unix has many text-editing applications for use at the command line. Some of the more popular ones include nano, vi, and emacs. Each of these text editors has its pros and cons — and say "thanks" to the thorough folks at Apple because all three are included with Mavericks! For my examples here, however, I use nano because it's simple to use and sufficient for our needs.

Creating a new document

To create a text file in nano, simply type **nano** at the command line. The result looks like Figure 2-7.

Figure 2-7: The nano program is a full-strength text editor, right from the command line.

This is the rough-and-tumble world of Unix, which preceded the Macintosh by many years. Perhaps this also helps you appreciate why the Macintosh was so revolutionary when it was introduced. (You can just hear the designers crowing, "We'll call this a *menu!* Yeah, that's the ticket!" The only graphics that you'd see on your monitor were the comics and sticky notes you stuck to the bottom.)

At the bottom of the screen is a menu of common commands. Above the menu is a large empty space where you can enter text, much the same as the word processors you already know and love. (For those of us that remember the halcyon character-based days of DOS, think older versions of Word and WordPerfect — or, if you're a *real* computing dinosaur like I am, consider the original WordStar.) Type some text in that area. Anything will do . . . a letter to a friend, a grocery list, or your school homework.

After you finish entering your desired text, save the document with the WriteOut command in the nano menu. Directly next to each command in the nano menu is a keyboard sequence used to perform that command. (Refer to the bottom of Figure 2-7.) The ∧ character is shorthand for the Control key on your keyboard. Thus, to save a file, press ∧+O. This flies in the face of standard Mac keyboard conventions, where the letter O is traditionally used to mean Open.

After pressing the Control+O sequence, `nano` prompts you for a filename. As with most Unix files, you're permitted to enter a simple filename here or a full path to a file. For this example, save the file to your Documents folder, naming it `MyNanoDocument`.

After you complete and save the document, press Control+X to transport you away from Planet Nano and back to the command line.

Networking with the Terminal

Because Unix isn't a new phenomenon, it has many useful networking capabilities built into it. Unix was instrumental in creating much of what we now take for granted: e-mail, the Internet, and the World Wide Web. Thus, you'll be happy to know that you can communicate over networks with the Terminal in practically any manner that you can dream of . . . and then some!

WWW and FTP

If you've used the Internet for any time, you're probably familiar with the various means to transport data over a network. From File Transfer Protocol (FTP) and Telnet to e-mail and the web, Unix can handle it all. Unix has a command for each of these functions (and many more that have passed into historical obscurity). Rather than use each individual command to send and retrieve data with the Terminal, Apple has conveniently provided a command that can handle them all: `curl`. The `curl` command is competent at all the standard network protocols. To see it in action, pass a web address (or *URL,* to The Enlightened) to the `curl` command:

```
curl http://www.mlcbooks.com
```

You see the HyperText Markup Language (HTML) page that's located at `www.mlcbooks.com`. Because this isn't particularly useful for most people (it's not very easy to read), you need to add the letter `o` as a flag. This specifies where you would like to save this file upon download. To save the HTML page to your Home directory, add the `-o` flag and a path to the destination file.

```
curl -o ~/mlcbooks.html http://www.mlcbooks.com
```

Don't forget to precede all flags with a hyphen.

If you now perform an `ls` command, you see that `curl` downloaded the HTML found at `www.mlcbooks.com` and saved it to a file named `mlcbooks.html` in your Home directory.

How do you spell success? c-u-r-l!

Sure, HTTP and FTP are handy, but did you know that you can use many other protocols for network communications? One of the niftier ones is the *Dictionary protocol*. With it, you can look up words from any server that understands the protocol. Suppose, for example, that you want to know the meaning of the term *DVD*.

Enter the following command to find out:

```
curl dict://dict.org/d:DVD
```

With `curl`, Dictionary, and your Dictionary Dashboard widget on the same Macintosh, you might never use a paper dictionary again!

The beauty of `curl` is that it does much more than just retrieve web pages: It's equally comfortable with FTP transfers. FTP is used to *download* (receive) files from a server as well as *upload* (send) them. Like the previous HyperText Transfer Protocol (HTTP) examples, you only have to provide an FTP address in Universal Resource Locator (URL) format, and `curl` takes care of the rest. Of course, most people want to save any files they download via FTP — not view them in the Terminal as I did the HTML file. Therefore, as in the previous example, you should add the -o flag and a path to the destination of your download. This time, I download a README file about `curl` directly from the makers of `curl`. (*Note:* Most FTP servers require a valid user ID and password before you're allowed to download.)

```
curl -o ~/Desktop/README.curl ftp://ftp.sunet.se/
    pub/www/utilities/curl/README.curl
```

If you're familiar with FTP, you might be wondering whether `curl` can upload, too. Yes, indeed! Instead of using the -o flag, you need to use two flags: -T and -u. The -T flag denotes which file you want to upload. The -u flag denotes the username and password. Then, specify the FTP destination address of where you want to upload it. Because this example deals with an upload, the remainder of this example is for an imaginary FTP server. In real life, you'd use the appropriate FTP address, username, and password for an FTP server where you are allowed to upload.

```
curl -T /Desktop/README.curl -u username:passwd ftp://
    ftp.yoursitehere.com
/myfiles/README.curl
```

This example uploads the README.curl file from the Desktop folder that I downloaded earlier to an imaginary FTP server.

**Book VIII
Chapter 2**

**. . . . And Unix
Lurks Beneath**

Chapter 3: AppleScript Just Plain Rocks

In This Chapter

✔ Simplifying your life with AppleScript

✔ Letting AppleScript create scripts for you

✔ Writing scripts on your own

✔ Using Automator to create your own applications

✔ Searching for AppleScript help elsewhere

Using a Macintosh is supposed to make your life easier — and in many ways, it does. But there's a limit to how much your Mac can do by itself, right? After all, you still have to move the mouse, press keys on the keyboard, and read information on the screen to get things done . . . or do you? Why not let your computer do the dull chores — say, renaming a thousand digital photographs from your family vacation and organizing them into folders based on the subject of each photo — for you? Although most people are familiar with controlling their Macs with the mouse and keyboard, few realize that they can operate their machines without touching a key or a mouse button — or even glancing at the screen.

What's So Great about AppleScript?

If one word could describe what AppleScript is all about, it'd be *automation*. *AppleScript* is a technology for automating practically any action that you perform with your Macintosh, including both common tasks in Finder and those that you perform in other applications.

Automate common tasks in Finder

If you've ever found yourself repeating some task, you're an ideal candidate for becoming an AppleScript technowizard. AppleScript is particularly good at taking the boredom and tedium out of using your Macintosh by performing all sorts of tasks automatically. To illustrate, consider a few jobs that would take a fair amount of time to do by hand but are a snap with AppleScript:

✦ While writing your next best-selling Great American Novel — or *For Dummies* book on OS X — you make a mistake and misnumber the chapters. All the chapters have a filename bearing the chapter number, but they're all off by one. Sure, you could rename each file by hand, but your book is a large tome and renumbering dozens of chapters manually doesn't sound like much fun. (Take my word for it. *Please*.) It'll require several minutes and lots of tedious attention on your part, not to mention introduce the likelihood of human error. But wait, there's another way! When using a simple AppleScript of only a few lines of code, you can rename the chapters in seconds whilst you go grab another Diet Coke.

✦ You're a neat individual and think that your Mac should reflect your penchant for order — you like your Desktop icons to be placed just so. Being left-handed, you prefer the icons over on the left side of the Desktop, like that *other* operating system. In this situation, an AppleScript can help you do things that aren't humanly possible; not only can you rapidly rearrange the icons on your Desktop, but you can do so with pixel-point accuracy. Without AppleScript, it'd be nearly impossible to precisely align dozens of icons. And even if you could, it would take a long time and probably cause you to go blind.

✦ After a font-download binge, you find yourself with hundreds of fonts. You really want to organize them into separate folders based on the date that you downloaded them. AppleScript comes to the rescue again! With a brief script, you could knock out this challenge without ever looking at a single date. Add a couple more lines of code to the script, and AppleScript will take care of creating the folders, too. Right, you know the word: *sassy*.

Automate tasks in other applications

By using AppleScript, you can also often automate your work from beginning to end, despite the fact that you need multiple applications to do so. Look at a few scenarios, and you'll begin to appreciate why AppleScript is such a powerful technology:

✦ You just completed creating the ultimate library of bagpipe songs in iTunes — no, really! — and you want to share the list with your friends at the next Bagpipers Anonymous meeting. You could easily send everyone in the group an iTunes Playlist, but not everyone in the club has iTunes installed, let alone a computer. This is going to require creating a hard copy for those members without a computer. Because your bagpipe song list contains thousands of songs, you don't want to retype the name of each song. AppleScript can save the day by extracting the song titles for you and compiling them into a list just in time for your meeting.

✦ AppleScript can take care of your computer-owning bagpipe friends, too. With a few extra steps, you can e-mail all of them the list as well.

✦ Being so doggone fond of bagpipes, you want to send your bagpiping friends a special note during the holidays. To help manage your holiday greeting cards, you can create a record in Contacts, FileMaker Pro, or some other database listing the name and address of each person who should receive a card. If you've entered their street addresses in the Contacts section of your e-mail application, AppleScript can aid in transferring the addresses from your e-mail application to the database. Never again will your bagpiping friends miss a holiday greeting . . . and the world is a much better place.

As you can imagine, you can use AppleScript to automate your workflow in thousands of ways. (Whoops, I just used a BST, or *Business Software Term*. A *workflow* is a single document or project that one or more people work on using multiple applications. In other words, your document can be automatically manipulated in multiple applications using the same script.)

Running a Script

The easiest way to get started with AppleScript is to use some scripts that others have written already. *Scripts* are small files that contain a list of commands that tells your Mac what functions to perform and when. Fortunately, Apple is kind enough to provide you with several completed scripts with your installation of Mavericks. You can find a large cache of scripts in the scripts folder, found in the Library folder, under Scripts.

Many scripts (but not all) end with the extension `.scpt`.

Before you get started running scripts, however, you should know a few things.

Identifying scripts in the field

Each script that you encounter will be in one of these three formats:

✦ **Script application:** Some AppleScripts act much like an application. To use one, simply double-click it in Finder, and off it goes to perform whatever tasks it was meant to do. Depending on an internal setting of the script, it might quit when it's finished doing its thing. Most often, the script completes its mission and quits. Scripts are typically identified by the icon that you see in Figure 3-1.

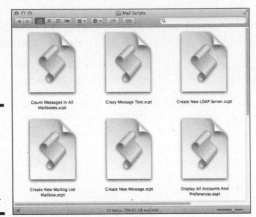

Figure 3-1:
A gaggle
of typical
script icons
caught by
the camera.

+ **Compiled script:** You might also encounter AppleScripts that won't
  run without the aid of another application. Apple calls these *compiled
  scripts.* Although they can't execute on their own, they do have the
  capabilities of a script built in. They just require a host application to
  use them.

+ **Text file:** The third category of AppleScript that you might encounter is
  a script stored in a text file. This kind of script also needs a host application before it can do anything. The main difference between a text file
  script and a compiled script is that you can read a text file script in any
  application that can open a text file.

The AppleScript Editor application

As I mention in the preceding list, compiled scripts and text file scripts
require some sort of host application before they can perform any action.
Luckily, Mavericks provides you with just such a host: AppleScript Editor,
which comes with OS X and can execute any AppleScript with ease. With
AppleScript Editor, you can also do much more, including

+ View or modify an AppleScript.

+ Create an AppleScript.

+ Check an AppleScript for errors.

+ Save scripts in one of the three possible formats.

To launch AppleScript Editor, click the Launchpad icon (which bears a rocket icon) on the Dock, click the Utilities/Other folder, and then click the AppleScript Editor icon. From the familiar iCloud Open dialog, click New Document — the AppleScript Editor application displays an empty, script-editing window, as shown in Figure 3-2.

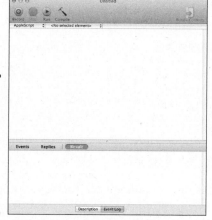

Figure 3-2: AppleScript Editor slices and dices . . . and even checks syntax. Order now!

Executing a script

With AppleScript Editor running, you can run any AppleScript that you can find. To get you started, Apple conveniently provides a handful of useful scripts. Navigate to the Scripts folder, which is located in the Library folder.

Scripts are divided into folders based on functionality, such as fonts, mail, and navigation. For example, open the Font Book folder, where you'll find a script named `Delete Empty Collections.scpt`.

Double-click the script to open it. Because it's a compiled script and not an application script, AppleScript Editor automatically loads the script and comes to the foreground (see Figure 3-3). This particular script opens the Font Book application and checks for empty font collections. If it finds any, the script displays a prompt asking for confirmation and then deletes the empty collection if you click the OK button. To see the script in action, click the Run button or press ⌘+R.

Book VIII Chapter 3

AppleScript Just Plain Rocks

Figure 3-3:
Click the
Run button
on the Editor
toolbar to
execute a
script.

Writing Your Own Simple Scripts

Using someone else's scripts is fun and all, but the real joy of AppleScript comes when you create your own. Not only can you customize a script to your own needs and desires, but saving all those keystrokes can really produce a feeling of euphoria. (Okay, perhaps only Mavericks power users will experience a heightened sense of existence . . . you'll be there soon.)

Create a script without touching a key

You needn't wear a pocket protector or tape the bridge of your glasses to become proficient with AppleScript. AppleScript Editor can get you up and running with AppleScript in no time at all. The secret weapon is the Record function of AppleScript Editor. Just click the Record button, perform one or more actions in a recordable application, return to AppleScript Editor, and click the Stop button. AppleScript Editor stores each action and then compiles the whole list into an AppleScript.

In theory, this is how it should all work. In reality, though, finding recordable Macintosh applications isn't always so easy. Finder is, perhaps, the most recordable application on the Mac. Although some other applications support recording, so few do that Finder could be the only recordable application most Mac users ever see.

To try it yourself, take the following steps to automate actions in Finder:

1. **Bring AppleScript Editor to the foreground.**

If AppleScript Editor isn't running, double-click its icon in a Finder window. If it is running, click its icon (which bears a script scroll and a pen) on the Dock.

2. **Create a new script by pressing ⌘+N.**

3. **Click the Record button.**

   The Record button is one of four buttons positioned near the top left of a new script window. (Refer to Figure 3-3.)

4. **Switch to Finder and perform the actions that you want to automate.**

   When Finder is active, you can select some icons on the Desktop and move them around, resize any open Finder windows, or navigate to your Home directory. Any action that you perform in Finder should be acceptable fodder for AppleScript Editor. As you now perform tasks in Finder, AppleScript Editor automatically generates a script that replicates your actions.

5. **Return to AppleScript Editor and click the Stop button.**

   To reactivate AppleScript Editor, click its icon on the Dock. Click the Stop button to cease the recording of your script.

When you're finished, you should be looking at a complete AppleScript. To test your work, return to Finder and return any icons or windows that you might have moved or repositioned to their original locations. (You don't want to run a script that doesn't appear to have any effect.) Then return to AppleScript Editor and click the Run button to watch your automated Finder tasks being performed.

Building your own scripts

An AppleScript novice can perform all kinds of amazing feats with the recording features of AppleScript Editor. Because AppleScript uses a kind of pseudo-English language, it's usually pretty easy to figure out what's going on behind the scenes. Consider the following script as an example:

```
tell app "Finder"
   activate
   set windowList to every window -- save open windows list
   repeat with theWindow in windowList
      tell theWindow
         if collapsed is true then
         -- do nothing, because the window is collapsed
         else
            set collapsed to true
         end if
      end tell
   end repeat
end tell
```

By the way, in the preceding code, I bold and italicize the commands you'll be working with, but they don't have to be bold and italic for the script to work.

The first thing that you might notice about this script is the first line: the `tell` command, which indicates that this script relates to Finder. This script activates Finder, creates a list of open windows, and then examines the state of each window: Is it collapsed or not collapsed? (By default, a *collapsed,* or minimized, window appears on the Dock.)

One of two possible results occurs:

✦ **If the window is already minimized,** nothing happens and the script continues through the list of windows.

✦ **If the window isn't minimized,** the script collapses it.

This process continues until the script has examined all open windows. The end result? All open windows end up minimized on the Dock.

Another thing to note about this script is that it contains two comments (`save list` and `do nothing`). Months later, when you open the script again, comments can help you remember what you were thinking. Although comments help us humans know what's happening, they don't have any other function. An AppleScript comment begins with two dashes (`--`).

Here's a big-time Mark's Maxim that every script author should remember:

Comments are your friend in any script!

One Step Beyond: AppleScript Programming

Creating AppleScripts can soon become involved, bordering on programming. Don't let that term *programming* scare you away, though. You needn't be a software developer to take advantage of AppleScripts. Apple provides a lot of help to get you started along the AppleScript trail.

Grab the Dictionary

Perhaps the greatest resource for AppleScript novices and experts alike is the AppleScript Dictionary. Although many applications are scriptable, not all are. To be scriptable, an application must contain an AppleScript Dictionary. An AppleScript Dictionary details the various commands and objects of an application that you can access via AppleScript.

The AppleScript Editor application allows you to peer inside an application and view its AppleScript Dictionary. To open an application's Dictionary in AppleScript Editor, choose File⇨Open Dictionary. OS X searches through your installed applications and presents you with the Open Dictionary dialog, as shown in Figure 3-4, which lists all applications that have an AppleScript Dictionary — and are therefore scriptable.

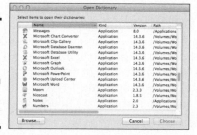

Figure 3-4:
Viewing the AppleScript Dictionary in AppleScript Editor.

If you don't see your favorite application in the list, alas, it's probably not scriptable. To make certain, click the Browse button and navigate to the application location. If the application is disabled, you're out of luck.

After you select an application and click Choose, AppleScript Editor displays that application's AppleScript Dictionary. An application's Dictionary lists all the features of that application that are scriptable.

Scriptable features are divided into categories called *suites,* which you can see on the left side of the AppleScript Dictionary. Every Mac application is supposed to support the required and standard suites, which list common terms that most applications should support.

Click an item in the suite on the left side of the Dictionary to view detailed information about its capabilities, as shown in Figure 3-5.

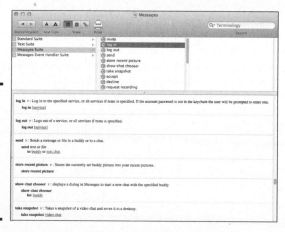

Figure 3-5:
Click an item in a suite to view details about its capabilities and syntax.

Look over the various suites of an application to see what tasks you can automate. Finder, with its huge AppleScript Dictionary, is perhaps the most scriptable of all applications, with iTunes, FileMaker Pro, and BBEdit (which I discuss in Book VII, Chapter 5) close behind.

Anatomy of a simple script

Although a full discussion of AppleScript programming is beyond the scope of this book — after all, we have other things to talk about, too — that doesn't mean that you can't produce some quick and useful scripts. Most AppleScripts begin with a command that addresses the application that you want to automate. Enter this command into a new AppleScript document, which you create by pressing ⌘+N.

```
tell application "Finder"
```

This is like saying, "Hey, Finder, listen up! I'm going to send commands your way!" The double quotation marks surround the application name that you're addressing in the command.

Similarly, after you finish instructing Finder what tasks you want performed, you must also tell it to stop listening. As such, typical scripts end with

```
end tell
```

With the shell of a script in place, all you have to do is add commands between the `tell` and the `end tell` commands of the script. If you want your script to force an application to the foreground, an `activate` command is usually the first line in the shell of your script:

```
tell application "Finder"
  activate
end tell
```

Believe it or not, the preceding code is technically a complete and valid script! It doesn't do much, though, so add some more functionality to make it accomplish something worthwhile. For example, suppose you want to perform some housekeeping chores each time you log in to your Macintosh. Some desirable tasks might include

+ Emptying the Trash

+ Having your Mac say, "Hello!" to you

(Okay, I'll grant that hearing your Mac say, "Hello!" isn't a housekeeping chore, but it makes the whole script that much more fun — and really impresses your visitors, too. No one ever said programming had to be boring!)

To add these functions, you can use a language you already know: English. As I mention earlier, Apple tries (and sometimes succeeds) to make AppleScript as English-like as possible. That way, you don't have to know some silly computer language; just use your native tongue. For example, to empty the Trash, tell Finder to do so.

```
empty trash
```

The trickiest line of code might be the speech, and that's only because you need to remember to add quotation marks. AppleScript thinks that anything without quotation marks is an AppleScript command.

```
say "Hello!"
```

The result is a super-simple script that anyone can read but that performs two powerful functions. The completed script looks like this:

```
tell app "Finder"
  activate
  empty trash
  say "Hello!"
end tell
```

After you complete the script, choose File⇨Save to save your script. Because you want the script to execute and then quit, use the File Format field to save it as an application. Also, make sure that the Stay Open After Run Handler check box and the Show Startup Screen check box are deselected. And don't forget to name your script in the Save As text field.

To have the script automatically run each time you log in to your Mac, save the script anywhere you want. (Assign its location in the Where field of the Save window.) Open System Preferences by clicking its icon on the Dock; click the Users & Groups icon. Make sure that your account is selected (if the pane is locked, click the padlock icon and type your admin password to continue) and then click Login Items. Click the Add button (which proudly bears a plus sign) and navigate to your script in the Open dialog that appears. After you click the Add button of the Open dialog, you see the script in the Login Items pane.

1 Summon Automator — the Silicon Programmer!

Okay, perhaps I've watched too much *Iron Chef* over the years. Anyway, Mavericks features *Automator* (as shown in Figure 3-6), and he's your own personal robotic automation assistant. Automator can help you create custom applications that can handle your repetitive tasks. Again, you're creating *workflows* here, which are sequential (and repeatable) operations that are performed on the same files or data. Your Automator application can automatically launch whatever applications are necessary to get the job done.

Figure 3-6:
Automator
is a dream
come true
for those
who hate
repetitive
tasks.

Here's a great example: You work with a service bureau that sends you a CD every week with new product shots for your company's Marketing department. Unfortunately, these images are flat-out *huge* — taken with a 16-megapixel camera — and they're always in the wrong orientation. Before you move them to the Marketing folder on your server, you have to laboriously resize each image and rotate it, and then save the smaller version.

With Automator's help, you can build a custom application that automatically reads each image in the folder, resizes it, rotates it, and even generates a thumbnail image or prints the image, and then moves the massaged images to the proper folder. You'd normally have to manually launch Preview to perform the image operations and then use a Finder window to move the new files to the right location. But now, with Automator, double-clicking your custom application icon does the trick.

You can run Automator from Launchpad, of course. Open the Utilities/Other folder and then click the Automator icon — it's also located in your Applications folder. Currently, Automator can handle specific tasks in more than 80 applications (including Finder), but both Apple and third-party developers can add new Automator task support to both new and existing applications.

Like other Mavericks applications, you'll initially see the iCloud folder Open dialog. (Don't forget, if you have Automator projects you want to store in your iCloud folder, you can simply drag them into this Open dialog.) If you're creating a new Automator application from scratch, however, click the New Document button to display the Automator window.

To create a simple application using Automator, follow these steps:

1. **Select Application and click Choose.**

2. **Click the desired application in the Library list.**

   Automator displays the actions available in that application.

3. **Drag the desired action from the Library pane to the workflow pane.**

4. **Modify any specific settings provided for the action you chose.**

5. **Repeat Steps 1–3 to complete the workflow.**

6. **Click the Run button (upper-right) to test your script.**

   Use sample files (copies) while you're fine-tuning your application lest you accidentally do something deleterious to an original (and irreplaceable) file!

   Figure 3-7 illustrates a workflow that will take care of the earlier example — resizing and rotating a folder full of images, and then moving them to the Pictures folder.

Figure 3-7: Now I'm ready to handle 10 or 1,000 images in a folder — my application does the work!

7. **When the application is working as you like, press ⌘+Shift+S to save it.**

8. **In the Save dialog that appears, type a name for your new workflow.**

9. **Click the Where pop-up menu and specify a location where the file should be saved.**

10. **Click Save.**

To find all the actions of a certain type in the Library list, click in the Search box at the top of the Library list and type a keyword, such as **save** or **burn**. You don't even need to press Return!

Help Is at Your Fingertips

If you want to explore AppleScript further, you have many resources on hand. Sometimes the easiest way to use AppleScript is to copy existing scripts and modify them as necessary; other times, it's a good idea to read the documentation included in Apple's Help system. Whichever approach you use, with a little practice and guidance, you'll soon be doing stupendous tasks with your Mac.

Built-in AppleScript Help

The most readily available AppleScript reference is built into OS X. From Automator, choose Help⇨Automator Help to launch the Automator Help Guide, or choose Help⇨AppleScript Help from AppleScript Editor. The latter is a great place to begin your AppleScript exploration because it includes detailed documentation about the AppleScript language and loads of demonstration scripts for you to try (or alter) yourself.

AppleScript on the web

In addition to the built-in AppleScript Help in Finder, the Internet has much to offer in the way of AppleScript training and examples. Like so many other excellent web resources, AppleScripts are free!

Not all AppleScripts are created equal: When downloading scripts from the Internet, make sure that they're compatible with Mavericks (OS X v. 10.9).

Mac OS X Automation

Although the built-in OS X help offers a lot, the Mac OS X Automation website (`www.macosxautomation.com/applescript`) offers even more scripts, tutorials, and general AppleScript and Automator goodness. Furthermore, the site maintains an extensive list of links to other useful AppleScript/Automator sites.

Automator World

Automator World (`http://automatorworld.com`) devotes its site to all Macintosh scripting. Because AppleScript is such a huge part of scripting the Mac OS, you can be certain that there's something here for you. Besides offering up-to-date news on Automator scripting for the Mac OS, Automator World also gives you access to many scripts, information about scripting books, and details on AppleScripts with interfaces. The sheer volume of information at this site makes it one you shouldn't skip.

Chapter 4: Talking with and Writing to Your Macintosh

In This Chapter

✔ Using handwriting recognition to control OS X

✔ Speaking to your Mac

✔ Having your Mac speak back

✔ Exploring assistive capabilities and devices

✔ Using VoiceOver to provide feedback in Mavericks

*I*f you're a hunt-and-peck typist — leaving you certain that there *must* be a better way to get information into your computer — Apple has you in mind. Ever since the first Mac rolled off the assembly line, Apple has had a keen interest in alternative modes of interaction between human and machine. OS X continues this tradition by offering three options for controlling your Mac without the keyboard:

✦ **Handwriting:** By using a stylus and computer tablet, you can enter text in your Mac by simply writing as you would on a sheet of paper.

✦ **Speech:** Talk to your Mac to make it obey your commands. It even talks back!

✦ **Assistive devices:** Use a number of third-party devices that can help Mac owners who have disabilities operate their computers, such as a head-mounted eye tracker.

This chapter guides you through the various options for controlling your Macintosh without using the keyboard. First, I cover the OS X *Ink* feature (also called *Inkwell*), which you use to write on a tablet to enter data into your computer. (Although it sounds a bit ironic, think of Ink as your digital paper for the new millennium.) Whatever you write on the tablet appears onscreen as text.

I also take a look at the more space-age speech capabilities available in OS X. With your voice, you can command a Macintosh to perform all sorts of interesting feats. And just so you don't get lonely, the Mac even talks back to you. (Now you can control your computer just like Captain Picard from *Star Trek*!) And the VoiceOver feature makes it easy for your Mac to read aloud all sorts of text, including web pages, Mail messages, and word processing documents.

So scoot away from your computer, lean that chair back, and let your Mac take care of the rest.

Using Ink with a Tablet

Typing on a keyboard can be tedious and error-prone for even the best typists. To help out, Apple includes some useful handwriting features in OS X. Based in part on some of Apple's handheld software for its ill-fated Newton (one of the first personal digital assistants, released before its time), the handwriting recognition in OS X gives you the ability to write text on a compatible tablet in your favorite applications.

The basic process of working with handwriting in OS X goes like this:

1. **Attach a tablet to your Mac.**

   Most tablets use a Universal Serial Bus (USB) connection, so connecting one to your computer is as simple as plugging in the cable from your tablet to a USB port on your Mac.

2. **Open the desired document on your Mac.**

3. **Write on the tablet with the stylus that accompanies it.**

   A *stylus* is the pen that accompanies most tablets. A stylus doesn't have any ink in it: It's just a pen-shaped tool with a plastic tip meant for writing on a tablet.

   Your Mac interprets your handwriting and places that text (at the cursor, where you would typically type with the keyboard) in the active application. You're spared the whole training bit, too.

You aren't restricted to writing just text on the tablet. You can use your tablet to control the interface of your Mac as you would a mouse. A tablet also works great for graphics applications, such as Corel Painter and Adobe Illustrator, Photoshop, and Photoshop Elements. Many artists are frustrated when drawing with a mouse; when you use a tablet, though, you can feel right at home with natural pen or brush movements.

Mavericks also offers a few settings in the Ink pane in System Preferences (accessible from the Dock). From there, click the Ink icon to adjust settings for your tablet.

If you don't have a tablet connected to your Macintosh, you can't view the System Preferences pane for Ink. OS X is smart enough to show you only the settings for your current hardware setup.

Computer, Can You Hear Me?

Remember that classic scene from the movie *Star Trek IV: The Voyage Home* in which Scotty picks up the mouse on a Macintosh and tries to talk directly to the computer? (We're not to that point yet, Scotty, but we're working on it.) Since the early days of the Mac Quadra computer line, Apple has included some form of speech recognition in its computers. Mavericks continues to improve on speech recognition by offering a host of tools that let you get more work done in a shorter amount of time as well as provide voice control for those Mac owners who have difficulty with or are unable to use a traditional keyboard, mouse, or trackpad.

Speak a word, phrase, or sentence, and your Mac translates what you said — and if it understands the phrase, it then performs an action associated with that phrase. The great part about this system is that you can say any phrase in continuous speech and have your Mac perform any action that you can imagine. You aren't limited to just one action: You can perform dozens of actions upon speaking a particular phrase.

Speakable Items are different from the Dictation feature, which simply types what you speak into an application. (I discuss Dictation later in the sidebar, "Mac, take a memo!")

Before you start using Speakable Items, make sure that you have a microphone with which to import sound into your Mac. Many current Macintosh models have a built-in microphone. An Intel iMac sports a microphone built into the monitor. MacBooks have a similar microphone built into the screen. If your Mac doesn't have a microphone, though, you can easily connect one via the microphone jack. (Apple's line of Cinema LED displays also includes a built-in camera and microphone.)

If you're looking for the best quality audio input from your microphone for use with speech recognition (as well as Messages, which I cover in Book V, Chapter 3), check out a microphone with a USB connection. You'll get far better sound quality than afforded by either your Mac's built-in microphone or a microphone that connects to your audio jack.

The Speakable Items controls

To get started with speech recognition in OS X, open the System Preferences window by clicking its icon on the Dock and then clicking the Accessibility icon. Click the Speakable Items entry in the list to the left to display the settings shown in Figure 4-1.

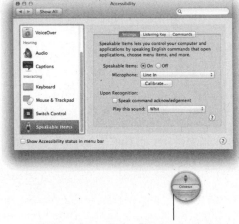

Figure 4-1:
Hail and well met, good Speakable Items settings (and Feedback window)!

Speech Recognition Feedback window

Two different panes in System Preferences make up the speech settings of OS X:

✦ Speakable Items (appears in the Accessibility pane)

✦ Text to Speech (appears in the Dictation & Speech pane)

In this section, I'm concerned only with the Speakable Items settings. Later, in the "Your Mac Talks Back!" section, I explore the Text to Speech settings.

The Speakable Items display in the Accessibility pane consists of three subtabs:

✦ **Settings:** Here you find a number of settings that control how your Mac listens to Its Master's Voice (meaning you, friendly reader). From here, you can toggle Speakable Items on and off, set the sound input, change microphone settings, and specify the action that your Mac should take when a command is recognized.

✦ **Listening Key:** On this tab, you can adjust the key on the keyboard that toggles speech recognition on and off (the *listening key*), specify when your Mac should listen for commands, and name your computer with a keyword. (You *do* want to call your computer by name as any technowizard does, don't you?)

✦ **Commands:** When Speakable Items are active, your Mac can understand any number of commands. From the Commands tab, you tell the Mac what type of command it should expect you to give. You can configure any number of specific applications and menus with speakable items, such as contact names in the Contacts application.

The Settings tab

Crowning the Settings tab are the Speakable Items On and Off radio buttons. You've probably already guessed how to use 'em to switch the Speakable Items feature on and off.

When you select the On radio button, the small circular Speech Recognition Feedback window appears on your screen, floating above all other windows. Know this face well because the Feedback window (refer to Figure 4-1) is your friend and partner. If you use Speakable Items often, it'll become a constant companion on your Desktop (more on Speakable Items in the next section).

You can select the microphone you want to use from the Microphone pop-up menu — a great feature if you have more than one microphone connected to your Mac. Click the Calibrate button to adjust the sound volume for better recognition.

At the bottom of the Settings tab is the Upon Recognition section. When your Mac comprehends one of your stentorian commands, you can set it to respond by playing a sound, speaking an acknowledgement, or both. This feature is helpful when you're not sure whether your Mac understands you. Like handwriting recognition, 100 percent speech recognition isn't a reality on any computer at this point, so sometimes it helps to have feedback. Otherwise, you might feel silly shouting at your machine while it sits there doing nothing. (Or perhaps not if you're into inexpensive anger management.)

The Listening Key tab

You can choose between two styles of listening with the Listening Method options:

✦ **Listen Only While Key Is Pressed:** Speakable Items works only while the designated key is held down.

✦ **Listen Continuously with Keyword:** When you speak the keyword, listening turns on and remains on.

To change what key must be toggled or held down, click the Change Key button.

Why change the keyword? Instead of saying, "Computer, empty the Trash!" you might prefer, "Elrond, empty the Trash!" This adds a little bit of personality to the interaction and also gives your computer a slightly longer time to react to your command. (As a general rule, the longer the spoken phrase, the more likely your Mac will understand it.) If you select the Listen Continuously with Keyword feature, you can change your computer's name via the Keyword text box.

The Commands tab

When Speakable Items are active, your Mac listens for whatever phrases appear in your Speakable Items folder (a directory on your hard drive that holds a number of scripts). The Commands tab — shown in Figure 4-2 — allows you to view the contents of this folder. When you speak a phrase that matches one of these filenames, your Mac automatically executes that script. The script can perform any number of actions, which is what makes Speakable Items so powerful. Apple includes a large number of scripts with OS X, but you're free to create your own, too.

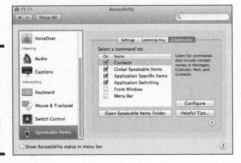

Figure 4-2: Specify the commands that your Mac should "hear."

To make something speakable, select the item and then speak the command, "Make this speakable." The new speakable command is based on the item's name.

To view the contents of the Speakable Items folder, click the Open Speakable Items Folder button on the Commands tab. Finder comes to the foreground and navigates to the folder that holds the scripts.

To the right of the Open Speakable Items Folder button is the Helpful Tips button. Click it to get some pointers on how to get the best performance from your microphone.

Mac, take a memo!

The Dictation feature in Mavericks is yet another idea borrowed from the iOS world — in this case, the iPad, where Dictation made its debut. You can use Dictation to enter the text you speak directly into a text field in any application that supports this feature.

To use Dictation, open System Preferences and click the Dictation & Speech icon. Then on the Dictation tab, select the On radio button. If you have more than one microphone available, click the pop-up menu button at the left side of the pane and choose the microphone you want to use with Dictation. By default, pressing the Function (FN) key twice starts the text entry; however, you can click the Shortcut pop-up menu to choose another shortcut.

In Mountain Lion (the previous version of OS X), an Internet connection was required to use Dictation — however, if you choose to use Enhanced Dictation in Mavericks (which requires a hefty but free one-time-only download of nearly 800MB), you can use Dictation while you're offline. To add this functionality, click the Use Enhanced Dictation check box to enable it.

When you're ready to use Dictation, click in the spot where you would normally begin typing, press the keyboard shortcut, and begin speaking. You can press the keyboard shortcut again to turn off Dictation.

The Speakable Items feature isn't restricted to items in the Speakable Items folder. Any application that supports Speakable Items is also fair game for your verbal manipulation. To control commands in other applications, use the Commands tab (refer to Figure 4-2). Here you can select the following check boxes:

+ **Contacts**
+ **Global Speakable Items**
+ **Application Specific Items**
+ **Application Switching**
+ **Front Window** (requires that you activate assistive devices at the bottom of the Accessibility pane)
+ **Menu Bar** (requires that you activate assistive devices at the bottom of the Accessibility pane)

Select any of these options to allow your Mac to listen to those kinds of commands.

The Feedback window

After you activate Speakable Items, you instantly see the Feedback window. You can click and drag the edge of the window to position it anywhere on your Desktop.

**Book VIII
Chapter 4**

Talking with and
Writing to Your
Macintosh

The Feedback window includes controls and displays of its own:

✦ **Microphone Level Meter:** View indicators to let you know how loud the input level to your microphone is.

✦ **Visual Indicator:** See visual feedback to let you know the active mode: idle, listening, or hearing a command. When the microphone isn't dimmed but there are no arrows on either side of the microphone, you're in listening mode. When the microphone is flanked by animated arrows, your computer is hearing a command spoken. When Speech Recognition is idle, no arrows are present and the microphone is dimmed.

✦ **Quick Access Menu:** You can quickly view the Speech Commands window or open the Speakable Items pane in System Preferences. Just click the downward-pointing arrow at the bottom of the Feedback window, and a menu appears.

As soon as you disable Speakable Items, the Feedback window disappears.

The Speech Commands window

Because Speakable Items might be listening for different sets of commands from Finder or many other applications, OS X provides you with the Speech Commands window, which contains a single listing of all commands that you might speak at any given time. To open the Speech Commands window, click the triangle at the bottom of the Feedback window and choose Open Speech Commands Window from the menu that appears.

The Speech Commands window is a simple one, but it serves an important purpose: to let you know what commands OS X understands. The Speech Commands pane, as shown in Figure 4-3, organizes commands into categories that match the settings in the Commands tab.

Figure 4-3:
The Speech Commands window, hard at work.

If you launch another application that supports Speakable Items, OS X adds that application's commands to the Speech Commands window. Speak any of these commands to make your Mac execute that function. For example, OS X ships with speech commands for Contacts, such as Mail To and Meet With.

Apple might be a big, serious, computer company — yeah, right — but it isn't without a humorous side! With Speakable Items enabled, say the phrase, "Tell me a joke." Your Mac replies with a random joke. Say it again, and your Mac tells you another joke. (Brace yourself, these jokes were likely written by preschoolers . . . they're really, really bad.) Oh, and if you get a "Knock, Knock" joke, remember that you have to actually say, "Who's there?"

Your Mac Talks Back!

OS X is great at listening to your speech, but the fun doesn't stop there. Your Mac can talk to you, too! Choose from one of many available voices — including the default Mavericks voice, *Alex* — and you can make your computer talk or even sing (not as well as Sinatra, but better than Bob Dylan). And whereas Speakable Items lets you speak to your Macintosh, the VoiceOver feature enables your Mac to speak text. This is an especially useful feature for listening to your e-mails, web pages, or even your homework — sometimes the eyes need a break. The text-to-speech capability gives you the opportunity to lean back in your chair or even get up and walk around while still using your Macintosh.

Text-to-speech settings appear in three places in System Preferences: the Dictation & Speech pane, the Date & Time pane, and the VoiceOver settings in the Accessibility pane.

Setting Text to Speech options

The text-to-speech engine that comes with Mavericks has a collection of many voices to choose among, including male, female, and (um) nonhuman. To select your Mac's voice in OS X, follow these steps:

1. **Click the System Preferences icon on the Dock.**

2. **Click the Dictation & Speech icon.**

3. **Click the Text to Speech tab, as shown in Figure 4-4.**

**Book VIII
Chapter 4**

**Talking with and
Writing to Your
Macintosh**

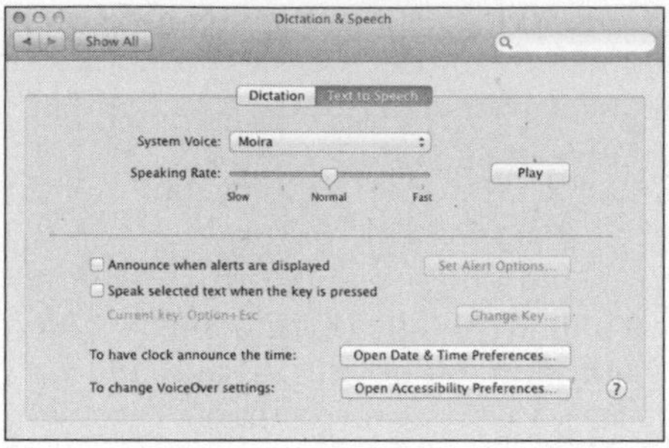

Figure 4-4:
Select
your Mac's
voice.

4. **Open the System Voice pop-up menu to choose a voice for your Mac.**

   To hear the voice, click Play; Mavericks speaks a sentence as a demonstration. To the left of the Play button is a slider for adjusting the speed of the speech. Move the slider right to increase the speed and left to slow it down.

Naturally, Alex receives the most attention these days because he's the default voice for Mavericks, and Alex definitely provides the most natural-sounding tone and the best pacing of the bunch. However, I also think that the old-school voices, such as Bruce and Vicki, are still quite intelligible. (I'm a Vicki kinda guy, myself.)

With your voice selected, turn your attention to enabling talking alerts and having your Mac speak selected text at the press of a key.

Talking alerts

You have these options for setting talking alerts:

✦ Announce when an Alert dialog pops up

✦ Announce when an application needs your attention

✦ Announce the time (more on that in an upcoming section)

You enable either of the first two check box options (or both) on the Text to Speech tab; refer to Figure 4-4.

Alert dialogs come in two levels of importance, but the key word here is *importance*. You don't want to miss these messages:

✦ **Stop sign:** Something particularly important requires your attention — usually an error or a dire warning.

✦ **Yield sign:** Not as severe as the Stop sign, but important nonetheless. Proceed cautiously.

Note that these two traditional types of alerts are different from *Notification Center* alerts. Notification Center alerts are configured in the Notification pane in System Preferences.

If you select the Announce When Alerts Are Displayed check box, click the Set Alert Options button to set alert-specific options:

+ **Voice:** Choose the voice that should speak alerts. (By default, it's any voice you opted for earlier.)

+ **Phrase:** Click this pop-up menu to choose a prefix phrase that's spoken before the actual alert text. By default, Mavericks speaks the name of the application that displays the alert, but you can also choose a phrase from the list or choose to mix up the phrases for a little variety. To add or remove phrases, click the Edit Phrases item.

+ **Delay:** Drag this slider to control the time that passes before Mavericks speaks.

To hear what your spoken alert settings sound like, click the Play button.

In addition to spoken alerts, you can even allow your Mac to announce the time! If you, like me, are constantly getting lost in time while immersed in your work — not to mention your favorite game — set your Mac to announce the hour. This feature always keeps my time sense firmly planted. More on this topic in the upcoming section "The Date & Time pane."

Have your Mac read to you

Ready for your Mac to read text aloud? Although perhaps not as soothing as a parent's gentle voice, your Mac can indeed read any text you can select with the cursor, in any application — including Safari, Preview, Notes, and even third-party applications such as Microsoft Word.

If you have a child who's learning to read, the Mac can help her by reading a selection of text. (Often, kids can figure out how to drag and select text more quickly than they can read the text itself.) And for those with less-than-perfect eyesight, selecting a large amount of text and having it read aloud can prevent headaches and eye strain.

To have a selection of text read to you when you press a particular key, enable the Speak Selected Text When the Key Is Pressed check box. By default, the keyboard shortcut to read text is Option+Esc, but you can click the Change Key button to assign your own shortcut.

The Date & Time pane

There you are, deep in concentration as you finish the final chapter of your Great American Novel, when you glance at the clock in the Finder menu bar and realize that you were *supposed* to pick up your kids at soccer practice an hour ago!

In the future, you can avoid this shameful lapse of parental responsibility by turning on the automatic spoken time feature, which you control from the Date & Time pane (in System Preferences). Click the Open Date & Time Preferences button on the Text to Speech tab, and Mavericks immediately switches to display the Date & Time pane. (Or click the Clock on the Finder menu bar and then click Open Date & Time. Again, it's all about convenience when it comes to the geniuses at Apple.)

From the Date & Time pane, click the Clock tab. Select the Announce the Time check box to enable your Mac to speak the time; use the Period pop-up menu to choose spoken time at the quarter, half, or full hour. You can also customize the voice for spoken time as well.

After you're done, zip back to the Dictation & Speech pane by clicking the Back button at the top-left corner of the System Preferences window.

Configuring VoiceOver in the Accessibility pane

With the VoiceOver utility, your Mac can give you all sorts of verbal feedback, creating a spoken English interface with Mavericks — a valuable addition to the OS for the physically impaired. The feedback includes

✦ **Announcing when certain keys are pressed:** Tells you when a modifier key (such as Control, Option, or ⌘) is pressed or when the Caps Lock key is pressed.

✦ **Announcing cursor movements:** You hear an audible alert when your mouse cursor switches among windows or when you click a menu.

✦ **Announcing the position of the VoiceOver cursor:** VoiceOver can audibly identify all OS controls (such as buttons, sliders, and list boxes) by using a special onscreen cursor.

✦ **Reading documents, web pages, and Mail messages:** VoiceOver can read aloud the contents of all sorts of documents and application windows.

✦ **Speaking the characters you type:** You can set VoiceOver to speak every character or each word you type.

To enable VoiceOver (or launch the VoiceOver utility), follow these steps:

1. **Click the Open Accessibility Preferences button on the Text to Speech panel (refer to Figure 4-4).**

2. **Click the VoiceOver item in the list at the left, as shown in Figure 4-5.**

Figure 4-5: You can customize the VoiceOver audible feedback with the VoiceOver Utility.

3. **Select the Enable VoiceOver option (or press ⌘+F5) to enable VoiceOver. (If you're using one of the latest Apple keyboards, press ⌘+Fn+F5 instead.)**

   Click the Open VoiceOver Training button to display a helpful interactive tutorial designed to help you understand and use VoiceOver. To customize how VoiceOver operates, click the Open VoiceOver Utility button.

Speaking text through applications

Although VoiceOver provides a comprehensive text-to-speech interface for OS X, it might be more than you need. If you simply want to hear text spoken in your applications, a number of alternative methods are available in Mavericks that don't require VoiceOver. As I mention earlier, your Mac can read selected text: Enable the Speak Selected Text When the Key Is Pressed check box on the Text to Speech tab, select the desired text, and press the keyboard shortcut.

Ah, but what if you don't want to select a huge text document? Another way to hear spoken text in OS X is by using *TextEdit,* the simple text processor that accompanies every copy of OS X. Besides its handy word-processing features, TextEdit can also speak text, which can be a helpful document review tool. To hear spoken text with TextEdit, follow these steps:

1. **Click the Launchpad icon on the Dock and click the TextEdit icon.**

2. **Select the desired text document and click Open.**

3. **Choose Edit⇨Speech⇨Start Speaking.**

Your Mac begins speaking the text from the document. The speech engine has some intelligence, so you can enter dollar amounts (such as $25,423.12) or Roman numerals (such as Chapter XIV), and the speech engine reads them back in plain English. The result of these two strings would be "twenty-five thousand, four-hundred twenty-three dollars, and twelve cents" and "chapter fourteen."

4. **Choose Edit⇨Speech⇨Stop Speaking.**

Your Mac stops speaking. It also stops speaking when it reaches the end of the text.

Index

N

O

X

Y

Z

About the Author

Mark L. Chambers has been an author, computer consultant, BBS sysop, programmer, and hardware technician for 30 years — pushing computers and their uses far beyond "normal" performance limits for decades now. His first love affair with a computer peripheral blossomed in 1984 when he bought his lightning-fast 300 BPS modem for his Atari 400. Now he spends entirely too much time on the Internet and drinks far too much caffeine-laden soda.

With a degree in journalism and creative writing from Louisiana State University, Mark took the logical career choice: programming computers. (Go figure.) However, after five years as a COBOL programmer for a hospital system, he decided there must be a better way to earn a living, and he became the Documentation Manager for Datastorm Technologies, a well-known communications software developer. Somewhere in between writing software manuals, Mark began writing computer how-to books. His first book, *Running a Perfect BBS*, was published in 1994 — and after a short 20 years or so of fun (disguised as hard work), Mark is one of the most productive and best-selling technology authors on the planet.

Along with writing several books a year and editing whatever his publishers throw at him, Mark has also branched out into Web-based education, designing and teaching a number of online classes — called *WebClinics* — for Hewlett-Packard.

His favorite pastimes include collecting gargoyles, watching St. Louis Cardinals baseball, playing his three pinball machines and the latest computer games, supercharging computers, and rendering 3D flights of fancy with *TrueSpace* — and during all that, he listens to just about every type of music imaginable. Mark's worldwide Internet radio station, *MLC Radio* (at www.mlcbooks.com), plays only CD-quality classics from 1970 to 1979, including everything from Rush to Billy Joel to the *Rocky Horror Picture Show* soundtrack.

Mark's rapidly expanding list of books includes *iPhone 5 First Steps For Dummies*; *MacBook For Dummies,* 4th Edition; *Macs For Seniors For Dummies,* 2nd Edition; *iMac For Dummies,* 7th Edition; *Build Your Own PC Do-It-Yourself For Dummies*; *Building a PC For Dummies,* 5th Edition; *Scanners For Dummies,* 2nd Edition; *CD & DVD Recording For Dummies,* 2nd Edition; *PCs All-in-One For Dummies,* 6th Edition; *Mac OS X Tiger: Top 100 Simplified Tips & Tricks*; *Microsoft Office v. X Power User's Guide*; *BURN IT! Creating Your Own Great DVDs and CDs*; *The Hewlett-Packard Official Printer Handbook*; *The Hewlett-Packard Official Recordable CD Handbook*; *The Hewlett-Packard Official Digital Photography Handbook*; *Computer Gamer's Bible*; *Recordable CD Bible*; *Teach Yourself the iMac Visually*; *Running a Perfect BBS*; *Official Netscape Guide to Web Animation*; and *Windows 98 Troubleshooting and Optimizing Little Black Book*.

His books have been translated into 15 different languages so far — his favorites are German, Polish, Dutch, and French. Although he can't read them, he enjoys the pictures a great deal.

Mark welcomes all comments about his books. You can reach him at mailto:mark@mlcbooks.com or visit MLC Books Online, his website, at www.mlcbooks.com.

Dedication

This book is dedicated with love to Frank and Vera Judycki. They might have started out as my in-laws, but now they're MawMaw and PawPaw.

Author's Acknowledgments

Once again, the good folks at Wiley have made things easy on a demanding technology author! It's time to send my appreciation to those who helped make this book a reality.

As with all my books, I'd like to first thank my wife, Anne, and my children, Erin, Chelsea, and Rose, for their support and love — and for helping me follow my dream!

No project gets underway without the Composition Services team at Wiley. Starting with my words and adding a tremendous amount of work, Composition Services has once again taken care of art, layout, and countless other steps that I can't fathom. Thanks to each of the team members for a beautiful book.

Next, my appreciation goes to my superb technical editor Dennis Cohen, who checked the technical accuracy of every word — including that baker's dozen of absurd acronyms that crops up in every technology book I've ever written. His eagle eye for detail and encyclopedic knowledge of everything Mac ensures that this finished book is the best it can be!

Finally, I come to Susan Pink, my exceptional project editor, and Bob Woerner, my top-of-the-line acquisitions editor (both of whom are also long-time friends)! My heartfelt thanks to both of them, for without their support at every step, this book wouldn't have been possible. With their help, yet another *For Dummies* title was guided safely into port!

Publisher's Acknowledgments

Acquisitions Editor: Bob Woerner

Project Editor: Susan Pink

Copy Editor: Susan Pink

Technical Editor: Dennis Cohen

Editorial Assistant: Annie Sullivan

Sr. Editorial Assistant: Cherie Case

Project Coordinator: Patrick Redmond

Cover Image: ©iStockphoto.com/EpicStockMedia